THE RISE AND FALL OF THE
BRITISH ARMY
1975–2025

OSPREY
PUBLISHING

DEDICATION

To fallen comrades who marched to the guns
and loved the Army, but not blindly.
They taught me more than I realized at the time:

Lieutenant James Barry
Lieutenant Colonel Bryan Elliott
Brigadier Professor Richard Holmes
General Sir Mike Jackson
Sir John Keegan
Sir Hilary Synott

BEN BARRY

THE RISE AND
FALL OF THE
BRITISH
ARMY
1975–2025

OSPREY PUBLISHING
Bloomsbury Publishing Plc
Kemp House, Chawley Park, Cumnor Hill, Oxford OX2 9PH, UK
Bloomsbury Publishing Ireland Limited,
29 Earlsfort Terrace, Dublin 2, D02 AY28, Ireland
Bloomsbury Publishing Inc.
1359 Broadway, 12th Floor, New York, NY 10018, USA
E-mail: info@ospreypublishing.com
www.ospreypublishing.com

OSPREY is a trademark of Osprey Publishing Ltd

First published in Great Britain in 2025

A catalogue record for this book is available from the British Library

ISBN: HB 9781472856340; PB 9781472856388; eBook 9781472856395; ePDF 9781472856371;
XML 9781472856357; Audio 9781472856364

25 26 27 28 29   10 9 8 7 6 5 4 3 2 1

Title page image: iStock.
Plate section image credits and captions are given in full in the List of Illustrations (pp. 9–11).
Maps by www.bounford.com
Index by Mark Swift

Typeset by Deanta Global Publishing Services, Chennai, India
Printed and bound in Great Britain by Clays Ltd, Elcograf S.p.A.

Osprey Publishing supports the Woodland Trust, the UK's leading woodland conservation charity.

To find out more about our authors and books visit **www.ospreypublishing.com**. Here you will find extracts,
author interviews, details of forthcoming events and the option to sign up for our newsletter.

For product safety related questions contact productsafety@bloomsbury.com

CONTENTS

ACKNOWLEDGEMENTS

Some of the ideas expressed in this book have already been aired in publications by the International Institute of Strategic Studies (IISS): the Adelphi books, *Survival*, *Strategic Survey*, *The Military Balance* and its blog. It also draws on my previous book *Blood, Metal and Dust: How Victory Turned into Defeat in Afghanistan and Iraq*. There is some overlap with that book's discussion of Basra and Helmand, but this book incorporates new insights, particularly from recently published US accounts.

Artificial intelligence was not used in the writing of this book. I would particularly like to thank the following people for supporting my research: my IISS colleagues Field Marshal Lord David Richards, Lieutenant General H.R. McMaster, Professor Sir Hew Strachan, Dana Allin, Desmond Bowen, Dr Bastian Giegerich, James Hackett, Nigel Inkster; and IISS' excellent librarians Graham Ivory and Kevin Jewell. Also Dr Simon Anglim, Sir Max Hastings, Allan Mallinson, Professor Brian Holden-Reid, Professor Theo Farrell and Dr Frank Hoffman.

Since 1975 many serving and retired members of the British Army have informed the development of this book. I am very sorry that I cannot name them all, including some who do not want to be named. But I would particularly like to thank Lieutenant General Dick Applegate and General Sir Nick Carter for sponsoring field trips to Afghanistan. I want to 'mention in dispatches' General Lord Richard Dannatt, General Sir Roly Walker, Major General James Bowder, Major General John Clark, Major General Charles Vyvyan, Brigadier Philip Pratley, Brigadier John Ridge, Brigadier Chris Coton, Brigadier Will Strickland, Colonel Alex Alderson PhD, Colonel Tom Archer-Burton, Colonel Caroline Emmett, Lieutenant Colonel Jim Storr, Major Jonty Kennon, Major Neil Croft, Captain Callum Fraser, and Corporal Wilf Owen.

Thanks are due also to Marcus Cowper, Gemma White, and Elle Chilvers at Osprey; the copyeditor Margaret Haynes and proof reader Guy Croton, and Robert Dudley, my excellent agent.

Finally, to my wonderful family: Liz, Charlotte and Jamie, for bearing the opportunity costs of my writing.

LIST OF ILLUSTRATIONS

Chieftain tanks assembled for Cold War training. From the mid-1960s to mid-1980s, the Chieftain was NATO's best-armed and best-protected tank, but it suffered from chronic unreliability. (Photo by Jacob SUTTON/Gamma-Rapho via Getty Images)

An Army 'snatch squad' in early 1970s Northern Ireland. They are weighed down by helmets, protective shields and flak jackets, requiring a very high standard of fitness to catch unencumbered rioters. (Photo by Popperfoto via Getty Images)

A soldier on patrol in Northern Ireland in the late 1970s. Operation *Banner* often featured surreal clashes of normal and abnormal circumstances. (Photo by John Roca/NY Daily News Archive via Getty Images)

Heavily laden soldiers of 2 Para gather for a helicopter in the Falklands. Their battalion was the only land unit to fight two battles in the campaign. (© IWM, FKD 2124)

Margaret Thatcher, prime minister from 1979 to 1990, drives an Abbott 105mm self-propelled gun. (DPA/AFP via Getty Images)

The battle of Mount Tumbledown was the only opposed attack conducted by the 5th Infantry Brigade in the Falklands War. Here, Scots Guards celebrate the Argentinian surrender. (© Regimental Headquarters Scots Guards)

Battlegroup training in Canada provided a strong foundation for the Army's armoured warfare capabilities. Here, 1st Battalion, the Scots Guards leads a battlegroup of two Chieftain tank squadrons, two mechanized infantry companies and an armoured engineer troop in 1990. By 2025, this training had ceased. (Crown Copyright)

In December 1995, the weak UNPROFOR in Bosnia was succeeded by the better armed and more robust NATO IFOR. Here, Warrior fighting vehicles of 2nd Battalion, the Light Infantry secure a front-line crossing point, supported by 105mm light guns and Lynx helicopters. (Author's Collection)

Chieftain tanks were replaced by the better protected Challenger, deployed on Operation *Granby* in 1990–91. The tanks' unreliability was a considerable constraint on operational planning. (Photo by PATRICK BAZ/AFP via Getty Images)

British troops entering Kosovo were greeted as liberators by the majority Albanian population. (Photo by TIM OCKENDEN/POOL/AFP via Getty Images)

A Parachute Regiment patrol in Sierra Leone. (Photo by ISSOUF SANOGO/AFP via Getty Images)

In August 2001, 16 Air Assault Brigade led a NATO mission to Macedonia to defuse a civil war. Here a paratrooper guards Albanian guerrillas who are surrendering their weapons. (Photo by PETER ANDREWS/REUTERS POOL/AFP via Getty Images)

The battle of Basra, 2003. A Warrior infantry fighting vehicle and a sniper of the Irish Guards cover armoured engineers extinguishing oil well fires. (Photo by Giles Penfound/MOD/Getty Images)

A British soldier prepares to jump from a burning Warrior during the September 2005 incident at the Jameat police station in Basra. (Atef Hassan/Reuters)

Prime Minister Tony Blair arrives by Chinook helicopter to meet Major General Jonathan Reilly. Reilly also played key roles in Bosnia and Sierra Leone. By tolerating Chancellor Gordon Brown's cuts to defence spending, Blair ensured that the Army would have insufficient helicopters in Afghanistan. (ADRIAN DENNIS/AFP via Getty Images)

A British soldier from 16 Air Assault Brigade shakes hands with a young Afghan boy during a foot patrol in Lashkar Gah, Helmand province, 16 May 2006. On the right is a lightly armoured Snatch Land Rover. These were easily defeated by roadside bombs in Iraq and Afghanistan. (JOHN D MCHUGH/AFP via Getty Images)

The Rifles was a new infantry regiment formed in 2007. Here, a rifleman from 1st Battalion takes cover in a ditch in Helmand's irrigated Green Zone in March

2009. The soldier in front is carrying a Vallon mine detector. (POA(Phot) Dave Husbands/Crown Copyright)

Army Apache helicopters, seen here leaving Helmand in 2014, provided invaluable fire support to ground troops, without which casualties would have greatly increased. (Cpl Daniel Wiepen/Crown Copyright 2020)

The self-organized tributes to dead troops at the small town of Royal Wootton Bassett captured the national mood of increasing respect for the Army's determination, combined with a growing sentiment that the Iraq and Afghanistan wars were not worth the increasing casualties. (Photo by Matt Cardy/Getty Images)

A gunner of the Royal Horse Artillery distributes a Covid-19 test kit in May 2021. From the mid-1970s onwards, restrictions on the employment of women in the British Army were gradually reduced, before being removed completely in 2018. (Photo by Christopher Furlong/Getty Images)

Paratroops snatch some much-needed rest during the 2021 evacuation from Kabul. Operation *Pitting* was dangerous, difficult and exhausting, and marked the end of Britain's unsuccessful war in Afghanistan. (MARCUS YAM / LOS ANGELES TIMES / Getty Images)

After the 2022 Russian attack on NATO, British Army exercises in Eastern Europe greatly increased. Here, a British engineer squadron, part of a German Army bridging unit, uses its M3 ferries to carry Challenger 2 tanks. (Photo by Dominika Zarzycka/SOPA Images/LightRocket via Getty Images)

The government and British people expected the Army to play a major role in state ceremonial events. Here, guardsmen of Queen's Company, 1st Battalion, the Grenadier Guards carry the coffin of Her Majesty Queen Elizabeth II into St George's Chapel, Windsor, 19 September 2022. (Crown Copyright)

Armoured infantrymen and a Warrior from the British battlegroup in Estonia guard NATO's borders with Russia. Since the end of the Cold War, the Warrior had acquired digital communications and thermal sights, and the infantry had better combat uniforms and body armour and improved SA rifles. (NATO)

LIST OF MAPS

INTRODUCTION

This book tells the important, but neglected, story of the British Army over the half century between 1975 and 2025. This is as rich a period in the Army's history as any other half decade – a period of great change, a mixture of peace and war, in which society, technology and the character of conflict altered significantly. The Army changed a great deal. Some of these changes were successful. There were also failures, some imposed from outside, others of the Army's own making. I aim to bring some fresh insights to the Army's recent history and its plans for the future.

Many histories of the Army approach the topic from a linear, arithmetical point of view. This book is about change, shaped more by calculus than arithmetic, because war is characterized by constant change. Use of new technology or tactics by one actor usually results in attempts by its opponents to develop countermeasures. If successful, these countermeasures often prompt further adaptation. Therefore, most wars feature complex action–reaction dynamics that constantly change their character. The late Professor Williamson Murray, one of the greatest experts on military innovation and adaptation wrote that:

> War is a contest, a complex, interactive duel between two opponents ... which presents the opportunity for the contestants to adapt to their enemy's strategy, operations, and tactical approach. But because it is interactive, both sides have the potential to adapt to the conflict at every level, from the tactical to the strategic. Thus, the problems posed by the battle space do not remain constant; in fact, more often than not, they change with startling rapidity.[1]

Murray identifies a complementary process in peacetime – military innovation, change in anticipation of future wars and operations. I show examples of the British Army attempting to seek advantage by both adaptation and innovation. Sometimes these initiatives were successful. Some innovations put the Army in a leading position in NATO, and even globally. But on other occasions, the Army failed to innovate or adapt fast enough, to its subsequent disadvantage both in operational effectiveness and in reputation.

Much of the Army's recent history is not as well understood as it could be, including by many currently serving. Some of it is directly relevant to the Army's current roles. For example, there are aspects of the Army's Cold War plans to defend West Germany against

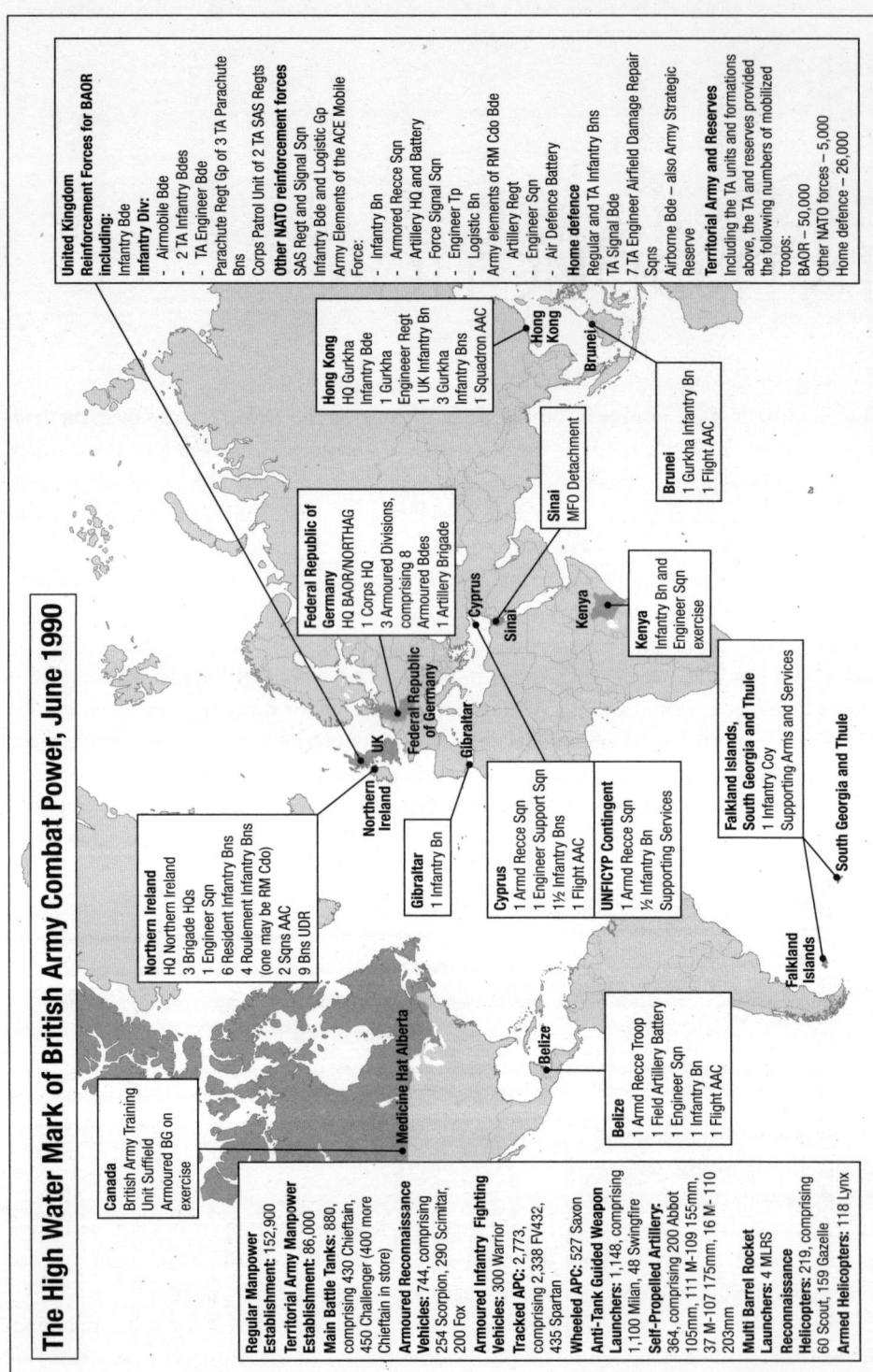

The High Water Mark of British Army Combat Power, June 1990

Canada
British Army Training Unit Suffield
Armoured BG on exercise

Regular Manpower
Establishment: 152,900
Territorial Army Manpower
Establishment: 86,000
Main Battle Tanks: 880, comprising 430 Chieftain, 450 Challenger (400 more Chieftain in store)
Armoured Reconnaissance Vehicles: 744, comprising 254 Scorpion, 290 Scimitar, 200 Fox
Armoured Infantry Fighting Vehicles: 300 Warrior
Tracked APC: 2,773, comprising 2,338 FV432, 435 Spartan
Wheeled APC: 527 Saxon
Anti-Tank Guided Weapon Launchers: 1,148, comprising 1,100 Milan, 48 Swingfire
Self-Propelled Artillery: 364, comprising 200 Abbot 105mm, 111 M-109 155mm, 37 M-107 175mm, 16 M-110 203mm
Multi Barrel Rocket Launchers: 4 MLRS
Reconnaissance Helicopters: 219, comprising 60 Scout, 159 Gazelle
Armed Helicopters: 118 Lynx

Northern Ireland
HQ Northern Ireland
3 Brigade HQs
1 Engineer Sqn
6 Resident Infantry Bns
4 Roulement Infantry Bns (one may be RM Cdo)
2 Sqns AAC
9 Bns UDR

Belize
1 Armd Recce Troop
1 Field Artillery Battery
1 Engineer Sqn
1 Infantry Bn
1 Flight AAC

Gibraltar
1 Infantry Bn

Cyprus
1 Armd Recce Sqn
1 Engineer Support Sqn
1½ Infantry Bns
1 Flight AAC

UNFICYP Contingent
1 Armd Recce Sqn
½ Infantry Bn
Supporting Services

Federal Republic of Germany
HQ BAOR/NORTHAG
1 Corps HQ
3 Armoured Divisions, comprising 8 Armoured Bdes
1 Artillery Brigade

Hong Kong
HQ Gurkha
Infantry Bde
1 Gurkha Engineer Regt
1 UK Infantry Bn
3 Gurkha Infantry Bns
1 Squadron AAC

Sinai
MFO Detachment

Brunei
1 Gurkha Infantry Bn
1 Flight AAC

Kenya
Infantry Bn and Engineer Sqn exercise

Falkland Islands, South Georgia and Thule
1 Infantry Coy
Supporting Arms and Services

United Kingdom
Reinforcement Forces for BAOR including:
Infantry Bde
Infantry Div.
- Airmobile Bde
- 2 TA Infantry Bdes
- TA Engineer Bde
Parachute Regt Gp of 3 TA Parachute Bns
Corps Patrol Unit of 2 TA SAS Regts
Other NATO reinforcement forces
SAS Regt and Signal Sqn
Infantry Bde and Logistic Gp
Army Elements of the ACE Mobile Force:
- Infantry Bn
- Armored Recce Sqn
- Artillery HQ and Battery
- Force Signal Sqn
- Engineer Tp
- Logistic Bn
Army elements of RM Cdo Bde
- Artillery Regt
- Engineer Sqn
- Air Defence Battery
Home defence
Regular and TA Infantry Bns
TA Signal Bde
7 TA Engineer Airfield Damage Repair Sqns
Airborne Bde – also Army Strategic Reserve
Territorial Army and Reserves
Including the TA units and formations above, the TA and reserves provided the following numbers of mobilized troops:
BAOR – 50,000
Other NATO forces – 5,000
Home defence – 26,000

Labels on map: Canada · Medicine Hat Alberta · Belize · Falkland Islands · South Georgia and Thule · UK · Northern Ireland · Gibraltar · Federal Republic of Germany · Cyprus · Sinai · Kenya · Hong Kong · Brunei

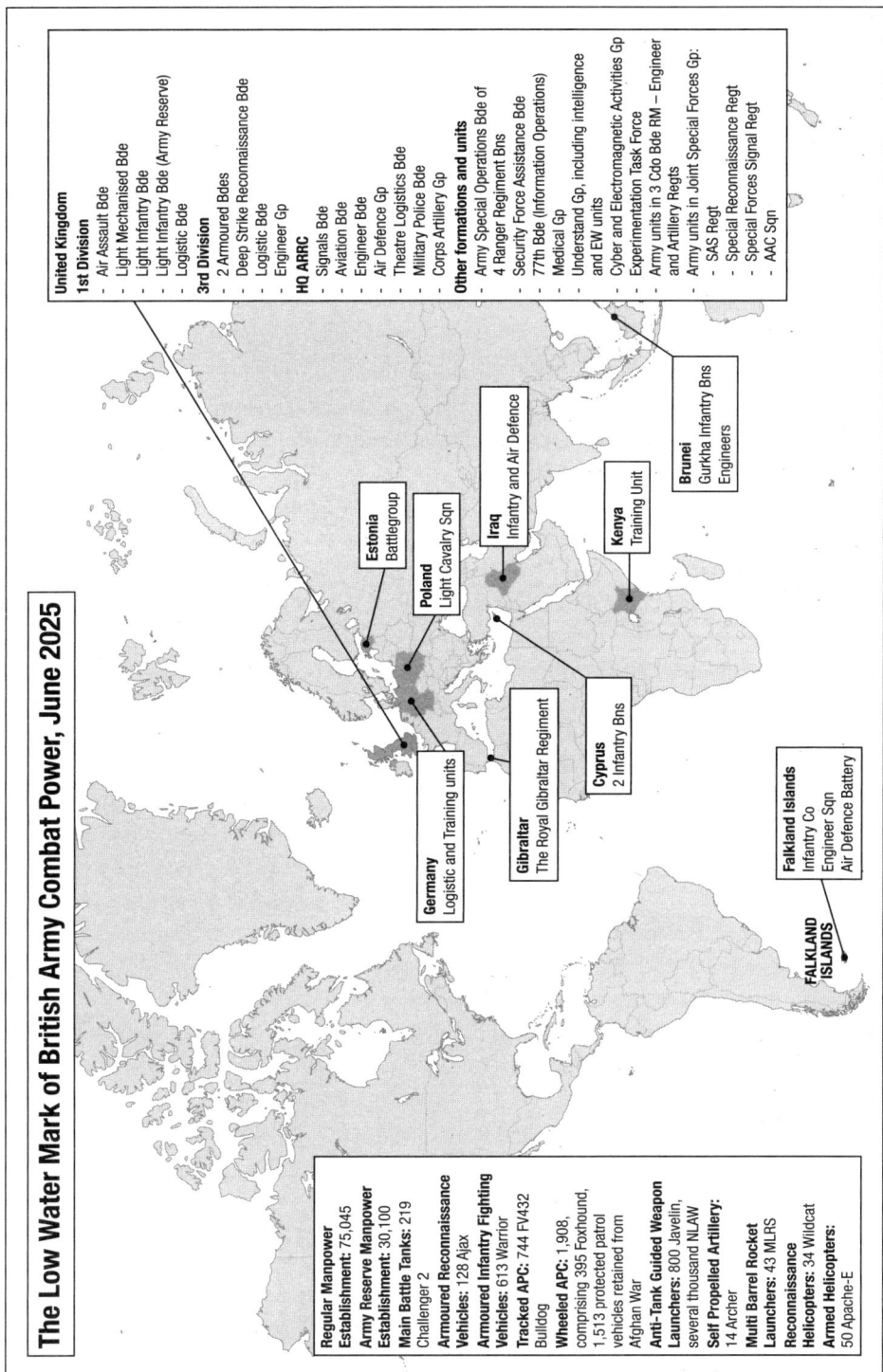

The Low Water Mark of British Army Combat Power, June 2025

United Kingdom

1st Division
- Air Assault Bde
- Light Mechanised Bde
- Light Infantry Bde
- Light Infantry Bde (Army Reserve)
- Logistic Bde

3rd Division
- 2 Armoured Bdes
- Deep Strike Reconnaissance Bde
- Logistic Bde
- Engineer Gp

HQ ARRC
- Signals Bde
- Aviation Bde
- Engineer Bde
- Air Defence Gp
- Theatre Logistics Bde
- Military Police Bde
- Corps Artillery Gp

Other formations and units
- Army Special Operations Bde of
- 4 Ranger Regiment Bns
- Security Force Assistance Bde
- 77th Bde (Information Operations)
- Medical Gp
- Understand Gp, including intelligence and EW units
- Cyber and Electromagnetic Activities Gp
- Experimentation Task Force
- Army units in 3 Cdo Bde RM – Engineer and Artillery Regts
- Army units in Joint Special Forces Gp:
  - SAS Regt
  - Special Reconnaissance Regt
  - Special Forces Signal Regt
  - AAC Sqn

Brunei
Gurkha Infantry Bns
Engineers

Estonia
Battlegroup

Poland
Light Cavalry Sqn

Iraq
Infantry and Air Defence

Kenya
Training Unit

Germany
Logistic and Training units

Gibraltar
The Royal Gibraltar Regiment

Cyprus
2 Infantry Bns

Falkland Islands
Infantry Co
Engineer Sqn
Air Defence Battery

FALKLAND ISLANDS

Regular Manpower
Establishment: 75,045
Army Reserve Manpower
Establishment: 30,100
Main Battle Tanks: 219 Challenger 2
Armoured Reconnaissance Vehicles: 128 Ajax
Armoured Infantry Fighting Vehicles: 613 Warrior
Tracked APC: 744 FV432 Bulldog
Wheeled APC: 1,908, comprising 395 Foxhound, 1,513 protected patrol vehicles retained from Afghan War
Anti-Tank Guided Weapon Launchers: 800 Javelin, several thousand NLAW
Self Propelled Artillery: 14 Archer
Multi Barrel Rocket Launchers: 43 MLRS
Reconnaissance Helicopters: 34 Wildcat
Armed Helicopters: 50 Apache-E

a Soviet attack that seem relevant to the Army's role helping NATO deter and defend against any Russian attack on Europe. With the increased pace of change in the strategic situation and the opportunities and threats from ever-accelerating technological development, there are lessons from successful and unsuccessful changes made by the Army. These topics should also be of interest to civilian defence officials, the defence industry and journalists.

THE STORY ARC

Why does this book's title begin with the phrase 'Rise and Fall'? Because it is the simplest way of explaining that the half century saw the Army's fighting power grow to a high point followed by a plateau; and that its size and relative capability then declined, a decline that has yet to be arrested, let alone turned around.

The book shows how from the mid-1970s, the Army committed many of its troops to supporting the police in Northern Ireland and helped to bring that conflict to an end. The Army was tested against the unanticipated challenges of peace operations in Zimbabwe and the Falklands War. In the 1980s, the Army's fighting power for the possible war between NATO and the Warsaw Pact considerably increased. This was a period of technological and tactical innovation, as well as a revolution in the Army's doctrine and thinking about modern war. These modernized capabilities were tested by a scenario that was unanticipated in the Cold War: Operation *Desert Storm* in Iraq in 1991. The Army's contribution was a considerable success, albeit with the Army's three armoured divisions having to be cannibalized to generate the single modernized, but small, armoured division that fought in Iraq.

Straight after that operation, the so-called Options for Change defence review was driven by budgetary cuts. But the foundations that the Army laid in the 1980s provided a firm base for success in the unanticipated, difficult and complex UN and NATO campaigns in Bosnia. The 1998 Strategic Defence Review had a sound policy foundation and resulted in the Army reorganizing in order to better conduct joint and expeditionary operations, but it was never adequately funded by the unsympathetic Chancellor Gordon Brown. Interventions in 1999 in Kosovo, 2000 in Sierra Leone, 2001 in Kabul and 2003 in Basra were all successful. These again exploited the Army's strengths that had been built from 1981 onwards.

The period from 1990 to 2003 represents a high plateau of military achievement. These successes gave the Army a justified sense of self-confidence. But this led to over-confidence and complacency in the Army, Ministry of Defence (MoD) and British government.

There then followed two decades of descent from this peak of operational effectiveness. This included a continual series of cuts of the Army's budget and troop numbers and mistakes made in Iraq and Afghanistan. These reflected poor leadership by prime ministers Blair and Brown, the rapidly rotating cast of New Labour defence ministers, and senior staff in the MoD. The increasing unpopularity of the Iraq and Afghanistan wars and the apparent lack of success of the US and UK resulted in a decline in political, public and media support for putting British troops in harm's way. This was a slow-burning strategic shock.

From 2010, cuts to defence funding resulting from the 2008 economic crisis, botched equipment procurements and persistent failures to fund sufficient training, stockpiles of ammunition and spare parts all eroded Army capabilities. The cumulative effects of the reductions of the Army's conventional capability by a third in 1991 and 2010, followed by a further decade of decline meant that the Army that began this book with an establishment of 155,000 regular troops, eight armoured and four regular infantry brigades now had an establishment of 75,000 regular troops, two armoured and three infantry brigades – an overall reduction of combat power by more than 50 per cent.

The strategic shock of the 2022 Russian attack on Ukraine forced defence ministers and the government to confront the fact that the Army's capability had greatly reduced – and particularly to recognize the shortages of the essential combat supplies required to fight a high-intensity war. The Army had long told the MoD that of the three British services, it was the least modernized, with much key fighting equipment either obsolete or approaching obsolescence. This 'inconvenient truth' was now undeniable.

In 2025 another strategic defence review was announced by Sir Keir Starmer's new government, and a modest increase of the defence budget was announced in 2025. But without a significant injection of additional money, it is unclear how the decline in the Army's strength and fighting power can be reversed.

Similar stories could be told about the Royal Navy and RAF. But the inconvenient truth was that in 2025, their equipment was more modern than that of the Army. And the Army lacked the support of the shipbuilding and aerospace industries that represented important industrial political lobbies.

APPROACH TO BATTLE

A country can have any number of defence policies, strategies and management plans, as well as rhetoric by its politicians and senior military leaders. But if its armed forces cannot successfully fight, the money spent on them is wasted.

So, the centre of gravity of this book is the British Army's campaigns, operations and battles.[2] The chapters are arranged in a sequence that tells this story. Defence and Army policy and resourcing are important factors. I mention them when there are significant changes or issues. For example, the chapter on the Army's role in Bosnia from 1992 begins with the Options for Change policy review, which reduced the size of the Army. And discussion of Iraq and Afghanistan is interspersed with the many defence reviews that took place between 2001 and 2014. Much of my discussion of Afghanistan centres on the Army's operations in Helmand up to 2014. But I continue the story of Helmand and Afghanistan until 2021, so as to better understand the causes of Britain's strategic defeat.

There is one exception to this linear narrative. Northern Ireland was the Army's longest single campaign during this period, lasting from 1969 to 2007. I have put the chapter explaining Operation *Banner*, as it was called, outside of this sequence. It sits to a flank, as a self-contained story.

Many campaigns, battles and operations are described. But there is not room for all. I also describe major exercises in the 1980s. These were not real battles, but simulated ones in which tens of thousands of British and NATO troops manoeuvred over the autumnal West German countryside. They allowed plans, tactics, deployment logistics and commanders to be tested. So, there was a real fog of war, friction and much pressure on commanders. Many lessons were learned. Exercises were as important to the development of the Army in the 1980s as operations and battles were in other periods, so I make no apologies for their inclusion. I also describe some operations that were planned, sometimes rehearsed, but never conducted. These also generated lessons.

This book does not say as much about the Army's people and its relations with society as do Richard Dannatt's *Boots on the Ground* and Richard Holmes' books, particularly *Dusty Warriors* and *Soldiers*. Instead, it follows the excellent example of Saul David's *All the King's Men* and General Sir David Fraser's *And We Shall Shock Them*, which concentrate on the Army's campaigns and battles, as well as its equipment, training and tactics. It also looks at the Army's interactions with the MoD and British government, sometimes successful, other times failing.

We are all prisoners of our experience. I served in the Army from 1973 to 2010. And my subsequent career in the International Institute for Strategic Studies gave me much contact with the Army. I learned a great deal. And I salute those who soldiered in the operations I describe, particularly the unexpectedly difficult and unpopular wars in Iraq and Afghanistan.

I have refrained from making this book a military autobiography, only occasionally drawing on personal perspectives. Some histories of the Army and memoirs, especially those by senior officers, sometimes read like love letters to the Army. My position is more that of a critical friend. I make many judgements, some positive, some negative. Some conform to conventional wisdom, others contradict it.

I analyze many Army successes and identify success factors. But there were also Army failures. I make no apologies for identifying failures by the Army, MoD and British government that produced sub-optimal outcomes, including avoidable casualties. I don't hide these, nor the key factors that prevented success. I am afraid that the Army's operations in Iraq and Afghanistan fall into the latter category. There were many tactical successes, but from the viewpoint of 2025, both wars saw more failures than successes, although many of the factors that led to strategic failure were outside the Army's control. I know that for those who fought in both wars, particularly those who were wounded, as well as the families of the deceased, these will be very bitter findings.

There is a relevant historical parallel – the fall of France in 1940. Here, superior German strategy, doctrine, morale, training and leadership defeated the French Army. The British Expeditionary Force (BEF) was a very small part of much larger French land forces. The BEF managed to escape destruction by evacuation from Dunkirk. The collapse of the French Army was probably inevitable. But after Dunkirk, the British Army accepted that it had not been nearly as ready for war as it should have been. A remarkable programme of modernization, reinforced by lessons of early failures in North Africa, Greece and Crete, turned what had been a defeated force into the British Army that played a leading role in

D-Day and the Normandy campaign. If the Army had not accepted the mandate to learn the harsh lessons and greatly improve its military capability, it would not have succeeded in 1944–45.

I have covered all the major Army operations, and some smaller operations that have especial significance. But I have not covered all the non-combatant evacuation, disaster relief, engineering, advisory and training operations conducted in that period. For those who participated, I apologize for the omission.

SOURCES

There is a wide range of books on the Army during this period. There are many memoirs from those who took part in the Army's wars, particularly Northern Ireland, the Falklands, Iraq and Afghanistan. At the other end of the telescope are the memoirs of four of the Army's chiefs: Generals Guthrie, Jackson, Dannatt and Richards. These provide an invaluable perspective on the Army in which they served, its operations and the highest levels of planning and decision-making. There are also many historical accounts, particularly of battles and campaigns. These all have invaluable perspectives. In the Select Bibliography I list the books I find most illuminating. There is also much useful material on the internet, including official reports and a selection of videos and TV programmes; these are listed, with the website links at the time of writing.

CHAPTER 1

NAMING OF PARTS

An army exists to fight on land. This chapter sets out to introduce the structure of the British Army, the training of its people and the idiosyncratic system of regimental identity that distinguishes it from many other armies and from the Royal Navy and Royal Air Force (RAF).

Readers who are familiar with the British Army may choose to skip the section on organization. But they may find the sections on training, the regimental system, culture and leadership of interest. Readers may find it useful to read a short piece by the Army that sets out its role, purpose, foundations and employment – the Joint Doctrine Publication *UK Land Power*.[1]

At the heart of the Army's organization is the principle of combined arms warfare. This uses the strengths and capabilities of different fighting arms combined together to achieve an effect greater than the sum of its parts. It can be seen as a lethal version of the children's game Paper, Scissors, Stone.

No single part of the land force can operate entirely independently of other parts. The core components are infantry, necessary to capture and then hold terrain, and armour in the form of tanks that can both combat other armoured vehicles with anti-tank ammunition and provide direct fire support to infantry with high-explosive shells. They are supported by artillery, firing high-explosive shells or rockets that can suppress enemy in defensive positions and destroy infantry in the open. And the enemy can emplace land mines and construct obstacles to stop attacking infantry and armour from moving. These can be breached by combat engineers, who can also lay mines and construct obstacles to assist with defensive operations.

Armies operate in and across terrain. This is infinitely variable and is usually inhabited by people. As terrain changes so do the capabilities of the combat arms. For example, infantry in open country can often be vulnerable to armour, especially when it has insufficient anti-armour capability. In wooded and urban terrain, armour is very vulnerable to infantry. Over such ground, when infantry and armour combine, armour becomes less vulnerable to enemy infantry and infantry supported by armour can exploit their firepower to greatly increase their effectiveness.

HOW IS THE ARMY ORGANIZED?

The British Army is organized into units called battalions or regiments, commanded by lieutenant colonels, aged between 37 and 42, and containing between 400 and 1,000 men and women. The British use the term 'regiment' to describe battalion-sized units of many of its branches. Armoured regiments are equipped with tanks, whilst armoured reconnaissance regiments are equipped with lighter, smaller armoured vehicles, optimized for gathering information and intelligence. Engineers and artillery are also formed in regiments.

Infantry battalions and armoured regiments are usually grouped into brigades – formations of anything from 3,000 to 10,000 troops, commanded by a brigadier. A brigade has a signal squadron to provide brigade communications, but all Army units have many radios for their own communications. Sometimes brigades have direct command of reconnaissance, engineers and artillery, at other times these are centralized at higher levels of command. To match the brigades' capabilities with their mission and the terrain of operations, units are grouped together – an activity called 'task organization'. A battalion or regiment organized in this way is called a battlegroup.

Brigades are often grouped together in a division, commanded by a major general, supported by a divisional signals regiment. Exact organization varied from 1951 to 1992. Divisions usually included armoured reconnaissance, aviation, artillery and engineers, transport, supply regiments, medical and military police units.

The next level of command is the corps, with a lieutenant general in command. Until 1992 most Army units in Germany were part of 1st British Corps (1 (BR) Corps). This had three or four divisions and a wide range of combat support and logistic brigades and units. It had a strength of around 50,000 troops in peacetime, but reinforcements would more than double its strength for war.

Above this sits higher command. In the Cold War all Army units in Germany were part of the British Army of the Rhine (BAOR). And those in the UK were part of UK Land Forces (UKLF). Both were commanded by full generals. After the Cold War, these two commands were merged into Land Command, the Army's command structure further contracting into a single much smaller Army Headquarters as troop numbers fell.

The Head of the Army was the chief of the General Staff (CGS). He would be assisted by the Adjutant General, responsible for personnel; the Quarter Master General, responsible for logistics; and the master General of the Ordnance, responsible for procurement. These were all historic titles, redolent of the previous two hundred years of Army history, but their roles and responsibilities were continually modernized.

CGS would also delegate much responsibility for co-ordinating Army business to an assistant, initially a Vice Chief of the General Staff, later reduced to an Assistant Chief. These officers, the Army's top commanders and a senior civil servant would often exercise their responsibilities through a small committee, the Executive committee of the Army Board. The Board itself was a rarely used mechanism that allowed defence ministers to exercise their constitutional control over the Army.

These mechanisms and appointment titles could seem old-fashioned and bureaucratic. In practice they could often be more flexible and agile. And CGS and his principal subordinates all had a culture of getting out of their offices to see the Army for themselves, gathering invaluable 'ground truth', including by talking to troops.

During this period, there were neither enough resources nor enough people to meet all the Army responsibilities, nor equip it with all the fighting equipment and supplies it would have liked. Juggling resource gaps would never be easy. On top of these challenges, for most of this half century CGS would be the strategic commander of forces supporting the police in Northern Ireland – a major responsibility.

Being CGS was no sinecure. He could have much confidence in his senior Army colleagues, but the effectiveness and support of defence ministers could not be guaranteed, and senior civil servants could often have agendas that diverged from the Army's, particularly the reduction of spending and the centralization of authority away from the Army. CGS had to sustain the confidence of the Chief of Defence staff, the MoD's senior civil servant, the Permanent Secretary and defence ministers as well as the Army's senior leadership and its troops. This required broad shoulders, the ability to think and lead strategically, and rising above the detail to concentrate on the really big issues, where he could make a difference.

ASSEMBLING A UNIT

All these organizations would be useless without people to fill them and employ their weapons and equipment. Army units are organized in a hierarchical fashion. All vary in the detail of organization, weapons and equipment and the detailed rank structure. To bring this to life I use the example of 2nd Battalion, the Light Infantry (abbreviated to 2 LI), an armoured infantry battalion based in Paderborn, Germany in 1994. I wrote a description of the battalion's organization and equipment at that time. I use it to illustrate how a combat unit is assembled:[2]

> 2 LI is equipped to take part in high-intensity warfare as part of an armoured brigade. Armoured infantry are battlefield partners to tanks in armoured regiments.
>
> The most important component of the battalion is the infantryman. Equipped with an SA 80 assault rifle, he is grouped into a fire team of three or four men led by a lance corporal or a corporal (the next step up the promotion ladder). All members of the fire team are capable of engaging targets out to a range of three hundred metres with their rifles.
>
> A corporal is the section commander, responsible for both fire teams. The section lives and travels in the thirty-two-tonne Warrior armoured infantry fighting vehicle, augmented by a vehicle crew of three soldiers, a driver, a gunner and the deputy vehicle commander.
>
> Warrior is two-thirds the size of a tank. In the centre of the vehicle is a squat turret, mounting a machine gun and a 30mm 'Rarden' cannon. The machine gun can engage

infantry and soft targets, as well as suppress bunkers and fortifications at ranges of up to 1,100 metres [3,609 feet]. Targets can be engaged at longer ranges by high-explosive shells from the cannon, which also fires armour-piercing rounds to destroy light armoured vehicles. Commander and gunner have excellent optical sights, with powerful magnification. At night image intensification sights amplify moonlight and starlight several thousandfold.

Despite having armour sufficiently thick to defeat small arms fire, the vehicle is fast and more reliable than any other armoured vehicle in service with the British Army. But it still requires the crew to maintain it regularly. Replacing old, worn track with a new one is a tedious and backbreaking task.

The back of the vehicle contains a rectangular crew compartment for the passengers. There is space for storing equipment, weapons, food and ammunition. Even so a Warrior carrying ten soldiers and a full load of combat supplies is extremely crowded. The infantry whose job is to fight on the ground (who we habitually call the 'dismounts') and their vehicle should be considered as a single fighting system. Much of our training is devoted to integrating both of these components.

A platoon comprises three such sections, each in a Warrior. The platoon commander is a second lieutenant or lieutenant. He and his platoon HQ, who travel in their own Warrior, comprise two sergeants, one his deputy for dismounted operations and one 'Warrior sergeant' who co-ordinates the maintenance, training and husbandry required by the armoured vehicles.

Three of these platoons comprise an armoured infantry company. All of 2nd Battalion, the Light Infantry's company commanders are in their early thirties. A Company commander, Major Jan de Vos, B Company commander, Major Stuart Mills, and C Company commander, Major Rex Sartain, are all experienced and respected officers. Jan de Vos is the only Light Infantryman in the battalion to have war experience, having served as a staff officer in the 1991 Gulf War.

Armoured infantry companies have two captains. One is the company second-in-command, the commander's deputy and responsible both for co-ordinating the company's logistics and for running the company headquarters (HQ). The other officer is the company 'second captain'. Often known as the 'Warrior captain', he oversees the management of the company's fleet of armoured vehicles. If the company commander dismounts to lead the battle on foot, the Warrior captain commands and fights the Warriors.

All companies have a warrant officer as company sergeant major, supporting the commander in many functions, including discipline and administration. The company HQ has two Warrior command vehicles with the same turrets, weapons and sights as the platoon Warriors; the crew compartment is configured as a command post, with additional radios, tables and map boards. The vehicles are crewed by the small company signals detachment commanded by a corporal.

The company also has a small logistic team commanded by the company quartermaster sergeant (CQMS). He and his storemen have a Land Rover and truck which they use to supply the essential commodities required by sustained operations.

All the vehicles and equipment need both maintenance and repair. Many of the simple routine tasks involved are the responsibilities of the soldier, weapon crew or vehicle crew.

The company is invariably accompanied by its affiliated 'fitter section' of two Warrior repair and recovery vehicles crewed by expert tradesmen of the Royal Electrical and Mechanical Engineers (REME). Commanded by a staff sergeant artificer or 'tiffy', they repair the company's vehicles and equipment and can use power winches to recover vehicles bogged in soft ground or stuck in ditches or culverts.

The Royal Electrical and Mechanical Engineers (REME) Light Aid Detachment (LAD) carries out more complex repair tasks. This seventy-strong group of electrical and mechanical engineers is fully committed to keeping the maximum amount of equipment 'on the road'. Our forward repair and recovery capability is invaluable in minimizing the amount of time that the company's vehicles spend 'off the road'.

The battalion has its own combat support grouped in Support Company, commanded by Major Ian Baker. The reconnaissance platoon has eight lightly armoured Scimitar reconnaissance vehicles. Although these look like small tanks, armed with a 30mm cannon and machine gun, they are lighter than Warrior, with thinner armour. The platoon's role is to gain information, and it fights only as a last resort.

The anti-tank platoon has twenty MILAN anti-tank missile launchers. The missile can knock out any armoured vehicles to be found in Bosnia, including tanks, that cannot be destroyed by the cannon of our Warriors. Like LAW 80, it also has a useful capability against bunkers and fortifications. An anti-tank detachment consists of six men in a Warrior with two MILAN systems. Three detachments make up a section, the platoon having three sections.

The mortar platoon gives the battalion its own indirect fire support. It has nine 81mm mortars, each firing an extremely effective anti-personnel bomb with a range of over five kilometres. They can also fire smoke and illuminating bombs. The mortars travel in the ubiquitous FV432 armoured personnel carriers, known universally as '432s', which are little more than steel boxes on tracks. Their fire is directed by mortar fire controllers (MFCs) equipped with laser rangefinders and hand-held thermal sights, who travel in a Spartan, an armoured personnel carrier based on the same chassis as Scimitar. Each MFC party and mortar section is affiliated to an armoured infantry company, although the mortar lines are usually controlled at Battalion HQ.

The signal platoon mans all the vehicles of Battalion HQ. These consist of a 'command' variant of the FV432, equipped with more radios and configured inside as a cramped armoured office. The platoon also has a few Spartan APCs [armoured personnel carriers] and the commanding officer's Warrior.

These men, weapons and armoured vehicles have to be capable of continuous operations for however long it takes the battalion to accomplish its mission. It is essential that ammunition, food, water, spare parts and other supplies reach the companies and platoons as and when they are needed. Obtaining these from dedicated logistic units and arranging distribution within the battalion is the role of our in-house logisticians in Headquarters Company, overseen by the battalion's two quartermasters. Fetching, carrying and delivering these supplies requires a fleet of trucks and fuel dispensers manned by the mechanical transport (MT) platoon.

Headquarters Company is commanded by Major Dave Wroe, the longest-serving member of the battalion. An immensely experienced officer, he and I had served together some years earlier in Northern Ireland, where I had acquired great respect for his logistic expertise and good-humoured common sense. The company also contains a small platoon of cooks from the Royal Logistic Corps and a team of clerks and pay specialists from the Adjutant General's Corps. At this time, women are not permitted to serve in roles involving direct combat, and the only women in the battalion are five clerical staff. The battalion has its own doctor and small medical section, maintaining health in peace and dealing with casualties in war.

Most Army regiments and battalions are organized along similar principles. As units they are all composed of sub-units. The terminology varies, with platoon-sized units sometimes called troops and companies sometimes named batteries or squadrons. The terms used for soldiers often vary. Whilst many regiments have private soldiers, there are other terms. In the infantry these include guardsman, fusilier, ranger and rifleman. Terms used in other arms and services include craftsman, driver, sapper, gunner and signaller.

RECRUITING AND TRAINING

Soldiers joining the Army undergo basic recruit training, to equip them with the skills necessary to survive on a battlefield, to fight and to protect themselves. Common skills imparted to all soldiers include survival, shooting, weapon handling, first aid, navigation, constructing field fortifications and concealment. This period, which lasts for about four months, saw the recruits undergo a great deal of character building and moulding. The key attributes were unhesitating and instant obedience to orders, the ability to work as a team member and the ability to fight.

Neither fighting nor unconditional obedience to orders in life-or-death situations are qualities routinely found in British society. So there is a considerable element of conditioning. Part of this is imparted by training in close order drill, by intensive physical training and by field exercises. Throughout their service, troops are expected to exercise the profession of arms with an unlimited liability to be killed or wounded in the course of their duty.

Once recruit training is completed, recruits move to specialist training where they are taught their role in the arm or service they have joined. For example, signallers are taught to operate communications equipment and the necessary protocols and procedures. Gunners are taught how to operate their guns. Infantry soldiers are taught how to conduct close combat, including attack, defence and patrols. The infantry requires the highest level of fitness in the Army, exceeded only by special forces, so more time is needed to achieve this.

Many soldiers leave the Army after a few years. But those who want to serve for a full career require more training. There are courses for section and vehicle commanders, sergeants, colour sergeants and warrant officers and for those commissioned from the ranks.

It is possible to directly join the Army's middle management by earning a commission at the Royal Military Academy Sandhurst. Attendance depends on passing a test of leadership ability at the Army Officer Selection Board. This uses practical problem-solving and leadership tests to assess whether or not the candidate officer displays the character to lead a platoon or troop of soldiers.

Those who pass join Sandhurst as officer cadets. Cadets are not only taught all the skills taught to soldiers; they also learn and practise leadership skills, using infantry platoon tactics and field exercises as a vehicle for practising combat leadership. After graduating from Sandhurst they are all trained in the role and equipment of the branch that they have joined.

COLLECTIVE TRAINING

Prussian military theorist Carl von Clausewitz outlines two foundations of war: its nature, which remains constant under all circumstances; and its character, which encompasses the varying ways and means by which war is fought. War's nature is inherently human, often chaotic. It is a highly dynamic contest in which opponents are constantly seeking an advantage over one another. Activities which are easy in peacetime can become very difficult in war. There can be much uncertainty, often called the 'Fog of War', fear, stress and physical effort. These factors combine to create friction – the multitude of factors that can interfere with military operations.

Even the best-trained troops have little military value, unless the team they belong to is trained in its role. This begins at the basic level such as the infantry fire team, armoured vehicle crew or gun crew. Training then needs to build up, climbing the levels of command, This is known as collective training. It not only increases the effectiveness of the unit or formation, but also builds teamwork, comradeship and cohesion.

This approach, of course, applies to the way fitness training improves human physical performance; and to practice by sports teams. But the majority of team sports are not lethal. Imagine a game of soccer or rugby in which both sides were allowed to physically attack the other side's players. The fear and uncertainty would rise considerably.

Sport teams without training are easier to beat by a trained team. So armies need to conduct collective training. The Army's method of doing this is described in the next chapter, and its approach to training of specific operations is discussed in the chapter on Northern Ireland.

THE REGIMENTAL SYSTEM

The Army's practice of recruiting and individual and collective training is similar to the approach used by many other armies. But unlike many of them, it has a 'regimental system' that helps foster a sense of identity. This helps promote unit and sub-unit sense of identity, morale and cohesion. It is particularly valuable in battle, doubly so in adversity. Simon Mayall, a cavalry officer who served with three different regiments, the 15th/19th The King's Royal Hussars, the Light Dragoons and the Queen's Dragoon Guards, observed that:

Every troop, squadron or regiment is the best in the Army to those who serve in it. That certainly is how it should feel if an organization is 'cooking on gas'. War and close combat are at the core of the profession of arms, and everything we did was directed at giving the individual the moral and physical courage to hold his place in the line under fire, when every other human instinct might say 'run'. Regimental colours, standards, and guidons, battle honours and regimental days, honours and awards, military and sporting competitions, squadron dances, regimental balls, everything was designed to generate a shared sense of pride, self-confidence, purpose and endeavour.

We expected the officer corps to respond to the call of 'God, Queen and Country' but our soldiers also need that sense of trust and confidence in the organization, their equipment, their leaders and above all each other, to underpin the more esoteric appeals to 'loyalty and duty'. It was a robust time when 'custard soldiers', those deemed to be upset by trifles, were disparaged and tough senior NCOs would exhort the less aggressive officers just to tell the soldiers what to do! 'Good God sir, we are here to defend democracy not to practise it!'

I loved the Army's combination of hard physical exertion, intellectual challenge and camaraderie. I embraced the team spirit, the 'band of brothers' philosophy that made the most tedious or terrifying activities such bonding experiences. It was by no means a 'caste system', indeed the mark of a good regiment and a good mess was precisely its openness and its welcoming hospitality, but it was delightfully 'tribal' in that thoroughly British way that is recognizable, but which at times defies definition.[3]

Regimental identity creates a close connection between the Royal Family and the Army. Every regiment has a 'royal patron' as its head, usually a core member of the Royal Family. There are outliers, such as the Green Howards, whose royal patrol is the King of Norway, and the Light Dragoons, who have as their royal colonel the King of Jordan – who after training at Sandhurst had served with the regiment following his commissioning. Prince Philip and Prince Andrew had served with the Royal Navy, and both had fought in war. Princes William and Harry attended Sandhurst and served with the Household Cavalry, Prince Harry serving in Afghanistan in 2007 and returning for a tour crewing an Apache helicopter.

This factor adds value by reinforcing the moral component. A well-run visit would give many soldiers, officers and family members the opportunity to meet and converse with their regiment's royal patron, something very rarely achieved in other walks of life.

In return the Army provides large numbers of troops to support royal occasions by conducting 'state ceremonial'. This includes providing ceremonial guards on royal palaces in London and Scotland and supporting events such as the state opening of Parliament and visits by foreign heads of state by providing ceremonial guards and escorts by the Household Cavalry Mounted Regiment. Every summer a battalion of Foot Guards, the Household Cavalry Mounted Regiment and the Kings Troop Royal Horse Artillery parades to mark the sovereign's birthday.

As well as the term 'regiment' defining a unit, in many arms and services, the function was also the regiment, for example the Royal Artillery, Royal Engineers, Royal Signals and

Royal Army Medical Corps. But regimental identity is more complex in the infantry and Royal Armoured Corps. In the 19th century the Army was large enough that it was possible to have infantry and cavalry regiments that were directly linked to the counties of the UK. But as the Army contracted, this link became more difficult to sustain. A tipping point was crossed for the infantry when the number of battalions fell below the number of counties.

The Army in 1975 had a regimental system for the infantry and armoured corps that contained a number of different models of regiment, some large, with three or four units bearing a single identity, others small, with an identity confined to a single battalion or regiment. This added value by improving morale and cohesion, particularly at unit level. But it sometimes subtracted value, for example by hindering formation cohesion. However, on the whole, between 1975 and 2005 the system worked, though sometimes imperfectly.

There are many books that explore the regimental system. Many of these are histories of regiments. Many have been written by authors wearing rose-tinted spectacles who are too generous to the regiment concerned, emphasizing its strengths and downplaying its weaknesses.

The British people are intensely clubbable. They take comfort from being in a small group, where people know and trust each other, and from being part of a larger successful group with a distinct and positive identity. My experience was that the sense of identity induced by the strengths of the regimental system was often a powerful contribution to morale. But even more important were the leadership and skills of those in positions of command, from lance corporal to commanding officer. The latter are particularly important, as their leadership and personality can rapidly permeate a unit, shifting the key factors of its culture and behaviour of its people. I explore the role of brigade commanders in Chapter 4.

These factors, as well as training and experience on exercises and operations, powerfully shaped the culture of the Army as a whole, its components, down to fire team and vehicle crew, and its people. It includes attitudes, habits, behaviours and formal and informal traditions that support tactical functions and group identity. The expression 'band of brothers' has real substance. But it should now be 'band of brothers and sisters'.

Another sporting analogy can help. A naval warship's crew is rather like a rowing eight – fit, determined, but effectively under command of the cox. An air force squadron is similar to a motor racing team, where the fitness, stamina and skills of the driver or pilot are supported by a trained, drilled and flexible supporting pit or ground crew.

A team in the Army is more like a rugby team. It requires fitness, stamina and individual initiative as well as the ability to bring together a sum of parts that is greater than the whole, seeking to frustrate its opponent's plans and seize the initiative.

Rugby games often involve accidental injuries. But in war the opposing teams are attempting to kill each other, greatly increasing fear, uncertainty, unpredictability and friction. War is an ugly, vicious, terrifying activity in which group cohesion and morale and the leadership skills of commanders help reduce fear and reinforce the essential shared sense of purpose to overcome the enemy and other difficulties to achieve the mission.

When training, leadership and culture mutually support each other, they can spur ordinary people to do extraordinary things. This has happened many times during the last 50 years. Compared with the majority of other national armies, the British Army sets a very high bar for bravery and merit that qualifies a soldier or officer for an operational award.

Even so, the wars in the Falklands, Iraq and Afghanistan produced many medal winners. Afghanistan, for example, led to the award of the following medals: two Victoria Crosses, four George Crosses, 40 Conspicuous Gallantry Crosses, 211 Military Crosses, 30 Distinguished Flying Crosses, seven Air Force Crosses, 840 Queen's Commendation for Brave Conduct, 13 George Medals, 38 Queen's Gallantry Medals and 42 Distinguished Service Orders.[4]

The current war in Ukraine provides a powerful reminder of the importance of training, leadership and culture in sustaining morale and fighting spirit. When the Russians planned to subjugate the country in a few days, they clearly underestimated these factors. It also reminds us that only soldiers in armies can control ground, by defending or attacking it – as demonstrated by Ukraine's successful defence of Kyiv in early 2022 and its successful counterattacks later that year.

CHAPTER 2

THE CRUCIBLE OF THE COLD WAR (1)

1970–80

Armies that wish to be effective over time must *innovate,* changing themselves to better meet the challenges of future conflict. Even so, wars and operations often turn out differently to an army's best predictions of the future. In this case, the army must *adapt,* changing its capabilities in reaction to the unique circumstances of that conflict.

In the first 70 years of the 20th century the Army had a proud record of adaptation in war. In World War I, the Army went from unsophisticated attritional attacks on the Somme in 1916 to the 'Hundred Days' offensive in 1918. This was an operational-level counteroffensive against the German Army, demonstrating principles of modern combined arms tactics that have endured to this day.

The first three years of World War II saw the Army outfought and often defeated, in Norway, North Africa, Malaya, and Singapore. But it reconstituted the combined arms approach of the Hundred Days and successfully used it at the battle of Alamein and thereafter. With the RAF it developed intimate air/land co-operation and jointly fielded airborne capability that was completely new to both services; and it took amphibious operations with the Royal Navy to new levels, culminating in the D-Day landings in Normandy. It invented three special forces: the Commandos for raiding, the Special Air Service (SAS) and the Special Boat Service (SBS).

After 1945, the unforeseen war in Korea saw a conflict very similar to World War II. The insurgencies in Malaya and Kenya caused the Army to refine its approach to counterinsurgency, especially in tactical intelligence and exploiting captured insurgents. And the 'confrontation' between Indonesia and Malaysia saw new tactics, including exploiting helicopters and mounting covert cross-border raids and ambushes.

Following the diplomatic, political and military debacle of the 1956 Suez Crisis – the Anglo-French attack on Egypt, which was vetoed by the US application of economic power – the then Defence Secretary Duncan Sands masterminded the 1957 Defence Review. This increased the role of nuclear deterrence in British military strategy. Overseas garrisons were reduced, as was the RAF fighter force. National service, which had conscripted young adult males since the end of World War II, was ceased.

The Army began the 1960s adjusting to the ending of conscription. It had substantial forces deployed overseas. As well as in Germany, there were troops deployed in Malta, Cyprus, the Gulf, Aden, Singapore, Malaysia, Hong Kong and Brunei. The defence budget represented 7 per cent of Gross Domestic Product (GDP).

An almost permanent economic crisis during the middle and late 1960s resulted in the Labour government of Prime Minister Harold Wilson conducting three successive rounds of contractions in the defence budget in 1966, '67 and '68. These are often known as the Healey reviews after the then Defence Secretary Denis Healey. All of these reduced the size of the armed forces and their programmes for future equipment, including aircraft carriers and aircraft programmes.

The government declared that it would concentrate the majority of all three services on the defence of Europe. Forces in the Mediterranean were greatly reduced and troops departed from Aden and the Gulf. British land and air forces would withdraw entirely from the Middle East and from Singapore and Malaysia. The only Army forces based 'east of Suez' would be the two brigades in Hong Kong and the Gurkha battalion in Brunei. The Army's reserves were reduced by half and modernized, forming a new Territorial Army (TA).

In 1948 and again in 1954 London had committed to the Brussels Treaty, agreeing to base 55,000 troops in West Germany until 1994. With the withdrawal of troops from 'east of Suez', this became the largest peacetime deployment of the Army and contributed to NATO's deterrence of a Soviet-led attack on West Germany.

This was the basis for the deployment of the British Army of the Rhine (BAOR). Its main combat formation was the 1st British Corps (1 (BR) Corps), the other parts being British forces in Berlin and a small number of logistic and communications units. The four-star general commanding BAOR would in war command NATO's Northern Army Group (NORTHAG). This multinational HQ commanded four national corps running across northern Germany from north to south: 1st Netherland Corps (1 (NE) Corps), 1st German Corps (1 (GE) Corps), 1st British Corps (1 (BR) Corps) and 1st Belgian Corps (1 (BE) Corps).

From its formation in 1949 NATO (the North Atlantic Treaty Organization) had sought to deter a Soviet attack on its member states. Soviet and Warsaw Pact forces had a considerable numerical superiority over NATO forces. Norway, Denmark and West Germany felt particularly vulnerable, to an attack from forward deployed forces in the Soviet Union around the northern city of Murmansk, in East Germany, and across the Baltic Sea in Poland. These had numerical superiority. In an attack with little or no warning they might seize a considerable amount of NATO territory.

NATO employed a 'tripwire' strategy. This planned that any Soviet attack on the alliance's states would trigger a response with nuclear weapons. The initial role of NATO ground troops would be to identify Soviet attacks and their main axes of advance. Their subsequent role would be subordinate to that of nuclear weapons. Conventional ground forces would have the primary role of delaying enemy advances, seeking to canalize attacking columns into 'Nuclear Killing Areas', for attack by tactical nuclear weapons. For the British troops in 1 (BR) Corps in the 1960s, the plan was to fall back from defensive line to defensive line, eventually taking advantage of the major obstacle afforded by the River Rhine.

NATO's strategy required yielding much of West German territory, its industry and citizens to control by Russian occupiers. More problematically, it depended on exploding nuclear weapons over much of the country. Even if these were targeted at Soviet troops in rural terrain as opposed to major towns and cities, exercise, operational research and simulations showed that this would result in millions of civilian deaths. As time went on, the German government and military became increasingly uncomfortable with this. As West Germany provided three of the eight corps stationed in the country, as well as an increasingly capable air force and navy, it had an influential voice within NATO's political and military machinery. It insisted that NATO change its military strategy to one that was much less reliant on nuclear weapons and moved NATO's planned defence to the east, as close to the Inner German Border (IGB) as practicable.

FLEXIBLE RESPONSE, FORWARD DEFENCE – IMPLICATIONS FOR THE ARMY

In 1968 NATO adopted a new strategy of flexible response and forward defence. It sought to deter a Soviet attack by making Moscow think that the costs of any aggression greatly outweighed its potential benefits. If deterrence failed, NATO would use its conventional forces to defend NATO states' territory as far forward as practicable. This aimed to slow down the attack sufficiently to buy time for political negotiations.

Should this fail, or should the Soviets inflict sufficient attrition on the NATO conventional defences for their attack to succeed, NATO had the option to use tactical nuclear weapons. This would have two aims. Firstly, to inflict sufficient damage on the attackers to allow NATO forces time to stabilize the battlefield and to rebuild their defences. Secondly, to demonstrate to Moscow that NATO was in deadly earnest about its defence of Western Europe and might well be willing to escalate the war, including the use of strategic nuclear weapons. NATO hoped that the shock of nuclear use would cause the Soviets to see reason and abandon their attack. This strategic concept was the foundation of the British Army's role in Europe from 1970 to 1990.

For the German, British, US, Dutch and Belgian forces based in West Germany, this meant an increased emphasis on deterring any Warsaw Pact attack, by being prepared to fight a conventional defensive battle in West Germany that yielded as little German territory as possible. No longer would the Northern Army Group fight its defensive battle

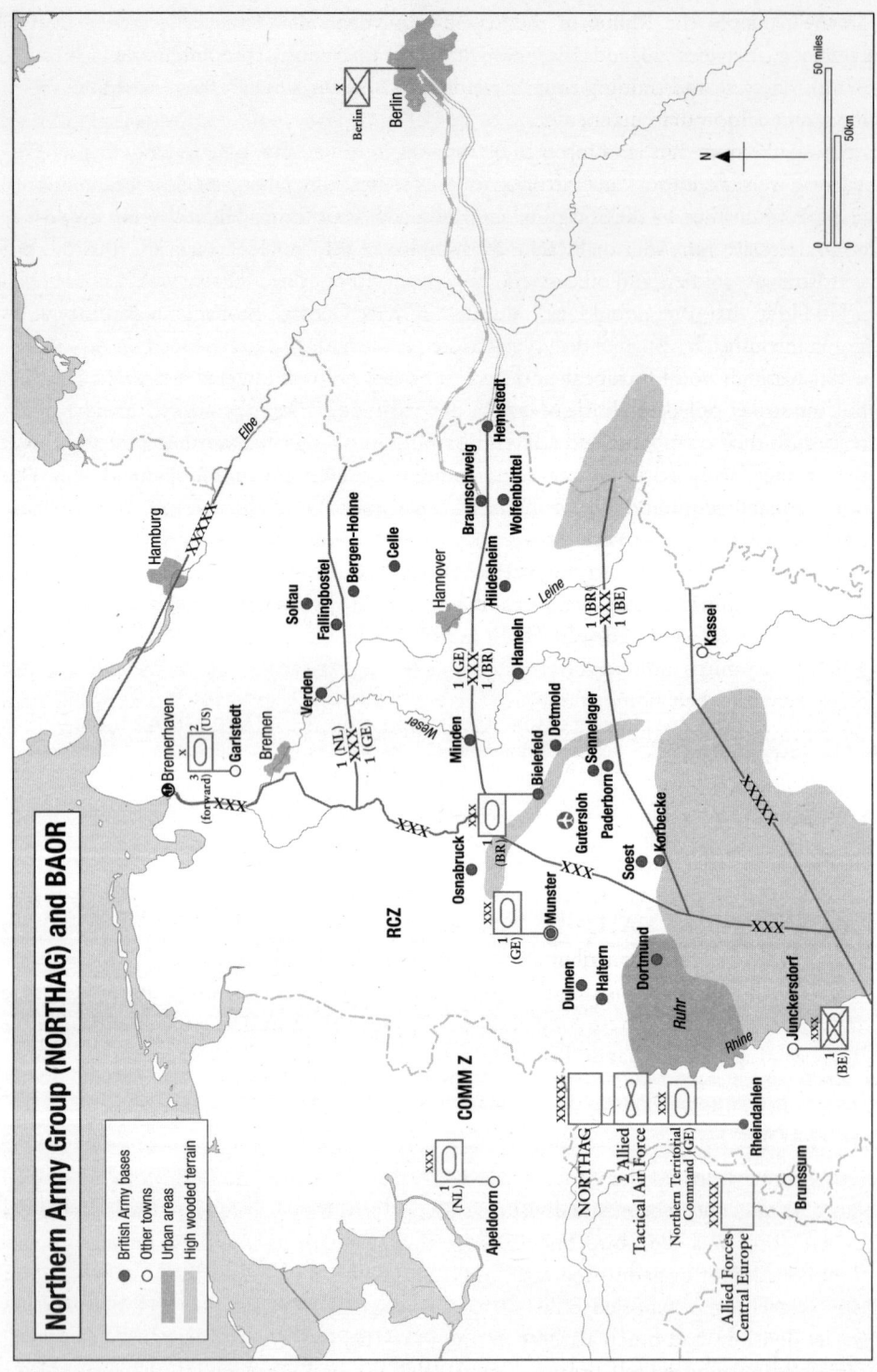

Northern Army Group (NORTHAG) and BAOR

British Army bases
Other towns
Urban areas
High wooded terrain

on the banks of the Rhine, or the Weser, but its forward defences would be west of Hannover, between 43 and 12 miles from East Germany. Throughout the 1970s the Army's doctrine and training concentrated on the tactical level and appeared to be based more on attrition than manoeuvre.

NATO required its land forces to be able to fight for at least a week. After then NATO might have suffered so much attrition that its defences would stand a serious chance of being overwhelmed by the Soviet-led juggernaut. When this happened, NATO would face a stark choice: surrender or escalate by using battlefield nuclear weapons. This did not perturb many soldiers and officers, most of whom either hoped the war would not happen or thought that they would not survive, if it did. Many probably held both views simultaneously.[1]

Increasingly vocal European anti-nuclear groups pointed out that if the initial NATO nuclear strikes failed to shock Moscow into abandoning its attack, Soviet forces might reply with their own battlefield nuclear weapons, possibly escalating the range and size of their strikes. Many British officers considered this a likely possibility, and one which would most probably result in rapid escalation to a nuclear world war. But this did not stop them training as hard as they could to deliver an effective initial conventional defence of NATO territory.

Whilst the British corps was manned in peacetime by professional troops, the other three corps in NORTHAG were all manned by conscripts. The Dutch and Belgian corps only had a limited number of formations forward deployed in Germany, with the rest being based in their home countries. The German corps was at least based in northern Germany. And throughout the 1970s and 1980s it was seen as relatively well equipped.

The British corps had three armoured divisions, each of two armoured brigades of mechanized infantry battalions and tank regiments. Combat support included brigade-sized formations of engineers, artillery and signals contained within the divisions and held at corps level. The priority of the TA was the reinforcement of BAOR.

In the UK there was the 3rd Division, largely comprising air portable light infantry, assigned to reinforce NATO. The 16th Parachute Brigade had a similar role. The Army also provided a major contribution to NATO's Allied Command Europe Mobile Force (Land), including an infantry battlegroup and the framework of the force's communications and artillery, forces that were Arctic trained – as were the Army gunners and sappers of the Royal Marines' 3 Commando Brigade, a formation optimized for amphibious operations.

THE THREAT

East Germany hosted the Group of Soviet Forces Germany (GSFG). This consisted of some 20 tank and motor rifle divisions subordinated to five armies. Directly facing the British corps was the Third Shock Army of four divisions. All these formations and their constituent brigade-sized regiments had many tanks. All the infantry was 'motor rifle', travelling in wheeled BTR APCs or tracked BMP-1 infantry fighting vehicles. Soviet divisions had much artillery. In the 1970s this was mostly towed, but was being replaced by armoured self-propelled guns. Each division also had a battalion of BM-21 multi-barrelled rocket launchers, a modernized version of the famous Soviet Katyusha rocket launcher of World War II.

The corps assessed that a short-notice attack would see the Soviets and the six divisions of their East German allies establish a 3:1 numerical superiority over the eight NATO corps of the Northern and Central army groups in West Germany. If GSFG concentrated its forces on a few selected narrow axes of advance it would be feasible for them to achieve local force ratios against NATO defences of up to 9:1. Such concentration of force had been a key tactic used by the Red Army in its successful offensive in the Great Patriotic War from the battle of Stalingrad onwards.

Also in East Germany was the 16th Air Army of the Soviet Air Force. This outnumbered the forward deployed NATO tactical air forces in Germany by a ratio of about 2.5:1. The Soviet Army was lavishly equipped with anti-aircraft weapons, with its divisions and armies having more than comparable NATO formations. These included the ZSU-23-4 anti-aircraft armoured vehicle with four radar-controlled 23mm anti-aircraft guns as well as a formidable array of anti-aircraft missiles. These factors meant that the corps could not expect the lavish degree of air support that the British Army had enjoyed in the closing years of World War II.

It was often feared by the British and German corps and by HQ NORTHAG that any Warsaw Pact attack on northern Germany might plan to overwhelm NORTHAG by attacking where it was weakest – through the Dutch and Belgian sectors – while mounting sufficient attacks on the German and British corps to fix them in place; more powerful attacks to the north and south of these corps would break up the cohesion of the army group, even resulting in the surrounding and destruction of its two most powerful corps.

CORPS ORGANIZATION AND PLANS

The corps was to defend a sector of northern Germany about 40 miles wide. It lay across the southern part of the North German Plain, bounded in the north by the south side of the city of Hannover and in the south by the northern edge of the Harz mountains, a range of forested high hills. In 1970 it had seven armoured brigades and one mechanized brigade, grouped into three armoured divisions each of two brigades, as well as an engineer regiment, artillery regiment and logistic units. The corps also had two armoured reconnaissance regiments, an artillery brigade, an air defence brigade, a signals brigade and logistic formations.

Armoured brigades had two tank regiments and two mechanized infantry battalions, as well as assigned artillery and engineer regiments and maintenance, supply and transport units. The single mechanized brigade had three mechanized battalions and a single tank regiment. In peacetime the infantry battalions and tank regiments lived separately in different barracks and worked under their appointed commanding officers. But for tactical training and operations they would regroup to form combined arms battlegroups, with tank squadrons joining mechanized battalions, who would donate companies in return. Each battlegroup would also be affiliated to a close support artillery battery, which would be joined by an artillery 'tactical group' comprising the battery commander and his forward observation officers. These would in turn join affiliated companies and squadrons. Often squadrons and companies would themselves gain a troop or platoon of their opposite arm, donating troops and platoons in turn.

This practice of 'battle grouping' was an enduring feature of the Army's approach to organizing for operations and training. Brigades would, as much as they could, practise it in peacetime training, keeping groups as stable as possible over the year. The Life Guards in 20th Armoured Brigade in Detmold habitually exchanged a squadron with 1st Battalion, the Light Infantry, receiving a company in turn, and were supported by the Chestnut Troop, a battery of 1st Royal Horse Artillery. They fondly recalled that they 'went to their parties and they came to the Life Guards' parties'. The regiment had returned to Germany in 1971 from a decade based in the UK and the Far East. Its members found that 'the Army's approach to soldiering had become much more professional over the decade and there was no room for those who failed to adapt, although most made the transition.'[2]

THE TERRITORIAL ARMY AND MOBILIZATION

The Territorial Army and Volunteer Reserve, TA for short, comprised part-time volunteers who trained to join the Army on mobilization. They were rooted in their communities, with company-sized training bases, known as 'drill halls', spread across the country.

Soldiers and officers trained in their spare time, in weekday evenings, weekends and at annual two-week camps. They were paid for every day's training. If they conducted the required minimum amount of training, TA members earned a substantial bonus known as the 'bounty'. The vast majority of personnel in TA units were reservists, but a small number of regular staff would provide a slim backbone for TA units.

The TA numbered over 80,000 reservists and grew to 86,000 troops by the late 1980s. The roles of TA units covered a wide spectrum of Army capabilities, apart from armoured and mechanized units. For example, they provided many of the field hospitals and medical personnel that were needed for war. They provided air defence, engineer and signals brigades to reinforce the corps and the lines of communications.

The majority of TA units had war roles in Germany, assigned to specified formations. There was a close association between the units and their 'parent regular formations'. For example, TA infantry battalions assigned to armoured divisions would plan and train with them, the TA unit HQs deploying on regular command post exercises, as well as the whole battalion taking part in brigade, division and corps exercises.

TA units had a unique atmosphere – often reflecting the community from which they were recruited. And their soldiers and officers would often be drawn from a wider social spectrum than their regular equivalents. Major General John Strawson, then Chief of Staff UK Land Forces, described a visit to a TA unit on a training weekend where he was:

> met by the commanding officer and the regimental sergeant major. Both are regular soldiers but fully part of their TA regiment. You go to the dining hall where all ranks are having lunch, many have motored through the previous night to be there on time. The atmosphere is one of

cheerful comradeship, mixed with an understanding of what service and duty are worth. There is a hubbub of discussion about the 24 hours to come, when adventurous, challenging, necessary exercises are to be done. For the next 12 hours you tour the regiment. In the field in small groups they are practising and perfecting their military skills – planning an airborne drop and an operational task, establishing communications with HQ and passing messages, learning to live and survive in the open, displaying mastery of guns and explosives, reviving a near-dead man (simulated), crossing at night a fast flowing icy cold river with only their customary kit to aid them. You talked to one of the patrols. The sergeant in charge is a London taxi driver, his subordinates a mixture indeed – a doctor, a don, a cabinetmaker, an underwriter. They set about their task quietly determined, full of spirit and enthusiasm, committed to using their leisure to add something to their country's security and their own fulfilment.[3]

Territorial Army units all had plans to mobilize and deploy to their operational locations. In the 1980s these were mostly in Germany (50,000 reservists) but also on NATO's flanks (5,000 reservists) and the remainder mobilized for UK defence. These were regularly tested and constantly updated.

As well as mobilizing the TA, the Army had plans to disband units that would not contribute to the war, to release over 20,000 regular troops to reinforce Germany. Former soldiers and officers would be mobilized to provide battle casualty replacements, the Army anticipating that up to 3,500 seriously wounded troops could need evacuation to the UK for each day of the war.

There were plans for further mobilization for a longer war. These included using training units as the corps of new units for home defence and for training volunteers who might present themselves after the war started. These new units could allow more regular troops to move to Germany.

FIGHTING EQUIPMENT

ARMOURED WARFARE

During the 1960s the Army's key equipment had been modernized. This included the Chieftain tank. In the 1960s and 1970s this was the best-armed and best-protected tank in NATO. Under development since the late 1950s as a replacement for the World War II-era Centurion tank, Chieftain entered service in 1967, over a thousand being delivered to the Army.

Chieftain's gun was optimized to defeat enemy armour at long range. When it was introduced into service in 1967 it had the most powerful tank gun in NATO, with a calibre of 120mm. The gun was rifled, its ammunition coming in three parts: the projectile, a bagged charge of propellant and an initiating cartridge. At this time all the other NATO armies' tanks had guns of 105mm calibre.

Survivability features included a reclined driver's seat, which lowered the height of the tank's forward glacis plate. This and the turret were of specially cast steel, which was contoured to maximize the chances of deflecting an enemy anti-tank shell.

But the Chieftain in British service was one of the least reliable tanks in NATO. Those delivered to the Army came with a poorly performing engine. The tank quickly acquired a reputation for generating huge clouds of smoke that often gave away its position, as well as large numbers of oil leaks. The tank weighed 55 tons and for it to fulfil its potential it desperately needed an improved engine and gearbox.

A series of upgrades were fielded during the 1970s. These improved engine performance and increased acceleration. Even so the tank's reliability remained much lower than required. Several factors contributed to this: the reduced output of British industry in the early 1970s because of industrial action, poor quality control and the parlous state of the defence budget resulting in insufficient spare parts being purchased. These all led to considerable restrictions on armoured vehicle movement. The tool used to implement this was 'track miles', the number of miles that vehicles were allowed to travel. Many unit commanders argued that if the tanks were used more, reliability would improve, and crews would become more experienced in maintaining their vehicles. This was not achieved in the 1970s.

The guns' firepower was improved by fitting a laser rangefinder. This replaced a machine gun used for ranging fire to establish the range to the target. Establishing the range was done almost instantaneously by the laser – with consequent improvement in accuracy and speed of engagement.

The Israeli Army had wanted to replace their Centurion tanks with Chieftains, the tanks' protection being a major factor. Israel had signed a contract to purchase the Chieftain in 1968, only for the order to be cancelled by Prime Minister Harold Wilson in 1969. This decision forfeited the likely reduction in unit cost of the tanks that would have resulted from an increased production run. Chieftains were subsequently sold to Kuwait and Iran, but the majority of armies using Centurion tanks replaced them with Soviet, US and German armour, the Leopard 1 tank being particularly popular with NATO armies.

Since the early 1960s the Army had been seeking to develop a family of light reconnaissance vehicles to replace the existing Saladin wheeled scout vehicle. The new vehicles had to be light and small enough to be transported by air as well as fit between trees in rubber plantations in Malaya. When Belgium joined the project a requirement to move along the tops of dykes in low-lying terrain was added. But the core British requirement was for reconnaissance, with the vehicles to be used by armoured reconnaissance regiments and the close reconnaissance troops and platoons of tank and mechanized infantry.

The resulting Combat Vehicle Reconnaissance (Tracked) CVR(T) family contained two different turreted armoured reconnaissance vehicles: the Scorpion with a 76mm gun and the Scimitar with a 30mm Rarden cannon – a revolutionary design which was smaller than similar contemporary weapons in other armies. The Striker carried long-range Swingfire anti-tank missiles. There was a small APC, the Spartan, a command vehicle, the Sultan, and an ambulance, the Samaritan. And a repair variant was issued, the Samson.

To meet the demanding weight target, the vehicles were made of aluminium, the first British Army vehicles to be so constructed. They were so light that they had less ground pressure than a soldier on his feet, giving them exceptional performance over soft ground and snow. They entered service with a powerful Jaguar 4.2-litre petrol engine. Speeds of about 70 miles per hour were achievable on good roads – resulting in widespread rumours of drivers being stopped by British police for speeding. More importantly the vehicles had higher tactical mobility than any other tracked armoured vehicles, which along with their smaller size would make them harder to hit.

The compact size of the vehicles was evidence of remarkable design. But with a full load of ammunition and combat supplies, as well as a full crew, the interiors of the vehicles were exceedingly cramped. Operating in them for any length of time became an exercise in paring personal equipment, clothing and bedding to a bare minimum and then shrinking it again. By the mid-1970s, both corps reconnaissance regiments were fully equipped with CVR(T) and a multitude of different roles were found for the vehicles across the Army.

The vehicles were an export success, particularly the Scorpion reconnaissance vehicle, which many other armies employed as a light tank. By the mid-1980s, over 1,800 were in service and the Belgian Army had over 700. Vehicles were also in service with the armies of Botswana, Brunei, Chile, Honduras, Indonesia, Iran, Ireland, Jordan, Malaysia, New Zealand, Nigeria, Oman, the Philippines, Spain, Tanzania, Thailand, Togo, the United Arab Emirates and Venezuela, making the CVR(T) the most widely exported British armoured vehicles family ever.

The corps' infantry had previously travelled in wheeled APCs, but during the 1960s, they were issued with the new FV432 tracked APC. A very simple design – essentially a steel box on tracks – it had a similar appearance to the contemporary US Army M113 armoured personnel carrier but had greater protection. The 432, as it was universally known, was designed for a crew of two, with ten passengers – giving it greater internal volume than the M113. Battlegroup commanders found that 432s had sufficient cross-country mobility to keep up with British tanks, improving tactical options. By 1971 all mechanized battalions had been equipped with 432s, including variants that carried mortars and Wombat recoilless anti-tank guns.

Many 432s were used as support vehicles. These included variants for command posts, signals, mortar-locating radar, artillery command posts, repair and recovery and ambulances. The engineers' FV432s could tow a special plough for laying mines. Armoured regiments were also issued with the FV438, which fired Swingfire long-range anti-tank missiles. Over 2,500 432s and their variants served with the Army through the Cold War and beyond.

At this time, infantry platoons were relatively well armed with short-range anti-tank weapons, the 66mm US light and anti-tank weapon and the 84mm Swedish Carl Gustav recoilless rifle. Against static vehicles, the weapons had a reasonable chance of achieving a hit out to 300 metres but accuracy against moving vehicles was reduced. In practice this meant that infantry platoons using these weapons would have little effect against moving enemy armour beyond about 200 metres. And firing both weapons created a large backblast that meant they could not be fired from inside bunkers or rooms. So, infantry could only fire them from relatively exposed positions, increasing their vulnerability.

In the 1970s, longer-range infantry anti-tank weapons were limited to the Wombat recoilless gun. This was fitted with a spotting rifle and had a theoretical capability to engage static targets at ranges of up to 2,000 metres. Its 120mm HESH ammunition could destroy any contemporary Soviet tanks, but as the ammunition had lower velocity than high-velocity tank rounds, the Wombat's ability to hit moving vehicles was reduced under field conditions to 600–800 metres. The size of the gun meant that it could not easily be protected from artillery fire by trenches or bunkers. Its back blast was much greater than that of the platoon weapons, making it even more difficult to site and to protect its crew. Infantry commanders considered it unlikely that Wombats would last for long against any all-out Soviet assault. Battalions had only a handful of Wombats – usually two or three per company.

For most of the 1970s these limitations of the infantry's anti-tank weapons meant that in practice infantry platoons and company positions would struggle to attack enemy armoured vehicles more than 300 metres away. This greatly limited the ability of infantry battalions and companies in defensive positions to interfere with advancing enemy armour.

ARTILLERY

The FV432 chassis was also used as the basis of a self-propelled gun, the Abbot. This had the advantage of logistic and training commonality with the mechanized infantry. But it mounted a gun of 105mm calibre. As Abbot was being rolled out to the artillery in the mid-1960s, many other NATO armies were purchasing US M109 self-propelled guns with a 155mm gun. This fired a heavier, more lethal shell over a greater range. The British purchased these too, initially equipping half their close support artillery with the heavier system.

The corps employed two other US self-propelled guns, the M107 175mm self-propelled gun and M110 203mm howitzer, both used to engage long-range targets. These were complemented with batteries of the US-supplied Honest John short-range unguided missile, primarily intended for delivering US-owned tactical nuclear warheads.

At the beginning of the decade the corps' organic air defences comprised the Thunderbird radar-guided anti-aircraft missile and the World War II-era Bofors 40/70 gun. Both were relatively immobile weapon systems, and neither was thought to have a high hit probability against the modern fighter bombers that were increasingly entering service with the Soviet Air Force.

Development of the Rapier anti-aircraft missile began in 1960. It entered service in 1971. It was optimized for the attack of low-flying jets. Unusually for missiles of that time, it was manually guided by an operator and had a direct fuse, rather than a proximity fuse. It was designed to be very accurate, and there was very high confidence that artillery gunners would be able to hit all the aircraft that were engaged. The system incorporated a warning radar and could be transported in two Land Rover vehicles.

COMBAT CLOTHING

There was one area where the Army led NATO and many other armies – its combat clothing. In the 1960s it wore olive green combat clothing, NATO nations having earlier agreed that their armies' fighting uniforms would share that colour. But at the end of the decade the British unilaterally decided that they would break with NATO policy and adopt a camouflage-patterned combat uniform. This was driven not by operational effectiveness, but by a desire to improve recruiting, by making soldiers appear more distinctively modern. However, trials in the early 1970s showed that that the camouflage pattern also improved concealment, especially for troops in woods, jungles and hiding in hedgerows.

A four-colour pattern of dull yellow, lime green, dark brown and black was devised, all printed in irregular blobs of colour. Close up the pattern appeared an abstract simplification of the British terrain, but from any distance, the eye simplified the pattern into an irregular series of dark and light splodges. This made it much more difficult to distinguish soldiers in woods, hedges and jungle.

The pattern was called Disruptive Pattern Material, universally known by its abbreviation – DPM. The British were the first major army in the world to adopt a camouflage pattern for their combat uniform. Throughout the next 30 years an ever-increasing number of armies would follow suit. The British DPM pattern would be adopted by other armies, including those of Indonesia and the Netherlands.

Another item of Army uniform increasingly widely adopted was the Army's woollen sweater. Made of heavy duty wool with reinforcing patches on the elbows and shoulders, the 'woolly pully' was widely worn in barracks and the field. Its simplicity, flexibility and comfort led to the design of the sweater being adopted by the Royal Navy and RAF. The design was also increasingly adopted by a wide range of other armies and police and security forces.

Even so there were weaknesses in the Army's clothing. Most troops were not issued with any waterproof clothing. And both socks and gloves were knitted from cheap polyester, which performed poorly in cold and wet weather.

TRAINING FOR WAR

1 (BR) Corps was the focus for the Army's training and thinking. It had to plan and prepare for a high-intensity defensive battle against an attack led by the armoured and mechanized formations of the GSFG. Training for this became the principal activity of all the units in the corps. Some of this took place throughout the year; other activities were seasonal, resulting in distinct yearly and multi-yearly rhythms of activity.

UNIT TRAINING

The corps had a small national training area at Soltau as well as access to the large NATO ranges at Bergen-Hohne and Munsterlager in north Germany. These allowed artillery and armoured regiments to practise live firing at up to squadron and battery level. On behalf of NATO, it managed the Sennelager training area; this was optimized for infantry, allowing field firing at platoon and company level, both for dismounted infantry, and for live fire manoeuvre with armoured vehicles.

One of the strengths of the British Army was its approach to the use of live ammunition. It insisted that all soldiers could effectively employ their personal weapon, be it rifle, machine gun or pistol. Every soldier had to pass an annual personal weapon test, and the infantry had a culture of spending as much time on ranges as practicable. The artillery and armoured corps with their more powerful guns needed bigger ranges. As their ammunition was much more expensive than small arms ammunition, it would be expended in an annual firing period, often known as 'range camp'. The climax of this would be firing under simulated battle conditions. For example, whole armoured squadrons would fire their tank guns on large ranges that allowed them to practise advancing, defending and withdrawing as they might in war. Artillery batteries and regiments would rehearse the kind of missions they would be assigned in war.

Known as 'field firing', this type of tactical training had a level of intensity and ambition greater than that displayed by the majority of other armies. It was enabled by the infantry, armoured corps and artillery all training their officers to plan, conduct and supervise field firing. The use of live ammunition created noise, physical impact and degrees not only of fear and stress, but also of sheer excitement, that were absent from tactical training against an enemy simulated by other troops.

Several times in my career I took part in very ambitious and exciting field firing exercises. At Bergen-Hohne, for example, my infantry company climbed onto the tops of tanks that advanced for several miles, the lead vehicles firing as they went. One of the most ambitious live firing exercise I participated in was at Sennelager, where my battalion organized a company live firing attack. While US Air Force jets attacked the simulated enemy position with cannon fire, the battalion flew by helicopter. With the simulated enemy now suppressed by live mortar and artillery fire, the company advanced. As it closed with the enemy its own machine guns and Milan missiles provided fire support. And then the infantry conducted close assaults on the enemy, where the all-enveloping sound of machine-gun fire and the crump and shock waves of grenades exploding in simulated enemy trenches created a real sense of momentum. In the immediate aftermath of the exercise, all the participants, from the dirty and sweaty infantrymen to the mortar and artillery fire controllers, to the officers who organized the exercise, shared a real sense of achievement and mutual confidence – in their weapons, themselves, the battalion and its supporting artillery. Exhilarating does not begin to describe the experience.

In the Cold War, it seemed that no other NATO armies had either the ambition or the necessary competence to conduct such demanding manoeuvres with live ammunition. Indeed, to the present day there are many armies who apply such rigorous training only to their elite forces. Nowhere was this training more evident than in Canada. Previously the Army had conducted large-scale training for armoured warfare in the vast, empty deserts of Libya, deploying battlegroups there for field firing, drawing on a stockpile of tanks and other *matériel* held in the country. Army training in Libya ceased abruptly in 1969 after a coup. A substitute location was found at the vast Canadian forces base at Suffield in Alberta, which could be used for live firing armoured manoeuvre training. In July 1972, the 4th Royal Tank Regiment became the first battlegroup to exercise on the vast training area, seven times the size of Salisbury Plain, a larger manoeuvre area than any other the British had access to.

The British Army Training Unit Suffield (BATUS) had an area of 2,700 square kilometres, about the size of the county of Lincolnshire. The very harsh Canadian winter created Arctic conditions, so between May and October up to seven armoured and mechanized battlegroups would train on the enormous training area at Suffield, spending a month on the bleak prairie conducting demanding exercises with live ammunition – combined arms training conducted at a level equalled by very few other armies.

BATUS was a centre of excellence for armoured warfare, although never designated as such. Exercises there produced armoured regiments and mechanized infantry battalions that were well trained to conduct combined arms warfare at battlegroup level and below. Occasionally battlegroups performed less well at BATUS than was expected. This was often, but not always, fatal to the commander's career prospects.

It is hard to describe the value of BATUS to those who have not participated in the training. I had the privilege of commanding an armoured battlegroup there. After a month on the prairie, I wrote that the exercise required the battalion:

> to train on the Canadian prairie as the framework of an all-arms battlegroup of more than two hundred vehicles and twelve hundred men. Formed around Battalion Headquarters, two armoured infantry companies and our recce platoon, the battlegroup included two squadrons of tanks from the Queen's Dragoon Guards, our affiliated artillery battery, engineers, logistic troop and reconnaissance helicopters. All training was conducted with live ammunition (of which a prodigious amount would be expended) against a sophisticated target array.

The aftermath of the Gulf War, the reduction of the Army after the Cold War and the battalion's Northern Ireland tours meant that this was the first time the battalion had achieved a concentrated period of all-arms war fighting training since 1990. The battlegroup spent a month on the vast and desolate prairie, mastering individual and collective skills and living in the harsh arid environment, little dissimilar to a desert. The single component of the battalion least prepared or 'worked up' before the exercise had been Battalion Headquarters. To put this right required the replacement of one officer who was not meeting the demands of his appointment.

I spent a lot of time during the first two weeks on the prairie training the headquarters and myself in the critical functions of command and control, without which the battlegroup could not function. We achieved a great deal and battalion HQ improved beyond all recognition. It had to climb a steeper learning curve than the other components of the battlegroup, but on the final part of the training, Exercise *Gazala,* everything suddenly seemed to gel. This exercise was a continuous six-day operation in which the battlegroup fought eight separate battles, including all the phases and operations of war that might be required of it.

We all learned a great deal about war-fighting tactics, our machines and ourselves. I was delighted with the way everyone thrived on the challenge, working extremely hard through the sweltering heat and choking dust. The exercise had thoroughly tested all parts of the battalion and all had passed with flying colours.[4]

FORMATION TRAINING

Just as important as battlegroup training in Canada was the training of formations: brigades, divisions and the corps itself. This required three other components to be trained: the commanders and staffs of the HQs, the Royal Signals units responsible for formation communications and the formations themselves.

The corps was able to exercise over the West German countryside, where it would defend against attacking Soviet forces. Areas over which this could occur were known as '443 areas' from the number of the BAOR form that was used to apply for such training. Throughout most of the year exercises were limited to movement of vehicles on roads and tracks and to infantry moving by foot across country. But each autumn, after crops had been harvested, armoured vehicles would be allowed to manoeuvre across country. This allowed armoured and mechanized units and formations to exercise at battlegroup, brigade, division and corps level.

Throughout Germany, the months of September, October and November would see large-scale corps and divisional exercises, accompanied by air force exercises. Together these simulated the air/land battles that might have occurred if the Cold War had turned hot. These could last a fortnight, a month or six weeks. Brigade and divisional exercises might begin with a period of unit tactical training, followed by increasing the level of operations. The exercise season would begin in early September with warm balmy days, but as the autumn unrolled nights would get longer and colder and sunshine would increasingly be overtaken by rain, mist and fog. Troops could leave barracks in the golden warmth of early September and return in October in distinctly autumnal weather.

Companies, squadrons and batteries would spend much time in hides, usually in woods. On sunny days these could be glorious places to live, thronged with wildlife and wild garlic. In the rain they could be dull and depressing.

HQs, communications and logistic units would often conceal themselves in farms and barns. In war, units would have made much more use of urban terrain to hide. In peacetime, German farmers could be persuaded to share some of their barns, not least as they would be paid a modest rent, but it was virtually impossible to displace businesses from the industrial buildings, garages and warehouses that would be useful for units in war.

Most exercises would take place in the sector that the corps planned to fight over. These would become rehearsals of assigned missions, allowing the plans to be tested against a live enemy. So as to ensure that this did not lead to over-familiarity and complacency, or provide too many clues to Warsaw Pact intelligence, a proportion of exercises were conducted outside the corps area.

There was a regular programme of staff rides and command post exercises and a high level of field training, with an objective of a complete division exercising every year and a corps field exercise every fourth year. This included not only troops based in Germany, but also regular and TA units based in the UK that were assigned to reinforce the corps.

1 (BR) Corps had a formation exercise cycle. Its principle was that each year one of the corps' divisions would conduct a field training exercise (FTX). Often this would include a

brigade from another division acting as enemy forces. Usually, TA units assigned to the division would deploy to Germany to take part. And units from other nations' corps would normally deploy to join the exercise. Reciprocating, British units or brigades might well take parts in other corps' field exercises.

There was also an annual corps-level training programme. It would begin with signals exercises where the corps signal brigade would deploy its signals regiments. Every summer there would be a corps command post exercise (CPX) where the corps HQ would deploy to field sites, supported by the signal brigade. The corps HQ would then be tested in commanding a simulated battle. For this the subordinate HQs of all the corps formations would provide 'lower controls', representing the information flow that they would generate in war. This would require several hundred officers and soldiers to gather in a large gymnasium in British barracks. Similar but smaller command post exercises would be used at all levels from division down to unit.

Corps exercises took place in 1980 and 1984, with most of the corps deployed into the field, apart from units deployed to Northern Ireland or training at BATUS. Regular units and formations based in the UK with a war role of reinforcing the corps would travel from the UK through the Low Countries to Germany by sea, air or both, as would assigned TA units. This allowed the mobilization and movement of units along the strategic line of communication across the Channel and through the Low Countries and across the Rhine into the corps area and forward to divisions and brigades.

In addition to this constant training, units and formations studied the ground over which they planned to fight. At least once every year unit commanders would visit the terrain and consider the operations they would have to conduct in war. Sometimes field exercises would take place over the very same ground. And often command post exercises would simulate the real plans over the expected terrain of operations.

An officer of the Queen's Regiment, Mike Reynolds, had served in Germany in 1958 as adjutant of an infantry battalion, whose planned battle positions had been on the west bank of the River Rhine. By 1964, when Reynolds commanded a mechanized infantry company, the planned defensive line had moved west along the River Weser. Commanding a mechanized battalion in 1971, he planned to fight the main defensive battle along the River Weser, some 30 miles from East Germany. He observed that the corps 'still trained for nuclear war, but it was felt in the higher echelons that, if we could hold the Soviets conventionally for a reasonable period, commonsense would prevail and they would draw back, rather than risk a nuclear exchange.'[5]

In 1975–76 Reynolds was commanding 12th Mechanized Brigade. He saw one of his prime roles as ensuring that the brigade was 'well trained for its wartime role and that our general deployment plans were thoroughly sound and understood – at least by all the senior ranks.' By then the main defensive position of the 2nd Armoured Division had moved to east of the River Leine. Together with his chief of staff, Major Mike Regan, they reconnoitred:

the whole brigade position east of the Sibesse Gap, blocking one of the main routes for an advancing Red Army. There with my chief of staff, we sited every minefield, battlegroup, combat team and artillery gun position together with their alternative positions. We pretended we were on tactical exercises without troops doing this, but I have little doubt that Soviet agents were monitoring us. Many years later, after the collapse of the Soviet Union, I was able to visit the former East Germany and drive towards and through what had been my brigade position, I was delighted to find that we would have presented the Soviets with a major problem, providing that we had reached our positions in time, had been given time to prepare them and had been supplied with sufficient ammunition.[6]

This high level of training activity combined with regular study and refinement of operational plans tested both tactical doctrine and the capabilities and plans of the corps from company, battery and squadron level, through all the intermediate levels of command to the corps itself. Commanders felt that they had a good understanding of the ground over which they expected to fight. And units and formations were constantly learning lessons about their effectiveness and how it might be improved.

It also led to a very high degree of mutual understanding within brigades and divisions. This would be disrupted by two factors. The armoured corps, artillery, engineers and logistic corps had most of their units in Germany. For these branches of the Army, Germany became the overriding way of life; they developed corporate expertise of the approach to forward defence practised by the armoured formations in Germany. This could sometimes lead to boredom and complacency, but overall, the advantages outweighed the disadvantages.

But the infantry was different. Only about a dozen of the Army's 55 infantry battalions were based in the corps – just over 20 per cent. The Army rotated infantry battalions through various different roles and locations. For the majority of the Cold War this meant that battalions might spend perhaps three or four years in the corps. It took them time to convert from light to mechanized infantry, often only reaching full effectiveness after a year in role. Armoured and mechanized formation commanders who came from the armoured corps constantly complained that the infantry had a shallower overall understanding of armoured warfare than the rest of the Army. The infantry sometimes displayed a resulting inferiority complex.

From 1970 onwards, operations in Northern Ireland suddenly resulted in large numbers of the corps' units being deployed to operational tours in Northern Ireland. As well as infantry battalions, which were the unit of choice to operate in the most dangerous areas, the corps provided artillery and armoured regiments to the province to act as infantry, and engineer and aviation squadrons. This had positive and negative implications. It provided an operational focus with a 'live enemy' that was impossible to replicate in peacetime training. Soldiers and commanders were tested and grew in confidence, particularly the young corporals, sergeants and junior officers who were tested on streets and in the fields of the province. On the debit side, preparation and leave after the tour would occupy eight or nine months. This was disruptive to brigade cohesion, but most formation commanders considered that the advantages of Northern Ireland Service outweighed the disadvantages.

READINESS

The corps planned that, in the worst case, it would have to be ready to transition from peace to war in a maximum of 48 hours. Achieving this in two days would be a formidable challenge. Many formations and units were based outside the corps area of operations. For example, much of the 1st Armoured Division was based in the I (GE) Corps sector, with two brigades' worth of combat power based in Hohne, Fallingbostel and Soltau. And German units were based inside the corps area, including a German armoured brigade based in Augustdorf in the middle of the corps rear area. Co-ordinating the movement of British and German units heading in opposite directions would be difficult and a potential source of friction and delay, even before any German civilians took to the roads and autobahns as they attempted to flee the fighting. At the same time, wives and children would be evacuated on civilian and military aircraft returning to the UK from Germany.

Units in Germany had to be capable of no-notice rapid deployment into survival areas where they would disperse and seek to conceal themselves in hides. The ability to do this would be tested by Exercise *Active Edge*, where units would be given a few hours to return married troops to barracks and then move to a local wood to camouflage their vehicles and weapons. Sometimes this would be ordered by the formation HQ. On other occasions rapid deployment would be assessed by a NATO inspection team. Failure to correctly deploy in time could damage the careers of commanders found to be at fault.

THE ARMY'S LIFE IN GERMANY

Lieutenant General Sir Christopher Wallace served in Germany as a battalion, brigade and divisional commander. He describes life in the BAOR during the Cold War:

It was not our job to worry about preparing to fight a war which privately we feared we might not win. On the contrary, the better prepared the better trained and the more professional we were, the more likely – or so we were told – that NATO's strategy of deterrence would succeed. War would not be required. And so we trained hard on exercise areas such as Soltau and Sennelager, to hone our individual and collective military skills. There were also frequent exercises entitled 'Quick Train' and later 'Active Edge' to test our preparedness at all times of the day and night, to move swiftly from our barracks to predesignated deployment areas.

Such activities all added to a prevailing sense of competitiveness, in which battalions and their commanding officers tried to be the best in the brigade, brigades to be the best in the division, and divisions vied to be the best in the corps. The annual exercise cycle involving command post exercises in the early part of the year and full-blown exercises with troops in the autumn, both established in destroyed reputations. To manoeuvre armoured formations around the battlefield successfully was perceived to be the acme of military skill. Thus – or so it was thought – aspiring generals had to be posted to Germany if they were to stand a chance of reaching the top.

But there were compensations. The married men enjoyed living allowances, better quarters and the quality of life which led some later to marry and settle in Germany. There was also plenty of opportunity for single men who were so minded to engage in sport, travel and adventurous training.[7]

Just as it had done in India and throughout the British Empire, the Army put down roots in Germany. Service there allowed for wives and families to accompany their husbands. (The Army in the 1970s was overwhelmingly male and the few female soldiers were required to retire on marriage.)

There was an archipelago of barracks, garrisons, logistic installations, ranges and British-run training areas, of which those at Soltau and Sennelager were the largest. At the height of the Cold War there were the best part of 200,000 British troops and civilians based in Germany. The largest group was the 55,000 troops in the corps, with another 3,000 in Berlin and about 12,000 airmen in RAF Germany. The remainder were civilian employees, including clerks, accountants, administrators, schoolteachers and many family members. There were schools for 33,000 children, British shops and a network of Army buses providing basic public transport.

Families' housing was largely in flats, with some officers in houses. These were often better maintained than the many houses in married quarters in the UK. And total take home pay could often be larger in cash terms than in the UK, due to a local overseas allowance designed to make up for the exchange rate and additional costs of living overseas. Moreover, the 'status of forces' agreement with the Bonn government exempted many goods from German taxes. This meant that many items including alcohol, cigarettes, cameras, consumer electricals, motorbikes and cars were significantly cheaper than in the UK.

For some soldiers and officers this made service in Germany attractive. For others these factors were not sufficient to overcome the downsides of living in Germany, including physical separation from friends and families and the language barrier. These factors particularly bore on young soldiers and wives, who could often suffer from deep homesickness.

Attitudes could be greatly influenced by the local geography of the archipelago of barracks and married quarters. Some garrisons such as Munster and Paderborn were based around large towns, but others such as Bergen-Hohne and Fallingbostel were completely artificial communities sited on the edge of a large NATO training area. A further factor was the standard of the barracks. Many were well found, housed in former Wehrmacht barracks, but others were less satisfactory, being camps originally constructed from temporary huts thrown up decades earlier.

INNOVATION AND EXPERIMENTATION

Throughout the 1970s and 1980s the Army tried out new ideas to increase the corps' effectiveness in this most demanding of potential battles. For example, the Army closely followed the US Army's fielding of attack helicopters. The Vietnam War saw the US Army rapidly field a purpose-built attack helicopter, the Hueycobra; and in 1972, it used the newly developed tube-launched, optically tracked, wire-guided (TOW) anti-tank missile to attack North Vietnamese armoured vehicles. At the same time the US Army conducted extensive trials to examine an anti-tank role for Hueycobra attack helicopters armed with TOW missiles. This saw Hueycobras attacking groups of German tanks, protected by US anti-aircraft tanks. It indicated that helicopters concealing themselves in folds in the grounds or behind trees and buildings could ambush advancing armoured vehicles.

The trials were widely briefed to the Army, arousing great interest. The Army ran Exercise *Hell Tank* to study the potential value of firing anti-tank missiles from helicopters. This showed that tactically sited helicopters could successfully attack tank columns moving in the open, sometimes achieving kill ratios of over 40:1. It also suggested that against static tanks in defensive positions helicopters flying forward were very vulnerable,

As a result, the Army Air Corps' Scout helicopters were fitted with SS11 anti-tank missiles and a concept for attacking Soviet armour was developed. Known as HELARM, it was convincingly demonstrated in the field. For example, I attended a September 1974 briefing to the officers of 4th Guards Armoured Brigade. After a presentation in a village hall, the audience were taken to the edge of a village overlooking open agricultural land surrounded by low wooded hills. We were told that a squadron of Scout helicopters armed with SS11 missiles were concealed in positions from which they could attack us with missiles. We were invited to find them. Even using binoculars no one could. The helicopters then rose above the trees they had been hiding behind and switched on their landing lights. All six were in excellent firing positions. They would have been much harder to detect by commanders of armoured vehicles, particularly if they were closed down with vehicle hatches shut and peering through narrow slits of armoured glass.

Another example was the evaluation of the unconventional Swedish S tank. This was the Swedish Army's main battle tank. It was radical in design having no turret but a fixed gun that was aligned on the target using the tracks and suspension. At the time there was a significant body of British officers who considered that such a turretless tank would make a very useful contribution to anti-armour defences, particularly in the corps sector's abundant and wooded terrain. Still serving were some senior officers who had fought in tanks in Europe in 1944–45, where the German Army had made very effective use of self-propelled turretless *Jagdpanzers* in exactly this role.

So, in 1973 an armoured squadron of the Royal Tank Regiment was equipped with S tanks. Having trained for a month in Sweden the squadron took part in firing trials and two-sided battles in which a force of S tanks and Chieftains opposed a force of Chieftains. The Army concluded that the S tank had performed well and was in many respects an ideal defensive weapon, but the lack of turret meant that it would be much less effective in the type of offensive operations the British planned to fight. The S tank was not purchased.

But Swedish Army staff attached to the British squadron saw things differently. Their official report is now declassified.[8] The Swedes saw British tank crews as less well trained than their own and displaying a much lower standard of tactical proficiency than Swedish crews. They also observed that at the end of the tactical trials 90 per cent of the S tanks were serviceable, compared with only 50 per cent of the Chieftains.

This latter statistic was an accurate reflection of the Chieftain's chronic unavailability in the 1970s. The corps' ability to manoeuvre was constrained by the low standard of reliability of many of its armoured vehicles, as well as a shortage of spare parts, a reflection of both defence spending cuts and weaknesses in the largely nationalized British defence industry. Both factors constrained the Army's ability to train for high-intensity warfare required by its NATO role.

Another potential innovation was an effort to improve the firepower of mechanized infantry battalions. By now Soviet motor rifle battalions had much more organic firepower on their armoured vehicles. About half of the brigade-sized motor rifle regiments travelled in wheeled BTR APCs. These had a large turret mounting a 7.62mm light machine gun and a 14.5mm heavy machine gun – the latter weapon being capable of penetrating the FV432's armour. Other motor rifle regiments were equipped with the tracked BMP infantry fighting vehicle. This had a turret with three weapons: a light machine gun, a 73mm low-velocity gun firing anti-tank shells and the *Sagger* anti-tank missile that had been used to considerable effect against Israeli armour in the 1973 Yom Kippur war.

The sole firepower of the infantry's FV432 APCs was a single machine gun fitted on a pintle that required the vehicle commander to expose half his body outside the vehicle's armour. This was a good way to use the gun as an anti-aircraft weapon, but those using the weapon to provide fire support would be very vulnerable to enemy fire, much more exposed than if they were on the ground. British mechanized infantry therefore had far less firepower than Soviet mechanized battalions. As British mechanized battalions were then equipped, neutralizing these threats, especially from the BMP, would have been almost impossible without extensive support from tanks. The infantry and the corps were also acutely conscious that the Bundeswehr had issued its panzergrenadiers with the Marder infantry fighting vehicle. It had a turret with a 20mm cannon that was also able to fire Milan missiles. This meant that German brigades were better able to defend against Soviet armour.

A trial was therefore conducted of upgrading mechanized infantry firepower, carried out by the infantry demonstration battalion, a specialized training support unit. The battalion trialled FV432s fitted with two different types of turret. Some FV432s were modified by adding small one-man turrets that mounted the general purpose machine gun (GPMG) which were fitted to some of the APCs. The trial judged that these were a useful addition to the vehicle's firepower.

The second type of turret trialled was the two-man turret that was used by the Fox wheeled armoured reconnaissance vehicle. It had a machine gun and 30mm Rarden cannon. The idea was that this would greatly increase the mechanized infantry's ability to counter massed armour by neutralizing BTR and BMPs, allowing tanks to concentrate on destroying enemy tanks. A dozen such vehicles were made.

This trial was only partially successful. The heavier Rarden turret was technically capable of improving vehicle firepower, as intended, but it was assessed that the space taken up by the turret reduced the number of infantrymen carried by at least two soldiers. And the added weight of the turret, above the vehicle's centre of gravity, reduced the APC's cross-country mobility, particularly on slopes.

At the end of the trials, the small GPMG turret was accepted, with two being issued to each mechanized platoon. The dozen FV432s with Rarden turrets were allocated to the Berlin Infantry Brigade. The infantry would not acquire a turreted infantry fighting vehicle until the late 1980s.

Light forces with NATO roles also conducted experiments. For example, an area of experimentation was to develop the ability to move infantry rapidly by helicopter. Several exercises were held to develop airmobile manoeuvre using RAF battlefield helicopters. In 1972 Exercise *Sky Warrior* was held in northern England, where 5 Airportable Brigade was supported by an array of Royal Navy and RAF support helicopters. This climaxed with the move of a battalion and two batteries of artillery over a distance of 50 miles, lifted by a force of 40 RAF Wessex and Puma helicopters. But such was the pressure on the RAF helicopter force and the infantry imposed by operations in Northern Ireland that it would be over a decade before the Army's airmobile capabilities were further developed.

Another experiment was conducted by 19 Airportable Brigade. The idea was to gain advantage when defending against a Soviet armoured formation by creating a tactical 'stay-behind' force. The 1st Battalion, the Light Infantry trained one of its rifle companies to conceal themselves several miles in from the brigade's forward defences. Dug into well-concealed underground hides in section-sized patrols, the company would emerge at night and seek out Soviet forces to attack under cover of darkness. Particular attention would be paid to seeking out armoured vehicles.

The company was trained by the SAS to construct covert hides. The idea was then tried out on exercises, including a battalion exercise in Canada. This demonstrated that the concept was, in principle, feasible. It was assessed that the 'stay-behind' company might be able to fight for two successive nights, after which it might well have run out of ammunition or be hunted down by Soviet troops. But to make the concept work properly, the stay-behind force would require the best junior leaders in the battalion. It was perfectly feasible to concentrate the most capable NCOs and officers in that way, but it would lower the quality of commanders across the rest of the battalion. It was judged that the potential gain from the actions of the stay-behind force would be outweighed by the reduction by one-third in fighting strength of one of the brigade's battalions, particularly if, at the same time, the quality of leadership of the rest of the battalion was reduced. The disadvantages of the concept were assessed to outweigh the advantages, so it was not implemented.

WIDER ROLES IN NATO

In the event of Soviet attack almost three-quarters of the Army's regular and reserves personnel would be committed to NATO. The Army's main effort was very much 1 (BR) Corps in Germany. But in the UK there were almost two divisions' worth of troops assigned to other roles in NATO.

The UK-based 3rd Infantry Division and 16th Parachute Brigade were assigned to reinforce NATO. Both formations had previously had roles as a global strategic reserve, but the defence reviews of the 1960s had seen strategic ambitions reduced and reinforcement of NATO was made the formation's priority role. The division had three airportable infantry brigades and a single armoured regiment.[9] Although 3rd Division was the largest NATO-reinforcing formation, it was not the only one. The 16th Parachute Brigade also had a role in reinforcing NATO, including the Baltic Approaches. In addition, it was considered to be employable for any contingencies outside the NATO area.

British Army units also contributed to two other formations with NATO roles. The first was the Royal Navy's 3 Commando Brigade Royal Marines. This formation was the designated landing force for UK amphibious operations and the Royal Navy retained a flotilla of amphibious shipping and helicopters to deliver it ashore. The core of the formation was its three Royal Marine commandos; organized on a similar fashion to an infantry battalion, with a similar size, the marines were given longer and tougher training than Army infantry recruits. They were required to pass the demanding commando tests, developed for the original commandos, elite coastal raiding units fielded by the Army and Royal Marines in World War II.

Whilst most of the commando brigade was manned by marines, it had two Army units – an artillery regiment and an engineer squadron. There was also a commando logistic regiment that included Army logistic soldiers and officers. The brigade was assigned to NATO's eastern Atlantic command. It had many potential roles, of which the most likely and most demanding option was reinforcing the defences of north Norway.

Also with a role in north Norway was the Allied Command Europe Mobile Force (Land), known as the ACE Mobile Force (Land), abbreviated to AMF(L). This was a multinational force, held at high readiness to reinforce NATO. The idea was that it could be rapidly deployed early in a crisis to symbolize NATO political and military resolve and reassure a NATO nation where the military threat was felt to be greatest. It was essentially a light infantry brigade with up to 5,000 troops. Various nations, including Canada, Germany and the US, assigned infantry battalions and combat support. The HQ was multinational and based in Heidelberg, Germany.

The British Army provided much of the force's architecture – the signal squadron, artillery HQ and a dedicated force armoured reconnaissance squadron. It also assigned combat engineers, an artillery battery, air defences, light helicopters and a light infantry battalion. Logistics being a national rather than NATO responsibility, there was a UK national logistic battalion.

The AMF(L) had deployment options in Norway, Italy, Greece and Turkey. It had a high level of operational reconnaissance and exercise deployments to all these areas. Both it and 3 Commando Brigade had to be prepared to fight in North Norway the whole year round. This required both formations to be fully capable of mountain and Arctic warfare, which was achieved by frequent training in north Norway in winter. Troops with an Arctic role had a complete suite of Arctic clothing, based on a lightweight combat suit and a multitude of special gloves and footwear, as well as skis and snowshoes, the use of which had to be mastered. Units were also equipped with specialist tracked over-snow vehicles. A proportion of these vehicles were stockpiled in Norway.

Personnel and units would be trained to survive and fight in the teeth of the deep winter. The training was tough and required a very high standard of physical fitness and leadership. But mastering the unforgiving environment of an Arctic winter was an immensely satisfying achievement – for soldiers, officers and units as a whole. A signals officer told me that 'there was nothing quite like skiing across a frozen lake illuminated only by the Northern Lights'. At a time before mass market package ski holidays became affordable, it was also for many a great adventure – something that many had joined the Army to achieve.

The only constraint on the training was money. At a time of repeated defence cuts, it was all too easy to reduce Arctic training to make budgetary ends meet.

THE 1975 DEFENCE REVIEW – REDUCED CAPABILITIES AND NEW STRUCTURES

Throughout the first half of the 1970s, Britain's economic performance continued to decline. In 1974 when the new Labour government of Harold Wilson took power, it conducted another defence review. This review began in 1974. It became known as the Mason Review, after Roy Mason, the defence minister who led it, although the military input was masterminded by Field Marshal Sir Michael Carver, the Chief of the Defence Staff (CDS). Reporting in 1975, this declared that over the next decade defence spending would drop from 5 per cent of GDP to 4.5 per cent. This was to reflect the UK's straitened economic circumstances and then current strategic optimism that détente between the West and Russia would defuse military tension between NATO and the Warsaw Pact. So 'some reduction in our current NATO contribution is inevitable if the strain on the British economy is to be eased by bringing the burden of British defence expenditure more into line with that borne by our major European Allies.'[10]

The Soviet Union and Warsaw Pact were identified as the overriding threat to national security, so 'NATO should remain the first and overriding charge on the resources available for defence'.[11] The review identified four major commitments of UK defence: the nuclear deterrent, land/air forces based in West Germany, the maritime defence of the Eastern Atlantic and home defence of the UK.

The review reduced the manpower of the armed forces by 10 per cent. Commitments outside NATO were greatly reduced, with the Hong Kong garrison diminishing from two brigades to one. This garrison would have the principal role of supporting the Royal Hong Kong Police in maintaining the colony's internal security, so the Hong Kong tank squadron would be cut. British forces would leave the Caribbean and Mediterranean, apart from British forces in Cyprus, which were reduced. The withdrawal from overseas bases continued, with troops leaving Malta and Singapore, the Army retaining small garrisons in Belize, Gibraltar and Cyprus, and a Gurkha battalion in Brunei, this funded by the Sultan. It was decided that the UK would no longer have significant numbers of forces assigned to 'out of area' intervention operations beyond NATO territory. Savings would be made by cutting the RAF air transport fleet by half.

The review required a significant reduction in Army manpower. Rather than cut more infantry battalions and armoured regiments, the Army chose to remove armoured brigade

HQs and their signal squadrons from 1 (BR) Corps. It was also planned to improve firepower and reduce manpower overheads by centralizing some combat functions. For example, armour and infantry units would lose organic reconnaissance troops or platoons, which would be provided from the divisional reconnaissance regiments. Infantry battalions would grow a fourth rifle company. And Swingfire long-range anti-tank missiles would move from the armoured corps to the artillery.

The corps would reorganize from three divisions, each of two large brigades, to four smaller armoured divisions and the new 8th Field Force. This had the primary role of rear area security but could be deployed forward into a defensive position. The corps strength would remain at 55,000 troops. In war it would be joined by the 7th Field Force and some 45,000 personnel from the TA and mobilized reservists. About 20,000 TA troops exercised in Germany each year.

The new armoured divisions would be organized as followed:

- an armoured reconnaissance regiment
- two tank regiments
- three mechanized infantry battalions
- two artillery regiments, one with four batteries of Abbot 105mm self-propelled guns, the other with three batteries of M109 self-propelled guns and an air defence battery
- two engineer regiments with a total of five field squadrons, a support squadron and an armoured engineer troop
- a divisional HQ and signal regiment
- an army aviation regiment
- logistics comprising a transport regiment, armoured workshop, ordnance company, two field ambulances and an ambulance squadron.

It was envisaged that on mobilization for war each division would be reinforced with a light infantry battalion carried in trucks as well as anti-aircraft batteries. Together with mobilized reservists, the size of the division would increase from 10,000 to 14,000 troops.

The centre of gravity of the formation would be five battlegroups, formed from the armoured squadrons and mechanized infantry companies, under armoured regiment or mechanized battalion HQs. The exact mix of armour and mechanized infantry would depend on the terrain and divisional commander's plan. Brigade HQs and their signal squadrons would be abolished. Instead, the divisional HQ would directly command all five battlegroups.

It was also announced that the infantry would replace their Wombat recoilless anti-tank guns with the Franco-German Milan medium-range anti-tank missiles, 16 for each battalion with a NATO role. This was a significant increase in anti-armour firepower.

The Army's radios were modernized. The 1950s-era Larkspur radios required frequent retuning and demanded a high level of operator skill. From 1976 they were replaced by a new radio family, Clansman. This incorporated new frequency synthesizer technology. They were much simpler to operate, with frequencies being set on simple dials that clicked into position. This made it much quicker and easier to change frequency, with the benefit that sub-units could more quickly regroup from one HQ to another, greatly speeding up the time taken to resubordinate a squadron or company from one battlegroup to another, increasing flexibility and adaptability.

Logistic arrangements were adjusted. With the demise of brigades, their logistic capabilities were centralized at division level. Some transport was removed from battlegroups and centralized in the divisional transport regiment. There would be more pushing forward of combat supplies to battlegroups, artillery and engineers.

The 3rd Division would now re-role to become one of four smaller armoured divisions based in West Germany as part of 1 (BR) Corps. Its infantry would be re-arranged into four brigade-sized infantry formations, retitled as 'Field Forces':

- 5th Field Force. This new formation would be part of 1 (BR) Corps, responsible for the security of the corps rear area, and available as a reserve for forward deployment.
- 6th Field Force. This assumed the UK Mobile Force role of reinforcing NATO's Baltic Approaches that had previously been assigned to the 3rd Division.
- 7th Field Force. This was assigned to reinforce 1 (BR) Corps from the UK.
- 8th Field Force. This had a primary role of military home defence as a secondary role of operations outside the NATO area.

The 5th Field Force had three regular infantry battalions. The 6th and 7th field forces had five battalions: three regular and two TA. The 7th and 8th field forces had little in the way of organic logistics. To operate in the Baltic Approaches the 6th Field Force had considerable assigned logistic support. Most of it was found from the TA.

With the significant reductions in RAF transport aircraft and the reduced priority of operations outside NATO, the 16th Parachute Brigade was disbanded. The brigade HQ and signal squadron re-badged to become the HQ and signal squadron of the 6th Field Force. But whereas the parachute brigade was a full airborne all-arms formation, the parachute capability was reduced to that of a 'Parachute Contingency Force' of a single parachute battalion with limited all-arms support – a greatly diminished capability to conduct airborne operations.

In actions that appeared calculated to demonstrate reduced capability and ambition, two of the three Parachute Regiment battalions were assigned non-airborne roles, one sent to join the Berlin Infantry Brigade, the other assigned to the 5th Field Force in Germany. Many of the regiment's officers and senior ranks wondered if this meant that the Army valued them less.

TESTING THE NEW STRUCTURES

As soon as the new divisional organization was announced, many middle-ranking and senior officers questioned the wisdom of abolishing brigade HQs. There was much speculation that the divisional commander and his HQ would get too involved in tactical co-ordination of battlegroups, a function previously performed by brigade commanders, while not being able to think and plan the battle days ahead of current fighting in a way that had previously occurred. This was essential, not least for the logistic plan to support the tactical plan, especially for the supply of ammunition to the division's artillery. And if the Army had no armoured or mechanized brigades, how would it have a pool of brigadiers who had proven their abilities in armoured or mechanized formations from whom future armoured divisional commanders could be selected?[12]

The new divisional structure was tested in 1975 on Exercise *Wide Horizon* and in autumn 1976 on Exercise *Spearpoint*.[13] Ostensibly a corps exercise, the number of troops was 18,000 with 376 tanks, 1,400 other armoured vehicles and 3,300 wheeled vehicles, most from the 2nd Armoured Division, commanded by Major General Frank Kitson. The exercise took place over three weeks over an area of 150 km by 60 km.

Some simulation was used. Simfire, a laser weapon effects simulator, was fitted to some tanks and Milan missile fire was simulated. When a tank was hit, the simulator released a small cloud of red smoke, greatly satisfying the crew that had knocked the tank out. The tactics employed featured armour and mechanized infantry fighting while widely dispersed. Infantry in FV432s was extensively used to defend woods and during counterattacks to clear them. Extensive use was made of the divisional aviation regiment for reconnaissance. Logistics were tested with more than 9,000 tons of combat supplies being delivered to units in the first week of the exercise.

Throughout the exercise the artillery's nuclear experts had been planning the potential use of nuclear weapons. On the final day of the exercise, nuclear strikes on the enemy were simulated, with warheads being delivered by howitzers, Honest John rocket launchers and RAF aircraft. As was typical for exercises of the era, the manoeuvres ended shortly after the simulated nuclear strike.

The corps analyzed the lessons of the exercises. The manoeuvres had demonstrated that the sceptical officers who predicted difficulties with command and control of the restructured divisions were right. As a result, a level of intermediate command was re-introduced. Each division was allocated some additional manpower to form two new 'task force' HQs. The divisional signal regiment generated two small signal troops, allowing the TF HQ to command a small or short operation. Brigadiers to command each task force would act as deputy divisional commanders, and were given a small tactical staff. The brigadiers would in peacetime command the corps' major garrisons. For example, HQ 3rd Division commanded two task forces – Task Force Echo, in Paderborn, and Task Force Foxtrot in Soest.

The task force HQs improved divisional command and control. But there was an anomaly that gave rise to weaknesses. Many garrison commanders administered units that were not part of their assigned task force, these units being under the peacetime command of a different task force HQ. That meant the familiarity, cohesion and confidence within the previous permanently constituted brigades that was so essential to a brigade's effectiveness in war would not necessarily apply to the eight task forces. The Army felt that having task forces was better than not having them, but divisional command and control was still not as effective as it should be.

THE CORPS PLAN FOR WAR

How did the corps plan to fight in the late 1970s? The corps assessed that there would be several axes along which concentrated tank and motor rifle divisions would advance. These would be supported by very heavy levels of gun and rocket artillery as well as fighter bombers and attack helicopters. Electronic warfare would jam British radio nets. The British assessed that from the outset the Soviets could well employ chemical weapons.

The aim would be to rapidly penetrate or envelop NATO defensive positions, exploiting gaps that were created. Soviet special forces, known as Spetsnaz, might conduct sabotage or diversionary attacks throughout Europe. Within the corps area, airborne forces might be landed by parachute or helicopter, to seize key terrain or choke points.

A division-sized covering force right up to the IGB would delay the initial Warsaw Pact advance. Behind this, the corps' remaining three armoured divisions would fight the main defensive battle. Finally, having reconstituted itself, the covering force division would act as the corps reserve. The British took great confidence from their detailed knowledge of the potential battlefield's terrain, which enemy commanders would lack.

THE COVERING FORCE BATTLE

The 4th Armoured Division would deploy forward as the corps covering force, to protect the other three divisions as they were preparing their defensive positions, by identifying and delaying the enemy advance westward from East Germany.

The corps wanted to ensure that from the very beginning of the war enemy columns were subject to attack from the ground, by artillery, and attack from the air, by both missile-firing helicopters and NATO fighter bombers. It was intended that this would sow fear, uncertainty and delay, putting enemy commanders under pressure, not least that imposed by armoured vehicles having to operate 'closed down' with all hatches shut. Seeing the outside world through narrow slits of armoured glass, their vision would be further diminished by smoke and dust. All this, it was felt, would impose friction on units and formations, increasing delay.

The most easterly elements of the division would be up to 40 km forward of the main British position. The division would use armoured reconnaissance to act as a screen, right up on the international border. This would seek to identify the initial crossing of the border, then the enemy's main axes of attack. Thereafter it would monitor the enemy advance as it developed.

Behind the screen would be a guard force of armoured and infantry battlegroups in defensive positions that sought to impose delay on leading enemy units along their main line of advance. This put a premium on tanks and anti-tank missiles. Although infantry might hold choke points and key terrain, including bridges, the aim was not to get embroiled in close-quarter defensive battles, but to force the enemy to deploy to clear British defensive positions, only for them to find that by the time they arrived at the places the British had been fighting from the defending squadrons and companies had broken contact and withdrawn to the west. In practice this required planning of some north–south lines from which delaying battles would be fought. The 4th Division planned that these would be short, sharp and effective.

But they had two major concerns. The first was that given preparation time the Soviet artillery would deploy to firing positions very close to the border, where they could be supplied with considerable quantities of shells and rockets. This could allow the Soviets to fire very intense artillery barrages on likely and actual British defensive positions, with the potential to inflict considerable casualties on troops, vehicles and equipment. It would be very difficult to counter this overhang of enemy artillery.

The covering force's second concern was the air battle. As with artillery, Soviet air defences could be deployed close to the international border. This would be a considerable threat to any RAF or NATO fighter bombers attempting to provide close air support to the covering force. And in the early stages of any war, NATO air forces would be seeking to gain air superiority over the Soviet Air Force, both by a defensive air battle and by direct attacks on airfields in East Germany. As NATO's belt of fixed radars and Hawk anti-aircraft missiles was deployed at least 60 miles west of the international border, it would be relatively easy for Soviet fighter bombers to attack the covering force. And in the 1970s Soviet forces in Germany received increasing numbers of heavily armed Hind attack helicopters. Indeed, at a presentation in 1979 the commander of the 4th Division named these helicopters as the threat that most concerned him.[14]

If the scenario involved a longer period of warning of a Soviet attack, the corps would have more time to prepare. This might allow the covering force to thin out, reducing its strength. This was the 'best case' scenario. But the 'worst case' was of a surprise or very short-notice attack. In this case the longer the enemy were delayed, the more time the rest of the corps would have to prepare, including out-loading supplies from logistic depots, forward infantry digging defensive positions, engineers laying minefields and preparing demolitions, let alone the receiving and deploying of regular and TA units from the UK. But this worst-case short-warning scenario carried the greatest risk of the covering force being greatly damaged, even of it being cut off and destroyed.

BREAKING CLEAN AND RECONSTITUTION

Having delayed the enemy advance the division would shake off the attackers by 'breaking clean'. This would have to be achieved just in front of the main defensive positions. The other three divisions would need to assist the covering force with artillery and anti-tank fire. In the worst case they might have to mount counterattacks to separate the covering force from closely pursuing enemy forces.

Having broken clean, the covering force would move back through the forward divisions to concentration areas sited well in the depth of the corps. Here they would be met by ordnance, maintenance and medical units. The force would then reconstitute itself and its effectiveness by replacing personnel, vehicles and equipment lost with fresh troops, vehicles and equipment, as well as refuelling its vehicles and rebuilding its ammunition stocks.

This aspect of reconstitution was comparatively simple to plan for. But it would be less complex and challenging than rebuilding the fighting spirit of the division, particularly if it had received a mauling at the hands of the attackers, battering morale. And there would be every chance that many surviving troops would be exhausted.

Those involved in planning the covering force battle wondered how much of it might survive. Destruction of the covering force would have been a major blow, as the corps planned for it to act as the corps reserve. It was fortunate that this part of the corps plan never had to be conducted for real.

THE MAIN DEFENSIVE BATTLE

The main defensive battle phase would seek to destroy attacking enemy formations. The 1st, 2nd and 3rd divisions were deployed from north to south in numerical order. The corps assessed that its divisions were well suited for a defensive battle. The Forward Edge of the Battle Area (FEBA) would be a broad line of forward defensive positions where most battlegroups would be deployed in well-prepared defensive positions, sited to exploit the terrain of the corps sector.

The many woods, towns and villages would provide concealment. The whole corps area was traversed by many streams and small rivers, flowing from south to north, getting deeper and faster as they flowed. Much of the terrain in the southern part of the corps area featured wooded hills with relatively narrow gaps between them. All these features favoured the defender.

The practical difficulties of moving attacking armoured columns suggested places where an advance could be slowed down. To delay the enemy units, to force them to bunch up, thus providing better targets, and to protect infantry defensive positions, maximum use would be made of obstacles. In planning these, likely enemy axes of advance would be identified. Places where enemy armour could best be attacked would be determined, known as 'killing areas' or 'killing zones'. These would be sited in depth along likely enemy axes of advance between the FEBA and the Rear Edge of Battle Area (REBA). This line might also have obstacles, sited to make it difficult for armoured columns to advance further west. Although not identified in surviving unclassified documents, this was probably the River Weser.

The corps defences would make use of a canal and two rivers that flowed from south to north across the corps area. In the east, the River Leine was narrow and relatively small but surrounded by areas of low-lying terrain that could be boggy in winter or after heavy rain. But in dry conditions it would be much less of an obstacle that in places could be forded. Further west was a canal and in the centre of the corps area was the much wider River Weser. Soviet reconnaissance and motor rifle units would cross rivers in light armoured vehicles that could swim. The Soviets planned to get their heavier tanks across such rivers by fitting them with tall schnorkel towers and driving across the bottom of the river. Attempting to do so while under fire would be a very hazardous operation. British doctrine was that obstacles must be covered by observation and fire to maximize the attrition that would be inflicted on the enemy.

The corps planned to construct defensive positions of great strength. Natural obstacles, principally rivers, would be reinforced with minefields. And where there were no natural obstacles, more minefields would be laid. Enemy attempts to find a way around the obstacles or to breach them would impose delay. Their large columns of armoured vehicles would inevitably bunch or concertina, offering lucrative targets for the defenders' firepower.

Infantry companies, Milan missiles and tanks would be sited to channel the enemy onto ground where they could be destroyed by concentrated firepower from complementary layers of anti-armour weapons in combination with artillery, anti-tank helicopters and air strikes. Mortars and artillery fire plans would support this. Those units and formations that were subject to the main enemy attacks would receive the greatest amount of artillery support.

At the main defensive positions, infantry battlegroups and companies would fight from well-prepared defensive positions in woods, villages or towns, with their anti-armour weapons sited to attack enemy attempting to avoid or breach natural and artificial obstacles. In laying out these positions, the aim was pose a dilemma for enemy commanders. Should they slow down and stop to dismount infantry to clear British defensive positions in wooded and urban terrain? Or should they seek to press on, either crossing obstacles or finding ways past, to push as rapidly as they could through open terrain? When the enemy reached the British defensive positions a high-intensity battle would be fought. The emphasis was on using firepower to destroy enemy armoured columns, although tactical manoeuvre would be needed for local counterattacks and to deploy reserves to prevent the enemy unpicking the British defences. Any enemy that made it through the defensive network would be blocked by battlegroups sited in depth or attacked by anti-tank helicopters.

The centre of gravity of tactical plans was the need to slow down and then stop enemy armour. The widespread issue of Milan anti-tank missiles to the infantry meant that this would be easier than it had been in the early 1970s, reducing the need for the anti-armour defence to make extensive use of tanks intimately supporting infantry defensive layouts. But Milan still had limitations. These included a much slower rate of fire than tank guns. Until a thermal imaging night sight was issued in the early 1980s, missile firing at night required using mortar or artillery illumination; and the missile guidance system found it difficult to work through smoke and dust.

So tanks would still be an essential part of infantry battlegroups. This greatly increased the anti-armour firepower of infantry battalions. Exercises and scientific simulation of combat showed that even a squadron of tanks could double the tank-killing capability of a contemporary infantry battalion. But Milan's new capabilities freed up more armoured squadrons from static defence to more mobile counterattack roles. About half of a division's tanks might be employed in this role.

The Chieftain tank's 120mm gun and thick shaped armour meant that it overmatched the firepower and protection of the main Russian tank of the time, the T-62, as well as the German Army's Leopard 1 tanks, the US Army's M60 tanks and the British-manufactured Centurion tanks of other NATO armies. But it was considerably slower across country than the Leopard 1; and throughout the 1970s its reliability was consistently well below that of the Leopard 1.

This meant that an armoured brigade's ability to concentrate its tanks to mount counterattacks was limited. As most of the brigade's mechanized infantry would be occupying static defensive positions, few mechanized infantry companies would be available to group with armoured squadrons for any all-arms counterattacks. So, whilst defensive battles might feature tactical counterattacks by some armour and mechanized infantry, the majority of the fighting was going to be relatively static and attritional. The defensive battle of the first echelon was certain to feature intense Soviet artillery fire. And the corps had insufficient air defence weapons, a weakness acknowledged by Major General Bramall when he commanded 1st Armoured Division.[15]

The corps plans recognized that sooner or later the Soviets might develop such strength where they were attacking that the first defensive echelon might be overwhelmed, risking its defeat and destruction. In that case, the forward formations would seek to break contact with the enemy and withdraw rearwards, through a second defensive line, held by formations sited in depth. Although these positions would have fewer armoured and mechanized forces than the first line, they would have had more time to prepare their positions, trenches, bunkers, fortified buildings and minefields, increasing the resilience of their defensive positions. And reinforcing infantry battalions, both regular and TA, might by then have reached the corps.

For the forward formations to successfully withdraw, they would have had to first break contact from attacking Soviet forces, an operation easy to state, but very difficult to execute while being attacked by a numerically superior enemy. It was not clear how many brigades and units might be able to do this. And even if they did so, units would have to move west while harried by Warsaw Pact aircraft which would be opposed by insufficient numbers of British Army air defence weapons. Assuming that units from the forward defensive positions had achieved this and had successfully moved back well behind the second defence line, they would need to be reconstituted for future operations.

The three divisions deployed in defence had areas of operations that were much longer than they were wide. The width of the divisional sector meant that there were not enough mechanized infantry to be strong everywhere and there was a danger of battlegroups being spread dangerously thin. Together with the relatively limited air defence capability allocated, divisional commanders were very concerned about the potential threat from Soviet infantry landing by helicopter in the depth of the divisional area, possibly seizing key terrain or blocking routes for forward movement by reserves and logistic convoys.

One way to prevent this would be to use light infantry, supported by armoured reconnaissance, and minefields to deny wooded terrain to enemy armour. This could make the woods extremely difficult for the enemy to push through, allowing the divisional commander to concentrate his armour and mechanized infantry, not only to defend terrain where the enemy might make more progress, but also to counterattack advancing enemy where they were most vulnerable.

A need was identified for a unit to be dedicated to security of the divisional rear area. This could be provided by the divisional armoured reconnaissance regiment, or an infantry battalion, but only at the expense of employing them for forward defence.[16]

The new divisional structure was less capable of offensive operations, but the corps plans envisaged these being limited to local counterattacks and 'exploitation of such reverses as the enemy may sustain'. A major limitation was the smaller number of tank squadrons, eight, compared with 12 mechanized infantry companies.

THE COUNTER-MOVE PHASE

In the counter-move phase, reserve units and formations initially deployed behind the REBA would move forward. They might be used for counter-penetration, to block any enemy force that looked as if it was going to break through, threatening the corps rear. Such a breakthrough might also threaten the integrity of the entire army group defensive plan, potentially as one arm of a Soviet encirclement of one or more corps. Alternatively these units might be used to counterattack enemy that had penetrated the Main Defensive Zone and threatened to greatly weaken the British defensive positions. Such a counterattack was the only major offensive move that the corps plans contemplated.

Should any large groups of enemy armour break through this defensive network, armoured reserves and missile-firing helicopters would be deployed to block the enemy advance, possibly supported by air attacks where the situation made them desirable and feasible. And the corps had a brigade-sized force: the 5th Field Force, comprised of three infantry battalions, supported by artillery and armoured reconnaissance. This might be sent forward by road or helicopter to conduct 'counter-penetration', the blocking of any particularly threatening advance. It planned and trained to do this, with a primary option in the heart of the 2nd Armoured Division's sector. This was the 'Sibesse Gap', a natural choke point between two large woods with the small town of Sibesse, in the middle of this potential thoroughfare from east to west.

THE GOODWOOD DEFENCE – INNOVATION AND EXPERIMENTATION

The advent of Milan created conditions for another innovation – the development of a defensive tactic known as Goodwood. It was led by General Sir William Scotter, first as Vice Chief of the General Staff (VCGS) and secondly as Commander in Chief BAOR.

As commander of 19 Airportable Brigade in the late 1960s, Scotter had used a NATO exercise in Jutland to try out a new approach. The exercise area was agricultural terrain but peppered with villages and small woods. Scotter deployed the brigade's infantry to defend the villages and woods, in co-operation with German and Danish armoured forces that manoeuvred between the British positions. The aim of Scotter's defence was to force the attackers to stop to dismount infantry to clear the British defences, thus providing ideal targets for attack by allied tanks and mechanized infantry.

In the MoD Scotter was concerned that the Army was not fully exploiting the capabilities of its light infantry forces to be better able to counterattack Soviet armoured forces. He searched for a historical example of light infantry defending against a numerically superior armoured force, supported by abundant air and artillery support.

The example of Operation *Goodwood* in July 1944 was selected. This was well known to many senior officers. Not only were there veterans of the Normandy campaign still serving in the Army, some in senior ranks, but the battle was one of those featured in the Army Staff College's annual staff ride to Normandy.

The battle was an attack by a corps of all three British armoured divisions in Normandy, aiming to break through German defences to the east of the city of Caen. The attack was preceded by a bombardment by over 2,000 RAF and US Air Force (USAF) bombers and an artillery barrage fired by over 500 guns. This heavy firepower greatly damaged the German defences, but did not destroy them. As the leading British armoured brigade advanced, it suffered heavy losses of tanks from surviving German anti-tank guns sited in French villages, many engaging from the sides of the villages. The Germans also rapidly assembled a line of anti-tank guns and tanks on the ridgeline overlooking the network of villages. British tank casualties were heavy, 437 of the 850 committed. In addition, the inevitable delay to the leading brigade caused great congestion, which was attacked by German mortar and artillery fire.[17]

A new concept, christened Goodwood, was developed based on the German defence that had so effectively stopped the British in their tracks. Some of the terrain in the northern part of the corps sector was covered with a network of small villages and woods. The idea was to hold these with infantry platoons, each protecting a team of two Milan missile launchers, sited to engage enemy armoured columns from the side and rear.

The concept was refined through a series of three computer-assisted wargames. The simulations showed that like the German layout in 1944, the concept had the potential to greatly slow down attacking Soviet forces. It could be applied by light infantry fighting from trenches and fortified buildings, but the likely weight of Soviet artillery fire meant that once battle was joined their lack of protection would make it very difficult for them to move around the battlefield. Mechanized infantry with their FV432 APCs would have more flexibility. Another limitation of the concept was that, effective as the Milan missile was, it had a much slower rate of fire than a tank. So, it would be essential to complement the framework of infantry and anti-tank positions with tanks and mechanized infantry that could manoeuvre between and around the defended positions, delivering surprise attacks on the flanks and rears of Soviet units. The concept was then tested in the field on exercises, culminating in the 1980 corps exercise.

WEAPONS OF MASS DESTRUCTION

NATO policies of Flexible Response and Forward Defence meant that whilst NATO would fight conventionally for as long as possible, it had to be prepared to use nuclear weapons on the battlefield. In theory this could occur at little or no notice. British commanders considered that it was more likely that any Soviet attack would begin conventionally. They assessed that the corps could probably fight conventionally for about five to seven days.

In the early 1970s the commander of 1st Division, Major General Bramall, considered that if his division fought with skill, it might be able to defend against a major Soviet attack for about five days. By the second week of war, it would certainly have expended the lion's share of its ammunition and spare parts and suffered so many casualties of troops and equipment that its defences would be in danger of being overwhelmed by Soviet forces, particularly as attacking formations exhausted and depleted from combat might be succeeded by another echelon of Soviet formations.

If this happened, the only way to prevent the destruction of the corps or a Soviet breakthrough would be to use tactical nuclear weapons. The destructive power of even relatively small nuclear explosions would greatly exceed that of any conventional weapons the corps owned. So the role of divisions, brigades and battlegroups would change from using their own weapons to destroy the enemy, to canalizing enemy forces into nuclear killing areas.

To allow the nuclear strike to inflict maximum damage on the enemy and thus to have maximum benefit for the corps battle, the employment of nuclear weapons would be planned in peace and then continually updated from the outset of fighting. The artillery staff in corps and divisional HQs contained secret nuclear planning cells that would constantly follow the battle. They would plan the best places for nuclear warheads to be exploded.

Whilst RAF Germany had British-owned nuclear bombs, the corps depended on US-owned nuclear warheads that could be fired from Lance missiles, M110 howitzers or M109 self-propelled guns. On operations these had to be at very high readiness to fire.

The nuclear warheads were held by a US Army ordnance battalion, who would only pass them to the British on the order of Supreme Allied Commander Europe (SACEUR). The warheads themselves were in peacetime stored in bunkers within specially designed nuclear storage sites, known by the Army simply as 'sites'. 'Site guards' would protect the fence and ditch surrounding the bunkers in which the warheads were held.

The guard force would require the best part of a company of troops to secure its perimeter from attack, with soldiers standing guard in watchtowers. As the sites were in remote locations, surrounded by woodland, long hours were spent staring at dark forests, where almost nothing happened. The unrelenting monotony was rarely broken by anti-nuclear demonstrations by German protestors.

Maintaining soldiers' motivation whilst conducting such a tedious task was a real challenge for the leadership of the company, squadron or battery conducting the guard. And the sites and their guard forces were subject to random inspections. To fail such an inspection would have negative consequences for the career of the site guard commander.

In war, the warheads would be removed from the bunkers and placed on trucks, but controlled by the US ordnance troops. At the beginning of this period an infantry battalion was assigned the role of nuclear convoy escort, at constant high readiness to deploy. This made it unavailable to take part in Northern Ireland tours. In the late 1970s, to reduce the pressure on the infantry, the role was transferred away. A new unit, the 8th Transport Regiment, was formed with integral companies of pioneers providing the close escort for the convoys.

Once SACEUR had authorized release of the warheads to be fired by British artillery they would be handed over to the designated artillery battery. This would be in parallel with coded warning messages to alert the corps' formations of planned strikes, so they could take measures to reduce damage to themselves from the nuclear burst.

NATO planned that nuclear bursts above the most threatening Soviet formations would not only relieve pressure on hard-pressed NATO ground forces but would also deliver such a shock to the Soviet government as to force a pause in hostilities. To many soldiers and officers, the planning and training to employ nuclear weapons had a hallucinatory character. Most thought that Moscow would rapidly retaliate in kind, with interest, probably launching a larger and deeper strike in greater depth.

Given the UK nuclear deterrent, Great Britain might be spared from nuclear attack, but the Army and RAF on the European mainland would not necessarily be excluded from the likely Soviet theatre-level strike. In the 1970s many exercises, both command posts and field training, would begin with a conventional battle, then practise the planning and conduct of a nuclear strike, the exercise then ending – which reinforced some participants' sense of unreality.

The British saw a serious threat from Soviet chemical weapons, not least as the Soviet-supported Egyptian forces had used them to attack royalist insurgents in the 1960s in Yemen. Some members of the TA SAS who had joined a privately funded operation to support the insurgents were said to have seen their impact, up close. A particularly challenging threat was assessed as nerve agents that had been thickened to make them persistent – sticking to the ground, vegetation, equipment and clothing, releasing their lethal toxins over hours and days.

Although the US had stocks of chemical bombs and shells that might be used for retaliatory attacks, the British had none. But at the MoD's research centre at Porton Down they had a remarkable centre of excellence in defence against chemical, biological and nuclear attacks. By the 1970s, while the Soviets and many other armies used heavy rubber one-piece suits to complement respirators by protecting the body against chemical agents, British troops had protective suits that bonded activated charcoal to much lighter polyester fibres, producing a suit that was much lighter, reducing heat stress. Coupled with a respirator that was as advanced as any in the world, rubber gloves and rugged over-boots, this provided a good balance between protection and reducing the friction and heat burden suffered by the soldier. Indeed, during exercises in German winters, troops often preferred to be wearing their protective NBC (nuclear, biological and chemical) protective suits.

Throughout this period, the new generation of armoured vehicles had NBC protection designed in. These were NBC packs which used filters to scrub air for toxins, which would be blown around the vehicle's interior at slightly greater pressure than the air outside. This was a degree of protection in advance of that achieved by many other contemporary armies.

THE MORAL COMPONENT

The Army considered that the defensive battle that they planned to fight against a numerically superior enemy would impose great strain on all the troops taking part. The Army had to be ready for what would be an extreme test. Deterrence meant that it had to be seen as ready, both by the Warsaw Pact and by the rest of NATO. In the 1970s the Army's very senior officers had fought in World War II. They knew how combat challenges leadership and morale. They understood how easily plans could go awry, often because of the pervasive presence of friction and uncertainty. In battle much would depend on small teams, some on their feet, others in defensive positions and many in vehicles. Necessary battlefield dispersion meant that many small groups would be relatively isolated. They would be led by NCOs and young officers.

The Army saw three factors as particularly critical to supporting the moral component and fighting effectiveness. First was a high level of training. Coupled with staff rides to familiarize commanders with plans and the terrain over which they would be executed, individual, unit and formation training was considered the indispensable foundation.

Second came the sense of individual and collective identity that would help bind small groups together. Some of this would come from the soldiers' and officers' sense of regimental identity – a feeling that every regiment and corps had a heritage of success and overcoming adversity. But battlegroups, task forces, divisions and the corps itself all depended for success on combining a large number of different arms and services together.

As well as the cohesion that came from frequent demanding training, the Army placed great emphasis on leadership. This was built on the character of the leader – their ability to inspire their subordinates to carry out their missions, despite the dangers. To achieve this, commanders needed to be trained in their operational role; much of this was done at Army schools in the UK. It was just as important that commanders be selected from those with the greatest leadership ability. A comprehensive system of annual reports and selection boards existed to achieve this. It usually worked well, but occasionally leaders failed and had to be removed.

The Army considered that in battle the greatest stresses and strains would be felt by commanders. The new night vision and surveillance equipment entering service throughout the 1970s and the more reliable Clansman radios increased the level of information flowing to HQs, more than in previous years. To cope with this, commanders needed training in the art of command. And they needed staff to support them, particularly to take care of all the many necessary details to allow the commander to concentrate on the big picture and make key decisions in a timely manner.

Before battle was joined commanders would have a key role, in leading planning and preparation. Once fighting began, battlegroup commanders would concentrate on fighting the enemy. They might be thinking only a short period of time ahead, perhaps an hour. Task force commanders, acting as brigade commanders had done and would do again, would be deploying battlegroups and arranging artillery and air support. And the divisional commanders would be anticipating the longer-term threat, including from the flanks and air, and planning for the commitment of divisional reserves and anti-tank helicopters. Overall, the battlegroup and task force commanders would be fighting the enemy in the short term, while the divisional commander would be fighting the battle over a longer term.

Despite the thoroughness of the formation and unit plans and the commanders' intimate knowledge of the ground over which they would fight, the enemy would create surprises and dilemmas. Commanders would need to spot enemy weaknesses and exploit them. This meant that they would need to be forward in their area of operations, seeing the battle for themselves, taking the pulse of the battle and visiting subordinates – and if necessary, reassuring or energizing them.

1977 saw the Queen's Silver Jubilee. All three British services celebrated this with royal reviews. The Army staged a major parade in Germany. Assembled on the Sennelager training area were the armoured vehicles and helicopters of the 4th Armoured Division. Over 500 vehicles and 3,000 troops took part, the largest such parade of an armoured division since World War II.

As the Queen arrived, she was saluted by the colours and guidons of all the regiments taking part. The Queen then reviewed the parade by driving past the assembled guards. Both activities were accompanied by music from Army bands. Then the tanks, armoured personnel carriers and self-propelled guns drove past the Queen on a saluting dais, the tanks dipping their guns in salute. A resulting vast cloud of dust enveloped the parade.

So far so conventional. But as the last armoured vehicle drove past, an innovative final flourish took place. The division's armoured reconnaissance regiment drove past at a much greater speed, illustrating how much faster the Scorpion reconnaissance vehicles were than the rest of the Army's armour. And over it flew the new Gazelle helicopters of the division's aviation regiment, barely 30 feet above the ground. As with many parades, much of the event had been dull. Those present thought the combined rapid drive past and low-level fly past was breathtakingly spectacular. And all the troops participating thought it to be a memorable event. Nothing like this had been done on an Army parade before. And no parade of this size was ever arranged again.[18]

Another royal jubilee tradition was the issuing of a special Jubilee medal. Thirty thousand medals were issued in the UK, of which 9,000 were awarded to members of the armed forces. Previous jubilee medals had been awarded to all those serving in the armed forces at the time. This limited issue was a source of great disappointment and much resentment. The lion's share of Army medals went to personnel on parade at Sennelager. There were fewer for the rest of the Army. This created anomalies. For example, 2nd Battalion, the Light Infantry, who paraded at Sennelager, received 22 medals. In contrast, 1st Battalion, the Light Infantry in Hong Kong took part in the Jubilee parade in that city. It saw as many troops participating as in Germany. The battalion received four Jubilee medals. Why a battalion of the same regiment should have received far fewer medals for the same activity was impossible to explain. Many troops felt that this was yet another of too many examples of the Army being starved of necessary funds.

NOT ENOUGH MONEY

Another symptom of shortage of defence funding at that time was the considerable restrictions in supply of spare parts. This inevitably led to restrictions on the mileage for armoured vehicle training and the amount of ammunition that could be fired, particularly by tanks, artillery and guided missile launchers. There was no way to disguise that this was a result of a squeeze on the Army's budget.

This was a result of the dire state of UK public finances. Another effect was an unprecedented constraint of pay. When national service had ended, the government committed to the concept of the 'military salary', in which pay would be set at comparative levels to equivalent civilian jobs. This was complemented by setting up an independent body to recommend armed forces pay – the Armed Forces Pay Review Body. Previously this had produced recommendations that the government had broadly honoured. But from 1975 the Labour government had imposed considerable limits on the rises in public sector pay. So the recommendations of the pay review body were not implemented. Instead pay of all ranks was increased by £3 a week.

From this time, pay of all the Army fell well below comparable civilian wages. Then Major Mike Jackson, a student at Staff College, observed that his 'one abiding memory of that year at Camberley is that hardly any of us seemed to have any money ... we seemed to be always worrying about how we were going to manage'.[19] The CGS in 1978, General Sir Roland Gibbs, saw the Army as facing 'something of a crisis. We are losing skilled manpower to civilian life at a rate that we can ill afford and are likely to continue to do so until pay comparability is fully restored'.[20]

These pay constraints and reduced funding for the maintenance of barracks and families' housing eroded morale, resulting in an increasing considerable outflow of expensively trained personnel. The Army became undermanned. As the decade went on, these constraints posed ever-increasing challenges to morale and retention. By early 1978, there was a 37 per cent gap between armed forces pay and that of their civilian equivalents. Following an unsatisfactory meeting between the Chief of Defence Staff, Marshal of the RAF Sir Neil Cameron, and Prime Minister James Callaghan, the Chiefs of Staff decided that selected journalists should be privately briefed on the facts of the matter.

This fell to General Bramall as the Vice Chief of the Defence Staff for personnel and logistics, who provided a factual briefing to the media. The briefing was followed by amplification of the detail in a private briefing by the Army's director of public relations. Associated Press released the data from the briefing so rapidly that the opposition were able to challenge the Prime Minister in the House of Commons, much to Callaghan's disadvantage. Sensing that this had gone too far and too fast, the Chiefs of Staff took responsibility for the error of judgement, but there was a modest upwards adjustment in forces pay.[21]

MILITARY HOME DEFENCE OF THE UK

The war role of the Army in the UK was updated. Previously it had focussed on helping the country recover from the effects of a nuclear attack. In this scenario the British government would be devolved to regions, each supported by an Army military district. A signal brigade, mainly composed of TA regiments, provided secure communications for home defence. The brigade HQ was at Corsham in Wiltshire, the seat of a large government bunker sited in underground limestone quarries. As this was to be the emergency seat of government if London were destroyed by a nuclear strike, it was the best place for the signals brigade HQ to be – alongside the surviving seat of government.

It was considered unlikely that the Soviets would pose a threat of a conventional airborne or amphibious landing on the UK mainland. There were too many layers of NATO and UK air and maritime defence to penetrate. But missiles or bombers might reach the UK mainland and attack RAF and USAF air bases or key command and control, radar or signals intelligence sites. A more immediate threat was foreseen from Soviet special forces or Spetsnaz: Moscow's equivalent of the SAS. These might be used to gather intelligence, guide in air and missile strikes or conduct sabotage or small-scale attacks on strategic targets.

The military districts in the UK would all have at least one TA battalion under command. And training and logistic unit HQs would take command of counties. For example, the county military HQs for Gloucestershire, Hampshire and Somerset would be provided for by the Central Vehicle Depot, the Rifle Depot of the Royal Green Jackets and the School of Infantry, respectively.

The 8th Field Force was the Army's sole strategic reserve formation. It was also the only formation available as an Army reserve for home defence. In 1979 and 1980 it analyzed the Spetsnaz threat and trained to neutralize it. The brigade had very limited combat support and logistics.

FURTHER EQUIPMENT MODERNIZATION

Modernization of the Army's equipment continued in the second half of the 1970s. As new equipment entered service, it was issued first to regular units in Germany, followed by regular units in the UK with a NATO role, then TA units with a NATO role, then Army units without a NATO role, followed by TA units assigned to home defence.

Shorts, an aircraft company based in Northern Ireland, had begun developing a man-portable anti-aircraft missile. Initially there was scepticism in the MoD that such a weapon was necessary, but from 1968 development was funded. The Blowpipe missile was guided by the operator using a small joystick, with commands being sent over a radio link. This, it was claimed, would allow attacking aircraft to be engaged before they dropped their bombs. Blowpipe had a protracted and difficult development, entering service with the Army in 1975. The Blindfire all-weather radar system was acquired to improve the utility of the Rapier anti-aircraft missile.

During the 1970s, the size of the Army Air Corps increased, and it was fully integrated into the new armoured divisions, with each having an aviation regiment. These were re-equipped with two new light helicopters. The small French-designed Gazelle helicopter was used for reconnaissance and moving key individuals around the battlefield.

The Gazelle was complemented by the larger Lynx helicopter. This could be used as a small utility aircraft, carrying up to six troops in its cargo compartment. The Army fitted 60 Lynx helicopters with launchers and sights for eight TOW anti-tank missiles, which were already in service with the US Army. These had a bigger warhead than the SS11 missiles of the armed Scout and a more effective guidance system. The operator no longer had to fly the missile to the target, but simply needed to hold a crosshair on the target. This was a much more accurate way of guiding the missile. At this time Lynx was one of the most agile helicopters in the world and was capable of performing loops and rolls. In the 1980s it set several helicopter speed records.

EXERCISE *SPEARPOINT*

The biggest troop deployment of this period was Exercise *Crusader*. A total of 95,000 British troops took part, including RAF personnel operating and supporting Harriers and helicopters. This included reinforcements from the UK of 10,000 regular troops and 20,000 members of the TA. This was a larger scale of reinforcement of the corps than had been previously exercised.

Two other exercises ran concurrently. Exercise *Square Leg* in the UK tested the ability of the United Kingdom Land Forces (UKLF) to mobilize these reinforcements and move them to airports and the Channel ports. Once this had been done the exercise continued, testing the plans for military home defence. This saw the home defence chain of command activated and regular and TA units deployed to protect key military installations. The 8th Field Force was deployed as the UK national reserve and moved around several UK training areas counterattacking simulated concentrations of enemy Spetsnaz. The exercise also tested the military plans for managing the aftermath of a nuclear attack on the UK.

Exercise *Jog Trot* tested BAOR's ability to receive reinforcements by air and sea from the UK and move them to their deployment positions in the corps area by road. The majority of UK-based units that took part reached their positions within 48 hours.

Within this exercise testing mobilization and deployment, between 1 and 26 September 1 (BR) Corps conducted Exercise *Spearpoint*, a full-scale field training exercise that took place over the terrain in which the corps was likely to fight. Previously corps exercises had been conducted every few years, but this was the most ambitious and largest so far. Some 63,000 British troops took part. Equipment deployed included 471 Chieftain tanks, 295 US tanks and 90 German tanks. Another 2,900 armoured vehicles, 18,000 wheeled vehicles and 360 helicopters took part.

In addition, some 22,000 US Army troops participated. The US Army's 2nd Armoured Division travelled from the US by air, taking over vehicles and equipment pre-positioned in Germany. This was part of the US Army's annual programme of exercises that brought reinforcing troops to Germany to exercises with pre-positioned equipment, known as Exercise *Return of Forces to Germany* (*REFORGER*).

Previously Army exercises had designated the units exercising in their NATO roles as 'Blue', and the opposing enemy forces, invariably representing Soviet and Warsaw Pact

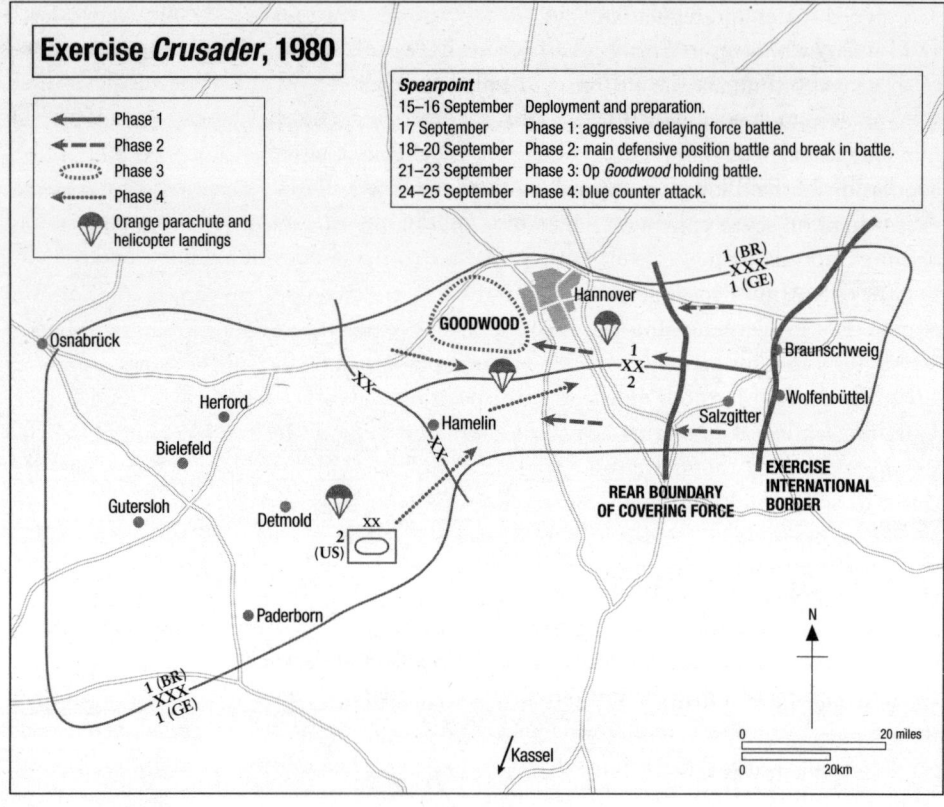

Exercise *Crusader*, 1980

← — — Phase 1
←--- Phase 2
:::::::::: Phase 3
←········· Phase 4
Orange parachute and
helicopter landings

Spearpoint
15–16 September   Deployment and preparation.
17 September   Phase 1: aggressive delaying force battle.
18–20 September   Phase 2: main defensive position battle and break in battle.
21–23 September   Phase 3: Op *Goodwood* holding battle.
24–25 September   Phase 4: blue counter attack.

forces, were 'Red'. By 1980, 'Red' was adjusted to 'Orange' as a minor measure to de-escalate Cold War tension.

The Blue force comprised three of the corps' four armoured divisions: 1st, 2nd and 4th. The 3rd Division provided exercise control and umpires. The laydown of the divisions was like the plan for war. The 4th Division provided the covering force to delay the enemy. The two other divisions deployed for the main defence positions. The 1st Division was in the north and the 2nd Division in the south, both divisions' boundaries being close to the boundaries they would have in war. Also taking part were the UK-based 7th Field Force of three regular and two TA infantry battalions and an armoured regiment, as well as the TA's 30th Engineer Group – an engineer brigade in all but name. The umpire organization was commanded by the 3rd Armoured Division, augmented by the 5th Field Force and German and US umpires – a force of 5,000 troops.

The Orange force was initially provided by the 2nd (US) Armoured Division. In addition, a US airborne brigade HQ led a specially assembled 'Disruption Brigade' to contact parachute and heliborne attacks. This included a regular British battalion and a TA battalion of the Parachute Regiment from Scotland, as well as a company of US Army Chinook helicopters. Special forces were simulated by a 'diversionary brigade' of

US special forces and regular and TA SAS units and a US parachute battalion, the latter flying all the way from Fort Bragg in North Carolina. Its parachute descent into the exercise was but one of the airborne threats posed to the corps.

The exercise began with British and US troops deploying to their field locations. For example, over the night of 12 September the 130 tanks of 4th Division were moved from Detmold to a field location 100 miles to the west. The corps tank transporter regiment lifted them on seven convoys, each some 4 miles long, that departed Detmold at seven-minute intervals.

The US Army had large numbers of vehicles and weapons stockpiled in enormous warehouses in Germany and the Low Countries. Known as Prepositioning of Materiel Configured in Unit Sets (POMCUS), the equipment was sufficient for several armoured divisions. As British troops moved to battle positions, a US Army National Guard artillery battalion landed at Frankfurt airport, picked up their 12 howitzers from a POMCUS depot, and loaded themselves on a train that took them to Brunswick, from where they drove to an assembly area in a forest to join the enemy forces.

PHASE 1, 17 SEPTEMBER: AGGRESSIVE DELAY BATTLE

The exercise began on 17 September with the enemy conducting reconnaissance of the exercise's simulated IGB, between Brunswick and Salzgitter, advancing from east to west the next morning, with two large armoured columns north and south of Salzgitter.

Facing them was the 4th Division, tasked to fight a covering force battle to delay the enemy attack by at least 24 hours. At this stage of the exercise armoured vehicles were restricted to roads and tracks, to reduce environmental damage. Even so, an intense armoured battle developed that day and night, with the covering force finding it difficult to stop massed attacks by US armour. The division had to take great care to avoid being cut off, encircled and destroyed. Considerable close air support from RAF Harriers and Jaguars was used to attack the enemy, which was itself supported by its own AH1 Hueycobra attack helicopters and A10 attack aircraft.

PHASE 2, 18–20 SEPTEMBER: BLUE MAIN DEFENSIVE POSITION BATTLE AND ORANGE BREAK-IN BATTLE

The 4th Division change sides to join the enemy force, and together with the and 2nd (US) Division it stages a demonstration of an armoured attack for the media and visiting VIPs. After this both enemy divisions moved to attack the main defensive positions of 1st and 2nd Divisions. The attackers quickly came up against strong infantry defensive positions to the east of the River Leine in woods and villages, which used the launching of flares to simulate the firing of Milan anti-tank missiles. The US division made extensive use of its organic Hueycobra attack helicopters, while Blue subjected the attackers to many close air support attacks by RAF Harrier and Jaguar fighter bombers.

That afternoon, to secure crossings over a canal to the north of Hildesheim, a US Army airborne battalion staged a parachute drop. It had flown in ten C141 Starlifter transport jets direct from Fort Bragg in the eastern US, refuelling in the air. The troops and supplies dropped a height of 1,000 feet, from waves of aircraft, the descent being completed in six minutes. The parachute landing succeeded, but the airborne battalion had too few anti-tank missiles to prevent the paratroops being neutralized by British armoured and mechanized forces.

The disruption brigade also landed forces by helicopter to seize bridges across the River Weser. Over the night of 19/20 September, the 1st and 2nd divisions began to withdraw their forces from the east bank of the Leine, protected by Rapier air defence missiles. They were pressed by the Orange armoured units and further heliborne attacks by the disruption brigade on bridges across the Leine. But Blue had prepared military bridges of their own and successfully used them to withdraw across the river. Blue now aligned the forward defensive positions along a line heading south from the centre of Hamburg.

In the early hours of 19 September another battalion of US paratroops landed north of Hildesheim, seeking to capturing a canal bridge. This plan was again thwarted by an immediate counterattack by British mechanized forces. Having fought off attempts by Orange to trap them, the Blue forces successfully withdrew across the River Leine.

There was then a change of phase. The 2nd (US) Division joined the corps and moved to a concentration area in the west of the corps area. The 4th Armoured Division became the enemy. On 20 September the Bundeswehr's 3rd Panzer Brigade moved by rail to join the Orange forces, replacing the US division.

The tactical battle died away during the weekend of 20–21 September. It was customary that NATO field exercises did not move heavy armour, conduct tactical combat or stage air battles between Friday night and Monday morning. The weekends therefore provided an opportunity for rest, vehicle and equipment maintenance and logistic replenishment and a welcome opportunity to catch up on much-needed sleep. But commanders and staffs would inevitably be receiving orders, planning and issuing direction for the next phase of the exercise. They would often be no less busy than they had been during the exercise proper. As would be the technicians of the REME, working all weekend to repair key vehicles and equipment that had broken down, particularly the Chieftain tank, on which so much of the corps plan depended.

PHASE 3, 21–23 SEPTEMBER: OPERATION GOODWOOD *HOLDING BATTLE*

Over the weekend Orange also refurbished and planned. It planned to envelop and surround the corps. In the south, the 2nd Division would be attacked by the 3rd Panzer Brigade. Beginning its advance west on the morning of 22 September, it was supported by a parachute drop by the disruption brigade, this time featuring 300 paratroopers of the 15th (Scottish) Battalion of the TA Parachute Regiment. Also jumping were parachute gunners with man-portable Blowpipe anti-aircraft missiles and a Scots piper. While he played 'Scotland the Brave', the paratroops worked furiously to set up a hasty defensive position. This furious military activity was overlooked by the castle of Schloss Marienburg, whose fairytale architecture sat on a prominent hill overlooking the river crossing.

Rapidly linking up with the airborne bridgehead the German brigade used US Army floating bridges and ferries to get its Leopard tanks and Marder infantry fighting vehicles over the river at four crossing places. But the brigade's efforts to rapidly advance west were thwarted by strong defensive positions that the 2nd Division had prepared in the wooded hills that overlooked the German advances. The defences were reinforced by Lynx helicopters firing anti-tank missiles and close support by USAF A10 attack aircraft, as well as heavy simulated British artillery fire. The umpires judged that the panzer brigade had suffered such attrition that it could not advance further.

This was a supporting attack to the Orange main effort, the northern attack on the 1st Division by the 4th Division. In its operational planning, the corps assessed that the relatively flat and open terrain in its northern sector would be the most vulnerable to a mass attack by Warsaw Pact armour. Operational plans allocated this sector to the 1st Armoured Division, as did Exercise *Spearpoint*.

By now the 1st Armoured Division's main defensive position had been reinforced with the 7th Field Force that had deployed from the UK. This brigade-sized formation with three regular and two TA infantry battalions deployed into the north-west sector of the division's area. Bounded in the north by the city of Hannover and in the south and west by a large, forested hill, the Deister, it was an area of relatively flat mixed terrain, open fields and many small towns and villages. Here the formation deployed its infantry companies and their Milan anti-tank missiles in a defensive position that applied the Goodwood concept. It had been given the time to prepare trenches and bunkers and get to know the terrain throughout its sector.

The exercise was choreographed to allow the armoured and mechanized battlegroups of the attacking 4th Division to test the Goodwood-style defensive layout of the 7th Field Force within the 1st Division. A total of 5,000 regular and 2,000 TA troops of the 7th Field Force with no armour of their own would face 9,000 troops of the 4th Division along with 200 tanks and 400 APCs.

Initially, 1st Division used an armoured guard force to fight an aggressive delay battle to slow down the 4th Division. After this withdrawal the attackers launched heavy simulated artillery strikes and then attempted to advance through the Goodwood defence. The infantry battalions had made extensive use of Carl Gustavs and Milan missiles sited in villages and woods to kill attacking armour moving in the open.

A favoured tactic was to allow Orange armoured reconnaissance to advance unmolested past concealed defensive positions. These held fire until tanks and APCs moved into pre-planned killing areas, where they were ambushed by the well-concealed infantry. Orange armoured and mechanized columns were subject to much delay, forming excellent targets for the full weight of the artillery of the 1st Division. The umpires assessed that the Goodwood defence had successfully absorbed the Orange attack and that the 4th Division had suffered such casualties that it would not have been able to advance further.

Meanwhile, in the south, another Orange attack by heliborne infantry sought to disrupt the 2nd Division's defences, to support an advance by the 3rd Panzer Brigade. But the British defences, supported again by USAF A10 Warthogs, proved too strong for the attackers.

PHASE 4, 24–26 SEPTEMBER: BLUE COUNTERATTACK

Judging that the Orange forces were incapable of further advances to the west, the corps mounted a counterattack to drive the enemy back to the east and restore the exercise international border. In the north, 1st Armoured Division attacked east towards Hildesheim. In the centre, 2nd (US) Armoured Division pushed east, grouped with a British battlegroup and two infantry battalions of the 7th Field Force. These conducted a heliborne attack into bridgeheads on the east side of the River Leine. Two infantry battalions were lifted by RAF Wessex and US Army Chinook helicopters. And the 2nd (UK) Armoured Division pushed east in the southern part of the corps area. This was supported by another battalion-sized heliborne attack. The Orange forces withdrew to the east. The exercise ended on 26 September.

EXERCISE SPEARPOINT ASSESSED

This was the Army's most ambitious corps exercise since NATO had adopted Flexible Response and Forward Defence. The Army's report stated that the exercise 'tested our operational techniques on a scale previously untried'.[22] This was an understatement.

The deployment of regular and TA units from the UK yielded important lessons on mobilization of the reserves and deploying forces by sea, road, rail and air. For example, a high tempo of raids into the corps rear area by the disruption brigade not only tested the alertness, defence plans and command and control of the many logistic units deployed there. The command and control of the three British armoured divisions had also been thoroughly tested. The Army assessed that task force structure had again proved to be sub-optimal and less resilient and capable than the previous brigade HQs and determined to revert to the previous structure as soon as it could.

Other weaknesses were demonstrated. The Chieftain tank was not reliable enough. And it was far less agile than the German Leopard 1 tanks. British mechanized infantry were envious of the German panzergrenadiers. Their Marder infantry fighting vehicle was equipped with a 20mm cannon, providing much more firepower than the British FV432s with their single machine gun. So the panzergrenadiers had more organic firepower and could use their cannon to attack Soviet light armour, allowing them to concentrate Milan missile fire on enemy tanks. The Marder also appeared to be more agile and reliable than the FV432.

The British were also jealous of the German brigade's close air defence company. This had Gepard anti-aircraft tanks. These boasted a turret with two radar guided anti-aircraft cannon, all mounted on the chassis of the Leopard 1 tank. Although the handheld Blowpipe air defence missiles had entered service, they were slower into action than the Gepards, which deployed well forward supporting the German armour. The exercise saw extensive use of the new British Rapier anti-aircraft missiles, but towed as they were by

Land Rovers, they lacked the cross-country mobility and protection of the Gepards. And whilst the Gepards could provide air defence while moving, it required at least 15 minutes to bring a Rapier into action, so it was less suited for a battle of armoured manoeuvre. It would not be until the early 1990s that all British armoured forces had tanks, infantry fighting vehicles and armoured air defences that were as capable of rapid armoured manoeuvre as German panzer and panzergrenadier brigades.

The British artillery delivered a lower weight of fire than its US and German counterparts. These were all equipped with the US M109 self-propelled gun with a calibre of 155mm, but half the British guns were lower calibre 105mm weapons mounted on the Abbot chassis, with a shorter range, and less lethal shells.

The RAF Wessex squadrons based in Germany had great utility throughout the battle, including evacuating casualties and moving key equipment forward. But each aircraft struggled to carry more than an eight-man infantry section. The Chinook helicopters that the US Army brought to the exercise could carry at least 30 troops and could lift much more freight.

The Army assessed that its tactics had succeeded. The three-day-long main defensive battle had stopped the Orange assault. The divisions had sought to make maximum use of infantry holding hills, woods and villages, exploiting their new Milan missiles. Fewer tanks were allocated to the mechanized infantry battlegroups, allowing more tanks to be held in reserve for local counterattacks. The Army judged that the Goodwood battle had demonstrated how light infantry could use a network of well-sited positions to absorb and stop a large, armoured force. And artillery, anti-tank helicopters and close air support had all succeeded in imposing additional casualties and delay on Orange's armoured columns.

Orange forces had been allocated a signals intelligence capability to monitor the corps radio nets. At the time, radio security was generally poor throughout the corps. It was comparatively easy for Orange's listening posts to gather considerable intelligence from Blue radio nets. Information that could be acted upon was passed to Orange forces. Several officers were prone to very long-winded radio transmissions. Some of these were recorded, to be played back to students subsequently attending training courses at Army schools in the UK. The Army decided that it needed to greatly improve its radio security.

Significantly, the exercise had not practised the use of nuclear weapons by either side. Previously it would probably have concluded with a simulated British nuclear strike. That this did not feature was a significant milestone – although apparently unremarked at the time.

The exercise had not subjected the Army's logistics systems to the same pressure as war; the only combat supplies being moved in realistic quantities were fuel and rations. Inevitably spare parts had been used, but as no equipment had been damaged by enemy action the repair of battle-damaged equipment had not been required, lowering the demands for spares. Quietly, in the background, the Army re-evaluated the corps' logistic support.

CHAPTER 3
RAPID INTERVENTION (1)
THE BIRTH OF ZIMBABWE, THE IRANIAN
EMBASSY SIEGE AND THE FALKLANDS WAR

OPERATION *AGILA* – THE BIRTH OF ZIMBABWE

Through the 1940s, 1950s and 1960s London dismantled much of the British Empire, granting independence to many colonies and setting up democratic constitutions.[1] In the mid-1960s the government of Rhodesia, a British colony in Africa, defied this trend by unilaterally declaring independence. The country disenfranchised its majority African population and Prime Minister Ian Smith faced down all British efforts to negotiate a transition to democracy.

Two different guerrilla movements formed, combining under the banner of the Patriotic Front. Initially Smith's forces contained the insurgencies. But Portugal's granting independence to its colony Mozambique greatly improved the insurgents' position, as did the late 1970s removal of military and economic support from South Africa. By now the issue had become diplomatically toxic for Britain, with the majority of Commonwealth and UN member nations calling for the dispute to be resolved in favour of majority rule. In late 1979 the new Prime Minister, Margaret Thatcher, sought to break the logjam. Foreign Secretary Lord Carrington convened the Lancaster House Conference. Against many predictions, a deal was negotiated for a ceasefire followed by elections.

The Army was tasked to lead a new Commonwealth Monitoring Force (CMF), to include small contingents from Australia, New Zealand, Kenya and Fiji to a total strength of 1,548 personnel, supported by Army Air Corps and RAF helicopters and Hercules transports. A ceasefire was agreed by the warring parties, so the force was deliberately small and armed only for self-defence, so as to not appear to be a combatant party.

There was very little solid information or intelligence to plan the mission. A small reconnaissance party deployed from late November 1979. It discovered that the guerrillas made extensive use of land mines, so it was decided to add mine protection to the force's Land Rovers – a modification carried out by the REME. The Rhodesian authorities and security forces voiced strong opinions that the mission would fail and that many monitors would die in the resulting bloodbath.

The force was commanded by Major General John Acland, the General Officer Commanding (GOC) of South West District, whose staff forced the nucleus of the joint force HQ. The land tactical HQ was provided by 8th Field Force, the formation designated for operations outside the NATO area. Commanded by Brigadier John Learmont as monitoring force deputy commander, it was required to provide teams to monitor 20 rendezvous points where guerrillas would assemble. After doing so the guerrillas would move to 16 assembly point camps. These rendezvous points and assembly places would be monitored by small teams from the CMF, who would also have a presence at agreed border crossing points and government forces bases. When these teams flew into the airport at Salisbury, the Rhodesian capital, they were deploying at range over a country several times larger than the UK, into an unknown and unpredictable environment.

Learmont needed plenty of officers and senior NCOs for the mission, but did not require many fighting troops. So the small teams were rank heavy, drawing not only on the field force's units, but on 30 other battalions and regiments from all over the UK. The CMF was assigned an Army Air Corps squadron, RAF Puma helicopters and Hercules transport aircraft, as well as the Army's air despatch squadron – experts in preparing loads for delivery by parachute and pushing them out of transport aircraft. The logistic requirements to sustain the teams were thought to be relatively small, so it had limited logistic support – principally a combat supplies platoon and some specialists.

RAPID DEPLOYMENT INTO THE UNKNOWN

Troops arrived by RAF and US aircraft between 20 and 25 December. General Acland personally briefed each party of monitors before they deployed from Salisbury. He set up his HQ in Government House alongside the governor, whilst the forces' main HQ, including the HQ of the 8th Field Force, was sited in a school. The force had to deploy teams by midnight on 28 December, when the ceasefire was to take effect, moving to a hundred different locations across a country the size of France. Its troops were deployed in mine-protected Land Rovers or by helicopter to remote locations where they apprehensively waited. Those at rendezvous points were joined by officers from the Patriotic Front. There were incidents, including torrential rainstorms, an RAF Puma crashing, killing the crew, and both an RAF Hercules and a monitoring team being shot up, fortunately without any casualties.

As the Rhodesian Army wore camouflage uniforms, the monitors dressed in plain green or khaki clothing. In many places it was some time before the guerillas appeared, as they were anxious not to walk into a trap set by the Rhodesian forces. A breakthrough was achieved when a small team led by a second lieutenant suddenly realized that:

the forest around them was alive with armed men. 'What do you think we should do?' the subaltern asked the wiry little company sergeant major sitting beside him. 'Put your rifle down on the table sir' he advised, 'then walk forward, hold up your arms and shout "welcome, welcome"'. The subaltern did as suggested, and the guerillas came out of the forest in hundreds.[2]

It was not long before parties of guerillas appeared, in groups of up to 300 fighters, greatly outnumbering the small monitoring teams. Although they were armed to the teeth, the great majority of guerrillas carried little or no food and their survival equipment was often limited to the clothes they stood up in.

The teams set out both to welcome the guerrillas and to appear as unthreatening and neutral as possible. This required determination, patience and finely tuned leadership. It had been predicted that 13,000–16,000 guerillas might emerge from the bush. In the event some 22,000 guerillas and 35,000 refugees appeared. Moving guerillas from the rendezvous points to the assembly areas in yellow civilian buses, along roads considered to be mined, on routes that took up to 20 hours to travel, was no ordinary journey. There was concern that the monitoring teams were in danger of being taken hostage, but the threat never materialized, in part because of the confidence that the monitors had established with the assembled guerillas.

The camps had little or no tents or logistic infrastructure. An example was Assembly Area Foxtrot where 6,000 people assembled, monitored by 50 Commonwealth troops. And the guerillas brought little food with them. The Rhodesian security forces refused to provide logistic support to the camps. So the monitoring force had to. This was a task none of the Army planners had foreseen, the force having only enough logistic support for itself. But it rose to the challenge.

Without food, supplies or tents, there was a great danger that assembled guerrillas might mutiny or melt back into the bush. This could lead to mission failure. Some supplies were rapidly flown to the country from South Africa, the UK and the US. These were delivered to the far-flung assembly areas by helicopter or parachute drop from RAF Hercules transport aircraft. Many necessary items were locally purchased, including tents, blankets, underwear, plates and cutlery – many guerrillas not even having plates to eat off. Initially these were delivered by air drop, but gradually land routes were opened and local contractors hired to make deliveries. Some of the rations initially supplied were very unpopular with the guerrillas, who forcibly demanded meat. Rhodesia did not have enough, so 450 tons of meat were purchased in South Africa, 90 tons of which was rapidly delivered to the guerrillas by air.

A key role was played by senior guerilla officers who had been appointed as 'peace commissioners'. They often helped to defuse tension. But the guerillas' suspicions were easily triggered. Captain Hugo Grenville of the Coldstream Guards observed that 'there was equal mistrust and suspicion with the guerrillas and the Rhodesian security forces. They knew their day had long gone, but were reluctant to relinquish what they thought was rightfully theirs. The rebels for their part were sometimes drunk and high, often too far gone to unload their AK47s.'[3] Many guerrilla fighters refused to make their weapons safe. Negligent discharges were common, with 12 guerrillas killed and 53 wounded as a result.

On 28 December 1979, Assembly Point Papa was established by 13 members of 3rd Battalion, the Light Infantry, a vehicle mechanic and three signalmen. Two insurgent liaison officers from Lusaka joined them. Captain Richard Hodson, the commander, takes up the story:

> During the first week the guerrillas poured in by busloads, laden with vast quantities of assorted ammunition and a whole host of mainly obsolete Soviet weapons, including mortars and anti-tank and anti-aircraft guns. Hercules aircraft clearly marked with white crosses droned constantly overhead, dropping supplies and equipment to house, feed and heal these reluctant, suspicious and temperamental men who constituted Joshua Nkomo's ragged 'Army of liberation'.
>
> Our initial priorities were to establish some form of working relationship with them and a semblance of order. Muster and sick parades got off the ground. Medicine became a great healer for them and for their attitude towards us. The sick numbered some 250 a day. The walking wounded were badly infected through lack of proper medical attention and had to be evacuated six days after their arrival.
>
> Establishing cordial relations with them wasn't an easy proposition. The entire operation ran on a shoestring for the first month. Shortages of food and water supply and promised camp stores that arrived long after they were due, prompted accusations of 'dirty British' or 'Rhodesian collaborators systematically starving the forces of liberation'.
>
> By the time we left, relations between ourselves and the Patriotic Front had become excellent. Patience, time and cinema shows had seen to that. The Rhodesian security forces arrived at long last to commence the initial integration process between the armed forces, once bitter enemies. The two opposing sides were now drinking beer and recounting their war experiences together and toasting the new Zimbabwe.[4]

The monitors were delighted to find that many guerilla medical assistants had been given months of effective medical training in the Warsaw Pact. They were very effective at dealing with minor injuries and local diseases. The British deployed military doctors who complemented the guerrilla medics, acting as a powerful incentive for fighters to stay at the assembly areas.

After successful elections, the CMF withdrew, leaving a British military training team in place, to assist with the formation of new armed forces.

Why had this extremely risky operation succeeded? Firstly, because the Lancaster House Agreement enjoyed support from all its signatories. And this policy was translated into explicit direction to the Rhodesian government forces and guerillas to conform with the military requirements of the treaty. Secondly the CMF had a successful concept of operations, and the monitoring teams used no small amount of courage, good humour and pragmatism to make it work on the ground. And thirdly, when more people turned up at the camps, the CMF, supported by the US and the RAF, moved quickly to forward deploy the necessary tents, infrastructure and supplies to accommodate the guerillas and refugees.

General Acland was later to reflect that success required 'the courage, sense of judgement and degree of self-control on the ground, to deal with a hitherto unexperienced situation in which the use of military force would mean the operation had failed'. And that unusually 'god had been on the side of the small battalions.' After the operation Acland was offered a knighthood. He accepted on the condition that all members of the monitoring force received a campaign medal. The medal was awarded.[5]

Other success factors included the actions of the Rhodesian government, security forces and the Patriotic Front itself. They had all signed up to the Lancaster House Agreement and directed their forces to comply. But there was such mutual suspicion that without the open-handed and scrupulously neutral endeavours of the monitors, the process would have broken down. And if the force had not rapidly provided logistic support to the assembled guerrillas, they would probably have dispersed, with fighting probably restarting.

The military provisions of the Lancaster House Agreement had proved workable. General Acland had been a very successful theatre commander and a key member of the ceasefire commission, displaying enormous quantities of both patience and political skill. The operation had been well led by Brigadier Learmont and the HQ of 8th Field Force. This type of operation was not one that was covered by Army doctrine and training, but Learmont and the HQ had rapidly produced a successful plan for this unforeseen scenario. The relatively new Clansman radios used by the force performed extremely well and communications across Rhodesia were excellent.

Learmont felt very well supported by the UK, particularly in providing the additional logistic support that the force requested, publicly commending 'the speed and efficiency with which the MoD and UK met our every request, without which we would have been in severe difficulty'. As this story progresses, it will be interesting to see how much Learmont's observations applied to other British Army operations. We shall call this the Learmont Test – was every request by the Army commander in the operational theatre met by the Army HQ and MoD?

OPERATION *NIMROD* – THE SAS AND THE IRANIAN EMBASSY SIEGE

In the Western Desert in the early 1940s a specialized raiding unit had been formed.[6] Commanded by David Stirling, it had successfully mounted raids on German airfields. It then took part in the Italian and Normandy campaigns. After the war the regiment was removed from the Regular Army but retained in the TA. In the 1950s it was re-formed to lead long-range patrols in the jungles of Malaya. It then fought with some success in Oman and Borneo, and during the insurgency in Dhofar it formed and led an irregular force that included surrendered enemy, the Firqat.

In the late 1960s the SAS had been allocated a NATO role, assigning squadrons to NATO's regional commanders. This reflected its core role, of operating deep in hostile territory to conduct intelligence surveillance and reconnaissance, carry out offensive operations or work with indigenous forces. It preferred to operate at the strategic or operational theatre level, where it could be applied to the highest priority missions and where it could draw on the highest levels of intelligence. Apart from SAS deployment to Northern Ireland, most of the Army had little or no contact with the regiment. And for officers, service with the SAS was not considered particularly career enhancing.

So, what was 'special' about the SAS? The answer was its people. Getting into the regiment was very difficult. Those who volunteered would undergo a selection and training process so demanding that not more than 5 per cent of soldiers and officers normally passed it. It began with cross-country marches over the unforgiving hills and mountains of Wales, carrying rucksacks of ever-increasing weight. As well as meeting the essential standards of physical endurance, the regiment was looking for people who could work for long periods in small groups or even on their own. Officers would be tested on their ability to assess a situation and form a plan under pressure.

There would then come training, including in the very demanding conditions of the jungle, followed by survival training that included resistance to interrogation, both skills tested on an escape and evasion exercise. Remaining volunteers would be given parachute training before being 'badged' – receiving the sand-coloured beret with its distinctive badge of a winged sword and motto 'who dares wins'.

Further training would follow. The building block of the regiment was a four-man patrol, with each trooper trained in one of four individual skills; as a signaller, advanced combat medic, demolitions specialist or linguist. Four patrols made up a troop and four troops a squadron. Each troop specialized in a different 'method of entry': the way to move into and through an area of operations. The air troop would become experts in free-fall parachuting, the boat troop in using canoes and small boats, the mountain troop in moving through mountainous areas, and the mobility troop in moving long distances overland in small vehicles. The design was such that an SAS squadron could offer a wide variety of operational options to a theatre commander.

Just as important were the SAS' cultural characteristics. These included a very high level of operational security, in which the 'need to know' principle was ruthlessly applied, as well as the relentless pursuit of excellence and a thirst to create and sustain advantage over the enemy. These characteristics produced an organization that could sometimes behave in a much more egalitarian fashion than the rest of the Army. Sometimes this grated with the Army's default hierarchical settings with resulting friction, but it worked for the SAS.

In the late 1960s the SAS saw an increasing threat from terrorism, both internationally and domestically. In 1972, the threat was brought home at the Munich Olympics. Palestinian terrorists took Israeli hostages, but a German police operation to free them spectacularly failed, with the deaths of five of the eight terrorists as well as all nine Israeli hostages and a German policeman. The German police and authorities had been ill-prepared for the challenge.

In the UK an agreed government-level approach was formulated. Police chief constables faced with a hostage crisis beyond their capabilities to resolve would request military assistance. Subject to agreement by the defence and home secretaries, the SAS would deploy the so-called 'Special Projects' team. This was a squadron on extremely high readiness to deploy. It would comprise groups of snipers and assault troops, wearing characteristic black flameproof overalls and carrying pistols and sub-machine guns. They would have access to a wide variety of equipment, including ladders, abseiling ropes and gas and 'flash-bang' stun grenades. The necessary tactics and drills had been rapidly developed and were regularly tested and refined during exercises.

But just as important was the supporting machinery. The SAS embraced the chief constables, running a programme of regular briefings and demonstrations for senior police officers at their Hereford base. They had also partnered with both police intelligence and MI5 to use a wide variety of technical and non-technical means to be able to rapidly gather information and intelligence about the terrorists, the hostages and the buildings in which they were held.

This was complemented by developing political/military command and control. The default setting was that the commanding officer would put himself alongside the police commander at the police incident control point, while the Director SAS, a brigadier, would be in the Cabinet Office Briefing Room (COBRA) where the required senior ministers would give political direction.

A regular programme of counterterrorist exercises gave the SAS practice in this role. Just as important, it practised the mechanisms of gathering intelligence and political/police/military planning and command and control.

So, when in May 1980 the Iranian embassy was seized by dissident Iranian terrorists, the well-practised machinery rapidly swung into action.[7]

But as with all military operations, there was risk, good and bad luck and friction, particularly when one of the SAS soldiers was trapped in tangled ropes and badly burned by flames. And in 1980, the tactics of hostage rescue operations were not widely publicized. They are now. The assault could have been much more difficult if the terrorists had had more military training, used more grenades, worn body armour or rigged the embassy building with explosives.

The SAS would much rather that the assault had gone in under cover of darkness or been less well covered by the international media, including the famous live broadcast of the attack on BBC TV. But the success of the assault immediately increased the military credibility of the UK, especially since a US effort to rescue hostages held in Iran had failed. Many media commentators failed to point out that whilst the police had complete control of the outside of the embassy in West London, the US did not have such purchase in Tehran. The US mission was very much more difficult.

The SAS' success resulted in a surge of requests from foreign governments to train their hostage rescue teams. Where the government accepted these requests, the SAS did all they could to help, but often found that many foreign forces focussed excessively on creating an elite assault force but underemphasized the need to integrate the forces' activity with intelligence gathering and the essential political military and police command and control that had been such important success factors in resolving this siege.

The siege also had a wider effect in the Army. In combination with the assignment of SAS teams to Northern Ireland and the role of the SAS in Falklands War, the regiment partially emerged from its closet, particularly with the Army's officers. Previously service in the SAS had been seen as a sideline that disadvantaged officers' careers. From the early 1980s service with the SAS was seen as advancing officers' careers, with mutual benefit to the Army, the SAS and the officers concerned.

Operation *Corporate* – the Falklands War

The April 1982 invasion of the Falkland Islands by Argentine forces came as a strategic surprise to the British government and its armed forces. But its recapture on 14 June was a significant victory, accomplished against challenges that many commentators had thought insuperable. These included the great distance over which the war was conducted and an apparent numerical superiority of the Argentine forces, who were fighting much closer to home.

Prior to April 1982, very few British people knew anything about the Falkland Islands, their location some 8,000 miles from Britain and their small population of British citizens. They were unaware of a lengthy festering dispute with Argentina, which claimed the Falklands as its own territory. Or that the 1981 Defence Review (the Nott Review) had announced that HMS *Endurance*, the patrol vessel that operated in the South Atlantic, which had an undeclared signals intelligence capability, would retire and not be replaced – a move seen by Buenos Aires as weakening Britain's military commitment to the Islands.

To learn that Argentine forces had attacked the Falklands and South Georgia and taken the small Royal Marine garrison prisoner came as a profound shock to the British media, public and parliament. Initially the MoD and Defence Secretary John Nott assessed that the British lacked the military capability to recapture the islands. An ad hoc meeting of Prime Minister Thatcher, Nott and other officials in the House of Commons was joined by the Chief of the Naval Staff, Admiral Sir Henry Leach. He vigorously refuted Nott's pessimism, starting that he had a plan to send a naval task force to recapture the Falklands, needing only the Prime Minister's direction to activate it. When asked by the Prime Minister if recapturing the islands was feasible, Leach replied, 'Yes, we can recover the islands, because if we do not, or if we pussyfoot in our actions and do not achieve complete success, in another few months we shall be living in a different country whose word counts for little.'[8]

She readily agreed. Leach's bold intervention had decisive strategic effect. But at a stormy emergency session of the House of Commons on 3 April MPs heaped humiliation on the government. The one positive announcement that Thatcher could make was that a naval task force had been ordered to sail. The mood in Parliament that day was such that subsequent failure to recapture the islands would have probably led to the demise of her government.

It was fortunate that plans made by Defence Secretary John Nott to retire the Royal Navy's aircraft carriers had not yet been implemented. Carrying Sea Harrier jump jets, both HMS *Hermes* and HMS *Invincible* would be at the core of the naval task force that was despatched on 5 April. At the same time an amphibious force was rapidly assembled and despatched. The landing force comprised the Royal Marines' 3 Commando Brigade. It took with it its three marine commandos and its integral Army artillery regiment and engineer squadron, as well as the Commando Logistic Regiment, a unique unit manned by marines, sailors and Army logisticians and technicians, all of whom had passed the commando course and earned the coveted green beret.

The marines understood the islands well, having long provided a company as a small garrison. They knew well that outside of Port Stanley, the capital, the terrain was comprised of very rough moorland. Apart from some terrain around the few settlements and a very few tracks that could accommodate a lightly loaded Land Rover, most of the terrain was inaccessible to wheeled vehicles, other than tractors. The marines were confident that the highly mobile Bandvagen over-snow vehicles that they used in the Arctic would be capable of traversing much of the terrain and took with them those Bandvagens that were not stockpiled in Norway.

Brigadier Julian Thompson, the Royal Marine officer leading 3 Commando Brigade, requested that the Army's Arctic warfare trained and equipped units join the commando brigade. These included the infantry battalion, artillery battery, reconnaissance squadron, engineers and logistics assigned to the NATO ACE Mobile Force. All exercised in North Norway every winter, alongside the marines. This request was denied.[9] Instead, the Army rapidly assigned the spearhead battalion 3rd Battalion, the Parachute Regiment (3 Para) as well as two troops of the Blues and Royals with Scorpion and Scimitar reconnaissance vehicles. A welcome addition was a battery of Rapier air defence missiles and a second engineer squadron, as well as the necessary engineer material to construct a short airstrip for Harrier jump jets. Subsequently 2nd Battalion, the Parachute Regiment (2 Para) was added to the force.

The Royal Navy's existing amphibious shipping would now be insufficient to carry the additional troops, equipment and supplies. So merchant ships were hired, as was the *Canberra*, a luxury cruise liner. At the same time ships were being rapidly loaded with both supplies and troops. The existing plans for the delivery of the commando brigade's ammunition to ports by rail were thwarted by the lack of notice to pre-position the necessary wagons. So the Commando Logistic Regiment sent its own vehicles, rapidly augmented by trucks from across both the regular and territorial armies and a hundred chartered flatbed trucks, augmented by hiring 44 special trains. Over 39,000 tons of supplies would be moved by road to the docks for loading on task force shipping. As soon as ships were loaded, they sailed in a blaze of military bands, publicity and emotion. The national mood was an extraordinary mixture of pride and apprehension, best summarized by the headline of the US magazine *Newsweek* 'The Empire Strikes Back'.

THE GREEN BERETS

The commando brigade itself was part of the Royal Navy. It was assigned a role to reinforce NATO in Northern Europe. Deployment options included Denmark and Norway. The latter role was the most demanding. It was considered the training priority, as it required the brigade to be capable of living and fighting in the mountains and wildernesses of north

Norway. To be able to do this the whole year round, the brigade was required to master the demanding skills of Arctic warfare. Since the brigade had returned to the UK from the Far East in 1972, it had vigorously trained itself in north Norway for as many winters as the defence budget could afford.

The Royal Marines were an elite force. All marines were required to complete commando training. This was a demanding process, based on the selection and training of specialized amphibious raiding units in World War II. Churchill had named these units 'commandos' after the irregular Boer units that had been so effective against the British in the Boer War. Initially commandos had comprised volunteers from the Army, but from the middle of the war the Royal Marines also formed commando units. After 1945 the Army commandos had been disbanded, but the Marines retained the demanding selection and training regime for their post-war amphibious forces. The commando brigade included many soldiers who had passed the commando course.

The commando tests have not changed in substance since the 1980s. The first day requires a 6-mile endurance run including moving through a series of tunnels, one of which is full of water. The next day sees a speed march of 9 miles to be completed in 90 minutes. Candidates have then to pass the Tarzan course, a series of high and vertiginous obstacles, followed by Lympstone's formidable assault course of lower, but no less tough obstacles, completing both in 13 minutes. Those who have passed the first three tests spend a final day conducting a 30-mile speed march across the high hills and moorland of Dartmoor. If they traverse the boggy and rocky uplands in eight hours or less, they are awarded the coveted green beret. The Army gunners, sappers and logisticians and naval personnel that serve with the brigade must all pass the commando tests, entitling them to wear the green beret and the badge 'Army Commando'.

These tests and the tough training that preceded them produced troops that were fitter and more robust than average Army soldiers. I vividly remember working alongside two different Royal Marine commandos in Northern Ireland in 1978. The marines were notably tougher and more self-reliant than the soldiers in my company. And their NCOs were more confident – a result of the better training given to Marine NCOs at the time. The commando course and the high level of Arctic training produced a brigade that had a high level of physical toughness and robustness. It was well prepared to operate in the demanding conditions of north Norway, a quality that would have great utility in the Falklands.

An amphibious landing is a difficult enough operation in peacetime. In war the difficulties posed by the enemy multiply the complexities and risk. Such a landing requires an amphibious force of naval shipping and a landing force, with both forces' commanders and HQs having expert understanding of their roles and a high level of mutual confidence. The commando brigade HQ, commanded by Brigadier Julian Thompson, had this, as did the Royal Navy's small amphibious warfare HQ, commanded by Commodore Michael Clapp. Both were well experienced in amphibious operations, landing from the Royal Navy's two amphibious assault ships, HMS *Fearless* and *Intrepid* and the six logistic landing ships of the Royal Fleet Auxiliary, as well as making best use of landing craft, small boats and the Royal Navy's amphibious helicopters. Both HQs were well used to working together on NATO exercises.

THE RED BERETS

Equally demanding selection and training applied to the two battalions of the Parachute Regiment that joined the brigade. Like the commandos, the regiment was a World War II innovation, this time for airborne operations. It too had a distinctive beret, maroon instead of green, and a challenging selection and training process, which looked for soldiers of greater toughness and resilience than the rest of the Army. This was based on the experience of airborne operations, that troops landing by parachute were of necessity less heavily equipped than conventional units and had to be prepared to fight for several days with only the weapons and ammunition that they carried or could be dropped from the air.

Selection for Army parachutists is conducted by Pegasus Company, known universally as P Company. The final eight tests take place over a week. They include a speed march completed in an hour and 50 minutes, a steeplechase of 1.8 miles across country and an obstacle course both completed in 18 minutes. Candidates then face a speed march across 20 miles of difficult terrain completed in four hours and ten minutes. Teamwork is tested by a stretcher race in which groups of 16 soldiers carry a 175-pound stretcher 4 miles across country and a log race where teams of eight soldiers carry a telegraph pole across 1.9 miles.

There are two tests of individual aggression and determination, the first being a minute's milling, an unsophisticated version of boxing with fewer rules. The second is the 'trainasium', an aerial assault course 55 feet off the ground, designed to test the candidate's ability to overcome fear of heights, an essential quality of military parachutists. Those who pass the course are awarded the coveted red beret. They then are taught by the RAF to parachute, initially without military equipment, but subsequently with their weapon, rucksack and a container of equipment, by day and night.

The two parachute battalions were joined by two artillery batteries from 7 Parachute Regiment, Royal Horse Artillery and 9 Parachute Squadron, Royal Engineers. P Company and parachute training meant that their physical toughness, robustness and resilience was equivalent to those of the marines. So reinforced, 3 Commando Brigade was a genuinely elite formation, containing most of the toughest troops the British forces had to offer. Also sailing south were the even tougher SAS soldiers of the regimental HQ and two squadrons of 22nd Special Air Service Regiment (22 SAS) as well as the equally tough marines of the Special Boat Service (SBS). The brigade was also joined by a battery of Rapier air defence missiles and additional gunners, sappers and light helicopters, giving it a strength of about 5,500 men.

Many of these troops, including 3 Para, boarded the ocean liner *Canberra* for their voyage south, finding the luxury of the ship a surreal experience. They were joined by the Royal Navy's dedicated amphibious shipping. HMS *Fearless*, a Landing Platform Dock (LPD), hosted the amphibious and landing force HQs. Designed for amphibious operations it carried four large Landing Craft Utility vessels (LCUs) stored in an internal dock. It could also carry four helicopters. The second LPD, HMS *Intrepid*, had been in storage. It was rapidly activated and joined the amphibious group in mid-May. The ships carried helicopters to support amphibious operations.

To lift troops, weapons and supplies the Royal Navy provided five Wessex helicopters and 12 Sea King aircraft. Four helicopters had crews trained in the use of passive night vision goggles, then a relatively new application of image intensification technology, that could be fitted to an aircrew helmet. Requiring an adapted cockpit and special training, these would allow helicopters to operate at night in darker conditions than had been previously possible. The commando brigade had its own helicopter squadron of Gazelle and Scout light helicopters, the latter able to fire the French SS11 anti-tank missiles. Reinforced by Army helicopters, it would have nine Gazelle and nine Scout helicopters.

Also part of the amphibious force were six Landing Ships Logistic (LSLs), crewed by civilian seamen of the Royal Fleet Auxiliary. These had bow and stern doors for rapidly offloading troops and supplies as well as two helicopter decks. The size of the landing force exceeded the capacity of these vessels, so five ferries and more cargo ships were hired. The SS *Atlantic Conveyor* was loaded with more Harrier fighters, five large Chinook helicopters and six Wessex helicopters, as well as tents and rations.

As the ships travelled south, negotiations to find a diplomatic solution were paralleled by UK military measures to put pressure on Buenos Aires and to make it easier to begin hostilities. These included the 12 April announcement of a 200-mile maritime exclusion zone around the islands. The troops constantly trained, with a particular emphasis on fitness and first aid.

APPROACH TO BATTLE

By now Ascension Island was a major air and logistic base. The commando brigade and amphibious ships arrived at the island over several days, starting on 13 April. The weeks at Ascension provided an opportunity to re-stow supplies to reflect the likely tactical plan for the landings and subsequent operations. This period also provided an opportunity to practise the necessary techniques and procedures that would be needed for the amphibious landing. Whilst the commando units were well practised in landing from ships by landing craft and helicopters, the parachute battalions and other Army units were not.

In despatching the shipping carrying the commando brigade and its logistic supplies of ammunition and spare parts the overriding need had been speed – driven by the political need to be seen to be despatching the task force as quickly as possible. Doctrine for amphibious operations recommends that supplies and equipment should be loaded in the reverse order to the priorities for the landing – so that the material to be unloaded first is loaded last. But in the rush to get the brigade loaded and despatched from UK, supplies had been loaded into the ships as quickly as they arrived at the docks, without regard to the operational priorities of a brigade plan. So the brigade's overriding priority at Ascension was to adjust the distribution of equipment and supplies in the ships to support the amphibious landing.

Ascension Island became a scene of intense activity as landing craft and helicopters moved troops and supplies between ships and carried commandos and paratroops ashore to conduct fitness training and test-fire their weapons on improvised ranges. New tactical ideas were tried out. These included parachuting from Sea King helicopters, as well as positioning the Scorpions and Scimitars at the front of landing craft, to provide suppressive fire as they approached the shore. Neither of these tactics had been tried before. The brigade also planned to unload the Rapier battery and its anti-aircraft missile launchers to test them, including firing missiles, but a signal from Northwood unexpectedly arrived placing the amphibious force at such short notice to sail that the Rapier could not be unloaded. And the recently arrived 2 Para had only time for a single daylight rehearsal of embarking from its ferry into landing craft.

COMMAND AND CONTROL

The overall task force commander was the Commander in Chief Fleet, Admiral Fieldhouse. Based at a bunker in the north London suburb of Northwood, his operational HQ was configured in peacetime not only to command Royal Navy ships around the world, but also to lead NATO's campaign in the eastern Atlantic, the English Channel and the North Sea. He had six subordinate commanders:

- **Commander Carrier Battle Group:** Rear Admiral Woodward in HMS *Hermes*
- **Commander Amphibious Task Group:** Commodore Clapp in HMS *Fearless*
- **Commander Landing Force Task Group:** Brigadier Thompson RM, initially in HMS *Fearless* later ashore at brigade HQ. Succeeded by Major General Moore RM in HMS *Fearless*
- **Commander Submarine Task Group:** Admiral Herbert at Northwood London
- **Air Commander:** Air Marshal Curtiss at Northwood
- **Commander South Georgia Task Group:** Captain Young in HMS *Antrim*.

SOUTH GEORGIA

A small joint task force was assigned to evict the Argentine troops that occupied the small settlements on the isolated island of South Georgia. It comprised several warships, a company of Royal Marines, an SBS section and D Squadron, 22 SAS. The latter had joined the force out of its own initiative. South Georgia was isolated with unpredictable and dangerous winter weather and the SAS' plan to set up observation posts on a glacier was defeated by the weather, resulting in the loss of two precious helicopters. Just as the mission seemed lost, an Argentine submarine arrived and was neutralized by a missile-firing naval helicopter. The Marines and SAS conducted a hasty improvised landing and used naval gunfire and their organic firepower to overawe the defenders, who surrendered.

Despite an unclear command structure, and the SAS underestimating the extreme weather, the success of the engagement was significant. It demonstrated that London was not only willing to use lethal force, but also had forces that could fight. It created political confidence that the armed forces could outfight the Argentinians. In British hands South Georgia provided a large anchorage outside the range of Argentine aircraft.

5TH INFANTRY BRIGADE – AN UNREADY FORMATION

It was decided that more land forces were required. Brigadier Thompson's commando brigade had five manoeuvre units. He advised that it could not effectively command any more forces. The Army's strategic reserve, the 5th Infantry Brigade, would also be assigned to the operation, to work under the land force HQ, commanded by Royal Marine Major General Jeremy Moore.

5th Infantry Brigade was the Army's designated brigade for any operations outside the NATO area. The brigade had been formed after the 1975 Defence Review as the 8th Field Force. Its role was the military home defence of the UK, for which its priority was countering parities of Soviet special forces, or Spetsnaz, that would attempt attacks in the UK. It had been used successfully as the land component HQ for the 1980 operation in Rhodesia. And later that year, it had deployed as a brigade on a UK-wide home defence exercise.

In 1981 two parachute battalions were resubordinated to the brigade, allowing it to mount limited airborne operations. The most likely scenario for this was seen as a non-combatant evacuation operation, in which a parachute battalion might be used to seize an airfield from which civilians could be flown to safety. The MoD planned that such an operation would only face 'light opposition'. In late 1981, the brigade began practising the conduct of such an evacuation operation.

The inconvenient truth was that of all the Army's deployable brigades, it was the lowest priority, for example being the last to receive new weapons and equipment. The brigade was probably the Army's regular formation with the lowest level of readiness. It was much less well trained than the Army's other brigades, and was short of organic combat support and logistics. It was much less capable of expeditionary operations than the commando brigade.

As the need to reinforce the land force had become clearer, the Army's staff considered which forces to deploy. Aware of the weaknesses of 5th Brigade, other options were examined. The 1st Infantry Brigade was an extant all-arms formation with a full complement of infantry battalions, artillery and engineers. Given its role outside 1 (BR) Corps as an independent expeditionary force to reinforce NATO's Baltic approaches, it had a substantial logistic group – albeit with a significant proportion of its capability delivered by the TA.

Garrisoned in Bulford alongside 1st Brigade was the British Army element of the ACE Mobile Force (Land) (abbreviated to AMF (L)), comprising an infantry battalion, an artillery HQ and gun battery, an armoured reconnaissance squadron and the force signal squadron. All these were supplied by a dedicated logistic battalion. The whole contingent was trained and equipped for Arctic warfare, holding over-snow all-terrain vehicles. Their annual winter deployment to Norway meant that they were well used to deploying by sea and sustaining themselves in cold weather and harsh terrain. At the start of the war, Brigadier Thompson had requested that these forces join the commando brigade.

Some of Army staff advised that instead of 5th Brigade the reinforcing formation should be 1st Brigade, using its own units and the units assigned to the AMF (L), as

Thompson had originally requested. But the decision of General Sir Edwin Bramall, then CGS, was that 5th Brigade would deploy instead, with its remaining Gurkha battalion, and be reinforced by 1st Battalion, the Welsh Guards and 2nd Battalion, the Scots Guards to replace the two parachute battalions. Why the Army had not earlier assigned units to replace the gaps in 5th Brigade left by the removal of the two parachute battalions, was a question that was never satisfactorily answered.

Once the brigade was warned for the Falklands, the Army belatedly sought to expand its capabilities. For example, its obsolete Larkspur radios were rapidly replaced by the newer Clansman, transferred from TA units that were assigned to NATO and had previously had a higher priority. Unlike the paratroopers and marines, the brigade's troops did not even have rucksacks, but the cheap and inadequate '1958 pattern' canvas large pack. Eventually the brigade was issued with several different models of civilian rucksacks produced by outdoor clothing and equipment companies. All were greatly superior to the large pack, but many were brightly coloured, requiring painting in green or camouflage colours (though not before some guardsmen had boarded ships with bright blue rucksacks).

The Scots Guards had their ceremonial bayonets replaced by new ones in dull gunmetal, which they immediately sharpened. They would later use them. The battalion also decided not to deploy its obsolete heavy Wombat anti-tank guns, but to replace them with .5-inch heavy machine guns, which were supplied. It also received Arctic socks, which were much better than the cheap polyester socks that troops were normally issued with. But the battalions often found the rest of the Army slow to respond. For example, it took questions in the House of Lords to unlock the supply of rucksacks. Lieutenant Colonel Mike Scott, the commanding officer, was told by General Bramall that 'you're in reserve and will be used'. Scott was not sure that he believed him. Some in the brigade and in the Army felt that the formation might only arrive after the war had been won, and would act as a post-war garrison for the islands.

The formation had precious little time for training and preparation for the Falklands. It was ordered to rapidly deploy to the uplands of the Sennybridge training area in Wales. The area was notorious throughout the Army for its wet weather and the difficult terrain, which in foul weather was a reasonable simulation of the tussock of the Falklands. But the brigade training period basked in balmy sunshine. For the three infantry battalions, the exercise revealed many problems with the brigade. Lieutenant Colonel Scott was astonished to be asked by the brigade commander, Tony Wilson, to lead the planning of a brigade attack – a function that Scott rightly believed should be performed by Wilson and the brigade HQ.

In peacetime, 5th Brigade was commanded by HQ South East District. Its commander, Lieutenant General Sir Richard Trant, visited the exercise and was greatly alarmed. He recommended that Wilson be removed from command. But concerned for the brigade's morale, General Bramall, the CGS, disagreed and left Wilson in place. Why Trant's HQ had not already known about the brigade or Wilson's weaknesses has never been satisfactorily explained.

Whilst the commando brigade had its own logistic regiment, 5th Brigade had very few logistics of its own. It was rapidly assigned two ordnance companies, with ample stocks of supplies, but no vehicles to move them, a transport troop with 20 Snowcat over-snow vehicles, a REME workshop and 16 Field Ambulance. The troops boarded another luxury liner, *Queen Elizabeth II*, at Southampton, in another spectacular and emotional send-off. As the ship sailed south, with soldiers again living in luxury conditions, the units trained as best they could, like the marines earlier, concentrating on fitness and first aid.

But 5th Brigade's commanding officers found themselves increasingly underwhelmed by the brigade HQ, particularly its commander, Brigadier Tony Wilson. Wilson appeared to be a showman and was observed by a commanding officer 'to be good with pen, but not with the sword'. Shortly after the brigade landed, he told his commanding officers that 'the intelligence will be so good that you'll know the name of every Argentinian soldier in every trench': a claim that he should have known better than to make.

Brigadier John Waters accompanied the brigade as the deputy land forces commander. Before embarking Waters had been told by a senior naval officer that, given the friction between Northwood and Brigadier Thompson, Waters might have to replace the Marine brigadier. Waters had also been told by General Bramall that there were some doubts about Wilson's ability. So Waters might have to sack him and take over command of 5th Brigade. Waters kept these directions to himself.

ADVANCE FORCE OPERATIONS

The carrier battlegroup began landing special forces reconnaissance patrols onto the islands to gain intelligence. Working to intelligence priorities set by Thompson and Clapp, the SBS sought to identify beaches that could be used for the amphibious landing and to determine their suitability for use by landing craft.

SAS patrols were tasked to gather information about enemy positions and the effectiveness of the defenders. The patrols travelled in low-flying Royal Navy Sea King 4 transport helicopters whose crews had been trained and equipped to use new image-intensifying passive night vision goggles to operate at night without using artificial light. It was particularly important that the defenders be unaware of the patrols, so as not to reveal the areas where the British were considering landing.

So the SAS landed at least a day's march from their targets. Their patrols moved stealthily by night to find covert observation posts, where they could watch Argentine forces. These were often positions in the open where the soldiers lay covered only by a camouflage net, staying as still as possible and with little protection from the elements.

The SAS patrols relied on morse and paper codes to report back to HMS *Fearless*. The enemy was thought to have had a radio direction-finding capability that would be able to pinpoint the locations of any but the briefest radio messages. So the SBS patrols examining potential beaches had to be extracted by helicopter for face-to-face debriefs, in order to provide the necessary details the planners needed to minimize the risks of the landings.

Both the SAS and SBS patrols required great stamina and endurance in the enduring cold, damp and high wind. For example, an SAS patrol landed by night on 1 May took five nights to reach the location from which it would observe Goose Green. Movement across the bleak tussock moorland was slow. And when crossing the many runs of rock boulders, it got even slower too – sometimes the patrol covered as little as 200 yards in an hour. Establishing an observation post amongst such rocks, the patrol had a good overall view of the settlement, observing Argentine personnel moving around and arriving and departing helicopters, but was too far away to determine the layout of defensive positions.

The patrols assessed that many of the defending troops appeared to be less well led and militarily proficient than the British. SAS reporting, combined with signals intelligence, showed that the majority of the 11,000 Argentine troops on the islands were based in and around Port Stanley, with smaller detachments based in settlements on East and West Falklands and at an airfield on Pebble Island. The overall level of military skill and morale seemed low.

There were two substantial groups of enemy forces on East Falkland. The main Argentine force of about 10,000 troops was the strong garrison of Port Stanley, equivalent to a small infantry division. The possession of the island's only concrete airfield and political significance of the island capital meant that Stanley would be the centre of gravity of the land operation. To the south of San Carlos, the small settlements of Darwin and a grass airstrip, Goose Green, straddled the narrow isthmus that connected East Falkland with the landmass of Lafonia to the south. There was thought to be an infantry battalion-sized force there. A 'strategic reserve' of about a thousand troops was believed to be based near Fitzroy.

Throughout April and May, Brigadier Thompson, Commodore Clapp and their staffs worked together in the cramped planning rooms in HMS *Fearless*, examining all the potential places to land. Over 50 beaches were assessed. In this they were greatly assisted by an expert on the islands and their inshore waters, with their complex networks of peninsulas, islands, bays, beds of kelp seaweed and the beaches themselves. This was Major Ewen Southby-Tailyour, a Marine officer who had spent an earlier tour in the Falklands sailing around the islands and preparing a guide for sailors.

The force had not only to land where there were sufficient beaches, but also where there was sufficient depth of water to accommodate the amphibious ships and escorting warships. Its terrain had to have room for the whole reinforced brigade to land, offload and organize its logistic supplies and suitable ground on which to build a fuel installation and operating base for helicopters and Harriers.

Clapp and Thompson jointly decided that the best place to land was San Carlos Water at the west end of East Falkland. Surrounding hills would provide excellent sites for Rapier and Blowpipe anti-aircraft missiles. The distance of about 50 miles from Port Stanley would make it more difficult for Argentine ground troops to organize a rapid counterattack. But this distance would also prove to be a disadvantage.

As the amphibious force sailed south, on 1 May the Falklands were attacked, beginning with a bombing raid against the main airfield at Port Stanley by a high-flying RAF Vulcan strategic bomber that in a complex feat of repeated air-to-air refuelling had been refuelled seven times by converted Victor bombers, which themselves required refuelling. This was followed by further bombing raids by Sea Harriers.

These initial attacks were intended to simulate a British landing near Port Stanley, to provoke an Argentine reaction and gather intelligence on Argentine defensive tactics.

Although the main British attacks were from the air, frigates and destroyers sailed close to the islands to bombard enemy positions with their 4.5-inch naval guns. This fire was controlled by the naval gunfire observation parties of 148 (Meiktila) Commando Forward Observation Battery. Unique to the commando brigade, the battery was led by Royal Artillery officers supported by naval and artillery personnel. All had not only passed the commando course but also qualified as parachutists. Ironically the battery had been listed for disbandment as a result of the 1981 Defence Review, but the war was to demonstrate just how vital they were to co-ordinating the powerful guns on most of the frigates and destroyers with fire and manoeuvre by land forces. Initially, the observers from the battery controlled fire from naval helicopters, but after the landings, they were deployed with battalions, commandos and special forces teams.

As Sea King helicopters ferried special forces into the islands and 148 Battery observers controlled naval gunfire, the British and Argentine naval and air forces sought to control the waters and skies around the Falklands. In rapid succession on 2 May a British submarine sank the Argentine cruiser *General Belgrano* and an air-launched Exocet missile sank the British destroyer HMS *Sheffield*. The war had begun in earnest, with deaths on both sides. After these sinkings, the mood amongst troops shifted, with land combat seeming increasingly probable. Minds were concentrated and attendance at church services steadily increased.

THE SAS AGAINST ENEMY AIRPOWER

The Exocet was a French-manufactured radar-guided sea-skimming missile.[10] It was in the Royal Navy's inventory, fitted to several warships, including some in the task force. But up to March the Navy's anti-missile defences had been optimized against Soviet anti-ship missiles, a less challenging threat. The cutting-edge performance of the Exocet meant that they would be difficult to stop, particularly if launched in a salvo. London launched a major operation to prevent more missiles being purchased by Buenos Aires. This used diplomacy and covert action by intelligence agencies.

The most acute threat to the task force was thought to be the Argentine Navy's small force of French Super Étendard jets carrying air-launched Exocets, assessed as being based at Rio Grande in southern Argentina. Both Northwood and the carrier battlegroup examined options to neutralize this threat. Admiral Woodward favoured sailing the whole battlegroup to attack the airfield from the air. This would have had a high payoff, but also carried considerable risk, should the battlegroup be detected by the enemy and subject to the full force of air and missile attack at close range to mainland air bases.

Instead, the Director SAS, Brigadier Peter de la Billière, was directed to attack the air base, destroying the jets and missiles and killing the aircrew. The SAS planned to achieve surprise by a tactical air land operation. Two C130 Hercules would fly from Ascension Island, the only two such RAF aircraft then fitted for air-to-air refuelling. They would land at night on the airfield's runway, carrying B Squadron, 22 SAS. They would fan out over the airfield, destroying aircraft and missiles and killing as many Argentine military personnel as they could find. If surprise had been achieved and any Argentine defenders neutralized, the two aircraft would fly the force to an airfield in Chile. If this was impossible, the SAS and RAF aircrew would attempt to secretly exfiltrate westwards to the Chilean border some 50 miles away.

The plan was daring, offering a high payoff, but at a very high risk, not least that of the Argentinians detecting the approaching Hercules. It appears that some key personnel in B Squadron failed to display the wholehearted aggression of the regiment's motto 'who dares wins', apparently considering the attack to be a potential suicide mission. De la Billière found it necessary to sack the squadron commander and replace him with the regiment's second in command. The attitude of the squadron rapidly improved. This is one rare example of a sub-unit of the Army coming close to a mutiny, an ironic development considering the elite status of the SAS.

Meanwhile, Admiral Woodward was greatly concerned by the Argentinian aircraft based on the islands, particularly a squadron of Pucará attack aircraft. Based at Pebble Island, these had turboprop engines and were originally designed for counterinsurgency strikes. But with their low speed and cannon and rocket armament, they could be a potent threat to the helicopters and landing craft that would be so important for the landings – as might be the smaller Turbo Mentor armed trainers based on the airfield.

Having helped recapture South Georgia, D Squadron, SAS itself conducted helicopter-borne raids. It deployed a patrol to Pebble Island that succeeded in observing the airfield. On the night of 14/15 May the rest of D Squadron was landed by helicopter. The raiding force needed to leave before dawn and time was tight. It force-marched to the airfield and, supported by naval gunfire, destroyed six Pucarás, four Turbo Mentors and a transport aircraft. This was a daring raid that returned the SAS back to its original role, that of destroying enemy aircraft on the ground.

Meanwhile, a patrol from B Squadron tasked with reconnaissance of the Argentinian air base was parachuted to the task force. Over the night of 17/18 May HMS *Invincible* steamed as far west as it dared to launch one of its precious night vision goggle-equipped Sea Kings to deliver the patrol, which would get into position to covertly observe the airfield. The helicopter would then to fly to Chile, where it would be abandoned and destroyed by the aircrew.

The four-hour helicopter flight ran into difficulties over Argentina, where unexpected fog made navigation difficult. The patrol eventually landed, but its members were uncertain of their location. The patrol commander abandoned the mission and walked into a town in Chile, where, by chance, he spotted some SAS soldiers sent to look for them. In the meantime, the helicopter and crew that had landed in Chile were discovered. Although London claimed the helicopter had accidentally strayed into Chile, no one was fooled. The operation was abandoned.

The planning to neutralize the Exocet was evidence of British determination to reduce the considerable threat the missiles posed. But in retrospect, the lack of direct attack on the Argentinian mainland probably benefited the British. If an attack had been mounted, there was a probability of civilian casualties and collateral damage. Even if by some miracle these did not occur, a direct British attack on mainland Argentina would probably have been exploited by Buenos Aires diplomatically to change the balance in the United Nations and influence the attitude of other Latin American states in Argentina's favour. This could have increased pressure in the UN General Assembly and the Organization of American States, having a diplomatic effect on the US: all factors tilting the international battle for the narrative away from London.

Meanwhile, on the night of 19 May a Sea King helicopter transporting D Squadron between two ships crashed into the sea. Of the 27 people aboard, 22 were drowned, 18 from the SAS – the largest single number of casualties ever suffered by the regiment in one day. This accident, the failure to insert the patrol to observe the Argentinian Exocet base and the inability to insert a patrol onto the glacier in South Georgia were powerful reminders not only of the inherent hazards and friction of war, but of how the Navy, its helicopter crews and the SAS were operating close to the very limits of human and aircraft capability.

An SAS patrol had landed by helicopter in the Mount Kent area. It was not only observing the terrain to the west of the capital but was also seeking to identify the field site being used by enemy helicopters thought to be in the area, probably dispersed from their original base at Port Stanley to reduce the risk of British air attack.

Led by Captain Aldwin Wight, a Welsh Guards officer, the patrol was heavily laden, carrying enormous rucksacks. The combination of weight and the difficulty of the terrain meant that in darkness they might travel 400 yards in an hour. It took them three nights to reach their observation post. Here they constructed a hide in a fold in the ground, covered with an improvised roof constructed out of a poncho, chicken wire and a camouflage net. Here they lay for 26 days, two men awake and two resting as best they could. The soldiers would only emerge from the hide during darkness. The weather was extremely demanding, randomly cycling through clear sunshine, drizzle, gale force winds and freezing rain. On 21 May the patrol located an Argentine helicopter basing site. Using target data from the patrol two Harriers attacked the aircraft, destroying a Chinook and a Puma.[11]

The British assessed that the Argentinians had a strategic reserve force of up to 1,000 troops, planning to move it around the Falklands using helicopters. The loss of the Chinook and Puma would make this more difficult.

The Harriers that made the attack were RAF ground attack aircraft. These had recently joined the aircraft carriers. Some flew direct from Ascension Island, refuelling in the air. Others had embarked on the *Atlantic Conveyor*, a British merchant navy ship that had been requisitioned for the Falklands War. Their arrival meant that the Sea Harriers could concentrate on air defence, the task for which they had been designed.

THE BATTLE OF SAN CARLOS WATER

On 12 May Thompson and Clapp were directed to 'repossess the Falkland Islands as quickly as possible.' Marine Major General Jeremy Moore was designated the overall land force commander, assuming command when he and 5th Brigade landed in the islands. Moore's directive to Thompson told him:

to secure a bridgehead on East Falkland, into which reinforcements can be landed, in which an airstrip can be established and from which operations to repossess the Falkland Islands can be achieved. You are to push forward from the bridgehead area, so far as the maintenance of its security allows, to gain information, to establish moral and physical domination over the enemy, and to forward the ultimate aim of repossession … It is then my intention to land 5 Infantry Brigade into the beachhead and to develop operations for the complete repossession of the Falkland Islands.[12]

On 20 May Moore flew to Ascension Island to embark on the liner *QE2*. But the secure radio equipment fitted to the liner rapidly failed and could not be repaired. Moore could not therefore communicate with Woodward, Northwood or Thompson.

The commando brigade successfully landed at San Carlos on the night of 21/22 May. This was complemented by a diversionary raid on Goose Green by D Squadron, SAS. Supported by naval gunfire, they subjected the Argentine positions to a sustained attack. Radio traffic intercepted by the British indicated that the defenders thought they were under attack by a full battalion. As the squadron withdrew to San Carlos it used a newly acquired US Stinger man-portable anti-aircraft missile to shoot down a Pucará aircraft.

The landings of the commando and parachute battalions went well, but it took 2 Para longer to embark in their landing craft than planned, resulting in some hours delay. As the battalion had the least practice at embarking in landing craft of any of the brigade's units, this was an unsurprising friction.

When the brigade landed, their supplies were initially limited to what could be carried by the marines and paratroopers. At dawn the Wessex and Sea King helicopters and the landing craft began taking the artillery's guns, Rapier missile launchers and ammunition ashore. Most ammunition, food and spare parts were aboard the LSLs and civilian ships. For example, the MV *Elk* held 2,000 tons of ammunition. If it the ammunition caught fire, the resulting explosion would be that of the size of a small nuclear warhead.

Argentinian jets attacked the ships deployed in Falkland Sound opposite San Carlos Water. The pilots of the fighter bombers flew fast and low, displaying bravery and determination, but most of their attacks were made on the warships, rather than the amphibious and merchant ships. Even so the toll was heavy, with two frigates sunk as well as three ships with unexploded bombs lodged aboard.

The offloading of Rapier missile systems, artillery and ammunition was delayed by Argentine air attacks, with helicopters seeking cover by landing. Even so, by the end of the first day the brigade had all its battalions and commandos, its Rapier battery and some of its ammunition ashore. It was confident that it would be able to beat off any Argentinian counterattack.

The air defence of San Carlos Water was not helped by weaknesses of the Rapier anti-aircraft missile system. It had never been designed for amphibious operations, was fragile and took a long time to be ready to fire. For some time, it failed to perform to expectation. The brigade also had a Royal Marine air defence troop equipped with Blowpipe man-portable missiles, reinforced by some Royal Artillery teams. The system was less fragile than Rapier, but it was even more difficult for the operator to guide. To a watching

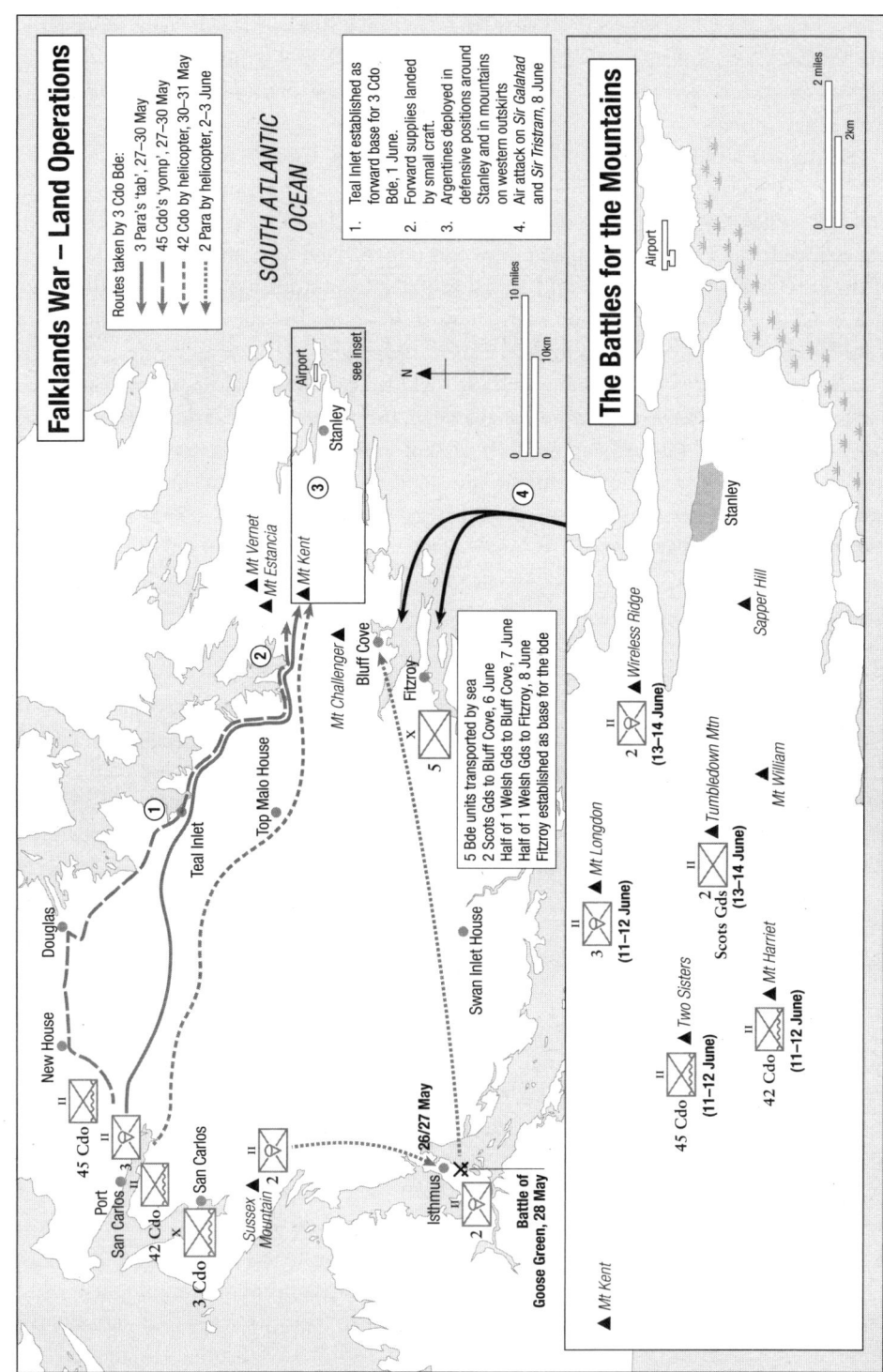

Falklands War – Land Operations

Routes taken by 3 Cdo Bde:

→ 3 Para's 'tab', 27–30 May
→ 45 Cdo's 'yomp', 27–30 May
→ 42 Cdo by helicopter, 30–31 May
→ 2 Para by helicopter, 2–3 June

SOUTH ATLANTIC OCEAN

1. Teal Inlet established as forward base for 3 Cdo Bde, 1 June.
2. Forward supplies landed by small craft.
3. Argentines deployed in defensive positions around Stanley and in mountains on western outskirts
4. Air attack on *Sir Galahad* and *Sir Tristram*, 8 June

The Battles for the Mountains

see inset

N

0   10km   10 miles
0   2km   2 miles

Airport
Stanley
▲ *Mt Vernet*
▲ *Mt Estancia*
▲ *Mt Kent*

▲ *Mt Challenger*
Bluff Cove ▲
Fitzroy

Top Malo House

Teal Inlet

Douglas

New House

Port San Carlos
45 Cdo
42 Cdo
San Carlos
3 Cdo
Sussex Mountain ▲

Battle of Goose Green, 28 May

26/27 May

Isthmus

Swan Inlet House

5 Bde units transported by sea
2 Scots Gds to Bluff Cove, 6 June
Half of 1 Welsh Gds to Bluff Cove, 7 June
Half of 1 Welsh Gds to Fitzroy, 8 June
Fitzroy established as base for the bde

5 ✕

▲ *Mt Kent*

45 Cdo ▲ *Two Sisters*
(11–12 June)

42 Cdo ▲ *Mt Harriet*
(11–12 June)

3 ▲ *Mt Longdon*
(11–12 June)

Scots Gds 2 ▲ *Tumbledown Mtn*
(13–14 June)

▲ *Mt William*

2 ▲ *Wireless Ridge*
(13–14 June)

▲ *Sapper Hill*

Stanley

Airport

journalist it looked like a defective Space Invaders game. And the requirement to keep the aircraft carriers out of range of Argentinian air-launched Exocet missiles meant that the combat air patrols mounted by the limited numbers of Sea Harrier fighters could not be everywhere at once.

Lieutenant Colonel Ivar Hellberg, the Army officer commanding the Commando Logistic Regiment, had originally planned to keep most of the brigade's supplies afloat on the LSLs, offloading them when required. After the first day of air attacks the logistic plan was changed. The LSLs and merchant ships carrying the land force supplies would stay out of the anchorage by day, but would return at night for unloading. A force maintenance area would be established ashore with supplies for both brigades. It took six days to complete the logistic offload into San Carlos. The Army's logistic doctrine laid down specific requirements for such an area. These included plenty of buildings, metalled roads and hard standing. None of these were available on the shores of San Carlos Water. Colonel Ian Baxter, General Moore's deputy chief of staff, explained that the force maintenance area 'was muddy, it was disorganized, it had no hard standing, it had no cover. But my goodness me, the flexibility of the men there, their hard work, both day and night, meant that we were able to sort it out'.[13]

'WE'LL BLOODY WELL HAVE TO WALK'

Having successfully landed the brigade at San Carlos, Thompson and Clapp planned to follow Moore's directive by establishing a force closer to Port Stanley. This would be their main effort. The key feature was Mount Kent, which dominated the terrain around it. The brigade planned to seize control of it and then fly the marines and paratroopers to secure Port Salvador and Teal Inlet to the north-west of Stanley. This would allow LSLs to sail inshore and offload the supplies they carried into a brigade maintenance area. The amphibious force had deployed with 16 support helicopters – five Wessex and 11 Sea King aircraft. Loaded onto the freighter *Atlantic Conveyor* were six more Wessex helicopters and five RAF Chinook helicopters. This would provide Thompson with sufficient air lift to fly his troops to the area of Teal Inlet and Mount Kent and then to rapidly offload the brigade's supplies from ships in Teal Inlet.[14]

Thompson saw enemy forces at Goose Green as a minor threat to a flank. The Argentines there could safely be screened by the force protecting San Carlos. Any ground attack on Goose Green would be a diversion from getting to Port Stanley. Thompson therefore planned to mask the isthmus while his brigade invested Stanley by seizing control of the large hills to the west of the town. The area was dominated by Mount Kent. First D Squadron, SAS inserted by helicopter would secure the feature. They would be followed by commandos and battalions, flown by helicopter from San Carlos.

With General Moore incommunicado on the *QE2*, Thompson was still dealing directly with Northwood. They were unsympathetic to Thompson's approach, regarding it as over-cautious. Northwood ignored his concerns about the risks of air attack outside the umbrella of Rapier and naval missiles and the vulnerability of helicopters to air attack as they flew forward, as well as the risk that if the enemy strategic reserve were deployed it could pose a major threat. They wanted more action all round. Thompson was unequivocally ordered to move the brigade out of its bridgehead and 'invest Stanley' and to attack Goose Green.

But on 25 May the *Atlantic Conveyor* was hit by an Exocet missile and sunk. Down with it went all its helicopters, apart from a single Chinook that had been readied for operations as it was conducting a test flight. Also lost were tents sufficient to accommodate several thousand troops. When the news broke in the brigade HQ, a staff officer was heard to say 'we'll bloody well have to walk'. The commando brigade HQ re-examined its options. Thompson concluded that the considerable reduction in helicopter lift meant that the only way for 45 Commando and 3 Para to move east to secure Port Salvador and Teal Inlet would be for them to walk there.

Both units set out on 27 May, a march over very difficult terrain in constantly changing weather. Outside settlements, the ground was very rugged moorland with peat bogs and large tussocks of grass making movement by foot slow and tiring enough for civilians. 3 Para used two civilian tractors and trailers requisitioned from San Carlos to carry their mortars, Milan missile launchers and heavy ammunition. They left their Bergen rucksacks in the beachhead, to be flown forward by helicopter. They all carried their personal weapon, helmet, first-line ammunition and a minimum of personal equipment, including a day's worth of rations, as well as image-intensifying night sights, radios and necessary batteries. This so-called 'assault order' would weigh anything between 40 and 100 lbs, so marching was very tiring. And crossing the many abundant stone runs, great corridors of stones and boulders, could be extremely slow by foot and impossible by vehicle. The weather of the South Atlantic winter was startling in its variation, from short periods of sun and great clarity to frequent mists, fog and rain. The wind was an energy-sapping constant.

The marines and paratroopers were very familiar with this kind of terrain and weather from training in the Welsh uplands and on Dartmoor, but there was no training camp to retire to after a few days in the field. Many started the march with wet feet and their boots remained soaked for the rest of the war. Waterproof clothing was issued, with Arctic waterproofs supplied to the Marines being much more effective than the thinner waterproofs issued to the Army. And both marines and soldiers found it very difficult to keep their sleeping bags dry. The physical toughness that was so much a part of the selection, training and culture of the marines and paratroopers would be severely tested but would not be found wanting.

The manoeuvre secured the northern approaches to Port Stanley. It entered the folklore of the war, particularly the contrasting terms for such a march used by the marines and paratroopers, 'yomping' and 'tabbing' respectively. These extremely arduous journeys exemplified the physical toughness of both marines and paratroopers.

THE BATTLE OF GOOSE GREEN

Thompson tasked 2 Para on Sussex Mountain with conducting a raid on the enemy at Goose Green. Over the night of 26/27 May the battalion marched to Camilla Creek

House from where it conducted reconnaissance and prepared for battle. Concurrently, a troop of artillery and its ammunition was flown to support the battalion. This diverted helicopter lift from the operation to seize Mount Kent. And the brigade maintenance area in San Carlos was bombed, killing and wounding valuable logistic personnel and destroying ammunition.

The battalion marched overnight on 26/27 May and lay up at the head of the isthmus. RAF Harriers struck Goose Green. But one was shot down. Battalion patrols and a captured Argentine soldier all reported that the defenders were alert to an impending British attack. As this unwelcome information reached battalion HQ, the BBC World Service short wave news was heard to report that 2 Para were advancing on Goose Green while 3 Para and 45 Commando were moving to Teal Inlet and Douglas. This made the commanding officer, Lieutenant Colonel 'H' Jones, extremely angry. An officer transferred to the Parachute Regiment from the Devon and Dorsets, Jones exuded a restless energy and a thirst for action.

No government official was ever to admit to feeding the information to the BBC, but it is likely that a thoughtless politician or senior official was the source of the briefing. This would not be the only time that off the record briefings by anonymous, and therefore unaccountable briefers would be to the Army's disadvantage.

Jones intended to attack before dawn, planning to break through the enemy defences in darkness, then clearing Darwin and Goose Green in daylight to reduce the chances of civilian casualties. Before dawn on 28 May, 2 Para began its attack on the enemy north of Darwin. It was a hard fight. A frigate providing gunfire support had to cease fire when its gun jammed. After dawn had broken the battalion was held up by defenders in well-sited trenches that lay across the isthmus from Boca House in the west to Darwin Hill in the east, combined with artillery fire. A Company was pinned down in front of this line and Jones launched his tactical HQ into an attack on an enemy trench but was killed. By now B Company was also pinned down by the defenders' fire in the Boca House area and the British artillery was having difficulties with high gusts of wind, while Harriers were unable to provide close air support, the carriers being surrounded by fog.

The battalion second in command, Major Chris Keeble, moved forward to take command. As he did so, the battalion was attacked by Pucará aircraft, which shot down one of a pair of Marine Scout helicopters bringing ammunition forward and taking wounded back. Having withdrawn from exposed ground Keeble orchestrated B Company, using machine guns and Milan anti-tank missiles to suppress enemy defences. The missile operators fired them straight into the Argentine defensive positions, killing or wounding the soldiers inside. D Company crawled along the isthmus' western shore to launch a successful flank attack that rolled up the enemy defences. As they did so, A Company was able to break into the line of enemy trenches around Darwin Hill, which it captured. The use of Milan anti-tank missiles into 'bunker busters', combined with D Company's manoeuvre, regained momentum for the attack.

Keeble then ordered D and C companies to push south towards Goose Green. The terrain was open, and the companies were subject to fire from artillery, machine guns and anti-aircraft cannon firing in the ground role. After capturing the schoolhouse, where an officer was killed attempting to negotiate the surrender of Argentinian defenders, the companies were attacked by Skyhawk and Pucará aircraft, the latter dropping napalm, which failed to ignite. A Pucará was shot down by a marine-operated Blowpipe, its falling wing coming so close to a paratrooper as to slice pouches off his belt.

But now the attack was held up by the enemy anti-aircraft guns outside Goose Green. The battalion's naval gunfire observer directed strikes by three RAF Harriers. The jets used cluster bombs and cannon fire to silence both the anti-aircraft guns and the enemy artillery. Civilians in Goose Green saw Argentine troops screaming in terror and sobbing. As light fell, the paras saw Argentine helicopters land an infantry company to the south of Goose Green.

After a cold and worrying night spent in the open, 2 Para girded themselves to attack Goose Green. But learning that over a hundred of the settlement's civilians were being held hostage by the enemy, Major Keeble, accompanied by BBC reporter Robert Fox, attempted to liberate them without further fighting. He arranged to meet the Argentine commander under a white flag and through skilful negotiation persuaded him to surrender the settlement. John Crossland, one of 2 Para's company commanders, observed that:

> I believe a lot of credit should go to Robert Fox, who speaks Spanish and understands the Spanish-American attitude. They wanted to sing their national anthem and have a parade, with which we had no problem provided they laid down their arms. Very few of us were privy to this plan, so suddenly seeing 1,200 or so Argentine soldiers come marching out of Goose Green Garrison was a very sobering moment. There were far more than we thought. But we'd completed our mission and taken the objectives we'd been given.[15]

Some 200 of the defenders had been killed in the battle. The company from the Argentine strategic reserve that had landed by helicopter also surrendered.

LESSONS OF THE BATTLE

Thompson had been reluctant to mount the attack. But its success had several benefits. It ramped up pressure on the Argentine defenders, and the battle must have done nothing for the morale and confidence of the Argentine commanders in Port Stanley. Secondly it was a considerable boost to the confidence of the British troops and to those in the chain of command above them, all the way up to Northwood, the MoD and Downing Street.

The British victory had been achieved by a force half the size of the defenders. The battalion had twice been pinned down, firstly by the bunkers around Darwin Hill and secondly by the anti-aircraft guns outside Goose Green. Success had come from the Paras' sheer determination and the high level of fighting power they generated. And the battalion had prevailed over several frictions: the death of their commander, enemy air attacks, insufficient fire support and almost running out of ammunition on several occasions. Even so, the attack had been 'a close-run thing'. Brigadier Thompson concluded that any future attacks should take place at night, when the cover of darkness would reduce the lethality of Argentine firepower.

After the war Thompson was to state that he should have concentrated more force on Goose Green, leading the attack himself from his tactical HQ and committing a second battalion or commando, more artillery and all of the brigade's light armour. Had even a single troop of Scimitars and Scorpions joined the paras to act as light tanks, the defences at Darwin Hill and anti-aircraft guns at Goose Green might have been more quickly neutralized. But at the time, neither Thompson nor any of his staff realized just how mobile the armoured vehicles would be.

ADVANCING TO THE EAST

While the battle had been raging at Goose Green, Teal Inlet and Douglas were captured by 3 Para and 45 Commando. By 29 May the final patrols of D Squadron arrived on Mount Kent. The squadron had begun deploying five nights earlier. The time taken was a product of two factors: the shortage of helicopters with night-vision equipment and the frequent periods when poor weather made night flying impossible. The brigade planned to follow up the SAS the next night, by flying marines and artillery to take control of the feature, but bad weather and the diversion of helicopters to support the raid on Goose Green meant that the fly-in of 42 Commando and an artillery troop could not begin until the night of 30/31 May. They arrived to witness a firefight between the SAS and Argentine commandos. It was just as well that Thompson had not given into pressure from Northwood to deploy the Marines to Mount Kent without waiting for a reconnaissance.

By first light a company of 42 Commando had secured the top of the mountain and their attached artillery opened fire on some enemy targets around Stanley. Together with the move of the commando brigade HQ to Teal Inlet, the north-west approaches to Port Stanley were now controlled by the British. By now Major General Moore had arrived at the islands and established his HQ on HMS *Fearless*. Neither his HQ nor the newly arriving units had experienced the six days of heavy air attacks and resulting ships sunk that had followed the initial landings.

Moore told the newly arrived 5th Brigade to take command of 2 Para at Goose Green. Here they were joined by 1st Battalion, the 7th Duke of Edinburgh's Own Gurkha Rifles, who marched from San Carlos. Major Keeble proposed sending a large patrol by Scout helicopter to Swan Inlet, where there was thought to be an intact civilian telephone line. Two days later Wilson agreed. A small force from B Company 2 Para flew there in three Scout helicopters, escorted by two Gazelles. The telephone worked and a call revealed that there were no enemy at the small settlements of Fitzroy or Bluff Cove. Keeble took advantage of the arrival of the only RAF Chinook helicopter to fly A and B companies and a mortar team to Fitzroy. The two sorties by the huge helicopter each carried 80 troops, 50 more than its peacetime load, standing up in conditions similar to a rush hour underground train. The rest of 2 Para flew in the next day.

Somehow neither the land forces HQ, nor the commando brigade HQ had been told of the move. A Marine patrol on Smoko Mountain, observing a Chinook landing troops, assumed it was an Argentinian aircraft and two batteries of British artillery prepared to shell this tempting target. Fortunately a check by the commando brigade HQ revealed that this was 5th Brigade, not the enemy. This would not be the only dangerous miscommunication on the southern axis.

The move was controversial and remains so. Some felt that it diverted logistic support from the commando brigade. And that the heliborne seizure of Fitzroy had been designed to present Moore with a *fait accompli* that would prevent 5th Brigade from being excluded from the attacks on the defences outside Stanley. General Moore himself refrained from ever commenting on this in public.

From Moore's viewpoint, 5th Brigade's leap along the coast had the advantage of complementing the commando brigade's seizure of the mountains and reduced the threat to the Marines' southern flank. But it created logistic imbalance and risk, as all the land logistic capability and helicopter lift was then sustaining the commando brigade in its forward positions and building up its logistic stocks, particularly of artillery ammunition. To move one artillery battery by helicopter required 15 sorties for the guns, gunners, and essential equipment, including generators and radios. Each Sea King helicopter would carry pallets of 105mm shells, swinging precariously on nets slung underneath the helicopters, increasing the height they had to fly above the ground, increasing their visibility and vulnerability and reducing their speed. To build up ammunition stocks to 400 rounds per gun would require another 20 sorties.

This posed major headaches to the logistics staff. The Navy assessed that the carrier task group and its Harriers would have great difficulty in sustaining its operations for more than a month after the initial landings. The harsh weather in the mountains was starting to take a toll on the health of the troops living in the open, with trench foot cases starting to rise. The full force of the South Atlantic winter was yet to arrive, but there were no additional tents, all having gone down with the *Atlantic Conveyor*. So it was imperative that the attack on the Argentine defences begin as soon as possible. A key constraint was the need to build up artillery ammunition. Thompson and the gunners were determined that the attacks should be much better supported than at Goose Green, with each gun having at least 500 rounds ready for use as the attacks began.

But now that the 5th Brigade had seized Fitzroy, how was it to get the rest of its forces there? The two guards battalions were protecting the bridgehead at San Carlos and the brigade HQ and the Gurkha battalion were at Goose Green. The Welsh Guards tried to march from San Carlos to Goose Green, taking their heavy weapons and ammunition with them. But without promised all-terrain vehicles, they made very slow progress. Feeling that without support weapons and full ammunition the battalion would not be effective, the commanding officer abandoned the march.

It was decided to send both battalions by sea, along with 16 Field Ambulance, 5th Brigade's medical unit. Moore wanted to move them over one night to Bluff Cove in HMS *Intrepid*. This was vetoed by Admiral Fieldhouse at Northwood as carrying too much risk, both military and political.

The Scots Guards were moved first, embarking on HMS *Intrepid*. They were to land at Fitzroy by the ship's landing craft. The battalion were told that the craft would be launched 13 nautical miles away, a journey of two hours. In the event the ship's captain decided that launching that close was too dangerous and they would be launched 35 miles out, but there were no other British ships in the area. The landing craft were suddenly illuminated by star shells from HMS *Cardiff*, who was unaware of their presence. The voyage took seven long hours, expertly navigated by Major Southby-Tailyour. In the choppy waters the troops were quickly drenched, and many were seasick.

The next night a similar manoeuvre was attempted by the Welsh Guards and HMS *Fearless*. But the ship had just two landing craft which could only lift half the battalion. The remaining half of the battalion moved the next night in the *Sir Galahad*, an LSL, along with another such vessel, the *Sir Tristram*. Here the friction of war intervened. The ships arrived at Port Pleasant Harbour, not Bluff Cove where the guards had been ordered by their commanding officer to disembark.

This was a surprise to HQ 5th Brigade, who had arrived at Fitzroy, but without key communications vehicles that had been lost in a landing craft sunk by air attack. There were no reliable communications between the brigade and the amphibious warfare commander. Up to now 5th Brigade had only experienced overcast weather and no enemy air attacks. But on 8 June the weather was clear and bright and the British ships were clearly visible to enemy positions on the mountains surrounding Stanley. Both Major Southby-Tailyour and Lieutenant Colonel Hellberg, commanding officer of the Commando Logistic Regiment, attempted to persuade the guards that such was the Argentine air threat that they should immediately disembark, but the guards insisted that they had to stick to their orders. At noon 5th Brigade ordered them to disembark, but the details were unclear.

That afternoon the ships were accurately bombed by low-flying Argentine Skyhawks. Two bombs hit *Sir Galahad*, resulting in a massive fireball. Despite valiant rescue efforts by naval helicopters, 51 troops died and 57 were wounded. The survivors of the two Welsh Guards companies on the ship had lost all their weapons, ammunition and equipment, so were rendered ineffective for operations, as was the advanced dressing station of 16 Field Ambulance which had been on the ships.

THE BATTLES FOR PORT STANLEY – MOUNT LONGDON, TUMBLEDOWN AND WIRELESS RIDGE

In planning the attack to seize Stanley the British had to overcome two lines of defences. The first comprised Mount Longdon, Two Sisters and Mount Harriet. Between these positions and Port Stanley was a second line of defences: Wireless Ridge, Mount Tumbledown and Sapper Hill. Between the ridges, the terrain was very open, terrain that was best attacked at night. Capturing each would require at minimum a battalion or commando supported by at least a battery of artillery and naval gunfire from a frigate or destroyer.

General Moore and his staff thought that the Argentinians expected a major attack to come from the south-west along the main track from Bluff Cove to Stanley. Moore wanted to reinforce that impression in the minds of the enemy HQ. He decided that the outer ring should be attacked from the west and north-west.

On the night of 11/12 June, 3 Commando Brigade attacked. 42 and 45 Commandos captured Two Sisters and Mount Harriet. This is not the place for a discussion of their successful attacks, but key roles were played by the commando gunners of their assigned artillery batteries and the battery commanders, forward observation officers and naval gun fire observers.

---

3 Para was to attack Mount Longdon, a rocky spine dominating the approach to Stanley from the north-west. Since arriving at Teal Inlet, the battalion had sent night patrols forward, both to map out the enemy defences and to harass them. During this period, the paras were intermittently shelled, attacked by Pucarás and subjected to night bombing by Canberra bombers, whose bombs missed and exploded harmlessly in the soft peat.

Lieutenant Colonel Hew Pike, the commanding officer, formulated a plan to approach the mountain in darkness. The attack was to initially be silent, without active fire support, but would go noisy, with the full use of mortars, artillery and naval gunfire, once close-quarter fighting began. To begin with, the advance was undetected by the defenders, but as the moon rose a soldier stepped on a land mine. The enemy rapidly opened a heavy fire, 3 Para bringing down its indirect fire as quickly as it could.

The battle lasted the rest of the night and was extremely hard fought. B Company got into a tough close-quarter fight amongst the rocks. A platoon commander was hit and Sergeant MacKay, the platoon sergeant, assaulted an enemy position, neutralizing it but dying in the attempt. The company had to withdraw, reorganize and wait for a barrage of fire from artillery and naval guns. They made some progress, but Pike, who was close to the assaulting troops, decided to push a fresh company through.

Once attacks started, commanding officers had to monitor the fighting, where necessary taking control, particularly when events diverged from the plan. Brigadier Thompson described the role of commanding officers in the night battles:

> It is hard for the layman to imagine how much information commanders at all levels in an infantry battle at night have to carry in their heads. The commanding officer orchestrating the whole is not sitting in a warm well-lit operations room, surrounded by staff, powerful radios and radar displays showing the positions of friend and foe; or even in a relatively warm armoured command vehicle. He is walking, crouching, running, lying, probably in pouring rain, under fire, trying to update his mental picture of the battle by conversations on a man-pack radio and going to see for himself if he can. The flashing of torches to read maps or look up codes can be unwise.[16]

The battle on Longdon continued through the night. It was slow work, with pauses to allow the British guns to suppress the enemy amongst the large rocks. Once this was achieved the paratroopers then attacked; crawling, shooting, dashing forward in short rushes, throwing grenades and finally using their bayonets. This was infantry close-quarter battle at its bloodiest.

By daylight the rocky ridge was controlled by the battalion. Initially it was shielded by morning mist but as this lifted accurate Argentinian artillery fire inflicted a steady stream of British casualties. Of all the six deliberate attacks conducted by the battalions and commandos, this took the greatest toll on British casualties. The battalion had 17 killed in the night attack. A further six were to die from shelling in the next two days. More would have died had not so many shells had their lethal effects reduced by landing in peat. Two of those killed were married to sisters. A wounded soldier was evacuated by a helicopter piloted by his next door neighbour in married quarters in Aldershot. Both are examples of how tightly knit a military unit or formation can be. Reflecting on the end of the battle, Lieutenant Colonel Pike observed that:

> The enemy dead lay everywhere, victims of shell, bullet and bayonet. The sour odour of death lingered in the nostrils long after many of the corpses had been buried. It was a slow job and eventually the task was abandoned when their artillery and mortars started again. The enemy bunkers proved an Aladdin's cave of Camel cigarettes, bottles of brandy, huge cakes of solid cheese, and of course bully beef! Standing amongst the shell-holes and shambles of battle, watching the determined, triumphant, shocked and saddened faces of those who had lost their friends on this mountain, the Iron Duke's comment was never more apt: 'there is nothing so melancholy as a battle won – unless it is a battle lost.'[17]

General Moore's original plan had been for momentum to be maintained by attacking the inner ring of defences on the next night. But commanders argued for more time for units to prepare the attacks, including conducting reconnaissance and battle procedure. And it was necessary to replenish shells on the artillery's gun lines. So a pause was agreed.

On7 June Brigadier Wilson ordered the Scots Guards to attack Mount Tumbledown in daylight. After his reconnaissance Lieutenant Colonel Mike Scott, the commanding officer, assessed that the vertiginous rocky mountain and open terrain around Tumbledown gave the defenders such excellent fields of fire that a daylight attack would probably fail. He recommended that the attack be mounted at night. He also argued for a day's delay to allow more time for reconnaissance and planning to rebuild stocks of artillery ammunition at the guns, where the holdings of shells had run dangerously low. To his credit, Wilson agreed. This and the tactical pause allowed the Scots Guards company, platoon and section commanders to see the mountain for themselves.

The battalion attack began at 2200hrs. Scott decided to use deception to make the defenders think that the attack would come by the most obvious route: the main track into Post Stanley. An ad hoc force was assembled from the battalion along with two CVR(T)s to conduct a diversionary attack along that route. This succeeded, but at a high cost in casualties.

Meanwhile G Company achieved surprise, gaining a foothold on the western end of Tumbledown. This was followed by Left Flank[18] Company, commanded by Major John

Kizeley, advancing through them to seize the summit. But, as Kizeley was to later describe, 'almost everything that could go wrong did'.[19] The defending 5th Argentine Marine Infantry Battalion opened a withering defensive fire, pinning down Kizeley and much of the company, who were unable to suppress the defenders with their own weapons. Kizeley was to describe the challenge of commanding his company during the battle:

Incoming artillery and mortar rounds, grenades exploding near you, have your ears ringing and at times you become almost completely deaf. You realize this only when you shout at someone to do something and it's quite clear they can't hear you. The only way to get your message across is to run over to them, grip them by the arm, and shouting into their ear. Then there is the effect in the dark and intensely bright flashes of light, as the shells and grenades explode. You are blinded and just as your eyes get accustomed to the dark again the same thing happens. You also tend to become over-focussed on the enemy immediately to your front. The result of all this is disorientation and confusion. At the same time you have a mass of information, much of it contradictory, coming into you over the radio net, such as casualty reports. Not just exercise casualties, but real people – your family. And yet there is no time for emotion, that can wait: and hardly any time for much fear you're too busy, and you're responsible for so many people's lives.[20]

Although the battalion was supported by artillery, naval gunfire and mortars, it took the best part of two hours to bring down accurate artillery fire where the guards needed it. This allowed a platoon to manoeuvre from a flank. The enemy were pushed back, but the company was so disrupted by casualties that only ten men reached the summit, three of whom were immediately wounded.

It took ten minutes for Left Flank's reserve platoon to join Kizeley on the summit. At that moment if the enemy had had a reserve able to counterattack, the guardsmen would probably have been pushed back off the mountain. The British might have lost the summit, and, with daylight approaching, the battle. However, although the defending Argentine marines had demonstrated considerable fighting spirit, their leaders had neglected to plan to counterattack. This was not the only elementary mistake. Daylight showed the natural defences of the mountain were even greater than the British had anticipated. Kizeley assessed that if the defenders had reinforced this natural fortress with properly sited barbed wire and minefields, the Scots Guards' attack might have been defeated. As it was, the only full battalion attack conducted by 5th Brigade succeeded.

On the afternoon of 12 June, as 2 Para were preparing for their night attacks, four Argentinian fighter bombers attacked the commando brigade HQ. The peat muffled the power of the bombs; no one in brigade HQ was hurt and no helicopters were shot down.

Later that same night 2 Para attacked Wireless Ridge, making it the only conventional land unit to conduct two major attacks. Unlike the daylight fighting at Goose Green, this would be at night. Lieutenant Colonel David Chaundler had parachuted into the sea to replace 'H' Jones in command of the battalion. While the battalion was at Fitzroy, he spoke to as many of them as he could. He was deeply impressed by the fighting spirit it had displayed at Darwin but agreed with Thompson that more artillery and the light tanks would have improved tempo and reduced the battalion's casualties. He was determined to make full use of all the firepower he could at Wireless Ridge. The commando brigade's attacks on the outer ring had begun silently but become noisy when the enemy had opened fire. Chaundler decided that tactical surprise was unlikely, so the attack on Wireless Ridge should be noisy from the outset, using the maximum firepower of the Scorpions and Scimitars, as well as mortar and artillery illuminating rounds and handheld flares. This would make command and control at company, platoon and section level much easier.

The battle opened with fire from two artillery batteries, two mortar platoons and HMS *Arrow* bombarding the positions, while the battalion's support weapons and the light tanks provided direct fire. A and B companies rapidly occupied their objectives, finding equipment rapidly abandoned, including radios still switched on, signs that the enemy had fled. D Company was able to rapidly clear its first objective. It went on to fight through a deep enemy position, later recognized as an HQ and two companies. D Company suffered from shellfire, both from misdirected British artillery and from enemy guns. As dawn broke a small Argentinian counterattack was attempted. D Company were almost out of ammunition, so fixed bayonets and prepared grenades, but the enemy manoeuvre was broken by artillery.

After the war, many in the Army considered Wireless Ridge to be a model attack, achieved at low cost, and the battle was used by the Staff College as an example of a battlegroup attack. Of the six such attacks in the war, it was the only one that made full use of the Scorpions and Scimitars as light tanks. Their excellent sights had identified many Argentine firing positions and their machine guns and 30mm and 76mm shells had rapidly silenced the defenders. This gave them particular value in providing fire supporting after artillery and mortars had to lift fire for fear of hitting British troops.

These attacks on Wireless Ridge and Tumbledown not only broke the ring of Argentine defences outside Stanley but also precipitated a collapse of Argentine morale. As dawn broke on 14 June, Argentine troops between the British and Port Stanley abandoned their positions and fled towards the town. An Argentinian cameraman filmed vehicles streaming east through the town and soldiers arguing with their officers – a sure indication that morale was breaking down.

As 3 Commando Brigade advanced into the town, Lieutenant Colonel Mike Rose, the commanding officer of 22 SAS, flew forward to negotiate the surrender of the Argentine troops remaining in the islands. This was the result of an earlier initiative. Based on his experience of counter-terrorism, he had learned a great deal about negotiation with hostage takers. He sought to apply this to the Argentine command in Stanley. Assisted by Captain Rod Bell, a Spanish-speaking Marine officer, and drawing on advice from a captured Argentinian officer, Rose used a civilian radio net designed for medical support to outlying settlements that still worked. This connected them to Captain Hussey, an officer in the Argentinian HQ, opening a channel of communication. After the Argentinian defences collapsed, Rose deployed to the Argentine HQ in Stanley, successfully negotiating the terms of their capitulation. The surrender document was signed by General Moore, while the exhausted paratroopers and marines of 3 Commando Brigade took shelter in the buildings of the eastern half of Port Stanley.

SUCCESS FACTORS

For the British forces the war was politically and morally uncomplicated. The great majority of the British people, parliament and media supported the action to eject Argentinian forces. The British had won, and the Argentines had lost. For many in the Army and elsewhere this was a just war, if ever there was one. Apart from Goose Green, civilians were not in the terrain being attacked, the enemy collapse preventing the need for urban combat in Stanley. Although the media was present, their reports, particularly film, took time to reach the UK.

There was much about the war that the forefathers of the marines, guardsmen, paratroopers and Gurkhas would have recognized. For example, the long marches, carrying heavy loads over very difficult terrain, living in the open in foul weather, the utter dependence on logistics and the irreducible need to close with enemy fighting positions and kill or capture the defenders.

They would also have recognized factors that led to British success: higher standards of British training, leadership, and command, as well as the ability of paratroopers and marines to endure long periods in bad weather and difficult terrain, in addition to British competence at combined arms tactics, especially the way that battalion and commando attacks integrated artillery, mortars and naval gunfire with the fire and manoeuvre of infantry companies. Those who fought in World War II would have been positively surprised by the image-intensifying night sights available to the marines and soldiers, as well as the relatively light and easy to use Clansman radios. They would have marvelled at the daring and determination of the helicopter pilots that so rapidly lifted casualties back to Ajax Bay. But they might have wondered why such little use was made of the Scorpions and Scimitars, which not only had the firepower to act as light tanks, but also had superb mobility that enabled them to master the Falklands' bogs, upland moors and tussocks, allowing them to go almost anywhere in that difficult terrain.

The British had defeated a much larger force. They were very lucky that the attack had not occurred a year later, when the Royal Navy's aircraft carrier capability would have been greatly reduced. They were also lucky to have a base on Ascension Island halfway to the Falklands. Had the bombs dropped on British ships in the first week of the war been properly fused, more British ships would have been damaged and sunk. And if an Exocet missile had struck an aircraft carrier, the operation would have become much more difficult. If both had been sunk, the British would probably have lost the war.

Land operations could have turned out very differently. For example, Argentine aircraft could have exploited the gaps in British Rapier coverage to attempt more attacks on the vulnerable slow-moving helicopters. And in April and May no one, not least the Argentinian commanders, knew that the defensive positions to the west of Port Stanley would each fall to British attacks on a single night. Or that there would not be successful air, Exocet or submarine attacks on the carrier battlegroup. Or that forces on West Falkland or landing by parachute from Argentina would not pose a serious threat to the amphibious anchorage and logistic facilities at San Carlos.

There was also much adaptation to the unforeseen circumstances of the conflict. This included the two parachute battalions and the SAS seamlessly blending into the commando brigade, the artillery adapting to the terrain and complete dependence on helicopters for movement and ammunition supply, and the sappers building the forward operating strip for the Harriers, greatly extending their effectiveness.

Perhaps the greatest adaptation by the land forces was in logistic support. The Commando Logistic Regiment with its integral contingents of marines, sailors and soldiers was undaunted by the Argentinian air attacks. The regiment rapidly rose to the challenge of changing the original plan to keep logistics afloat, instead landing supplies into the improvised maintenance area at San Carlos. As if this were not enough, the arrival of 5th Brigade with insufficient logistic support of its own, meant that the logistic regiment was now supporting two brigades, instead of the one for which it had been designed. And the combination of the regiment's commando medical squadron with the airborne medical units that came with the Parachute Regiment into a joint 'Red and Green Life Machine' was a key factor in the survival of the great majority of the wounded – both British and Argentinian; as was the very high standard of first aid administered to the wounded by their comrades in their sections coupled with the lifesaving skills of the regimental medical officers and their small teams at battalion aid posts.

But those who fought in World War II would not have been surprised by the human factors on display, particularly the much higher level of morale and combat cohesion displayed by the British troops. This was the product of a high standard of basic training in infantry skills in the battalions and commandos; and the higher standard of professional training of British NCOs and officers.

With the exception of the bravery of fighter-bomber pilots who pressed home their attacks against British ships and the tenacity of the enemy marines on Mount Tumbledown, these characteristics were signally lacking from the Argentinian forces. Although many Argentinian conscripts often held their fighting positions with courage, sometimes dying where they stood, others hid at the bottom of their trenches. And their defensive schemes often lacked aggression and initiative. The British were lucky that many of the Argentine forces displayed less professionalism and determination than they did. A more competent and determined enemy could have caused great difficulties, imposing greater delay and more casualties.

After the war ended, the British dealing with the thousands of surrendered prisoners of war discovered that there was a considerable gap between Argentinian officers and soldiers. The officers had better clothing and received better ration packs, that included a miniature bottle of whisky. They appeared disinclined either to mix with their soldiers or to share their hardships. In the British battalions, regiments and commandos, the opposite applied.

Officers were in and amongst their troops, wearing the same uniforms, eating the same rations and battling the same elements. In battle they led from the front. For example, Right Flank company of the Scots Guards' total of 27 casualties on Mount Tumbledown included the company sergeant major, a platoon commander, two platoon sergeants and three section commanders. British Army and Royal Marines tactical commanders led from the front, while too many Argentine officers led from the rear.

After the war, a joint forces' garrison remained in the Falkland Islands. Initially the Army element was an infantry battlegroup and a substantive engineer and logistic presence. When a long runway and dedicated camp was built south-east of Port Stanley, the infantry element was reduced to a single company group and an air defence battery. Only once has the rapid reinforcement of the islands' land component been exercised – in 1988.

LESSONS LEARNED AND DENIED

In December 1982, the MoD published a command paper: 'The Falklands Campaign: the Lessons'.[21] The first part of the paper set out a short narrative history of the war. The second half set out the MoD's assessment of the lessons.

In an operational staff appointment in the MoD in the late 1980s, I unearthed the original, classified paper on the war's lessons considered by the Chiefs of Staff in late 1982. Much of the paper's content was used in the command paper, the main exclusions being text on special forces and intelligence. The published report correctly assessed that:

> the most decisive factors in the land war were the high standard of individual training and fitness of the land forces, together with the leadership initiative displayed especially by junior officers and NCOs ... The present types of weapons proved effective, but the infantry need to be supported by a greater direct and indirect firepower in attack. There is also a requirement for an area attack weapon such as a grenade launcher.[22]

The issue of the SA80 rifle from 1985 did improve the firepower of the infantryman, mainly because he finally had a rifle that could fire bursts. But the firepower of light infantry battalions was not otherwise improved. It took another 20 years before the infantry were issued with a grenade launcher.

The command paper stated that the 1981 Defence Review had been validated. The four core pillars of UK defence policy would not change. But plans for the Royal Navy would be adjusted. The frigates and destroyers would be replaced, and the planned reduction of aircraft carriers cancelled. The Treasury funded these costs and those of replacing equipment that had been lost and the operating costs of the new Falkland Islands garrison.

The RAF would accelerate the fitting of station-keeping equipment to sufficient C130 Hercules transports to deliver a parachute battalion group. This allowed 5th Brigade to be designated 'airborne' instead of 'infantry'. The brigade would be assigned an armoured reconnaissance regiment, an artillery regiment, an aviation squadron and some logistic capability. A small stockpile of supplies and specialized equipment for out of area operations was assembled.

In the paper the MoD deliberately concealed the poor performance of the Blowpipe and Rapier anti-aircraft missiles. It said that Rapier had 'performed well', and stated numbers of enemy aircraft shot down that were subsequently shown to be in excess of the numbers actually destroyed. This emerged in an extensively researched book on the air war that checked British claims with credible Argentinian sources.[23]

A subsequent independent study by the Defence Operational Analysis Establishment showed that whilst the MoD had claimed that British anti-aircraft missiles had shot down 72 aircraft, the total was actually 41. It comprehensively showed that for the MoD's claim that Blowpipe had shot down nine aircraft, the evidence showed only one or two downed. The claim of 14 kills for Rapier was downgraded to a single proven kill, with several possible hits. The Royal Navy's air defence missiles had also performed less well than they should have.

The evidence suggests that once the MoD learned that Rapier and Blowpipe had performed much less well than initially claimed, this assessment was seen as a challenging 'inconvenient truth', particularly as BAE, the Rapier manufacturer, was being privatized. The report remained highly classified. A 1985 investigation by the House of Commons Defence Committee into weapons performance in the Falklands threatened this. Humphrey Atkins, the committee chair, was quietly persuaded by the MoD not to disclose the evidence, at least until the weaknesses identified with the missiles had been overcome.

This was institutional dishonesty. If the Army had again gone to war against an enemy that achieved air superiority, the poor performance of both missiles would again be a strategic shock. The Army deserved better than this.

The war also demonstrated a need to better organize and command special forces. This resulted in the 1987 establishment of a new joint formation; the Directorate of Special Forces brought the Army SAS and Royal Marines Special Boat Service under unified joint command. This was a success.[24]

5TH BRIGADE – AN ACCOUNTING AVOIDED

Perhaps the most significant lesson for the Army that was not addressed in the command paper was the considerable weaknesses displayed by 5th Brigade. The 3 Commando Brigade was a well-led and coherent all-arms formation, who were experts in both amphibious operations and living, moving and fighting in difficult weather and harsh terrain. Whilst the Army had reacted with commendable speed to many of the challenges of the unforeseen war, for example in rapidly out-loading the commando brigade's ammunition and overcoming daunting logistic challenges, 5th Infantry Brigade appeared much less effective than the commando brigade. Not only was it at a lower level of training, but its coherence was reduced by replacement of its parachute battalions by two guards battalions, both less combat ready than the paratroops and marines.

It seemed that the Army's attitude to the war had been inconsistent. By adding to the commando brigade the extremely tough parachute battalions, as well as the Rapier battery and artillery, engineers, helicopters and light armour, it had done all it could to maximize the chances of the commando brigade succeeding. Indeed, General Bramall was quoted as saying that the First XI had been despatched. But the way the Army put together 5th Brigade seemed to demonstrate the opposite approach, that minimized its chances of success. It was more like the Fourth XI. Bramall's biographer Michael Tillotson, who was Chief of Staff of UK Land Forces at the time, observed that when 5th Brigade was warned for operation the Army view was that '5 Brigade would not be required except to relieve 3 Commando Brigade of occupation duties.'

The Army was not maximizing the chances of achieving the 'complete victory' that Admiral Fieldhouse had told the Prime Minister was essential. Before the war the brigade was often described as the Army's strategic reserve. It seems odd that this role was performed by the least ready brigade of the Army with the lowest combat power. Allan Mallison considered that the apparent haste with which 5th Brigade was put together and despatched exemplified how:

> so much of the Army's response was desperately improvised (and some say amateurish) that invites comparison with the way the Crimea expedition was thrown together – not least in the way that the failings of the commanders and logistics would in the end be redeemed by the sheer fighting courage of the field officers and soldiers. There had been no serious fighting anywhere in over a decade, but Northern Ireland had sharpened basic soldier skills and junior leadership. There was an unaware complacency from political top to military bottom, in part no doubt a result of the distraction of Northern Ireland ironically in the very experience that had given junior leaders and soldiers their edge.[25]

It was not that a second brigade was unnecessary. The decision to send a second formation was vindicated by events, not least the enemy air strike on the commando brigade HQ. Had the bombs been slightly more accurate, been set to explode as an airburst, or dispensed cluster munitions, the HQ could have been neutralized or even destroyed.

Some wondered if the senior leadership of the Army lacked enthusiasm for the war? Or was the Army assuming that the Royal Navy and reinforced commando brigade would be able to defeat the Argentines on their own, and that 5th Brigade would only be needed after the fighting to garrison the islands? To many in 5th Brigade and the wider Army these questions were never satisfactorily resolved.

But many of those involved in the land war could not avoid comparing the Army and Royal Marine brigades. Major Cedric Delves, then commanding D Squadron, SAS, judged that:

> Three Commando Brigade was in superb shape, a shining example of organizational stability. Comprising the one commando 'clan', whether Army or Navy, it was blessed with an intense, near spiritual, fighting ethos that made it surprisingly well able to absorb additional units. The Paras fitted in notably well, Marine and 'Airborne' instinctively trusting and respecting one another, recognizing kindred things deeply shared, including a wholly healthy professional rivalry. And of course, the Brigade was expert in the theories and practices of fighting from the sea, including under harsh climate conditions …

A unit could be expected to behave well on operations, because that was what it had always done, and would forever continue to do, or strive to do, whatever the circumstances, whatever the company. This could be expected to compensate for any lack of esprit at formation level. However, the full preparation of a specifically task-organized brigade takes time, a good six months to ready a formation for operations in Afghanistan recently. But the Falklands War was a come-as-you-are party, with no time for exhaustive, pre-deployment training. It would take a very special brigade commander and staff to sort 5 Brigade without benefit of a thorough period of pre-deployment training: while in contact; under the wholly unfamiliar circumstances of amphibious warfare and out in the open of a South Atlantic winter … But there was fragility. It would show.[26]

Many of those involved in the Falklands War, including those who served with 5th Brigade, agreed with Delves. If the British had lost the war, or even suffered many more casualties, it is likely that the brigade's weaknesses would have received much more public, media and political scrutiny. But after victory, there were few outside the Army prepared to ask awkward questions about inconvenient truths.

A significant number of officers involved in the war were critical of Brigadier Tony Wilson, the commander of 5th Brigade. These included the commanding officers of the brigade's three infantry battalions, who during the voyage to the Falklands lost confidence in him. To many, Wilson appeared to be a showman who came up with plans that did not fit the circumstances of the war. And although many frictions contributed to the successful Argentinian air attack at Bluff Cove, ultimately the responsibility for the forces on the logistic ship was Wilson's.

Wilson had established a formidable reputation as an infantry officer, earning the Military Cross in Northern Ireland. It is much less widely known that when commanding his battalion in Hong Kong in 1977, he came within an inch of being sacked, as a result of his soldiers' display of football hooliganism at an international football match.[27] But Wilson had already been selected for promotion to colonel and was allowed to continue to an important staff job in the UK.

Wilson is dead, so cannot defend himself. But with the benefit of hindsight, there are questions to ask of the Army's senior leadership. Did they have sufficient confidence in Wilson? If they did not, why did they let him take the brigade to the Falklands? In early 1980 the brigade, in the form of HQ 8th Field Force, had been highly successful in leading the previously unforeseen and risky operation in Rhodesia – an operation well outside the framework of Army doctrine and training. But just over two years later, the same formation had come close to failure in the Falklands. And its mission there, conducting a brigade attack, was a core part of Army doctrine and training. The one factor that appears to have changed between the two deployments was the brigade commander.

Applying the test of the Learmont question, the Army could answer with a resounding yes to the provision of the SAS and its support and reinforcement of the commando brigade. But it failed to provide a properly trained, equipped and led second brigade to the force. Ultimately, the responsibility for this lay with General Bramall. As CGS, he was a figure of enormous stature, subsequently promoted to become Chief of the Defence Staff.

And right at the end of his life he was subject to a highly intrusive and distressing police investigation, prompted by wholly false allegations that he was a member of a secret network of paedophiles. Bramall rightly gained enormous sympathy when the charges from an apparently incompetent police investigation were eventually dropped.

Bramall was later reported as saying that not replacing Wilson as brigade commander was the worst decision he had made in over 40 years as a soldier.[28] There appears to be no evidence that Bramall was ever held to account for the weaknesses of 5th Brigade. In the aftermath of the war there were rumours in the Army and Royal Navy that both services had identified officers whose performance in war had been found wanting. But the same rumours also alleged that since the war was the result of a failure of deterrence by Mrs Thatcher's government, it would be unfair to take any action against those judged to have failed in their duties during the war. Some said that Mrs Thatcher herself had directed this approach. And whether the Amy acted after the war adjusted its processes for selecting brigade commanders is unknown.

This would not be the only time when officers were not held to account for their failings on operations. And it would not be the only occasion when a brigade commander lost the confidence of people above and below him.

CAPABILITY OF BRIGADE COMMANDERS

After the Cold War, the Army made great efforts to prepare brigades for operations. Examples of this, including preparing formations for the wars in Iraq and Afghanistan, are described later. But whether it sought to better select officers for brigade command was less clear.

I served in ten different British Army brigades. Seven were well led by the commander and both he and the formation's units were well supported by an effective brigade HQ with competent and helpful staff officers. A friend who commanded a brigade described the brigade staff and unit commanders as a 'merry band of brothers'.

But this happy state did not apply to three brigades that I served in. In the first, the commander underwhelmed not only the brigade's fiercely competitive commanding officers, but also the brigade's mid-ranking officers, the majors and captains, who were uniformly unimpressed with him. Fortunately, the brigade HQ contained two outstanding officers – the chief of staff and deputy chief of staff. Both acted as excellent co-ordinators of operations, applying robust common sense and infinite amounts of patience to ensure the wheels did not come off.

A decade later the chief of staff, now a colonel, was fulfilling the same role in a multinational formation with an ad hoc staff and a mercurial commander, with a very short fuse prone to outbursts that manifested themselves as unpleasant tantrums. Again, this officer displayed industrial quantities of quiet patience and again the show was kept on the road.

I later served in an infantry brigade, whose commander was not an infantry officer. This should not have been a handicap. But it was painfully obvious that he understood neither how infantry fought, nor their culture, nor how he could best support them. And whilst the brigade had an excellent deputy chief of staff, running logistic and personnel matters with an assured touch, the chief of staff appeared less effective. Whether this was through a lack of personal competence, or because the brigade commander would not let him be effective, I could not say. After a year the commander and chief of staff departed. Shortly after the replacements assumed their posts, the quality of leadership, decision-making and mutual confidence in the brigade rapidly improved.

In Northern Ireland, I served in a brigade where the commander was suddenly sacked. Later it emerged that his approach had greatly unsettled both the police and the Commander Land Forces. He was formally warned to adjust his approach. When he failed to do so, he was removed from command. He did not leave the Army and served with notable distinction in a non-operational role, going on to have a fruitful civilian career.

These three examples, as well as 5th Brigade's role in the Falklands War, all happened in the 1980s and early 1990s. I had thought that the impact of the Higher Command and Staff Course and the reduction of numbers of brigades to command meant that the standard of brigade commanders had improved. But at least two brigadiers were sacked in 2021, one for apparent financial misdemeanours and another for mistreating his subordinates. The Army reacted by setting up a new selection and training programme for potential brigade commanders, called the One Star Command Assessment.[29] All this shows that the senior leadership of the Army have important roles not only in selecting officers for brigade command, but also in closely monitoring their performance. And in identifying those that are not up to the job and dispassionately removing them.

CHAPTER 4
THE CRUCIBLE OF THE COLD WAR (2)
THE BAGNALL REVOLUTION

PROJECT MERCURY AND THE 1981 DEFENCE REVIEW

Mrs Thatcher's Conservative government took power in 1979 on an election pledge to increase defence spending. Its first action was to implement the recommended pay awards that had not been honoured by the previous government. A noticeable increase in all ranks' pay packets was very welcome.

But the spending plans of the MoD were in considerable excess of the money available in the defence budget. Suddenly in late 1980 the MoD imposed a 'moratorium' on expenditure. Money for training, ammunition and transport was greatly reduced and many other short-term cost savings were imposed on the Army. Some of these measures smacked of financial desperation, including sending troops home early on Christmas leave to reduce the cost of heating barracks. With typical ingenuity, units and formations found ways to exploit loopholes and boundaries in financial procedures to lessen some of the worst impacts of the freeze.

In January 1981 John Nott, a former Gurkha officer, took over as Defence Secretary. Nott decided that he must hold a defence review to bridge the gap between plans and expenditure. The 1981 Defence Review took a hard look at UK defence strategy and resulting commitments. Four 'pillars' of defence capability were identified: the nuclear deterrent, maritime operations in the East Atlantic, the home defence of the UK and the air/land contribution to NATO in Germany. Nott concluded that of these roles, the role where money could be saved was the maritime contribution to the East Atlantic. Forces allocated to this were reduced, resulting in significant cuts to the naval surface fleet. Army and RAF forces assigned to NATO would not be cut.

For the Army this was a fortunate alignment of the planets. Since Exercise *Spearpoint* the Army had been planning how it might adjust its structure to overcome the weaknesses that had resulted from the 1975 restructuring. These had been clearly demonstrated in exercises and operational planning between 1975 and 1980, especially the weakness of the task force level of command between division and battlegroup. The Army therefore commissioned Project Mercury, to redesign itself to eliminate these weaknesses, including restoring the brigade level of command. It was able to present this restructuring to Defence Secretary John Nott as a package of enhancements, to be announced in the 1981 Defence Review White Paper.

The corps restructured into three armoured divisions based in Germany. The two forward divisions had three armoured brigades each. The 3rd Division was to be the corps reserve. It had a heterogeneous composition of two armoured brigades and the UK-based 19th Infantry Brigade. Exercise *Spearpoint* had deliberately featured a significant threat to the corps rear area from special forces, helicopter-borne air assault units and parachute-delivered airborne forces. The exercise showed that there were insufficient forces to secure the area, which measured about 5,000 square kilometres – equivalent to the combined area of the English counties of Cornwall, Somerset, Dorset and Wiltshire or the US state of Connecticut. Within this sector were based many British logistic, medical, air defence and support units, plus the RAF forces of Harrier jump jets and support helicopters, as well as German troops and all required better command and control.

The existing 5th Field Force of infantry brigade strength would be joined by three TA brigades from the UK – one engineer and two infantry. To command these formations and co-ordinate security across the corps rear area, the HQ of the 2nd Armoured Division would move back to the UK, to be redesignated HQ 2nd Infantry Division, leaving an operational planning team based in Germany.

THE INCREASING SOVIET THREAT

By now it was clear that the Soviet Army was rapidly improving its capability. Particularly noteworthy were its tanks; all of these now fielded the powerful 125mm gun, which fired a powerful finned anti-tank round. Its artillery was being rapidly converted from towed to self-propelled guns. Hind attack helicopters were being deployed to East Germany, at a time when the only NATO army with a dedicated attack helicopter was the US Army. Overall in any likely scenario of a Warsaw Pact attack on West Germany the British corps would probably be outnumbered and outgunned, particularly if it lay in the path of a Soviet main effort thrust.

As well as improving its equipment, the Soviet Army was seeking to improve its effectiveness by adapting its tactical and operational doctrine. It had always emphasized the value of breaking through enemy defence lines to disrupt them in depth, something it had developed in World War II in its massive offensive operations against German forces from the battle of Stalingrad onwards. It considered that improved artillery, armoured vehicles and air support would create new opportunities to achieve this.

The Soviet Army was developing the concept of the Operational Manoeuvre Group (OMG) a formation of at least divisional size that was designed and trained for breaking through a linear NATO defence and rapidly moving into the corps rear area. The Soviets considered that this formation would not only be capable of attacking key objectives in NATO rear areas, including HQs, logistic units, airfields, nuclear artillery and river crossings, but also had the potential to assist in the encirclement of NATO formations. At the same time Soviet exercises featured increasing use of air manoeuvre with parachute and heliborne forces landing in NATO rear areas. Intelligence showed that Soviet forces in East Germany were augmented by a new air assault brigade and that there were also Spetsnaz units in East Germany.

HQ BAOR watched these developments through three different windows. One was intelligence, a proportion of which was gathered by BAOR itself, using the SIGINT capabilities of 13 Signal Regiment. Another view came from unclassified reports and analysis that were produced in-house by the Soviet Studies Research Centre. This was a small team of Russian-speaking military experts, who translated and analyzed Soviet military publications – of which a surprising number were openly available. These were made available throughout the Army; and the staff often lectured to Army courses and to formations. In the 1980s, their assessments of Soviet military capability were widely circulated throughout the Army. Being based entirely on open-source material, they were unclassified, so were much more accessible than classified intelligence assessments. The centre's staff regularly lectured to Army training courses and formations. Their assessments had a considerable influence on tactical thinking.[1]

The third perspective came from HQ BAOR's unique unit for gathering intelligence in East Germany, the British Commander in Chief's Mission to Soviet Forces. Abbreviated to BRIXMIS, the mission descended from the military missions exchanged by British and Soviet Forces in the last year of World War II to co-ordinate operations, particularly to avoid accidental clashes as the two armies approached each other.[2]

These missions continued throughout the Cold War. A Soviet Mission to the British commanders (SOXMIS) based itself in Bunde, where its personnel were sometimes seen shopping in the local British families' NAAFI shop. BRIXMIS was based in West Berlin. Both missions created opportunities for Soviet and British commanders to meet each other – a unique channel for military-to-military messaging.

But both missions spent most of their time gathering information and intelligence about each other's forces. Neither the British nor the Soviets made this easy, banning the missions from areas around training areas and major exercises, and having dedicated units to monitor and disrupt the missions' intelligence gathering. Whilst the Royal Military Police did not use force to obstruct SOXMIS, both Soviet and East German forces engaged in deliberate ramming of BRIXMIS vehicles and did not use kid gloves when they sometimes detained BRIXMIS personnel.

Major General Peter Williams, then a BRIXMIS Tour Officer, was showing a new mission commander around East Germany. Discovering a new East German surveillance site, their Opel saloon car was rammed by a 10-ton truck: 'The noise was incredible as the truck ploughed into us as we braced ourselves for the deadly roll that I knew would certainly kill us. The side of the Opal caved in as it was violently shunted off the road sandwiched between the truck and a fruit tree.'[3]

Emerging from the wrecked vehicle, the BRIXMIS team were surrounded by heavily armed East German troops and plain clothes officers of the Stasi, the notorious East German secret police.

BRIXMIS had about 80 troops, 40 per cent from the RAF. Headed by a brigadier, they mounted patrols continuously, until October 1990. This included an officer bravely getting onto a Soviet BMP-2 fighting vehicle, to measure the calibre of its cannon, which was then unknown. Having no tape measure, he took an apple from his pocket, and pressed it into the gun's muzzle to get an impression of the barrel. Brigadier John Foley described some other intelligence coups: 'When I was chief, we were urgently tasked to get an explosive reactive armour box recently introduced onto the Soviet tanks – by a stroke of luck one of our sharp-eyed NCOs spotted one on a tank firing range and grabbed it.'[4]

BRIXMIS had great success in gathering intelligence that eluded both US satellite observation and British electronic eavesdropping. They provided 'ground truth' that was otherwise unobtainable to HQ BAOR.

IMPROVING EQUIPMENT

The British had long been developing a new type of tank armour. Previously this had been thick steel plate. At the Fighting Vehicle Research and Development Establishment scientists and engineers had pioneered a new approach which was given the name Chobham Armour, after the nearest town. The technical details remain secret but it is clear that the armour used extremely hard ceramic armour plates, within a metal matrix. These not only offered improved protection against kinetic energy shells, but also better neutralized the effects of the hollow charge warheads of rocket-propelled grenades (RPGs) and anti-tank missiles.

The technology was shared with the US, who fielded it on the M1 Abrams tank that entered service in 1979. Initially it was planned that the technology be introduced into the British Army much later. Before this, it would have been used on the British-made Shir Lion tank that had been ordered by the Iranian Shah's government. This was an evolution of the Chieftain with the same gun and fire-control system but with Chobham armour attached to the turret and hull. With the fall of the Shah of Iran in 1979, the order lapsed, but the tanks were diverted to the Army as the Challenger.

Only enough Challenger tanks were funded to replace half the Army's tank fleet, with Chieftain soldiering on. The priority was to allocate the new tanks to brigades more likely to counterattack, brigades with a primarily defensive operational role and those in the UK and Berlin retaining the less well-protected Chieftains. Challenger and Chieftain continued to use the same 120mm gun and ammunition, the same day and night sights and fire-control system, simplifying logistics and training. Challenger tanks were supplied between

1983 and 1990, quickly gaining a reputation for indifferent reliability, particularly of the engine and gearbox.

The Army had three UK-based infantry brigades with a NATO role, two assigned to 1 (BR) Corps and one assigned to reinforce NATO's Baltic Approaches Command. At the beginning of the decade these relied on trucks and Land Rovers for mobility. A modicum of protected mobility was provided by issuing these formations with Saxon wheeled APCs. Initially developed by GKN Sankey as an internal security vehicle, these were relatively simple and easy to operate. But, with only four wheels and a pintle-mounted machine gun, they lacked the tactical mobility and firepower of the many wheeled APCS in both NATO and Warsaw Pact armies. Even so, they were a relatively cheap way of improving the utility of light infantry where there was an adequate road network.

Helicopter capability also improved. The Gazelle was fitted with an improved sight. And the RAF replaced elderly Wessex helicopters with new US-made Chinook helicopters. These huge twin rotor aircraft were a quantum leap in lift capability, lifting up to 60 troops, four times as many as a Wessex, and able to carry up to 10 tons in weight as underslung loads. Both Army and RAF helicopters also had their night-flying capability greatly improved by the fielding of night-vision goggles for the crew. At the same time the RAF Regiment field squadrons assigned to defend the Harrier and support helicopter squadrons in Germany were given Scorpion armoured vehicles, improving their mobility, firepower and ability to protect the aircraft from ground attack.

The Rapier anti-aircraft missile was initially fielded with only a day sight. But in the early 1980s it was given a radar, Blindfire, that allowed engagement in poor weather and at night. And another spin-off benefit of the fall of the Shah was the acquisition of the Tracked Rapier system that had been ordered by the Shah's government. This fitted the missile system to a tracked chassis, improving the ability of Rapier to deploy alongside armoured forces, as well as a much swifter ability to come into action.

In a harbinger of the breaking wave of information technology, a computer system was fielded to the corps. Named Wavell, it was by today's standards slow and limited. It collated and displayed key battle information, including personnel and equipment strengths, ammunition holdings and locations. There was some resistance to its use, overcome when the corps commander announced that when he visited units on exercises he would travel to the location listed on Wavell as the unit rendezvous.

THE BAGNALL EFFECT

Lieutenant General Nigel Bagnall was corps commander from November 1980 to July 1983. In this role, he would shape the corps structure, thinking, planning and training. In his subsequent appointments, as the commander of both BAOR and NATO's NORTHAG and then as CGS, he would profoundly influence the British Army, more than any other officer in this period.[5]

Bagnall was commissioned into the Green Howards, an infantry regiment, in 1946. Two years later he volunteered for the Parachute Regiment, where he was given early responsibility, commanding a company, at an age much younger than his peers. Returning to the Green Howards, he served on counterinsurgency operations in Malaya and earned the Military Cross twice, gaining a reputation for tireless energy, great bravery and an innovative approach. In 1956 he transferred to 4th/7th Royal Dragoon Guards, an armoured regiment in Germany.

In his spare time, he studied military history, ranging from the Punic Wars to the war between Israel and its Arab neighbours. He took a particular interest in armoured battles between German and Russian forces fought between 1941 and 1945, teaching himself German to better do so. He sought to identify what made these forces so successful in holding off a numerically superior enemy. He identified the key factor as commanders that concentrated force at decisive points whilst accepting risk elsewhere, delivering surprise counterattacks that disrupted Russian advances.

In 1970 Bagnall, now a brigadier, took command of the corps reconnaissance regiments. Their role was that of corps covering force, acting as a screen to identify the main Warsaw Pact armoured thrusts into the corps area. The NATO policy of forward defence required the corps to yield as little terrain as possible, which meant the lightly armoured Scorpion, Scimitar and Striker fighting vehicles had to be initially deployed within line of sight of the border, to be able to identify the initial Warsaw Pact thrusts. They would then fall back, attempting to maintain contact with enemy armoured columns as they advanced, until they reached the armoured brigades' forward positions.

Given the large amount of artillery the Soviets could bring to bear from firing positions sited just to the east of the border and the few British air defence weapons likely to be deployed to support the regiments, this would be a difficult and dangerous mission. To better understand how it might be achieved, Bagnall researched the approaches of the other NORTHAG corps. He discovered that there was very little, if any, co-ordination of the battle plans of the four national corps. This had adverse implications for the British corps screen. If the German or Belgian corps screen withdrew more quickly than Bagnall's small formation, it risked being outflanked and cut off. If the British withdrew faster than the German or Belgian screens, they would subject them to the same risk.

At a corps' study day, Bagnall told the audience that he had discovered that the army group did not have a co-ordinated plan for battle. This outspoken assessment made many of the more senior officers present uncomfortable. For a time, there was a possibility that Bagnall would be dismissed. This threat passed, but the corps commander noted on Bagnall's annual report that he could 'either go to the top or be shot down in flames'.

A subsequent fellowship at Balliol College, Oxford, saw Bagnall study the Israeli victories against Arab forces. He analyzed the factors that made them so successful against a numerically superior enemy. He assessed that the Israeli Army was of a much higher quality than the Arab armies that it defeated. Key factors that explained this qualitative superiority were individual and collective training and the selection, education and training of commanders. The Israeli Army had adopted a philosophy of manoeuvre warfare that saw commanders deploy well forward on the battlefield, to better identify and exploit fleeting opportunities.

Returning to the corps in 1975, Bagnall commanded the 4th Armoured Division, which was restructured into the post-1975 *Wide Horizon* structure. He sought to practise armoured manoeuvre warfare but saw for himself the weaknesses of the new formation, particularly the loss of properly constituted brigades.

Appointed to command the corps in 1980, he was now senior enough to put his ideas into practice. At a time when NATO and the US sought to make the use of battlefield nuclear weapons less likely, he set out to maximize the ability of the corps to impose greater delay on attacking Soviet forces, thus delaying resort to nuclear weapons. Bagnall accepted the general approach of the previous corps plan – a covering force protecting the preparation of the main defensive positions of the defending armoured divisions and brigades. But he thought the extant corps plan was too defensive in character. If the corps was subjected to a major Soviet attack that concentrated armoured formations and artillery on a narrow thrust, its defences would be overwhelmed. Instead Bagnall directed development of a more aggressive plan, with a less linear and much deeper defensive layout. This would accept enemy penetrations on selected routes, in order to set the conditions for rapidly delivered surprise armoured counterattacks. These would dislocate both the attacking formations and the plans of the Soviet commanders, thus regaining the initiative. The new plan carried more risk than the previous, more attritional plan, but the greater emphasis on offensive manoeuvre would, if successful, impose greater delay on the enemy.

With its divisions now organized into coherent brigades, the corps was better poised to implement this approach. There were now only two armoured divisions, the 1st and 4th, defending the Forward Edge of the Battle Area positions with two brigades each. Each division's third armoured brigade was available as a covering force, but Bagnall intended that soon as possible the covering force would withdraw so as to be each division's reserve, thus escaping the heavy attrition they would suffer if they stood and fought under the overhang of Soviet artillery. This would allow each division to mount its own brigade-sized tactical counter moves. And the whole of the 3rd Division would be the corps reserve.

As well as directing the formulation of a new corps plan, Bagnall produced new tactical doctrine for 1 (BR) Corps. This was the Corps Battle Notes,[6] a short document that set out at the lowest level of security classification Bagnall's approach to the corps battle and the way it was to be fought by the divisions, brigades and battlegroups. The notes required a more offensive spirit and more agile command. Defensive operations must be offensive in concept, with formations carefully choosing the ground to fight from and reinforcing this with obstacles, as well as being able to form and employ reserves.

Bagnall expected the doctrine to be 'clearly understood and implemented by commanders at all levels, only in this way can the need for long, explanatory orders be dispensed with. There is no time for them on the modern high-intensity battlefield.' An early section on the issue of orders set out Bagnall's approach to command:

> Orders are the means by which a commander conveys his intentions to his subordinates, either in detail or as short directives. Detailed orders should only be issued when close co-ordination is necessary, or subordinate commanders lack the ability to work on their own

initiative. Whenever possible orders should be given as a single directive together with any executive co-ordinating details, such as timings and boundaries. In a fast-moving battle commanders will control events by giving personal direction over the radio and by visiting subordinate commanders to see what is going on for themselves.

The mission is the essence of every order. It is the starting point for the actions of subordinates and must therefore be realistic and expressed clearly and unequivocally. The mission should leave the subordinate commanders as much freedom of execution as possible and should contain only those constraints essential to cooperation with other units.

If a subordinate does not understand his commander's instructions he must say so. However, the situation will seldom be clear, and commanders at all levels having been given their task must use their own initiative in effecting its prompt execution. Determination and drive will resolve most situations. Dithering over details, when these are not fundamental to the task, leads to delay and lost opportunities.

THE COUNTERSTROKE INITIATIVE

British doctrine had always stated that any defensive layout should be offensively minded, not least because a purely defensive attitude was poor for morale and forfeited opportunities to strike at the enemy, handing them the initiative. It considered that formations should be prepared to conduct counter moves to frustrate an enemy advance. The first operation would be counter-penetration – deploying a force to block an enemy advance. The second option would be a counterattack to recapture key positions that had fallen to the enemy. British doctrine also foresaw higher tactical or operational-level counterattacks to exploit NATO nuclear strikes.

Bagnall's concept for corps operations admitted of these types of counter moves, but went further, advocating more ambitious offensive operations. This was to set enemy columns up for destruction by surprise counterattacks at times and places that the British, not the Soviets, would choose. These were to be attacks by complete armoured brigades, into the flank of an enemy formation.

To do this would require the armoured brigade to move secretly into a position to mount a surprise strike. The attack would begin with a short but intense artillery strike by all the artillery within range. The armoured brigade of two tank regiments and a mechanized infantry battalion would attack on a narrow front with tanks leading. Infantry would remain mounted in their APCs. The intent was to maintain momentum with concentrated tank fire being the primary method of destroying the many enemy armoured vehicles in the target areas. Only if substantial enemy defences were encountered would the infantry be brought up to clear them. The operation was not to recapture the terrain occupied by the enemy forces, so once the counterstroke had achieved the desired effect, the attacking brigade would move away, to reconstitute for subsequent operations.

This was a challenging role: attacking into the flanks of enemy armoured formations required speed and aggression to surprise and shock the enemy. To achieve this the brigade had to be able to move rapidly, usually at night, invariably observing radio silence, then stealthily assemble in a position from which to mount the attack. This would include a major effort to synchronize the ground manoeuvre with concentrated artillery fire, and the use of armed Lynx helicopters, not only to protect the brigade's flanks, but also as highly mobile anti-tank reserves.

NATO airpower had an important role to play in reinforcing the ground attack. For example, in late 1982, I took part in a 3rd Armoured Division command post exercise. Following a divisional defensive battle, there was a simulated counterstroke by the 4th Armoured Brigade. This began with a short sharp carpet bombing by a flight of USAF B52 bombers, flying from Fairford in Gloucestershire.

Training for counterstrokes greatly energized the armoured brigades that were assigned the missions. The 4th Armoured Brigade felt this the most. At the time it was part of the 3rd Armoured Division. This was the corps' reserve division. But at the time two of its brigades were of non-mechanized infantry, leaving the 4th Brigade as its only armoured formation. So it would play the leading role in any corps counterstroke.

For then Brigadier Charles Guthrie, the brigade's commander, this new role was an opportunity for the brigade to seize with both hands. Guthrie's previous tours in Germany had frustrated him as collective training 'had become far too much of an accustomed regime and the major BAOR exercises were neither challenging nor memorable.'[7] He thought that:

Any institution can become moribund after time. People can become complacent and lethargically content with a routine and a way of doing things that does not stretch them. An example of this was the BAOR warrior type who had served in Germany for too long, knew every training area backwards, and had become accustomed to exercises that were predictable and unimaginative. Under Bagnall, a gifted thinker, BAOR became fresh, fun, and exciting.[8]

Guthrie described how Bagnall's concept energized him, his brigade and the whole corps:

In essence this meant allowing the Soviet Third Shock Army to run its course, run out of fuel and supplies as its logistical tail sought to catch up, and then we would catch them on the hop with bold and aggressive armoured thrusts from their flanks ...

At a Corps study day Bagnall summarized this as 'shock action along the line of least expectation'. It was all exciting stuff, particularly for the squadron commanders and company commanders of the brigade on whose shoulders the success or failure of such an operation would fall ... The Royal Armoured Corps had rather lost their dash and verve in the inertia of BAOR in the 1970s. But I did feel the counter stroke was just the tonic they needed to shrug off their lethargy and regain their natural elan ...

The concept of building a team around a common endeavour was to some senior officers at the time an alien concept. They relied too much on their rank to get their message across and would brook little opposition to their views. I used to have regular days when all the key players in the brigade would meet, and we would debate how to best execute counter strokes quickly and emphatically. I would select a clear aim for the day and made sure that we kept to it but apart from that I would allow free rein to our discussions. Shared ownership of a challenge is a great boost to morale and motivation.

The counter stroke operation was a special role for the 4th Armoured Brigade, the jewel in the corps' crown, and made life for us all a lot more worthwhile and enjoyable than that experienced by others in BAOR. We even began to look forward to the ritual dance of BAOR autumn exercises, usually heavily choreographed, where we would execute the counter stroke operation in the glorious landscape of Nord Rhein Westphalia. We practised and rehearsed until we were close to pitch perfect. The sense of renewal began to spread through the whole of BAOR.[9]

THE AIRMOBILE BRIGADE EXPERIMENT

As Bagnall's concept meant that the corps could not be strong everywhere, there was an inevitable risk of enemy columns breaking through the forward divisions' defensive positions and debouching into divisional and corps' rear areas.[10] Divisions and the corps itself had to accept that enemy tank and motor rifle formations would be allowed, even encouraged, to penetrate the British defensive network along selected routes, so as to be attacked from their flanks. And the impact of a counterstroke would be increased if the target divisions had been slowed down or even stopped – resulting in congestion. From the point of view of corps and divisional commanders, the more enemy there were in the target area, the better.

The Army decided that the corps needed a dedicated formation for counter-penetration operations, that could rapidly deploy to delay and block any enemy force that threatened to penetrate through British defensive positions, both to protect rear areas from enemy breakthroughs and to make them better targets for counterstroke attacks.

If such a force were trained and equipped to move by helicopter, it could reach its positions more quickly than moving by road, especially if bridges were damaged or destroyed, or roads were congested with NATO troops or refugees. And the RAF Germany support helicopter force would greatly increase in lift capability in 1983, as it received the US Chinook helicopter, with a much greater payload than the Wessex helicopters it would replace.

The 6th Armoured Brigade of the 3rd Division was selected for this role. The Army's long-term plans were for the brigade to become a modernized armoured brigade with two armoured infantry battalions and a tank regiment. But there would not be enough new armoured vehicles to achieve this before the late 1980s. So the brigade would conduct a novel experiment, giving up its armoured vehicles to become an airmobile brigade for five years, trialling the new concept.

This was a more radical departure than the counterstroke, which used three existing armoured brigades to conduct offensive operations – something they already had the capability to do – albeit in a more ambitious way. The airmobile brigade initiative took an existing armoured brigade, radically changed its organization and equipment, partnered it with the RAF support helicopter force and tasked it with a role that was completely new to the British Army. The new 6th Airmobile Brigade (Trial), to give the brigade its full title, would be the first experimental brigade fielded by the Army since the Experimental Mechanized Force, which almost 60 years earlier had trialled the concept of an armoured brigade on Salisbury Plain. This airmobile trial was forgotten in the flurry of interest in experimentation and innovation that occurred in the early 2020s.

In 1982 and 1983, the brigade HQ planned how it would deliver this new capability. Much was learned from the Bundeswehr. Each of its three corps had an airborne *Luftlande* brigade. The primary role of these brigades was counter-penetration. They had well-developed tactics and techniques for this, flying forward in the Bundeswehr's CH53 transport helicopters, then rapidly preparing defensive positions, making use of the brigade's many Milan and TOW anti-tank missiles.

The first task for the 6th Brigade HQ was to design itself. Its allocated forces included its signal squadron, two infantry battalions and an engineer squadron. All the brigade's armoured vehicles were withdrawn and replaced by lorries and Land Rovers. The brigade artillery regiment would retain its Abbot self-propelled guns, but the regimental HQ and battery HQs and forward observation teams would give up their armour. An Army Air Corps squadron of Gazelle and Lynx helicopters, the latter armed with TOW missiles, was assigned to the brigade. And for the duration of the trial, the brigade would have priority call on the RAF's support helicopter squadrons. Based at RAF Gutersloh, inside the corps area, these comprised a squadron of Pumas and another of the newly issued Chinooks. The arrival of the latter aircraft greatly increased the volume of troops, equipment and supplies that could be moved by air. Without them, the necessary speed of air movement could not have been achieved.

Learning from their study of 27th Luftlande Brigade, the brigade HQ designed the organization and equipment they thought they would need. These included a significant increase in Milan missile launchers, which would rise from 16 per battalion to 42, with each battalion having three instead of one anti-tank platoon. The number of machine guns would double. Unlike the rest of the corps, units would own large numbers of the nets and slings required to transport vehicles and cargo under helicopters. Many soldiers were trained in the necessary skills to operate helicopter pick-up points by day and night. All these measures were agreed by the Army staff in the MoD.

From autumn 1983 the brigade would have a year to develop its new capability. The brigade was given a simple mission by the corps – to reach an initial operating capability to conduct airmobile counter-penetration operations for the corps, in time to take part in the September 1984 corps field exercise.

Both the corps and 3rd Division HQ provided their support, and the necessary resources, but then stood back and let the brigade get on with developing its new capability. In late 1983 the brigade began the trial, with the issue of new equipment and people going on necessary training courses. In December all the formations' officers were assembled for a two-day briefing on the new role and equipment, as well as the brigade's new concept of operations. Throughout 1984 the brigade's units worked out and practised how they would move by air and the necessary tactics for rapidly preparing defensive positions to counter an enemy penetration. Three brigade-level exercises were organized, the first exercising HQ and logistic capabilities, the second a week's exercise for the full brigade, and the third a short exercise to improve the brigade's ability to move by night. All these saw full use of the brigade's assigned Army and RAF helicopters.

BAGNALL'S IMPACT AS CORPS COMMANDER

Bagnall's leadership of the corps catalyzed a revival of the Army's doctrine for better fighting an armoured battle at divisional and corps level, especially by increasing the agility of commanders. To develop and refine his thinking he formed an informal committee, the Tactical Doctrine Discussion Group. Given Bagnall's hair colour and sometimes fiery temper it was rapidly nicknamed the 'Ginger Group'. Its membership was defined by Bagnall and included trusted subordinates and some relatively junior officers that he personally selected. The group would regularly meet under Bagnall's leadership to discuss and refine the Army's approach to its NATO role, especially tactical doctrine. In his subsequent two appointments, Bagnall would continue to use the group as an agent of change.

A significant number of middle ranking and senior officers in the corps, many with much service in Germany, found the changes uncomfortable. But an equal number of officers welcomed them. In late 1982, as he approached the end of his time as corps commander, Bagnall set out his thinking in a signed note entitled 'Tactical Training'. It appears to have been the text of a talk he gave to his commanders and key staff.[11] It began with his addressing a body of opinion in the corps that did not embrace either the principles of Bagnall's thinking or his intentions for the corps battle:

> I am told that there are some people who express the view that the emphasis on mobility, quick reaction and an offensive spirit which we have been placing on our tactical thinking, does not reflect the British way of waging war. If such views are seriously held in some quarters, and from what I hear, I must assume they are, they reflect a very shallow knowledge of our military thinking. Though it is true to say that with the expansion of the Army in 1914–18, detailed planning and a methodical approach to warfare became firmly established as British military characteristics, they have not always been so and have never been universally accepted.

He went on to commend Marlborough's campaigns for displaying 'boldness, offensive mobility and his strategic thinking, conduct of operations and tactical handing on the battlefield'. The same could be said of Wellington's Peninsula campaign, especially his handling of reserves at the battle of Salamanca. And:

> during World War I, the achievements of the Australians under Monash, even under conditions of near stagnant trench warfare, shows what can be done under vigorous, well-led troops. While Allenby's Palestine Campaign portrays how boldness, mobility and surprise achieve results, with a minimum of casualties, that costly head on battles of attrition had singularly failed to produce. In the 1939–45 war, O'Connor showed what can be accomplished against a numerically superior but supine opponent by

acting offensively and exploiting success. There were others as well but, on the whole, the British commanders at the higher level in World War II never matched their German counterparts.

This obsession for detailed planning on every occasion, instead of only when necessary, is in reality little more than an excuse for some commanders not to have to take decisions in mid-battle on their own initiative, or to act as the situation demands, rather than as the textbook lays down. Our methodical and pedestrian approach is not a truly national way of waging war, but rather a sad reflection on our lack of professionalism at the higher level of command and restricted teaching in many of our training establishments. We have not trained the teachers and not enough officers have taken the trouble to train themselves in any depth. This results in a perpetuation of mediocrity in our tactical thinking above the regimental level. The British soldier is a resourceful and courageous fighter who, when well led is a match for any opponent. The 2nd Parachute Battalion's attack at Goose Green exemplifies what I am saying …

What is to be done? In my opinion, nothing will be achieved by producing all-embracing tactical publications. Spoon feeding individuals with tactical template models does not develop self-reliant commanders, but unimaginative stereotypes. If you try to explain everything or in tactical planning cover everything in detail, you will lose simplicity and once you have lost that, you have as good as lost everything of importance: vitality, urgency, initiative, and surprise. In the absence of sufficiently competent teachers, self-education is unavoidable, and this can only be done by selective reading and study …

To those of you who think about your profession, I hope this note will encourage you to persevere. None of us can afford to stop learning. If you have any comments, queries or suggestions as to how we can develop this 'feeling in one's finger tips' to which Kannengiesser refers, speak up, but be brief.

EXERCISE *LIONHEART*

The corps' new organizations, equipment and tactical doctrine were tested on the 1984 exercise *Lionheart*, the Army's largest field manoeuvre of the Cold War. Compared with the previous exercise, *Crusader*, it was a larger and more dynamic exercise with a greater degree of free play. It was planned that over130,000 troops would take part in the exercise as follows:

- Already in Europe: 42,000 from 1 (BR) Corps, 6,000 from British Rear Support Command, and 12,000 RAF personnel
- Reinforcing from UK: 17,000 Regular Army, 39,500 TA and reserves, and 1,000 RAF personnel
- Allied Forces: 165 Commonwealth troops and a German-led multinational NATO division of 6,300 German troops, 3,500 Dutch troops and 3,400 US troops.

The exercise lasted a month from 3 September, when the lines of communication activated, until 5 October, when all the reinforcing units had returned to the UK. The first part was Exercise *Full Flow*. This tested the plans for deploying reinforcements from UK to the corps. This was no small undertaking. The command, support and protection of the lines of communications for BAOR came under a two-star HQ, British Support Forces. It had two subordinate formations:

- The Communications Zone spanned the posts of Ostend and Zeebrugge, northern Belgium and Southern Holland, with a one-star HQ in Antwerp. The British would like to have used the shorter sea crossing to Calais and Boulogne, but French withdrawal from NATO's integrated military structure in the 1960s meant that NATO was excluded from its soil. This increased the time required for the Channel crossing.
- The Rear Combat Zone ran from the west border of Germany to the rear boundary of the corps and was commanded by a one-star HQ in Antwerp.

In peacetime, these HQs were small, commanding few troops. In war an early reinforcement would be a regular infantry battalion based in the Channel port of Dover. As mobilization began, it would cross to Belgium and deploy along the line of communication to provide a modicum of security and command and control. Thousands of troops would follow to deploy along the lines of communication to provide essential command, control logistics and force protection. These included a large number of TA units, including seven infantry battalions, an air defence regiment and many transport, maintenance and medical units. As well as getting units and combat supplies forward to the corps, they would in war also manage the return of casualties to the UK and establish a camp for enemy prisoners of war. For Exercise *Lionheart* 6,500 troops would support the lines of communication.

The exercise tested the mobilization of the reserves. Of the 32,000 TA volunteers that had been planned for mobilization, some 29,385 (92 per cent) reported for duty. A new feature of the exercise was the voluntary mobilization of individual reservists, former soldiers and officers. Out of a planned 4,500 volunteers, 75 per cent reported for duty, allowing the mobilization system to be tested. The mobilized troops were deployed across the exercise. Arriving in 1st Battalion, the Light Infantry, a recently retired guards officer turned out to have been a cadet in the commanding officer's company at Sandhurst four years before. Both knew each other well and had considerable mutual respect.

Fifty thousand troops were moved from the UK to Germany and the Low Countries in 290 flights and 150 sailings across the North Sea and English Channel, using civilian ferries. RAF transport aircraft and chartered civilian airliners carried a further 27,000 troops from the UK to Germany. Sitting at the western part of the corps area, the RAF base at Gutersloh received the majority of flights, including, for the first time, wide-bodied airliners. To minimize vulnerability to air or missile strike whilst concentrated at the airport, much effort had been put into rapidly unloading these large aircraft, matching troops up with their weapons and equipment and getting them out of the airfield, travelling to their field locations by road and helicopter. This was often achieved in an hour or less.

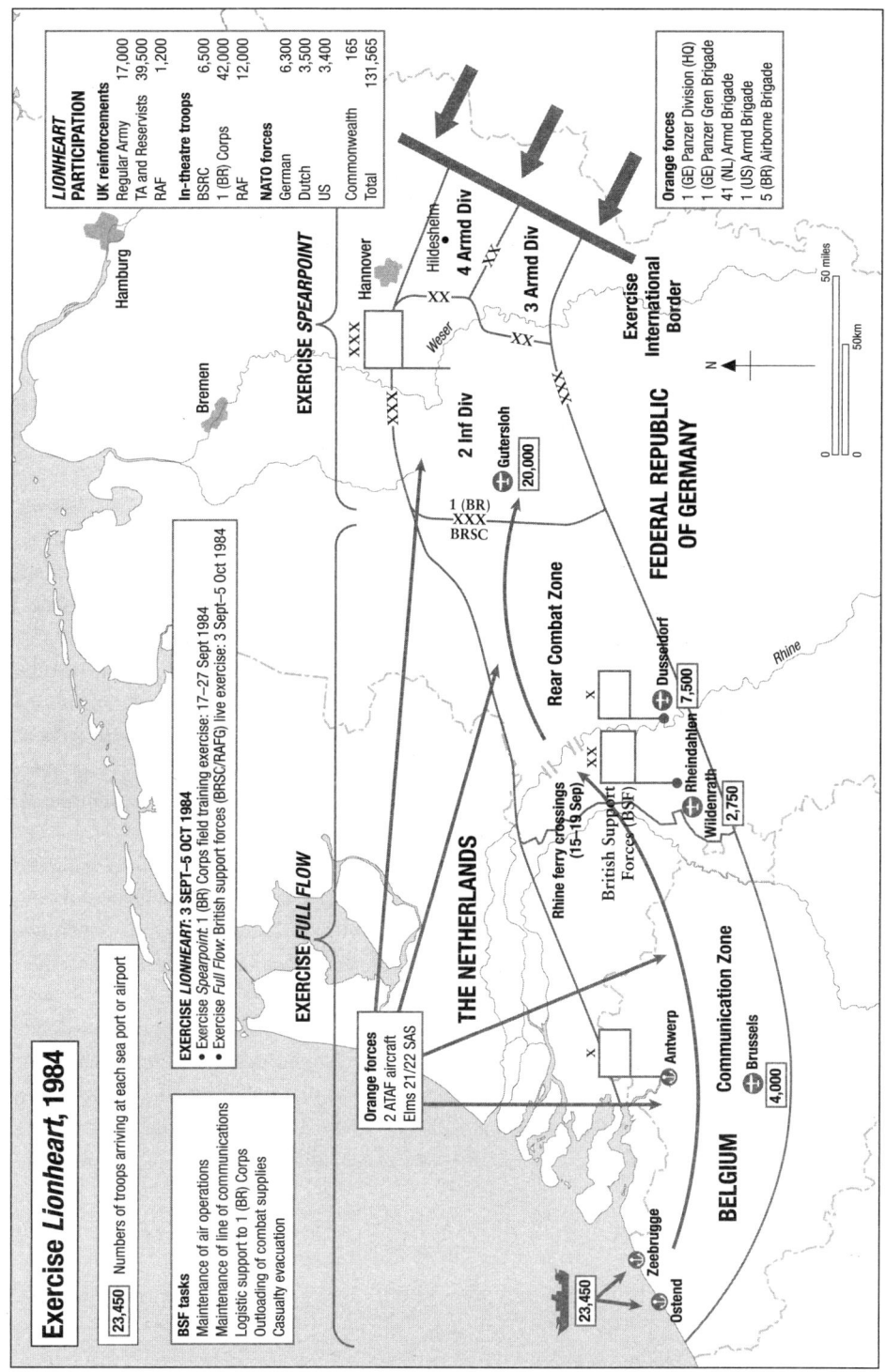

At the same time, 23,000 personnel with 14,000 vehicles and trailers crossed the English Channel and North Sea in chartered civilian ferries. After disembarking, a large number of vehicles and combat supplies were moved westward on the continent by rail, on a total of 260 trains. To simulate the friction of war and test commanders, one of these trains was deliberately misdirected by the exercise organizers, but the resulting disruption was easily managed.

For TA personnel, their participation in the exercise would count as their annual two-week camp. Soldiers reported to their drill hall on Saturday 15 September, to move out as soon as possible. They needed to be in their deployment positions 48 hours later. This meant that the weekend of 15–16 September was the peak of the deployment, testing the lines of communication. Over 13,000 personnel landed at RAF Gutersloh over the weekend.

Intelligence assessments suggested that the bridges over the Rhine could be high-priority targets for Warsaw Pact air or missile strikes, attacks by airborne troops and sabotage and diversionary attacks by Spetsnaz, as well as potential blockages by anti-war demonstrators. The exercise simulated the closure of the main Rhine road bridges that the British planned to use. The Bundeswehr maintained a flotilla of large landing craft to provide alternative ways of crossing the river; many of the British convoys were re-routed to cross the river using German landing craft, ferries and military bridges. Further enemy activity was represented by attacks by regular and TA SAS troops and by air strikes.

The exercise included the reinforcement of the corps by a US-based armoured brigade. Its personnel flew from Texas to the Netherlands and Northern Germany, where the brigade took over its pre-positioned vehicles and equipment. As it did this, it was subject to sabotage attacks by the SAS, simulating Soviet Spetsnaz. Evidence of this was a Bradley fighting vehicle seen later on the exercise bearing the slogan '22 SAS' in large whitewash letters.

There were storms in the channel, which delayed ships. Fog in the Low Countries slowed down air transports and road moves, as did peak traffic levels on the busy motorways and autobahns. As a result of these frictions, delays built up. These were not cleared until the reinforcement phase was complete. Even so, all regular and TA units reached their deployment positions in time, although there were some close calls. The RAF's new Chinook helicopters were a particularly useful way of rapidly moving troops forward.

The purpose of Exercise *Full Flow* was to get reinforcements into the corps area in time to join the corps. Some of these arrived early, for example a platoon of newly trained recruits from the training depot at Winchester, which secured some key logistic installations. The corps field training exercise proper would run from 17 to 27 September.

EXERCISE *LIONHEART*

The order of battle of the manoeuvre formations taking part was as follows:

BLUE FORCES

HQ 1 (BR) Corps

2nd Infantry Division

15th Infantry Brigade (TA)

49th Infantry Brigade (TA)

53rd (GE) Home Defence Brigade

3rd Armoured Division

4th Armoured Brigade

19th Infantry Brigade

24th Infantry Brigade

4th Armoured Division

11th Armoured Brigade

20th Armoured Brigade

33rd Armoured Brigade

Corps troops

6th Airmobile Brigade

1st Artillery Brigade

1st Signals Brigade

14 Signal Regiment (Electronic Warfare)

Corps Patrol Unit of 23rd SAS TA

RAF

RAF Support Helicopter Force

18th Squadron, RAF, Chinook helicopters

230th Squadron, RAF, Puma helicopters

RAF Harrier Force

RAF Harrier squadrons

RAF regiment armoured squadron

RAF logistic units

Royal Engineer squadron

Royal Signals squadron

ORANGE FORCES

HQ 1st (GE) Panzer Division

1st (GE) Panzergrenadier Brigade

1st (US) Armored Brigade

41st (NL) Armoured Brigade

5th (UK) Airborne Brigade

UK Special Forces

EXERCISE CONTROL AND UMPIRES

1st Armoured Division

This overall force comprised five divisions, a total of seven armoured and seven infantry brigades. It was commanded from corps HQ. The 1st Armoured Division provided the exercise control HQ and many parties of umpires.

Armoured vehicles included 750 Chieftain tanks. New armoured vehicles took part in their first corps exercises. These included the Tracked Rapier air defence missile launcher, a regiment of Challenger tanks, an infantry battalion of Saxon wheeled APCs and a platoon of new Warrior infantry fighting vehicles on their troop trials. The Orange forces also had new armoured vehicles; the US fielded new M1 Abrams tanks and Bradley infantry fighting vehicles and the Germans had new Leopard 2 tanks.

A major effort was made to brief and host British, German and international journalists. At a press briefing at the start of the exercise, a briefing officer told the assembled journalists that *Lionheart* was the biggest Army exercise since D-Day. Reporters with a sense of historical irony pointed out that D-Day had not been an exercise.

CORPS DEFENSIVE BATTLE

By 17 September, the corps was deployed in its exercise positions. In 1980, Exercise *Crusader* had seen 1st and 2nd armoured divisions deploy into the operational areas where it was planned that they would fight. For Exercise *Lionheart* the corps layout was radically altered. The 4th Division would normally defend the southern part of the corps area. Instead, it was deployed into the north, the southern half of the corps area being defended by the 3rd Armoured Division, in a different role from its planned task as corps reserve. The corps reserve would instead be provided by 6th Airmobile Brigade, which would be replaced in the 3rd Division by 24th Infantry Brigade from the UK. That brigade was normally the reserve formation of the 2nd Infantry Division, but this gap was filled by the assignment of a Bundeswehr home defence brigade.

This rearrangement of the corps order of battle and deployment positions provided the divisions with new challenges, including fighting in new tactical groups and over unfamiliar terrain, to get commanders tackling new and unforeseen challenges. It also evaluated whether there was a role for more infantry in the south of the corps, to release armoured battlegroups for manoeuvre.

One of the aims of the exercise was to practise manoeuvre warfare with fewer restrictions than previous corps exercises, to allow commanders at all levels to make more use of their initiative. Orange forces were controlled, but less so than on previous corps exercises, being encouraged to use their initiative to gain advantage over the corps.

For the first 36 hours of the exercise, intelligence portrayed a rapidly deteriorating international situation and the enemy making overt preparations for war. I attended an orders group at HQ 6th Airmobile Brigade in a wood near Hameln. Suddenly the brigade was instructed to move to NBC State Black. There was urgency as we all wrenched our respirators from their cases, pulled them onto our heads, raised the hoods of our chemical defence suits and jammed our helmets onto our heads. The meeting then proceeded as normal albeit with people straining to hear voices necessarily muffled by respirators.

After this flurry of activity in a gloomy cramped tent, the sky filled with the sound of jet engines. This was deafening, making conversation impossible. It had a shuddering, breathtaking impact, which together with the gathering darkness created a great sense of unease. Some people found it frightening. After a few minutes the visceral intensity of this roaring wall of sound reduced to reverberating echoes that died away in the threatening darkness. 'What the fuck was that?' someone asked.

The senior umpire for the brigade strode to the front of the tent. Unencumbered by NBC suit or respirator, he explained that the exercise had a simulated IGB, west of the real international border along the River Leine. The radars used by the corps' Rapier air defence systems had detected a large gathering of potentially hostile aircraft assembling over enemy territory, the corps HQ ordering NBC State Black as a precaution. The subsequent noise was a mass air strike on the corps by at least 60 fighter bombers. This had been accompanied by simulated missile strikes, targeting the main bridges across the River Weser, some of which were now unusable. Comparing notes with fellow officers as the meeting dispersed, we all agreed the exercise had truly started with a bang!

Orange forces crossed the border shortly after the air strike, with German armour moving in the north and Dutch units in the south. The corps reconnaissance screen rapidly fell back, handing the battle over to the two covering force brigades, one for each British division.

In the north, the 4th Division was attacked by the Dutch and German brigades. Both quickly closed to the River Leine. On 19 September the 3rd Division was attacked by the US brigade but the many hills and woods greatly favoured the defence, inflicting casualties on the enemy armour and slowing it down.

HQ 4th Division deployed 20th Armoured Brigade to mount a counterstroke against an Orange armoured brigade. It had a mechanized infantry battalion, a tank regiment with Chieftain, the 4th/7th Dragoon Guards, and the Royal Hussars, the Army's single regiment of new Challenger tanks. Overnight it moved into the wooded hills to the south of Pattensen, a large village in a bowl of open country surrounded by wooded hills. The plan was that after first light the next morning the brigade would launch a surprise counterstroke against the vulnerable flank of an Orange armoured brigade that it was anticipated would be moving through the Pattensen bowl. This would be destroyed by the surprise use of concentrated force, a whole armoured brigade and strikes by the full force of the division's artillery with supporting air attacks.

Initially some Orange armour advanced towards Pattensen along the expected routes from the east, going around the north of Pattensen. But as the night wore on, 20th Brigade's units started observing Orange units swinging south instead of west. The enemy started probing the woods in which 20th Brigade were hiding. By now the brigade chief of staff was telling divisional HQ that all was not going to plan. He was told to stay calm.

As the night wore on the British hides in the woods were probed by Dutch infantry. Running battles developed that caused havoc amongst the British brigade. The brigade commander in his forward tactical HQ was captured and the enemy rapidly closed in on the brigade main HQ. The chief of staff of the formation was then Major Richard Dannatt, who would go on to become CGS in 2006. He takes up the story:

Hearing firing in the village, I ordered my command vehicle to break out of the HQ so that in the event of the disaster we could still exercise some form of command over the brigade. We roared down the street, as only the tolerant West Germans in those days would have allowed and headed for a wooded ridgeline. Grinding to a halt, I jumped out to see where we were. 'Hello, Sir', came a familiar North Yorkshire voice. 'I thought you were doing some fancy job on the staff. What are you doing here then?' My flight from the battle had taken me into the adjacent brigade's area of responsibility and I had arrived on the mortar fire support positions of 1st Battalion the Green Howards – my own regiment. The embarrassment was complete.[12]

Orange continued to attack westwards over the next two days. A British brigade defending the Sibesse gap, an area of flat farmland between two large woods, was attacked by the Bundeswehr. A column of panzergrenadiers in Marder infantry fighting vehicles sped through woods held by a TA battalion, outmanoeuvring the defenders. As this happened a squadron of German CH53 helicopters flew over the brigade, landing infantry that captured a bridge over the River Leine, cutting the formation's supply line and preventing it from withdrawing.[13]

But in the south of the corps' area, a vigorous Orange effort to break through to the River Weser was blunted and enemy armour was unable to achieve a breakthrough, in part because one of the routes it might have used to achieve this was blocked by the rapid air deployment of the 6th Airmobile Brigade. The Orange units were now very extended and were not able to bring to bear sufficient combat power to break through the airmobile brigade's guard forces, let alone attack its main position. The 3rd Division used its armoured brigade to counterattack Orange armour advancing along its southern boundary, There was a hard-fought battle with the US armoured brigade in open country between the Harz mountains and the River Weser.

Orange used the British 5 Airborne Brigade to land troops by helicopter to seize bridgeheads over the River Weser. A helicopter-borne raid by paratroops destroyed the HQ of 6th Airmobile Brigade. As was standard procedure for such an event, one of the battalion HQs took over temporary command of the brigade, until umpires allowed the brigade HQ to come back to life.

The next evening 6th Airmobile Brigade was ordered to fly to the very north of the corps area to block any move that the enemy might make around the southern edges of Hannover. Halfway through the night air move, fog stopped flying and almost 200 soldiers had to drive like fury to catch up with the rest of the battalion.

IMPRESSIONS OF SIMULATED BATTLE

How realistic was the exercise? As realistic as the corps could make it. With more free play than on any previous corps exercise, there was more uncertainty and friction in the exercising forces. A perceptive account of morale throughout the exercise was written by a Captain Gene Vincenti, a medical officer serving at a dressing station supporting one of the two British divisions.[14] He observed that the first week of Exercise *Spearpoint* saw the division withdraw 'under increasing conditions of chaos and confusion from the Orange Force offensive.' He observed:

> general rumours that abounded among the soldiers of many different units who passed through the dressing station … The chaos was quite realistic. Hussars were observed walking along the roadside. A column of tanks speeding left to right, was passed by another tank column going the other way and there was even a real casualty from a local formation HQ that had been 'taken out' by enemy special forces …
>
> As the pressure rose, so did the rumours. Suddenly ambulance crews reported being stopped many times by enemy infiltrators. Battle casualties reported enemy tanks always 'only a village away'. The helicopter that was expected for a quick casualty evacuation was suddenly an enemy air cavalry unit about to descend into the vicinity.
>
> Casualties filled the dressing station with rumours of an unstoppable flood of enemy armour. 'They came round the other way Sir', became the most often-quoted phrase that was heard. The Bundeswehr, who were the immediate opponents, were invested with a quality of invincibility. A feeling of their opponents' material superiority seemed to be building up in the minds of the young soldiers.

It was an inconvenient truth that Orange's German brigade had material superiority over British armoured brigades: the Leopard 2 tank, being better protected, more reliable and more manoeuvrable than Chieftain tanks. And all the British mechanized infantry battalions' FV432 APCs were greatly overmatched by the German Marder infantry fighting vehicles, which were much faster and more reliable, with a 20mm cannon turret that considerably surpassed the single externally mounted machine gun of the British APCs. And the British mechanized infantry knew it.

Vincenti also noted other evidence of fragile morale during defensive operations. When the fighting was intense, 'sizeable batches of real casualties would arrive. At these times the proportion of cases with frankly dubious organic pathology would rise'. A liaison officer was so pestered by soldiers seeing his vehicle, marked with the Red Cross, as a source of medical supplies, that he had the emblem removed. And many real casualties were brought into the dressing station 'escorted' by fit colleagues. An unwelcome surprise was the appearance of the regimental sergeant major of a hard-pressed infantry battalion, escorting a young soldier who on examination appeared to be perfectly fit. The warrant officer was both aggressive and disruptive. It was unclear how he had been able to remove himself from his battalion in the midst of battle. Both men were returned to their unit.

CORPS OFFENSIVE OPERATIONS

The customary weekend exercise pause took place over the weekend of 22–23 September. Units and equipment that the umpires had ruled to have been destroyed were brought back to life and the corps prepared for a counteroffensive. Soldiers caught up on sleep, which many had been deprived of during the previous week's fighting. So did HQ staff, but they were also involved in planning the following week's operations.

For 1st Battalion, the Light Infantry in 6th Airmobile Brigade, this was the exciting high point of the exercise. The brigade was ordered to mount an overnight helicopter assault to seize bridges over the Mittelland canal, to protect the northern flank of the 4th Division's advance. To pinpoint enemy positions and locate helicopter landing sites, the reconnaissance platoon was clandestinely inserted by Lynx helicopters 18 miles behind the enemy lines. It was successful and the next night the brigade flew forward to seize the bridges and surrounding villages. After an extremely successful night attack which took the Orange defenders by surprise, the battalion found itself in two villages surrounded by marauding German armour. During the day fierce anti-armour battles splintered into exhilarating street fighting while ammunition was brought in by Puma and casualties evacuated on returning aircraft.

Concurrently on the morning of Monday 24 September, after the morning rush hour had subsided, both armoured divisions moved eastward to attack. As did the TA brigades of the 2nd Infantry Division, corps rear area security being handed over to the Bundeswehr home defence brigade. This manoeuvre was not entirely unexpected, but the corps plan had all the armoured and infantry brigades again advancing over territory with which they were unfamiliar. From his post in a dressing station, Captain Vincenti observed that this period was 'the complete opposite of the first. The chaos and confusion seemed less. They had the initiative, they enjoyed success. Rumours quietened down … The flow of real casualties lightened and the percentage with dubious organic pathology seemed less.'

The corps advanced to the simulated international border by the morning of Thursday 27 September, when the end of the exercise was declared. It would take the best part of a week to move all the participating units back to their barracks in the UK and Germany.

TA units on their annual camps took full part in the exercise. For example, 5th Battalion, the Light Infantry was part of 2nd Infantry Division, responsible for securing the corps' rear area. It began the exercise defending key points astride the wooded hills of the Teutoburger Wald. After an enemy ground attack, the battalion then cleared enemy from a village, then moved 60 miles by road overnight to relieve a regular battalion on the River Leine. After supporting an assault river crossing, it conducted a battlegroup wood clearance operation and was joined by tanks to attack another village, before the exercise ended and it returned to the UK two weeks after it had mobilized.

Accidents happened; three British soldiers died and seven were seriously injured. For some troops the exercise seemed as boring and predictable as many previous periods of field training in Germany. But for others it was an adventure – albeit with very real casualties. A soldier in an armoured reconnaissance regiment observed that:

My squadron were pulled from the Corps Recce role to be armoured umpires during *Lionheart*. It was certainly an interesting experience. We were often engaged by both sides even though our CVR(T)s were adorned with white crosses and flying white flags and mine tape.

Highlights were umpiring the brigade bridgehead over the River Weser and spending an exercise without weapons, which felt really strange. Copious bottles of Herforder Pils were consumed of an evening, in moderation, and a dhobi run[15] back to camp became particularly exciting when we found out that our barracks had a field hospital on the square and the NAAFI was full to bursting with TA nurses.

We had to umpire an imaginary chemical attack and were at a dressing station. I had wandered off just prior to the NBC alarm being sounded to give the chemical sentry the nod, feeling sorry for him in some sort of empathetic 'we've all been there' kind of way, when the Dressing Station OC [Officer Commanding] came blustering out accusing me of distracting his sentry. A cry of GAS! GAS! GAS! rang out just at that very moment and the aforementioned OC was stood there sans respirator. I couldn't help but smile and I rose in height two inches as I delivered the words 'You're dead sir'.[16]

The Army conducted a thorough lessons-learned exercise. This began with units writing post-exercise reports, which were aggregated together with observations made by brigade HQs and on up through divisions to corps HQ. The two theatre HQs, BAOR and UKLF, added their observations and the military operations directorate in the MoD assembled the complete document. The report was put to the Executive Committee of the Army Board. A redacted version was placed in the House of Commons library. It is three-quarters of the length of the original report.[17]

The Army assessed that the exercise had demonstrated that the plans for the rapid reinforcement of the corps had worked.[18] This helped reinforce deterrence of the Warsaw Pact and reassurance to NATO, particularly the German, Dutch, Belgian and US armies that had invested so much in NORTHAG. An identified weakness of the exercise was that apart from the crossing of the Rhine by ferry and landing craft, the full vulnerability of the lines of communication to air attack was not tested.

The report identified some weaknesses. The lines of communication through the Low Countries and Germany were assessed as 'fragile'. They were vulnerable to enemy air attack and depended on rather ad hoc command and control arrangements. Logistics were not fully tested – a result of live ammunition not being used – but bottlenecks were identified. Enemy troops landing by parachute or helicopter could often melt into nearby wooded hills, making them difficult to find. Although over 29,000 TA troops had deployed on the exercise, the Army assessed that their effectiveness would be less than that of regular troops. But the longer the period they had to prepare for war, the more effective they would become.

The Army thought that many of these weaknesses had already been identified. Some would be addressed by the fielding of new equipment. But others were exposed by the numbers of troops deployed and by the inevitable fog and frictions of war. For example, the movement of long trains or vehicle convoys could never have been fully simulated by a command post exercise. The chief of staff of BAOR observed that 'the arrangements made between allied generals do not always get transmitted down to part-time private soldiers at the roadside'.

The manoeuvre phase of the exercise was judged to have met or exceeded all its aims. The Army was particularly gratified that its effort to make the exercise less stage managed, with much more freedom of action allowed to both sides, had provided more challenges to commanders. Armoured reserve brigades and battlegroups had successfully moved quickly and sometimes achieved surprise. The concentration of artillery and airpower and its co-ordination with armoured manoeuvre had been successful, as had the essential airspace control to reduce the chance of mid-air collisions and air–ground blue on blue strikes, the result of a considerable amount of pre-exercise planning and training with the RAF. Massed attacks by Lynx anti-tank helicopters were judged to have been particularly successful.

Orange had been given a greater signals intelligence capability than had been allocated during Exercise *Crusader* in 1980. The exercise report said that Orange's electronic warfare capability was 'used to good effect'. But it also assessed that there had been a distinct improvement in radio security, a result of greater emphasis in individual and collective training and the introducing of the new tactical cypher – Battle Code (BATCO). This worked reasonably well for armoured, mechanized, and logistic units that had vehicles in which the paper-based code could be used with relative ease. But dismounted infantry found the codes awkward and time consuming to use. Not all were convinced that the notable improvement in security was worth the price of slowing down the passage of time-sensitive information and the passing of urgent orders.

The published report did not acknowledge that there had been failures – such as the destruction of the 20th Armoured Brigade. However, there was a sense amongst the corps' senior leadership that in launching counterstroke attacks, timing was all. Attack too early and the blow might fall in front of the enemy main body; too late and the attack might fall where the enemy had been and fail to prevent them advancing into the depth of the corps position. In either case the brigade or division that mounted the attack might itself be very vulnerable to enemy counterattacks by ground and air forces. Indeed, a general who spent two years in the 1980s commanding an armoured division and a further two commanding a major training organization privately wrote that he had never seen a counterstroke launched at the right time and place.[19]

The Army assessed that the new structure of the corps with the divisions each having three strong brigades had worked well, with divisions being better balanced for their likely missions. But the unredacted report noted that the 3rd Division with a single armoured brigade and two infantry brigades was less capable of offensive action than the 4th Division. The 3rd Division had given up its 6th Airmobile Brigade to act as corps reserve. The brigade's two airmobile deployments to counter-penetration positions in the depth of the two forward divisions were judged to have succeeded. But offensive airmobile operations conducted by the brigade, such as the two mounted during the corps counteroffensive, were judged in the Delphic language of the full report to 'require further study'.

The 2nd Infantry Division was considered to have succeeded in its new role securing the corps rear area, particularly by improving command and control. The division deployed with its two complete TA infantry brigades and customarily deployed with an engineer brigade of TA sapper regiments and an air defence brigade of TA artillery regiments equipped with Blowpipe missiles. It had successfully integrated the German home defence brigade that had reinforced it. But the report identified that 'enemy troops who were inserted into the rear areas by parachute or helicopter were difficult to locate once they landed and dispersed'.

Large numbers of TA logistic, engineering and maintenance units helped keep the lines of communications open and freely flowing. Mobilizing most of these units on a Friday evening, moving them over the weekend to their deployment positions and expecting them to be fully operational on the Monday was always going to be a demanding task for units with lower levels of individual and collective training than regular units. But this complex choreography of road and sea transport, picking up equipment and vehicles from logistic storage sites and marrying people, vehicles, equipment and supplies was well executed.

The report assessed that 'TA units noticeably improved during their fortnight on the exercise. Any measure that will allow them training before General Alert will pay great dividends'. This reflects that TA combat units tended to be less well practised and thus slower into action than their regular equivalents. And when there were direct regular and TA equivalent logistic units, such as transport squadrons, the TA could not produce the same output at the same work rate as regulars.

There were of course exceptions. For example, the stay-behind observation posts manned by the TA SAS provided invaluable reporting of enemy movements that were otherwise unavailable to the corps. And a TA artillery observation party that joined 1st Battalion the Light Infantry added considerable value. But the Army senior leadership knew that a war that erupted with little or no notice would be an extremely demanding scenario for the whole Army, both regular and reserve. The Army had to be ruthless about this and accept that in this event soldiers, officers, units and formations would be severely tested, and not all would withstand the pressure. But in a longer warning scenario it would be essential to allow TA units the opportunity to 'work up'.

The report failed to boldly state that this was the Army's second corps exercise not to conclude with nuclear strikes, but with a corps-level conventional counterattack. It notably omitted to identify the widespread perception in the corps that the three enemy armoured brigades had much more capable modern armour than the British. The Dutch and German Leopard 2 tanks outmanoeuvred British Chieftain tanks. In comparison the British had a single regiment of Challenger tanks, the remainder being Chieftain. Although this still had a powerful 120mm gun, the tanks' lower level of mobility and reliability was painfully obvious.

All three Orange brigades had infantry fighting vehicles. The German Marders and Dutch YPR vehicles were faster, more agile and equipped with cannon that were completely lacking in British mechanized companies. And the US Army's Bradley not only had a similar speed and agility but also had a turret with both a 25mm cannon and TOW missiles. British battlegroups and brigades that tangled with the three enemy armoured brigades found them tough opponents that moved faster and rapidly generated more firepower than their British opponents. This was observed by the *Economist*'s defence correspondent who entitled his report on the exercise 'Blue got the Reds'.

In these and many other ways *Lionheart* had tested the corps and three of its four divisions. The two armoured divisions had practised Bagnall's design for battle: the new defensive layout that accepted penetration by enemy armoured columns, to set them up for counterstrokes by armoured brigades. It also tested the corps' two new formations, the 2nd Infantry Division and 6th Airmobile Brigade, as well as the generation of the force and its deployment from barracks and TA centres to the battle positions. And 6th Airmobile Brigade had been used by both divisions to rapidly deploy to counter-penetration positions in both forward divisions to block further advances by enemy armour, thus improving the chances of successful counterstrokes.

Although the second week of the exercise had seen the corps mount a counteroffensive against the enemy, this had the character of a general advance on a wide front. This was a useful manoeuvre, but it was not a corps-level counterstroke as Bagnall had envisaged it. Indeed, with the 3rd Armoured Division only having a single armoured brigade, it would have required the corps to bring together both the 3rd Division and an in-place division to deliver the kind of concentrated blow of massed armour that Bagnall envisaged for a full corps-level counterstroke. And the exercise had focussed on the threat to the corps coming directly from the east. Neither of the corps flanks had been faced with a significant threat. In addition, although the enemy chemical threat had been simulated, the nuclear threat had not.

NORTHERN ARMY GROUP AND THE OPERATIONAL LEVEL OF WAR

Although Exercise *Lionheart* had tested the new corps and divisional concepts and plans that Bagnall had developed, by the time of the exercise he had left the corps, promoted to full general to become Commander in Chief BAOR. This appointment carried with it command of NATO's NORTHAG of four national corps: British, Belgian, Dutch and German. Also based in the corps area were the forward elements of III (US) Corps, with several heavy divisions' worth of equipment in POMCUS storage sites and an armoured brigade based in the northern German port of Bremen. And the rear part of the army group's area would in war be protected by the German Territorial Command North.

In his previous service in Germany, Bagnall had already seen for himself that the army group plan was insufficiently coherent, which carried the risk of it being defeated by a concentrated Warsaw Pact attack. Bagnall set out to make the formation more capable of fighting a campaign of operational-level manoeuvre. This would increase the chance of the army group repelling the first echelon of an attack. Achieving this would extend the time that northern Germany could be defended, before NATO would be faced with a stark choice between defeat or the use of tactical nuclear weapons.

As army group commander Bagnall would in war command the assigned four corps. But in peacetime he only had full authority over the British corps, the other formations being under national command until authority was transferred to NATO. So, in peace he had less authority over his four corps than he had had as corps commander over his four divisions.

Overcoming this lack of formal authority would require Bagnall to persuade the German, Dutch and Belgian corps commanders and the national hierarchy above them to support his new ideas for an army group concept of operations. He would also have to sell the idea to his superior at the HQ of NATO's Central Front.

In peacetime, the HQs of BAOR and NORTHAG were based in a camp at Rheindahlen, close to Germany's western border with Holland. The camp also contained the HQ of RAF Germany, which commanded all RAF forces in Germany. In a similar fashion to NORTHAG, its commander also had a NATO role, commanding the multinational Second Tactical Air Force (2ATAF), made up not only of RAF units, but also of units from the Luftwaffe and Belgian and Dutch air forces. It was already standard practice for both NORTHAG and 2ATAF to work closely together, but Bagnall sought to increase this partnership into a fully integrated joint land/air campaign.

Achieving this required two major initiatives: developing a joint and combined concept for a land/air campaign; and generating an army group reserve that could be used for counterattack operations. Speaking in 1984 Bagnall assessed that the army group had interpreted forward defence in an over-literal fashion. The four in-place corps tended to defend too passively and too close to the IGB. They had previously been ordered to fight a corps battle in isolation, reflected by the rigid allocation of defensive sectors to divisions, brigades and battlegroups with overall tactical direction to the higher formation schemes of manoeuvre.

Bagnall set out an army group concept with three phases that resembled his previous corps concept of three phases:

1. Covering force
2. Main defensive battle
3. Employment of reserves.

The distance between the IGB and the main defensive positions could vary from 65 km to 7 km. Some of the terrain in the area was suitable for defence, but much was not. In the early 1980s, the four corps planned to deploy significant combat power to delay an attack. This would be very exposed to heavy Warsaw Pact artillery fire and would suffer considerable attrition. After the covering force battle, most of the formations concerned were to be refurbished to form reserves. Bagnall considered that this would, in practice, be 'impossible' (his words). So strong covering forces would only be deployed for as long as it took for the army group to deploy to its main defensive positions. As soon as this was achieved, corps' covering forces would reduce in size, to screens of reconnaissance units.

The main defensive battle would be where the initial enemy advance was halted. But Bagnall found little in the way of an army group design for this. Corps had been told to fight their own battle within their boundaries. An example of this was the contrasting national approaches to mine warfare. The British defensive positions were encased within a strong network of deep minefields. This would greatly constrain the British ability to mount rapid countermoves. The German corps took an opposite view, with defensive plans with much less dependence on minefields, but with no capability to breach minefields, thus constraining their ability to conduct offensive manoeuvre.

Army group direction was previously confined to a co-ordinating line behind which corps were not to withdraw without the army group commander's authority. The Warsaw Pact was likely to exploit the boundaries between the corps, both with direct advances and potentially by conducting manoeuvres designed to attack one corps from another's area. So, the army group needed to fight a co-ordinated battle.

Bagnall put much thought into the role of airpower in this battle. He worked jointly with his RAF opposite number Air Chief Marshal Sir Patrick Hine, the commander of RAF Germany and NATO's 2ATAF. They both agreed that at the outset of war, the air forces had two priorities: air defence to keep Warsaw Pact aircraft from neutralizing NATO airfields and launching a campaign of offensive counter air operations by attacking airfields in East Germany.

Both Bagnall and Hine agreed that routine use of NATO aircraft for close air support should be minimized. This was a very difficult mission to perform against the formidable array of Soviet Army air defences. It should be reserved only for a major emergency. It was not that NATO aircraft should not be used to attack advancing enemy ground forces. Once the initial Warsaw Pact air offensive had been blunted, the air forces would conduct battlefield air interdiction to slow down enemy reinforcements, particularly by attacking bridges and other choke points. But key formation countermoves should be supported by concentrated use of ground attack aircraft, fully integrated with artillery, attack helicopters and 2ATAF's allocation of EW and defence suppression aircraft.

Bagnall assessed that a static defensive battle against an enemy with superior numbers would inevitably lead to defeat. So a more offensive concept was needed. The army group would fight a more mobile battle of manoeuvre, that sought to gain the initiative from the start of the war:

I wish to stress that there is no such thing as a NORTHAG concept of operations in isolation. There can only be a joint Land/Air battle which means a joint NORTHAG/2ATAF battle. I know it is easy to make a statement like that, in the same way as it is easy to go round talking about the need for close cooperation between the five national corps that make up NORTHAG …

What is harder, is to give substance to these expressions of faith. Let me try. To my mind, the only way one can develop a truly integrated Land/Air battle is to have a concept of operations, or design for battle, for the army group which the air forces have agreed and use as a basis for their own planning and allocation of scarce resources … unless we are ready to fight a truly joint Land/Air battle on the Central Front from the outbreak of hostilities we will have failed in our peace-time duties …

The practical answers to most problems are considerably harder to achieve than their theoretical solution. Money, real estate, capability limitations and international considerations severely limit our freedom of action; especially when fear is not present to act as a spur. Swift and resolute decision-making is sometimes frustratingly hard to achieve in times of peace. Nevertheless, we must all endeavour to achieve progress but pragmatically and at a realistic pace.[20]

THE ROLE OF ARMY GROUP RESERVES

The army group needed to be able to call on powerful reserve forces to mount counterattacks or counterstrokes to dislocate the enemy advance. To find several reserves, the army group could not be strong everywhere, but should concentrate on defending the truly vital ground and accepting more risk elsewhere. Reserves therefore should be used in strength to conduct concentrated attacks, supported by the maximum amount of gun and rocket artillery and airpower.

The concept depended on having sufficient reserve formations. These needed to have high levels of combat power and to have a high chance of being available to the army group commander when they were needed. Given the difficult initial air battle that would be fought over northern Germany against numerically superior Warsaw Pact air forces, the reserve formations needed to be in situ in northern Germany, on the east side of the Rhine.

The Dutch corps would find this difficult to achieve, as would the Belgian corps, to the south of the British. In peacetime this corps had a single brigade and reconnaissance group stationed around Soest. The terrain in their sector largely favoured the defence, with woods, hills and the River Weser all likely to slow down attackers, but only if defenders were physically present in enough strength. This would not be achieved until the Belgian corps was fully reinforced by formations coming from Belgium.

So the British had a plan to detach a brigade to cover the deployment of the Belgian corps by acting as a covering force. There is evidence of a British corps plan to move its reserve division to the area south of Paderborn, to prevent a successful enemy thrust from breaking through the Belgian positions and turning the southern flank of the British corps. This contingency provided the scenario for the week-long final exercise of the Junior Division of the Army Staff College that I experienced in early 1984. And the many British field exercises in this area had the useful bonus of familiarizing British units with terrain over which they might have to fight – at short notice and in difficult circumstances.

The army group's northern corps provided by the Dutch was stronger than the Belgian corps, but most of it was stationed in Holland. III (US) Corps was largely based in the US. But several divisions' worth of American equipment and supplies were pre-positioned in enormous logistic installations in northern Europe under the POMCUS programme. An armoured brigade was forward-based near the German port of Bremen. The US Army regularly exercised reinforcing NORTHAG, such as the deployment of the US armoured brigades that joined Exercises *Spearpoint* and *Lionheart* in 1980 and 1984. Throughout the 1980s there was ever-increasing co-operation between the army group and the US corps.

So, from the outset of war the corps could only rely on the in-place British and German corps to generate reserve divisions that it could control. During Bagnall's tenure as commander, the army group greatly depended on the German corps to provide one, or even two of its strong armoured divisions as potential army group reserve formations. Each division had three brigades equipped with Leopard 2 tanks and Marder infantry fighting vehicles. These were more powerful formations than the British 3rd Division. In the mid-1980s this still lacked an infantry fighting vehicle and was mostly equipped with older Chieftain tanks with less mobility and reliability than Leopard 2. Nevertheless, the army group designated that although the 3rd Division was the British corps reserve, it should be available to the army group as well.

Bagnall was prepared to reduce the strength of the German and British corps to create sufficient reserves to mount strong offensive operations. It may be that he reasoned that unless the Warsaw Pact concentrated its main effort against the army group, there would, in practice, be only one or two major thrusts against the formation. And if there was sufficient warning time, the Dutch and Belgian corps would reach their battle positions. Whatever the scenario, having up to three divisions available to the army group would allow it to mount a counteroffensive operation of up to corps size.

The reserves might be used for division counterstrokes, both in corps sectors or across corps boundaries. If two or more divisions were used, they could deliver a concentrated corps level counterattack that would stop a Soviet first-operational echelon in its tracks, greatly damaging it. Such an operational-level attack might reach into East German territory, to disrupt subsequent enemy echelons, in conjunction with interdiction by NATO airpower. Since NATO aircraft would from the outset cross the international border to attack airfields in East Germany, Bagnall reasoned, once the shooting started the IGB should be 'considered no more than a line on a map'.[21]

In the 1970s the Army had considered that the decisive battle would be the defensive phase. Now its thinking had shifted to the decisive phase being the counteroffensive. For the corps this increased the importance of co-operation with the army group's other national corps, particularly the German corps and Belgian corps to the north and south respectively.

By the time the army group launched any counteroffensives, fighting would already have been heavy. The NATO forces would probably have suffered significant casualties, both of troops and of equipment. And large amounts of ammunition would have been expended. Another Warsaw Pact operational echelon might be bearing down on the corps, and in circumstances where the army group reserves had been worn down. And NATO troops might well be approaching physical exhaustion.

This was why reinforcement of the army group by III (US) Corps was so important. Its armoured divisions were equipped with new modern Abrams tanks, Bradley fighting vehicles and Multiple Launch Rocket System (MLRS) rocket launchers. Both the corps and its component divisions had powerful combat aviation brigades abundantly equipped with Apache attack helicopters and Blackhawk and Chinook transport helicopters.

EXERCISE CERTAIN STRIKE

In 1985, Bagnall moved to become the CGS. He was succeeded by General Sir Martin Farndale. In 1987 Farndale and the army group HQ oversaw Exercise *Certain Strike*. This tested the deployment of III (US) Corps to its POMCUS sites, the issue of the stored equipment and a corps-level counteroffensive operation. A total of 78,300 troops, 2,200 tracked vehicles, 20,000 wheeled vehicles, 383 helicopters and 300 combat aircraft took part. III (US) Corps commanded the following formations:

- 1st Cavalry Division (despite this celebrated title, the division was a heavy armoured division)
- 2nd Armored Division
- 6th Cavalry Brigade (Air Combat), a brigade of attack and transport helicopters
- 3rd Armored Cavalry Regiment, a brigade-sized reconnaissance force
- corps troops: artillery, intelligence and surveillance signals, military police, infantry, engineer and logistic brigades
- 1st (GE) Panzer Division
- a French regiment.

The enemy forces comprised:

- HQ 4th (NE) Mechanized Division
- the Belgian Army's reconnaissance brigade
- 1st (BE) Mechanized Brigade
- 4th (UK) Armoured Brigade
- 43rd (NE) Mechanized Brigade.

On 21 August, as part of the US exercise *REFORGER*, US reinforcements began to arrive at the port of Rotterdam, the first ships bringing Apache helicopters. Troops flew into airfields in the Netherlands and moved to the POMCUS storage sites to pick up their pre-positioned vehicles and heavy weapons. US units then moved to staging areas in existing NATO barracks and training areas.

Over 7–9 September the corps moved to an assembly area in huge road convoys along six different routes. The exercise scenario was that an enemy corps were advancing south-west to seize a crossing across the River Weser. This was to be blocked by the 1st German Panzer Division along the line of the rivers Aller and Weser. The US corps moved to an assembly area about 18 miles to the west of the Germans. As the Orange forces closed with the river line, putting the German division under considerable pressure, the US corps was attacked by enemy aircraft.

III (US) Corps was ordered to move east, to cross the river line and counterattack Orange forces. The corps planned to use the extant bridges and its own military bridging to get across the river, but as planning was underway, British infantry landing from German helicopters seized the main road bridge over the river by helicopter assault. Supported by depth fire from their MLRS artillery batteries, the US troops began crossing the river and landed an infantry brigade by helicopter on the far side of the river. Having seized four bridgeheads, US engineers quickly built ten floating pontoon bridges across the rivers. The corps crossed the rivers, but the exercise then halted for two days, to allow for the weekend.

The second week saw both US divisions advance. Orange was forced onto the defensive and there were some intense battles. The exercise controllers had stage managed the exercise so that these occurred on existing NATO training areas. A large-scale battle against Orange forces in prepared defensive positions took place near Soltau, while US Apache helicopters hunted Orange armoured forces and Orange special forces attacked US HQs and rear areas. By 23 September the US corps had reached its limit of exploitation, the eastern boundary of the NATO training area.[22]

This had not been a British exercise; rather it had been a NATO exercise run by the British-led HQ NORTHAG in which the centre of gravity had been the III (US) Corps. As far as HQ NORTHAG and the British and US armies were concerned it had successfully tested and demonstrated the US' ability to rapidly reinforce northern Germany with a heavy armoured corps, as well as NORTHAG's ability to provide the necessary command and control to direct it on a corps-level counterattack, passing through a hard-pressed German division to do so. It was a vindication of Bagnall's design for operational manoeuvre.

LATE 1980S EQUIPMENT MODERNIZATION

By now the Army's equipment was benefiting from the defence spending increases of Margaret Thatcher's government. There was a major improvement to command and control, with the delivery of Ptarmigan, a new formation communications system that connected brigades, divisions and corps. This used microwave relays to link up formation HQs from corps to brigade. It also created a secure cellular radio network for mobile users down to battlegroup level, a precursor of the cellular telephone networks that were to revolutionize mobile telephones in the next decade. It took over a year to issue the new system to the whole corps. It would also be issued to the units running the lines of communications from the Channel ports, greatly improving the fragile and ad hoc command and control that had been identified during Exercise *Lionheart*. Exercises showed that Ptarmigan greatly improved the corps' communications.

An improved version of the Wavell battlefield computer was issued. The 3rd Division pioneered the use of ruggedized laptop personal computers to aid command and control. In the late 1980s this was cutting edge capability!

Personal protection was improved by the issue of a new combat helmet. Up to now troops had used the Mark 4 steel helmet first issued in 1945. It could never have been considered comfortable and required the user to make their own camouflage cover. It was universally unpopular. Airborne troops used a different helmet, without the extensive rim. A similar helmet was issued to armoured corps vehicle crew. Many soldiers sought to acquire these. Others, myself included, had purchased surplus US Army helmets, which were much more comfortable. All three types of unofficial helmets could easily be camouflaged to look like the standard helmet.

From 1986 these were replaced by the Mark 6 helmet. This was made of ballistic nylon. It was the same weight, but was much more comfortable, owing to a modern harness that included internal cushions and better straps and fastening. It came with a camouflaged cover and was comfortable and popular.

A new rifle was issued. In the mid-1970s the Army had decided that the infantry sections' SLR (self-loading rifle) rifles and GPMG machine guns were too large, cumbersome and slow into the action. This applied both to the mechanized infantry who were constantly getting in and out of their APCs and soldiers in Northern Ireland who found the SLR cumbersome in the complex urban environments of the province. And NATO decided that the standard calibre of small arms ammunition could be reduced from 7.62mm to 5.56mm. The alliance selected a new bullet design containing a steel core, to improve penetration of enemy helmets and body armour.

A new rifle, the SA80, was designed. It had an unconventional 'bullpup' design, with the trigger grip in front of the magazine, making it much shorter than the SLR. It was provided with an innovative sling, based on those used in the Arctic, that allowed it to be strapped across the body or hung against the upper leg. It was also fitted with an optical sight, the SUSAT, that improved accuracy and magazines that carried 30 of the smaller and lighter 5.56mm bullets, a 50 per cent increase over the SLR. It was demonstrably more compact and more accurate than the SLR. Unlike the SLR, it could fire automatically, giving the infantryman a burst-fire capability that in comparison with most NATO and Warsaw Pact armies the British had previously lacked.

To replace the GPMG each infantry section was provided with two light support weapons (LSWs). These were heavier versions of the rifle, but with a bipod and longer barrel. They were less accurate than the GPMG and were prone to overheating. Most infantry soldiers and commanders much preferred the 7.62mm GPMG which had longer range and a higher rate of fire and were more resistant to over-heating.

The SA80 rifle and LSW combination was a great concept but was flawed in execution. There is evidence that the weapons trials were rushed, in part because of the need for the Royal Small Arms Factory at Enfield to have a full order book to assist with its already announced privatization. The weapons were far less rugged than the SLR, the GPMG and the US M16A3 rifle that had been adopted by the SAS. Build quality was poor and too many components broke too often. The weapons performed reasonably well on exercise in the UK, Germany and Canada, but their weaknesses would be exposed in the future.[23]

THREE REVOLUTIONARY CAPABILITIES – WARRIOR, MRLS AND DROPS

By the mid-1980s many armies in Europe had infantry fighting vehicles. Like APCs, these provided protected cross-country mobility for an infantry section. But with turret-mounted cannon they had much greater firepower. Half of all Soviet infantry were equipped with the BMP infantry fighting vehicle, which was itself being fitted with a new cannon and anti-tank missile. German armoured brigades already had the Marder, with a 20mm cannon and the ability to fire Milan missiles; Dutch armoured brigades were acquiring YPR 375 cannon-armed vehicles; and the US armoured brigades were rapidly replacing their M113 APCs with the Bradley infantry fighting vehicle, which had better protection and greatly improved firepower, from a 25mm cannon and a launcher for TOW anti-tank missiles.

From the early 1970s the Army had recognized the need to replace the FV432 APC with an infantry fighting vehicle. The Army looked hard at purchasing the US Army's Bradley fighting vehicle. For reasons that are obscure they asked for a version without the powerful TOW anti-tank missile. But from the British viewpoint, the vehicle had important handicaps including insufficient capacity for troops and supplies and inadequate NBC protection. And the price quoted by the US manufacturer was higher than the price that GKN Sankey quoted for an infantry fighting vehicle of UK design and manufacture.

This was adopted. It had a crew of three, commander, gunner and driver, and carried seven infantrymen in the back. Its turret had then cutting-edge image-intensifying night sights. As well as a machine gun, it had the 30mm Rarden cannon that was already fitted to the Scimitar and Fox reconnaissance vehicles. As the gun was manually loaded it had a slower rate of fire than the belt-fed cannon fitted to many nations' infantry fighting vehicles. But it was simple to use, a very accurate weapon and much easier to maintain and repair than belt-fed weapons. By the early 1980s prototypes of the vehicle were being tested. It began troop trials in 1984, including a platoon of four vehicles deploying on Exercise *Lionheart*. The first batch of over 700 vehicles was ordered in 1984.

Replacement of Chieftain by Challenger had been an evolutionary improvement in the capability of armoured regiments. But for the British infantry, Warrior was a revolutionary improvement in capability. So much so that as battalions were issued with it, their names were changed from 'mechanized infantry' to 'armoured infantry'. The firepower and sights in its turret allowed Warrior to destroy the many light armoured vehicles with which Soviet forces were equipped. When combined with the 24 Milan missile launchers now held by infantry battalions in Germany, armoured infantry would need much less assistance from tanks in the defence, freeing up armoured squadrons for manoeuvre and surprise counterattacks.

In offensive operations, Warrior had much better mobility than the FV432. Previously Challenger tanks would often leave the FV432 in the dust – literally – in exercises on the training area at Soltau or in Canada. But Warrior could easily keep up with Challenger. It had better armour, although not nearly as effective as that of Challenger. And when armoured infantry closed with the enemy, their greater speed reduced their vulnerability, while the machine guns in the turret could effectively suppress the enemy defenders. In my own battalion, during live firing attacks well-trained Warrior crews could hosepipe concentrated machine-gun fire at individual enemy trenches, often literally blowing them away. And the Rarden cannon's 30mm shell could neutralize well-constructed bunkers and fortified buildings that were strong enough to deflect machine-gun fire. Exercises in Canada and Germany showed that companies equipped with Warrior were faster moving, more lethal and suffered fewer casualties than those with the FV432.

Previously, armoured corps officers had often chafed at being shackled to slower infantry in FV432s. They would sometimes claim that in comparison to fast-moving, quick-thinking powerful tank squadrons that were experts at manoeuvre warfare, the infantry's culture was pedestrian and slow. The infantry therefore resolved that it should make the most of Warrior.

Two battalions a year would convert to the vehicle. A comprehensive plan was made for their conversion to the armoured infantry role. The size of battalions was increased, with extra instructors, particularly in vehicle gunnery, which was also supported by issuing simulators. The battalion's many specialists were trained on extra courses and the armoured vehicle ranges at Sennelager were upgraded. Troops were also briefed on the theory and practice of armoured manoeuvre warfare, the tactics for employing Warrior and the new attitude needed to exploit its revolutionary capabilities. Just as importantly, battalions were given the time, spare parts and ammunition to convert.

In 1987 1st Battalion, the Grenadier Guards became the Army's first armoured infantry battalion. Battalions and brigades that converted to Warrior developed a new confidence and displayed tangible excitement. There was a particular sense that counterattacks and counterstrokes now stood a significantly greater chance of success.

Most NATO armies were outnumbered and outranged by Warsaw Pact artillery. As well as large numbers of towed and self-propelled guns, Soviet forces had many multi-barrelled rocket launchers (MBRLs). Descended from the fearsome Katyushka rocket launchers used in World War II, these could rapidly deliver a considerable amount of high explosive in a short time, giving them the ability to both suppress targets and cause shock.

In the 1980s the US Army developed their own MBRL. The MLRS was based on the M270 lightly armoured tracked rocket launcher that fired 12 227mm calibre rockets at targets up to 20 miles away. All 12 rockets could be fired in about a minute, after which the highly mobile launcher could move away to reload. The rockets came pre-packed in pods of six and the fitting of an ingenious remote-controlled reloading system meant the launcher could be quickly back in action.

Each rocket dispensed 644 small bomblets that had a hollow charge sufficient to penetrate the thin top armour of Warsaw Pact armoured vehicles. On detonation they also scattered shrapnel, killing and wounding troops in the open and greatly damaging soft-skinned vehicles. A single 12-round launcher could neutralize a kilometre wide grid square.

The Army aimed to have three regiments of MLRS, replacing the M110 and M107 self-propelled guns. They would greatly enhance the ability of 1 (BR) Corps to conduct counter-battery fire against Soviet artillery. And their rapid area attack capability would be invaluable at critical times, such as in slowing down an enemy breakthrough or as sudden fire strikes just before counterstrokes were launched.

The Royal Artillery were optimistic that MLRS would cause a revolution in artillery firepower. France, Germany, Italy and the UK entered a collaborative programme with the US to manufacture M270 launchers in Europe and first deliveries to the British began in 1988.

Just as important as the transformational fighting systems, Warrior and MLRS, was a quiet revolution in battlefield logistics. It began with a fresh study into attrition likely to be inflicted during a NATO/Warsaw Pact war. The Battlefield Attrition Study (BAS) reported in the early 1980s. It used evidence from the 1973 Arab–Israeli War, in which the

Israelis suffered unexpectedly heavy attrition, and new computer simulation techniques, including evidence from a long-term programme of divisional and battlegroup wargames. It reflected earlier decisions to phase out 105mm artillery in BAOR and replace it with larger heavier 155mm guns and to increase the number of land mines laid.

The British Army had signed up to meet a NATO target of holding sufficient ammunition for 30 days of fighting. But the British thought this target was too low. The study confirmed that the fully mobilized corps could resist and contain a major Soviet attack, but after eight days of fighting it would probably be at about 40 per cent of its capability. It still needed to be able to fight for two more days. This became known as the '8+2' target. This would require more ammunition to be held in Germany.

Exercise *Lionheart* and other tests and trials had shown that the existing ammunition could not be moved quickly enough from the ammunition depots. This was inhibited by the speed at which fixed body trucks could be loaded and unloaded by forklift trucks. This was too slow, exacerbated by ammunition depots being too cramped for rapid out loading. It was also planned to send ammunition forward by train, but the railheads at ammunition depots were too cramped and the conventional mechanical handling equipment was too slow. Too many ammunition depots were too far to the west of the corps.

The Army analyzed how outloading and distribution of ammunition could be accelerated. Its solution had three parts. Firstly, new ammunition storage sites would be built in the corps area, including to the east of the River Weser. Secondly, new mechanical handling equipment was needed to speed up offloading from ammunition brought forward by rail.

The third pillar was a new concept for a large heavy military truck. This would have the ability to carry a standard 20-foot ISO container. It would use ingenious large pallets, known as 'racks', onto which pallets of ammunition could be fixed. A motor-driven hook on the vehicle would allow it to load and unload full racks. The vehicle became known as the Demountable Rack Offload and Pickup System, DROPS for short. The basic vehicle was to have some cross-country capability and improved medium-mobility DROPS trucks were issued to the artillery and engineers to allow them to carry ammunition and mines over more difficult terrain. A thorough competition was run, including a year of trials. As a result, 1,400 basic DROPS lorries were ordered; first deliveries took place in 1990, with improved mobility lorries being delivered in the mid-1990s. Both vehicles revolutionized the supply and distribution of ammunition and mines to artillery and engineers.

THE CORPS' LAST HURRAH, 1988–90

In the late 1980s, the corps reorganized again. The 4th Division gave up the 33rd Armoured Brigade, which was replaced by the 19th Infantry Brigade based in Colchester. It was judged that the heavily wooded terrain in the south of the 4th Division's sector favoured the defence sufficiently for an infantry brigade to amount a strong defence. And this sector was one that was unlikely to initially lie on a major enemy axis.

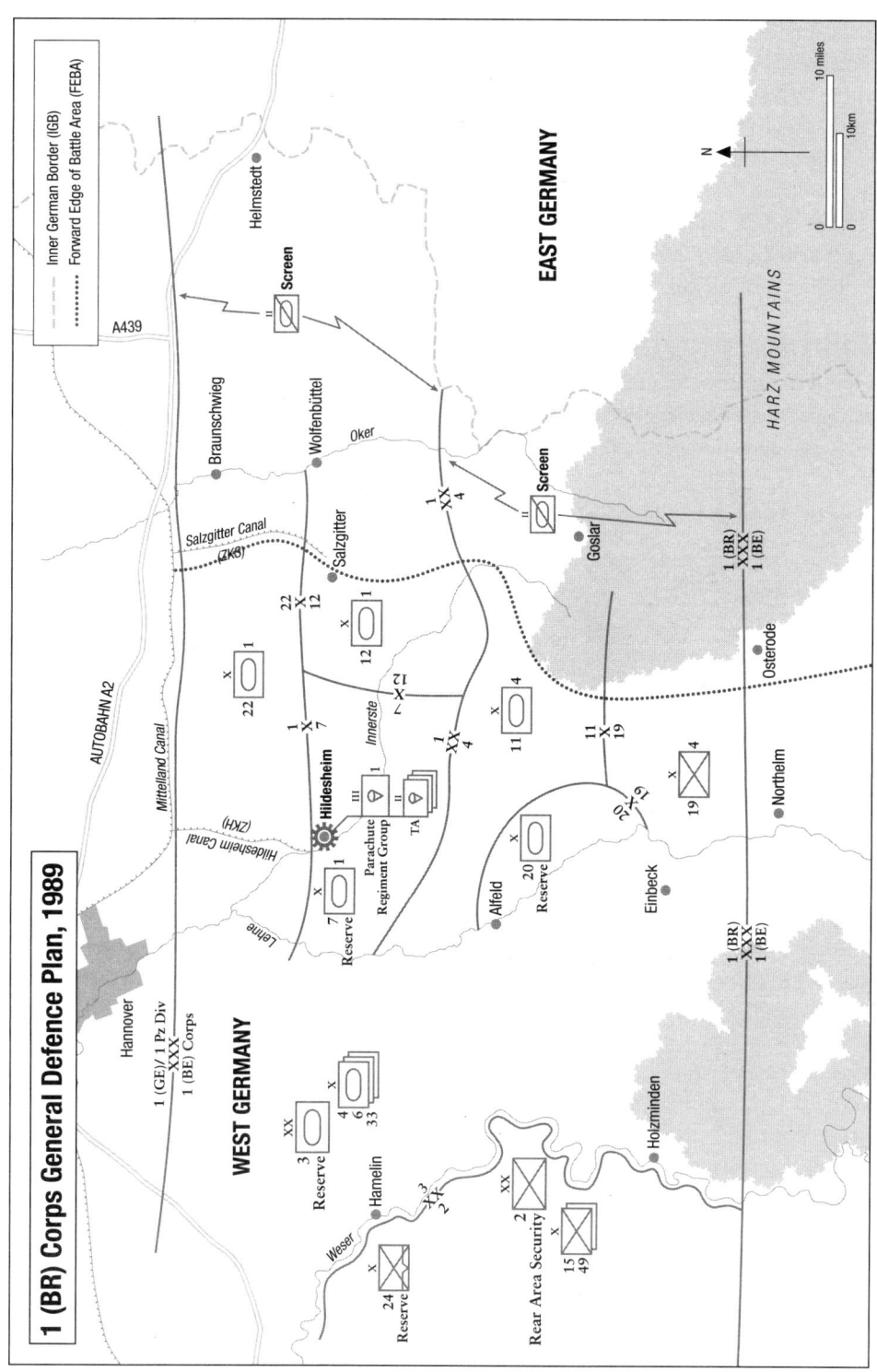

1 (BR) Corps General Defence Plan, 1989

It was also decided that 1st Armoured Division needed more infantry, particularly to hold the key town of Hildesheim. There were no more regular infantry battalions available, so the three battalions of the TA Parachute Regiment were grouped into a brigade-sized 'Hildesheim FIBUA Force', FIBUA being the acronym for fighting in built-up areas. The battalions were allocated 16 Milan missile launchers each and a small tactical HQ for the force was improvised out of the regimental HQ of the Parachute Regiment.

The Army decided that the airmobile brigade trial had succeeded, and that the capability should endure. But it would be transferred to the 24th Infantry Brigade of the 2nd Infantry Division, based in Yorkshire. This would allow 6th Airmobile Brigade to re-equip as an armoured brigade of a Challenger tank regiment and two Warrior-equipped armoured infantry battalions. 3rd Armoured Division would therefore have three armoured brigades: 4th, 6th and 33rd. By the early 1990s, the division would be completely equipped with Challenger, Warrior and the new MLRS, making it well suited to conduct division-sized counterattacks and counterstrokes.

EXERCISE IRON HAMMER

Autumn 1988 saw the Army's last ever field exercise in Germany by a full armoured division. This was Exercise *Iron Hammer*, testing the reorganized 3rd Division.[24] By now the division's four tank regiments were fully equipped with Challenger tanks and 4th Armoured Brigade had the Grenadier Guards fully equipped with Warriors, whilst 6th and 33rd brigades' infantry remained in FV432s. The division also had the first artillery battery to be equipped with MLRS. As well as the division's assigned TA reinforcements for UK, the exercise included the British corps reconnaissance regiments, as well as Belgian, Canadian and German troops, the exercise involving 35,000 NATO troops and 8,000 vehicles.

For the first week of the exercise units and formations conducted their own training. The Saturday of the middle weekend saw units refurbish themselves and divisional HQ issue orders for a divisional defensive battle. Commanders conducted reconnaissance during Sunday. Over the Sunday night the division deployed to defensive positions. The 4th and 6th brigades were forward, with 33rd Brigade in reserve.

Orange forces comprised the Bundeswehr's 20th Panzer Division, 1 (BR) Corps' three armoured reconnaissance regiments and a Belgian reconnaissance battalion. On the Monday these sought to force the 3rd Division's covering forces across the River Weser. Concurrently 2nd Battalion, the Light Infantry conducted a helicopter landing onto high ground in the rear of the divisional area. This threat was neutralized by a counterattack by 33rd Brigade. On the Tuesday the enemy concentrated their forces against 4th Brigade, who mounted a counterattack to drive them back. The next day saw 33rd Brigade conduct a counterattack.

The 3rd Division was now ordered to mount a counterstroke into the enemy flank. To assist with this, 20th Panzer Brigade changed sides to secure the start line from which the division would attack. As the division moved, the weather greatly deteriorated, with an expectedly heavy snowfall. This resulted in the German police placing great restrictions on armoured vehicle movement. Despite this, the division made it to the start line in time to attack at dawn on Friday with the 4th and 33rd brigades leading and 6th Brigade following as divisional reserve. By now the weather was so bad that both road and cross-country vehicle movement was difficult, so the exercise was ended at that point.

Many found the curtailment of the exercise just as it was getting to its most challenging and exciting battle disappointing. This was frustrating, particularly for commanders, as it prevented the division from practising how it would fight the counterstroke battle, an aspect of the division's role that had not yet been exercised in the field. The Grenadier Guards were not the only unit to rename the exercise from *Iron Hammer* to *Rubber Mallet*. The earlier ending of the exercise meant that it had not been possible to demonstrate how the improved mobility of Challenger tanks and the firepower and mobility of the Warrior infantry fighting vehicle could be fully exploited to wreak havoc on the unsuspecting enemy formation. But the exercise convincingly demonstrated the constraints on manoeuvre resulting from the lower mobility of the increasingly elderly FV432 APCs.

This was the only time in the 1980s that a counterstroke by a full division was conducted on a field exercise. It would also be the last exercise in Germany in which a full British armoured division would deploy for a field manoeuvre and the Army's last ever exercise with a division of three armoured brigades.

Autumn 1989 was to see two more divisional exercises in Germany. The first was Exercise *White Rhino*, conducted by 1st Armoured Division. It was an ambitious manoeuvre for the whole division of three armoured brigades. But under pressure from the German government, considerable restrictions were put on the movement of tracked armoured vehicles. These meant that battalion and regiment HQs commanded batteries, companies and squadrons with fewer than half of their vehicles, perhaps one per troop or platoon. Whilst this still exercised and tested HQs down to unit level, the restriction greatly reduced the value for sub-units.[25]

The second was Exercise *Key Flight*. This was to test 24th Brigade in its new airmobile role against an enemy provided by 20th Armoured Brigade. It practised deploying by helicopter to defensive positions and offensive air assault attacks. Further developing the airmobile brigade concept, it used newly issued Supacat light all-terrain vehicles. It also practised laying anti-tank mines from Chinook helicopters and using Lynx anti-tank helicopters to attack the flanks of attacking enemy armour.[26]

BAGNALL IN LONDON

In 1987 Bagnall left Germany and moved to the MoD in London to become CGS. Here he continued to view the Army and defence through his historical perspective, intellectually probing assumptions and challenging conventional thinking. He sought to improve the education and training of the Army's officer corps. Critical to this was the Army Staff College. Modernizing its teaching would not only influence the 120 Army officers who were taught there every year, but also impact the many more senior officers who instructed on the course.

Bagnall saw a particular need to improve the competence of the Army's senior officers. He directed the Army Staff College to create a new Higher Command and Staff Course to better educate and train selected senior officers. This began in 1988, modelled in part on the US Army's School of Advanced Military Studies. The Army's top echelon, about a dozen officers, lieutenant colonels, colonels and brigadiers, underwent three months of intense education and training, focussing on the operational level of war, the level that Bagnall had found so wanting in Germany.

Central to this was using military history to inform and illuminate. The course made use of two military historians, Brian Holden-Reid of King's College London and Richard Holmes, a Sandhurst historian who was also a TA officer. Both had great influence on the course and students. Bagnall and successive Army chiefs took a great interested in those who had blossomed on the course and those who struggled. The Higher Command and Staff Course also had a 'trickle down' effect on the wider Army, as graduates of the course who increasingly populated the senior leadership of the Army sought to apply what they had learned.[27]

The Army chief had great powers of patronage. He chaired the board that selected all generals and key brigadiers for their appointments. As Commander-in-Chief BAOR Bagnall had been a member of the board; as CGS, he presided over it. As CGS, Bagnall had the final say on officers' appointments. This gave him considerable influence over the character of the Army. He gave the Army a legacy of officers that outlasted him.

ARMY THINKING ABOUT ITS FUTURE

In the late 1980s, no one in the Army foresaw an end to the Cold War. So it was planning to continue to develop its capability over the next two decades. It thought that the corps would continue to need numerous armoured vehicles, although replacement of the elderly Chieftain tanks was becoming very urgent. It was confident that the three regiments of MLRS it would receive would have a great impact on artillery depth fire, against both enemy artillery and concentrations of enemy armour.

To achieve this, it would be important to gather real-time targeting data. So specially selected and trained gunners would man a new Special Observation Post battery, deploying covertly into enemy territory to find targets for the depth fire battle. The Army also had CL-289 drones – small pilotless aircraft that flew a pre-programmed path taking photographs. It wanted to replace these with much more flexible unmanned aerial vehicles, that could be flown in real time, beaming pictures back to a ground station, for real-time surveillance target acquisition and fire control. This was the genesis of the Phoenix drone, which would enter service in the late 1990s.

The US Air Force was fielding ground surveillance radars aboard large, manned aircraft, and the French Army had smaller radars carried by modified Puma helicopters. The Army considered that such capability would be extremely useful at corps level. By 1989 they were very clear in their articulation of such a requirement. But it would take almost two decades before the RAF fielded such a capability in the Sentinel aircraft.

The Army also wanted to better exploit the third dimension by improving helicopter capability. Airmobile infantry lifted by transport helicopters were seen as having great utility for defensive tasks, especially counter-penetration. This assumed that their lack of inherent protection could be complemented by combined arms support, especially from artillery and anti-tank helicopters.

But the Army had greater ambitions to move from the armed Lynx used as an anti-tank helicopter to a purpose-built attack helicopter. This was to be able to deliver powerful surprise attacks, both in the brigade or division close defensive battle and more ambitiously for attacking follow-on forces in the enemy's tactical depth. They were greatly influenced by the US Army, which was replacing the Hueycobra in its attack aviation units with the much more capable Apache helicopter. The Army was debating with itself whether future attack helicopters should be held in divisional aviation regiments or grouped together on a corps-level aviation brigade. This thinking was to result in the fielding of the Apache attack helicopter a decade and a half later.

In the medium term, 1 (BR) Corps had identified a need for more infantry to hold key terrain. The Army saw that this requirement could be met by the Gurkha Infantry Brigade. With the return of the colony of Hong Kong to Chinese control in 1997, the Army planned to bring the brigade to UK and assign it to 1 (BR) Corps.

This measure had other utility. The Army in the late 1980s was undermanned, especially the infantry. The personnel staff were concerned that demographic trends meant that the Army would find it increasingly difficult to recruit in the 1990s. This was addressed by a programme named MARILYN (manning and recruiting in the lean years of the nineties). But this programme would be overtaken by the end of the Cold War.

BRITISH MILITARY DOCTRINE

As Bagnall changed the character of the Army, some members of the 'Ginger Group' became increasingly concerned that although the Army's tactical doctrine was improving, it was not based on a solid foundation of thinking that set out the Army's purpose and approach to modern war. At the end of 1987, General John Waters, Commandant of the Staff College, wrote to Bagnall proposing that such doctrine be written, to provide the baseline for all doctrine and teaching throughout the Army. A very small team spent a year doing this. But by the time the *British Military Doctrine* was published as a small book and sent to every officer in the Army, Bagnall had retired.

The doctrine had impact in providing the foundation for the Army's thinking about war in the 1990s. It had been drafted during the last two years of the Cold War, but was written with sufficient breadth that it was not made obsolete by the fall of the Berlin Wall.

Some of its analysis was based on tried and tested historical principles of tactics and the operational art. But it also contained new thinking, for example in the new concept of 'air manoeuvre'. Based on the Army's experimentation with the airmobile brigade and thinking about the potential value of the attack helicopter, it sought to develop a unifying idea to consider the movement of land forces through the sky – embracing operations by airmobile, airborne and attack helicopter units and formations.

It set out a new way of thinking about combat capability: the concept of 'fighting power'. It saw this as consisting of three components: a conceptual component (the ideas behind how to fight); a moral component (the ability to get people to fight); and a physical component (the means to fight). The idea was deceptively simple but provided a new way of assessing the foundations of military capability. The idea gained considerable traction, being adopted by the MoD as a central element of British Defence Doctrine. It went on to be adopted by NATO.[28]

The publication of the *British Military Doctrine* was followed by *Army Doctrine Publication Operations*. Written by then Colonel Richard Dannatt, it set out the Army's general approach to operational art and tactics. It was published in 1994 and helped commanders frame their approach to the novel challenges of unforeseen operations in Bosnia.[29]

BAGNALL'S IMPACT

Many key factors were in Bagnall's favour. Prime Minister Margaret Thatcher instinctively supported defence and the armed forces, a factor reinforced by the Falklands War. Defence spending rose throughout the first half of this period, before levelling off in the middle of the decade. An immediate and sustained rise in previously constrained military salaries helped retention. The TA, which rose in strength to 83,000, provided considerable resilience to the mobilized force structure.

Both the MoD and Army prioritized 1 (BR) Corps' capabilities. The Army benefited from considerable equipment modernization. Key programmes included the replacement of Chieftain by Challenger and FV432 by Warrior, the introduction of the Ptarmigan trunk communications system, Tracked Rapier and SA80 rifle, as well as the significant impact of RAF Chinook helicopters, without which air mobility would have been impossible.

Bagnall's influence on the Army was profound. He changed it more than any other CGS since World War II. This had not been part of a formal change programme, rather it had been Bagnall using the levers available to him at corps, army group and MoD to shape the Army to his personal vision. His initiatives, clarity of thinking, analysis of military history, revival of doctrine, and promotion of mission command, manoeuvre warfare and the operational level, all revolutionized the Army's thinking about modern war and its role in NATO.

This created a bow wave of military thinking and an Army that was much better equipped to fight, as well a generation of commanders infused with Bagnall's approach. Bagnall retired in 1988, the year before the fall of the Berlin Wall, not knowing that the change programme that he had set in hand would put the Army in a much better shape to meet the unexpected challenges of Operation *Desert Storm*, the Balkans, Sierra Leone and the initial interventions in Afghanistan and Iraq.

CHAPTER 5
OPERATION *BANNER*
THE ARMY IN NORTHERN IRELAND

Between 1969 and 2007 the Army conducted Operation *Banner*, providing support to the police to counter the twin threats of public disorder and terrorism. The campaign was an ever-present backdrop to the Army during the last two decades of the Cold War and for much of the period from 1990. During this period, units, officers and soldiers went back and forward to Northern Ireland, both on short operational tours of four to six months and on longer tours of 18 months to two years. The locally raised part-time Ulster Defence Regiment (UDR) and its successor the Royal Irish Regiment Home Service battalions spent their whole careers there. This chapter considers the campaign as a whole and its effects on the Army both positive and negative. It makes use of many sources[1] and of the author's experience both in the province and in the wider Army, as well as much discussion of operations there with many soldiers and officers. It has four sections:

1. A narrative of the campaign between 1969 and 1979.
2. A section titled 'Learning under fire' that analyzes the Army's major innovations and adaptations.
3. The campaign from 1979 to its end in 2007.
4. A concluding overall assessment of the campaign.

The year 1968 was unusual for the Army. It had no troops killed or wounded on operations. At the time many officers worried that this lack of operational activity would continue for the 1970s and beyond. Had the series of wars that had occupied the Army from the Korean War to the end of the confrontation with Indonesia really come to an end? If so, the Army would have no active operations to conduct.

In the 1960s training for a war between NATO and the Warsaw Pact could often be routine, predictable and stereotyped, particularly for the 'heavy' Army stationed in

Germany. More enterprising officers and soldiers wondered how without real adversaries the Army could maintain a sense of challenge and hone its cutting edge. Those who were comfortable with a predictable life did not see this as a challenge, but those who had more of a sense of adventure and a thirst for action saw the 1970s as potentially becoming disappointingly dull.

This uneasy sense of looming stagnation would be swept away by the unforeseen challenges of operations in Northern Ireland. These would combine large-scale rioting and lethal attacks by ruthless and agile terrorists, mostly in Northern Ireland, but also sometimes in the UK and Europe. There would be no part of the Army that would not be touched by the conflict.

Operation *Banner*, military operations in Northern Ireland, began in 1969 and would last until 2007, with some specialist support to the new Northern Ireland Police Service continuing afterwards. Over 250,000 members of the armed forces took part in the operation. Fatal casualties from terrorist action included 478 from the Regular Army, 210 from the UDR, nine members of the TA, 21 from the Royal Marines, five from the Royal Navy and four from the RAF. Three hundred police officers were killed.

1969–72 – WIDESPREAD DISORDER AND INSURGENCY

Before 1969, Northern Ireland had been a military backwater. It had a small garrison of two infantry battalions and a reconnaissance regiment. The Army was welcomed by the Protestant population and usually lived a relatively congenial and undemanding life. But the province had a deeply unfair political system, in which the Protestant majority controlled the local parliament at Stormont. Most Protestants were loyalists, seeing themselves as an integral part of the UK and strongly opposing any changes that might increase the chance of a united Ireland. The overwhelming majority of the police service, the Royal Ulster Constabulary (RUC), were Protestants, especially the relatively poorly trained and ill-disciplined police reserve, the B Specials.

The political architecture of the province institutionalized discrimination against the Catholic minority. Influenced in part by civil rights protests in the US, in 1968 and 1969 Catholics increasingly demonstrated against the wide range of discriminatory measures they suffered. Many Catholics identified themselves as nationalists, seeing the transfer of Northern Ireland to the Irish Republic as their political objective. In 1969, increasing civil rights protests by the minority Catholic population led to ever-increasing public disorder and strife between Catholics and Protestants, the latter viewing any concessions to Catholics as undermining the political status of loyalism. This clash of irreconcilable political aims would bedevil the province for many years.

The RUC's approach to crowd and riot control was often heavy handed and made the situation worse. An escalatory cycle of public disorder grew in intensity. People who were a minority in an area where the majority were of a different religion were forcibly evicted from their homes, including by burning. Barricades went up, and the police were soon overwhelmed by the scale of the problem and were getting exhausted.

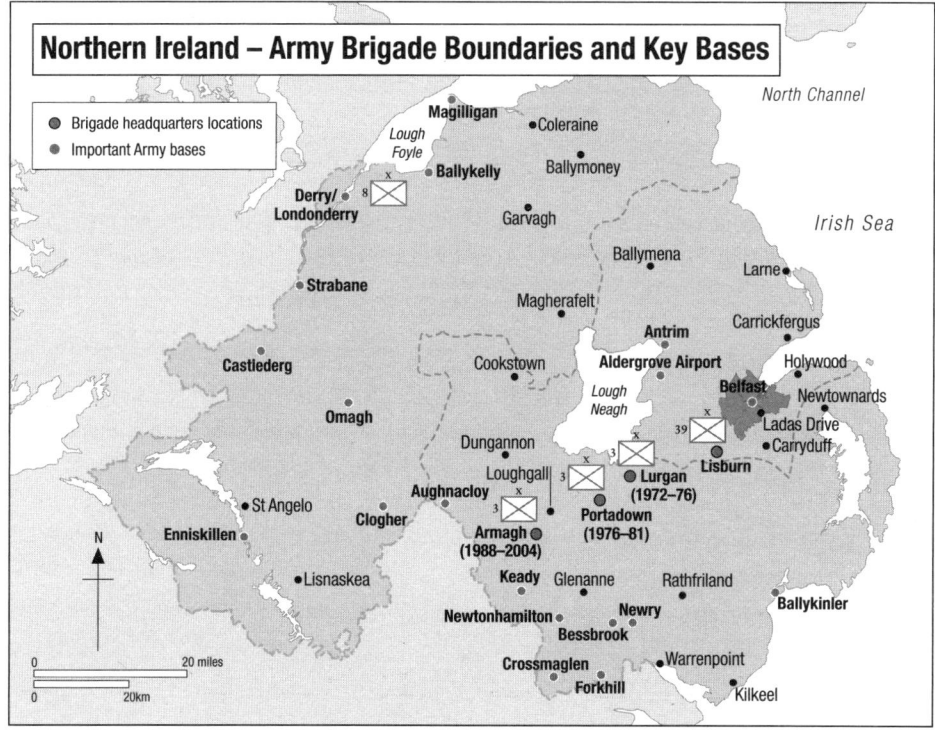

Northern Ireland – Army Brigade Boundaries and Key Bases

- Brigade headquarters locations
- Important Army bases

North Channel

Irish Sea

Magilligan
Coleraine
Lough Foyle
Ballykelly
Ballymoney
Derry/Londonderry
Garvagh
Ballymena
Larne
Strabane
Magherafelt
Carrickfergus
Antrim
Castlederg
Cookstown
Aldergrove Airport
Holywood
Belfast
Newtownards
Omagh
Lough Neagh
Ladas Drive
Carryduff
Dungannon
Lisburn
Loughgall
Lurgan (1972–76)
Aughnacloy
St Angelo
Clogher
Portadown (1976–81)
Enniskillen
Armagh (1988–2004)
Lisnaskea
Keady
Glenanne
Rathfriland
Ballykinler
Newtonhamilton
Newry
Bessbrook
Crossmaglen
Warrenpoint
Forkhill
Kilkeel

N

0   20 miles
0   20km

An outbreak of serious rioting in Londonderry on 12 August saw large-scale clashes between Catholics and Protestants. Petrol bombs were thrown and barricades built, violence spreading to Belfast and other towns. Even though half of the 3,000-strong RUC were in Londonderry, by 14 August they were overwhelmed and lost control of the city. The Chief Constable requested Army assistance.

On 15 August the Army was deployed to provide a neutral force between Catholics and Protestants by keeping both sides apart and deterring sectarian violence. The province's small Army garrison was rapidly mobilized, 1st Battalion, the Prince of Wales's Own Regiment of Yorkshire being the first Army unit to deploy on what became known as Operation *Banner*. The province's small force was insufficient to stabilize the situation and more units from UK and Germany were rapidly deployed by air.

The troops moved into areas of which they had little understanding. The RUC were unable to help much. Not only were they exhausted and demoralized by the preceding strife, but they were utterly discredited in the eyes of the Catholics. The Army fell back on its experience of public order in former colonies, troops often deploying in the 'box formation' that had been used for riot control in Hong Kong in the 1960s. This was certainly imposing, but its utility would not last in the province.

Initially, the presence of the Army on the streets of Belfast and Londonderry was welcomed by both Protestants and Catholics. Troops were often brought tea and cakes by well-wishing inhabitants of the working-class estates. For a few very short months there

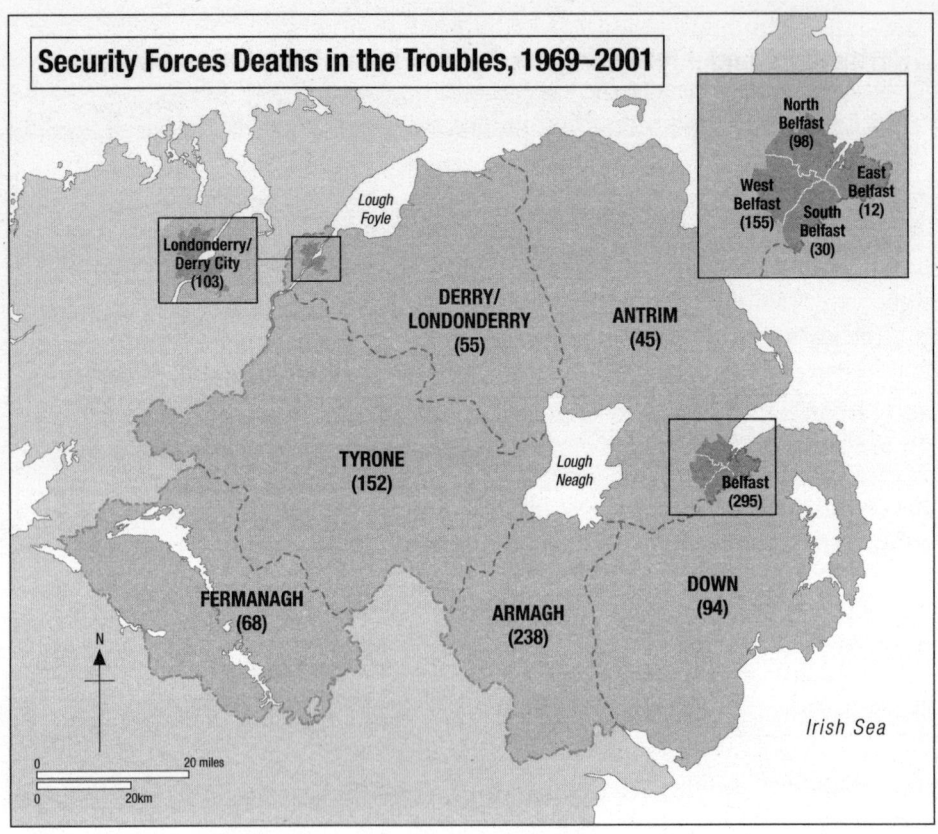

Security Forces Deaths in the Troubles, 1969–2001

was a honeymoon period. But there was considerable friction between Protestant and Catholic communities that gave rise to shooting and rioting. The 3rd Battalion, the Light Infantry was made responsible for the Shankill Road area. Violence broke out on Shankill Road in mid-October, and the battalion was engaged for four consecutive days and nights. The most serious was the evening of Saturday 11 October. Major Keith Hitchcock described the disorder, which became known as the 'Battle of the Shankill':

> A crowd of Protestants was moving towards the Catholic Unity Flats at the city end of the Shankill. The RUC had a strong cordon across the road but it was obvious they would not be able to hold the vast mob. The RUC were backed up by a company of ours around the flats, but the brigade commander told us to thump the crowd from the flank. Then began a memorable night.
>
> We moved into the Shankill down two parallel streets and cordoned the road 50 yards in front of the RUC. Bricks and bottles were rained at us, and after warning that CS gas would be used, we donned respirators. The noise from the mob was thunderous and only increased when we fired our first CS canister. At this time some shots were fired from the

crowd, resulting in one policeman shot dead, two injured and one soldier shot through the leg. After more CS and shots from the mob, it was obvious they were more determined than on previous occasions, and different tactics must be employed.

We took cover in side streets and doorways while the 'heavy squad' was used for the first time. The first charge covered by a blanket of CS accounted for two arrests and was quickly followed by more charges. By this time petrol bombs were being thrown, and more varied weapons were joining those already in use by the mob. It is difficult to describe this utterly incredible scene in a British city; a howling drunken mob, half bricks and broken flagstones bouncing down the street, petrol bombs and automatic weapons joining the fray.

This was the pattern for the remainder of the night, an advance behind the armoured cars smashing through the new barricades erected by the crowd, parties detailed off to cover side streets and the heavy squad constantly raising their score of arrests. We estimated that over 1,000 rounds were fired at us, plus a couple of hundred petrol bombs.

We reached the junction of Northumberland St and the Shankill at about 0400 hours, where brigade told us to go firm, which we did under constant sniper fire which eventually faded away. Dawn brought a look of the blitz to Belfast.[2]

The 52 hours the battalion spent on the Shankill saw an unknown number of snipers and petrol bombers shot and over 70 rioters arrested. The battalion had fired 78 rounds of 7.62mm and almost 450 rounds of CS gas.

After the August disorder the British government commissioned Baron Hunt to produce an advisory report on policing in Northern Ireland. Hunt recommended major changes. These included the disarming of the RUC and the disbandment of the B Special police reserves. They would be replaced by a new military part-time reserve force commanded by the Army, the UDR. There was an aggressive reaction from loyalists, including the fatal shooting by loyalist gunmen of Constable Victor Arbuckle, the first member of the RUC killed in what became known as the Troubles.

Strategic command and control was complicated. The British government distrusted the province's government at Stormont. In London, the CGS exercised strategic command over the GOC. He also had to respond to requests from Stormont. The RUC were independent, as were all the many British police forces. Neither London nor Stormont had any appetite to formulate a cross-government comprehensive strategy. Elements of a strategy would emerge over the years, but for much of the campaign the important pillars around which a campaign plan could be constructed were notably absent.

By now the Army was the only security force in the Catholic working-class areas of Belfast and Londonderry. It was increasingly seen by Catholics as an agent of the Protestant majority Stormont government. Extremists on both sides began to see the Army presence as thwarting their political aims. This was particularly the case in the Catholic community, where a new more militant faction of the Irish Republican Army (IRA), the Provisional IRA, quickly grew and armed itself.

The lack of political progress increasingly frustrated Catholics. There were increasing eruptions of disorder and rioting, particularly triggered by traditional Protestant marches. Barricades would be built and the Army would move in with sappers to remove them, triggering both riots and shooting attacks. For example, over the night of 27/28 June 1970 six civilians died and 61 were wounded by paramilitary gunfire. Three soldiers were wounded and the Army used large amounts of CS gas to disperse rioters.

THE FALLS ROAD CURFEW

In July 1970 a search operation in West Belfast triggered serious rioting. The Army responded by using CS gas to disperse crowds. This was another tactic that had worked in colonies like Hong Kong, but in the province it was counterproductive. Rioters could easily run away from the clouds of the gas, but the intensely irritating material quickly made its way into homes. And the gas discriminated by age, the young and elderly disproportionately suffering.

The Army sealed off the Lower Falls Road, an area of some 3,000 homes, imposing a curfew and conducting hundreds of house searches. Soldiers were angry and many were in no mood to behave with any empathy. There were widespread complaints of aggressive and wanton destruction during searches. Many of these complaints were justified, but large amounts of weapons and ammunition were found.

The 'Falls Road curfew' lasted 36 hours. When it was lifted, gun battles had claimed the lives of four civilians and 18 soldiers had been wounded by shooting, grenades or rioters. Some 1,600 CS gas cannisters had been used and almost 1,500 rounds fired by the Army. Much ammunition and many weapons were seized during searches. The operation was a tactical success, but a strategic failure. The Army was now seen by Catholics as an arm of Protestant repression and the IRA as their brave defenders. The situation greatly worsened during the rest of 1970. Protestant paramilitaries and the IRA began to use violence against communities on the other side. In October 1970, the IRA began a campaign of bombing directed against commercial targets to disrupt the functioning of the province and its economy. In early 1971 the Provisional IRA declared that it would use lethal force against the troops. And this came in the form of petrol bombs, grenades and shooting attacks.

The first British soldier to be killed, Gunner Curtis, died on 6 February 1971. During a serious riot on the New Lodge Road the crowd suddenly dispersed. A nail bomb was thrown, followed by a burst of automatic fire. The IRA also murdered off-duty soldiers. This began with three soldiers drinking in Belfast being lured by young women to their murder. By Easter 1971, in Belfast and Londonderry the Army was dealing with major riots and many nail bomb and shooting attacks. For example, 1st Battalion, the Royal Anglian Regiment, deployed in Belfast for four months during that period, had 177 rounds fired at it. Four of its soldiers were killed and 36 wounded.

INTERNMENT

Stormont agitated for the introduction of imprisonment of terrorist suspects without trial. This was resisted by the Army, but London eventually agreed. On 9 August 1971 a large number of dawn raids were mounted on houses in Catholic areas all over the province.

Operation *Demetrius* came as a surprise to those detained. But it made the situation worse. The Army's post-conflict analysis concluded that internment set the Catholic areas aflame with pro-IRA sentiment:

> The Army and RUC were poorly prepared: suspect lists were badly out of date and detention facilities were inadequate. The former led to many of the wrong people being arrested and the latter meant that those arrested could not be properly segregated during screening. In addition, the Army subjected a small number to deep interrogation techniques which had been developed in other theatres during the 1950s and 1960s.
>
> The introduction of internment was in practice an operational level reverse. A considerable number of terrorist suspects were interned: the net total of active IRA terrorists still at large decreased by about 400 between July and December 1971. A very large amount of intelligence had been gained: the number of terrorists arrested doubled in six months. However, the information operations opportunity handed to the republican movement was enormous. Both the reintroduction of internment and the use of deep interrogation techniques had a major impact on popular opinion across Ireland, in Europe and the US. Put simply, on balance and with the benefit of hindsight, it was a major mistake.[3]

The deep interrogation techniques included hooding, white noise, placing detainees in physically stressing positions against the wall, deprivation of sleep, and a bread and water diet. These methods, known as the 'five techniques', had been used by Army interrogators in previous colonial campaigns. They were also used in training British servicemen, such as pilots and SAS, who were considered at particular risk of capture. As detainees were released from internment, stories of ill-treatment rapidly reached the media.

Their use reflected the inconvenient truth that police intelligence, the RUC Special Branch, had also been overwhelmed by the rapid growth of disorder and insurgency and was also not trusted by the Army. Indeed, the weakness of Special Branch was one of the major factors that contributed to the inadequacy of the intelligence used for internment. Special Branch interrogators had been trained by the Army intelligence school. And Army interrogators assisted in the running of the interrogation centre where these techniques were used. This was examined by an independent inquiry commissioned by the government. In 1972 Prime Minister Edward Heath banned the use of the 'five techniques'. This was implemented but by 2003 the Army had forgotten the policy …[4]

BLOODY SUNDAY AND DIRECT RULE

Violence continued to increase. On 30 January 1972, a banned nationalist march in Londonderry was blocked by troops from 8th Infantry Brigade. It was assessed that this would trigger rioting. It was therefore planned that 1st Battalion, the Parachute Regiment (1 Para) would move against the crowd to arrest rioters. As they did so, a shot was heard. The Paras opened fire and 12 civilians were shot dead. The exact course of events was and remains contested. The incident was subject to two judicial inquires, the second criticizing

1 Para for reckless behaviour. 'Bloody Sunday' was another strategic defeat, fanning yet more violence. It was exploited in the province, Eire, the US and around the world by the IRA and its supporters,

By spring 1972 the British government had lost patience with Stormont's inability to make meaningful reforms. This led to the March 1972 suspension of Stormont and the return of Northern Ireland to direct rule, to be conducted by the Secretary of State and a new Northern Ireland Office. This was followed by secret but fruitless negotiations with the IRA. To encourage IRA co-operation, the Army was directed to adopt a low profile in Catholic areas of Belfast and Londonderry. Parts of both cities were allowed to fall under IRA control, becoming 'no-go' areas, surrounded by barricades, which the Army did not cross.

BLOODY FRIDAY AND OPERATION MOTORMAN

The IRA took advantage of these 'no-go' zones as base areas, particularly for launching bombing attacks. The worst of these occurred on 21 July, when, without warning, ten large bombs exploded in Belfast city centre. In what became known as 'Bloody Friday', ten civilians were killed and 130 wounded, many seriously. Most were Protestants, the event leading to increased support for Protestant paramilitaries.

The bombings greatly darkened the mood in the province and London. This shifted government opinion to favour restoring control over the province. General Carver suggested an operation, named *Folklore*, to establish greater security by disarming the province, including loyalists. Such an operation would have required 47 battalions or regiments. This option was rejected, the government preferring an operation to restore control over the no-go areas in Belfast and Londonderry. The Army planned to quickly swamp the areas with overwhelming force, giving the enemy the option of standing to fight or withdrawing. Operation *Motorman* was the result. The Cabinet agreed and the Army was rapidly reinforced to its peak force level of 28,000 regular troops, while Centurion armoured engineer vehicles were brought in by Royal Navy amphibious shipping to bulldoze barricades.

The operation began at dawn on 31 July 1972. The night before, the Northern Ireland Secretary asked the public not to interfere with major troop movements, effectively telegraphing the impending operation. This was one of the few successful information operations in the campaign. The IRA chose not to stand and fight, so the expected intense firefights never happened. The barricades were quickly swept away, but the insurgents continued to attack the Army and police as well as conduct a bombing campaign. 1972 was the height of the conflict, with 239 civilians, 123 soldiers and 17 police killed.

1973–78 – COUNTER-TERRORISM

From 1973 to 1975 the IRA continued to mount a high level of attacks, but large numbers were arrested: almost 1,800 between May and December 1973, for example.

There was usually a pattern to operations. Units would incessantly patrol their area. While doing so they would check the identities of people they encountered and stop and search people who were behaving suspiciously. This not only deterred terrorist activity but could also sometimes interdict it. For instance, in the early 1970s a street patrol in Belfast spotted a young man carrying a guitar case. Not only was the man concerned not known to play any musical instrument, but the case appeared much heavier than it would be if it contained an acoustic guitar. He was stopped and the case was found to contain two assault rifles.

A typical infantry company would adopt a routine. For example, the company I was a member of, deployed in West Belfast in the late 1970s, had three platoons. One would be conducting patrols throughout the assigned company area, employing most of the platoon in mounting five or six patrols of several hours' length every day. Another platoon provided the company quick reaction force, with one section at instant readiness to deploy, another ready to deploy at ten minutes' notice and a third at 30 minutes' notice. Only members of the third section could remove their boots and have time to shower, or sleep in their beds. The third platoon was guarding the base, with typically four soldiers in protected sentry towers, known as sangars, and one or two soldiers guarding the heavily fortified entrance. Soldiers in this platoon would have a modicum of time to catch up on sleep and wash their clothes.

With platoons changing roles every two days, this type of routine would in theory allow a reasonable balance between operations and time for sleep and rest. In reality, this only held true when there were no incidents or major operations. These could involve most or all of the company. Any period of sustained operations would see fatigue rapidly accumulate across the whole sub-unit. Fortunately, Army chefs would provide very high-quality food in large quantities, something that was good for both morale and personal energy levels.

The company base had been purpose built and featured a perimeter of concrete blast walls, thick enough to stop small arms fire. The sangars were more heavily fortified, with windows of thick armoured glass. People lived in Portakabins that were hot in summer and cold in winter. Soldiers were crammed into four-man rooms and slept on bunk beds. In the heavily fortified bases in South Armagh the hardened accommodation allowed even less room, with soldiers in three-tiered bunk beds.

A 1973 referendum showed that most people wished to remain part of the UK. London attempted to restart political progress, with the election of a new Northern Ireland Assembly and the Sunningdale Agreement between Dublin and London. Sunningdale was strongly opposed by loyalists. The Ulster Workers' Council staged a province-wide strike of essential services. The Army was ordered to conduct fuel distribution, but this resulted in the strike escalating. The new assembly government collapsed.

THE IRA ADAPTS

By the mid-1970s the Army and RUC were penetrating the IRA with informers and improved intelligence and surveillance capabilities were starting to have an effect. This was aided by the IRA's structure of a conventional military hierarchy of companies, battalions and brigades. Its internal security was weak. For example, successful attacks were often celebrated in republican drinking clubs.

The IRA adapted by reorganizing from a conventional military organization to a network of smaller so-called active service units (ASUs). These adopted a cellular structure with much greater operational security and a ruthless application of the need-to-know principle. The IRA's reorganization increased its terrorists' security. This resulted in a reduction in attacks. But those that occurred were much better organized, with extensive planning, reconnaissance and getaway plans. And ASUs sometimes trained in remote areas in Eire. The result was that the IRA could no longer be seen as conducting a widespread insurgency but was now masterminding a terrorist campaign designed to raise the cost to the British government of retaining control of the province. Initially this was not supported by a meaningful republican political strategy.

MOVING TO POLICE PRIMACY

Concurrently with the IRA's reorganization, the British developed a new strategy, sometimes described as 'normalization'. It was intended that as security improved the Army's de facto primacy for security would pass to the police. The special emergency legislation in the province would, over time, be reduced and eventually ended. The special category of prisoners interned without trial would end and those convicted of terrorist offences would be jailed under the same conditions as common criminals. This policy of police primacy was formally agreed in January 1977 as the GOC and Chief Constable signed a joint directive:

> which placed the RUC at the forefront of security operations. Under this rubric, the Secretary of State for Northern Ireland was responsible for deciding the security policy in Northern Ireland and the RUC 'was to be fully consulted' with Army operations, agreeing to the frequency and tasking of Army patrols and vehicle checkpoints, and the Army seeking authorization from the police for house searches, identity checks and arrests ... Security policy was now firmly centred on separating terrorists from their communities and dealing with acts of political violence through a criminal justice approach.[5]

At the time this policy was announced, many in the Army were sceptical that the strategy would work. And in the so-called hard republican areas, including Londonderry, West Belfast and South Armagh, the Army continued to have effective primacy. The Army's considerable caution about police capability was balanced with an equally strong institutional desire to reduce the negative impact of Northern Ireland on the Army, particularly on training for the Army's NATO role.

A four-month operational tour would occupy a unit for the best part of a year. From three months before the tour key commanders and staff would conduct reconnaissance trips. The ever-increasing numbers of specialists would attend courses, for example intelligence and photography. Units would reorganize from their normal structure to a special Northern Ireland organization. Training would occupy at least another month. And during this period leave would need to be taken.

After the tour, units would usually hold commemorative events, often a parade to hand out Northern Ireland medals to those whose first tour it was. There would frequently be a large party, followed by several weeks' leave. Then the unit would return to its normal organization. But there would now be a requirement to retrain for its war role. Very few troops would have been able to leave the province for their routine career courses, so there would be a backlog to catch up on. No matter how well a unit had performed on its operational tour, its formation commander in the UK or Germany would have lost it for a year.

Between 1969 and the late 1970s, many units deployed on multiple four-month tours. For example, between 1969 and 1975, 1st Battalion, the Light Infantry deployed six times on emergency tours, two of which occurred with little or no notice. To measure the disruptive effects of operational tours, the Army used the concept of the 'tour interval'. This was the time between two successive operational tours. Recognizing that a tour interval of zero would represent an army conducting no operations, the Army would later judge that its target should be an average tour interval of 18 months between tours of four-month lengths. In 1972, when the Army's strength in the province was at an all-time high, the tour interval for the infantry was eight months.

Throughout the 1970s the Army struggled to reduce this disruption. For example, in the mid-1970s, the Army assumed that by the end of the decade there would be a significant reduction in the requirement for the Army in the province. By early 1978, it was clear that this would not happen, and the Army was in danger of having insufficient infantry. So to reduce the pressure on the hard-pressed infantry, four additional battalions' worth of infantry capability were created. This saw the raising of an extra Gurkha battalion, to take on other infantry commitments, and the Royal Marines generating an additional commando. Both these units had a life of five years. In addition, the role of nuclear convoy escort was transferred from the infantry to the Royal Corps of Transport and the role of supporting the School of Infantry, previously conducted by an infantry battalion, was transferred to a static demonstration battalion. This freed up two more battalions to go to the province.

Even so, the disruptive effect of Northern Ireland lasted until the end of the campaign in the next century. And the bald statistics of the tour interval over-simplified Northern Ireland's considerable effects on the infantry. For example, between January 1990 and September 1992, 2nd Battalion, the Light Infantry (2 LI) deployed twice on planned operational tours to South Armagh; but it was also deployed in November and December 1990 to help thwart any expected IRA Christmas bombing offensive and again in September and October 1991 to reinforce South Armagh. The 1st Infantry Brigade, to whom the battalion belonged, saw very little of the unit. By the end of the campaign 2LI had conducted 16 roulement tours and two resident deployments, more tours than any unit in the Army – an average of an emergency tour every 2.1 years. But it was just one of 30 infantry battalions to conduct more than ten operational tours in the province.[6]

Northern Ireland emergency tours had negative effects on troops' families. Not only was there the absence of the spouse, with all the challenges that resulted, not least in looking after young children, but there was the justified fear that the spouse could be killed or wounded. And many wives came from parts of the UK that were some distance from their families and friends. These problems were exacerbated for wives and families living in Germany, with its unfamiliar language and culture and greater distance and expense of travel to and from their home area of the UK.

Units had families' officers and small families' offices. These played an important role in supporting their families, including much troubleshooting. And many units had a culture of officers' and warrant officers' wives pitching in to assist. Troops welcomed the challenge and chance to practise their skills against a real enemy. But as people got older and acquired wives and children the separation became more difficult to bear.

LEARNING UNDER FIRE – ARMY ADAPTATION TO NORTHERN IRELAND

Throughout the 1970s the Army had made many tactical, technological and training adaptations to better operate in the province. Crowd and riot control was an early area of adaptation. In 1969 troops moving to separate Catholics and Protestants had used tactics applied in colonial conflicts, including the late 1960s riots in Hong Kong. For example, the troops would march forward in a box formation with fixed bayonets. A police officer or magistrate would order rioters to disperse. A banner would then be displayed ordering the rioters to disperse. There are credible stories of platoons initially using this tactic, carrying banners written in English on one side and Arabic on the other.

Widespread civil disorder was a major feature of the campaign in the early 1970s. This ranged from casual rock throwing by youths, known as 'aggro', to full-scale riots where large angry crowds confronted the Army, throwing bricks, rocks and petrol bombs and hijacking buses and lorries to form barricades, often setting them on fire. Riots could provide cover for gunmen and for efforts by mobs to separate a soldier from the rest of his comrades, disarm him, rush him away and find an IRA gunman to kill him.

It is all too easy for those who have never been on the receiving end of a hostile rioting crowd to pass judgement on the security forces combatting it. In reality, facing an angry and aggressive mob can be terrifying, even before it begins to project lethal force by using bricks, petrol bombs, nail bombs or grenades. As physical and verbal threats, tension and pressure on the security forces increase, it can be tempting to respond with lethal force, particularly firearms, but the Army had learned from much hard experience that simply killing rioters would make the situation worse, often much worse.

So the Army sought to counter riots using less than lethal force. Troops were equipped with riot guns firing rubber bullets that would administer painful bruising to those hit. But experience showed that the best way to disperse crowds was to grab hold of rioters, arrest them and hand them over to the RUC for prosecution. Tactics were devised to deal with larger riots. Some soldiers would act as a base line, standing and receiving the bricks, bottles and petrol bombs. They would protect themselves with riot guns. Specially trained 'snatch squads' would dash into the crowds. Usually lightly equipped and armed only with batons, they would seek to grab rioters and drag them back behind the base line.

Key to this was the morale, discipline and leadership needed to withstand the bricks and petrol bombs and then to instantly turn on the speed and controlled aggression required for snatch squads to sprint to crowds, seize hold of rioters and drag them away for arrest. These qualities were usually displayed in abundance on the hostile streets of Belfast and Londonderry. They made the events of Bloody Sunday so exceptional.

This approach was evidence of two overriding operational principles that the Army had learned in previous counterinsurgency and internal security operations. The first was adherence to the law, albeit modified by emergency legislation. This linked to the second principle of using the minimum necessary force, an enduring principle of British law. It was legal for the police and Army to use force, but only where necessary to save life or counter an immediate threat. These principles would be strongly emphasized during training. And when a civilian or terrorist was killed by the Army, the police would investigate. On a few occasions soldiers were tried in court.

Small 'Yellow Cards' were issued to all troops in the province. The cards set out the circumstances in which fire could be opened. These were when the soldier, his colleagues or civilians were under lethal attack, or imminent threat of lethal attack. But from the point of view of the law, the decision to apply lethal force was for the soldier to make for themselves.

FORCE PREPARATION AND TRAINING

Army units operating in Northern Ireland were a mixture of 'resident units' and 'roulement units', those temporarily deployed on operational tours from the UK and Germany. By now the most demanding areas of operations saw battalions and regiments from the UK and Germany conduct emergency tours of four months' duration. The roulement units would usually live in makeshift bases within their area of operations. Initially these were often ad hoc, including community halls, police stations, schools and disused mills and factories. But temporary accommodation such as Portacabins was soon added to make locations less cramped.

Resident units lived in pre-existing barracks, in accommodation similar to that in barracks in the UK or Germany. These units would be accompanied by families living in married quarters, either inside the barracks or outside of it. Most of these barracks were situated in Protestant areas, where the threat from the IRA was much less. This allowed a modicum of normal life. But the work rate of resident units was often intense.

Initially, the units sent to Northern Ireland went with little or no time for preparation. There was much reliance on institutional memory of recent counterinsurgency campaigns, including Malaya, Kenya and Aden. For planned deployments key unit commanders would conduct a reconnaissance, creating an important opportunity for learning from the unit they would relieve. But this essentially informal and ad hoc approach to unit preparation had considerable weaknesses.

In 1972, the Army sought to improve unit preparation by formalizing pre-deployment training of those deploying to Northern Ireland, establishing dedicated training facilities and ranges. This helped to ensure that training was as up to date as possible. To assist unit training specialist NITATs were formed in England and Germany.

Following a reconnaissance by key commanders and intelligence personnel, the NITAT would brief the whole unit on the situation and a wide range of important issues. NITAT would then conduct a 'train the trainers' package where the units' leaders down to section commanders would be taught the necessary tactics, techniques and procedures then used in the province. Desmond Hammill described some of the key teaching:[7]

> They were taught how the Provisional set up an incident. They were taught never to establish patterns that the 'dicks'[8] would notice where they would stop for a smoke on a particular bit of waste ground or where they might shelter in a particular shop entrance. They were taught that they were watched all the time.
>
> They were also taught to be courteous but firm. Slowly it was sinking in that the way a battalion behaved made a big difference to its overall success. Toughness was acceptable, roughness was not.

The unit would then have a period of training itself in barracks. Priorities would include fieldcraft, low-level tactics, first aid and shooting. There was never any shortage of small arms ammunition, prodigious quantities of which would be fired before units deployed. The unit would then move to a specialist training area in either Kent or Sennelager in Germany. Here there would be specially constructed ranges where the types of shooting required would be practised. Companies and squadrons would also spend several days in a simulated housing estate known as 'Tin City'. Here they would go through a period of simulated high-intensity operations amongst a civilian population.

For three days troops would be faced with a multitude of incidents representing the likely challenges they would encounter. These could include riots, shootings and bomb attacks. They would also have to conduct planned operations, such as arrests and searches. The exercise was not entirely scripted. For example, an alert patrol could, if it moved fast enough, capture a gunman. As a platoon commander I was tasked with conducting a search of a couple of adjacent houses. I chose to cordon not just the two houses, but to seal off the whole of a busy street. Understandably this irritated those who lived and worked there, resulting in a riot, which a less restrictive cordon would have avoided. I learned the lesson. Battalions going to rural areas would then move to Stanford training area in Norfolk, where they would practise company- and battalion-level rural operations.

These exercises put commanders under the pressure they would feel during operations in the province. And the very high tempo of operations in Tin City created challenges. On a few occasions commanders crumbled under pressure. They were quietly replaced before the tour.

There was a very close connection between the operational theatre in Northern Ireland and this training. It was kept constantly up to date and changes made in Northern Ireland could be applied quickly to training.

The relief in place of units would begin with intelligence staff going ahead of the unit, several weeks beforehand, to better understand the intelligence picture. A week before the unit handover, commanders and specialists would arrive, to prepare to take over. This created considerable continuity and minimized the chances of dips in both understanding and operations.

URBAN PATROLLING

One way the Army adapted to the threats of shooting, grenade, or bomb attack was to change its patrolling tactics. Previously troops had often patrolled in platoon-sized groups moving on a single route. These were predictable and relatively easy for terrorists to target. When attacked, the troops would attempt to capture the gunmen or bombers, but the IRA fighters would have made good their escape. Trial and error quickly showed that moving in small groups on different routes was much less predictable. If one team was attacked, the others could quickly move to attempt to cut off the terrorists' withdrawal. Richard Beath, a platoon commander in 1st Battalion, the Light Infantry, described his experience when the battalion was sent to Belfast in 1972:

> The battalion was going into the no-go areas in Operation *Motorman*. We didn't really know how to patrol safely and shortly my platoon was caught in a three-sided ambush where a soldier was shot in the back.
>
> Next day I asked Captain Rex Rice if we could cease patrolling until we had worked out something better. I sat down with Sergeant Reah and Corporal Vargas. We worked up the idea of having four four-man groups or patrols commanded by a corporal or lance corporal. Each patrol would be leapfrogging with the other covering. The two four-man patrols would work in parallel with the other two.
>
> As we put this into practice, I could tell immediately that the junior commanders loved it and were enthusiastic. It proved its worth and we had no further casualties whilst on patrol although many shootings took place. We left the province, and on our return nine months later, I discovered that the 16-man patrol technique had been adopted by the whole British Army.[9]

This tactic, called 'multiple patrolling', was quickly adopted throughout the province. Often a platoon would be divided into two 'multiples' of three four-man 'bricks', the overall patrol commanded by an officer or sergeant and the other bricks commanded by corporals or lance corporals – all carrying radios. In June 1979 a multiple patrol of 2nd Battalion, the Royal Green Jackets, encountered terrorists preparing a lorry-borne attack in the border town of Keady. Phillip Mostyn, the platoon commander, tells the story:

> Having just completed a vehicle checkpoint Corporal Barnfield was taking his section into mutually covering groups across some rough boggy ground to Victoria Street. Lance Corporal Mitchell was climbing over a gate onto Victoria Street, when he noticed a small

gathering of people watching something besides a house some 50 metres up the road. When they saw him, the spectators rushed inside. His suspicions were sufficiently high for him to cock his weapon. Looking up the road, he found himself staring at a masked gunman at the side of the lorry, feeling behind him for the door of the cab. Shots were exchanged and Lance Corporal Mitchell dropped behind cover, only to have to move immediately because he could not see his target.

By this time a considerable weight of fire was coming from the back of the lorry. Rifleman Ashort moving up behind Mitchell, found himself unable to see what was happening and ran up to the side of the house beside the lorry to adopt a more useful fire position. By the time that they had reached their new position the lorry was pulling away. They both fired as rapidly as possible into the back and side of the lorry. Lance Corporal Mitchell heard screams as the lorry pulled away.

Having passed through the centre of the town the lorry was driven out towards the border. Later in the evening one dead and two wounded terrorists were admitted to hospital in Monaghan, south of the border.[10]

If available, a helicopter could fly over the patrol to observe the ground below, looking out for suspicious activity and talking to the patrol commander by radio. There were never enough helicopters to support all the patrols on the ground. But the Army Air Corps would make every effort to scramble helicopters to provide top cover to serious incidents. And both they and the RAF would also lift reserves to quickly reinforce troops in difficulty on the ground. These tactics would later be applied in other operations further afield, including Bosnia, Kosovo and Iraq.

EARLY EQUIPMENT ADAPTATIONS

Troops deploying in 1969 had no more protection than their issued steel helmets and cotton combat clothing. As rioting increased, they were rapidly issued with anti-riot equipment. This included plastic visors for helmets, batons and riot shields. The threat of shrapnel from bombs, shotgun blasts and low-velocity bullets was countered by body armour in the form of flak jackets.

Weaknesses in combat clothing were countered by several initiatives. At that time the Army did not routinely issue troops with waterproof clothing to keep out rain. Waterproof nylon jackets were quickly issued. And soldiers were ordinarily issued with cheap green polyester gloves. These offered little in the way of warmth or protection and were a fire hazard. So units on winter tours were issued with excellent black leather gloves. The general issue footwear of short ankle boots and woollen puttees was less than ideal for urban operations. A new lightweight 'Northern Ireland Boot' was issued. It reduced fatigue and was quicker to put on than the issued boots and puttees – an invaluable characteristic when rapidly preparing to deploy.

In 1969 the Army deployed with its then range of tactical VHF radios. These were bulky, heavy and depended on an abundant supply of batteries. They were also difficult to re-tune to a new frequency. So civilian radios, as used by police forces, were procured.

Using only a few fixed frequencies, these were much smaller and could easily fit on a belt or in the pocket of a flak jacket.

COUNTERING THE BOMBERS

The IRA increasingly made use of a wide variety of IEDs. These ranged from improvised hand grenades, often known as 'nail bombs', to roadside bombs set off remotely using a command wire, and a range of bombs for use against static targets, the larger of which would be carried in cars. These were usually set off by a timer. Sometimes coded warnings would be given by telephone, sometimes not. In the early 1970s terrorists often blew themselves up when assembling, moving or emplacing IEDs. For example, in 1972 at least 30 IRA men and nine civilian bystanders died in so-called 'own goals', but as the campaign went on, IRA engineers became more competent.

To deal with the IEDs, the Army formed a new unit, 321 Explosive Ordnance Disposal (EOD) Company. The company's Royal Army Ordnance Corps Ammunition Technical Officers (ATOs) had the dangerous role of defusing bombs to make them safe. These were the Army's in-house experts on ammunition, from small bullets to the largest guided missiles, who also received specialized training on IEDs. Known by their radio callsign of Felix, they gave themselves a badge of the cartoon cat.

The Army rapidly developed a remotely operated robot to assist them. Initially improvised from a lawnmower, the 'Wheelbarrow' had an arm that could carry a variety of tools, including a mechanical claw and a shotgun to disrupt the bombs. Wheelbarrow would undergo a very rapid evolution to retain its utility against a constantly evolving threat, with a new remotely operated bomb disposal system entering service as this book was written.

Even with the aid of Wheelbarrow and other technology, the ATO's job was very risky, not least as the IRA bomb makers constantly refined their devices to counter the work of ATOs. Seven of these were killed in 1971 and 1972, with 321 EOD Company dealing with an average of 40 incidents a week.

When bombs were captured or defused, they could yield valuable intelligence and forensic information that could improve the effectiveness of counter-IED efforts and could also improve the chances of successful prosecution. To assist with this effort, the Army set up a weapons intelligence section that worked closely with Army and police intelligence and other agencies. It performed the same function for captured conventional weapons and ammunition. As the Northern Ireland campaign continued, there was a technological and tactical campaign against IRA bomb makers; the specialized technology required became increasingly refined, assisted by scientists working alongside Army.

SEARCH

From 1970, the Army devoted considerable effort to searching for illegally held arms, ammunition and explosives, to interdict the supply of these, reducing the threat. Increasingly it would also help provide intelligence and forensic evidence.

Initially, searching was conducted with little or no training, and with little or no intelligence on which to target the searches. This made a major contribution to alienating Nationalists. The situation quickly changed as intelligence improved, and the Royal Engineers became the Army's lead for search capability. They not only provided search teams for areas where there was a high risk of IEDS but also conducted training for the search teams of units deploying to the province.

Improving search capability was both a bottom-up and top-down activity. An important initiative in the early 1970s came from Captain Richard Winthrop. He put himself in the minds of terrorists seeking to hide weapons to be used by other terrorists. They would, he thought, use simple small rural landmarks. He used this approach of thinking like a terrorist to target his searches. This was very successful and the company he served in rapidly discovered more hidden munitions than the rest of the brigade. This was spotted by a brigade HQ staff officer, who got Winthrop to explain his approach more widely, greatly improving other units' success rate.

The approach was rapidly shared across the rest of the Army in Northern Ireland and fed into the training system. As a result, the Army developed a way of systemically analyzing terrorist hides and munitions storage on a map. This became the discipline of 'search analysis'. Each sub-unit and unit acquired a search advisor who would be an expert in this approach.

Throughout the campaign, search equipment and techniques were constantly adapted and refined. Maximum use was made of specially trained sniffer dogs, with their uncanny ability to detect ammunition and explosives. Every soldier with a patrol role was trained in basic search techniques. If they had to stop moving for any length of time, they would conduct a quick search of the area around them. This tactic sometimes led to the discovery of concealed arms, ammunition, bombs or command wires. This technique was more effective than the IRA liked. If the 'find' had happened outside the public eye, it might be usable as the target of a covert surveillance operation, so procedures were devised to allow this to happen.

INTELLIGENCE

The Army had entered the conflict with considerable experience of integrating intelligence with counterinsurgency operations. Brigadier Frank Kitson, commanding 39th Infantry Brigade, which was responsible for Belfast from 1971 to 1973, had great experience of this from Kenya and Malaya and had applied the same techniques to UN peacekeeping in Cyprus. He had written about this in detail in his book *Gangs and Counter-gangs*. He followed this with a second book *Low Intensity Operations*, which was based on an academic fellowship he had held.[11]

Kitson's approach had two principles. First was achieving the greatest possible co-operation between Army and police intelligence. Second, troops should be used to develop intelligence to create opportunities to detain or kill insurgents. He had remarkable success doing this as a company commander in Malaya. The technique was also applied with some success in Northern Ireland in the early 1970s, as Kitson described:

My job involved working with the police within my area of responsibility to ensure that law and order was preserved. I had frequent and regular contact with the Assistant Chief Constable of Belfast and my battalion and company commanders worked harmoniously with their opposite numbers in the police.

At this time the Army relied on the RUC for intelligence; it was disseminated initially from Special Branch of the RUC to HQ Northern Ireland, who would pass it on to the relevant Brigade HQ who would then pass it on to relevant units as necessary. Most intelligence was passed in writing or by word of mouth because the telephone was insufficiently secure.

During my time in command of 39 Brigade, the Army set up a more effective network of information gathering. It was not intelligence as such (this was the role of the specialized intelligence agencies and the RUC) but troops on the streets collected and collated as much overt information as possible to allow the Brigade to do its job.[12]

In Northern Ireland there was much useful information that could be gathered by observation by sentries and from patrols. To analyze and collate the information gathered and turn it into intelligence required units to field an expanded and decentralized tactical intelligence organization down to company level and use it to drive operations. In 39th Brigade, Brigadier Kitson's direction was that every company commander should identify and disrupt the terrorist organization in his area of responsibility. Journalist Desmond Hamill described how Kitson's approach:

pushed each company into becoming a low-level intelligence unit. It also pushed these companies into developing a real understanding of the terrorists and the local people. This policy was continued by his successor and eventually it spread to Londonderry and the rest of the province.[13]

I was a battalion intelligence officer in West Belfast and commanded over 30 soldiers who assisted with this, including company intelligence sections of half a dozen people and some specialists from outside the battalion. These included continuity NCOs, known as CONCOs, from the Belfast resident battalion, who were on a two-year accompanied tour to act as a long-term source of institutional memory.

Initially records were kept on paper, maps and index cards. But the Army quickly developed a database of all cars registered in Northern Ireland, which could be interrogated and updated at company level. This was based on a central computer, and it was accessed by dedicated teleprinters issued down to company intelligence sections.

The system was known as Vengeful and was relatively quickly developed, as vehicle registration numbers represented a fairly simple dataset. But records on people and places contained much more variable data and were more complex to digitize. This was not an insuperable challenge and in the late 1970s a computer database system, Project 3702, was developed, which allowed analysis of the data held to be conducted much more quickly across the whole province.

HUMAN INTELLIGENCE (HUMINT)

Unlike former colonies, in Northern Ireland there were no language or cultural barriers to overcome. From the beginning of Operation *Banner* local people were willing to talk to the Army. And some were recruited as secret informers. Some soldiers and officers had a remarkable degree of empathy and conversational skills and proved very successful at recruiting 'sources', as informers were known. By 1978, there was formalized training for those handling sources at battalion level and above, who would often meet their sources in civilian clothes in safe areas.

By the early 1980s the handling of Army sources had become more regularized. All sources were now managed by the Army's Force Research Unit (FRU).[14] The commander and key staff were all professional human intelligence operators from the Intelligence Corps. The unit also accepted volunteers from the rest of the Army and the Royal Marines. They went through much more thorough training than the now disbanded unit handlers had done. But troops from battalions and regiments still developed empathic conversations with local people and some of these would be targeted for recruitment. There was a proportion of people who distrusted the RUC so much that they would not talk to police officers but would talk to British handlers. And the Army found it much easier to operate in the most hostile nationalist areas than did the RUC.

This was a very dangerous activity for both source and handler. Both the IRA and Protestant terrorists were paranoid about informers, or 'touts' as they were called, promising to execute any they discovered. The IRA developed a much-feared internal security unit known as the 'nutting squad'. It conducted extensive investigations after any security force success that might have been based on human intelligence. People found guilty of passing information to the security forces would be killed and their bodies dumped on a remote road. This was often accompanied by an IRA statement that the person concerned had been a 'tout'.

Understandably, both the FRU and RUC Special Branch went to great lengths to protect the identity of their sources. Simply meeting the sources required meticulous planning to ensure the source could not be identified, either by the terrorists or by other members of the security forces.

Gathering HUMINT was not only a very dangerous and stressful activity but one that carried a degree of moral hazard. It could be very uncomfortable to deal with people who were members of a terrorist organization. Informers needed to be persuaded to put themselves in considerable danger. Money could assist with this, but only up to a point. And when an informer was unmasked by terrorists, the resulting interrogation, torture and callous murder could be very distressing for the handler.

For much of the campaign there was little government policy or guidance to provide a regulatory framework for HUMINT conducted in the province, whether by the Army, Special Branch or MI5. It was only after implementation of the Regulation of Investigatory Powers Act promulgated in 2000 that HUMINT was put under a proper legal and policy framework.

In the meantime, some very difficult judgements had to be made by handlers and their command chain in the FRU. For example, Brian Nelson, a notorious loyalist terrorist, was recruited by the FRU. He provided invaluable intelligence that saved lives but claimed he had been given assistance by the Army in his role as an intelligence officer for loyalist vigilantes. And in the informer known as 'Stakeknife', the FRU had a source inside the IRA 'nutting squad' itself. The Army claimed that he saved lives, but an independent inquiry considered that by employing Freddie Scappaticci, the alleged informer, more lives had been lost than saved.[15] Both cases remain very controversial and illustrate the very thin line that the FRU walked upon.

From the mid-1970s RUC Special Branch rebuilt its capability. The Security Service, MI5 and Army assisted with this. Senior NCOs and officers were deployed to increase connectivity between Special Branch and the Army, but in the 1980s the increasing capability of Special Branch resulted in these posts reducing. Nevertheless, there was considerable tension between the FRU and Special Branch. Inevitably, this resulted in friction, mistrust and competition.

SURVEILLANCE AND COVERT OPERATIONS

The sangars of Army bases offered a considerable ability to gather information on people and activity in the area they were sited in. This was increasingly exploited as the campaign went on. Elevated observation posts (OPs) were built inside bases. And some isolated OPs were constructed just for surveillance. For example, in West Belfast an OP was built on top of the Divis Flats and an elevated OP built atop a 30-metre-high tower in Fort Whiterock.

In the early 1970s units experimented with hiding small teams to secretly observe for terrorist activity. Derelict houses in urban areas were ideal for this. Sometimes the lofts of occupied buildings were used. Entering and leaving the buildings undetected required high standards of fieldcraft. And living in silence for days at a time, consuming only cold rations, was a real test of motivation and self-discipline. Covert surveillance in rural areas often required hiding in ditches or hedges. Sometimes these covert OPs spotted terrorists about to conduct an attack or moving openly with weapons, in which case Army marksmen could engage them.

Most of the small teams used to conduct covert OPs were usually found from battalion reconnaissance platoons, due to their training in observation and the high quality of their soldiers. By the late 1970s this type of static covert surveillance conducted by troops in uniform had become more formalized. In 1977 battalions were directed to form 'close observation platoons' (COPs) that received the necessary specialist training.

These developments were paralleled by developing more covert methods of surveillance by troops in civilian clothing. For example, the Army conducted an ingenious operation in West Belfast. It set up the Four-Square Laundry company. This not only collected and delivered laundry but tested it for explosives residue. This deception was penetrated by the IRA, who attacked the laundry van, killing the soldier driving it, although a female soldier managed to escape. This is the first known example of women serving in an Army covert unit.

The dangers for Army personnel in civilian clothes were also illustrated by a senior NCO working on community relations. He was captured by the IRA. Finding his army ID card they shot him, but he twisted away and the five bullets that hit him went into a leg. Luckily for him, the IRA rapidly departed, not checking whether he was alive or dead.[16]

In 1971 to counter the IRA bombing campaign a few joint Army/RUC covert teams were established to gather intelligence and evidence but these were unsuccessful. So, the Army established a Military Reaction Force (MRF) of troops operating in civilian clothes and cars to conduct surveillance, protection arrests and counter-hijacking. Most personnel were drawn from units in the province on an ad hoc basis. Its activities appear to have been relatively unco-ordinated and insecure. Training was limited, as was administration and command and control. There are many accusations of MRF personnel operating outside the rules of engagement, including conducting illegal killings, but these are very difficult to prove or disprove.

In late 1973 the MRF was replaced by a new covert surveillance unit, the Special Reconnaissance Unit (SRU).[17] This was surrounded by a cloak of operational security. The unit was later renamed 14th Intelligence Company. It had three main detachments, covering Belfast, Londonderry and the south of the province, and rapidly became known simply as 'the Det'.

Volunteers were sought from across the Army and armed forces, including women. The Det used a thorough process of selection and training of its operators, firstly to find out if they had the physical and mental aptitude to work for long periods in small teams in hostile areas and then to develop the necessary skills and tactics to follow suspects through these areas on foot and in cars and use surveillance equipment of ever-increasing sophistication. They also needed extremely high standards of marksmanship to be able to fight off terrorist attacks to kill or capture them.[18]

The IRA was determined to do all it could to capture or kill undercover soldiers or police, and at least four members of the Det were killed during the campaign. Driving or walking through areas of high terrorist activity was therefore inherently dangerous. To do so, passing oneself off as an ordinary civilian, required a very high level of tradecraft, as well as nerves of steel.

Unsurprisingly, the Army often struggled to find sufficient volunteers able to complete selection and training, particularly women. Fortunately, the Royal Marines generated many volunteers, a high proportion of whom went on to serve with distinction. And the SAS provided a small quota of their troops to serve with the Det.[19]

The RUC also developed a covert surveillance organization with similar capabilities to the Det, known as E4A. In setting up the organization they were given considerable advice and assistance by the Det and SAS, who ran the first selection and training course to provide the essential cadre of police officers on which the unit could be built.

The SAS themselves had briefly been deployed shortly after the disorder of 1969, conducting Land Rover-borne reconnaissance operations in uniform in rural areas. But in 1976 a rise of sectarian killings in the south of the province led Prime Minister Harold Wilson to announce that the SAS would deploy to Northern Ireland. Defence Secretary

Roy Mason later announced an increase in the number of SAS in the province. Thereafter the Army maintained a very high level of security, its default position being to never comment on the SAS or other special forces.

Initially focussed on South Armagh, the SAS were soon to be employed all over the province. The key to making best use of them was to gather the type of very high-quality intelligence that would allow their unique skills to be best used, for example in pre-planned ambushes of terrorists in the act of preparing or mounting attacks.[20]

THE TCG SYSTEM

In 1978 I was a company intelligence officer in West Belfast. I had contact with Army source handlers and the Det. I provided some limited support to a couple of SAS operations that failed. I also saw from the sidelines a couple of undercover operations by the Det. I could not help becoming aware of considerable mutual distrust between Special Branch and Army intelligence and source handlers. If there was an HQ guiding these covert operations, I was unaware of it.

In Dunloy in July 1978, a farmer stumbled across some weapons that the IRA had hidden on his land. This intelligence was passed to the SAS who mounted an ambush on the weapons hide. But the farmer's son, not knowing of this, visited the hide and removed a weapon. Thinking he was a terrorist who was about to open fire, the SAS shot him dead.[21]

In the late 1970s a mechanism was created that greatly improved co-ordination of Army and police covert operations. It was known as the Tasking and Co-ordinating Group (TCG). Each of the three assistant chief constables who ran the three RUC areas – Belfast, East and South – was supported by a regional head of Special Branch who acted as their intelligence chief. He also used the TCG to approve, direct and co-ordinate covert intelligence-gathering operations by both police and Army, thus creating previously absent unity of effort.[22]

The approach was that terrorists were best defeated by gathering highly precise intelligence to conduct highly focussed operations. This would be the antithesis of the very imprecise way the Army had operated in the early 1970s. By not repeating the mistakes of the Falls Road curfew or internment, excessive inconvenience to the local people and the resulting resentment could be avoided.

By the early 1980s there would be a considerable level of covert activity with human intelligence gathered by the region's Special Branch source handlers and the regional detachment of the Force Research Unit. The Army's Det and close observation platoons would be conducting covert surveillance operations, as would the police's E4A. There were also some specially trained and equipped Army and RAF helicopters that conducted airborne surveillance and provided 'top cover' to covert operations.

Many operations were mounted to seize ammunition and explosives. Others sought to arrest terrorists assembling or moving weapons and bombs. When terrorists were armed and intent on violence, the SAS were available. For operations where it was intended to arrest terrorists, the police had a special unit that had all the appearance of an ordinary police unit. This was usually known as the HQ Mobile Support Unit (HMSU). As the campaign continued it became increasingly capable.

I returned to West Belfast in 1983 as a battalion intelligence officer to find that the TCG system meant that Army and police human intelligence and covert operations were now much better co-ordinated than in my 1978 tour.

All this sounds routine. It was not, especially when intelligence indicated an imminent attack. On other occasions the various units would be combined. For example, a human source might indicate a major terrorist attack and identify some of those involved. Close observation platoons, the Det and E4A would seek to identify the movement of the terrorists and weapons concerned with the SAS deployed in ambush positions.

To maximize the chances of success, it was important to minimize the chances of an accidental encounter between covert forces and other police and Army units, not least to avoid uniformed security forces accidentally opening fire on covert forces in civilian clothes. The essential deconfliction of covert and overt forces was explained by Mike Jackson:

> the real war of attrition against the IRA was carried out by covert forces working on a very 'close hold', meaning on a strict need to know basis. Some of the time we didn't even know when they were around. To avoid the risk of mistaken identity and a 'blue on blue' friendly fire contact, the standard procedure was to impose a so-called out of bounds area. For example, we might be told that an area of two or three square kilometres was out of bounds to us. Sometimes a quick reaction force would be put on standby in case things went wrong.[23]

The TCG system's intelligence-led, covert, counter-terrorism operations had considerable successes. Some of these were visible in public as bombs and weapons seized, or terrorists arrested or occasionally shot. But terrorist operations disrupted were usually invisible to the public and often hidden from the police and wider Army. On other occasions terrorists slipped through the invisible net. The IRA became even more paranoid about the security of its operations.

The covert units of the Army and RUC used unconventional tactics and equipment. But at its heart it was a combined arms force, where different components were brought together to produce a capability greater than the sum of its parts. Today the TCG system would be described as an 'interagency task force'.

FRAMEWORK OPERATIONS BY THE GREEN ARMY

The Army took to describing the majority of resident and roulement units as the 'Green Army'. Covert forces became known as the 'Black Army', in part because of the black coveralls worn by SAS counterterrorist teams. But the dependence of the TCG approach on very sensitive high-quality intelligence reduced the amount of intelligence passed to Green Army units. Commanders often felt that they were being deprived of intelligence that could be used for their own operations. This was often a source of considerable frustration to commanders of Green Army units. However, the Special Branch and Army covert units were adamant that they could not risk their sources being compromised. Managing this frustration required firm but sympathetic leadership by commanders, particularly at unit and brigade level.

Even if battalions and regiments in Northern Ireland did not form the main effort in the intelligence-led counterterrorist campaign, there was plenty for them to do. Their role became described as framework operations, principally patrolling to gather information and intelligence and to deter and disrupt terrorist movement and attacks. Stopping and checking vehicles was an important part of this. There were many occasions when alert soldiers detected some suspicious sight or activity that led to weapons or bombs being found or terrorists detained. And without large amounts of background information gathered by Green Army units, both human intelligence and covert operations would be less successful.

At times this could all be very monotonous. But IRA information gathering could be both patient and thorough. They were particularly good at identifying patterns set by the security forces and exploiting them to increase the chances of a successful attack. So Army units took considerable precautions to avoid setting patterns by varying the time and level of their activity. This could often lead to friction with the uniformed police, whose modus operandi was regulated by shifts. It could require much tact and diplomacy for commanders both to lead their units and sub-units and to support the police, whose culture was quite different from the Army's.

COUNTERING RADIO-CONTROLLED BOMBS

Earlier in the 1970s the IRA had developed ways of setting off bombs by radio command link, in part as a reaction to the Army's ability to find command wires. And some intelligence had been gained, both from signals intelligence and from captured IEDs. Initially the Army deployed intelligence-gathering and jamming equipment to EOD teams. This was large, power hungry and required a dedicated vehicle. But the deaths at the 1979 Warrenpoint attack, described below, generated a major acceleration in efforts to counter the threat from radio-controlled IEDs by rapidly developing electronic countermeasures (ECM) equipment to detect and jam the command signals.

Much of the detail of this capability and the IRA's attempt to counter it rightly remains classified. But it was an extraordinarily successful programme masterminded under conditions of great secrecy. Much is often made of US 'black programmes', such as reconnaissance satellites or stealth aircraft. The rapid fielding of ECM was a very successful British 'black programme' that not only saved lives but imposed opportunity costs on IRA bomb makers. It deserves to be more widely celebrated as a remarkable military, technological and industrial achievement. Equally remarkable is the way in which soldiers and officers kept the capability secret for so long. And for most of Operation *Banner* no other army in the world had such a capability.

I saw this for myself in 1983 when 1st Battalion, the Light Infantry took over the West Belfast area of operations. After a classified briefing and a package of specialist training, we took over two types of ECM equipment. Boxes the size of large suitcases were installed in our patrol vehicles. And each four-man brick had a man-portable ECM device. Looking like an existing Army radio, the equipment was continually scanning the frequency bands used for command signals that would set off the bombs. If it detected such a signal it would very rapidly jam it. This created a 'bubble' of protection against radio-controlled bombs. Patrol tactics were therefore adjusted to ensure that soldiers stayed within the maximum distance the protection allowed.

The capability depended on a very close relationship between intelligence staffs, HQ Northern Ireland, research and development establishments and trusted industrial partners. As this part of the campaign progressed there was a very close connection between technology and the tactics necessary to maximize its effectiveness. The process became very sophisticated.

COMMAND AND CONTINUITY

CGS, as strategic commander, answered to CDS and the Defence Secretary. He was supported by the Director of Military Operations and a small staff in the military operations directorate. HQ Northern Ireland at Lisburn acted at strategic, operational and tactical levels. The GOC, a lieutenant general, worked closely with the Secretary of State for Northern Ireland and the RUC's Chief Constable. Working to him were senior RAF and Royal Navy commanders as well as the Commander Land Forces – a major general who acted as the land component commander, directing the brigades and Army covert forces support to the regional TCGs.

At the peak of the campaign most units were on four-month operational tours, leaving their families back in the UK or Germany. But there were a considerable number of units and people based in the province on a longer-term basis, located in Protestant areas where the threat of terrorist attack was much lower. They were normally on postings of about two years' duration and were encouraged to bring their families with them. This particularly applied to brigade HQs and HQ Northern Ireland. It meant that at formation level there was a considerable continuity of knowledge and understanding as well as essential contacts with key police officers. This also applied to many high-level intelligence capabilities. On all my Northern Ireland tours I saw the value this added.

HQ Northern Ireland added value in many other ways. It controlled pre-tour training conducted by the two NITAT units in England and Germany, and a small NITAT in the province that trained personnel posted there as individuals. It set the objectives and monitored the output of training conducted by other establishments, for example by the Royal Engineers and Intelligence Corps.

It held the budget for the command and would plan on a multi-year basis. For example, it would develop and then manage a plan for upgrades to security force bases to improve protection against mortar attacks. This required it to think and plan for the long term.

From the early 1970s it was determined to exploit technology, both to gain advantage and improve protection of soldiers. Some key equipment adaptations have been described above. For example, troops were rapidly equipped with body armour. Initially this was conventional simple flak jackets. In the early 1980s these were placed by specially developed body armour using Kevlar fabric fitted with ceramic plates that could stop a high-velocity bullet. On several occasions they did so.

There was a small staff section in the MoD that began the necessary work to turn requirements into equipment in the hands of troops, working closely with equipment staff in HQ Northern Ireland. The HQ also had a senior defence scientist who acted as the command's scientific adviser (SCIAD). A key actor in HQ Northern Ireland, he was supported by a small multi-disciplinary team of scientists, analysts and engineers. He had the authority of the commander, considerable connectivity with intelligence operations and training staff and the MoD's research and development establishments, and the authority and budget to conduct trials and experiments on operations. In 1992 I saw how SCIAD play a key role in developing technology to counter IEDs and conduct surveillance.

HQ Northern Ireland was thus able to control the generation and training of units and personnel that deployed to theatre, shape where resources were invested, formulate the requirements for equipment and manage its introduction into service. This created a virtuous circle that optimized the military capabilities in the province. The system could be mobilized to move very quickly – something I saw for myself on several occasions. The Army's internal study of Operation *Banner* identified that:

An enduring lesson is the need for a comprehensive, multi-disciplinary all arms joint and interagency approach to countering threats, led by the chain of command. This produced a virtuous cycle of effectiveness in Northern Ireland as advances in any one discipline created benefits elsewhere.

Conflict is complex, adversarial and evolutionary, which suggests that in the longer term the advantage goes to the side whose military and non-military processes adapt and evolve fastest. In NI we saw a very closely linked loop responsible for the development of counter terrorist response measures, all of whose components were effectively under command of the theatre HQ, HQ Northern Ireland. This evolved from the very earliest days of the campaign and was a war winner. That loop included all aspects of intelligence (including technical intelligence); forensics; scientific research and development; the development of organizations and minor unit tactics; the conduct of operations; procurement; training; constant review and feedback. It was very much threat-driven, although where possible commanders and staff sought to predict changes to the threat and thereby gain the initiative.

Such speed of reaction had an operational benefit. It continuously undermined the terrorist's apparent initiative, eroding his will to pursue new developments. It also boosted security force confidence and morale. The close linkages between response measures and the fact that the key agencies were under command of the operational level HQ was mentioned above. It would not have been possible, for example, had NITAT not answered to HQ Northern Ireland on issues of tactical doctrine, or if SCIAD had not been an integral part of the same HQ. This overall lesson would seem to be applicable to other theatres. The key is not the scale or variety of the threat, nor the breadth of agencies needing co-ordination. It is the organization and the co-ordination processes which make them work together efficiently.[24]

1979–81 – TWO CRISES

In late August 1979 two IRA bomb attacks administered strategic shocks. The first occurred in Eire, with the assassination of Lord Mountbatten, a cousin of the Queen and former CDS, along with family members and friends.

On the same day lorries carrying troops of 2nd Battalion, the Parachute Regiment (2 Para) were travelling by road to support 1st Battalion, the Queen's Own Highlanders at Bessbrook in South Armagh. They were attacked by a large radio-controlled bomb killing six paratroopers. The Highlanders' commanding officer, Lieutenant Colonel David Blair, and a quick reaction force flew to the site to assist, provide protection and take control of the incident. They set up an incident control point at a nearby gateway, where casualties were being assembled. This place was attacked by a second bomb, killing ten more members of 2 Para, a Highlander and Lieutenant Colonel Blair, bringing the death toll to 18.

Major Mike Jackson, commanding B Company of 2 Para, took charge of the incident. He described his role:

> I knew what I had to do as incident commander: deter further attack, put a cordon around the whole area, preserve the scene of the crime, help investigative agencies do their job, keep other people out. It was a horrifying scene. There was human debris everywhere, in the trees, on the grass verge, in the water. I had seen the effects of bombs before of course but never carnage on this scale. In these circumstances your emotions shut down and the training takes over. Soldiers try to remain as professional as possible. If anyone felt sickened by what he saw he would go into the bushes, so as not to be seen vomiting by his mates.[25]

The next day Prime Minister Margaret Thatcher flew to the province.[26] She first visited HQ 3rd Infantry Brigade at Portadown. She was briefed by the brigade commander, Brigadier David Thorne, who voiced reservations about border security and police capability. He concluded by holding out a single epaulette bearing lieutenant colonel rank badges, saying 'Madam Prime Minister, this is all I have left of a very brave officer, David Blair'. The epaulette was all that could be found of him after Warrenpoint bombing.

The GOC, Lieutenant General Sir Timothy Creasey, had commanded the Sultan of Oman's armed forces as the Dhofar War was successfully concluded. He had two major frustrations that he shared. The first was with the police. Over the preceding three years the Army had at times been sceptical that the RUC would be able to take over from the Army. And there was lingering friction with Special Branch over intelligence.

The second frustration was with the high-level direction of the campaign. Creasey and other senior officers felt that the Malaya campaign had been much better directed, particularly the necessary political, social and economic measures that were needed to complement the security operations of the police and Army. The appointment of a 'supremo' with both political and security authority had been a crucial measure that had directly led to success there. Creasey keenly felt the lack of such an individual, directing not only the Army and police, but also the whole machinery of government.

He put these points to Thatcher. She was non-committal but gave every impression that she better understood the Army's work. She then asked to visit Crossmaglen, even then the Army's most besieged base. Arriving by helicopter she spent time in the operations room and talked to soldiers. This was the first of her many meetings with troops and was greatly appreciated.

Thatcher then visited the RUC chief constable in Armagh. Kenneth Newman took a different line to Creasey. He saw deaths in the province as reducing and the police as increasing in capability, with greatly improved covert surveillance capabilities. As security continued to improve and conditions in the province normalized, policing itself would have to become more normalized. The Army's proposal for a supremo would bring movement to police primacy to stop. Newman told Thatcher he needed a thousand more police officers, which could allow a proportionate reduction in troop levels. Thatcher agreed this measure.

After Thatcher returned to London, she found that most official opinion in the MoD and Northern Ireland Office agreed with the chief constable that the 'supremo' proposal should not be agreed. Instead, a new Director and Co-ordinator of Intelligence would work in the Northern Ireland Office, specifically tasked with co-ordinating intelligence gathering by the Army, RUC and MI5.

The first holder of the new role was Sir Maurice Oldfield, an extremely experienced senior civilian intelligence officer. He quickly earned a reputation as a very good listener. By all accounts he added value by harmonizing intelligence gathering and reducing the friction among the three organizations that conducted it. Friction between Army and police further reduced at the end of 1979 when General Creasey departed the province to return to Oman. He was succeeded by Lieutenant General Richard Lawson. He supported police primacy both with words and deeds, as did successive GOCs. It is probable that displaying the emotional and interpersonal skills necessary had been a factor in their selection.

THE IRA HUNGER STRIKES

In 1981 the security situation deteriorated again. The efforts to criminalize terrorist activity undermined the terrorists' legitimacy as 'freedom fighters'. Previous nationalist efforts to halt this process having failed, IRA prison members in Northern Ireland jails embarked on a hunger strike. This greatly resonated with nationalists across the province.

The first prisoner to refuse food was Bobby Sands. Other prisoners joined the strike at regular intervals to maintain pressure on London. Sands died on 5 May. Major rioting in Belfast rapidly broke out, the first for many years, leading to two civilian deaths. For the first time the RUC also made a large-scale deployment to counter the rioters. They were successful and did not have to withdraw from the streets, a development welcomed by both the Army and police.

Tension rapidly rose and disorder in Catholic areas greatly increased, amplified by Prime Minister Thatcher's unwillingness to countenance concessions. Polarization between the two communities increased, as did IRA attacks, particularly against off-duty UDR personnel.

The key result of the strike was political. Six weeks after beginning his strike Bobby Sands was elected MP for the Fermanagh–South Tyrone Westminster constituency. Sands' funeral was reported to have been attended by 100,000 mourners. After ten men had starved themselves to death, the strike was eventually called off following quiet British concessions. The effect on Sinn Fein was decisive. Previously a niche political party, seen as nothing more than the political wing of the IRA, its leadership came to embrace a dual strategy of political activity and armed action. At the October 1981 Sinn Fein conference activist Danny Morrison asked, 'who here really believes we can win the war through the ballot box? But will anyone here object if, with a ballot paper in this hand and an Armalite in the other, we take power in Ireland?'[27]

1982–2007 – THE LONG TAIL

It would take 25 years from the end of the hunger strike until the end of Operation *Banner*. The first half of this period would be spent in continual conflict with the IRA. The second half would see the first and second IRA ceasefires and the negotiations leading to the Good Friday Agreement, followed by its implementation and finally both policing and the Army presence 'normalized'.

Increasing sophistication of the undercover counterterrorist campaigns helped reduce the IRA's advantages in Northern Ireland. By the early 1990s the RUC effectively had the lead for security. In urban areas most Army patrols had an accompanying police officer. The RUC would still require military support until the end of Operation *Banner* in 2007 though.

In 1987 General Sir Nigel Bagnall became CGS. He had never deployed on Operation *Banner*. This meant that Bagnall was unencumbered by the tramlines of conventional wisdom. Bagnall was troubled by what he found, particularly the relatively attritional nature of the campaign and the limitations that the policy of police primacy imposed on the Army's ability to gain asymmetric advantage over the IRA. The police often wanted to use troops as if they were simply low-quality police, guarding checkpoints and police stations, rather than exploiting soldiers' training, motivation and desire to use their initiative to gain advantage over the terrorists. Army operations needed greater coherence and co-ordination.

He set in hand a strategic assessment. It was conducted in conditions of great secrecy by the Director of Military Operations and a small group of four officers: a brigadier, a colonel, a Royal Marines major and a captain. Bagnall and the team identified four areas where the Army could gain advantage. The first was to upgrade the capabilities of Army special forces in the province. The second was to improve the Army's intelligence capabilities. The third was to better exploit technology to protect troops and gather intelligence. These three initiatives were complementary, each seeking to gain advantage, but simultaneously amplifying each other's effects – the whole becoming greater than the sum of the parts. Bagnall assigned a protégé of his, Lieutenant General John Waters, to the role of GOC, with directions to 'wake the place up'.

Bagnall's strategy had a fourth pillar, a new approach to the province's border with the Irish Republic. The permeability of the border had been a constant frustration since 1970, the Republic providing a safe haven for terrorists. By the 1980s Mrs Thatcher had become so frustrated with this that she agitated for building a border fence. In great secrecy a Royal Engineer colonel was despatched to Israel to assess the use of fencing by the Israeli security forces. The Army assessed that for the fence to effectively interdict movement of terrorists and their equipment into Northern Ireland, it would have to be under continuous observation and backed up by quick reaction forces to intercept suspicious movement, as well as deal with any efforts by civilians to breach the obstacle. This would require assigning a large number of troops to both roles, requiring a significant increase to the size of the Army in Northern Ireland, with a resulting reverberating impact on the Army, including disrupting training and readiness. The General Staff breathed a collective sigh of relief when the idea was dropped.

But the border still needed addressing. Bagnall decided to assign an entire Army brigade to border security. The HQ of 3rd Infantry Brigade was reactivated. Existing Army units were assigned areas of responsibility along the border. Great energy was put into implementing the new concept and organization. But the police were strongly opposed to the idea. To them it ran counter to the existing police divisions, who regularly dealt with the border and whose practical co-operation with the Gardai, the Republic's police, was slowly improving. Sir John Hermon, the RUC chief constable, opposed the initiative and the formation never received the intelligence co-operation from Special Branch so essential to operational success. The border brigade initiative had the effect of eroding the unity of effort between police and Army – a principle of counterinsurgency. After Bagnall retired, 3rd Brigade's role was changed so that instead of being a border brigade it was responsible for the south-east of the province, its borders aligned with the RUC Southern Region. The police welcomed this re-alignment.

However, the rest of Bagnall's strategy increased the effectiveness of both the Army and police in the province. I saw this for myself in 1992, when I was second in command of 2nd Battalion, the Light Infantry, deployed to South Armagh. I observed that Bagnall's three other initiatives were all making a difference in that most dangerous part of the province, even if secrecy meant that the great majority of soldiers and officers were oblivious of them.

For example, there was a major effort to develop a long-term strategy to use emerging surveillance technology both to gain more intelligence and to provide better early warning of attacks. A package of high-technology sensors was installed on OPs across the province, fitting advanced radars and thermal imaging cameras to the network of watchtowers.

Another project, codenamed *Convertible*, aimed to greatly improve surveillance from the air. Large powerful surveillance devices would be mounted on three airships. These would be able to loiter above the province for days on end. An airship was purchased, and the concept was trialled in early 1990s. Had the IRA not moved to a ceasefire and peace talks, the airships would have entered service in the late 1990s.

For troops operating in the staunchly nationalist areas, operations could have a very high tempo. In 1991 1st Battalion, the Prince of Wales's Own Regiment of Yorkshire spent six months supporting the RUC in Belfast. The regimental sergeant major, then Warrant Office Class 1 Mick Haynes, remembered the battalion's role and the leadership of its commanding officer, Lieutenant Colonel Alastair Duncan:

> We deployed to Belfast in November 1991. In 180-plus days the Battalion had over 200 reported serious incidents – shootings, nail bomb attacks, Improvised Explosive Devices, riots and weapons finds. At times with reinforcements from other units our strength went up to 1,200 men with our area of responsibility covering all of West and North Belfast. The official mission was to assist the RUC in returning the province to normalcy. The implied task given to us by Alastair was to ensure we would not give the public any reason to support the men of violence. When on the streets we were to be smart, courteous and at all times be firm, fair and efficient, setting the standard for others.
>
> A serious incident usually involved the company commander getting on the ground to sort out the response and follow up. The RUC would invariably turn up and liaison with them was crucial. Alastair, keenly aware that his commanders needed to get on with their jobs whilst not displacing the RUC, had a strategy of deploying with his small rover group, eight of us, usually in two Snatch Land Rovers, so he could effectively manage the interface with the police, which he did with consummate skill.
>
> Sometimes I thought we got a little too involved in the action. In North Belfast there had been a nail bomb attack on an A Company patrol. The patrol had gone firm and were consolidating the position when petrol bombs began to be thrown. I had to caution Alastair that we were a little too far forward when the petrol bombs were landing behind us, Alastair chuckling, like a schoolboy, as we ran back through the flames.
>
> ... his overriding personal mission was to bring everybody back safe and sound, and near misses aside, he achieved that and the award of the OBE was testament to his exceptional leadership. He did say it stood for Other Buggers' Efforts, as always praising his officers and soldiers, but it was him that led the Battalion to excel.[28]

This is a moving tribute to an officer who later served with distinction in Bosnia. But many retired senior officers have reflected that whilst tours in the province would allow soldiers, low-level leaders and commanders to practise against a real enemy, there was an ingrained attitude of commanders to do all they could to bring their soldiers back alive. This was understandable, but over time it had an effect of sapping the Army's aggression and killer instinct and instilling a form of ingrained tactical caution. Field Marshal Lord Guthrie observed: 'Northern Ireland certainly kept the Army's blade sharp, but only at a junior leadership level. The strategy of no casualties and minimum force had blunted the Army's offensive spirit and meant that its step had begun to falter'.[29]

THE IRA RURAL CAMPAIGN

The police were now in the lead in West and North Belfast in 1992, supported by a single battalion – clear evidence of progress. (In the late 1970s the area required three battalions, and the police were most definitely not in the lead.) But as the Army and police gained advantage over the terrorist networks in Belfast, in the south-east of the province, the IRA continued to pose a more enduring challenge.

In the late 1980s the IRA in East Tyrone greatly increased their attacks. Their aim appears to have been to achieve such a tempo of successful attacks on the security forces, as to force a withdrawal, thus creating a rural 'no go area' controlled by the IRA. Security force bases would be destroyed by large bombs. Attempts to rebuild installations would be thwarted by attacks on the engineers and contractors working on them. In addition, there was an increased level of attacks against off duty personnel. There was a long-term contest across the region between the IRA and Army and RUC intelligence and covert forces.

An Army success occurred at Loughgall in May 1987. Intelligence indicated that a major IRA attack was planned to destroy a small police station. The IRA stole a digger and placed a large bomb in its bucket. Driving alongside a van full of armed terrorists, it was followed by 14 Company personnel in civilian vehicles. To do so in the narrow rural roads and lanes without arousing suspicions took surveillance skills of the highest order. Two police volunteers took the places of local constables. The van stopped outside the police station and IRA fighters with assault rifles got out and opened fire. At the same time the stolen digger crashed through the station wall and terrorists lit the fuse of a large bomb it carried. As this point a waiting SAS team opened fire from ambush positions, during which the bomb detonated badly, damaging the station and wounding a policeman. Eight IRA men attacking the station were all killed, as was an innocent civilian who was driving past the police station.

Despite the civilian death, this was one of the most successful intelligence-led ambushes of the campaign. One of those shot was Jim Lynagh, the charismatic and determined leader of the IRA in East Tyrone. It has been assessed that during the campaign the Tyrone IRA group lost at least 53 fighters. Twenty-eight of these were killed between 1987 and 1992, evidence of the intensity of the conflict between them and the security forces.

But this was not a one-way exchange. In late 1989 the IRA attacked a permanent checkpoint at Derryard. Crashing a dump truck fitted with improvised armour into the base, terrorists dismounted and moved forward using rifles, grenades and a flamethrower to clear the rooms inside. Two soldiers were killed, and the survivors withdrew to the sangars and fired into their own base.

This was one of the few occasions in which IRA fighters engaged in a direct close combat assault on an Army base. Had they continued to press forward the attack, there might have been more casualties to both sides. But the attackers had not identified that the defenders, soldiers of the King's Own Scottish Borderers, had a four-man patrol outside the base, with the mission of deterring any attack. As soon as the fighting started the patrol rushed to fire at the attackers. Surprised by an effective counterattack the IRA withdrew, abandoning their improvised assault vehicle. As a result of the attack, troops in rural areas were issued with a rifle-launched anti-tank grenade to give them a capability against improvised armoured vehicles. Such vehicles were also used in some of the IRA's efforts to shoot down helicopters.

The IRA had long had a very strong presence in South Armagh, where there was deep resistance to Belfast's authority, powerful family ties across the border and a long history of smuggling. Indeed, by the late 1970s the ability of the IRA in the area to place roadside bombs was so great that the Army ceased to routinely travel by road. Instead, all movement to and from Army bases forward of Bessbrook Mill would be done by helicopter, Prime Minister Thatcher visiting Crossmaglen in this way twice in 1979.

As well as the ingrained hostility of most of the people of South Armagh, the terrain was itself a formidable obstacle to movement on foot. Much of it was very boggy and there were many small hills. The fields of the many farms were delineated by thick Blackthorn hedges, which were difficult to cross – particularly for infantrymen on patrols several days long, where they carried food, water and ammunition for the duration of the patrol. As roads and tracks were avoided for fear of triggering a bomb, movement was very slow. And IRA gunmen knew how to shoot straight and were expert in laying ambushes.

To counter this threat, several permanent OPs were built on top of the region's high hills. And to dominate the border area between Crossmaglen and South Armagh and complicate IRA movement, four 'Golf Towers' were built, sitting on top of large bunkers in which a dozen or so soldiers would live. Initially, these overt OPs made use of powerful binoculars, telescope cameras and the first-generation image-intensifying night sights that the Army had in the early 1970s. But these were gradually replaced by surveillance devices of growing sophistication.

This initiative helped suppress terrorist attacks in the areas that was overwatched. But for the 1980s and 1990s South Armagh accounted for about a quarter of Army casualties. Before I embarked on an operational tour in the area as a battalion second in command, I sought out a friend for advice. He had just spent a year commanding the SAS in the province. I asked his advice about the region. 'The best thing you can all do in South Armagh is your very best to stay alive,' he told me.

Another ingenious IRA attack in South Armagh was mounted on the permanent vehicle checkpoint south of Newry that controlled the main Belfast to Dublin highway. The IRA converted a stolen van into a guided missile. In May 1992 a hijacked digger used under cover of darkness built a ramp from a road to the Belfast to Dublin railway line. The van, with a large bomb on board, had its wheels modified to travel on the rails. It was sent north, exploding close to the sentry post. The soldier inside was killed and much of the base badly damaged, although the rest of the occupants in heavily fortified 'hardened' accommodation were unscathed.

Perhaps the most ambitious IRA shooting attack in the region was the 'Battle of Newry Road' in September 1993. The IRA had assembled five armed trucks carrying gunmen armed with machine guns and assault rifles to shoot down an RAF Puma helicopter. But they had not reckoned with two Lynx helicopters armed with machine guns that were acting as escorts. These were reinforced with two other armed Lynxes and a running gun battle developed between the helicopters and the IRA vehicles. It lasted over half an hour, with the IRA claiming to have fired thousands of rounds. Between them, the Army Lynx aircraft and infantry that had landed from a Lynx who engaged terrorists that were thought to be armed, fired 200 rounds. The lower number was a product of the very tight rules of engagement under which the Army operated. This was the most intense gun battle in South Armagh during the whole campaign.

At irregular intervals throughout the 1990s the South Armagh IRA mounted sniper attacks, sometimes using assault rifles, sometimes with a heavy-calibre .5-inch Barrett sniper rifle. These claimed the lives of two policemen and seven soldiers, including Bombardier Stephen Restorick, the last soldier killed by the IRA. This threat was reinforced by an IRA information operation, which included road signs bearing the warning 'sniper at work'. Several attempts to catch the sniper team or teams were unsuccessful, but in 1997 a covert operation arrested four IRA men and captured a Barrett rifle.

In the later 1980s, the IRA extended attacks to the UK mainland and British forces in Europe. A 1988 covert operation where the SAS killed three IRA fighters in Gibraltar was controversial, as the IRA members were unarmed at the time they were killed. But the subsequent inquest accepted that the terrorists were on reconnaissance and that the soldiers had honestly believed that they were armed. The incident inflicted some damage on IRA operations, as the organization desperately searched for informers. Most of the attacks in Europe were against off-duty Army and RAF personnel. In one of them a member of the RAF was killed, as was his six-month-old baby daughter. The necessary security precautions added considerable friction to the Army's way of life in the UK mainland and Germany. Nevertheless, they could not completely prevent attacks, as shown in February 1991, when the IRA mortared Downing Street, narrowly missing killing Prime Minister John Major and other government members.

THE ENDGAME

From the early 1990s, brigade commanders arriving in Northern Ireland were graduates of the Higher Command and Staff Course. On arrival some asked to see the campaign plan. There was not one. So, in 1992, the GOC, Lieutenant General Roger Wheeler commissioned the writing of one by then Lieutenant Colonel David Richards, a name that will reappear later.

This increased effort to develop the military campaign coincided with beginnings of a peace process, although most of those involved in either activity were unaware of the other work. By the early 1990s the IRA was prepared to enter peace talks and an intermediary told the British government so. Begun by the Conservative government of John Major, these were taken to a successful conclusion by Tony Blair's New Labour government, resulting in a power-sharing peace agreement and decommissioning of terrorist weapons. But a small proportion of IRA members were dissatisfied with this political compromise. They formed a splinter group, the so-called Real IRA, which was responsible for the August 1998 bombing of Omagh that killed 29 people, the worst single bombing attack of the conflict.

During the period between the 1998 Belfast Agreement, also known as the Good Friday Agreement, and the return to a fully devolved government in 2007, the Army lowered its profile and gradually reduced the number of troops. The UDR and RUC were disbanded, the latter being replaced by a new Police Service of Northern Ireland.

During this period there were two occasions of large-scale disorder, where the police needed military support. The first was at Drumcree, where an illegal Orange Order march was blocked by the building of a large physical barrier and the deployment of hundreds of troops to deal with aggressive crowds. The second was at the Holy Cross primary school between June and November 2001, where Protestant extremists attempted to block Catholic children from attending a Catholic girls' school in a Protestant area. The Army provided troops and armoured vehicles to support the police.

Operation *Banner* ended in 2007. But there was some residual Army support to the police, with specialists including EOD teams remaining. And the conflict was not over, as shown by the killing of two sappers by dissident republican terrorists in 2009. The chief constable asked for a team from the Special Reconnaissance Regiment (SRR) to be deployed to assist the police in surveillance operations against such terrorists.

OPERATION *BANNER* ASSESSED

The conflict was not a total war, but a limited one. The republican and loyalist terrorists, as well as the British government, Army and RUC all deliberately limited their ends, ways and means. This certainly reduced casualties, compared with many less limited civil wars. This may have helped with the negotiated ending of the conflict.

Many who served in the second half of Operation *Banner* also consider that attrition of the IRA greatly contributed to the moves towards a ceasefire. By the 1990s anyone who became an IRA fighter stood a good chance of being killed, wounded or jailed. Some of the Army's experts on Northern Ireland have wondered if senior republican leaders, such as Gerry Adams and Martin McGuinness, looked forward to any of their children becoming IRA fighters against such odds?[30]

The truth may never be known, but there can be little doubt that the Green Army, Army intelligence gathering, the Det and the SAS must have greatly contributed to a sense of IRA vulnerability to Army and police intelligence, informers and surveillance. This slowed the rate at which attacks could be organized and increased the ability of the security forces to disrupt attacks before they were launched. With an apparent unwavering will of the British government, Army and RUC and ever-improving intelligence gathering and covert capabilities, the prospects for violence achieving a British withdrawal from the province must have seemed vanishingly small.

In the absence of other wars, Northern Ireland deployments had a positive effect on unit level-cohesion and developed the confidence of tactical commanders. But it reduced the Army's readiness for war, particularly at formation level.

CONDUCT OF THE CAMPAIGN

Some of the Army's actions made the situation worse. These included the imposition of a curfew in the Falls Road area of Belfast, mass arrests to intern suspected terrorists based on out-of-date intelligence, abuse of detainees during interrogations and the shooting dead of civilians in Londonderry during 'Bloody Sunday'. These all combined to greatly increase support for the IRA in the province's Catholic minority, in Eire and in the US. These were all serious mistakes, but the Army learned from these self-inflicted reverses. They were not repeated. Often the Army acted as an agile and learning organization. Many innovations and adaptations were driven from the bottom up rather than top down but were recognized and supported by the chain of command. The Falls Road curfew and Bloody Sunday were rapidly acknowledged by the Army as self-imposed strategic reverses.

From the Army's point of view the campaign was adequately resourced. Examples include the rapid reinforcement to build up forces for the major internment operation in 1972. And at the height of the campaign over half the helicopter hours available to the Army and RAF were being used in the province. Moreover, there is no suggestion that equipment was inadequate either in capability or in numbers. The Army's ends, ways and means were in balance. This would not be achieved in later campaigns.

This was assisted by the campaign continuity achieved by HQ Northern Ireland, the close coupling between operations and training through the vehicle of the NITATs and a mechanism that fused intelligence, scientific advice and a rapidly responding equipment organization outside the province to great success.

The Army's post-conflict analysis assessed that Operation *Banner* often seemed like 'a campaign without a campaign plan', particularly as the Army became increasingly attuned to the operational level of war after the late 1980s. But this was addressed in the early 1990s. This was late in the day, but those involved did not know that the campaign would end as quickly as it did.

The Army also considered that Operation *Banner* was limited by the lack of a 'campaign authority'. It assessed that:

> By 1980 almost all the military structures which eventually defeated PIRA [the Provisional IRA] were in place. It is revealing to examine why it then took another quarter of a century to end the campaign. In retrospect some signs are visible. There was no single authority in overall charge of the direction of the campaign, but rather three agencies, often poorly co-ordinated: Stormont followed by the Northern Ireland Office; the MoD; and the RUC. From a military perspective, for most of the campaign there was little coherence and synergy. There was little evidence of a strategic vision and no long-term plan. Below the level of Westminster White Papers there was no clearly articulated strategy or view of the future and how to achieve it which involved all the relevant agencies. As a result, the 'wheel was often reinvented' and progress was unnecessarily slow. Action against terrorists was not linked closely to addressing the causes of the problem.
>
> Ministers and civil servants were sometimes reluctant to engage in the comprehensive, fully co-ordinated cross-government activity which the Army would recognize as a campaign plan. That is a good reason for the need to take very firm action to ensure that they are engaged in, and convinced of the need to abide by, the process. This will not be easy.[31]

Of course, the late 1970s policy of police primacy did set out a security strategy. This was followed by the evolution of the TCG system of covert counterterrorist operations, complemented by framework operations by the Green Army – a broad operational design for security operations that underpinned the rest of the campaign. General Creasey's 1979 request for appointment of a 'supremo' with authority over all security and government action in the province was turned down.

If the Army was right to complain about the lack of interagency strategy and operational direction, who should have therefore been the 'campaign authority'? The answer is as clear as it is simple: it should have been the Cabinet minister with political authority for the province, the Secretary of State for Northern Ireland, supported by the Northern Ireland Office. But the evidence suggests that most secretaries of state did not fulfil this role as comprehensively as they should have done. This would not be the Army's only campaign where appointed political leadership failed to energize and combine together the necessary whole of government activity.

CHAPTER 6

OPERATION *DESERT STORM*

This story begins in 1945 and ends in 1991.

As the Soviets, US and British closed in on the Third Reich, they planned for the occupation of Germany. The British would occupy north-western Germany, the US the southern half of the country and the Soviets eastern Germany. Berlin, the capital, would be split into similar geographic sectors for three-power occupation. French sectors were later added.

Agreements were made for units and personnel of the three Western powers to travel to Berlin by road, rail and air. All four powers' forces, personnel and family also had freedom of movement throughout the whole city, regulated by a single checkpoint between East and West Berlin – Checkpoint Charlie.

As the Cold War worsened and East Germany became communist, Berlin became a flashpoint – a barometer of Cold War tensions, such as those demonstrated by the Berlin airlift in 1948–49 and the construction of the Berlin Wall in 1961.

By 1975 these crises were long past. For British troops in the Berlin Infantry Brigade, the city could have an electric atmosphere, with East Berlin occupied by a Soviet brigade, the four occupying powers taking it in turns to guard former deputy Führer Rudolf Hess and regular patrols along the Berlin Wall. The brigade was at very high readiness and units were regularly tested in their ability to get themselves and their equipment out of barracks and to battle positions in a couple of hours.

The British had a small urban training centre, the size of a small hamlet. A much bigger facility the size of a small city block lay on a US Army training area called Doughboy City. These facilities helped the brigade achieve a relatively high level of proficiency in the tactics and techniques of urban warfare. They could also manoeuvre troops and armoured vehicles in the city's large forest parks.

Berlin was an amazing city to live in. It had nightlife that ranged from glittering to sordid, catering for all tastes. For those with a thirst for culture, both West and East Berlin had magnificent museums and galleries and boasted no fewer than three opera houses. Going to the opera in East Berlin could be an inexpensive adventure. But for the combat arms, three infantry battalions, an armoured squadron and an engineer squadron, Berlin could be a military goldfish bowl, where minor failures or disciplinary incidents could lead to critical responses by the British HQ.

There was a loosely co-ordinated plan between the British, French and US forces to defend the city. It was anticipated that the Warsaw Pact would strike the city's three airfields and destroy the allies' signals intelligence-gathering facilities. It was certain that there would be some attacks to capture places of strategic significance, such as the Reichstag building just across the Berlin Wall. After these initial attacks the Warsaw Pact would have two options. The first was to launch an all-out attack on West Berlin. This would result in significant casualties. It could also destroy much of the city, thus rendering it difficult to exploit economically after the war ended. The second option was to mask the city with East German troops and paramilitary police. For much of the period, plans were incrementally refined and adjusted, but no significant innovations were made.

In the late 1980s, there was an effort to apply the growing body of manoeuvre warfare thinking in the rest of the Army to the Berlin Brigade. In what was at the time a highly classified initiative, both the British and US brigades looked at options to mount offensive operations from West Berlin. Tempting targets were a ring of autobahns similar to the M25 and an East German railway that also ringed the city. If the defenders secretly concentrated forces they might be able to mount raids in up to battalion strength to attack these routes, thus disrupting the flow of reinforcements and supplies to the Warsaw Pact forces fighting in West Germany.

I was a company commander in Berlin at the end of the Cold War. The US Berlin brigade was in deadly earnest about this, and had twice as many tanks and armoured vehicles as the British brigade, as well as the only artillery battery in Berlin. The British brigade had less combat power and seemed less interested in using Berlin as a platform for offensive action into East Germany.

In November 1989 the British troops in Berlin were astonished to find that the Berlin Wall had been breached by East Berlin citizens reacting to a surprise announcement by the East German government that restrictions on travel out of the country had been abandoned. Previously hostile East German border guards stood aside as East German citizens poured through the existing crossing point at Checkpoint Charlie and knocked holes in the concrete slabs of the wall. The British brigade was not put on a war footing, as such an action would have sent entirely the wrong signal. Instead, it deployed small parties of troops with containers of tea and coffee for the huge crowds of East and West Berliners that gathered on the western side of the Wall.

The 1st Battalion, the Light Infantry had a late entry officer serving who had been a private soldier in Berlin in 1961 when the Berlin Wall was constructed. For him the city had turned full circle. Little were he and the rest of the brigade to know that this unexpected shift of previously frozen strategic tectonic plates would allow the deployment of a British armoured division to fight in an unexpected war.

OPTIONS FOR CHANGE – A FALSE START

In early 1990, the MoD began another defence review. Called 'Options for Change', it was unashamedly an exercise to realize financial savings by reducing the size and cost of the armed services. Despite politicians' statements that this review was 'strategy led', no one in the MoD could convincingly pretend it was anything other than an effort to realize a peace dividend from the end of the Cold War.

On 25 July its initial findings were announced to parliament by Defence Secretary Tom King. As well as naval and air reductions, the Army would be about 120,000 strong, reducing to two divisions, one in Germany and one in the UK. There would also be 'a strategic reserve division bringing together amphibious, parachute, airmobile and armoured formations with roles also in Europe or in national defence.'[1]

THE UNFORESEEN IRAQI ATTACK ON KUWAIT

In August 1990, even as the Soviet Union was disintegrating and Germany was unifying, Saddam Hussein, the president of Iraq, launched a surprise attack on Kuwait. The US led an international coalition to defend neighbouring Saudi Arabia, rapidly moving ships, aircraft, a marine expeditionary force and XVIII (US) Airborne Corps, with airborne, air assault and mechanized divisions. The Coalition was an unprecedented international grouping of forces from 42 nations. It was commanded by the US Central Command (CENTCOM) led by US Army general Norman Schwartzkopf.

The initial British response was to deploy aircraft and ships to the region in Operation *Granby*. But on 14 September 1990, the MoD announced the deployment of 7th Armoured Brigade to join the US-led Operation *Desert Shield* defending Saudi Arabia from an Iraqi attack. The formation was assigned to the US Marines assembling in Kuwait to protect eastern Saudi Araba.

Neither the MoD nor the Army had any form of contingency plan for this. Such plans as existed for land operations outside NATO were for reinforcement of Cyprus or Belize, non-combatant evacuation operations or an operation along the lines of the Falklands, all using the Royal Marine commando brigade and 5 Airborne Brigade. So new plans had to be improvised.

Whilst the initial US Army deployment included two light divisions, it quickly became clear that the large number of Iraqi armoured and mechanized formations and the open desert terrain meant that any British Army contribution would have to come from the armoured divisions of 1 (BR) Corps. The corps commander, Lieutenant General Charles Guthrie, chose 7th Armoured Brigade for the deployment. It was well equipped with Challenger and Warrior armoured vehicles. Two of its three battlegroups had trained at BATUS during the summer and Guthrie considered that the brigade was well led.

The brigade's commander, Brigadier Patrick Cordingley, was summoned to HQ 1 (BR) Corps for a day of lengthy briefings. He was then sucked into a whirlwind of planning, preparation and a press conference, later describing the challenge faced by the brigade:

> No author writing an exercise for students at the Staff College could possibly have produced a more fanciful scenario than that given to me by the corps commander. He told me that during the next 26 days our establishment would double in size. We were then to move the brigade and its 117 Challenger tanks to Saudi Arabia, in order to counter Iraqi aggression. We would be operating under the tactical control of the US Marine Corps. 'Oh and by the way the first ship leaves in two weeks' time', he added …
>
> I thought long as I travelled back to Fallingbostel just south of Soltau, where the majority of the brigade was stationed. The magnitude of the undertaking was clear to me, but I had to make light of it. It was my job to be positive and give confidence. If there were concerns of an unusual nature, they were mine to seek a solution to and not to share unnecessarily with my subordinates. Command is an isolated position. However, I had been trained to cope when running my own regiment for three years. But then we had been guarding Western Europe. Now it was going to be harder.[2]

Three days later Cordingley and his staff departed on a reconnaissance. The brigade's heavy armour, particularly the Challenger tanks, would be greatly welcomed by the 1st (US) Marine Division. It had two tank battalions. But they were equipped with the M60, a less modern tank with a less powerful gun and less well protected. They had no infantry fighting vehicles and only three armoured engineer vehicles. The British brigade would become the Marines' counterattack formation.

But both the US Marine Division and US Army officers in HQ Central Command (CENTCOM) showed polite doubt about the reliability of British equipment. This was because the US military had formed adverse impressions of British armoured vehicles. These came from reports by US attachés in London, as well as the many contacts between the British and US armies, not only through the numerous exchange and liaison personnel, but also resulting from the many interactions in Germany, not least on exercises. These provided abundant evidence of the unreliability of British tanks and other armoured vehicles. There were also years of adverse comment in the British media. Whilst BATUS provided an excellent facility for field firing, unequalled by any other Army, the British had conspicuously failed to invest in force-on-force training with laser weapon effects simulators, as had the US Army. So, 7th Brigade would have to demonstrate the credibility of its combat capability.

Army planning for a war accepted that units would not be up to the strength necessary to fight in war. They would need to grow from 'peace establishment' to 'warfighting establishment'. This would be achieved by mobilizing regular reservists to fill gaps. The MoD decided that reservists would not be mobilized. So regular personnel were found across the corps to fill these gaps. Many soldiers and officers of the brigade's units employed elsewhere sought to rejoin their parent unit, to test themselves in war alongside their friends and close comrades. Some succeeded in this.

In addition, 7th Brigade HQ increased from 23 people to almost 80. The tank regiments acquired an extra troop of tanks and 16 people. The Staffordshire Regiment (The Prince of Wales's) grew by over 200 soldiers and officers. The brigade's artillery, 40 Field Regiment, expanded from almost 500 to over a thousand. Much of this growth was to allow the regiment to handle and fire large amounts of ammunition, something that did not happen in peacetime training.

Not all the brigade's equipment was the most up to date model. So a large amount of equipment was moved around by corps HQ. It was necessary to take spare parts from all over the corps to get enough to the Gulf to keep 7th Brigade operational. The reliability of some key equipment, especially Challenger tanks, was of great concern, all the way up the chain of command from the vehicle crews to the top of the Army.

Normally the brigade would receive logistic support from the 1st Armoured Division, which would have pushed forward combat supplies – ammunition, food water and fuel – as well as spare parts. These would have been stockpiled in divisional supply areas. And the division would receive casualties and broken equipment from the brigade. As 7th Brigade would be operating independently from the division, it would still need this logistic support.

This would now be provided through a Force Maintenance Area, which would deploy before the brigade, in order to receive the brigade's troops and equipment. Once the brigade had arrived, the area's support would allow the brigade to operate and fight within the Marine Expeditionary Force (MEF), without causing any drag on that formation.

By 28 September the brigade's armoured vehicles had been sent by rail to the German port of Bremerhaven, for loading onto chartered ships. On 7 October the HQ of the Force Maintenance Area arrived in the Saudi port of Al Jubail, with advance parties from the brigade arriving three days later and the main body of troops arriving by air from 15 October. The first ship arrived on 18 October and the majority of vessels arrived by the end of the month. Inevitably, some ships overtook others. Concurrently, combat supplies were arriving by sea. The ammunition was to be sufficient for 42 days' combat at normal planning rates, or 14 days at 'intense rates'.

Armoured vehicles unloaded at the port were taken by civilian low loaders to a concentration area 10 miles to the west at Fadili. Here they were married up with the units they belonged to. As soon as vehicles were ready, the brigade threw itself into an intensive regime of training exercises. The brigade had three combat units, each forming battlegroups that combined tank squadrons with armoured infantry companies. Two units that had trained that year in Canada, the 1st Battalion the Staffordshire Regiment, known as the 'Staffords', and the Scots Dragoon Guards, refreshed tactical skills that had been practiced there in a new environment. The Queen's Royal Irish Hussars had only moved to Germany in 1990, and had not trained in Canada, so were less well trained than the other two battlegroups. They used this period to catch up on working with the infantry and artillery. Like the rest of the brigade, they put great effort into learning to live and fight in the desert. The exercises also helped integrate the many new troops who had reinforced the brigade.

A large live-firing range was carved out of some empty desert. Named 'Jerboa Range', it was used by the squadrons, companies and battlegroups to fire their weapons, in order to test that their accuracy and functions had not degraded during the sea voyage. The brigade conducted very ambitious live-firing exercises. The US Marines were already doing this, but the brigade had much greater ambitions – to conduct live fire and manoeuvre exercises similar to those conducted at BATUS. This would help them master the unfamiliar desert terrain and practise tactical drills with live ammunition, in a way that the Army only otherwise did in Canada.

The safety rules were reduced from the rules applied at BATUS, to allow the greater freedom of manoeuvre so necessary in war. The principle was that soldiers and commanders were responsible for their own safety. Even so, five soldiers were injured, mainly from fragments from exploding grenades that they had hurled too close to their positions. The exercises worked up from platoon and troop to company and squadron level, incorporating artillery and mortars and engineers breaching obstacles.

The exercises finished by mid-November, by which time the brigade was very confident in its ability to fight a combined arms battle in the desert. Brigadier Cordingley declared 7th Brigade as ready for operations with the US Marines. The initial US deployment included the 24th Infantry Division (Mechanized). It had three armoured brigades. So 7th Brigade increased the Coalition armoured formations by a third.

Throughout the rest of the autumn the brigade's commanders and staff continued to plan with the Marines. This included integrating the Marines' artillery and airpower with the British artillery. To assist with this, the brigade was allocated a Marine naval gunfire liaison company (ANGLICO) team. This was a team of specially trained and equipped US Marine Corps personnel who were experts in controlling and co-ordinating fixed and rotary wing air support, naval gunfire and artillery. The initial US deployment included the 24th Infantry Division (Mechanized). It had three armoured brigades. So 7th Brigade increased the Coalition armoured brigades by a third.

Should the Iraqis attack south from Kuwait into Saudi Arabia it was planned that 7th Brigade would take its place in the western part of the MEF's defensive line. By October, CENTCOM and the MEF had planned how they might eject the Iraqis from Kuwait by a direct attack by the MEF and XV111 Airborne Corps. This would see the MEF advance northwards to cut the road from Basra to Kuwait City.[3] The British armoured engineer regiment greatly increased the MEF's obstacle-breaching capability. Both nations' engineers worked hard to develop a combined approach to breaking through the minefields and berms that the Iraqis were constructing on their side of the international border.

How would 7th Brigade have performed, had the Iraqis attacked? Its more powerful and better protected armoured vehicles would have given it an important role in the MEF's plans. The Challenger tanks would have outranged the Iraqi tanks and were much better protected. And the 30mm cannon on the Warriors and Scimitars would have easily destroyed the many Iraqi APCs, which all had very thin armour. The brigade would have been able to well integrate artillery and air and helicopter strikes. As the war later showed, Iraq troops would be much less well trained than the British and US Marines.

Throughout the autumn, there was an extensive programme of equipment modification for desert conditions, including sand filters and extra cooling systems. To increase protection additional armour was fitted, particularly to Warrior infantry fighting vehicles that originally had considerably less protection than the Challenger tanks with their integral heavy slaps of Chobham armour. Rapidly designed and developed additional panels of Chobham armour were fitted to the sides and front of the Warriors.

The Army worried about the reliability of the armoured vehicles sent to the Gulf, particularly the Challenger tank, whose reputation for unreliability was well deserved, especially in terms of its engine and gearbox, known as its 'power pack'. To bring 7th Brigade to full warfighting establishment, many tanks and power packs were removed from elsewhere in the Army.

Unlike the US Army and Marines, the British infantry lacked a grenade launcher. A simple rifle grenade, the 'close assault weapon', was rapidly procured. Initially all the troops deployed in existing British tropical uniforms. With their predominantly green pattern, these were very conspicuous in the desert. New uniforms in a desert pattern of sand and brown were rapidly procured. This was an area where the British did better than the US Army, many of whom did not receive desert uniforms until after the fighting had ended. And the British logistic system managed to keep up with the immense amount of mail sent to the Gulf, whilst US troops' mail was often very slow to arrive.

OPTIONS FOR CHANGE ON HOLD

The MoD declared that the review was 'suspended' for the duration of the war. But many troops realized that after the war finished a considerable reduction in front-line forces would be highly likely. For the infantry and armoured corps units participating, this added a distinct frisson to the operation. Many regiments saw an opportunity to demonstrate their fighting spirit and the operational excellence of their regiment in a way that might increase their chance of surviving Options for Changes with their identities unscathed. This amplified the already fierce competition between regiments and units to get out to the Gulf.

ORDER OF BATTLE OPERATION *GRANBY*, NOVEMBER 1990
HQ 7th Armoured Brigade
- signals: 207th Signals Squadron
- armoured reconnaissance squadron: A Squadron, Queen's Dragoon Guards
- armour: Royal Scots Dragoon Guards
- armour: Queen's Royal Irish Hussars
- armoured Infantry: 1st Battalion, the Staffordshire Regiment
- artillery: 40th Field Regiment
- air defence: 10th Air Defence Battery
- engineers: 21st Engineer Regiment and 21st Armoured Engineer Squadron
- electronic warfare: 640th Signal Troop (EW)

Second-line support

- military police platoon: from 201st Provost Company
- ordnance battalion: 3rd Ordnance Battalion
- armoured workshop: 7th Armoured Workshop
- medical unit: 1st Armoured Division Field Ambulance
- transport regiment: 1st Armoured Division Transport Regiment

Third-line support

- HQ Force Maintenance Area
- 659th Signal Squadron
- engineers: 39th Engineer Regiment and 49th EOD Squadron
- transport: 10th Transport Regiment and Tank Transporter Troop
- supply: 6th Ordnance Battalion
- medical: 33rd Field Hospital and 24 Field Ambulance
- maintenance: 7th Armoured Workshop
- provost: 203th Provost Company

The original UK national component commander had been an air marshal. But as 7th Brigade became the largest part of the British force in the Gulf, he was replaced by Lieutenant General Peter de la Billière. A former Light Infantry officer, de la Billière had spent most of his career in the SAS, culminating in being the Director SAS as a brigadier. This coincided with the siege of the Iranian embassy and the Falklands War. He spoke Arabic and had spent a year as the joint force commander in the Falkland Islands, where he gained the confidence of his naval and air components.

De la Billière relished the appointment and applied his considerable interpersonal skills to gaining the confidence of his two superiors, General Schwarzkopf commanding CENTCOM, and Air Chief Marshal Paddy Hine, the UK Joint Commander. These relationships worked well, but UK Defence Secretary Tom King was much more difficult to deal with. In the MoD and his dealings with de la Billière, he exhibited considerable micromanagement. To make matters worse, civil servants in his private office greatly amplified these micromanaging characteristics. To many of the military staff in MoD, at Joint Headquarters (JHQ) in High Wycombe and to commanders in the Gulf, they gave the impression that their convenience was more important than the success of the mission.

For example, as the CENTCOM and British plans evolved, so did the force structure necessary for British forces to achieve their missions. King and his office insisted on very tight control of force levels and appeared to want to micromanage the deployed forces. This required lengthy staff work, in exhaustive detail, which used up a disproportionate amount of staff energy, time and bandwidth and generated great frustration in the MoD, High Wycombe and at de la Billière's HQ in Riyadh.

Sometimes King's office would issue a demand that advice be very rapidly submitted to it, only for the work to the languish there for days before it was put before King. General de la Billière had directed SAS operations in the Falklands War. He and many other Army commanders and staff officers considered that in 1982, there had been far less obstruction, interference and micromanagement by Defence Secretary John Nott, his ministers and their offices, and far fewer unnecessary demands for excessive information and examples of delayed decision-making. For example, General de la Billière became very worried that the MoD's refusal to alter naval rules of engagement placed the Royal Navy's ships in the Gulf at great, and avoidable, risk. This created friction and eroded confidence, both in King and his office. At times it seemed that neither Tom King nor his office wanted to pass the Learmont Test.

EXPANDING THE MISSION AND FORCE

From mid-autumn the focus of CENTCOM's military planning shifted from the defence of Saudi Arabia to an offensive operation to evict Iraqi forces from Kuwait. This would require the existing XVIII (US) Airborne Corps to be joined by a corps of four US Army heavy divisions.

On 22 November the British government announced that it would deploy more troops to Saudi Arabia. These would join 7th Armoured Brigade to form 1st Armoured Division. As well as 7th Brigade it would contain:

- 4th Armoured Brigade with one tank regiment, the 14th/20th Kings Royal Hussars, and two armoured infantry battalions, the 1st Battalion, the Royal Scots and the 3rd Battalion, the Royal Regiment of Fusiliers
- an artillery group of an MLRS regiment, a regiment of M110, and two more regiments of M109
- three engineer regiments
- a reconnaissance regiment
- an aviation regiment
- a large force of support helicopters from the Royal Navy and RAF
- a combat service support group including two transport regiments and three field hospitals with a capacity of 1,400 beds.

To bring all the vehicles, troops and supplies from UK and Germany to Saudi Arabia required 400,000 tons of freight, carried in 146 ships. The division comprised all of the Army's most modern equipment and over 20 per cent of its troops. The Army wanted it to be employed on the ground war's main effort. Whilst the terrain in Kuwait was constrained, the Iraqi desert offered better opportunities for the British to practise armoured manoeuvre. The Army and General de la Billière wanted to adjust the role of the British formation away from the US Marines. De la Billière felt that the comparatively constricted area of operations would not allow the British to practise the armoured manoeuvre warfare that the division had spent the last decade preparing for. He was also concerned that breaching the defences that the Iraqis had constructed on the Kuwaiti border would carry a high risk of British casualties, particularly if the Iraqis used chemical weapons.

It took a while to persuade General Schwarzkopf of the wisdom of switching the British force from the Marines to VII (US) Corps, and of the ability of the British to logistically sustain the division over the greatly extended distances. De la Billière eventually prevailed, not least as he had invested considerable effort in building a relationship of mutual confidence with Schwarzkopf. It helped that both generals had fought in wars before and shared mutual determination to avoid unnecessary casualties.

The division would be commanded by Major General Rupert Smith, widely considered to be one of the Army's most able and thoughtful senior officers. After commanding a parachute battalion, he had been chief of staff of an armoured division, commanded an armoured brigade and been the deputy commandant of the Staff College, directing the newly established Higher Command and Staff Course. Both the division's brigade commanders and its artillery commander were graduates of the course.

This announcement triggered another wave of training in Germany and despatch of vehicles to Bremerhaven port. But there was now even more pressure of time. New equipment continued to be fielded. The 39th Heavy Regiment was in the process of introducing the US MLRS into service. These were being built by a European production line. When deployment was announced the regiment had five launchers. It needed 11 more. The other European nations then receiving launchers were asked if they would agree to the British taking the next launchers off the production line, so as to get them to the Gulf. They agreed. These were taken straight from the factory in France and modified for desert conditions, some only arriving in Saudi Arabia as the war began.

The decision to increase the force to division size also triggered another bout of friction with Tom King and the armed forces minister, Archie Hamilton. They insisted that the total British force be limited to 30,000 personnel. But as the division's plans evolved, new requirements emerged. These included electronic warfare and specialist fuel units. But the ministers appeared to hate the idea of sending necessary additional troops that were requested by the Army. Their deeply unhelpful attitude became known as 'rate capping'.[4] It appeared that they did not want to satisfy the Learmont criteria.

In December and January 1991, the US land force was doubled in size. But the new British units and formations were less ready for combat than those deployed in the autumn. Indeed the 14th/20th Hussars had given up all but one of their Challenger tanks to 7th Brigade in early autumn. The division was allocated all the Army's remaining Challenger tanks and Warrior infantry fighting vehicles. So that the poor reliability of the Challenger tanks and other armoured vehicles did not constrain manoeuvre, the Army's entire stock of spare parts for these vehicles had to be deployed. Although the force contained only two armoured brigades, the withdrawal of so much of its modern equipment and spare parts meant that the corps' remaining operational capability was limited to that of a single infantry division.

With the fall of the Berlin Wall and the unification of Germany, the government judged this an acceptable risk. But for the many battalions and regiments based in Germany that had most of their vehicles withdrawn to allocate to units in the Gulf, and the remainder stripped of spare parts, it was cold comfort indeed to live and work alongside the remains of their equipment. Once-smart vehicle parks now had the appearance of dilapidated scrap yards.

On a visit to a unit that had been stripped of its equipment to be sent to the Gulf, General Sir John Chapple, the CGS, was asked to explain how it was that the Army was having to cannibalize itself, to send a single division to war, particularly with vehicles and personnel. 'The sky is going dark with chickens coming home to roost', was his reply.[5]

The reinforcing Challengers and Warriors were fitted with additional armour and the other improvements were made to armoured vehicles. There was also widespread issue of Global Positioning System (GPS) satellite navigation systems.

The British division was re-assigned from the US Marines to the US Army's VII Corps. This would require a long move from eastern Saudi Arabia to a new assembly area, 350 km to the west. If the division had been fighting in north-west Germany, it was unlikely to have moved far from its assigned area of operations, with local counterattacks into neighbouring divisional areas of no more than 20 km being the limit of ambition. It would have been able to use ammunition and spare parts stockpiled at sites much closer to the intended battlefield. And its fuel would have been drawn from NATO's extensive pipeline array. But now the necessary supplies were close to the port of Al Jubail, much further away from the division's area of operations than they would have been in Germany.

The corps required the division to attack alongside its US divisions to protect the formations from any flank attack. It needed to prepare to fight over a distance of 350 km. This was a novel task that had not previously been part of British planning or training. But the division learned from the desert training conducted by 7th Armoured Brigade and evolved a novel plan to destroy Iraqi positions using successive brigade attacks with mass artillery and air support, as well as plans for logistics, engineers and chemical defence.

Detached from 1 (BR) Corps, the division would need to be much more self-sufficient. This also had considerable implications for logistic and medical support. The division would require stocks sufficient for 21 days of combat, some 50,000 tons of supplies. As well as spare parts, this included 21,000 tons of ammunition, 590 tons of rations, 5,450 tons of material and stores and over 1,500,000 gallons of fuel.

This meant that many more logistic units would be needed than the division had in peacetime. The government had only authorized the mobilization of TA and reserves for medical roles, so the many TA logistic units that would deploy to Germany in war could not be used. Instead, the majority of deployable logistic units and personnel in 1 (BR) Corps were sent to the Gulf.

THE MOVE UP

A divisional support area was established 350 km to the north-west of the port and airfield at Al Jubail. It was inside the US corps' Logistic Base Alpha, which had a width of 25 miles and a circumference of 100 miles.

Moving the supplies and division took four weeks. It took three transport regiments to complete this, with most trucks making 17 round trips.[6] As extra logistic backup, the

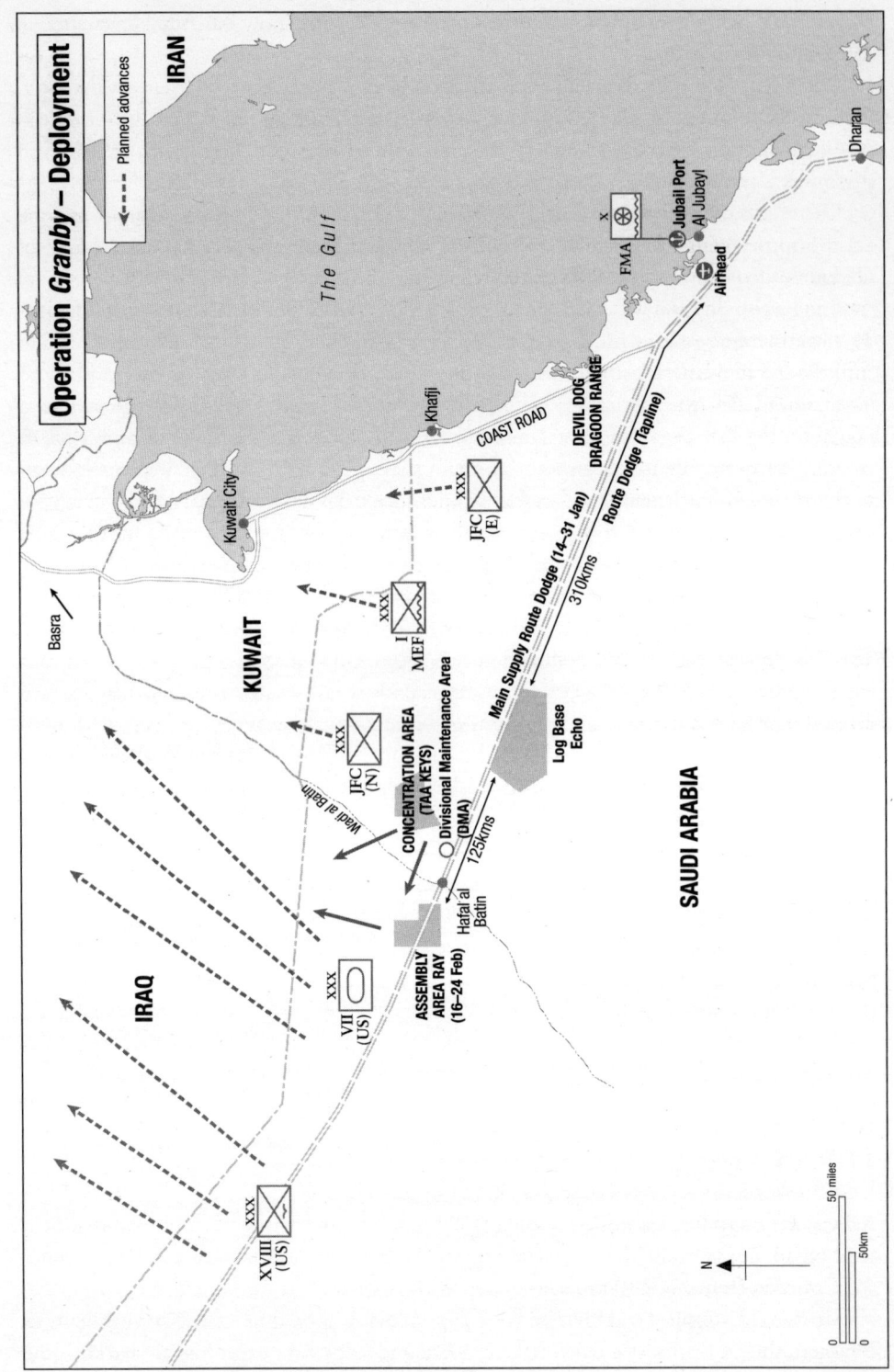

Operation *Granby* – Deployment

- - - - - Planned advances

IRAN

The Gulf

Dharan

Jubail Port
Al Jubayl

FMA

x

Airhead

Khafji

COAST ROAD

DEVIL DOG
DRAGOON RANGE

Route Dodge (Tapline)

Main Supply Route Dodge (14–31 Jan)

310kms

Kuwait City

JFC
(E)

XXX

I
MEF

XXX

KUWAIT

Basra

JFC
(N)

XXX

CONCENTRATION AREA
(TAA KEYS)

Divisional Maintenance Area
(DMA)

Log Base
Echo

Wadi al Batin

125kms

Hafar al
Batin

SAUDI ARABIA

VII
(US)

XXX

ASSEMBLY
AREA RAY
(16–24 Feb)

IRAQ

XVIII
(US)

XXX

N

50 miles

50km

Royal Navy task force in the Gulf had four logistic ships loaded with Army ammunition. These could be unloaded across beaches in Iraq and Kuwait, adding extra resilience to the logistic plan.

The division had 33,000 troops and 6,000 vehicles, 800 of which were armoured. To move the division, tracked armoured vehicles were carried by tank transporters and civilian low-loaders with their crews travelling by air in C130 Hercules to a desert air strip. The remaining vehicles, supplies and personnel travelled by road. This was a single corps main supply route being used not only by the British, but also by VII (US) Corps' three armoured divisions and vehicles delivering US combat supplies. The corps had a total of 140,000 troops, 32,000 wheeled vehicles and 6,600 armoured vehicles and only a fortnight to move them to assembly areas over 350 km to the west.[7] The British division had to fit into the US movement plans.

A round trip was 700 km long and took about 36 hours. It took three weeks to complete the logistic build-up and two weeks to move the division. There was a week's overlap between these two activities, so the total deployment took about four weeks. It took four UK transport regiments, augmented by local contractors, to achieve this, with most vehicles making 17 round trips. The daily British Army convoy that departed Al Jubail was 65 km long. One transport squadron calculated that during this period it had driven to the moon and back.

While this buildup of logistics and units was taking place the division was also training. The 7th Brigade had worked with the US Marines to create a bigger, more challenging range, named 'Devil Dog Dragoon Range', which allowed them to practise full battlegroup attacks. This they did, making attacks at night their priority. The practice greatly increased the confidence throughout the brigade and its units.

The 4th Brigade had had less time to train than 7th Brigade. As quickly as it could it deployed to the ranges to conduct its own tactical live-firing exercises. Many considered these to be the most realistic training they had ever done.

THE WAR

The US-led international coalition had its HQ in Riyadh, the Saudi capital. Commanded by the formidable US Army General Norman Schwarzkopf, the command structure drew on the existing US Central Command HQ. The air forces were commanded by the CENTCOM air component HQ. The same applied to the naval forces assembling in the Gulf.

The command of the land component was more complicated. US doctrine called for a land component HQ to command all land forces in such an operation. CENTCOM had such an HQ standing by, but Schwarzkopf chose not to use it. Instead, he commanded the land component himself.

Coalition forces were arrayed along the northern Saudi Arabian border. In the west was XVIII (US) Airborne Corps, with the 82nd Airborne Division, the 101st Air Assault Division, the 24th Infantry Division (Mechanized) and a French light armoured division.

Facing Kuwait were two US Marine divisions, under Schwarzkopf's command, alongside two groups of Arab forces, under command of Prince Khaled, Schwarzkopf's Saudi opposite number. As well as Saudi formations, these included Egyptian and Syrian divisions, and smaller contingents from Kuwait, Oman and the United Arab Emirates.

Between these two groups of forces would be VII (US) Corps. This was deploying by sea from Germany and the US. It would eventually comprise four US heavy divisions, the 1st Cavalry, 1st Infantry, 1st Armored, and 3rd Armored. Despite their historic titles these divisions were fully armoured and mechanized, fully equipped with the new Abrams tanks, Bradley fighting vehicles, MLRS rocket launchers and Apache attack helicopters. The British division would join the corps.

The Coalition plan was for a long air campaign to reduce the combat power of Iraqi forces in Kuwait and southern Iraq. Then a land attack into Kuwait from the south would give the Iraqis the impression that this would be the Coalition main effort. This would be reinforced by US Navy and Marine forces simulating an amphibious task force in the northern Gulf, preparing to land on Kuwait's coast.

Much further to the west both US corps would attack into southern Iraq. The land forces' main effort would be the attack by VII US Corps. This would initially attack north, and then pivot to face east and destroy the elite Iraqi Republican Guard formations deployed to the north of Kuwait, as well as cutting routes from Kuwait into Iraq. The Republican Guards were better trained and equipped than the regular Iraqi Army. They also had an important political role in bolstering Saddam's dictatorial regime. The British division was to protect the corps' southern flank, by attacking Iraqi Army tactical reserve formations. The corps' 1st Infantry Division would attack where the Iraqi border defences were weakest, an area defended by the Iraqi 26th Division. Having breached these defences, the British division would pass through to attack Iraqi tactical reserve formations, whilst the rest of the corps would move north and then east to envelop the Republican Guard.

The reception process for reinforcing British troops and equipment at Al Jubail and the necessary modifications of armoured vehicles benefited from lessons learned the previous autumn. Even so, 4th Brigade would have only three weeks to conduct the training and planning that had taken 7th Brigade three months. The overall unreliability of equipment and shortage of spare parts forced General Smith to make difficult decisions about the priorities for the use of track mileage. For example, to allow 4th Brigade and the artillery group to train, 7th Brigade's armoured vehicles movement was limited to 15 km per week.

All the division's activity since mid-January had been under the umbrella of Coalition airpower. Troops arriving at airfields in Saudi Arabia were astonished to see the large numbers of US aircraft of all types on the tarmac, as well as the huge number of helicopters that belonged to the US Army and Marine Corps. For many, this was the first time that they had seen the huge size of the fixed and rotary wing air fleets that the US was assembling in the region. On clear nights soldiers could hear the hundreds of aircraft heading north to attack Iraq. And they could be easily viewed using the many image intensifier night sights available to the troops.

General Smith described his concept of operations as follows:

The enemy had plenty of time to prepare their defence. They were deployed behind substantial obstacles along the Saudi/Iraqi border and in considerable depth in Iraq and Kuwait. The enemy forces in the depths of the defence were primarily the Iraqi Republican Guard. The VII Corps' plan involved breaching the obstacle with 1 US Infantry Division, then advancing north with the other divisions destroying the Iraq Republican Guard. 1 (UK) Armoured Division, having passed through the breach and conducted a forward passage of lines through 1 US Infantry Division, was to guard the east and south flanks of VII Corps' attack. I was to be reinforced by a US artillery group.

On the basis that over time small fights won quickly incur the least logistic penalty, my intention was to fight quick small battles concentrating all available firepower on each objective in turn to destroy, or if necessary and temporarily, delay the enemy. These small objectives were to be attacked sequentially and at a high tempo by each brigade or battlegroup in turn. Thus, if one got into trouble the other could come to its help and the one not engaged would be the focus of logistic support.

I intended to go in deep on a narrow front so as to gain the earliest possible contact with enemy elements moving towards the corps' flank. Advantage was to be taken of long range engagements and night, where the division had technical superiority. Static enemy positions were to be bypassed and if the enemy were then to counter attack or more, my groupings must be able to operate cut off from each other: they must be big enough in terms of firepower, logistic and medical support to stand in isolation.

This end I decided to fight in three simultaneous battles. This is not new now, but for a division to do this (at least in the British Army) was new then. I called them Depth, Close and Rear battles.

The Depth Battle was to be commanded by my artillery commander. He was to disrupt, divide, and destroy the enemy so as to present easily digested bite-sized targets for the Close Battle. All the artillery less that allocated to support the Close Battle, the Reconnaissance Group and the attack aviation were grouped to his command.

The Close Battle was to be fought by the two armoured brigade commanders, who, reinforced with artillery, engineer support and with their own logistic and medical elements, would be committed in turn to destroy enemy groupings.

The Rear Battle was to be commanded by my Rear HQ whose objective was to secure communications, establish area surveillance and, if necessary, convoy logistic and medical columns so as to ensure the maintenance of the depth and contact battles. Grouped group to this command were the Engineer Group (less those allocated to support of the close battle), the Air Defence Artillery Group, reserve armoured fighting vehicles and air portable infantry.[8]

Smith reorganized the division to support this concept of operations:

ORDER OF BATTLE OPERATION *GRANBY*, FEBRUARY 1991

HQ 1st Armoured Division with 1st Armoured Division Signal Regiment. Electronic Warfare Squadron 14 Signal Regiment

4th Armoured Brigade
- armour: 14/20th Kings Hussars
- armoured infantry: 1st Battalion the Royal Scots, 3rd Battalion the Royal Regiment of Fusiliers

7th Armoured Brigade
- armour: The Royal Scots Dragoon Guards, The Queens Royal Irish Hussars
- armoured infantry: 1st Battalion the Staffordshire Regiment

Divisional artillery group
- close support artillery: three regiments (2, 26 and 40 field regiments), with M109 guns
- heavy artillery: 32 Regiment with M110 guns. 39 Regiment with MLRS rocket system
- air defence: 12 Regiment with two batteries with Tracked Rapier and two with Javelin
- armoured reconnaissance: 16th/5th The Queen's Royal Lancers
- aviation: 4 Regiment, Army Air Corps
- artillery locating: a surveillance and target acquisition battery with a drone troop and a sound-ranging troop
- divisional engineer group: 32 Armoured Engineer Regiment and two engineer squadrons support helicopter force: two squadrons Royal Navy Sea King Mark 4 Squadron RAF Puma. Squadron RAF Chinook
- prisoner of war guard force: commanded by the commanding officer of 1st Battalion, the Coldstream Guards
  - 1st Battalion, the Coldstream Guards
  - 1st Battalion, the Royal Highland Fusiliers.
  - 1st Battalion, the Kings' Own Scottish Borderers

Smith's plan featured several innovative new organizations, for example the grouping of aviation and reconnaissance regiments under the command of the divisional artillery group.

In planning the attack, both the US and British assessed that large numbers of Iraqi troops could well surrender. The country that captured the prisoners would not only need to secure them, to prevent escape and to interrogate prisoners to gather intelligence, but would also have to meet the requirements of the Geneva Conventions, including medical treatment and life support. As planning went on, the division became increasingly concerned that with no dedicated force to handle prisoners, any more than a few Iraqis surrendering would require forces to be taken from the armoured brigades to handle them. In the worst case, this could greatly reduce tempo.

Unbeknownst to the division, the MoD had been seeking to find a force to guard prisoners from another nation. None was forthcoming, so at almost the last safe moment, three light infantry battalions from the UK were flown out to the Gulf. Designated the Prisoner of War Guard Force, it was an ad hoc force, commanded by the commanding officer of 1st Battalion, the Coldstream Guards.

The armoured brigades' capability centred on their armoured fighting vehicles and their crews. Some would certainly be damaged or destroyed, with resulting casualties to their crews. To maintain tempo after such casualties, it would be necessary to rapidly deploy armoured vehicles with trained crews. To achieve this, a new Armoured Delivery Group was formed. At the end of his reconnaissance in November, General Smith asked for an infantry battalion to be sent to run the new unit. This simple request became mired in the morass of delay and micromanagement around Tom King's office. It eventually deployed – only just in the nick of time, its commander reporting to Smith in mid-February. The unit was rapidly assembled and equally rapidly disbanded after the war.[9]

Commanded by the commanding officer of 1st Battalion, the Queen's Own Highlanders, it was an all-arms group with formed tank squadrons, armoured infantry companies and troops and platoons of specialist armoured vehicles. These were crewed by soldiers and officers who had been sent to the Gulf as battle casualty replacements. To keep up with the advance, all the armoured vehicles would be carried on tank transporters. The new organization was complemented by a new Divisional Reconstruction Group to repair battle-damaged equipment, formed by 7th Armoured Workshops. Should a brigade suffer significant casualties, both new units would join the brigade to regenerate its combat power.

Measures were taken to conceal the move west to the division's concentration area. It was not reported by British or international media. The great majority of the division did not know that the live firing training at Devil Dog Dragoon range in eastern Saudi Arabia had been recorded by a Royal Navy electronic warfare unit. The recordings made were replayed over the radio to simulate that training was still going on at the ranges. To reinforce this there was a high level of control over divisional communications, with the power of radios reduced. Additionally, a British Forces Broadcasting radio station established in eastern Saudi Arabia remained there, instead of moving with the division. This electronic deception was repeated until two days before the division attacked.

The division conducted four mission rehearsal exercises. The first was a map exercise with US staff present, to understand how the US 1st Infantry Division would breach the Iraqi defences and assist the movement of the British division through them. The second was a command post exercise with US staff. It included commanders and vehicle drivers practising moving through a mock-up of the lanes through the breached obstacles that the US division would lay out.

These were followed by two full divisional exercises, both designed to practise General Smith's plan. The first, Exercise *Dibdibah Drive* on 4–6 February, was an operational rehearsal of the breaching of the Iraqi border defences by the 1st (US) Infantry Division, followed by the British division's passage of lines through the US positions. The second, Exercise *Dibdibah Charge*, practised the divisional manoeuvre that General Smith planned to conduct. The move ended with the division present in Assembly Area Ray. The exercise was limited by the need to conserve spare parts for the battle, particularly tank engines, so the division moved through an enormous circle.

The division's artillery had not been able to participate fully in this. It was the last part of the division to arrive. It also had to take part in VII (US) Corps' preliminary programme of artillery strikes. These were limited by the need to sustain the deception plan. Reconnaissance missions were flown by the division's drones, which were able to generate some imagery of its objectives. But the artillery had been unable to exercise land/air integration with the US Air Force-led air component.

OPERATION DESERT SABRE

By the end of January, the 1st Armoured Division was complete in Forward Assembly Area Keyes. But it had not had the chance to train together in the way that 7th Brigade had. Its logistic units had been entirely occupied in supporting the division and its move. The artillery and engineers had arrived late because of shipping delays.

General Smith issued a planning directive to the division. He wrote that:

> Our purpose is the defeat of the enemy's mobile forces – to achieve this we must destroy his armoured mechanized and artillery units – and his HQs. We are not fighting for ground.
>
> I intend to fight the division by committing appropriately grouped brigades sequentially to the Close Battle while fighting a Depth Battle with the Artillery Group. By sequencing the committal of the brigades, we can prosecute an attack in depth while simultaneously allocating Combat Support to the brigade fighting the contact battle and Service Support to that out of contact thus maintaining the tempo momentum of our attack for as long as possible.[10]

Smith assessed that in the division's sector there was no ground of any importance at all. Using such intelligence that was available, concentrations of enemy forces were identified and named using metals. Operational analysis was used to assess how much combat power would be needed to destroy each enemy position. It was decided that to keep British casualties at 10 per cent or below, British combat power applied to each position needed to overmatch the enemy's by at least 6 to 1. Plotting these factors on the map allowed time, space, firepower and movement calculations to be made. This allowed each brigade to be allocated 'bite-sized' objectives that they could destroy.

Objectives in the north of the sector were allocated to 7th Brigade, those in the south to 4th Brigade. Smith wanted to keep his options open. For example, if the US breaching operation had thoroughly destroyed enemy defences, the division's advance would be led by 7th Brigade, which was more suitable to advancing in relatively open terrain. But if there were substantial enemy defensive positions just beyond the breach, then 4th Brigade would lead, as its greater numbers of infantry made it more suitable for clearing defensive positions.

Artillery raids begin on 18 February. These were conducted by the division's long-range guns, targeting Iraqi artillery. The guns deployed close to the international border on radio silence. They then fired for 15 minutes before withdrawing. The aim was to use intelligence and surveillance systems to learn about the speed of response of Iraqi artillery.

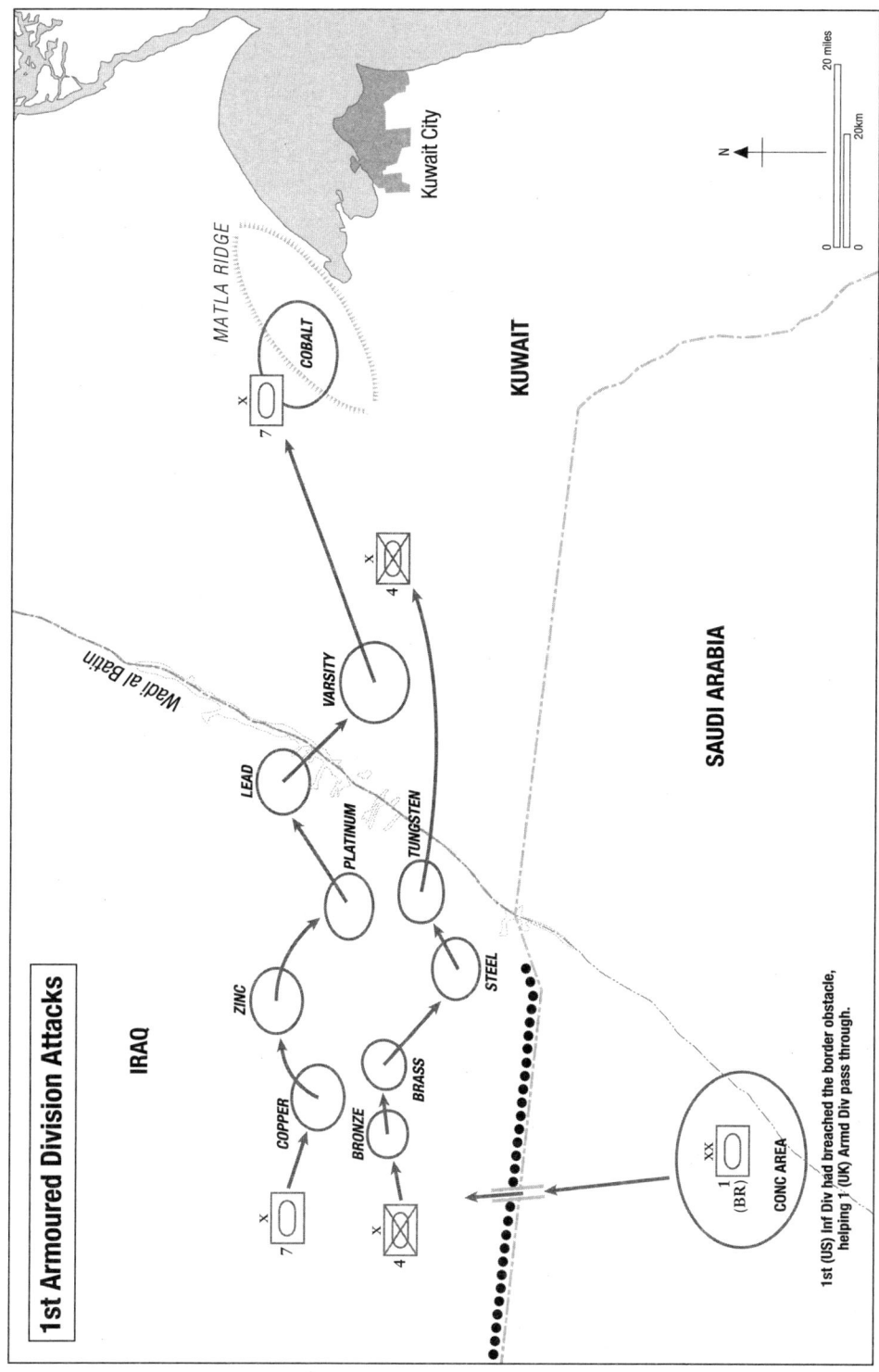

1st Armoured Division Attacks

IRAQ

KUWAIT

SAUDI ARABIA

Kuwait City

MATLA RIDGE

Wadi al Batin

COBALT

VARSITY

LEAD

PLATINUM

TUNGSTEN

ZINC

COPPER

BRONZE

BRASS

STEEL

CONC AREA

1 (BR)

1st (US) Inf Div had breached the border obstacle, helping 1 (UK) Armd Div pass through.

20 miles

20km

N

The Coalition land attack began on 24 February with attacks by XVIII (US) Airborne Corps in the west and the US Marines in the east. That morning General Smith gave formal orders to the division. It was originally planned that the VII (US) Corps attack would begin on 25 February. But the unexpected success of other land operations resulted in the British division's movement through the breach being brought forward by several hours. The British began moving through around midday, Smith having decided that 7th Brigade should lead.

Many troops found the movement through the breach an awe-inspiring experience. They were greeted by huge signs that read 'welcome to Iraq courtesy of the Big Red One', the latter term being the 1st Infantry Division's nickname. Everywhere there were huge numbers of British and US vehicles, destroyed Iraqi vehicles and fighting positions and US engineers clearing land mines. And the MLRS rocket launchers were firing at Iraqi positions ahead, the noise of the rockets like the roar of a gargantuan dragon.

As the brigade moved forward, the division's artillery group struck Objectives *Copper* and *Bronze*. The northern part of *Copper* was attacked by 7th Brigade, including a dismounted attack by an armoured infantry company of the Staffords. The brigade then moved west to attack Objective *Zinc*. This began with a large-scale preliminary artillery bombardment by the division's guns. They were joined by salvos from the MLRS rocket launchers. These were spectacular, with rockets roaring into the sky and showering down clouds of bomblets onto the enemy positions which were carpeted with a devil's garden of small explosions, lethal against troops, equipment and vehicles in the open. The British 39th Heavy Regiment with its MLRS quickly became known as the 'grid square removal company' – a typical example of macabre humour. The resistance at *Zinc* was light and it was quickly secured. 7th Brigade went firm and replenished, the division's main effort switching to 4th Brigade.

Although the divisional reconnaissance regiment, the 16/5th The Queen's Royal Lancers, had initially struggled to overcome traffic congestion at the breach, it was able to get ahead of the two brigades and move some 60 miles into the enemy's depth to begin directing artillery and air strikes onto Objective *Lead*. In the meantime, 4th Brigade crossed the breach at 1930hrs on 25 February. Its advance was delayed by poor weather and unexpected encounters with small numbers of enemy. By the early hours of 26 February, it had cleared Objective *Bronze*. It moved on to attack the southern part of Objective *Copper*. Intelligence had pointed to this containing an enemy artillery battery. In fact, it contained a full Iraqi battlegroup of over 20 tanks with infantry, artillery and logistics. This was cleared by the 14/20th Hussars, the thermal sights on their Challenger tanks providing a decisive advantage.

By now 4th Brigade was the division's main effort, advancing to and clearing Objective *Brass*, reflecting General Smith's concept of sequential punches alternating between the armoured brigades. During their attack on Objective *Brass*, B Company of the Royal Scots dismounted from their Warriors to clear Iraqi bunkers and armoured vehicles. The company commander, Major John Potter, described the action:

> We dismounted and commenced clearing through the bunkers to get towards the vehicle and that was the point where Private Gow won his Military Medal. There was a great deal of

confusion. It was slowing down and he took the initiative and went forward on his own. The area was covered in bomblets and there was an anti-personnel mine threat. He crawled to about 20 metres from the vehicle and hit it with the Close Assault Weapon rifle grenade. It started to burn and he followed it up with a white phosphorus grenade. He then went forward and cleared another two bunkers around it until I called him off because at that point a lot of ammunition was exploding around us from the Iraqi vehicle and I didn't want him to waste time on that. In fact, if I hadn't stopped him at that point God knows where he would have ended up.[11]

During an attack on Objective *Steel*, the 3rd Battalion, Royal Regiment of Fusiliers, was attacked by US Air Force A10 jets. Two Warriors were destroyed, with nine killed and 11 wounded – the largest single British death toll of any incident in the war.

The division assessed that it had gained the initiative in its sector. But there were considerable communication difficulties, including between the divisional and corps HQs. General Smith was concerned that enemy might move additional forces against the division, most likely Republican Guard forces moving from the division's northern flank. Some small local Iraqi counterattacks were defeated over the night of 26/27 February.

The next move planned was an attack by both brigades on Objective *Platinum*. But such had been the success of the earlier brigade attacks that Smith adjusted his plan to assign *Platinum* to 7th Brigade alone, following an artillery bombardment and attacks by US aircraft. The Irish Hussars and Staffords attacked *Platinum,* whilst the Scots Dragoon Guards quickly moved on to attack Objective *Lead*, which was cleared by last light on 26 February. 7th Brigade then went firm on its initial objective, designated Phase Line *Smash*.

The main effort then switched again to 4th Brigade. Following a heavy bombardment by both the division's artillery and a US Army National Guard artillery brigade, the brigade attacked Objective *Tungsten,* which was assessed to contain an Iraqi mechanized brigade. Using both of the brigade's armoured infantry battalions this was cleared by the morning of 27 February. With both brigades forward on Phase Line *Smash,* the division had succeeded in its mission of destroying the Iraqi tactical reserves to protect the southern flank of the US corps.

The division was then ordered to attack east again to capture Objective *Varsity.* By now Smith had to abandon his initial concept for deep attack. The reconnaissance regiment had found it difficult to get far ahead of the armoured brigades. Its Scorpion and Scimitar vehicles were no faster and often slower than the brigade's Challengers and Warriors. Both these vehicles were much better protected than the very thinly armoured reconnaissance vehicles. They also had more modern night sights, particularly the tank's thermal imagers. And the British could make less use of their aviation for deep reconnaissance and strike than the US formations, which had the Apache purpose-built attack helicopter with built-in armour, defensive aids and advanced sights and anti-tank missiles. These could fly further into harm's way than the British Lynx helicopters, which were essentially light utility helicopters with added anti-tank missiles. They were much more vulnerable than the Apache, so had to be used with less aggression and more caution.

So Smith stopped using the artillery group to fight the depth battle, and grouped much of the division's artillery to directly support 7th Brigade. He ordered that the brigade move to Objective *Varsity* as fast as possible, with 4th Brigade and the rest of the division following. The attack on *Varsity* began on the morning of 27 February and after a five-hour fight 7th Brigade secured it. It contained a brigade's worth of enemy equipment which had largely been abandoned by Iraqi troops. By now the almost non-stop fighting and moving meant that many in the division had had very little sleep. This was in part a consequence of the ability to fight at night that was conferred by the modern night sights of Challenger and Warrior and the improved navigational capabilities offered by GPS. Whilst a proportion of soldiers could sleep in the back of their vehicles when not fighting, drivers and commanders were afforded no such relative luxury. This greatly concerned General Smith. So he kept the plans and orders as simple as possible to reduce the chances of mistakes and accidents resulting from the deep fatigue felt by many in the division.

The US corps ordered the division to attack south-west down the valley of the Wadi al Batan, the border between Saudi Arabia and Kuwait. This was to clear the wadi so that a supply route could be used to support the four US divisions now north of Kuwait. No sooner had the division ordered 4th Brigade to do this, than the corps cancelled the order. Instead, at 2230hrs on 27 February the division was ordered to be ready to attack eastwards to seize Objectives *Cobalt* and *Sodium*, blocking the main highway out of Kuwait to the Iraqi city of Basra. Smith assigned the mission to 7th Brigade, supported by a reinforced artillery group. During the night, the attack was called off and then on again, while the media reported rumours of a ceasefire. But after a firm order was given, 7th Brigade raced forward, meeting minimal opposition. The brigade secured Objective *Cobalt* at 0725hrs on the morning of 28 February, rapidly moving forward to seize Objective *Sodium*.

The brigade now bestrode the so-called 'highway of death', the road north from Kuwait to Basra. The area was littered with abandoned and destroyed vehicles, victims of overwhelming US airpower. There were many dead Iraqi troops and the area was liberally strewn with body parts. The heavy dark smoke from burning oil wells gave the scene an apocalyptic feel. Some likened this to the dark wasteland of Mordor, from Tolkien's *Lord of the Rings*.

THE AUDIT OF WAR

Once the ground attack began, the division moved another 290 km. During this '100-hour war' it consumed 3,200 gallons of fuel per mile and 660,000 gallons of water per day. Meanwhile, the lower-than-expected level of Iraqi resistance resulted in lower expenditure of tank and infantry ammunition than planned. In 100 hours the division advanced 290 km, destroying three divisions' worth of Iraqi forces and capturing 7,000 Iraqi prisoners, but had only 19 British troops killed.

The division finished the war with the majority of its armoured vehicles still running, confounding many pessimists and armchair commentators. But it had struggled with the poor reliability of its armoured vehicles. The division had 211 Challenger tanks. During the operation some 279 power packs had been changed. That some 130 per cent of the power packs required replacement was a shocking demonstration of just how unreliable the tank was: an unreliability that had been tolerated by the MoD throughout the 1980s. Fortunately for the division, the Army's entire Challenger power pack repair capability had to be sent to the Gulf. Many soldiers, officers and commentators criticized this and other reliability problems as evidence that the Army and MoD had underinvested in this important area. They were right to do so.

Within the Army and in the media there was criticism of the number of logistic units deployed to the Gulf. This was unfair, as the division was acting in a role that required movement over greater distances than it would have had to do fighting a predominantly defensive battle in 1 (BR) Corps, where it would also have benefited from the pre-positioned supplies held in Germany.

The division had undoubtedly succeeded in its mission. It had maintained a rapid rate of advance and suffered remarkably few casualties in doing so. Why was this?

Firstly, the Iraqi defenders had low standards of morale, leadership and training. Their combat power and will to fight were further sapped by the Coalition air campaign, as well as the firepower of the British gun and rocket artillery that bombarded their positions before the Challengers and Warriors reached them. And Challenger's thermal sights meant that at night Iraqi armoured vehicles were often engaged and destroyed before their crews realized the threat. Even so, some pockets of Iraqis put up significant resistance. These were usually rapidly despatched by tank guns and Warrior cannon and by rapid attacks by determined platoons and sections of armoured infantry. Iraqi anti-tank weapons rarely hit British armoured vehicles, and such hits as occurred were defeated by Chobham armour.

Tying all this together was the high standard of British training, both individual and collective. Many of those who fought in the two armoured brigades identified that battlegroup live fire manoeuvre at BATUS had provided an important foundation. This was reinforced by the live firing training in Saudi Arabia, which was particularly important for individuals, companies and squadrons that had not recently trained at BATUS. There was a high level of mutual understanding between armour, armoured infantry, artillery and engineers.

As important as this mutual understanding was mutual confidence across the units and formations. This was also of a high standard. Key to this was leadership at every level from vehicle commanders through troop/platoon, company/squadron, battlegroup and brigade-level leaders. General Smith was a man who inspired with quiet confidence, as well as making great efforts to get his commanders to understand his general approach to battle. No mission like this had previously been envisaged. But the British division succeeded in its new offensive role, integrating into the US corps and keeping up with its advance. It is difficult to see how this would have been achieved if the doctrine and approach to command of the British Army had not been modernized by Bagnall. The divisional commander and both brigade commanders were graduates of the Higher Command and Staff Course.

The Army had done all it could to create the conditions for the division's success. Smith was later to say that '1st Armoured Division lacked for nothing that could be provided … And this point applies to the quality and quantity of men as well as the equipment, spares and so on that were made available to me'.[12] The contrast with the under-resourced and ill-prepared 5th Infantry Brigade in the Falklands War could not have been greater.

Although such a scenario had not been foreseen by General Bagnall, his reforms and the previous decade's modernization had laid the foundation for the division's success in this wholly unexpected operation. In particular, Bagnall's shaping of the Army's approach to command, doctrine and manoeuvre warfare had provided an excellent foundation for General Smith and his commanders and staff to think through the many novel challenges that the operation posed.

Without the new generation of fighting equipment procured in the 1980s – Challenger, Warrior and MLRS – the operation would have been much more difficult. There were many other lessons for the Army. Some would be implemented, others not. For example, armoured manoeuvre would continue to be constrained by the limitations of the aging FV432 and CVR(T) and armoured vehicles. These vehicles would still be in service 30 years later.

In general, the logistic support to the force had worked. No combat units ran out of ammunition, fuel or food, despite the unexpected speed of the advance, which resulted from weaknesses in Iraqi training, leadership, morale and technology. Had the Iraqis put up a more spirited and effective resistance, logistics would have been more tested.

Even so, a significant weakness was revealed. This was a major difficulty in 'asset tracking', that is monitoring where consignments were in the supply chain that flowed from depots in the UK and Germany to ports, airports to Saudi Arabia and then on through the deployed logistic chain to the front line. This worked much less well than it should.

But despite these problems the Army's logistic troops made sure that the battlegroups and brigades were well supported. Although the great majority of the Army's soldiers and officers were new to the desert and had never conducted such a long-range deployment before, many relished the challenge. And the Army's units had a high level of competence in their primary roles, including operating, fighting with and living off their vehicles, displaying an individual and collective skill born of a high level of unit and formation training in Germany. In the close combat arms, armoured infantry, tanks, artillery close support engineers and the battlegroup HQs that commanded and controlled them there was a very high level of expertise, acquired from training in Germany and particularly on the Canadian prairie, where the demanding exercises with live ammunition had no equal in any other army. And the brigade HQs and HQ 1st Armoured Division had a high level of expertise, forged on both field and command post exercises. The Army, including its constituent parts that went to Saudi Arabia and Iraq in 1990 and 1991, knew its business so well and was imbued with such a sense of mission command and pride in rising to challenges, that it took the many unforeseen demands of the campaign in its stride.

MORE THAN BRAVO TWO ZERO – THE SAS IN WESTERN IRAQ

Whilst the 1st Armoured Division had been the Army's main effort, the SAS had fought deep in western Iraq. But whereas the 1st Division succeeded in its mission, it is far from clear what the true impact of the SAS operations was.

After the Iraqi attack on Kuwait, 22 SAS were deployed to the Middle East. General Schwarzkopf was unenthusiastic about special forces. It took some effort and time for General de la Billière to persuade him that the SAS might have a role to play in the campaign.

But when the Iraqis began launching Scud ballistic missiles against Israel, the calculus in Riyadh and Washington changed. The Israelis threatened to attack Iraq to stop the attacks at source, preparing a force of commandos and strike aircraft to attack into Iraq. An Israeli attack would be politically disastrous, likely provoking Arab states to withdraw their forces from the Coalition. This would place Saudi Arabia in an impossible position.

To reach Israel, the Scud missiles had to be launched from western Iraq, a vast area of desert. Schwarzkopf tasked the Coalition air component with finding and attacking the mobile launch vehicles that carried the Scuds. He accepted with alacrity de la Billière's offer for the SAS to find and destroy Scud launchers.

Three patrols deployed into western Iraq to find Scud launchers. One with the callsign of Bravo Two Zero was discovered by Iraqi civilians and attacked. It attempted to evade pursuers by heading to Syria, including by hijacking a car. The patrol was forced to split up. Three SAS soldiers died. Andy McNab, the patrol commander, and one other soldier were captured by the Iraqis, kept in poor conditions and repeatedly and harshly interrogated, a fate they shared with captured Coalition air crew. Both SAS soldiers and the captured airmen were released by the Iraqi authorities shortly after the war ended.

The desperate fighting, exceptional physical endurance, determination and resistance to interrogation shown by the patrol and its soldiers are compelling evidence of the extreme toughness and fighting spirit of the SAS. But the Bravo Two Zero patrol must be regarded as a failure, as it survived in its planned position for too little time to gather any intelligence.

Why did the patrol fail? The simplest explanation is that McNab, the patrol commander, decided to deploy by helicopter rather than vehicle. Two other patrols given similar missions chose to deploy by Land Rover. The regimental sergeant major of 22 SAS tried to get McNab to travel by vehicle, as did the regiment's commanding officer. But he was adamant that he would not travel by vehicle, and neither were prepared to overrule him, as they preferred not to interfere with the plans of one of their subordinates. At the same time, Bravo Three Zero, which had deployed by vehicle, lasted much longer behind Iraqi lines. They had the mobility not only to escape from any attack but move to a new observation position from which they could resume their mission.

Bravo Two Zero joins the list of historical British military failures that are celebrated as if they were victories. These include the 1940 evacuation of British troops from Dunkirk, saving it from destruction by the surrounding German forces; and the battle of Arnhem, where 1st Airborne Division was destroyed, celebrated in the book and film *A Bridge Too Far*. The patrol was the subject of several books.[13]

As Bravo Two Zero was deploying, the SAS rapidly prepared a larger operation. There are a number of accounts of this. The best is *In the Eye of the Storm* by Peter Ratcliffe. Two SAS squadrons, A and D, would travel in modified Land Rovers. Named 'pinkies' after the slight pink hue of their desert camouflage paint, these long-wheelbase Land Rovers were fitted with long-range weapons. Each vehicle had a GPMG but was also fitted with a Mark 19 grenade machine gun, a .5-inch machine gun or a Milan missile launcher.

To enter from Saudi Arabia into Iraq required crossing the berm of sand that the Iraqis had created to mark the border. One squadron managed this relatively easily on the first night of operations. The other did not. There were other delays and messages that suggested hesitancy and anxiety on the part of the squadron commander. Despairing of this apparently hesitant leadership, the commanding officer decided to sack him. He was replaced by Peter Ratcliffe, who flew out with a letter signed by the commanding officer explaining that the outgoing squadron commander was to get on the returning helicopter.

Ratcliffe took the squadron deep into western Iraq. This included leading the squadron in an attack on an Iraqi military communications installation codenamed the 'Victor Two', for which he was awarded the Distinguished Conduct Medal. There were a number of other firefights with Iraqi forces. And on at least one occasion one of the patrols called in a US air strike on something they thought was a Scud missile launcher.

General Colin Powell, Chairman of the US Joint Chiefs of Staff, had ordered that US special forces deploy into western Iraq to join the SAS in Scud hunting. Delta Force took responsibility for the area of western Iraq north of the main highway, whilst the SAS operated south of the road. The SAS built on a long history of partnership with Delta Force, sharing the hard lessons they had already learned in western Iraq with the US commandos. In return, the US special forces offered that if the SAS bit off more than they could chew, they could call on US special forces helicopters.

Claims were made to the media that the UK and US special forces had destroyed a significant number of missile launchers, thus playing a decisive role in keeping Israel out of the war. The true picture is difficult to ascertain, particularly as there is no open-source evidence from the Iraqi side. But one US special forces officer was unpersuaded. Stanley McChrystal, then a mid-ranking officer in the US Army Rangers, observed the operation from the US Special Operations Forces (SOF) HQ. McChrystal concluded that the very short notice of Joint Special Operations Command's (JSOC's) deployment and other problems meant that:

> our intelligence simply could not generate enough clarity on Iraqi Scud operations to support an effective campaign to cripple the system. As a result, our efforts relied on thoughtful guesswork by intelligence teams and risky operations by the forces on the ground. We were largely dependent on luck. It was a position I never wanted to be in again ... I doubt our operations ever had much direct effect on Iraqi Scud operations. But in the end, Israel never intervened.[14]

This cautious assessment should not obscure the SAS' success in rising to a new challenge, well outside the parameters of the regiment's NATO role. Not since 1943 had it conducted long-range desert operations. Several factors accounted for its adaptability. It had kept alive the skills developed in the deserts of North Africa between 1941 and 1943. This included each squadron having a mobility troop trained and equipped for long-range operations by vehicle. The SAS' thirst for adventure meant that the regiment and its squadrons relished the challenges of these novel operations. As with the Falklands War, the SAS' section and training process had created a sound foundation for demanding operations in enemy-controlled territory.

CHAPTER 7

BLOODY BOSNIA

In 1991 after the US-led victory over Iraq, US President George Bush told Congress that:

> we can see a new world coming into view. A world in which there is the very real prospect of a new world order. In the words of Winston Churchill, a 'world order' in which 'the principles of justice and fair play ... protect the weak against the strong ...' A world where the United Nations, freed from cold war stalemate, is poised to fulfil the historic vision of its founders. A world in which freedom and respect for human rights find a home among all nations.[1]

Things were not to turn out as he anticipated. It was not long before many commentators started using the phrase 'a new world disorder' to characterize the strategic challenges of the 1990s. The Army was finding itself conducting stabilization operations throughout this period and on one occasion it would prepare to mount a large-scale attack. These operations were all unanticipated, posing challenges that the Army was to adapt to. The 1990s also saw two major reviews of defence policy and capability that would reduce the size of the Army by a third. This chapter and the next will explain the turbulent decade's impact on the Army.

OPTIONS FOR CHANGE CONCLUDES

Despite the Gulf War, the Options for Change review continued to be conducted by the MoD under conditions of great secrecy, as did the Army's work to identify the regiments and battalions that were to be disbanded or amalgamated. This drove a complex plan to close barracks, especially in Germany, and to move units to their new formations and barracks.

At the end of July 1991, unit commanding officers were given sealed letters, to be opened and read to units at the same time as Defence Secretary Tom King got up in Parliament to announce the review's outcome. He reduced the Army by about a third, from 144,000 to 116,000 regular personnel, fewer than announced the previous year. A total of 22 infantry battalions and armoured regiments would disband, with 13 new regiments resulting from amalgamation.

I paraded on the square at the barracks of 1st Battalion, Light Infantry in Berlin to hear that the Light Infantry would reduce from three battalions to two. Very few officers and soldiers were surprised to learn this. At the same time Lieutenant Colonel Richard Dannatt assembled 1st Battalion, the Green Howards in the battalion's gymnasium in Catterick Camp. He had been worried that the single-battalion regiment might be merged with two other infantry regiments that, like his, recruited from Yorkshire. In the event, the Green Howards were saved. Other infantry regiments were not so lucky.

Rumours were that the CGS, General Sir John Chapple, had managed to persuade defence ministers to retain more infantry battalions than originally planned. But the reasons why particular regiments had been selected for merger were never made clear. This prompted campaigns to save the regiments from amalgamation. The British media fixated on the infantry mergers and the voices of those opposing them. The media said much less about the armoured corps, which was to undergo an even greater proportionate reduction in size, with almost all regiments amalgamating and the Royal Tank Regiment halving in size. And there was virtually no media interest in the significant reductions being made both in deployable formations and in artillery, engineer, signals and logistic units. Restructuring included the merger of many separate logistic organizations into the new Royal Logistic Corps and many formerly separate personnel support branches into the new Adjutant General's Corps.

The Army's combat divisions reduced from four to two. The 1st Armoured Division would still be based in Germany, with three armoured brigades, each of four battlegroups – two armoured and two armoured infantry. HQ 3rd Division would return to the UK and command 5 Airborne Brigade, and two infantry brigades in the UK would convert to mechanized brigades. The airmobile brigade would be retained. The TA was considerably reduced, and the 2nd Infantry Division with its TA infantry and engineer brigades was disbanded. The overall number of regular deployable manoeuvre brigades fell from 13 to eight.

Both divisions would be fully equipped with Challenger tanks and new AS90 self-propelled guns. No tears were shed for the demise of the elderly Chieftain tanks. All the infantry in Germany would have Warrior fighting vehicles, but the mechanized brigades would each have only a single armoured regiment and armoured infantry battalion, though they would gain two more infantry battalions equipped with Saxon wheeled APCs.

Tom King claimed that the Army would be 'smaller but better'. No one believed this sound bite. But aspiring commanders of all ranks saw the reduction in numbers of formations and units as greatly reducing their promotion prospects, especially in regiments that were amalgamating. I had many friends serving in those regiments to be reduced or amalgamated. They reacted with bleak incomprehension, often flavoured with anger and a sense of unfair deals done behind closed doors. Why, they asked, was their unit to be scrubbed by the Army whilst others, no more deserving, were to soldier on? The Army chain of command could not provide convincing answers. Quickly the Army's cynical sense of humour rephrased Tom King's aspirational slogan as 'smaller but bitter'.[2]

Of the strategic reserve division announced the previous year, there was no sign. But there was to be an innovative new HQ. The Army persuaded the MoD and NATO that the alliance needed a deployable corps HQ. Both agreed and HQ 1 (BR) Corps became a new multinational NATO HQ, the HQ Allied Command Europe Rapid Reaction Corps (ARRC), the Army providing its commander and about 60 per cent of the staff, the rest coming from NATO nations. The Army would also provide the corps' integral signal brigade. This decision was to prove remarkably prescient.

THE CHANGING ROLE OF WOMEN IN THE ARMY

The early 1990s saw a step change in the role of women in the Army, when decisions taken in the late 1980s were implemented. The Women's Royal Army Corps was disbanded; and women were allowed to serve throughout the Army but remained excluded from the Royal Armoured Corps and infantry. Throughout the next two decades the proportion of women in the Army slowly increased, with female soldiers and officers becoming increasingly integrated into combat support and logistic arms.

However, the distribution of women was broadly aligned with the distribution of women in civilian employment. For example, there was a high proportion of women in medical roles and human resources and administrative roles. This was reflected by large numbers of women in the Army medical services and the Adjutant General's Corps. But the more front line the branch of the Army, the lower the proportion of women.

'FRONT LINE FIRST'

The defence budget continued to come under pressure from the Treasury to generate savings. This led to the 1994 *Front Line First: The Defence Costs Study*.[3] This sought to save more money by streamlining management structures across Defence, greatly increased use of the Private Finance Initiative, and reduced command, training and support structures to generate savings.

Initiatives included a new tri-service Defence Helicopter School. All three services' staff colleges were merged into a single Joint Services Command and Staff College. And all three services' responsibilities for commanding joint operations overseas were transferred to a new Permanent Joint HQ (PJHQ), including a new high-readiness deployable joint task force HQ. The services' high-readiness units and formations were assigned to a new Joint Rapid Deployment Force. This included the SAS, 5 Airborne Brigade and the Royal Marines' 3 Commando Brigade, including its Army units and personnel.

The Army was reduced by a further 2,200 posts. The regular medical services of all three services were cut and much of their peacetime training and employment assigned to the National Health Service. The services' remaining military hospitals were disbanded, the reasoning being that it would be easier and cheaper for medical specialists to sustain their knowledge and skills by working in the civilian hospitals. And most UK married quarters were sold and leased back – a decision that the Army and MoD came to regret.

A REVOLUTION IN TACTICAL TRAINING

At the same time the Army fielded a revolutionary improvement to collective training. Throughout the Cold War the Army considered BATUS to be the jewel in the crown of training for armoured battlegroups. They assessed that the performance of battlegroups on Operation *Desert Storm* had greatly benefited from the unique experience of BATUS. No other army in the world, they thought, conducted such demanding and realistic training entirely with live ammunition. The combination of Alberta's wide-open prairie and the expert BATUS staff created an armoured warfare 'centre of excellence'.

But the US Army had identified a new approach to collective training. This involved the use of weapons effects simulators. These fitted guns from rifles to tank main armament with simulators that fired coded pulses. Soldiers, vehicles and helicopters would be fitted with laser sensors that on receipt of laser pulses would determine the effect on the target.

The new MILES (Multiple Integrated Laser Effects System) would be used as the basis for tactical training that removed the guesswork of judgements made by umpires. At the new National Training Centre (NTC) in Fort Irwin, the US Army combined these with transponders that showed the locations of all the exercise combatants. It also had a permanent 'enemy'. The OPFOR (Opposing Force) was a cavalry regiment equipped with visually modified vehicles that represented Soviet armour. They were very experienced, knew the harsh terrain extremely well and fought to win. The final element was the observer controllers, who monitored all the troops' actions and contributed to extensive debriefing of commanders.

This approach was a central element of the US Army's effort to better train for future wars in Europe or the Middle East. The NTC opened in 1980. By 1981, whole brigades were deploying there to train in its arid desert. The complementary Joint Readiness Training Centre optimized for light infantry brigades opened in 1987.

The effect of these centres on US Army training was revolutionary. The combination of the laser simulators, professional OPFOR and thorough debriefing made exercises there very realistic. It was just as stressful as the live-firing exercises in BATUS, but in many ways it was more demanding on commanders, as they not only had to exercise their tactical drills, but also had to fight an agile enemy who were determined to win.

The British Army observed the NTC's revolutionary effects, but was very slow to replicate the capability. It may be that it was excessively satisfied with BATUS. It was not until 1987 that an experimental exercise was conducted at BATUS where a whole battlegroup and OPFOR were fitted with laser simulators. A similar experimental exercise for an infantry battlegroup was conducted on Salisbury Plain in 1988. These were both highly successful, but the Army found it difficult to find the money to invest in the necessary simulators.

In 1990, the then CGS, General Chapple, tired of delay, set up a special task force to drive through a new programme to provide an equivalent capability to the NTC at BATUS. By 1995, the necessary simulators were procured and training at BATUS adjusted, to conduct as much simulated combat against a permanent OPFOR as field firing. This had considerable effect, making training at BATUS even more demanding. But there was no doubt that the Army was 15 years behind the US Army in fielding such a capability.

THE DISINTEGRATION OF YUGOSLAVIA

During the Cold War, academics and journalists often speculated about how a NATO/ Warsaw Pact war might start. A frequently identified scenario was the death of the Yugoslavian dictator Marshal Tito. He had held together the nationalist tension between the country's main ethno-religious groups: Catholic Croats, Orthodox Serbs and Bosnian Muslims. Croats dominated Croatia and Serbs Serbia and there were more Muslims in Bosnia than in any other area. But minorities were spread all over Yugoslavia.

Many Western experts considered that when Tito died, tensions between Yugoslavia's different ethno-religious groups would erupt, and the resulting sparks would have the potential to ignite a superpower confrontation. In 1979 the academic staff at Sandhurst took this view. When Tito died in 1980, the anticipated detonation failed to happen. But throughout the 1980s the Yugoslav economy declined, and interethnic tension rose, especially after Slobodan Milošević became Serbian Prime Minister in 1989. He became a rabble-rousing populist champion of Serb nationalism.

Two years later the centrifugal forces of ethnic nationalism broke Yugoslavia apart. Slovenia successfully seceded from Yugoslavia following a short war. Croatia attempted to do the same, but this led to a much more intense and longer war, fighting being especially brutal and heavy in the Serb minority areas of Croatia, known as the Krajina. These areas seceded from Croatia and became the Serb majority 'Republic of Serbian Krajina'. A UN peacekeeping force was deployed to Croatia, to provide security in three designated 'safe areas'. Britain contributed 24th Airmobile Brigade's medical unit to the first rotation of force, but the increased tension in Bosnia resulted in the commitment ending as British forces concentrated on Bosnia.

Interethnic tension continued to rise in Bosnia. After Germany's recognition of Croatia's independence, Bosnia itself declared independence in April 1992. The Bosnian Serbs rebelled against this by declaring their own mini state: Respublika Srpska. Bosnia rapidly descended into a vicious civil war. Initially, the Bosnian Muslims, often known as Bosniaks, allied with the Catholic Bosnian Croats, against the Orthodox Bosnian Serbs.

This fighting was played out in front of the world's media. Images and reporting of the fighting around Sarajevo, 'ethnic cleansing' and the forcible eviction of civilians, mistreatment of prisoners and atrocities all greatly energized calls from activists, commentators and politicians that 'something must be done'. For the EU, the return of war after over 40 years of peace was a strategic shock. Many European politicians struggled to adjust to the dynamics of the war.

THE SO-CALLED UN PROTECTION FORCE (UNPROFOR)

The UN Security Council approved the formation of an international force to protect the delivery of humanitarian aid within Bosnia. They named it the UN Protection Force (UNPROFOR). The force was to protect the delivery of humanitarian aid – a very narrow mission. This term caused dangerous strategic misunderstanding. As the war got worse Bosnians, international media and activist international politicians took 'protection' to mean not just the protecting delivery of humanitarian aid, but also the protection of civilians. But this wider mission was not one that either the Security Council or the troop-contributing nations authorized.

With a strength of only 25,000 troops, many of which were restrained by their capitals from putting themselves in harm's way, UNPROFOR lacked the means to halt fighting. Some were from countries with great experience of traditional UN peacekeeping operations which emphasized neutrality and the minimum use of force. Many of these contingents did not display a culture of combat, the resolve to face down warlords, or the will to stop aid being stolen from UN convoys.

In London, Prime Minister John Major asked the Chiefs of Staff how many international troops might be needed to keep the warring factions apart. Four hundred thousand was their reply.[4] The British government decided to contribute a battlegroup to UNPROFOR. A reconnaissance in early autumn 1992 showed that fighting was heavy. This was definitely not a conventional peacekeeping operation with the consent of the warring parties, but was a more difficult and dangerous mission. The region assigned to the British in central Bosnia was full of high hills, low mountains, dense woods, fast-flowing rivers and narrow winding roads.

It was decided that the aid convoys should be protected by Warrior infantry fighting vehicles. So an armoured infantry battalion, 1st Battalion, the Cheshire Regiment with an armoured reconnaissance squadron from the 9th/12th Royal Lancers, was assigned the mission. It would be supported by an engineer regiment and signals and logistic units, a total of 1,800 troops. The battlegroup would work to the UNPROFOR HQ, while the national commander would be a British brigadier with his brigade HQ, reporting to the joint HQ in the UK, based on the Army HQ in Wilton. A logistic base and HQ was set up outside the Croatian port of Split.

The Cheshires prepared for deployment. Prudently, the huge slabs of additional armour added to Warriors for Operation *Desert Storm* had been stored. These were brought out of the warehouses and fitted to the Warriors, while the Cheshires rushed to refresh their live-firing skills on the range and conformed with the conventions of UK peacekeeping forces by painting all their vehicles white, wearing blue berets with UN badges and fitting blue covers to their helmets.

But there was no peace to keep. Instead, there was a vicious civil war. The Cheshires found themselves in a role the Army had never attempted before. The battlegroup was given little meaningful direction by the UN's HQ, nor did they have a UK national directive.

As they arrived in central Bosnia, the town of Jajce fell to the Bosnian Serbs. Thousands of its Muslim and Croat citizens were forcibly displaced and often robbed, as they fled to Muslim and Croat areas of central Bosnia. At the front-line crossing point of Turbe, the Cheshires did all they could to help the desperate and destitute refugees with immediate medical aid and arranged and guarded transport away from imminent danger. It was a shocking introduction to the war.

To get the convoys of humanitarian aid lorries through the war zone required the Cheshires to operate beyond the narrow boundary of the UN mandate. Lieutenant Colonel Bob Stewart, their commanding officer, found the UN mandate and rules of engagement frustrating and ambiguous. So he took advantage of the ambiguity to set out a battlegroup mission of 'creating the conditions by which humanitarian aid can pass freely' – an approach of attempting to stabilize the conflict and reduce fighting to create an environment stable enough to allow the aid convoys to move. BBC journalist Martin Bell assessed that Stewart:

> invented the concept of the 'implied mandate'. Since the mission was humanitarian, he would help the victims and broker local ceasefires wherever possible and so create the conditions under which aid could be delivered. It made more sense and was more likely to succeed than simply opening a road into a war zone, which was all that the original instructions would have allowed. These UN officers were soldiers of conscience deeply troubled by the inadequacy of their mandate. They pushed it to the limit.[5]

The Bosnian government's army was known as the Armija or ABiH. It professed multi-ethnicity and included a small number of Serbs and Croats, but the vast majority of troops were Bosnian Muslims. All three warring parties (known universally to the British Army as the 'factions') had many citizens under arms. Most had little or no understanding of the Geneva Convention and laws of armed conflict. Ancient ethnic hatreds reasserted themselves with a vengeance and spiralled into savage cycles of atrocity and reprisal. Troops were exposed to much evidence of war crimes, attacks on civilians and torture – both directly, by seeing the impact on fighters and civilians alike, particularly when the factions or UN invited the British to provide security for exchanges of prisoners or bodies, and also indirectly, when faction soldiers and officers boasted of their crimes. An officer told me he had never 'expected to see what happens when men are chopped up like logs in a sawmill.'[6]

A particular problem in the mountainous terrain was the proliferation of checkpoints, which the factions used to block movement on roads and tracks. They were usually manned by highly suspicious local soldiers, usually ill-disciplined, untrained, frightened, drunk, or a combination of these.

Checkpoints allowed the factions to restrict UNPROFOR's freedom of movement. Faction commanders suspected the UN would directly or accidentally pass information to their enemies. They wanted the UN out of their way as they got on with the fighting. And the commanders of checkpoints often seemed to relish making life difficult for the UN.

UN rules of engagement forbade the use of force to break through convoys, and the factions knew this. So getting UN vehicles and convoys through checkpoints required much patience and negotiation skills of the highest order, using a mixture of persuasion, bluff and charm.

Once Stewart had established a stable pattern of battlegroup operations, the escorting of convoys could be left to his company commanders to lead. Stewart found that he had a key role to play in dealing with local warlords. In this he had three assets that gave his force greater utility than many other national contingents within UNPROFOR.

Firstly, he had Warrior infantry fighting vehicles. These were better protected than any other vehicles in UNPROFOR, with excellent firepower. Even so, soldiers were sometimes injured in the crossfire, including Lance Corporal Wayne Edwards, a Royal Welch Fusilier serving with the Cheshires who was killed in January 1993. As a result, a Royal Navy aircraft carrier was sent to the Adriatic. It not only carried Harrier jets, but also a battery of light artillery, ready to reinforce the Cheshires.

Secondly, the battlegroup was led by commanders who were not overfaced by the considerable difficulties posed by the mission and chaotic and dangerous environment. Indeed, many relished the challenge. For example, commanders used their initiative to help the factions and Red Cross arrange the opening of crossing points between the front lines to allow refugees to cross, and prisoners and bodies to be exchanged.

The third asset was Stewart himself. In a war of warlords, he used his battlegroup and his outspoken personality to make himself one. Not to fight as such, but to cajole and even bully the Bosnian warlords in his area. He increasingly used the international media. Journalists found getting around Bosnia increasingly hazardous and many welcomed assistance from British troops to report, move and live. There was a shared interest in highlighting the plight of civilians, and the work that British troops were doing to alleviate this.[7]

Throughout the Cheshires' tour, relations between Bosniaks and Bosnian Croats steadily deteriorated. In the early months of 1993, the alliance collapsed and there was full-scale conflict between Croats and Muslims. In central Bosnia, there had been much geographical intermingling of Croats and Muslims, leading to nested pockets, enclaves and front lines of bewildering complexity. Civilians were often caught in the crossfire and on many occasions subject to deliberate killings.

An example of a massacre witnessed by the Cheshires was at the village of Ahmici. Accompanied by Martin Bell, the resolute BBC TV reporter, Stewart took his Warrior to this village, where over 90 Muslim civilians had been massacred by Bosnian Croat troops. Many bodies, including those of women and children, had been burned. Stewart berated the local Croat commander. His party came under small arms fire and Stewart returned more accurate fire from the turret of his Warrior. The Croat machine gun fell silent. All this was captured by Martin Bell's teams and broadcast on BBC TV evening news that night. It was powerful front-line reportage that exposed both the lethal malice of the Bosnian Croats and the way that Stewart and his battlegroup were putting themselves in harm's way to expose war crimes.

This kind of war was new to the British troops. Northern Ireland in the early 1970s had seen intimidation and forced displacement of civilians and murders by sectarian death squads, but from the mid-1970s that type of violence had greatly declined. All the battles in the Falklands were in rural areas. In Iraq, British troops had fought in empty desert, where the only inhabitants were Iraqi troops. But this war was truly amongst the people. Villages, towns and cities were regularly attacked by all three sides, with resulting civilian casualties and destruction of homes.

High-explosive weapons are brutally cruel to the human body and troops were often confronted by appallingly wounded civilians and dismembered bodies. If these sights were not distressing enough, there were many, far too many, refugees fleeing the fighting and 'ethnic cleansing'. Often these had few if any possessions. And all these sights were in a place where the towns and wooded hills were not too different from parts of Germany, Wales or Scotland. Nor did the people appear much different.

Where circumstances allowed, British units did what they could to help, including securing front-line crossing points for the passage of refugees and swaps of prisoners and bodies, often in conjunction with the International Red Cross. British troops could not hide from these distressing sights. I found it very difficult to forget the sight of refugee children in snow with no shoes and of body parts randomly hanging from trees resulting from a high-explosive shell literally blowing an unfortunate Bosnian soldier to pieces.

Some people found this easier to deal with than others. Many commanders found that allowing their people to unwind over a couple of cans of beer or glasses of whisky could help. Famous Grouse whisky certainly helped me. But just as important in countering the stress-testing of the moral component by the violent and unpredictable civilian suffering was morale, both of the individual and the team. Being in a group with a sense of purpose, which carried out difficult missions and had a shared sense of success in adversity and mutual confidence – up, down and sideways – was a strong source of comfort to commanders and soldiers.

While the Cheshires were operating under such difficult circumstances, the Army and MoD revisited the reductions in the infantry resulting from Options for Change. Bosnia looked as if it would be an enduring commitment for the foreseeable future and the infantry would be at the heart of whatever force was committed. This meant that the requirement for infantry battalions had increased beyond that planned in 1991. The CGS, General Sir Peter Inge, persuaded the MoD that two infantry battalions be 'added back' to the Army, by suspending the planned amalgamations of the Cheshires with the Staffords and the Royal Scots with the Kings Own Scottish Borderers.

INTO THE MAELSTROM

In May 1993 the Cheshires rotated out of central Bosnia, replaced by 1st Battalion, the Prince of Wales's Own Regiment of Yorkshire. They deployed into the full fury of the three-way civil war, where the Croat and Muslim communities of central Bosnia wanted UNPROFOR to live up its name by protecting them from their adversaries. Alastair

Duncan, the PWO's tough, but softly spoken, commanding officer, found that neither the UNPROFOR nor the UK chain of command, gave him any meaningful direction. So he wrote his own directive and had it endorsed by his UK superiors.[8]

Most of the British troops in Bosnia had very little previous experience of peacekeeping, other than from tours with the UN force in Cyprus. Since 1975 this had been a very static and pretty undemanding operation. Indeed, the UN Medal awarded to troops serving in the UN Mission in Cyprus was widely nicknamed the 'windsurfing medal'. But the Bosnian mission, in a complex, unpredictable, and lethal civil war, was of exponentially greater difficulty.

By early 1993 the political and military leadership of UNPROFOR was visibly struggling. The UN's HQs had many officers whose English was inadequate and its support was bedevilled by ponderous bureaucracy. Things got done, but often inefficiently and much too slowly. Those officers who got things done often came from a few nations, including France, the UK and Canada. The UN political leadership appeared desperate not to confront the warring factions. Many British officers found this intensely frustrating and disillusioning. It took some effort for commanders to act as a buffer, suppressing their frustrations, in order to sustain the morale of their soldiers.

Shortly after arrival, Duncan helped to remove the remains of a family with a small baby who had been burnt alive in their house. *The Times* reported Duncan as saying 'Someone told me I never smiled. It happened to be on the same day that I came across the remains of that family, so I didn't feel like smiling.'[9] Like Stewart, Duncan both led from the front and assisted the international media. This was memorably captured on film when Duncan's Warrior struck a land mine.

Duncan talked to legal experts at the UN's HQ in New York. They agreed with his idea that he could directly protect civilians at imminent risk. Where it was practicable to do so, he and his soldiers did. Carefully positioned Warriors sometimes acted as a deterrent to faction attacks, as warlords thought twice about attacking the well-protected vehicles and being on the receiving end of their firepower.

In June 1993 the Prince of Wales's Own Regiment discovered that amongst the swirling fighting, Croat civilians had taken sanctuary in a monastery at Guča Gora. Duncan's battlegroup rescued them from almost certain death, by bundling villagers into the back of their Warriors and taking them across the front lines to safety, deliberately going into harm's way and inviting the warring armies to fire at them, certain in the knowledge that if that happened the British would return accurate and effective fire. This was one of many occasions where British troops deployed in a way to use the essentially defensive UN rules of engagement to confront the warring armies.

The battlegroup saw many atrocities, much sniping at civilians and aid convoys being shot at and sometimes shelled. The battlegroup had 14 men wounded and returned fire on 69 occasions, estimating that between 30 and 40 faction fighters were killed. But as well as returning fire in self-defence, Duncan's troops did all they could to try to reduce the intensity of the fighting and civilian suffering in central Bosnia. Duncan told *The Times* that 'If it blows up again between the Croats and the Muslims, a lot of people are going to be killed and we can't give aid to dead people. I'm not proud of killing people but it was necessary at the time.'[10] Duncan's battlegroup left Bosnia feeling that had it been absent from the region, the number of people killed would have been much higher.

The Prince of Wales's Own were replaced by 1st Battalion, the Coldstream Guards. They too found themselves in the midst of a heavily armed conflict, but still managed to get 25,000 tons of aid delivered. Much of this travelled into central Bosnia along Route Diamond, a new road built by the Royal Engineers over the hills and mountains that led from Croatia to Gornji Vakuf, now a major British base.

The town had become a fulcrum of fighting between Muslims and Croats with much destruction of buildings. Shells, rockets and mortar bombs were constantly falling, and small arms fire was a continuous hazard. Most of the civilian population lived in deprived conditions, shown by sallow, unhealthy skin and tired, lined faces. There were few men aged between 16 and 50 to be seen; most of them were at the front, apart from invalids and a few men who appeared to be members of organized crime syndicates running the highly lucrative black market.

By now there was a pattern to British operations. Troops spent long periods operating from armoured vehicles escorting convoys – mostly convoys carrying humanitarian aid, but also British convoys bringing up fuel, food, spare parts and ammunition to the many British bases.

The winter produced copious amounts of ice and snow, especially in the high hills and low mountains. Movement on mountain roads could be difficult, dangerous and very slow. Not only would roads and tracks be poorly maintained, if at all, but there was Bosnian military and civilian traffic, with drivers often drunk and aggressive. And rockfalls and landslips would not only block roads and tracks but could also carry displaced land mines with them. Navigating the snow and packed ice could be a demanding test of drivers' skill, confidence and nerve. Snow chains fitted to wheeled vehicles gave some additional purchase. Warrior fighting vehicles with the additional armour weighed 37 tons. Great skill was needed on downhill stretches to avoid them becoming 37-ton sledges. The Army procured special winter track for the Warriors which had protruding steel to bite into the ice. This had some effect, but the drivers of the Warriors would often earn their pay the hard way.

In summer, the valleys were often smothered with blankets of humid air, effectively a tropical environment, in which soldiers sweltered, especially those inside armoured vehicles. The stifling heat did nothing for anyone's tempers, British or Bosnian. Where possible companies or squadrons would occupy larger bases, such as schools, disused factories or warehouses. But it often became necessary to deploy platoons and troops on their own. Such small outposts became known as 'platoon houses'. These would quickly be given nicknames. For example, a yellow house in northern Bosnia occupied by British troops was heavily pockmarked by direct hits from heavy machine-gun fire that stripped away the plaster yellow paint. Troops named it 'Spotty Dog'. Soldiers spent much time guarding their bases. Direct attacks were rare, but sometimes occurred, crossfire from fighting being a greater hazard. However, there was an ever-present threat of Bosnian soldiers and civilians and soldiers breaking into bases to steal fuel, food and weapons.

When they left central Bosnia in May 1994, the Coldstream Guards had come under fire almost 200 times. They had returned fire against identified targets on 70 occasions, firing almost 4,000 rounds of small arms and cannon fire. Troops had seen much suffering, with faction fighters and civilians killed and wounded, exchanges of prisoners and bodies and the sickening evidence of atrocity and war crimes. The commanding officer estimated that up to 10 per cent of the battalion exhibited signs of stress after they returned to Germany.

Each November and May the British armoured infantry battalion would be replaced by a new unit coming from England or Germany. The November relief in place could be a real challenge, with winter weather creating great difficulties. This was the case in November 1994 when the Royal Highland Fusiliers had a very difficult journey up country from Split to their bases. It required a great deal of determination to complete the move. The same applied a year later to the similar move conducted by my battalion.

1994 – GENERAL ROSE PUSHES FOR PEACE

In January 1994, the UNPROFOR commander, a Belgian general, unexpectedly resigned. It was widely reported that he was frustrated with the repeated refusals of national contingents to do what he asked. It was by then clear to the media that some national components of UNPROFOR not only had no appetite for risk, but often displayed corruption, selling supplies and equipment to the factions.

The commander was replaced by Lieutenant General Michael Rose, previously the commanding officer of 22 SAS in the Iranian embassy incident and the Falklands War. Rose was determined to make a difference. In early 1994 Colonel Richard Dannatt, running the Higher Command and Staff Course at the Army Staff College, was summoned to Sarajevo by Rose to develop a new campaign plan for UNPROFOR. This proposed a more robust approach to the factions.

Rose became a strategic actor in the conflict, doing everything he could to dampen down the violent conflagration. He was prepared for UNPROFOR to go further in taking risk. He also used NATO air support to signal resolution, but he did not want to cross the 'Mogadishu Line' as the US had in Somalia in 1993. The 1993 US mission in Somalia had taken sides in that conflict, resulting in a war with a key clan; this led to the 'Blackhawk Down' incident in which US special forces were tactically defeated, prompting a humiliating US withdrawal.

Rose did not want to do this, but through a combination of force of personality, brinkmanship and patient negotiation he achieved some success in promoting peace, particularly in the early part of his tenure. However, this success could not be developed into a final settlement between the Federation and the Bosnian Serbs.

Early in Rose's tenure the Bosnian Serbs blocked traffic from passing through their lines to Sarajevo. Rose sent a platoon of Warriors from the Coldstream Guards, his former regiment, to the Serb checkpoint. The BBC's Martin Bell observed that 'the Warrior is a high-impact vehicle and the nearest to a tank that the UN could muster at the time. The Serbs gave way and the general's "get tough" policy seemed instantly vindicated.'[11]

In February 1994 a mortar bomb exploded in a crowded Sarajevo marketplace. There was international outrage, stoked by the extremely effective information operation being conducted by the Bosnian governments and its diplomats. Who fired the bomb was never satisfactorily explained, but British officers in Sarajevo strongly suspected it had been fired by the Bosniaks. Over the next fortnight, against much expectation, Rose and the UN negotiated a ceasefire agreement. It included openingcrossing points across the Sarajevo front lines, an end to the city's blockade by the Serbs and the withdrawal of all heavy weapons within a 12-mile radius of the city to collection points run by UNPROFOR.

A ceasefire between Bosniaks and Bosnian Croats was negotiated by the US and cemented by the March 1994 Washington Agreement, which created a new Federation of Bosnia and Herzegovina. Both factions became allies against the Bosnian Serbs. This changed the roles of British troops in central Bosnia. There was still aid to get through checkpoints, but there was a new role, helping the nascent Federation reduce tension and conflict between Muslims and Croats through practical implementation on the ground. The UN sector commanders established Joint Commissions, to help co-ordinate the military and civil implementation of this fragile peace. This included mapping front lines, establishing zones of separation, identifying and marking minefields and opening roads that had been closed. They provided security for demilitarization of the previous front lines and supervised the opening of checkpoints and removal of land mines.

British troops did all they could to turn the Washington agreement into peace, including convening endless meetings between military commanders who had recently been fighting each other. These inevitably took place in rooms filled with deep clouds of tobacco smoke and involved consuming large amounts of dark intensely strong coffee and the equally strong traditional Bosnian plum liquor called *raki* or *slivovitz*, often known as 'slip-in-a ditch' by the troops. Those participating needed strong constitutions and industrial quantities of patience.

Previous operations had largely been confined to the road network, but monitoring and implementing the ceasefire required British troops to get out and around the former front lines. These were strewn with land mines, many of which had not been recorded. This increased risk was reflected in increased casualties from mine strikes. This was sad, but it was a risk that commanders reluctantly lived with, to achieve the goal of reducing the risk of renewed fighting between the Bosniaks and Bosnian Croats by making the new Federation work.

Rose needed his own independent observers who could operate throughout Bosnia, to provide him with accurate and speedy information, unfiltered by the UN chain of command. To achieve this, he set up a small unit of Joint Commission observers (JCOs). These were specially selected and trained soldiers and officers accustomed to operating in small groups deep in hostile territory for long periods. Operating with small arms for personal protection, Land Rovers and portable satellite radios, they had a key role in the remainder of UNPROFOR operations.

The JCOs proved invaluable. For example, one Bosniak enclave was holding out against the new peace process, its commander disbelieving the news of the Muslim/Croat agreement, thinking it was a trick by his enemies. JCOs were delivered to his HQ by a brave UN helicopter crew. Another party of JCOs was at the HQ of the isolated commander's superior officer. They were able to persuade both commanders to speak over the satellite radio. This was the first direct conversation they had held in over a year and the potentially lethal misunderstanding was quickly ironed out. The JCOs and Coldstream Guards played a key role opening a route for aid into the isolated pockets of Muslim and Croats in Maglaj, an enclave largely surrounded by Bosnian Serb forces. The guardsmen were welcomed as heroes.

UNPROFOR's British contingent grew in size. Previously the UN HQ in Sarajevo had commanded national contingents directly. But as UNPROFOR increased, the span of command became too great. So, an intermediate level of command, the sector, was formed, roughly equivalent to a brigade command. Most British troops were assigned to Sector Southwest, based in Gornji Vakuf. The brigadier commanding the British contingent became the UN sector commander, the sector HQ staff coming mainly from the nations that contributed troops to formation, with much of the British staff from the brigadier's parent brigade providing the UK national contingent HQ.

A squadron of Light Dragoons already in theatre was joined by a second squadron and the regiment's HQ to become a second battlegroup. The commanding officer was told to get his vehicles and people to Hannover airport, from where a stream of transport aircraft flew them to Croatia, testament to the strategic mobility of the Scimitar light armoured vehicles.

In April the UN Security Council reacted to pressure from the Bosnian government and its supporters to create so-called 'safe areas'. These were to be 'free from armed attack or any other hostile act'. The council designated Sarajevo, Bihać, Žepa, Gorazde and Tuzla as such areas. But having willed the ends, the UN did not apply sufficient means. Its members sent over 7,000 extra troops to UNPROFOR but these were not sufficient to defend these areas against attack by the Bosnian Serbs. And no troop-contributing nation, including the British, had the political will to actively fight the Bosnian Serbs for the control of the 'safe areas'.[12]

Like the name UNPROFOR, the very term 'safe area' reflected neither the reality on the ground nor any willingness of most troop-contributing nations to increase the risk to their troops. Both terms created expectations that could not be fulfilled. And Bosniak forces used the safe areas as firm bases from which to attack the Serbs, under a UN protective umbrella. This further eroded the credibility of UNPROFOR, both with the Bosnian Serbs and with many British officers.

A Serb offensive almost captured the Bosniak enclave of Gorazde, but was stopped by NATO air strikes. The UN brokered a ceasefire agreement. This created a Total Exclusion Zone (TEZ) of a nearly 2-mile radius from the town centre, which armed Serbs were forbidden to enter.

Britain rapidly deployed an infantry battalion with Saxon wheeled APCs. The 1st Battalion, the Duke of Wellington's, were to deploy to the isolated Bosniak enclave of

Gorazde. Driving through Serb-controlled territory to Gorazde, they acted boldly on the ground to defend the safe area, by pushing Bosnian Serb positions out of the TEZ. There were firefights with Bosnian Serb forces, including a 15-minute gun battle in which a soldier was killed and over 2,000 rounds were fired by the Duke of Wellington's Regiment, killing eight Serb soldiers. In another firefight a patrol led by Corporal Wayne Mills was attacked by the Bosnian Serbs. Two Serbs were killed but the heavy fire led to the British patrol withdrawing. To protect the rest of the patrol, Mills led a personal counterattack under heavy fire. He became the first recipient of the new Conspicuous Gallantry Cross.

Under the leadership of David Santa-Olalla, their determined commanding officer, the Duke of Wellington's Regiment acted with great robustness. If they had not done so, Gorazde might well have fallen to the Bosnian Serbs. Theres would probably have been a massacre and 'ethnic cleansing' of Bosniaks, not only increasing civilian suffering, but further eroding the credibility of UNPROFOR.

Gorazde continued to be a flashpoint. In April 1994, the small British garrison was provided by 1st Battalion, the Royal Welch Fusiliers. Their line of communication ran through 50 miles of territory over mountain roads from Sarajevo. It was controlled by the Bosnian Serbs, who applied severe restrictions on all UN traffic. Bosnian Serb checkpoints imposed draconian checks and inspections on what the UN could bring into the enclave. Soldiers developed ingenious techniques to hide military equipment in their vehicles.

Convoys regularly endured hours or even days of delay and abuse at the hands of Bosnian Serb troops, who were often ill-disciplined, abusive and frequently drunk. The British troops tolerated this as best they could, as neither the UN nor the UK were prepared to fight their way through. For example, a British convoy taking supplies to Gorazde was detained by Bosnian Serb troops at a checkpoint for ten days. Effectively hostages, the small force acted quickly to retain the initiative over their captors. This included a regime of parades, fitness training and constructing a make-believe television from a wooden box.

Bosnian Serb harassment of logistic convoys and the parlous state of the damaged civil infrastructure meant that the small garrison – the newly formed 1st Battalion the Royal Gloucestershire, Berkshire and Wiltshire Regiment having taken over from the Duke of Wellington's Regiment in September 1994 – was short of essential supplies, particularly fuel. Troops had to make maximum use of improvisation to survive and operate in an extremely austere environment. They had insufficient fuel to sustain radios and the medical facilities and to have enough fuel in vehicles to react to emergencies. So their REME craftsman built a water wheel to power a battery charger.

NATO was providing air support to UNPROFOR. But many in the alliance seemed to find UNPROFOR's reluctance to request massive air strikes frustrating. There were shrill cries that this reduced NATO's 'credibility'. Many US politicians and officials argued for a policy of 'lift and strike' – lifting the international arms embargo, supplying weapons to the Bosnian government and supporting them with air strikes. This was strongly opposed by London and Paris, who felt it would increase the threat to their troops in Bosnia.

There was strategic contradiction between Britain and France, both of which had troops on the ground in Bosnia who were at considerable risk, and the US, which had no troops on the ground but had no shortage of politicians volubly advocating the use of US airpower against the Bosnian Serbs. Strategic divergence between London and Washington was at its greatest since the Suez Crisis in 1956. To British commanders in Bosnia, it seemed that there was little political co-ordination between the US, NATO, the UN and the various nations attempting to negotiate a peace deal.

1995 – THE YEAR OF CRISIS

By the end of 1994 much of the tension between Croats and Muslims in central Bosnia had reduced, restoring some relative 'normality'. British troops played a major role in this. And a winter truce between the loose and uneasy Muslim/Croat Federation and the Bosnian Serbs was brokered. But in early 1995 this ceasefire collapsed, making peacekeeping impossible.

Much of UNPROFOR in central Bosnia was making only a very limited contribution. All three UN sectors included contingents that appeared to have come to Bosnia structured, equipped, trained and conditioned for peacekeeping in a benign environment, with their national governments being unwilling to allow them to go into harm's way. UN commanders had little or no effective authority to direct the operations of these forces, particularly for any new operations that increased risk.

All three factions sought to manipulate UNPROFOR. Most active was the Bosnian government, who seemed to want to draw the UN, NATO and the US into the conflict on the Bosnian side. They would often attack the Bosnian Serbs, and then suffer military and civilian casualties from retaliatory Serb artillery fire, after which they would exploit the international media reporting of the resulting suffering to generate international sympathy for themselves. The Muslims often succeeded in portraying themselves as victims of Serb aggression, thus achieving a high degree of public and political support in the West, particularly in the US.

The British commander of UNPROFOR was now Lieutenant General Rupert Smith, who had commanded 1st Armoured Division in Operation *Desert Storm*. He was widely regarded by the Army's more professional officers as a man who thought and spoke with exceptional clarity – clarity that some senior officers and politicians above him sometimes found uncomfortable. There were many 'inconvenient truths' about the UN operation that they would rather evade than grapple with. For example, Smith told the British commanding office in Gorazde that 'the Safe Area exists to safeguard the civilian population, so far as it is possible to do in a war.'[13]

The three factions seemed determined to resume full-scale war. They were making it increasingly difficult for UNPROFOR to carry out its missions, especially the protection of the safe areas. UNPROFOR was reaching the limit of its utility. Sooner or later the ever-increasing dissonance between its mandate and the hesitation and caution of most of its troop-contributing nations, would put UNPROFOR on an irreversible trajectory to failure.

On 25–26 May 1995, in response to a Bosniak offensive around Sarajevo, the Bosnian Serbs repossessed tanks and artillery from UN-controlled 'weapons collection points' outside the city. General Smith issued an ultimatum, demanding the return of the weapons and that the Serbs cease shelling the UN safe areas.

When they refused to comply, Smith authorized NATO air strikes against the Bosnian Serbs. The Serbs responded by closing Sarajevo airport and the road into the city. Their tanks and artillery attacked UN positions and convoys, including British vehicles travelling through Serb territory to Gorazde. They seized UN personnel as hostages, including by attacking a French position in central Sarajevo where Serb soldiers in French uniforms captured a dozen French troops. The French promptly counterattacked, killing four Serb soldiers and losing two of their own troops. In a blaze of Serb publicity, hostages were chained to Bosnian Serb military installations, to deter further NATO air strikes.

On 28 May the Bosnian Serbs attacked Gorazde. The British garrison was now provided by 1st Battalion, the Royal Welch Fusiliers. To the east, a ridge of high hills dominated the town. These were occupied by five observation posts manned by the Fusiliers in fortified trenches. They were surrounded by Bosnian Serb infantry who invited the Fusiliers to get out of the way. The Fusiliers declined and a major battle developed with a brigade of about a thousand infantry attacking them, supported by at least three tanks. The Bosnian Army was nowhere to be seen, so the Fusiliers fought for as long as they could to delay the attackers, to allow the Bosniaks to deploy their troops into defensive positions. There was a two-hour firefight in which the British fired over 1,600 rounds of small arms fire. Many Serb soldiers were killed.

Once the Bosniak troops deployed into defensive positions to block the Bosnian Serb attack, the Fusiliers withdrew, but 33 of their soldiers were captured by the attackers. To protect the civilians of Gorazde, the Fusiliers had temporarily abandoned impartiality and had used lethal force to slow the Serb advance. Their determined commanding officer, Lieutenant Colonel Jonathan Riley, was later to explain: 'This was a military defence. It was well beyond our mandate. We were buying time for the Muslims to take over our line. I did it with General Smith's knowledge and encouragement. The Serbs knew they were fighting the UN'.[14]

The Fusiliers' resolute defence of Gorazde and the French counterattack against the Serbs in Sarajevo were decisive moments. Neither action provoked Serb retaliation, demonstrating short-term deterrence. There were no further major Serb attacks on British troops in Gorazde, although at the time no one in London or Sarajevo would have dared to forecast this. The captured Fusiliers were released, in part as a result of diplomatic pressure from Russia. In their counterattack, the French had captured two special forces soldiers from the Yugoslav National Army. This provided General Smith with some much-needed additional leverage.

Riley was telephoned by Prime Minister John Major. In doing so he bypassed the MoD, joint HQ at Wilton and Brigadier Andrew Pringle, the UK national commander in Bosnia. He also left General Smith out of the loop. Many British officers in the chain of command were aghast that modern communications technology enabled Major to skip the formal levels of command. Some suspected that he was seeking reassurance before he spoke at a party conference in Wales. That was not what he got.

Instead, Riley was forthright in telling the Prime Minister that if peacekeeping was impossible where there was no peace to keep, then the troops in Gorazde served no purpose, and with limited supplies were best withdrawn. After the war Riley recalled that 'I asked the Prime Minister what was it we were to do?' Major gave no direction. In the absence of strategic guidance from the head of government, Riley went on to tell Major that 'everyone here knew their duty and would do it'. General Sir Peter Inge, then British Chief of Defence Staff, later commented that: 'The Welch Fusiliers did bloody well. The prime minister got a bit of a shock, but commanding officers are not in popularity contests. If I was in the same situation, I would have done the same.'[15]

British forces in central Bosnia responded rapidly to crises around Sarajevo and Gorazde. The 1st Battalion, the Devon and Dorsets, an armoured infantry battalion, had begun their tour in May 1995, conducting 'framework' peacekeeping operations. They quickly passed this role to other British troops, to move under command of the Brigadier Andrew Pringle and the HQ of 20th Armoured Brigade, to become the core of a British reserve force under national command. If UNPROFOR collapsed the force would play a major role in securing its safe withdrawal, which could well require combat.

The British planned an offensive operation to forcibly re-open the main road into Sarajevo. This involved no little danger, as the route led through the heart of Bosnian Serb-controlled terrain south of Sarajevo. There were several substantial checkpoints, which the Serbs could easily reinforce with landmines and other obstacles. Each would require an attack by an armoured infantry company to clear, and engineers would be needed to deal with mines and obstacles. One of the British field engineer squadrons with UNPROFOR had been assigned to the 20th Brigade, but it lacked dedicated armoured breaching vehicles. So Pringle asked the UK joint HQ at Wilton to send him armoured engineers, as well as artillery and extra secure communications.

This request was rapidly agreed and armoured engineers were sent from Germany. Also sent was 19 Field Regiment, 24th Airmobile Brigade's artillery regiment with 105mm light guns. They were on leave but reassembled at their barracks in Colchester within 24 hours. The regiment's two batteries and ammunition were rapidly flown to Croatia in RAF C130 Hercules, requiring 18 sorties a day until complete.

The UK Joint Commander General John Wilsey asked Brigadier Pringle for advice as to additional forces that could be usefully employed in Bosnia. London's thinking was to send either the Royal Marines' 3 Commando Brigade, which could deploy helicopter-borne marines from amphibious ships in the Adriatic, or the Army's 24th Airmobile Brigade, with its airmobile infantry and Lynx armed helicopters. Pringle counselled against both options, advising that both helicopters and infantry on their feet would be very vulnerable to shelling and land mines. Instead, he recommended deploying more armoured forces to make the 20th Brigade more capable of offensive operations. Pringle's advice was rejected and the airmobile brigade was sent instead. But the Serbs around Gorazde were unsettled by the brigade's arrival, with its potential to reinforce Gorazde and to block Serb offensive operations.

Simultaneously, the UN conducted intense negotiations with Bosnian Serbs. There were also rumours that France had done a deal with the Bosnian Serbs. Within a month, the British and UN hostages had all been released. But Gorazde remained a very dangerous place. For example, the battalion doused all lights at night as any illuminations were fired at by Bosnian Serb troops. At the time, this was the loneliest and most isolated British position in Bosnia, if not the world, not least because its supply lines were closed by the Bosnian Serbs. Eventually UNPROFOR was able to negotiate a new supply route for Gorazde.

The Bosnian Serbs had closed the main road into Sarajevo. The French and other UNPROFOR contingents in the city now depended on the exposed and difficult route down the north face of Mount Igman, under the eyes of Bosnian Serb tanks and guns.

Visiting Bosnia at the time, I saw for myself that HQ 20th Brigade and its British units had the combat capability, high morale and motivation necessary to fight their way into Sarajevo or Gorazde. But conversations with senior British officers made it equally clear that there was no political appetite in London to take the risk.

24th Airmobile Brigade was despatched to the port of Ploče in Croatia to become part of the new Rapid Reaction Force. But it took a long period to negotiate the necessary agreement with the Croatian authorities. It also took time to achieve full readiness, particularly in establishing an expeditionary base. The French Army did this more quickly, particularly in having rapidly deployable catering and sanitation capabilities.

Later that summer the UN Rapid Reaction Force was assembled from French, British and Dutch troops, with the role of 'protecting' UNPROFOR. The British elements repainted their vehicles from UN white to green to imply a combat role and removed their UN blue berets and helmet covers, replacing them with regimental berets and camouflaged helmet covers.

Bosnia deteriorated. In early July, the Bosnian Serbs attacked the Srebenica 'safe area'. They quickly overwhelmed weak Bosniak defences and forced Dutch UN troops out of the way. As the Dutch withdrew, they too were attacked by Muslim troops, who killed a Dutch soldier.

Like the British troops in Gorazde, the Dutch UN contingent in Srebrenica was isolated deep in territory controlled by the Bosnian Serbs and it was subject to similar levels of harassment and disruption. But when the Bosnian Serbs attacked, the Dutch seemed to have put up a much less determined resistance than the Fusiliers had in Gorazde. It was not long before the Bosnian government and international media started reporting evidence of a systematic massacre of male prisoners by the Bosnian Serbs.

General Smith reduced the number of UN troops in isolated positions that were exposed to further Bosnian Serb hostage-taking attempts. The 'international community' wanted UNPROFOR to keep the now non-existent peace between the Federation and the Bosnian Serbs. British troops in Gorazde were more isolated than ever. London announced that the Royal Welch Fusiliers would not be replaced, but did not warn the battalion, which was unsettling.

The deterioration in Bosnia, particularly the fall of Srebrenica, galvanized London, Washington, Paris and the Hague. On 14 July, Prime Minister John Major chaired an international conference at Lancaster House. He forged a degree of strategic consensus:

> The US abandoned their insistence on generalized bombing and the French had set to one side some fairly hair-raising plans for the recapture of Srebrenica. We agreed to send an Anglo-French Rapid Reaction Force of 1,700 to Sarajevo, to defend the city against attack, and also that Bosnian Serb aggression would be met by disproportionate and punitive military attacks'.[16]

The British, French and US governments persuaded the UN to agree that its tight controls on the use of NATO airpower should be relaxed. At the beginning of August, NATO warned that the existing threat to use airpower to deter attacks on the 'safe area' of Gorazde now applied to the other 'safe areas', including Sarajevo, and that any future air strikes would be on a much larger scale than before. A delegation of US Air Force and RAF senior officers secretly flew to Belgrade to warn military leaders that the UN and NATO were not bluffing about the increased use of airpower.

By now the Rapid Reaction Force amounted to an improvised multinational brigade. Commanded by an ad hoc French HQ, joined by British and Dutch staff officers, it comprised the Devon and Dorsets, with their Warriors and the armoured engineers that had been rushed out to Bosnia in the summer, the French Foreign Legion's 2e Régiment Étranger d'Infanterie in wheeled APCs and a squadron of Legion cavalry with wheeled light tanks. It also had substantial artillery: a French regiment of giant 155mm self-propelled guns, 19th Field Regiment with 105mm light guns, a heavy mortar battery from the Dutch Marines and Dutch Firefinder artillery-locating radars.

Escorted by the Warriors of the Devon and Dorsets, the best-protected armoured vehicles in Bosnia, it moved onto Mount Igman. The artillery deployed to fire positions and British, French and Dutch fire controllers found positions where they could observe and map the factions. Mount Igman, which overlooked Sarajevo, had been site of the ski events in the 1984 Winter Olympics. Soldiers established a modicum of shelter amongst battle-damaged, burned and looted hotels built for the event.

For the 'Highland Gunners', as 19 Field Regiment was known, this was a new role, for which no military textbook existed. So, they went back to artillery basics. They were within range of Serb artillery so proper gun emplacements were excavated. And to increase protection, their wheeled light towing vehicles were replaced by FV432 APCs. The commanding officer, Lieutenant Colonel Dick Applegate, and his regiment's HQ played a leading role in setting up a multinational fire-control centre in a disused hotel, to better co-ordinate target acquisition, fire control and planning between British, French and Dutch artillery and mortars.

Over the preceding year, NATO had developed a contingency plan for the failure of UNPROFOR's mission. In the event of a UN decision to end the operation, NATO would deploy a force to assist its withdrawal from Bosnia. The land component HQ for this operation would be the British-led HQ ARRC. It would involve major land forces from France, the US and UK entering Bosnia to assist the withdrawal of UNPROFOR. In the worst case, this could be a major combat operation in its own right. This plan would require NATO approval. Assembling the full force required could not be done quickly.

In the meantime, the British government was particularly concerned about the plight of the small British force in Gorazde. There was no doubt that further Bosnian Serb attacks would be met by a determined use of lethal force by British troops and NATO aircraft, weather permitting, but a large-scale Bosnian Serb attack could eventually overwhelm the British defenders, who had only limited supplies of fuel and ammunition.

So, a national plan was developed for an emergency extraction of the Fusiliers. Known initially as Operation *Screwdriver*, and subsequently as Operation *Haymarket*, the plan was evolved in conditions of great secrecy. The Director Special Forces would lead an air/land operation in which special forces Chinook helicopters would fly from Italy to rescue the Royal Welch. The SAS and a parachute battalion would secure a landing zone and escort the troops out of their bases. It was hoped that lethal force could be avoided, but the British planned to use electronic warfare to jam Serb air defences and command networks, and British fighter bombers and the ground force were prepared to attack any Serb forces or installations that might interfere with the operation.

The plan was secretly rehearsed in the UK. But the British military and political leadership considered it to be a high-risk operation, only to be launched if there was no alternative. Prime Minister Major wrote on his briefing paper on the operation: 'Not at all an easy option: cock-up factor clearly present.'[17]

Bosnian Serb forces were commanded by General Ratko Mladić. He had a formidable reputation for tough military leadership and was very popular with the Bosnian Serbs. He had an uncompromising attitude and was already being identified with war crimes, particularly the massacre of Muslim civilians at Srebrenica. Smith and Riley met Mladić on 20 August. Over a lavish Balkan barbeque lunch and display of Mladić's collection of white stallions, Smith persuaded the Bosnian Serb commander not to interfere with the withdrawal of the British from Gorazde. From Riley's viewpoint it seemed that Mladić simply wanted the UN out of his way, so he could more easily deal with the enclave.

There was now a military stalemate between the Federation and the Bosnian Serbs. UNPROFOR was obstructed by the Bosnian Serbs and despised by the Federation for its unwillingness to join their battles. There were plenty of politicians, warlords and black marketeers on both sides with an interest in keeping the war going.

On 29 August there was a mortar attack on a Sarajevo market that killed 39 civilians. UNPROFOR investigated and concluded that the bomb had been fired by the Bosnian Serbs. General Smith intended to order the Rapid Reaction Force to shell Bosnian Serb mortar and artillery positions around Sarajevo and for NATO to begin its coercive air attacks. But if those began with the Royal Welch still in Gorazde there was a very high chance that they would be attacked by the Bosnian Serbs. Armed forces minister Nicholas Soames was worried that British troops would not only be taken hostage, but might also be executed. So as soon as intelligence experts assessed that the mortars had been fired by the Bosnian Serbs, Smith ordered the Royal Welch to leave Gorazde.

To achieve surprise, no notice would be given to the Bosnian forces. Instead of travelling west to return to central Bosnia along the accustomed supply route, the battalion would travel east into Serbia. In case this went wrong, Belgrade refused entry, and the Royal Welch had to find another way back through Croatia, a small number of British officers were quietly deployed to key points with briefcases full of cash, to be used to overcome difficulties posed by obstructive officials.[18] In the event these measures were not needed. Riley recounted that General Smith:

> called me and said he was going to stall Mladić by saying that the investigation was ongoing and there was no clarity about who had fired the shell. Our withdrawal was well under way and there were only 80 of us left – although we had had to fight the Bosnians at one point and kill some of them who were obstructing and attacking us. I brought forward our departure at very short notice so as to beat Mladić's passage of information. We got out alright that night into Serbia – the relief was incredible, followed by the realization that we had done what no one thought we could, leave Gorazde in good order, with all our gear, and no casualties. No-one had told him we were gone – I would love to have seen his face when he realized! And God help the object of his fury!'[19]

OPERATION DELIBERATE FORCE

By now the French, British and Dutch artillery had, through weeks of painstaking observation, built up a detailed picture of Bosnian Serb positions between Mount Igman and Sarajevo. UNPROFOR's Rapid Reaction Force HQ had done a great deal of planning with NATO's air component and the artillery in the multinational brigade.

They put this to good use when the NATO air campaign, designated Operation *Deliberate Force*, began on the afternoon of 30 August. After two and half hours of air strikes around Sarajevo, the NATO jets departed, allowing the artillery fire plan to begin.

This French heavy artillery, the British light guns and Dutch heavy mortars bombarded Bosnian Serb artillery and tanks. They did great damage to the Bosnian Serb artillery, while resulting in relatively few civilian casualties and little collateral damage. The British artillery observers on the forward slope of Mount Igman proved invaluable. After an hour, the artillery fire ceased, so as to make way for more air strikes.

After a few days the UNPROFOR and NATO attacks were paused, to allow negotiations. These failed and the air campaign resumed, with increasing attacks against strategic targets. By now the Bosnian Croat army, revitalized by training provided by US government-funded contractors, had waged a highly successful offensive, evicting Bosnian Serb forces from a huge swathe of western Bosnia. Serbia's President Milošević seemed to have tired of the war and the opprobrium and sanctions it brought upon Belgrade. These factors, combined with NATO air and missile strikes and the Rapid Reaction Force's shelling around Sarajevo, brought about a ceasefire and the reopening of routes into Sarajevo. By now the British gunners had fired over 350 shells.

In late autumn, 2nd Battalion, the Light Infantry, which I had the privilege to command, replaced the Devon and Dorsets on Mount Igman. Bosnian Serb commanders around Sarajevo told me that they had greatly feared that the artillery fire was but a precursor to the British Warriors descending from the mountain to forcibly open routes to Sarajevo. They were particularly concerned that previous firefights with the British had shown that fire was rapidly and accurately returned by the Warrior's cannon, often resulting in Serb casualties. They told me that the Warrior was impervious to all the weapons that the Bosnian Serbs had used against the vehicle.

Though many British soldiers and officers with experience of the war hoped that an enduring peace deal could be negotiated, they were not optimistic. With the Bosnian Serbs controlling much of the country, all previous peace plans had foundered – neither their opponents nor the international community having much leverage. Now the Bosnian Serbs' share of Bosnia had been reduced to half, and they had experienced a full-spectrum artillery and air offensive. Would the US be able to exploit this to clinch a peace deal?

The US seized the opportunity, and the indefatigable diplomat Richard Holbrooke negotiated the Dayton Peace Agreement. British troops were relieved. There was also much reflection on UNPROFOR's operations. From the outset, it had been set ambitious ends by the UN Security Council, but member states consistently failed to provide adequate means. And they had also been unwilling to employ adequate ways of achieving its missions. The proclamation of 'safe areas' was perhaps the worst example of this, in which the UN was given insufficient troops and national capitals were unwilling for them to militarily confront the Bosnian Serbs. The British and French were partial exceptions to this, but London was unwilling to put British troops further in harm's way until the US became decisively engaged.

UNDER NATO COMMAND

The military annex of the Dayton Agreement gave the new NATO Implementation Force (IFOR) complete freedom of movement throughout Bosnia and unlimited authority to take any measures necessary to supervise and enforce compliance with the treaty, including the use of force – very assertive provisions that stood in stark contrast to the limited UNPROFOR rules of engagement. The agreement set out a timeline for separating the faction forces, their withdrawal to barracks and partial demobilization under an inspection regime, and required the forces of the warring factions to disengage and withdraw from the front line. The first key measure was the requirement for both sides to withdraw from their front lines creating a 2.5-mile-wide zone of separation. This had to be achieved by D plus 30 days.

On 20 December, the date designated as D-Day, military responsibility for Bosnia would transfer from UNPROFOR to IFOR. This quickened the pulses of British commanders and acted as a focus for planning. Understandably there was much political and military apprehension in Brussels and London. The considerable difficulties, tensions and uncertainties of 1992–95 had greatly frustrated the British.

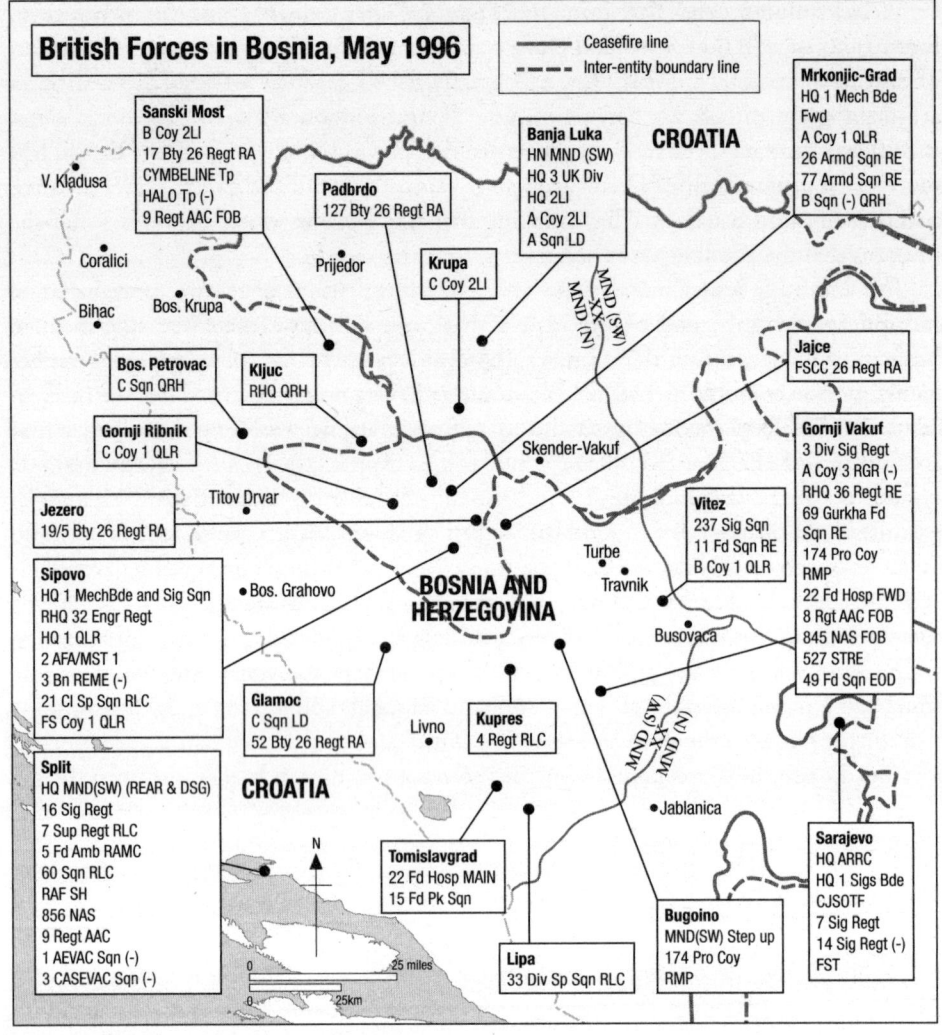

British Forces in Bosnia, May 1996

—— Ceasefire line
---- Inter-entity boundary line

Mrkonjic-Grad
HQ 1 Mech Bde Fwd
A Coy 1 QLR
26 Armd Sqn RE
77 Armd Sqn RE
B Sqn (-) QRH

Sanski Most
B Coy 2LI
17 Bty 26 Regt RA
CYMBELINE Tp
HALO Tp (-)
9 Regt AAC FOB

Banja Luka
HN MND (SW)
HQ 3 UK Div
HQ 2LI
A Coy 2LI
A Sqn LD

CROATIA

V. Kladusa

Padbrdo
127 Bty 26 Regt RA

Coralici

Prijedor

Krupa
C Coy 2LI

Bihac   Bos. Krupa

MND (SW) XX MND (N)

Jajce
FSCC 26 Regt RA

Bos. Petrovac
C Sqn QRH

Kljuc
RHQ QRH

Gornji Vakuf
3 Div Sig Regt
A Coy 3 RGR (-)
RHQ 36 Regt RE
69 Gurkha Fd Sqn RE
174 Pro Coy RMP
22 Fd Hosp FWD
8 Rgt AAC FOB
845 NAS FOB
527 STRE
49 Fd Sqn EOD

Gornji Ribnik
C Coy 1 QLR

Skender-Vakuf

Jezero
19/5 Bty 26 Regt RA

Titov Drvar

Vitez
237 Sig Sqn
11 Fd Sqn RE
B Coy 1 QLR

Turbe

Sipovo
HQ 1 MechBde and Sig Sqn
RHQ 32 Engr Regt
HQ 1 QLR
2 AFA/MST 1
3 Bn REME (-)
21 Cl Sp Sqn RLC
FS Coy 1 QLR

Bos. Grahovo

BOSNIA AND HERZEGOVINA

Travnik

Busovaca

Glamoc
C Sqn LD
52 Bty 26 Regt RA

Livno

Kupres
4 Regt RLC

MND (SW) XX MND (N)

Split
HQ MND(SW) (REAR & DSG)
16 Sig Regt
7 Sup Regt RLC
5 Fd Amb RAMC
60 Sqn RLC
RAF SH
856 NAS
9 Regt AAC
1 AEVAC Sqn (-)
3 CASEVAC Sqn (-)

CROATIA

Jablanica

Sarajevo
HQ ARRC
HQ 1 Sigs Bde
CJSOTF
7 Sig Regt
14 Sig Regt (-)
FST

N

Tomislavgrad
22 Fd Hosp MAIN
15 Fd Pk Sqn

Bugoino
MND(SW) Step up
174 Pro Coy
RMP

0   25 miles
0   25km

Lipa
33 Div Sp Sqn RLC

British troops in Bosnia then amounted to a small brigade, the 4th Armoured, commanded by then Brigadier Richard Dannatt. This comprised two batteries of light guns, an engineer regiment, a squadron of JCOs and two battlegroups: 1st Battalion, Royal Regiment of Fusiliers with Saxon wheeled APCs and 2nd Battalion, the Light Infantry (2 LI), which many foreign troops were surprised to find was a heavy armoured infantry battalion equipped with Warrior infantry fighting vehicles. I commanded the battalion, which together with an armoured reconnaissance squadron of Light Dragoons and an armoured engineer troop, had universally been seen as the most powerful battalion in UNPROFOR.[20]

Plans were quickly developed in London, Wiltshire and Bosnia to rapidly deploy British troops to their new NATO roles and areas of responsibility. IFOR's land component would consist of three multinational divisions, one each led by Britain, France and the US. These would be commanded by HQ ARRC and its signal brigade. The British contingent in Bosnia would be reinforced with heavy units, including an armoured regiment, more Army and RAF helicopters, the HQ of the 3rd Division and its supporting, engineer, logistic, signals and medical units and more JCOs. The reinforcing equipment would travel on six civilian ships, but on 20 December the only additional unit in Bosnia was the 3rd Division's HQ and its tough-minded commander, Major General Mike Jackson.

As I and 2 LI's leadership team planned our part in NATO's first-ever land operation mission we identified risks. Would the warring armies comply with the agreement so hastily negotiated at Dayton? Would NATO troops suffer the same non-cooperation, harassment, and attacks as UN forces? Would NATO have to use force? Would there be casualties? The best way to prevent these problems arising would be to give each side confidence that IFOR could provide security for them while they withdrew, so that their opponent could not make mischief. We therefore set out to reassure both sides. We patrolled in as many places as we could, moved out mortars and artillery around as much as we could. We deployed as much strength as we could around the front line.

BBC journalist Martin Bell played a distinguished role in reporting from front lines across Bosnia, being wounded in Sarajevo in the process. He called us a 'stage army, exiting stage left and reappearing stage right'. He was right. He reflected on the role of British troops that transferred from UNPROFOR to the NATO IFOR:

> They began their tours of duty as the UN's soldiers and ended them as NATO's – for which they were properly rewarded with two medals. Those medals were earned the hard way in hard weather. The troops enforced the military provisions of the Dayton Agreement, risked their lives to save the lives of others, swept away the roadblocks and restored a minimal peace in Bosnia after three-and-a-half years of war. It was NATO's first-ever ground operation, and it was substantially led by the British. At the time of the transfer of authority, on 21 December 1995, the Americans, for all their logistical power, had actually failed to arrive. I remember reflecting, not for the first time, on the extraordinary quality of the British troops participating, on the dangers they faced across a mine-strewn landscape, and on the unique and unprecedented nature of the task before them.[21]

Easier said than done. For the first 30 days of the operation, 2 LI had two armoured infantry companies, a squadron of Light Dragoons, a light artillery battery, some engineers and were assisted by a small patrol of JCOs. Our area of responsibility contained a front line 75 miles long, through very hilly country. Intelligence estimated that there were two Bosniak and two Bosnian Serb corps facing each other, with a strength of up to 120,000 troops. We numbered about 700 men and one woman.

We had no bases, other than those we found for ourselves, so lived in disused factories and empty houses on the desolate front line, usually with no electric power or running water. Bases were temporary, opened and closed in accordance with tactical priorities. This came to be known as 'manoeuvre peacekeeping'.

For example, a lonely platoon outpost in an abandoned village in the middle of the front line in north-west Bosnia was named by a surfing enthusiast as 'Bondi Beach' – an intentional irony, giving the complete lack of tropical weather, beach, breaking waves and surfing amenities. There was no electricity or running water, but an abandoned bath was placed on brick supports and had a fire lit beneath it – an improvised capability relished by soldiers whose last access to showers had been five weeks earlier.

In the event the deployment of 60,000 NATO ground troops proceeded successfully. The Bosnian warring factions were given the confidence they needed to withdraw from the front line, then concentrate in barracks and largely demobilize. There was no armed opposition to NATO troops and thus no NATO combat casualties, although land mines and the hazards of Bosnia's extremely dangerous roads took their toll.

On three occasions 2 LI were fired at. We responded with cannon and small arms, then followed up with a massive show of force around the incident. Although initially bullish, the local faction brigade commanders subsequently became contrite after a one-way 'interview without coffee'.

These were the only occasions in which British troops in the brigade opened fire. But we often had to consider the use of force to coerce the factions, particularly when one faction or another was threatening not to comply with a military timeline. So we would open negotiations, concurrent with an ostentatious movement of our forces into the contentious area. In every case where we did this the factions backed down, albeit often at the last minute.

We also got crossing points opened across the front line. For example, after a Bosniak complaint of a ceasefire violation by Bosnian Serb troops, Captain Tobias Ellwood[22] and Lieutenant David Livingston, assisted by a patrol of JCOs, arranged to bring the opposing commanders together in no-man's land to thrash out the problem under our protection. The JCOs would bring the Serb battalion commander from the east, B Company would provide security and Tobias Ellwood, escorted by David Livingston's platoon, would bring the Muslim commander. David deployed his Warriors to cover the site of the mine strike, to respond to fire from either side. David takes up the story:

> We were keen to get the two opposing commanders together in the middle to sort out the problem that had caused the letter of complaint and instil respect and trust. After discussion with both sides it was established that the minefield had been laid by the Muslims. They stated that we had cleared all their mines. The Serbs claimed not to have laid any at all. However, we still had three hundred metres of snow-covered track to clear to the Serb side. I decided the risk was acceptable and started to move down the track in my Warrior. We stopped several times for me to dismount and check suspicious lumps in the snow, all the time being watched tentatively by both sides. The route, as the commanders had said, was clear and we linked up with the JCOs on the Serb side.
>
> Having cleared the route, it was then up to us to coax both opposing commanders into no-man's land. They were put into the rear of the JCOs' Land Rovers, which in turn were escorted by Warriors from my platoon. Once in the centre I deployed riflemen to provide a close inner cordon round the group while the two Warriors sat close at

hand, traversing their turrets menacingly, as the liaison officer and JCOs conducted the negotiations.

It was a strange moment as the two commanders who had been fighting each other for so long met, discussed and resolved a problem, shook hands and then returned to their respective sides, all under close protection of British soldiers.[23]

David, Tobias and the patrol of JCOs exposed themselves to danger by accompanying the commanders into the zone between the two forces, giving both sides great confidence in the security that IFOR was providing. This was practical leadership, of the highest order.

The British division was much more capable than UNPROFOR had ever been. Our battalion's Warriors were soon joined by Challenger tanks and new AS90 howitzers. These self-propelled guns had only just entered service with the Army and went straight into service in Bosnia. And the British division brought its aviation regiment of Lynx and Gazelle helicopters as well as RAF Chinook helicopters. Although the factions had greater numbers of guns and tanks, these were of 1970s vintage and the armour of their Soviet-pattern tanks offered much less protection than that of Challenger and Warrior.

We were confident that in a military confrontation with the factions, our hardware and training would provide 'escalation dominance'. To demonstrate this the division set up an area where it fired heavy weapons. A large unpopulated area of Herzegovina was found. Named 'Glamoc Range', it allowed the firing of all the division's heavy weapons and attacks by NATO jets and US Army Apache helicopters. As soon as it could, the division staged a large-scale live firing exercise, to which it invited senior Bosnian officers from all sides. This was useful training for the British troops, but it had the key purpose of messaging British firepower and training to the three faction militaries. Glamoc Range would continue to be heavily used by NATO troops during subsequent years.

The combination of IFOR's unconstrained authority, the very tight military timelines of the agreement, the speed at which we redeployed from UNPROFOR and the way we concealed our relative weakness in the first month of NATO operations by constant redeployment meant that we seized the initiative and largely maintained it. We no longer saw our role as peacekeeping, a term that had become discredited by UNPROFOR's weaknesses, but as a new role of 'peace enforcement'.

There was no British or NATO doctrine for this, so we made one up for ourselves, while conducting operations. Many of the principles of manoeuvre warfare helped us, including our doctrine of mission command, which aimed to promote decentralized command, freedom and speed of action and initiative. The large areas covered by our forces, the complex nature of the task, the lack of hard intelligence, the often confused situation, the poor communications and the problematic passage of information necessitated a clear statement of mission and full understanding of the higher commander's intent in order to be able to react quickly to changing situations or fleeting opportunities. If mission command did not exist, it would have had to be invented for Bosnia.

For the British troops, the clear chain of command from HQ ARRC to 3rd Division and 4th Brigade was much tauter and more effective than UN command had ever been. In March 1996 British commanders were delighted to meet Gilbert Greenall, a contractor working for the UK Overseas Development Administration who arrived in the divisional area with British government money to spend on funding quick-impact development projects, including repairs to water, supply roads and schools that had been used as temporary bases by British troops. General Mike Jackson used:

> the analogy of rope to describe peace support operations in a post-conflict situation. The provision of security is only one strand; the other strands are political progress, humanitarian aid, demobilization of the factions' armies, reconstruction and economic progress. Once the strands are woven together the rope is stronger than the sum of its parts. It's essential to demonstrate that for the vast majority of people the future is going to be better than the past.[24]

In his memoir, General Richard Dannatt analyzed the failures of UNPROFOR, the success of IFOR and the difficulties of achieving progress in the civilian measures of Dayton as follows:

> Where military intervention is required, it must be strong, robust and timely. Where a fractured state needs help, the international assistance needs to be broadly based and to cover not just the military line of operation, but governance, the rule of law, justice, human rights, and economic support ... Perhaps of greatest importance is the requirement that strategic objectives set out by governments must be linked to tactical activity on the ground by soldiers and aid workers through a properly worked out operational-level plan – a campaign plan – drawn up by an appropriately trained and empowered theatre commander, be he ambassador or general. Strategic success is delivered by the soldiers on the ground, but is enabled by a properly thought through and resourced operational-level campaign plan. There are no short cuts.[25]

In Sarajevo, HQ ARRC had their work cut out establishing the multinational corps, not least as they found themselves literally on the front line coming under sniper fire in January and February 1991. At the time they were NATO's only rapidly deployable land higher HQ and they earned their pay, validating the Army's initiative five years earlier to establish the HQ. HQ ARRC, HQ 3rd Division and 4th Armoured Brigade all played key roles.

The IFOR Mission had intentionally been limited to a year. But towards the end of 1996 NATO countries agreed not to withdraw from Bosnia. Instead, NATO's military mandate was extended into a 'Stabilization Force' (SFOR).

The conflict shifted from the battlefield to politics. Elections were held for posts in the many layered government structures. But these allowed nationalist extremists to embed themselves in power. Extremists demobilized themselves from the entities' armies and moved into civil appointments, for example as mayors and police officers, often becoming a malign influence, obstructing progress and making a bad situation worse. In Republika Srpska the malign influence of Radovan Karadžić and his supporters threatened stability. They acted as a threatening break on the reforming actions of Republika Srpska's Prime

Minister Biljana Plavžić, who was opposed to the revanchist nationalism of Radovan Karadžić and his supporters.

The Bosnian Serbs had retained large numbers of paramilitary 'special police'. These were heavily armed, for example operating armoured vehicles. The ranks were populated by many hard-core extremists. There had initially been a dispute between SFOR and NATO HQ as to whether these units counted as armed forces or police. But in 1997 NATO agreed that they should be subject to the full provisions of the Dayton Agreement as if they were armed forces and should therefore be disarmed.

An attempted coup by hard-line Bosnian Serb nationalists in Banja Luka was foiled by British troops. Acting on intelligence that suggested the special police in Banja Luka were about to mount a *coup d'état* to remove Plavžić, British armoured infantry deployed at dawn and surrounded the city's special police station with their Warrior fighting vehicles. A sergeant major walked to the door to tell the special police that they had 30 minutes to leave. US General Eric Shinseki was later to tell General Wesley Clark, the new NATO SACEUR, that 'they came streaming out barefooted and in pyjamas. And we closed the station.'[26]

By now the US and NATO had changed their policy. Previously both had been extremely reluctant to involve the military in implementing the civil provisions of the Dayton Agreement: a policy that the British had often turned a blind eye to. But now they agreed that NATO would support those who supported the agreement and oppose those who opposed it, retrospectively endorsing the British seizure of the special police station in Banja Luka.

Streams of extreme propaganda were broadcast by Bosnian Serb radio stations. As a result of these challenges the Peace Implementation Council of France, UK, US, Russia, Turkey and Germany authorized the High Representative to remove Bosnian public officials and to impose legislation.

THE BATTLE OF THE BUSES

In September 1997, Bosnian Serb hard-liners called for 'all Intelligent and Courageous Serbs' to attend a political rally in Banja Luka. All the indicators pointed to this being a blatant effort to stage another coup, this time with about 10,000 people. Muscular males were being paid $250 to attend. Violence looked likely. British troops discovered a hidden cache of weapons and police uniforms, possibly intended for a raid to seize President Plavžić.

Those attending the rally were to travel in around 250 buses. NATO determined that the rally was a threat. But the International High Representative, who had the power to prohibit the rally, would not agree to NATO's requests that the event be banned. So, rather than stop the buses outright, potentially provoking a confrontation that would promote the extremist agenda, SFOR did everything it could to slow them down. Buses were stopped at NATO checkpoints, painstakingly searched for weapons, and identities checked. Buses were preceded by NATO armoured vehicles driving very slowly. In the

British area, troops ingeniously used caltrops, chains of spikes designed to puncture tyres. Wesley Clark later described the ploy:

> A single British soldier stayed behind to pull the cord to spring the spikes as the first bus passed over. Sure enough, the tyres blew and the bus halted blocking the narrow road. As the Serbs dismounted and recognized the trick they grabbed their lumber and sticks in the baggage compartment of the bus and searched for the soldier in the brush. This was no game. Fortunately, he had already escaped. The manoeuvre was executed at least once more.[27]

Police from Banja Luka who were loyal to Plavžić set up vehicle checkpoints on the city's approach roads. To support them, British troops deployed behind them with riot-control equipment. As it was getting dark, they also had artillery on call to fire illuminating shells. Throughout this tense day, NATO had been negotiating with the High Representative. He was eventually persuaded to ban the rally. The British troops then stopped the buses, turned them around and sent them home.

No shots had been fired, but NATO had defeated a second potential coup attempt that risked considerable potential violence. British troops and the British-led multinational divisional HQ at Banja Luka had again played a decisive role.

There were occasional outbreaks of public disorder and rioting. For example, in April 1998 interethnic rioting broke out in the town of Titov Dravar. The Canadian battalion responsible for the area needed help, so an armoured infantry company that had just arrived in Bosnia was warned to intervene and found itself rapidly loading its Warriors with live ammunition. Major Dick Ovey, the company commander, was flown by helicopter over the vast and bleak landscape to meet with Major General Cedric Delves, commanding the multinational division, who had himself assumed command only minutes before the rioting began. In a brief conversation he gave Overy direction:

> 'Have you been in Northern Ireland?'
> 'Yes Sir.'
> 'Good, then you'll know what to do'.[28]

After an overnight drive the company arrived and set about restoring order.

THE SECRET HUNT FOR WAR CRIMINALS

In 1997, some NATO states changed their approach to war criminals. The existing NATO policy of abstaining from hunting for war criminals was outweighed by the disadvantages of the impunity and malign influence they were exercising. Energized by the Dutch government, an international coalition was formed within NATO of nations that employed a more assertive approach. They and the International Criminal Tribunal for the Former Yugoslavia developed the 'sealed warrant', an indictment that would be issued to NATO, but otherwise kept secret, only revealed in public when the indictee was arrested and transferred to the court at the Hague. This informal 'coalition of the willing' within NATO comprised the US, the UK, the Netherlands, Germany and France. Each took on a number of 'targets'. At the height of the operation there were hundreds of military and civilian intelligence personnel and special forces personnel gathering intelligence and planning operations.[29]

The approach was not to mount large-scale searches and round-ups of suspects or aggressive offensive operations as had proved so counterproductive in Somalia. Instead it would be to use precision intelligence and surveillance, with a minimum of force, thus achieving the least possible civilian casualties, collateral damage and disruption. This began with intelligence being secretly collected, analyzed and fused. Once there was enough hard data to identify the suspect, special forces would conduct covert surveillance, often operating in civilian vehicles and clothes, and find an opportunity to make an arrest, quickly departing with the detainee.

The first two arrest operations were mounted by British troops. These drew on their approach to intelligence-led counterterrorist operations in Northern Ireland. There are many credible reports that the troops on the ground were from the SAS. The targets were hard-line Bosnian Serb extremists. One was arrested without a struggle. The other pulled a pistol and was shot dead. He was a hard-line paramilitary who had become a senior Bosnian Serb police officer in Prijedor. The previous year he had done everything he could to impose friction on my battalion's operations and actively oppose the implementation of the Dayton Agreement.[30]

Subsequent operations by British and NATO troops successfully detained other indicted war criminals. For the British troops involved, this required long hours spent on covert surveillance operations, as well as painstakingly developing plans for the arrest. It was essential to avoid civilian casualties.

For example, in developing an arrest operation in north-west Bosnia, extensive covert surveillance was carried out to identify the suspect's pattern of life, to select an option for an arrest. On the morning of the planned operation, all went to plan, with an arrest team covertly deployed. But as the suspect walked into the ambush location, he was seen to be carrying a young child, probably one of his grandchildren. The arrest operation was immediately suspended and took place at a later date. As time went on, the remaining fugitives became increasingly difficult to find. It was likely that they had left Bosnia.

THE MOSTAR BANK JOB

Operations in Bosnia continued for the next few years. The British presence gradually reduced, transitioning from being a British-led multinational division to a genuinely multinational formation, made up of equal numbers of British, Canadian and Dutch troops.

There was no armed opposition to NATO and bases were well developed. Indeed, for a year or so, the main British base in a metal factory at Banja Luka developed a reputation as something of a holiday posting and was nicknamed 'Banja Napa', after Ayia Napa, the hedonistic tourist resort in Cyprus. But a determined British brigade commander, Andrew Farquhar, a no-nonsense infantry officer from Yorkshire, used his sheer force of personality to reverse this trend, cutting the number of bars on the base by two thirds and instituting a tough alcohol-rationing regime.

One exception to the generally routine character of the operation was an incident that became known as the 'Mostar Bank Job'. The context was an effort by Bosnian Croat separatists to help the predominantly Croat area of Herzegovina secede from the Bosnian Federation. Many had links to organized crime groups that were funnelling black money through the Herzegovina Bank in Mostar.

The High Representative and SFOR commander in Bosnia decided that that all the branches of the bank should be raided by SFOR and their contents, including money and files, seized, in order to throttle the separatist network and subsequently prosecute the corrupt officials. In mid-April, all the branches of the bank were simultaneously raided across Bosnia. Raids by Canadian, Dutch, US and French troops were all successful.

But in Herzegovina the raid on the bank's HQ failed. A well-organized mob of Bosnian Croat militants seized several civilian auditors going into the bank and threatened to kill one – a Canadian lady. The Spanish battalion in Mostar had soldiers injured in the vicious riot, gave in to the militants' demands and withdrew. As the Canadian Major General Rick Hillier, commanding the multinational division put it, the failure of the raid had been 'a black eye for SFOR and would have undermined our credibility immensely'.

The deputy commander of SFOR was then Major General Richard Dannatt. He called for the British armoured infantry battalion with its Warriors: 2nd Battalion, the Princess of Wales' Royal Regiment. It had much Northern Ireland experience and was trained and equipped for crowd and riot control. It was tasked with mounting a second raid.

Special forces began surveillance operations of the area around the bank. These included Italian Carabinieri paramilitary police in civilian clothes. Surprise was achieved by the battalion moving in daylight not by the direct route to Mostar, but to Sarajevo. After dark it headed south for Mostar, drove past the town and then doubled back on itself. Surrounding the bank and immediate area, the doors were blown in with explosives by SAS experts flown in for the task. The troops found three safes. Two were small enough to be opened explosively, but the third was much larger, with much thicker walls and a complex lock. The experts advised that the amount of explosive necessary to open it would probably destroy the contents. In the event a chain was hooked up between the safe and a Warrior fighting vehicle. When the Warrior accelerated away, the safe came flying out of the building, taking part of the bank's wall with it.

It was not often that soldiers got to rob a bank as part of their duties. As General Dannatt said it was truly 'a night to remember'. The evidence seized enabled the High Representative to neutralize the conspiracy.

Above From the mid-1960s to mid-1980s, the Chieftain was NATO's best-armed and best-protected tank, but it suffered from chronic unreliability.
(Getty Images)

Centre An Army 'snatch squad' in early 1970s Northern Ireland.
(Getty Images)

Bottom Operation *Banner* often featured surreal clashes of normal and abnormal circumstances.
(Getty Images)

Above Heavily laden soldiers of 2 Para gather for a helicopter in the Falklands. (© IWM, FKD 2124)

Left Margaret Thatcher, prime minister from 1979 to 1990, drives an Abbott 105mm self-propelled gun. (Getty Images)

Below Scots Guards on Mount Tumbledown celebrate the Argentinian surrender. (© Regimental Headquarters Scots Guards)

Above Battlegroup training in Canada provided a strong foundation for the Army's armoured warfare capabilities. By 2025, this training had ceased. (Crown Copyright)

Left In December 1995, the weak UNPROFOR in Bosnia was succeeded by the better armed and more robust NATO IFOR. (Author's Collection)

Below Chieftain tanks were replaced by the better protected Challenger, deployed on Operation *Granby* in 1990–91. (Getty Images)

Above British troops entering Kosovo were greeted as liberators by the majority Albanian population. (Getty Images)

Left A Parachute Regiment patrol in Sierra Leone. (Getty Images)

Below In August 2001, 16 Air Assault Brigade led a NATO mission to Macedonia to defuse a civil war. Here a paratrooper guards Albanian guerrillas who are surrendering their weapons. (Getty Images)

The battle of Basra, 2003. A Warrior infantry fighting vehicle and a sniper of the Irish Guards cover armoured engineers extinguishing oil well fires. (Getty Images)

A British soldier prepares to jump from a burning Warrior during the September 2005 incident at the Jameat police station in Basra. (Atef Hassan/Reuters)

Prime Minister Tony Blair arrives by Chinook helicopter to meet Major General Jonathan Reilly. By tolerating cuts to defence spending, Blair ensured that the Army would have insufficient helicopters in Afghanistan. (Getty Images)

Top British troops dismount from a Snatch Land Rover to greet Afghans in Helmand, May 2006. (Getty Images)

Centre A rifleman from the newly formed 1st Battalion, the Rifles takes cover in a ditch in Helmand's irrigated Green Zone in March 2009. (Crown Copyright)

Bottom Army Apache helicopters, seen here leaving Helmand in 2014, provided invaluable fire support to ground troops. (Crown Copyright)

Above The self-organized tributes to dead troops at the small town of Royal Wootton Bassett captured the national mood of increasing respect for the Army's determination. (Getty Images)

Left A gunner of the Royal Horse Artillery distributes a Covid-19 test kit in May 2021. Restrictions on the employment of women in the British Army were removed completely in 2018. (Getty Images)

Paratroops snatch some much-needed rest during the 2001 evacuation from Kabul. (Getty Images)

Above After the 2022 Russian attack on NATO, British Army exercises in Eastern Europe greatly increased. Here a British engineer squadron uses its M3 ferries to carry Challenger 2 tanks.
(Getty Images)

Left Guardsmen of Queen's Company, 1st Battalion, the Grenadier Guards carry the coffin of Her Majesty Queen Elizabeth II into St George's Chapel, Windsor, 19 September 2022. (Crown Copyright)

Below Armoured infantrymen and a Warrior from the British battlegroup in Estonia guard NATO's borders with Russia. (NATO)

BOSNIA'S LONG TAIL

I returned to Bosnia in February 2003 to command NATO's Multinational Brigade Northwest. Its area of responsibility was the same as that of Multinational Division Southwest in 1996. Instead of the 20,000 NATO troops in the sector in 1996, the brigade had 3,500 troops, including battalions from UK, Canada and Holland. This reflected a greatly improved security situation. The entities' armies had greatly reduced in size. There had been progress in implementing the civilian provisions of the Dayton Agreement. For example, refugees of all three ethnicities had returned to the many towns and villages from which they had been evicted during the war.

The presence of our force had an important role in deterring the entities' armed forces from any military non-compliance. But the brigade had considerable excess capacity over and above the minimum required for this deterrence. So we sought to identify the options to widen the utility of the brigade.

We did what we could to support the energetic leadership of the new High Representative, the British politician Paddy Ashdown. He had an ambitious agenda to move Bosnia forward by improving its governance by embedding economic and political reform and greater interethnic co-operation. All of this was to make Bosnia self-sufficient economically and a credible candidate for membership of the European Union.

In Republika Srpska there was a still a nexus of ultra-nationalists, corrupt officials and organized crime networks. Money from organized crime and corruption was being used to fund the covert networks that were hiding the indicted war criminals Radavan Karadžić and Ratko Mladić from the attentions of NATO and the International Tribunal. The same applied in Bosnian Croat areas, where the indicted Croat general Ante Gotovina still commanded considerable support. We supported operations to arrest the remaining indicted war criminals, but no arrests resulted. It seemed that the fugitives were by this time in 'deep cover', if they were in Bosnia at all.

We sought other ways to disrupt the networks in Republika Srpska that intelligence suggested were supporting the concealment of key individuals indicted by the war crimes tribunal. This required a variety of activity, often covert. For example, intelligence and surveillance detected a network of police corruption centred on the town of Kneževo. After months of patiently building the intelligence picture the police station was raided, evidence gathered and the police chief replaced.

These initiatives were complemented by new tactics developed by 1st Battalion, the Highlanders. These adaptations created a new way of locating clandestine arms dumps dating back to the immediate aftermath of the war six years earlier. This was able to uncover vast stocks of weapons and ammunition that had been carefully hidden in Republika Srpska after the war. The battalion made ever-increasing discoveries of these caches, with growing evidence that they were being actively maintained by a secret network. There was convincing evidence that this was linked to hard-line extremists, including those supporting the concealment of Mladić and Karadžić. The operation became increasingly successful over the summer. It was assessed to have put increasing pressure on the extremist elements in Republika Srpska.

The brigade also sought to support and encourage political progress. An unexpected opportunity in this area was helping the Bosnian government and police conduct the security operation for the 2003 visit of the Pope to Banja Luka. A previous visit of the Pope to Sarajevo in the previous decade had seen heavy levels of security provided by NATO troops, but this time the Bosnian government and police would take the lead. As there were 12,000 NATO troops in the country, they would support the Bosnian security operation and the brigade would lead the operation. I found myself representing NATO on the Bosnian government committee planning the event, as well as leading the tactical operation in Banja Luka. If ever there was an example of the compression of the strategic, operational and tactical levels of command, this was it.

We supported the Bosnian police. They would lead the operation, but NATO would be available as a backup should the security situation deteriorate beyond their ability to control it. To guarantee the capability to do this the brigade received NATO reinforcements, doubling in size. Plans were developed jointly with the Bosnian police and extensively rehearsed.

In the event most of the visit went extremely smoothly. The majority of the people attending the event were Catholic Croats, both from Herzegovina and Croatia. But there were a surprising number of Bosnia Muslims and Serbs attending the large open air mass. Conversations with NATO troops and interviews by the Bosnian media suggested that these people wanted to see the Pope for themselves, a surprising and welcome return of the religious tolerance that had been a feature of the previous Yugoslav state.

The mass went smoothly, but as the Pope was departing the city for Banja Luka airport, an intelligence report suggested that a Chechen assassin would make an attempt on his life. Well-developed contingency plans were put into effect; reinforcements were rapidly deployed around Banja Luka airport and its approaches, and every available NATO helicopter was launched to cover the Pope's route. In the joint NATO/Bosnian police operations room the tension was palpable. When the papal aircraft successfully departed Bosnian air space there was much applause. The success of the operation greatly boosted the confidence of the Bosnian Serb police.

The Bosnian armed forces underwent a process of integration into a single organization under civilian political control. Efforts to integrate the entities' police forces achieved only limited success; but overall Ashdown's tenure successfully reformed and strengthened the Bosnian state sufficiently that a Stabilization and Association Agreement with the EU was signed in 2006.

In 2004, SFOR was replaced by a European Union Force. But after Ashdown's departure in 2006, political progress and reform stagnated. A 2009 US-led effort to rejuvenate political reform failed. The three ethnicities remained largely culturally and politically segregated and there was insufficient support for necessary reform. Meanwhile Bosnia's neighbours made progress in overcoming the legacy of the wars of the 1990s and became increasingly integrated into Europe. Croatia became a member of NATO in 2009 and of the EU in 2013. Serbia oriented itself towards the EU, becoming a candidate member in 2012. However, the 2022 Russian attack on Ukraine impacted both Serbia and Bosnia's Republika Srpska, energizing pro-Moscow elements.

As part of this progress, the Croat and Serb governments played an increasing role in the hunt for the major indicted war criminals. In 2005 Ante Gotovina, the former Croat military commander, was detained in Tenerife. In Serbia Radovan Karadžić was arrested in June 2008 and Ratko Mladić was detained in May 2011. Both were tried for war crimes, found guilty and imprisoned.

BOSNIA IN RETROSPECT

From 1992 onwards, the Army was heavily committed to operations in Bosnia. This commitment peaked in 1996 with an armoured brigade, divisional HQ, combat support, signals brigade and logistics deployed for the NATO Implementation Force. HQ ARRC commanded the land component, demonstrating the value of HQ. The Army sometimes struggled to sustain the forces required in Bosnia, particularly in engineers, signals and logistic personnel, resulting in short tour intervals, and increased overstretch and outflow. The CGS at that time, General Sir Charles Guthrie, did much to balance the Army's commitments, ensuring that the Army succeeded in Bosnia, whilst retaining its warfighting edge, particularly its armoured warfare training in Canada,

In the first five years, 1992–97, the operation was often very demanding with a disputed mandate, inadequate and dysfunctional UN strategic leadership, tensions with NATO and high-intensity fighting between ruthless warlords. The UN was severely tested in Bosnia and often failed. British units and formations did not. Troops were not usually fighting a war but they were definitely inside other people's wars.

Many soldiers and officers deployed in the first five years of British operations in Bosnia often told me that their operations had been a great adventure. And they often took away a sense of achievement from having made a difference. Afterwards, the operation in Bosnia became less exciting and much more routine. This carried with it a considerable danger, that of the Army becoming accustomed to a form of stabilization operations where the adversaries did not use violence.

In 2007 British troops left Bosnia. Fifty-nine had died in the country since 1992. Spring 2008 saw a memorial service at the new National Memorial Arboretum in Staffordshire. One of the lessons was read by Mollie Wormald, whose son Steven had died while serving with the Royal Anglian Regiment in 1994.

There are now very few people serving in the Army who experienced the challenges of the first few years of operations in Bosnia. The level of violence against the Army was much lower than in Iraq and Afghanistan. But it is all too easy to forget just how dangerous and difficult those operations were. How incredible it seemed in 1992 that a European state had disintegrated into a savage civil war which the best efforts of the international community seemed utterly incapable of preventing. And from 1992 to 1996 there was considerable strategic uncertainty and ambiguity, where the contractions in European, UN, NATO and British policy made circumstances confusing and difficult for the UN and British troops on the ground.

British units had played a key role, particularly in being prepared to go to the limits of the UN mandate and sometimes beyond it, as the Royal Welch did in Gorazde on 28 May. Given the considerable weaknesses and limitations of many national contingents in UNPROFOR, the Army often punched well above its weight. The contributions of Generals Rose and Smith as UNPROFOR commanders in 1994 and 1995 now seem underestimated by commentators and historians. Both were sent to Bosnia in an all too familiar role of a British commander assigned insufficient forces to achieve a very difficult mission in in a fiendishly complex situation, one in which many nations' governments and forces lacked the stomach for a fight.

Rose took over a mission that was on the verge of failure and regained sufficient initiative for the intensity of the war to reduce, this saving lives. And the British Army gave him significant reinforcements of infantry, cavalry and the determined small teams of JCOs. In 1995, in a constantly deteriorating situation, Lieutenant General Rupert Smith played an extremely weak hand with great skill. His contribution to the July Lancaster House conference and the way he integrated the multinational brigade and NATO airpower to coerce the Bosnian Serbs into the ceasefire that set the conditions for the Dayton Agreement was genuinely decisive. Many British officers felt that if there was any justice in the awarding of Nobel Peace Prizes, Rupert Smith and Richard Holbrooke should have shared one for ending the terrible war.

At the other end of telescope, battalion and regiment commanding officers had played decisive roles. Particularly noteworthy were Bob Stewart and Alastair Duncan, commanding the first two armoured infantry battalions, and David Santa-Olalla, commanding the first battalion in Gorazde; as well as Jonathan Riley, who found his battalion in a very challenging outpost, where both logistics and strategic direction were often very short, and Dick Applegate, who did so much to set the conditions for the success of British, French and Dutch artillery on Mount Igman. They led units at the very fulcrum of events and tilted the balance in ways that both saved lives and helped end the vicious war, making more of a practical impact on the ground than many politicians and officials in London.

Between 1994 and 1995, the British and French had often effectively acted as joint leaders of UNPROFOR, both being key NATO members and deploying the most combat capable contingents to the UN. Carl Bildt, the International High Representative, was to observe that:

> the British and the French had been the core of UNPROFOR in Bosnia taking responsibility for actions which had involved loss of life, as well as extreme risk. Their units had experienced numerous other low-level military confrontations around the world. British units often circulated between Bosnia and Northern Ireland, while some of the French units had seen substantial action in different parts of Africa. These units were the most forward leaning when it came to using force in order to achieve political ends. The fact that we had British forces in Banja Luka turned out to be of critical importance on a number of occasions.[31]

CHAPTER 8

KOSOVO

While Bosnia was absorbing much of the Army's commitments and attention, the world continued to become more unstable. The second half of the 1990s posed more unanticipated challenges and opportunities for the Army.

THE 1998 STRATEGIC DEFENCE REVIEW

The Labour government elected in May 1997 conducted a foreign policy-led review to re-assess the UK's defence strategy and military capabilities. Energized by the authoritative political leadership of new Defence Secretary George Robertson, it drew on the lessons of operations since 1991, including weaknesses in readiness, expeditionary and medical support and interoperability.

The central role in shaping the Army input to the review was played by the Army staff in the MoD in London, particularly the CGS, General Sir Roger Wheeler, his assistant, Major General Mike Willcocks, and Brigadier Anthony Palmer, the Director Army Plans in the MoD. A conceptual foundation was evolved by the Director General of Doctrine and Development, including an assessment of future conflict on land. This anticipated many features of the wars resulting from 9/11.

The armed forces were to become more expeditionary and more rapidly deployable. High-readiness units of all three services were assigned to a new Joint Rapid Reaction Force. The CGS explained that the Strategic Defence Review (SDR) required the Army:

> to be able to deploy a brigade quickly as part of the new Joint Rapid Reaction Forces (or
> JRRF), to be able to mount two brigade-sized operations concurrently (and to sustain one
> of them indefinitely), to deploy a warfighting division for operations such as the Gulf War,
> and to maintain our overall contribution to NATO. To meet these requirements whilst still
> meeting our other commitments in peacetime we have developed a structure for the Army
> comprising two deployable divisions at realistic peace establishment, each of three brigades

rotating through a three-year formation readiness cycle (the successor to our current formation training plot). To achieve this, we need to form a sixth mechanized brigade …

We should be able to implement the organizational changes necessary to meet key readiness targets within the first few years, but improvements in manning and sustainability will take longer. Implementation will be phased, so that whilst we reorganize, we can still prepare for and carry out operations.[1]

The airborne and air-mobile brigades were merged into the new 16 Air Assault Brigade, which combined armed helicopters and the Army's parachute capabilities. This would be at high readiness, as would the lead battlegroups of the armoured and mechanized brigades. The Army was to be able to generate one brigade at 30 days' notice, another at 60 days' notice and a third at 90 days' notice, with a divisional HQ and divisional combat support and logistics delivered in three echelons at similar readiness.

The Army would continue to field the 1st Armoured Division with three armoured brigades based in Germany. The 3rd Division would lose the airborne brigade but would have a third mechanized brigade in its place.

In parallel, collective training expanded, with exercises in Canada and Poland preparing armoured and mechanized brigades for their high-readiness years. And BATUS was used for an innovative experimental exercise by the 3rd Division, commanded by then Major General Richard Dannatt. This saw his HQ deploy to the prairie to develop its capability to conduct airmobile and attack helicopter operations. It took with it the 1st Reconnaissance Brigade and helicopters and infantry from 16 Air Assault Brigade. This was the first and only exercise at divisional level at BATUS.

Operations since the Cold War had shown that the Army was short of essential 'enablers', the logisticians, engineers and signallers necessary to mount new operations in new theatres and then sustain them. The size of the Army increased by 3,300 logisticians, engineers and signallers, reversing the reductions made. To generate a proportion of the new manpower required, the size of the TA was reduced, including its regular staff. The SDR envisaged a restructured TA that would integrate more closely with the Army. Its role in military home defence ended and it was cut from 56,000 to 40,000 reservists.

There were to be more joint forces and joint structures. The Joint Helicopter Command was created in Land Command for all three services' battlefield helicopters and the new air assault brigade. There would be a joint ground air defence HQ for Army and RAF Rapier units and a joint Army/RAF NBC regiment would form in Strike Command.

Strategic lift increased with acquisition of Ro-Ro ferries and C17 heavy transport aircraft. There were only small changes to the composition of the RAF and the Royal Navy. Two aircraft carriers and a new joint strike fighter were to be acquired.

All these measures were pretty much supported by the Army and the other services. The capability outcomes of the review were seen as an success for the Army. But new joint and centralized structures were created for setting equipment requirements, for procuring equipment and delivering logistic support. These reduced the services' ability to determine their future capabilities.

But after negotiations with the Treasury, the MoD accepted a settlement that underfunded the implementation of the review by about £500m per year – insufficient to resource the three services' future equipment programmes. The Treasury also set a rolling 3 per cent efficiency savings target that further constrained capability and activity. Many military and civilians in the MoD found Gordon Brown to be deeply unsympathetic to the requirements of the forces. General Sir Charles Guthrie, then CDS, wrote that:

> The strategic defence review was not the first time (nor was it the last) that I had to cross swords with the chancellor Gordon Brown. We got off to a poor start.
>
> It was clear soon enough that Brown would not fund what had been previously agreed.
>
> When I went to see him in 11 Downing Street to discuss the review he paid no attention to what I told him. It was not long before he interrupted and said with a smirk,
>
> 'General I do know a bit about defence you know.' I gave him a hard look and replied 'Chancellor, you know fuck all about defence.'
>
> His face turned red and his jaw slackened...
>
> I genuinely felt that the armed forces in the Army in particular suffered because of the damaging clashes between Blair and Brown at the time. If I raised the topic of funding with Blair he would look distinctly uneasy and just say 'well you need to take that up with Gordon.'[2]

Other defence, security and intelligence officials reported similar conversations with Blair during the Iraq war.[3]

Kosovo

The ripples of the disintegration of Yugoslavia spread through the Balkans. The former Yugoslav province of Kosovo had a Muslim majority, but was ruled by a Serbian establishment. Serbs regarded the province as the spiritual home of Serb nationalism.

In 1997 the Albanian government collapsed, and large numbers of weapons became available to the ethnic Albanians of Kosovo, where they were in a majority. An insurgency against Serb rule began. Violence rapidly escalated between the Kosovo Liberation Army (KLA), drawn from the majority Muslim population and the ruthless Serbian security forces. Atrocities and 'ethnic cleansing' were widely reported.

Negotiations were brokered by European diplomats. A force of unarmed international monitors was deployed. A small Anglo/French quick reaction force was stationed in nearby Macedonia, with a British armoured infantry company. But this failed to end the hostilities and civilian suffering. French-led negotiations with the Serbian government and the KLA envisaged a peace deal which was to be enforced by a NATO Kosovo Force (KFOR). These talks collapsed.

The unarmed monitors were withdrawn and NATO presented Serbian president Slobodan Milošević with an ultimatum demanding the cessation of Serb repression. This was ignored, so in March 1999, NATO began air and missile strikes to compel Milošević to change the behaviour of his government's forces.

The UK offered to play a leading role in KFOR. So the brigade HQ of 4th Armoured Brigade and two of its battlegroups were deployed to Macedonia. So were HQ ARRC and its signal brigade, under its commander General Mike Jackson, designated as the HQ for KFOR.

Shortly after the strikes began the Serb forces began to forcibly evict ethnic Albanians. Hundreds of thousands of desperate refugees moved south to the border with Macedonia. People were loaded onto trains and dumped on the international border. Three-quarters of a million people fled Kosovo. It was thought that Belgrade wanted this mass flow of ethnic Albanians to destabilize Macedonia.

Providing shelter to this stream of desperate humanity should have been the responsibility of the Macedonian government, assisted by the UN High Commission for Refugees. But both were overwhelmed. Jackson ordered KFOR to assist. They did most of the work to build the first camps, eventually handing them over to the UN and various NGOs. The work was led by the Army's 101st Logistic Brigade, commanded by Brigadier Tim Cross. After the campaign was over Cross took to wearing the Boy Scout badge for camping. Many staff officers from HQ ARRC also volunteered to help in such spare time as they had. It was hard physical work.

The refugee crisis was of intense interest to international politicians and the media. HQ KFOR was inundated with VIP visitors, many seeking photo-opportunities. Jackson wrote that: 'I became irritated with the constant refrain "I'm here to help". After hearing this for the umpteenth time I handed one of the worthies a spade. "Take this up to the camps" I said "and start digging latrines."'[4]

It took much longer than NATO had expected for the air campaign to force the Serbs to withdraw their forces from Kosovo. The Serb army and paramilitary forces were well versed in camouflage, concealment and deception and often did not need to concentrate to attack the relatively weak insurgents, or to conduct 'ethnic cleansing' and atrocities. US Army General Wesley Clark, then NATO supreme commander, noted that the US Air Force-dominated NATO air command often showed much greater enthusiasm for prosecuting 'strategic' targets than for attacking Serb forces in the field. Clark also made great efforts to bring US Army Apache attack helicopters into the campaign but was frustrated by considerable institutional resistance in the Pentagon.

Efforts were made to co-ordinate NATO air strikes with insurgent operations in Kosovo. It seems unlikely that special forces were deployed on the ground there, but both the CIA and US special forces established contacts through the Albanian Army in south-east Albania. It is likely that the SAS also operated there. This was highlighted by the crash of an RAF Hercules transport aircraft leaving a forward airstrip in the region.

OPERATION B MINUS – *THE SECRET PLAN FOR A GROUND ATTACK*

Early in the war President Clinton had publicly ruled out a land attack.[5] General Clark worried that without a complementary ground attack NATO's air-only campaign could well fail. He sought to persuade his US superiors, NATO Secretary General Solana, and European defence chiefs to support him.

In conditions of great secrecy, a small team of staff officers from the US and UK were assembled in Europe to plan for a land attack to evict Serb forces from Kosovo. A complementary US team was established at the US Army Europe's HQ. NATO procedures required the North Atlantic Council to direct SACEUR to begin military planning. There was not a majority for this amongst the diplomats in Brussels, so the US and UK planning effort had to be conducted in great secrecy.

A wide range of options were considered, from occupying 'safe areas' inside Kosovo, to arming the insurgents. Initially US commanders expressed a preference that the main ground attack be made on Serbia from the north, using Hungary as the assembly area. This would strike south to capture Belgrade, the Serb political centre of gravity. There could also be attacks from Bosnia or Bulgaria. All these directions of attack would draw Serb reserves away from Kosovo, which would be attacked by NATO forces from Albania and Macedonia. But Option B, as it became known, carried with it considerable risk, not least of the urban combat that would be required to occupy Belgrade.

A second plan was developed that was easier to link to protecting the refugees. Operation *B Minus* limited the ground attack to Kosovo and surrounding areas of Serbia. It envisaged ground formations advancing from the south from Albania, and two routes north out of Macedonia. The first was directly north up the main road from Skopje to Pristina and the second was to the east, heading north from south-east Serbia before pivoting to the west and entering north-east Kosovo, thus outflanking defending Serb forces in the south of the province.

By mid-May, the planners had developed a plan for Option *B Minus*. A key requirement was to evict Serb forces from Kosovo in time for refugees to return to Kosovo before the winter snows fell. General Clark had a concept that he could take to the Pentagon. In his memoir he explained that the ground offensive would:

> attack with decisive force to be certain that we could make the penetration and exploit to finish the operation within a few weeks. I wanted six divisions, some light some heavy, some mixed. US Marine as well as Army forces would be needed. We would use avenues of approach through Albania as well as Macedonia, moving and fighting through the mountains as necessary. Some would attack by infiltration, others would have to make a river crossing. In every area we'd be struggling with the difficult terrain as well as with the enemy. We would also exploit our helicopters and heavy armour at the appropriate time.
>
> We would make the deployment in about 75 days. Informally we were envisaging at least 35,000 to 50,000 British troops, 10,000 to 20,000 French and at least 3,500 Italians. If everyone else contributed, we would get other NATO troops. I figured with the American contribution we could assemble the 175,000 troops we would need for the campaign. The mission would be tough and it would take the wholehearted commitment to the nations to make it work. They would have to commit themselves to war, if the air campaign were to prove insufficient.[6]

Of the planned force about 100,000 troops would enter Kosovo and the remainder would support from Albania, Macedonia and Greece. At that time Albania was the least developed country in the Europe. Not only was the terrain bordering Kosovo mountainous, but also Albanian roads and transport infrastructure were suffering from years of neglect. A covert reconnaissance by a British engineer officer identified ways of using the roads and inland waterways to get the necessary forces to the Albanian border, provided that NATO engineers could make necessary repairs and upgrades. US, German and Italian engineers were deployed to Albania to start doing this, the mission being portrayed in public as improving the flow of humanitarian aid to refugees.

UK Defence Secretary George Robertson and CDS General Guthrie were strong supporters of this initiative, as was Prime Minister Tony Blair. Robertson instigated a meeting on 27 May in Germany with defence ministers from the US, France, Germany, Italy and the US. Defense Secretary Cohen from Washington had up to then been very sceptical of the political wisdom of a ground attack, and the other European defence ministers had displayed a similar lack of enthusiasm. But they all accepted Clark's, Guthrie's and Robertson's assessment that to get refugees home in time, the land campaign had to begin in the first week of September.

While many NATO nations prevaricated, HQ ARRC, HQ 3rd Division, 4th Armoured Brigade and 5 Airborne Brigade quietly began preparing to invade Kosovo to evict the Serb forces. The Army assigned up to 50,000 troops to the operation. This would include engineer and bridging units to make essential improvements to the deployment routes and help units get across rivers. To assemble the necessary US, British and NATO formations, a decision to start mobilizing and deploying them must be made by the beginning of June.

The MoD and Land Command started planning to mobilize and deploy the additional forces necessary to reinforce UK troops already in Macedonia. The small brigade in Macedonia needed building up to full divisional strength, using the HQ of 3rd Division to command British land forces, HQ ARRC would command the land component, supported by its signals brigade. The SAS would act as an advance force, going behind enemy lines to gather intelligence and call in air strikes.

At the time, I was a colonel in the arcane-sounding Directorate of Army Staff Duties in London, responsible for Army reserves policy. I came back early from a family holiday to begin secure video conferences from the MoD's underground bunker. The Army's integrated mobilization cell was activated, and the start button was pressed on the necessary machinery for compulsory call up of reserves. Once this began, the mobilization could not be kept secret.

Robertson and Guthrie were not concerned about this loss of secrecy. Instead they welcomed it. Inevitable leaks of the mobilization would be useful, as they would show Milošević's government and NATO that the UK was in deadly earnest about preparing for the ground attack. The same applied to planning for strategic deployment, with movement staff beginning to hire cargo ships and airliners to deliver troops, vehicles and equipment to Albania, Greece and Macedonia. These measures could not be concealed. Nor could the mobilization of the regular troops. With the Regular Army having a strength of about 100,000 and troops committed to Northern Ireland, Cyprus and Bosnia, most of the Army would be on operations.

How might Option *B Minus* have turned out? Although many of those involved in planning considered that the Serb troops and paramilitaries would not have a high standard of training, leadership or morale, the terrain offered formidable difficulties. Kosovo was ringed by hills and mountains that offered many opportunities to an enterprising defender. In particular, the British would have to advance through the Kacanik defile where the road twisted through high hills. There were plenty of places like this where some demolitions could close the few roads into Kosovo. Once through these difficult defiles advancing NATO forces would have to enter the flat plains of Kosovo. But these were densely populated with many small towns and villages and low wooded hills, all offering more opportunities to defending forces. And there would be great pressure to reduce civilian casualties, limiting the attackers' ability to make full use of their artillery, attack helicopters and airpower.

Before the war, NATO had demanded that the Serbs cease hostilities and withdraw from Kosovo, allowing KFOR to assume security responsibility. It took until 3 June for President Milošević to agree to NATO's terms. There is little doubt that Belgrade had learned that the US and UK were now in deadly earnest about escalating to a ground attack.

In this Blair, Robertson and Guthrie all played decisive roles. General Guthrie was later to observe that:

> we could put 50,000 into the field and I do not know of another European nation that could do that, even though some of them have much bigger forces than we do. The British had a lot of influence because of the way we approached it. We had a Prime Minister, Defence Secretary, and I hope a Chief of Defence staff that knew what they wanted.[7]

General Jackson and HQ ARRC became the fulcrum around which ending the war pivoted. Rather than holding government to government talks, NATO decided that Jackson would present the Serbs with a so-called Military Technical Agreement (MTA), setting out an agreed plan for KFOR to assume responsibility for Kosovo's security with a concurrent withdrawal of Serb forces out of Kosovo.

The MTA was drafted in NATO HQ, but Jackson was required to meet with a Serb military declaration and persuade them to agree to his proposed plan and sign the document. Serb officers were very suspicious of NATO, not least because their forces in Kosovo were still being bombed. They also wanted NATO to ensure that the Kosovo insurgents did not attack withdrawing troops.

There followed a week of extensive negotiations led personally by Jackson. It was complicated by the arrival of several different drafts of the MTA from NATO, by indicators that separate US-led negotiations were going on elsewhere, including between Washington and Belgrade, and by many random appearances by self-important international actors who had no value to add, including spin doctors from Tony Blair's office.

There was great pressure on Jackson and his staff, not least as a result of intense micromanagement displayed by General Clark, who often appeared unwilling to delegate control to Jackson. There were several false starts and breakdowns. At one stage during a walkout by the Serb delegation Jackson was conducting simultaneous telephone conversations with Clark, the US Vice President and a senior State Department official. But an endgame became clear. A UN Security Council Resolution would authorize KFOR's role, the MTA would be agreed between KFOR and the Serbs, and a verifiable plan for Serb military withdrawal would be agreed, with the Serbs all departing Kosovo over the next 11 days.

Then, and only then, would KFOR enter the province. There was an agreed sequence of Serb withdrawals from designated zones, followed by NATO entering these zones. The Serb forces would eventually leave through 'gates', the main roads crossing the border between Kosovo and Serbia proper.

In the week before the MTA was signed, Jackson spent long hours negotiating through translation and enduring considerable frustration with the Serbs, NATO and the British and US governments, whilst HQ ARRC were fully occupied co-ordinating the plan for KFOR to enter and then control Kosovo.

Most military doctrine sees clear distinctions between the political and military dimensions of conflict and between the military strategic, operational and tactical levels. During this period Jackson was acting at all four levels at the same time. The Army and NATO were fortunate that he had enormous reservoirs of personal stamina and had considerable experience of negotiating with the Bosnian Serbs from his time in Bosnia. It was also fortunate that HQ ARRC was an extremely capable HQ, well trained and well led, with a chief of staff, Major General Andrew Ridgway, in whom Jackson had complete confidence not only to run the HQ, but to routinely run KFOR. Jackson was to write that his HQ had a 'first-rate staff. It took as much off my shoulders as possible. I can't praise them highly enough for what they did'.[8]

ENTRY TO KOSOVO – WITH RUSSIAN AND AMERICAN COMPLICATIONS

The tactical plan for entry to Kosovo required six brigades, US, German, Italian, French and two British, to enter Kosovo from Albania and Montenegro. Not only did it have to be sequenced to the plan for transition agreed with the Serbs, but also the few roads across the mountains that fringed Kosovo had limited capacity, requiring expert planning and control, if monumental traffic jams were to be avoided. And although it seemed likely that the Serbs would withdraw as agreed, renegade elements could unilaterally decide to fight. And any attacks by the KLA on the Serbs as they withdrew might trigger a resumption of fighting. In the worst case the Serbs would suspend their withdrawal.

It was originally planned that KFOR should enter Kosovo on Saturday 12 June. The Serb military agreed. But on 11 June there began another extraordinary sequence of events that would again pose unexpected challenges to Jackson, HQ ARRC and British forces.

Russian forces in Bosnia unexpectedly detached a column of armoured vehicles to drive to Kosovo.

Clark, whose suspicion of the Russians bordered on an obsession, thought that this was to take over control of northern Kosovo, where there was a majority of ethnic Serbs. He ordered Jackson to send helicopter-borne troops to seize the airport that afternoon, before the Russians arrived.

This order greatly concerned Jackson. Firstly, it was not part of the carefully sequenced plan for Serb forces withdrawal and KFOR's advance. It could lead to the Serbs unilaterally abandoning the agreement. In the worst case, they could fire on KFOR, whose helicopters would be very vulnerable. Secondly there was a risk of a confrontation or even a clash between NATO and Russian troops. Russian diplomacy had played a key role in persuading Milošević to agree to NATO's demands and Jackson judged that keeping Russia onside was vital to the success of KFOR.

The 1st Battalion, the Parachute Regiment and RAF helicopters were stood by for the mission. And the French were willing to commit troops and helicopters. But the US was unwilling to commit ground troops or close air support, and NATO HQ were unwilling to give Jackson clear instructions about the purpose of the force or its rules of engagement. And the Serbs refused a request that KFOR enter Kosovo earlier than planned.

By 1500hrs Clark called a NATO video conference. By now Jackson was so concerned about the political and military risks of the operation that he was prepared to resign rather than conduct it. Jackson and his staff were very relieved to learn that the US and Russian presidents, Clinton and Yeltsin, were to talk, and the Pristina airport operation was postponed.

The next day, 12 June, Russian troops were at the airport. KFOR was due to enter Kosovo at 0500hrs – H Hour. In the early hours of the morning NATO ordered that this be delayed by 24 hours. Jackson refused to derail the complex synchronization plan agreed between KFOR and Serbs. Eventually after many frustrating phone calls, the order was rescinded, just in time for the plan to start on time.

'I'M NOT GOING TO START WORLD WAR 3 FOR YOU'

That morning a Russian military attaché called on Jackson, presenting a letter from the 'Russian KFOR Contingent', addressed to 'KFOR Commander'. By mid-afternoon 5 Airborne Brigade had reached Pristina airfield and established contact with the major general commanding the Russian battalion. Flying to the airport for a press conference, Jackson then met the Russian commander, and they shared a whisky together.

But General Clark then appeared to obsess again about a Russian plot to fly reinforcements into Pristina airport and ordered KFOR to block the runways. Jackson had considerable reservations about the political and military risks of this action. And if NATO wanted to keep Russian transport aircraft from Kosovo, all they had to do was deny them transit rights.

Clark arrived the next day and privately met with Jackson, who recorded that:

I made it clear to Clark that I was fed up with taking orders from Washington from people seemed to have no appreciation of the problems on the ground.

'Mike these aren't Washington's orders, they're coming from me.'

'By whose authority?'

'By my authority as SACEUR'

'You don't have that authority'.

'I do have that authority, I have the authority of the Secretary General behind me on this.'

'Sir, I'm not going to start World War 3 for you.'

Again, Clarke stated what he wanted done. I said to him: 'Sir, I'm a three-star general, you can't give me orders like this I have my own judgement of the situation and I believe this order is outside our mandate.'

'Mike I'm a four-star general and I can tell you these things.'[9]

Jackson then spoke to General Guthrie, the UK CDS. Guthrie told him 'For God's sake Mike, don't do that'. He then spoke to Clark, supporting Jackson and saying that General Shelton, Chair of the US Joint Chiefs of Staff, agreed with Guthrie.[10]

Clark then again ordered Jackson to block the runway with armoured vehicles. The nearest armour to the airfield were in the British battlegroups of 4th Armoured Brigade. Jackson told the brigade to block the runways. Unsurprisingly the British declined to act. Clark reluctantly accepted this and departed. Reflecting on the crisis, Jackson wrote that:

> my view was that Clark's people needed to get a grip and stop panicking in response to every unfounded rumour and ill-informed press report. The next ridiculous poorly thought-out order I received would be the last. In fact the crisis was over. We had avoided unnecessary and potentially dangerous confrontation with the Russians. But my relationship with my superior officer suffered. I had come to the brink of refusing a direct order, though in the end it did not quite come to that.[11]

Clark's memoir contains a very similar account of this confrontation, albeit from his point of view. He saw a deep cultural difference between US Army and British Army command styles:

> In the British system, a field commander is supported. Period. That is the rule. A field commander is given mission-type orders, not detailed and continuing guidance. It's a wonderful traditional approach, one that embodies trusting the commander and confidence in his judgement as the man on the scene. The American military has always aspired to this model, but has seldom seemed to attain it. My experience couldn't have been more different than Jackson's. In my service I had seen frequent oversight by higher headquarters, repeated questioning of seemingly insignificant details and surprisingly little autonomy for field commanders ... if higher headquarters could observe, supervise or control, then higher headquarters usually would observe, supervise and control.[12]

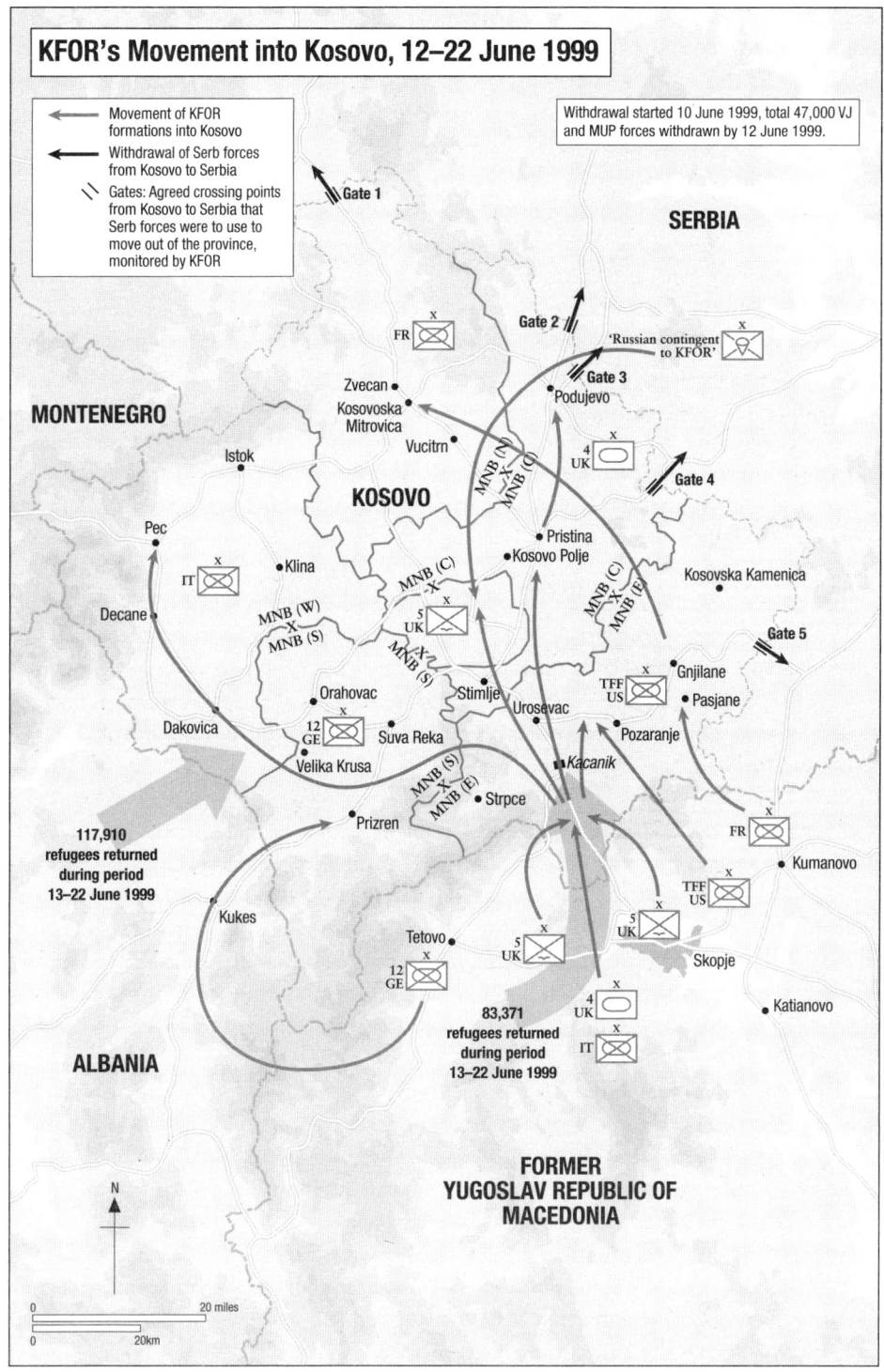

KFOR's Movement into Kosovo, 12–22 June 1999

Movement of KFOR formations into Kosovo

Withdrawal of Serb forces from Kosovo to Serbia

Gates: Agreed crossing points from Kosovo to Serbia that Serb forces were to use to move out of the province, monitored by KFOR

Withdrawal started 10 June 1999, total 47,000 VJ and MUP forces withdrawn by 12 June 1999.

SERBIA

Gate 1

Gate 2

'Russian contingent to KFOR'

Gate 3

Podujevo

FR

Zvecan

Kosovoska Mitrovica

Vucitrn

MNB (N)

MNB (C)

4 UK

Gate 4

MONTENEGRO

Istok

KOSOVO

Pec

Klina

MNB (C)

Pristina

Kosovo Polje

Kosovska Kamenica

IT

Decane

MNB (W)

MNB (S)

5 UK

MNB (C)

MNB (E)

Gate 5

Orahovac

Stimlje

Urosevac

Gnjilane

Pasjane

TFF US

MNB (S)

Dakovica

12 GE

Suva Reka

Pozaranje

Velika Krusa

Kacanik

MNB (S)

MNB (E)

Strpce

FR

117,910 refugees returned during period 13–22 June 1999

Prizren

Kumanovo

TFF US

Kukes

Tetovo

5 UK

5 UK

4 UK

Skopje

12 GE

83,371 refugees returned during period 13–22 June 1999

IT

Katianovo

ALBANIA

FORMER YUGOSLAV REPUBLIC OF MACEDONIA

N

0   20 miles

0   20km

As British troops entered Kosovo, they were greeted as liberators by the Muslim majority population. In much of the province flowers were thrown, troops were garlanded and there were scenes of great celebration; but there was apprehension in the Serb-majority areas in the north of Kosovo. The retreating Serb troops were understandably sullen and resentful. But they all left the province by the agreed routes and by the required deadline.

Tony Blair drew conclusions from the war. Even as it was underway in April 1999, he used a speech in Chicago describing the Kosovo intervention as:

> a just war based not on any territorial ambitions but on values. We cannot let the evil of ethnic cleansing stand. We must not rest until it is reversed. We have learned twice before in this century that appeasement does not work. If we let an evil dictator range unchallenged, we will have to spill infinitely more blood and treasure to stop him later.
>
> So how do we decide when and whether to intervene? I think we need to bear in mind five major considerations. First, are we sure of our case? War is an imperfect instrument for fighting humanitarian distress; but armed force is sometimes the only means of dealing with dictators. Second, have we exhausted all diplomatic options? We should always give peace every chance, as we have in the case of Kosovo. Third, on the basis of a practical assessment of the situation, are there military operations we can sensibly and prudently undertake? Fourth, are we prepared for the long term? In the past we talked too much of exit strategies. But having made a commitment we cannot simply walk away once the fight is over; better to stay with moderate numbers of troops than return for repeat performances with large numbers. And finally, do we have national interests involved?[13]

Blair viewed the war as a great success. There can be no doubt that he did a great deal to sustain NATO and shore up its cohesion, as it came under great pressure, as civilian casualties mounted and the air campaign foundered. Blair had stiffened President Clinton's sometimes shaky resolve. General Guthrie, his CDS, thought Blair had done a good job, not shirking from decision-making or providing strategic direction; Guthrie observed that 'in the Kosovo crisis he showed himself to be a man of courage and principle. Once he had been convinced that the course was right his attitude was "OK we'll do it".'[14]

Direction and support from Blair and Defence Minister George Robertson were key success factors, as was the command, control and leadership supplied by Jackson and the HQ ARRC. And the two manoeuvre brigades deployed – 4th Armoured and 5th Airborne – had rapidly deployed at speed. They had also rapidly transitioned their mindset from peace support to being prepared to fight a war and back again. Their training, experience and culture had given them great flexibility in this uncertain and difficult operation. No other major NATO army was as effective at moving rapidly back and forth across the spectrum of conflict. The entry into Kosovo operation had succeeded in a relatively short time, with no British casualties from enemy action.

STABILIZATION AND RECONSTRUCTION OF KOSOVO

Initially much of Pristina, the capital, was the responsibility of the Irish Guards battlegroup. Amidst the celebrations, there were sparks of intended or actual violence and score settling. For example, one Sergeant Matthews disarmed an Albanian about to attack some Serbs with a live hand grenade, with the pin already withdrawn. He later told his commanding officer, 'I saw he had a hand grenade and had removed the pin. Knowing this to be an unsafe condition I placed my hand over the grenade lever and moved him to a safe area.' A display of great coolness![15]

Throughout Pristina and the British area of Kosovo, there was much evidence of 'ethnic cleansing'. Many Serb civilians fled, burning their homes as they did so. Businesses and civilian installations were also torched. As KLA fighters came down from the hills and out of the forests, there was intimidation, beatings, looting and violent settling of scores. British troops did the best they could to damp down interethnic frictions, spending a lot of time talking to both factions. But the majority of civilian officials, managers, engineers and technicians in the province had been Serbs, most of whom rapidly departed.

As the UN administration of the province did not arrive until September, the British troops did all that they could to fill the gap. British Army experts did their utmost to keep the province running. For example, a signals squadron ran the main telephone exchange and Army medical staff worked in civilian hospitals that had been vacated by Serb medics. Most important of all was the electricity supply, which depended on an elderly lignite-fired power station. An engineer squadron was sent to assist. By great fortune the squadron commander's uncle worked for the UK Electricity Generation Board. Over the satellite telephone he was able to advise his nephew how to keep the long obsolete power plant running. This advice was followed by two of the board's civilian engineers, who added great value. These were but three of many examples of British efforts to jump-start reconstruction.

HQ ARRC and General Jackson did all they could to help the small team setting up the UN Mission in Kosovo (UNMIK), which was to provide an interim civil administration for the province. KFOR remained responsible for maintaining a 'secure environment'. So until a civil police force was established, KFOR were the police.

It was agreed that the KLA would demobilize within 90 days, weapons to be placed in KFOR-controlled storage sites. Many of the former insurgents were unwilling to do so. Jackson led lengthy and frustrating negotiations with the KLA. Eventually he had to escalate by threatening that any KLA members retaining weapons would be arrested. This reached an impasse and Jackson invited General Clark to join the talks in Pristina. Clark did so and played to his considerable strengths, effectively charming the KLA into agreement. The KLA became the 'Kosovo Protection Corps'.

THE LONG TAIL IN KOSOVO

Kosovo became another medium-sized enduring commitment. The Army already had one such commitment in Bosnia. So it was now operating at a level beyond that envisaged in the SDR. And most of the changes to the Army's structure required by the SDR were yet to be implemented. A particular problem was that it would take several years to grow the size of the Army to allow the second line of communications to be sustained. But two lines of communications were required to sustain both Bosnia and Kosovo. This inevitably put pressures on units and their people.

There was a particular problem with some specialist personnel, such as intelligence experts, who found themselves much in demand. The Army used a term the 'tour interval' to measure this. The term represented the time spent by an individual or a unit between operational tours. The Army judged that the optimum tour interval was at least two years. This would allow sufficient time to maintain personal and unit training and allow people to take all their leave, spend time with their families and attend necessary training courses.

For example, during the 1996 peak of the Army commitment to Bosnia and the Kosovo intervention in 1999–2001 the tour interval of the Royal Signals was particularly short. During this period the mobile phone industry was rapidly growing in the UK. It needed exactly the kind of technicians and operators that were essential to running Ptarmigan formation communications equipment, and was prepared to offer salaries and financial incentives considerably in excess of the pay offered by the Army. Understandably many members of the Royal Signals found the offer impossible to resist. This outflow led to signals units becoming undermanned. So, in peacetime the units' remaining personnel had to work harder than ever. And to send a full signals regiment on operations would require it to be reinforced by personnel from regiments that were not deploying. This of course forced the tour interval down, increasing overstretch across the Royal Signals – making service in signals units even less attractive.

The Army was very worried about this issue. It had seen similar problems in the 1970s, albeit exacerbated by the serial pay freezes in the late 1970s. From its viewpoint, it was essential to achieve a balance between operational commitments and the capability of the Army, so pushing up the tour interval for the Army's people and units was essential. The MoD agreed that one way to do this would be to reduce the British commitment in Bosnia from medium scale to small scale. This was achieved by turning the British-led HQ in north-west Bosnia into a multinational HQ, collaborating with the Dutch and Canadians. And the British contingent would reduce from a brigade to a single battlegroup.

In the meantime, the British handed HQ KFOR over to NATO. They concentrated on leading the security of Pristina. Gradually the brigade in the city became more multinational. But its core remained British battlegroups. Unlike most other national contingents, British troops were capable of crowd- and riot-control missions – a positive legacy of Northern Ireland.

The 2nd Battalion, the Royal Green Jackets was rushed to northern Kosovo's divided city of Mitrovica, where there were large-scale riots between Serbs and Muslims. At that time French government policy was that their army was not to conduct crowd and riot control, which was the express role of the Gendarmerie. The French Army contingent in the city was struggling to contain the widespread rioting and disorder triggered by Albanians attempting to cross a bridge into the Serb area.

The Green Jackets linked arms and formed a human wall to block the Albanian effort. Scuffles developed into a day-long full-scale riot that saw soldiers trampled underfoot. At the time KFOR could not arrest rioters but could at least drag ringleaders from the crowd! To maintain the 'thin green line' required great physical endurance, coolness and discipline. Things were not improved when, without warning, the French fired tear gas. But the Green Jackets held the line and eventually the riot fizzled out. The battalion was commanded by Lieutenant Colonel Nick Carter, a name that will recur in this story.

Increasingly, the British were able to hand over their roles in Kosovo to other nations. Quite early in the stabilization campaign, they recognized that threats were posed by organized crime and networks and hard-core nationalist extremists, groups that often overlapped. They could sometimes overmatch the Kosovo police.

So the Army set up an innovative new capability, which applied the approach that had been the core of covert counterterrorist operations in Northern Ireland. They established an Intelligence Surveillance and Reconnaissance (ISR) task force to gather covert intelligence, to counter threats to Kosovo's stability and security. The core of this unit was specially trained and equipped close observation platoons that conducted covert observation in similar ways to such platoons in Northern Ireland. They were also assisted by other British intelligence, surveillance and technical experts, as well as human intelligence teams. The Swedish contributed plain clothes surveillance teams and the Italian Carabinieri provided a useful arrest capability.

This initiative had great success. It was admired by the Scandinavian nations that increasingly provided units to the British brigade in Kosovo. They joined the force, providing very effective additional surveillance capabilities, not least as their troops were hardened to working in more severe winters than occurred in the UK or Germany. In 2003 the British brigade handed over to a Scandinavian multinational brigade, but NATO requested that the ISR Task Force remain and expand its operations from the Pristina area to the whole province. Security precludes describing their operations in any detail, but for the specially selected and trained elite members of the task force the role was an exciting one, particularly for the infantry cavalry and artillery soldiers who were given the demanding training and specialist equipment. It was a challenging role to relish. Reflecting on Kosovo, General Guthrie observed that:

> as far as the British Army was concerned, we learnt to operate flexibly and pragmatically where there is not only a powerful enemy threat but also a battle for the support of the civil community. We had become a master of operations other than war. We had learned what kit worked well and what was a waste of money.[16]

CHAPTER 9

RAPID INTERVENTION (2)

AFRICA, EAST TIMOR, SIERRA LEONE AND MACEDONIA

As well as the major intervention in Kosovo, the 1990s saw a number of short-notice small-scale operations conducted. There were also two stabilization operations, the first under Australian command in East Timor, followed by rapid intervention in Sierra Leone. Finally, 16 Air Assault Brigade conducted a peace support mission to support a fragile ceasefire in Macedonia.

All of these missions had their challenges for the Army and all are worthy of study. The most interesting of these is the intervention in Sierra Leone, in many respects, a groundbreaking operation. It saw a rapid evacuation, a challenging hostage rescue by special forces and a long-term training and assistance mission. It forms the central part of this chapter, bookended by the shorter operations that preceded and followed it.

SMALL-SCALE PEACEKEEPING MISSIONS IN AFRICA

Since the novel mission to Zimbabwe, there had been more British missions in Africa. In 1988, a peace deal ended the insurgency in Namibia against South African rule of the former German colony. A UN peacekeeping force was mandated to monitor the withdrawal of South African forces. The Army contributed engineer and signal squadrons to help the new force get itself established and set up its command and control.

These squadrons arrived well before the rest of the UN mission. Shortly after they did so, trust between the South African and insurgent forces broke down. It seemed likely that the South Africans would deploy to fight the insurgents. If they did so, the UN mission might well fail before it began. So the small British contingent made itself an ad hoc monitoring force, deploying to reassure both sides. This brave initiative was sufficient to nip the trouble in the bud and allow the rest of the UN force to arrive, allowing the engineers and signallers to resume their planned tasks.

In 1994 there was a mass outbreak of interethnic violence in Rwanda. In scenes of appalling savagery, several months of fighting had caused the deaths of nearly a million civilians. The violence had totally overfaced the small UN mission already in the country which had itself taken casualties.

The UK agreed to join the UN Mission to Rwanda (UNAMIR). Lieutenant Colonel Mike Wharmby commanded a task force formed around 5 Airborne Brigade's logistic battalion, assembled from the brigade's combat support, logistic and medical capabilities. Given five days' notice to deploy, they moved by air and found that the country was in a dire humanitarian emergency. Hundreds of thousands of people were crowded into refugee camps, where cholera and dysentery were claiming 600 lives a day.

23 Parachute Field Ambulance set up primary health clinics in refugee camps in the north of Rwanda, and its environmental health experts worked to counter the spread of disease. Some of its medical specialists deployed to Rwanda's three hospitals, which the British also helped defend, using an infantry company from the 2nd Battalion, the Princess of Wales's Royal Regiment.

After a month in Rwanda there was an unexpected mass exodus of refugees into Zaire. The field ambulance was deployed to this area to alleviate the suffering, to reduce the outflow of refugees. Over the four months of the deployment the field ambulance assessed that it had directly assisted over 125,000 civilians.

Before the conflict, Rwanda had reasonable civilian infrastructure, but much of it was devastated. The Royal Engineers' 9 Parachute Squadron worked to restore road communications, particularly river crossings, as well building latrines for refugee camps, rebuilding village clinics and restoring electricity supplies to towns and villages.

The force's logistic close support squadron helped transport refugees and humanitarian aid. Many of UNAMIR's vehicles were worn out by the difficult roads and had been abandoned all over the country. 10 Airborne Workshop recovered and repaired as many UN vehicles as it could, helping to restore the UN's road mobility. Most of the vehicles were of types that were not in service with the British Army and there were very few spare parts to be had. The REME craftsmen had to use great ingenuity and much engineering improvision and cannibalization to get as many vehicles back on the road as they could.[1]

In 1996, the Army supported the deployment of a UN peacekeeping force to Angola. The UN Angola Verification Mission (UNAVEM) was mandated to cement a ceasefire between the Angolan government and two different insurgent groups. 9 Supply Regiment of the Royal Logistic Corps formed the core of the force, which also included a contingent of Welsh Guards for force protection. The role of the regiment was to provide the necessary supply, support and logistic command and control for the 3,500-strong UN force to get itself into the country and deployed. Despite delays caused by renewed fighting, the mission was successful.[2]

These missions showed that the UK's expeditionary capability included not just combat units, but also combat support, logistic and medical units. Very few other European or UN nations had such capabilities, the US and France being notable exceptions. The

Angola mission demonstrated that the British Army was one of the few in the world that could set up an intervention force's reception in country and provide its initial logistic support. And the UK deployment to Rwanda showed that the UK could rapidly deploy by air a humanitarian relief and reconstruction task force into an extremely austere environment.

In 1996 the Joint Force HQ (JFHQ) was formed as part of the Permanent Joint Headquarters (PJHQ) as a high-readiness joint HQ for operations. In its early years it spent much time developing itself, including through a vigorous programme of exercises.

In 1996, another violent upheaval in the Great Lakes region produced millions of refugees, many in a desperate condition. The British government considered deploying a brigade to help stabilize the situation and support delivery of humanitarian aid. Planning got as far as deploying a reconnaissance team, and preparations were made to deploy either 3 Commando Brigade or 5 Airborne Brigade. But the crisis passed and the operation was cancelled.

The following year, a growing insurrection in Zaire generated great concern about the safety of British citizens in Kinshasa, the capital.

Commanded by the JFHQ, a detachment of RAF Puma helicopters and a company of the Princess of Wales's Royal Regiment were deployed to Brazzaville, poised to fly across the River Congo into Kinshasa to evacuate British citizens. In the event the resulting regime change was not as violent as expected, so no evacuation was required.

EAST TIMOR

In 1975, Indonesia had annexed the former Portuguese colony of East Timor. There was a resulting insurgency. In 1998 a new Indonesian government agreed to hold a referendum to establish whether the province should gain independence. This was violently opposed by pro-Indonesian militia, violence that was tolerated by the Indonesian Army. The referendum voted in favour of independence, triggering renewed violence by anti-independence militias. Civilians died and up to 500,000 were displaced.

The UN Security Council authorized a multinational force to restore peace and security and support humanitarian assistance, until a peacekeeping force could deploy. Australia led the force and provided the majority of troops. The British component was commanded by the JFHQ. It included a troop of SBS, who supported the Australian SAS in securing the airport at Dili, the capital. Battalion HQ of the 2nd Battalion, the Royal Gurkha Rifles and a troop of Royal Marines helped secure the capital. The Australian Army would later observe that of all the national contingents, the Australians, British and New Zealand forces were the most interoperable.[3] The UK force also included the destroyer HMS *Glasgow* and RAF Hercules transport aircraft.

Coming from Brunei, the Gurkhas were acclimatized and experts in jungle operations. They made an important contribution to the force, particularly in moving into areas where anti-independence militia had recently operated. Brigadier David Richards, commanding the JFHQ, was particularly impressed by the support of the Department for International Development (DfID), which had replaced the Foreign and Commonwealth Office's (FCO) Overseas Development Administration. The agency sent Gilbert Greenall, who had so impressed General Mike Jackson in Kosovo. Greenall again had money to spend on quick-impact projects, the authority to spend it and an instinctive thirst for civil/military co-operation.

The Australian HQ soon realized that to put East Timor on its feet, the country would need a new constitution, but their HQ had insufficient legal capability. Fortunately, the JFHQ staff included Lieutenant Colonel Lee Marler of the Army Legal Corps. Over a month he drafted a new interim constitution for the country, to apply for the necessary transition before the long-term constitution was written.

The force built up to a strength of over 5,000, with significant contributions from Australia and New Zealand. Eventually some 22 nations would take part. The JFHQ departed in October and the Gurkhas returned to Brunei in December.

SIERRA LEONE

Since the mid-1990s the former British colony of Sierra Leone had been in a state of violent disorder, principally driven by the brutally violent Revolutionary United Front (RUF).[4] Interventions by Executive Outcomes, a South African private military company, and Nigerian forces had pushed back the rebels, but the Nigerian forces outlived their welcome and the RUF had recovered afterwards.

The RUF had begun as a legitimate protest movement. But it soon fell under the influence of Charles Taylor, president of Liberia. Both parties saw that money could be made from RUF control of Sierra Leone's diamond mines. This set up a mutual dependency based on the RUF, destabilizing Sierra Leone.

By May 2000, the violent civil war had almost destroyed the former British West African colony. There was a large UN peacekeeping mission, the UN Mission in Sierra Leone (UNAMSIL), but it had been outfought and outmanoeuvred by the RUF. They had destroyed an African battalion of UNAMSIL and seized hundreds of Indian soldiers and UN military observers (UNMOs), including several British officers. An Indian battalion was surrounded by the RUF, who held the military initiative and overmatched the Sierra Leone Army (SLA). The RUF was rapidly advancing, prompting UNAMSIL to evacuate their HQ to the capital at Freetown, which seemed on the verge of falling.

In London it looked to the British government that the capital would be overrun by the RUF, with resulting atrocity and massacre. The MoD and FCO activated their crisis management machinery, which worked with unusual speed to formulate a plan and get their ministers to approve it.

To evacuate British, EU and Commonwealth citizens from risk, a non-combatant evacuation operation (NEO) was mounted by air. The commander of the JFHQ, Brigadier David Richards, was despatched, along with the high-readiness standby special forces squadron, to find out what was happening and prepare for the evacuation.

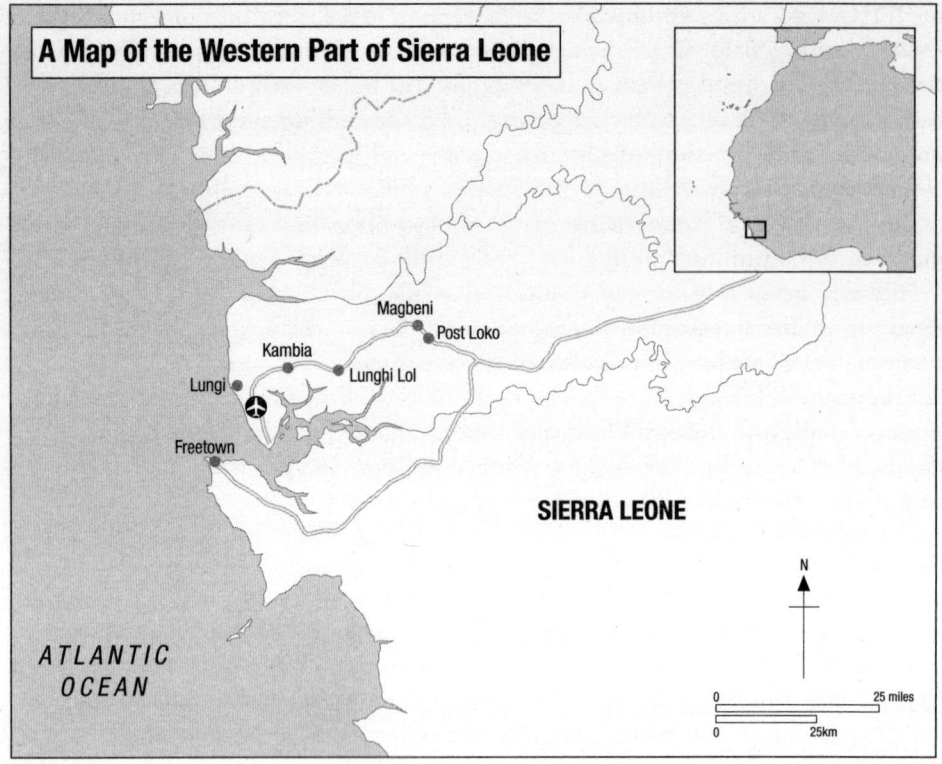

The Army normally had two battalions at very high readiness for operations: the spearhead battalion, found from the Army's light infantry battalions, and the lead airborne task force. But the infantry were over-committed to Northern Ireland, Bosnia and Kosovo. So, the two roles had been combined and were being conducted by 1st Battalion, the Parachute Regiment (1 Para) from 16 Air Assault Brigade.

1 Para was required to have its HQ and a company at 48 hours' notice to move, the rest being at five days' notice to move. When on Friday 5 May they were warned to deploy, from the commanding officer, Lieutenant Colonel Paul Gibson, downwards there was an infectious enthusiasm to get to Sierra Leone as soon as possible. The battalion thirsted for action and spared no effort to get itself airborne as quickly as possible. To save time, 1 Para took the calculated risk of deploying with 'light scales' of ammunition and equipment and leaving their rucksacks and much heavy equipment behind. By 0800hrs the next morning the battalion was complete at the Air Mounting Centre in Gloucestershire, the secure mounting base for military airlift, some four days earlier than their mandated readiness state required them to be.

Richards, his advanced reconnaissance team and some SAS troops landed at Lungi airport on the morning of Saturday 6 May. It became clear that the only force stopping the main RUF advance was a UN position some 30 km from Freetown. Their morale was very fragile and it seemed unlikely that they would stop a determined RUF attack. In the north the RUF were advancing in a direction that threatened Lungi airport. The sense of fear and panic amongst civilians was palpable. Richards requested immediate despatch of 1 Para to secure Lungi and conduct the evacuation. This was agreed by London.

The next day the HQ and a company of 1 Para, carrying enough ammunition for a short battle, arrived, not knowing what they might find. They were met by Richards, who directed them to secure the airport. The rest of 1 Para arrived on 8 May, but it took time for their full scale of ammunition, rucksacks and other logistic support to reach them. An SAS force also joined them.

Richards' initial mission was to evacuate British citizens. This required controlling Lungi airport and an evacuee assembly area in Freetown. 1 Para secured both. It took a couple of days for almost 450 evacuees to be flown from Lungi to Dakar by RAF Hercules transports; this was about half of those who were entitled. It seems likely that the rapid appearance of British troops persuaded many foreign civilians to stay in the country. One unexpected problem for 1 Para was that a number of UN military officers attempted to get themselves evacuated. The British refused to do this.

The force was quickly joined by a detachment of four RAF Chinook helicopters that flew from the UK via France, Gibraltar and the Canary Islands. The MoD ordered the aircraft carrier HMS *Illustrious* and the Amphibious Ready Group carrying 42 Commando, Royal Marines as well as two frigates all to make best speed to West Africa.

Richards knew Freetown, Sierra Leone's capital, well, having visited the country three times before, when he had also met key figures from the government and security forces. At one stage he had come under fire from rebels. He had seen for himself plenty of the horrific violence the rebels had inflicted on innocent civilians, including systematic amputations. Even before the Paras arrived, he was thinking through what else his small force might do to assist the country's threatened government. As he was doing so, members of the UN Security Council and other governments requested that the British join UNAMSIL.

On paper, this was a large force of over 9,000 troops that outnumbered the various rebel groups and was much better equipped, including with light armour. But it quickly became clear that UNAMSIL lacked the political and military will to confront the rebels. Its HQ displayed clear signs of panic and it was unclear whether UNAMSIL would be able to withstand an all-out RUF offensive. The best assessments from intelligence indicated that the RUF was rapidly approaching the capital. Whether government forces and UNAMSIL would be able to stop this advance was unclear.

The British declined to join the UN force, as they doubted its competence. Memories of the great weaknesses displayed by the UN in Bosnia ran very deep. And the Army was still heavily committed to Bosnia and Kosovo. The commitment of brigades to Bosnia and Kosovo meant that the Army was operating well beyond the SDR's planning assumptions. The MoD judged that there was not a spare British brigade to despatch to join UNAMSIL, without which the UN would not transfer leadership of the force to Britain.

During his first day in the country Richards developed a long-term plan to support both UNAMSIL and the SLA in defeating the rebel advance, and push them away from Freetown. Without waiting for direction from PJHQ, Richards initiated operations that would shift the balance away from the RUF and towards the government of Sierra Leone and UNAMSIL. There were three elements to this. Firstly, holding Freetown and Lungi airport and preventing any RUF attacks on them. Secondly, stiffening the resolve of UNAMSIL, to persuade it to stop the RUF advance and then move forward. Thirdly, to restore the Sierra Leone government's will and the capability of its armed forces and aligned militias to fight the RUF.

His formal orders from PJHQ, which arrived three days after him, were confined to the evacuation operation, but Richards pressed on with his more ambitious plans, confident that they would be supported by General Guthrie, Foreign Secretary Robin Cook and Prime Minister Blair.

The Indian major general in command of UNAMSIL felt strongly that the UN must be impartial to both the RUF and government forces. He seemed particularly unwilling to take any risk that might jeopardize the safety of the hundreds of Indian soldiers captured by the rebels. The UN's self-imposed inactivity was a near-fatal wound to the credibility of UNAMSIL. But by lucky coincidence, Bernard Miyet, Head of Peacekeeping Operations at UN HQ In New York, was visiting HQ UNAMSIL. He wanted the UN Mission to succeed, and Richards was able to sell his concept to him. Richards had propounded a campaign design that was well outside London's mandate. He later explained his thinking:

> I was convinced that a bit of elan, fighting power and cohesion would have a huge impact on the RUF, because, like most African rebel groups, they were disorganized and ill-disciplined. I had a sense that even though there were people in the Ministry of Defence chain of command who didn't want me to get involved, people at the very top political level probably did but I had no links to them. I couldn't exactly pick up the phone and talk to Tony Blair or Robin Cook … So what was driving me was pure instinct, reinforced by some analysis combined with my own determination not to let Sierra Leone revert to the horrors that I'd witnessed the year before. Taken together that's why I decided to chance my arm.[5]

Richards considered himself very lucky to have a competent, close-knit and entrepreneurial team around him. The staff of the JFHQ were well trained and experienced, having conducted many operations and exercises in the previous couple of years. And there was considerable mutual confidence between Richards and the two Army commanding officers in Sierra Leone: Paul Gibson commanding 1 Para and Jacko Page commanding 22 SAS, both of which did all they could to support the plan. Richards ordered the SAS to move west and within hours their vehicle-borne patrols were in Freetown, Port Loko, Hastings and Waterloo. This area around Freetown became known as the 'horseshoe' because of the shape. For Richards:

> The Paras and the SAS became my instructors and morale raisers. They went forward to UN or SLA positions, assessed their dispositions, stiffened resolve and made sure that the soldiers were doing what they were supposed to be doing. The SAS in particular, whose reputation preceded them to Sierra Leone, had a big impact on morale amongst troops who had been

poorly led, and in the case of the UN soldiers were confused about whether they should fight or not. The SAS were instructed to defend themselves if necessary, and did so.[6]

Richards established his HQ in the British embassy compound in Freetown, co-located with the special forces HQ and intelligence agencies. 1 Para took charge of the local defence of Lungi airport and deployed a company to Freetown. Having secured the evacuee assembly area, they began local patrols to reassure the locals and encourage the Sierra Leonean police. The need both to secure Lungi airport, the British line of communication and supply base, and also to have a presence in Freetown fixed many of his troops in place, limiting the numbers Richards could send forward.

The British also gathered information and intelligence to better understand the situation. An RAF Nimrod R1 signals intelligence aircraft deployed to Ascension Island to fly offshore, complemented by Army signals intelligence teams and GCHQ.

Meanwhile, the Royal Navy had mobilized a substantial task force to sail from the Mediterranean to Sierra Leone. This included the aircraft carrier HMS *Illustrious*, carrying Navy Sea Harrier fighters and some RAF ground attack Harriers. It also redeployed the Amphibious Ready Group. At the core of this was HMS *Ocean*, carrying 42 Commando, Royal Marines, their integral combat support including engineers, light guns from the Army's Commando Light Regiment and Lynx and Sea King helicopters. The force was joined by two frigates, HMS *Chatham* and HMS *Argyll*. These arrived on Thursday 11 May, with the remaining ships arriving on Monday 14 May. By then the RAF had four Chinook helicopters and two C130 Hercules at Lungi and further C130s at Dakar. By 14 May there were almost 4,500 British military personnel deployed, with almost 1,400 on the ground in Sierra Leone.

OPERATION KILL BRITISH AND THE BATTLE OF LUNGI LOL

The RUF reacted to the arrival of the British by escalating their already blood-curdling rhetoric. They announced Operation *Kill British*, signalling their intent to do precisely that. Intelligence pointed to the RUF moving from the east against the airfield. Since Lungi was surrounded by jungle, it was essential to gain early warning. Richards and Gibson decided to use the Pathfinder Platoon to do this. This was a small group of 27 expert parachutists whose primary role was acting as the air assault brigade's advance force, landing in enemy territory to mark out and secure parachute drop zones. They were an elite, who as well as passing P Company had undergone the platoon's further demanding specialist selection and training regime and were accustomed to operating for long periods in hostile territory.[7]

They were deployed to Lungi Lol about 30 km to the east of the airport. Here they established a defensive position, dug trenches and laid out defensive *punji* sticks of sharpened bamboo. They were to act as a lure to draw the RUF to attack them and be defeated by superior British combat power. In an extraordinary display of seamanship, HMS *Chatham* sailed up a treacherous uncharted estuary, but conditions made it too unsafe for it to stay.

Three light guns were flown ashore from HMS *Ocean* on an extraordinarily dark night – another hazardous operation. This was part of the disembarkation of 42 Commando. Travelling by sea they were a much heavier force than 1 Para, with more supplies, vehicles, heavy weapons, and ammunition than had been rushed out with the Paras. By now the paratroopers were exhausted, not least because of the debilitating heat. So the commandos would take over their positions. It was important not to allow the RUF any opportunity to disrupt this, so the move was conducted in secret, in darkness, as a combination of a relief in place and a withdrawal. This would allow 1 Para to return to the UK by air. Royal Marine Lieutenant Colonel Andy Salmon quickly bought into Richard's concept of operations.

The Pathfinder Platoon waited in their trenches outside Lungi Lol. After ten days, a much larger force of rebels attacked at night. There was heavy fire, but the Pathfinders were well protected in their trenches. At the climax of the battle, Sergeant Steve Heany and Royal Marine Captain Richard Cantrill, who happened to be visiting the position, crawled out from the trenches to fire illuminating bombs from a light mortar. Heaney made the mortar rounds fall behind the attackers, silhouetting them to make better targets for the defenders. Heaney was awarded the Military Cross for his bravery. At least 30 RUF fighters were killed and more drowned in a river as they fled.

This short, but intense, battle was a decisive moment. If the RUF had prevailed, killing or capturing any of the Pathfinders, the defeat would have greatly undermined the British position in country, weakening government resolve both in Freetown and in London.

Shortly after the battle of Lungi Lol the rebel leader, Foay Sankoh, was captured. Richards saw an opportunity to tip the balance of the conflict in favour of government forces. He took the initiative to create an informal coalition that he and staff called the 'Unholy Alliance'. This would comprise the SLA and the Kamajor tribal militias. There was another militia group, the West Side Boys, of uncertain affiliation, that had previously collaborated with the RUF. Richards sought out the commander, Johnny Paul Koroma, and in a scene from a dystopian apocalyptic movie, went to his lair to meet him, arguing that now was the time for his militia to side with the government against the RUF.

Koroma agreed and the British worked out how to supply them with arms and ammunition. They were also assisted by a helpful UN official who was persuaded to release food from the UN's stockpile, thus reducing pressure on the RAF's fragile airbridge to Lungi.

The three different groups – SLA, Kamajor and West Side Boys – would be encouraged by the British to go the offensive against the RUF, working separately, but to a common purpose. To help the SLA, the British provided a team to co-ordinate the different parts of the force and improve their communications and logistics. This included rapidly constructing an operations room.

A simple campaign plan was rapidly written. The key concept was that as the RUF were pushed back, UNAMSIL would be encouraged to move forward to occupy terrain that was now secure. The British persuaded the SLA and UNAMSIL to co-ordinate their actions by exchanging liaison officers and having both forces meet daily. By mid-May the JFHQ was effectively directing SLA operations and influencing those of UNAMSIL. At the request of the Jordanian government, 300 newly arrived Jordanian troops were flown by Chinooks to their area of operations along with essential supplies.

Russian-built Mil Mi24 Hind helicopter gunships operated by contractors hired by the Sierra Leone government represented a potent source of firepower that the rebels greatly feared. Richards used one for a personal reconnaissance of the country and 1 Para assigned an artillery officer to fly in it, as a way of conducting much-needed airborne surveillance, despite PJHQ explicitly forbidding such actions. This was not the only example of direction from London or PJHQ being seen in Sierra Leone as irrelevant at best, or at worst inhibiting mission success, and being ignored in theatre. There were times during the short campaign when staff officers in London criticized Richards' actions as outside his orders. At times he feared he might be sacked but relied on a small network of trusted contacts in PJHQ and in the CDS' office.

OPERATION BASILICA – THE TRAINING MISSION

London agreed that after the JFHQ departed, the UK should continue to train the SLA. The core of this would be a six-week training course, a compressed version of British recruit training, and support to the formation of new infantry battalions. Training would be conducted by short-term training teams, provided by a British infantry battalion, which would deploy its HQ, a bespoke group of trainers and a single infantry company for force protection.

The new British-led International Military Advice and Training Team of about 75 troops assembled in May 2000, commanded by a small HQ headed by a newly promoted brigadier from the Royal Signals. As well as the training package delivered by the infantry, it provided advisors to the SLA, including two British advisors in each battalion. Much work was done to set up logistic and administrative systems to ensure troops were properly supplied with food and ammunition and paid. The Sierra Leonean soldiers were supplied with obsolete British personal equipment and small arms.

In mid-July, the British supported a rare offensive operation by UNAMSIL. In May the RUF had released over 400 of the Indian troops it held. But over 200 Indian Army Gurkha soldiers and 11 UNMOs were still under siege deep in RUF-controlled territory. The Indian contingent in UNAMSIL assembled a brigade's worth of troops to rescue them. The core of this was the 18th Grenadiers, a well-led Indian battalion with recent combat experience. Other Indian troops included special forces, mechanized infantry in BMP fighting vehicles, engineers with bridging equipment, Indian Air Force Mi-8 transport helicopters and Mi-35 attack helicopters. There was also infantry from Ghana and Nigeria.

The British provided RAF Chinook helicopters and an SAS detachment. The Chinooks had an all-weather capability, which they used to insert the Indian special forces, who were also supplied with phosphorous grenades by the SAS. The UNMOS were recovered and taken away in Chinooks. There was heavy fighting as the besieged Indian contingent broke out of encirclement along with the relief column and the whole force withdrew. But the Indians prevailed, suffering only one casualty.

This operation showed that UNAMSIL could, if it wished, conduct combat operations and tactically defeat the RUF. But afterwards, the UN force returned to its posture of neutrality.

OPERATION BARRAS

The infantry short-term training teams were on relatively short operational tours of a few months. The second battalion to deploy was 1st Battalion, the Royal Irish Regiment. In late August, a British patrol led by a company diverted from its planned route to visit a village known to be occupied by the West Side Boys, to check reports that that particular militia group had begun to demobilize. At the village of Magbeni a group of militia, who were initially welcoming, blocked the British escape route with anti-aircraft guns and captured them, taking the troops across the Rokel Creek to the village of Gberi Bana where they were imprisoned.

High on homebrewed alcohol and heroin, the captors often mistreated and humiliated the troops. The commanding officer of the Royal Irish began negotiations, assisted by professional hostage negotiators from the Metropolitan Police. A deal was eventually agreed by which five soldiers were released for a satellite phone and medical supplies. Further negotiations proved fruitless, in part because the militia negotiators consumed so many mind-altering substances that they often forgot previous conversations.

In conditions of great secrecy London despatched a contingent of special forces. This was an uncomfortable moment for Prime Minister Tony Blair. General Guthrie, the CDS, advised him that 'if we don't take action there's a good chance our hostages will be skinned alive by the West Side boys.'[8] Blair was visibly shocked by this assessment. As a former SAS squadron commander, who had also flown to Sierra Leone to understand the situation for himself, Guthrie knew what he was talking about.

Using all the skills from their jungle training, and no little determination and endurance, special forces established observation posts. These were threatened by patrols of child soldiers into the jungle surrounding the village. But through expert camouflage and concealment, contact with the child soldiers was avoided. The special forces were able to establish the exact buildings that were holding the hostages in Gberi Bana. There were also many militia just across the river in Magbeni. These had sufficient combat power to interfere with any hostage rescue mission. The SAS' plan required Magbeni to be attacked simultaneously with their assault on Gberi Bana to rescue the hostages.

For this task A Company of 2nd Battalion, the Parachute Regiment, was flown to Sierra Leone. A deception operation portrayed this as a routine short notice exercise to test readiness. They joined the special forces task force assembled in Sierra Leone, which consisted of an SAS squadron, an SBS detachment and the special forces' dedicated Chinook and Lynx helicopters, both types of aircraft mounted machine guns. A Royal Fleet Auxiliary logistic ship acted as a secure mounting base and medical facility.

The SAS' plan to rescue the hostages was described by then Major Tim Collins, an SAS-qualified Royal Irish officer working in the special forces HQ. To take advantage of the rebels' drug and alcohol habits:

we would strike at dawn. The Chinooks would suppress known enemy billets on their approach and their door gunners would take down the 12.7 mm heavy machine guns as they landed on the football pitch. SAS teams already in place would provide covering fire. Simultaneously, Lynx helicopters from the special forces detachment would strafe the area to the south of the river, preventing the use of the captured vehicles and more importantly the captured machine gun, keeping reinforcements at bay and creating an opportunity for the Para distraction force to land and assault the rebel village of Gberi Bana to the South. The main assault troops, guided from the football pitch by the observation teams already in place would close in on the hostages and take them to safety.[9]

The attack took place largely as planned. The RAF helicopters achieved surprise by low-level tactical flying. As they arrived, they opened up with their machine guns and fired flares to confuse the enemy, helped by their downdraft taking the roofs off some of the nearby buildings. The soldiers descended by fast roping, which at least one rebel confused with bombs being dropped.

A West Side Boy named Corporal Blood later said that 'we never experienced anything like this. We saw the soldiers coming down to the ground. I fired my RPG two times but both times the helicopter swerved and I missed.'[10] Within 20 minutes of the landing the hostages had been rescued and loaded onto a Chinook. This included an SLA NCO, who had been subject to so much physical abuse that he might not have survived much longer.

Across the river, the attack on Gberi Bana began with strafing by Lynx helicopters and the South African-crewed Hind helicopter. One of the surviving West Side Boys later observed that 'the helicopters were almost on the water. They fired again and again until there was no more shooting'.[11] He hid, emerging four hours later to find most of his comrades dead.

As the Lynx helicopters fired on the village, the command team and half of A Company disembarked from Chinook helicopters, only to find that the landing zone that appeared as open terrain from the air was in fact chest-deep in water. A further early setback was a successful enemy mortar attack on the company commander's party, all being wounded. Captain Danny Matthews, the company second in command, took over. Ensuring that weapons, ammunition and radios were taken from the wounded as they were dragged into cover and rushed to a Chinook for evacuation, he assumed command of the attack:

> I cracked on to find the platoon sergeant pushing one of his sections through the attack at the time and he called to me 'Where's the boss?' I told him I was the boss. He said, 'Where's the OC?' I said that 'I'm the OC, let's push on.'[12]

Enough West Side Boys had survived the helicopter attacks to temporarily put up some stiff opposition, but the company successfully attacked through the village, clearing it of militia.

Unreported by the British media, the operation also freed 22 local civilians who had been captives of the West Side Boys. The men had been used for forced labour or trained as fighters. Five were women used as cooks or sex slaves. A total of 13 paras were wounded in the attack. More would have become casualties had the company not worn helmets and body armour. Early in the attack an SAS trooper, a former commando gunner, was killed – the only British fatality. At least 25 rebel bodies were counted. During the following week several hundred West Side Boys surrendered to UNAMSIL.

This was the first infantry company attack since Operation *Desert Storm*. As with that war, the Army considered it validated infantry training and leadership. A corporal who took part in the attack said: 'This is the only firefight I've ever been in. This company is a very young company and none of us had ever experienced it before. But when the battle started the training just took over'.[13]

The MoD was to claim that the success of the rescue administered a considerable shock to the morale and leadership of the RUF. Post-conflict research suggests that this was an over-estimate, but the operation reinforced the already formidable reputation of the SAS, both in Sierra Leone and elsewhere. For the rest of the campaign, the ability of the British to rapidly assemble such a credible force with its mixture of helicopters and special and conventional forces greatly complicated the rebels' calculations.

As with the initial evacuation and intervention, rapid deployment of special forces, paratroops and helicopters, overseen by a well-trained and very capable HQ, had achieved rapid effect, both militarily and in the information environment. But as with the May intervention, success had been far from guaranteed.

The ease with which troops had been taken hostage administered a considerable shock. As General Guthrie had unequivocally told Tony Blair, the rescue mission carried considerable risks. For example, had the hostage takers chosen a more easily defensible location and had they not been of such a low level of training and befuddled by alcohol and narcotics, the rescue mission might have incurred many more British casualties amongst the attackers and hostages, particularly if a helicopter had been shot down.

Land Command commissioned an independent analysis of the hostage taking by Brigadier Peter Pearson, a Gurkha officer. He concluded that in spontaneously choosing to visit the West Side Boys, the Royal Irish company commander had made a grave error of judgement. He also admonished the brigadier commanding the training mission for inadequate control of the force.

The report's judgements were controversial within the Army. Some supported them. Others felt that they were over-harsh, as there were many other circumstances in which similar British patrols could have been attacked and captured. To criticize a company commander for taking such initiatives was dangerous. As an anonymous officer put it:

> We rely on men such as these to stick their necks out on operations across the world. We must therefore be prepared sometimes for things not always to go according to plan. That is why we have contingencies, and they must have the confidence that we will back them up – come what may. The British Army punches above its weight in many areas. If we lose the courage and 'brass neck' of our soldiers we will all join the ranks of mediocrity and there are plenty of armies already in that vein.[14]

At the time, many of my colleagues echoed this sentiment. I well recall similar patrols that I led in Northern Ireland, Bosnia and the Middle East, that ventured close to harm's way. Any of these might have ended in equally difficult situations. Looking at these events from a quarter-century perspective, it seems that there were factors outside of these commanders' control. The force seems to have been seen by PJHQ and London as essentially a training mission in a relatively stable security situation. Although it was continuing some of the work done by the JFHQ, it lacked many of the JFHQ's capabilities and had no formal role in defeating the RUF. The mission's HQ was small and ad hoc, headed by a combat support, rather than combat, officer. Brigadier Richards observed that the UK had 'replaced an operational HQ with a bunch of trainers. We attempted transition too early. We took a risk and failed.'[15] Many in the Army agreed with this judgement.

REGAINING THE INITIATIVE

In August 2000 the UN Security Council adopted Resolution 1313. This not only increased the authorized size of UNMASIL, stating that 'the structure, resources and mandate of UNAMSIL require strengthening'. The mandate was shifted to allow direct support of the Sierra Leone government 'To deter and where necessary decisively counter the threat of RUF attack by responding robustly to any hostile actions ... To assist the efforts of the government of Sierra Leone to extend state authority, restore law and order and further stabilize the situation progressively throughout the entire country.'[16]

But shortly afterwards India announced the withdrawal of its contingent of over 3,000 troops, the second largest in the force, and Jordan declared that its 1,800 troops would withdraw. It was likely that New Delhi and Amman were unhappy with the shift to a more assertive mandate. These withdrawals reduced UNAMSIL's size by 40 per cent and removed two of the force's most capable contingents.

The RUF still controlled half the country. This included the diamond-producing areas. Diamonds were exchanged for arms, ammunition and supplies from the government of Liberia. This was the RUF's centre of gravity. There was no sign of the RUF wanting to negotiate. And it expanded its war into neighbouring Guinea.

On the positive side, British efforts to build Sierra Leonian military capability were having some initial effect. But PJHQ saw the situation as one of 'strategic muddle and operational impasse'.[17] Some senior officers privately described British operations at the time as being enough to prevent the government's defeat, but far from enough to deliver victory.[18] Both General Guthrie and the Army advocated deploying a well-trained and organized formation HQ to the country that could manage the training programme and also assist the government in Freetown and SLA in developing and executing a campaign plan. The HQ of 1st Mechanized Brigade was warned to deploy in this role. This time its readiness state of being at a month's notice to move was honoured, allowing it a short time to prepare itself to untangle the muddle and shift from impasse to initiative.

As an interim measure Brigadier Richards and the JFHQ were sent back to Sierra Leone. Working closely with the Sierra Leonean forces, their main effort was an information operation to convince the RUF that it would be defeated. This was a comprehensive interagency plan. It included diplomatic pressure on Liberia to cease supporting the RUF and exploited the growing capability of the SLA, announcing the increasing size of UNAMSIL and sending more British officers to the UN, both in New York and Sierra Leone, where the UNAMSIL chief of staff would be a British brigadier.

These initiatives were supported by the highly visible return of the Amphibious Ready Group to the country. It conducted a week-long demonstration of force, including the high-visibility landing of 42 Commando Group by helicopter and landing craft, followed by jungle training. This concluded with a demonstration of British firepower to a large invited audience.

These activities were deliberately conducted openly before local, regional and international media, creating a blaze of publicity. They had effect, as shown by statements by the RUF and President Charles Taylor of Liberia, deploring the intervention. They were also criticized by the acting commander of UNAMSIL, who saw them as destabilizing, claiming that Britain had more aggressive plans in Sierra Leone than the UN, reflecting the disconnect between the mandate set by the UN Security Council and the timid attitude of much of the force. These statements resulted in Sierra Leone's parliament passing a resolution supporting the British military and large public demonstrations, supporting the intervention.

In November there were negotiations between the Sierra Leone government and the RUF in Abuja. These resulted in a ceasefire deal which reduced military pressure on the RUF. Although the ceasefire held for some months, the provisions for UNAMSIL and disarmament by the RUF were ignored by the rebels.

Prompted by Liberia, the RUF then attacked Guinea, killing a thousand civilians and displacing a hundred times more. The Guinean government's response was ruthless, mounting a series of merciless cross-border attacks on the RUF inside Sierra Leone, including using multi-barrelled rocket launchers and attack helicopters. There were many casualties, both rebel and civilian. Guinean forces literally took no prisoners. Many of the most capable RUF commanders were killed in the fighting.

STABILIZING SIERRA LEONE – OPERATION SILKMAN

HQ 1st Mechanized Brigade deployed to Freetown in late November 2000, commanded by Brigadier Jonathan Riley, who had commanded the Royal Welch Fusiliers in Gorazde in 1995. The HQ was tasked to achieve a strategic end state of 'the establishment of sustainable peace and security, a stable democratic government, the reduction of poverty, respect for human rights, the establishment of accountable armed and police forces, and the enhancement of the UN's reputation in Africa and more widely.'[19]

The British military would play important roles in this, but would be complemented by the FCO and DfID, including a civilian police mission to reform the local police. Riley found that in London and PJHQ the prevailing sentiment was that the war was over. This was far from the case. Riley considered that his initial mission, whilst requiring him to ensure that UNAMSIL did not fail, did not require enabling Sierra Leonean government success. This point was accepted, and his mission was adjusted, to allow him to directly support government forces.

The British HQ had been expanded from the brigade HQ's establishment of 30 personnel to a size of 130, to allow it to function at the operational level. It developed a campaign plan to neutralize the RUF. This began with an operation in which three SLA brigades, acting in turn, cleared the immediate area of Freetown and moved over 180 miles to re-occupy Kenema, the country's third largest city. The operation was sequenced, with each brigade at a time moving and fighting, activity that would have been impossible at the start of the year. These operations greatly improved government and civilian morale and eroded that of the RUF.

Initially, London forbade British advisors embedded in SLA units to accompany RUF units moving more than 25 miles from Freetown – a considerable limitation. But when the Defence Secretary visited the country Riley persuaded him to lift the restriction.

In early 2001, President Kabbah opened the country's new MoD HQ. New Joint Forces and Joint Support Commands became operational – both initially led by British officers. The SLA was renamed the Republic of Sierra Leone Armed Forces (RSLAF), symbolizing that they were under government control, not the other way round, something that happened far too often in Africa.

The British made a considerable investment in equipping the RSLAF. This included supply of weapons, equipment and ammunition. But bureaucracy and interagency friction in London sometimes delayed this. Brigadier Riley found a partial way to overcome these frictions. He was approached by the Chinese embassy, the ambassador explaining that Beijing supported British efforts to restore stability, as Sierra Leone was a country which China wanted to do business with. They supplied a shipload of arms and ammunition.

The RSLAF with British support began attacking RUF command and control. By now the British intelligence architecture for the theatre was well developed. The RUF relied greatly on satellite phones. When the local telephone company cut off the service as a result of the RUF not paying its bills, Riley personally settled the account, so the British could continue listening to the RUF's calls. Through a combination of signals and human intelligence the British now had a very good insight into the RUF's leadership, capabilities and plans.

The RSLAF still controlled two besieged garrisons, isolated deep in the north of the country and under frequent attack by the RUF. The RAF used Hercules transport aircraft to deliver much-needed supplies to bush air strips. Supported by the British the RSLAF moved to successfully relieve both sieges. Both garrisons now became bases for further government offensive operations.

In March 2001 UNAMSIL moved into northern and western Sierra Leone. It did so, occupying the towns of Lunsar and Makeni. But it failed to establish full control of security, failed to disarm the RUF and obstructed the return of government authority. It was still behaving with self-imposed impartiality, ignoring the new mandate from New York, possibly because the troop-contributing nations were very averse to the risk of fighting the RUF.

In April HQ 1st Mechanized Brigade returned to the UK, replaced by a bespoke HQ commanded by a brigadier. In May there was a second peace conference in Abuja, backed by Nigeria and Britain, and with President Kabbah negotiating from a position of greatly increased strength. The RUF effectively capitulated, agreeing to withdraw from the contested areas of the Guinean border, and to recognize the RSLAF as the forces of the legitimate government.

In autumn 2001, the newly arrived Pakistani contingent of UNAMSIL restored government authority over the diamond-mining district of Koidu. By February 2002 RSLAF had full control of the country, effectively ending the war.

In 2001 and 2002 the international training mission was joined by contingents from Canada, France, Australia Bermuda and the US. At its peak it had over 300 troops. Britain signed a ten-year memorandum of understanding with the government and the British brigadier remained military advisor to the president of Sierra Leone.

The programme of reform, advice and training continued. The British did all they could to embed the concepts of democracy and of civilian control of the military. Commenting on the 2007 elections, the US ambassador observed that the British had 'insight into the attitude of the military, and that there was always the fear the British might call for their over horizon SAS troops to come in if the military acted inappropriately ... what was clear was the security forces were not going to intervene to influence the outcome of the election.'[20]

SIERRA LEONE IN RETROSPECT

The initial evacuation operation and the rescue of hostages had both featured rapid deployment of high-readiness reaction forces at long range, calculated risk taking, integration of land, sea, air and special forces, information operations and the selective use of force. The MoD considered that East Timor and Sierra Leone validated the JRRF concept. There had only been two relatively small battles: the Pathfinder Platoon at Lungi Lol and the hostage rescue mission. Operation *Basilica*, the summer training mission, had helped improve the SLA. But had the capture of hostages by the West Side Boys resulted in significant British deaths and casualties, it would have probably been seen as a strategic failure with negative military and political implications for the government, the MoD and the Army.

The stabilization of Sierra Leone and the re-establishment of its government's control required an interagency campaign, which was successfully developed and implemented by HQ 1st Mechanized Brigade, grown from a tactical to an operational level HQ, directing the military element of UK grand strategy, which succeeded.

There were a number of other factors that contributed to the campaign's success. The RUF's principal motivation was greed and it lacked an ideology that gained traction on the majority of the population. The Sierra Leone government strongly supported British operations. The police supported the government and stayed loyal throughout the campaign. And British diplomatic pressure, supported by the US, to throttle the flow of illegally mined diamonds from Sierra Leone greatly assisted. Counterinsurgency expert

David Ucko, who was later to be very critical of British failures in Iraq, summarized the campaign: 'Britain used a limited force to empower other actors, exploit shifting opportunities, and draw benefits from unanticipated occurrences.'[21]

For all the British personnel deployed, the campaign was challenging. Not only because of the humid tropical heat, but also because of the grinding poverty of many civilians and the appalling war crimes committed by the RUF. But many officers and soldiers who participated recalled it as a great adventure, engendering a sense of real accomplishment. Reflecting on Sierra Leone , General Guthrie wrote that: 'Sierra Leone was a good example of the kind of liberal military intervention, similar to our role in Kosovo, that gave our merch a good name and a renewed sense of self-worth. For that Blair deserves praise.'[22]

Guthrie also revealed that Blair became increasingly concerned about the situation in Zimbabwe, where President Robert Mugabe's regime was complicit in the murder of white farmers and seizures of their land, as well as committing human rights abuses on Zimbabwean people. It was a long time since the relative optimism of the early 1980s.

Mugabe antagonized Blair by calling his government 'a gangster regime led by gay gangsters', a direct attack on both Labour politicians and gay activists. Guthrie assessed that a British military intervention would ignite the embers of anti-colonial sentiment that lay dormant across Africa. He said to Blair 'hold hard, Prime minister, or you'll make it a lot worse'. Blair accepted the advice.[23]

It was ironic that Mugabe's homophobic slur came at a time when the British Armed Forces had lifted the ban on gay people serving in the armed services. In 2000, all restrictions on service in the armed forces by gay people were removed. There was some internal and external controversy about this. I had previously noticed the application of a certain amount of 'live and let live' quiet toleration of gay troops in the medical services and military musicians – provided those concerned stayed in the closet. But there were contemporaries of mine who found the new policy troubling. One brigadier resigned. However, the admission of gay people did not bring the Army to its knees. Far from it.

THE 2001 FOOT AND MOUTH CRISIS

In early 2001 there was a major outbreak of foot and mouth disease in England, the first since 1967. The disease rapidly spread across the country. The Ministry of Agriculture, Fisheries and Food (MAFF) initially struggled to understand the rapid spread of the disease. The character of agriculture had changed greatly since 1957, with animals being moved long distances around the UK.

Prime Minister Blair directed Army involvement. As MAFF were struggling to manage the situation, HQ 101st Logistic Brigade deployed to the ministry to assist them in organizing their response. The brigade set up a command and control and planning capability that the ministry otherwise lacked.

A plan was developed to slaughter animals within a 2-mile radius of an infection. At the height of the disease this required over 11,000 animals to be slaughtered a day. The scale of this challenge required mobilization of the military. At the time, the Royal Logistic Corps' catering branch had troops qualified as butchers, who could act as slaughterers. These were all deployed, as were other troops to collect carcasses and burn them in huge funeral pyres. Royal Engineers helped construct burn sites and large mass graves and assisted heavy vehicles in gaining access to difficult hilly and boggy terrain. At the height of the crisis some 2,000 troops were deployed to counter the disease.

This was a distressing task. Not just because of the loss of animal lives, but also because many farmers were losing their livelihoods as the animals went up in flames. This tested morale and leadership and required compassion. There was much activity in north-west England, under command of 42nd (North West) Brigade. Brigadier Alex Birtwhistle came from the region and served in the Queen's Lancashire Regiment. Setting up a command post in four vehicles in a car park, he became a welcome face of the operation on both national and local media. Richard Morris, the owner of Penrith Farmers' Market, itself turned into an operations centre, told the *Guardian*: 'So often the farmers have had contradictory information or misinformation from MAFF. The army have brought discipline and organization. They just make things happen. It is demanding keeping up with their pace, but that is how it should be.'[24]

By the summer the crisis had passed. The logistic brigade HQ departed the Department of Food and Rural Affairs, as MAFF had become. The UK had been challenged by a virus and the Army had played a major role in defeating the infection – not least in providing much-needed assistance to civil authorities overfaced by the challenge, including by adding a command-and-control and planning capability to a government department that was overwhelmed by events. This would happen again.

OPERATION *ESSENTIAL HARVEST* IN MACEDONIA – A FORGOTTEN SUCCESS

Although NATO and the UN were successfully stabilizing Kosovo, the conflict had rebounded on Macedonia – the state now known as North Macedonia. Thousands of refugees from Kosovo had destabilized the country, with fighting between majority Macedonians and minority ethnic Albanians. Some of these turned to violence and a new Albanian guerilla group, the National Liberation Army (NLA), began a full-scale insurgency demanding full civic rights for ethnic Albanians.

After the failure of negotiations led by the Organization for Security and Co-operation in Europe (OSCE), fighting intensified. But NATO Secretary General George Robertson and EU foreign policy chief Javier Solana successfully brokered a ceasefire deal signed in mid-August 2001. This not only set up a political settlement that protected minority rights, but required the NLA to voluntarily disarm, withdraw from the conflict zone and demobilize, by turning over its weapons at NATO-supervised collection points.

To support Robertson, London offered the recently formed 16 Air Assault Brigade for the mission. Operating under the KFOR Rear HQ in Skopje it became the multinational tactical HQ commanding NATO's Task Force Harvest. The brigade commander, Brigadier

Barney White-Spunner, would command some 3,000 NATO troops, including 2nd Battalion, the Parachute Regiment (2 Para).

The British troops deployed rapidly, helped by the RAF's newly acquired giant C17 airlifters. Operations began nine days after signature of the ceasefire agreement. White-Spunner and his team quickly formulated a concept of operations for this novel task. NATO was clear that it did not want a long-term stabilization operation in Macedonia.

The British brigade rapidly deployed small teams to the insurgent leaders, to liaise, reassure and gather information. These were grouped together in a special forces task force that included 16 Air Assault Brigade's reconnaissance teams and artillery fire controllers. This initiative succeeded and insurgents began coming forward to hand their weapons over to 2 Para and other units in the task force. The operation ended in late September, with the insurgents having handed over about 3,500 small arms and an assortment of heavy weapons.

The operation was an outstanding success, but it was not without its risks. Interethnic tension in Macedonia was high and a group of youths dropped a concrete block onto a British Land Rover, killing a sapper. But another Balkan war had been averted, particular by George Robertson's speedy personal diplomacy and by the rapid deployment of the air assault brigade.

THE CHANGING ROLE OF WOMEN IN THE ARMY

Progress on granting female troops full emancipation took longer. Throughout the 21st century, women gradually expanded their service in the Army. By 2020, 10 per cent of the Army was female, and six female cadets had won the Sword of Honour for best cadet at Sandhurst. The previous rules that excluded women from close combat had been rendered irrelevant by the Iraq and Afghan wars, where there had been no distinction between the front line, lines of communication and base areas. Female soldiers had come under fire and some had been wounded and killed.

A notable example was Private Michelle Collins of the Royal Army Medical Corps. For rescuing a wounded soldier under heavy fire she was awarded the Military Cross, the first woman to achieve this. And female medics, combat engineers and dog handlers in Afghanistan often earned great respect from their hard-bitten male comrades. For example, the commanding officer of the Light Dragoons reporting on Operation *Panther's Claw* observed that in the hot, exhausting, and intensely bloody combat of that most difficult operation the female soldiers had performed as well as the men.

The Chiefs of Staff had twice reviewed the policy of excluding women from ground close combat. In 2000 they decided to retain it. But in 2016 the policy was abandoned. It became possible for women to join the infantry and armoured corps.

There was not a huge surge of applications. And more women wanted to commission from Sandhurst than wanted to join as recruits. But there was a gradual surge of women applying for and passing the demanding commando course and P Company. This was no mean achievement.

However, integration of women still faced challenges. Some of these were practical, such as uniform and body armour, and could be easily solved. But a number of independent reports showed that there were weaknesses in Army culture and leadership that discouraged women from continuing to serve. And sexual harassment seemed troublingly difficult to eradicate. There was no easy solution to these issues, apart from first-class leadership.

THE WARM GLOW OF SATISFACTION

The British interventions in Bosnia, Kosovo, Sierra Leone all succeeded. Casualties to the intervening British forces were very low. Throughout the armed forces and defence ministries of the US, the UK and their allies that had contributed troops there was a sense of positive difference. The professional satisfaction and pride displayed by the armed forces contributed to widespread support from the public, media and politicians.

The British military were publicly praised by Prime Minister Tony Blair. Success in these diverse operations drew on the foundations laid down by General Bagnall in the 1980s, complemented by new doctrine – some of which was world leading. But despite its successes the Army was often overstretched, producing personnel shortages. And it constantly struggled to achieve the funding it needed.

CHAPTER 10
RAPID INTERVENTION (3)
AFGHANISTAN

BEFORE 9/11

In 2001 the Army had a 20-year record of successful operations from Northern Ireland, Rhodesia/Zimbabwe, the Falklands, Operation *Desert Storm,* Bosnia, Kosovo, East Timor, Sierra Leone and Macedonia. All these operations were supported by Parliament, the public and the media. The Army was confident that it was successful at stabilization operations. But the adversaries were usually of lower quality than British forces, were mostly unwilling to stand and fight and were overmatched by British and US all-arms and joint warfighting capabilities.

In the first part of 2001, the new administration of President George W. Bush did not appear to afford a high priority to countering Al Qaida. Neither Al Qaida nor Afghanistan was a high priority for the British government, nor for the MoD.

EXERCISE SAIF SAREEA 2 *DEPLOYS*

The SDR required the Army to be able to mobilize and deploy a division of up to three brigades and divisional troops, moving in three echelons at 30, 60 and 90 days' notice. The MoD had committed to a target of achieving a 'full Joint Rapid Reaction Forces Capability by October 2001'. It planned to test and demonstrate this capability by conducting a major exercise in Oman in autumn 2001.

Over late summer, a joint force deployed, commanded by the UK JFHQ. The RAF sent Tornado bombers, helicopters and transport aircraft. A maritime task group of one of the UK's pocket-sized aircraft carriers was joined by amphibious shipping carrying the Royal Marines 3 Commando Brigade, who were to initially play the role of enemy forces. The British land component was commanded by the HQ of 1st Armoured Division. As well as 102nd Logistic Brigade and combat support units, HQ 4th Armoured Brigade commanded two of its battlegroups. The brigade and division were also joined by Omani troops.

But in the land forces, both brigades were incomplete, the commando brigade having two rather than three commandos. And 4th Brigade had only two battlegroups, both at peacetime strength, rather than the normal allocation of four heavy battlegroups at warfighting establishment. So the brigade fighting element was at less than half the strength required for war. And the armoured division was supporting only one-sixth of the battlegroups needed for large-scale warfighting. This did not reduce the value of the exercise for the troops, the commanders and the HQs involved. But it meant that the strategic lift and logistics were faced with much lower demand than for the maximum size of operation envisaged by the MoD's planning assumptions.

STRATEGIC SHOCK

The 9/11 Al Qaida suicide attacks by hijacked airliners on the World Trade Centre and the Pentagon were a shock for the US, the greatest since Pearl Harbor. Thousands of its citizens had been killed. The 9/11 attacks might just be the first of many attacks that Al Qaida could have planned. Another successful attack could have been politically lethal to his government. The CIA Director George Tenet assessed with 'near certainty' that Osama Bin Laden had initiated the attacks.[1] This put immense pressure on US President George W. Bush, and the presidential TV address to the nation contained a clear warning to countries that might be harbouring anti-US terrorist networks: 'We have made the decision to punish whoever harbours terrorists, not just the perpetrators.'

That fateful day I was at a doctrine committee meeting at Upavon camp, a windswept cantonment high on the northern edge of Salisbury Plain. Amongst the half dozen brigadiers attending was the Director Special Forces. A clerk brought me a hastily telephoned message from my office in London, describing the initial attack. Like many British people we were inexorably drawn to rolling TV news, sucked into the trauma. The meeting was abandoned, the Director Special Forces packing up his papers to return to London, saying as he left the room 'this has all the hallmarks of Osama Bin Laden'. The remainder of us discussed the implications. We all felt that it was inevitable that war would be the result. Driving back to London where many more people were on the streets than normal, most apparently walking home, rather than using public transport, there was much to think about.

The UK was faced with new requirements. Firstly, domestic security had to be stepped up. Any further Al Qaida cells had to be found and neutralized. And border, airline and transportation security had to be upped to prevent further terrorist groups slipping into the UK undetected.

On September 13 at a Pentagon briefing for reporters, Deputy Secretary of Defense Paul Wolfowitz stated that US objectives included 'ending states who sponsor terrorism'. Wolfowitz subsequently pressed for attacking Iraq.[2]

For Bush, and Defense Secretary Donald Rumsfeld, public, political and media pressure to be seen to act against this new enemy was considerable. The imperative was to be seen to be taking rapid and decisive action against both Al Qaida and the state that harboured it. And the US needed to deter further terrorist attacks, not just from Al Qaida in Afghanistan, but more widely.

Neither the US nor UK had any contingency plan for an attack on Afghanistan. In theory it would be possible to use the strategy of Operation *Desert Storm* – building up large ground and air forces around Afghanistan, then at some stage launching an air campaign, followed by a ground invasion by conventional forces. This option was judged to be far too slow.

President Bush addressed a joint session of Congress, setting out the US government's demands on the Taliban:

Deliver to United States authorities all the leaders of al Qaeda who hide in your land. Close immediately and permanently every terrorist training camp in Afghanistan, and hand over every terrorist, and every person in their support structure, to appropriate authorities. Give the United States full access to terrorist training camps, so we can make sure they are no longer operating.

These demands are not open to negotiation or discussion. The Taliban must act, and act immediately. They will hand over the terrorists, or they will share in their fate … Our war on terror begins with al Qaeda, but it does not end there. It will not end until every terrorist group of global reach has been found, stopped and defeated.[3]

The Taliban refused these demands, so the US faced the unforeseen requirement of having to attack Afghanistan. In conditions of great secrecy but under great pressure to act quickly, the CIA developed a plan in which CIA teams would arm and fund the anti-Taliban Northern Alliance militias, with US Special Operations Forces (SOF) linking up with the CIA and the Northern Alliance to co-ordinate air strikes, multiplying the combat power of the anti-Taliban forces. US ground troops would be introduced to complete the destruction of the Taliban and Al Qaida. Once this was complete, there would be stabilization operations.

This was a period of intensive political, diplomatic and military planning. The full weight of US intelligence collection was applied to Afghanistan. The British rapidly began collecting intelligence on Afghanistan and sharing it with the US. The RAF deployed its signals intelligence capability, carried by ageing Nimrod aircraft, as well photo reconnaissance aircraft, the even older Canberra PR 9.

US Army General Tommy Franks exercised command and control from CENTCOM's main HQ in Tampa and decided to retain tight control over the operation. He was joined by a delegation of British military planners. The UK and the US had a long-standing military and intelligence partnership, the latter founded on the 'five eyes' intelligence collaboration arrangement between London and Washington, Australia, Canada and New Zealand. There was a very close working relationship between UK and US SOF. Royal Navy and RAF officers were already embedded in the HQs of CENTCOM's maritime and air components. A reinforced British military team was sent to join CENTCOM's main HQ in Tampa, headed by a three-star officer. And a British one-star officer deployed to the Pentagon to act as the Chief of Defence Staff's liaison officer to the Chairman of the US Joint Chiefs of Staff.

Lost in the noise of frenzied media speculation about war and a growing conspiracy theory that the British were part of a scheme to attack Afghanistan and the wider Middle East and that the US had faked the attacks on the Pentagon and World Trade Centre, the exercise continued.

On 9 September, most of the troops including the divisional HQ were in the desert of southern Oman. They had no televisions, but were aghast to listen to reports on the BBC World Service radio. Mixed with the apprehension and outrage was a strong sense that the world had changed. Many thought that the attack would have a similar effect on US politicians and people and that war would be an inevitable consequence. The same sense of shock and apprehension was shared by the division's 7th Armoured Brigade, then in Kosovo.

Shortly after 9/11, quietly, with no publicity, 1st Mechanized Brigade's HQ was flown out to Oman to replace the JFHQ that had been running the exercise. This was to free it up to plan and command any UK new operation to assist the US in Afghanistan, named Operation *Veritas*. The Royal Navy moved two nuclear submarines into position to fire Tomahawk cruise missiles at Afghanistan. Amphibious ships with Royal Marines embarked, and an aircraft carrier became floating bases in the Indian Ocean for helicopters, marines and special forces. The 1st Armoured Division departed Oman and returned to Germany.

The exercise had demonstrated that the UK could successfully deploy its forces to the Middle East and operate there. It showed that the additional strategic lift rapidly brought into service accelerated deployment. The MoD congratulated itself.

But the exercise had generated some important lessons. For example, before the exercise the Army had identified the need to modify the Challenger 2 tank, to better protect against dust. Requested funding for these modifications was denied. Unsurprisingly, on the exercise the tanks sometimes struggled with the desert dust, leading to consumption of spare parts at a rate much higher than planned, depressing the tanks' availability.

Although the exercise had been planned for three years, there was not enough desert clothing for all the troops deployed. A particular problem was a lack of desert boots, requiring a proportion of troops to wear the standard black leather boot. Unsurprisingly, many troops found the boots too hot, some boots literally melting in the heat, and a proportion of them developed infections as a result.

This British force had over 4,000 personnel. It was much smaller than the ever-increasing US military capability in the Gulf and Indian Ocean, but its value was as much political as military, as was the effort to garner international political and diplomatic support for attacking Afghanistan that Prime Minister Blair threw himself into.

TOPPLING THE TALIBAN

Offers to the US of intelligence-gathering and combat capabilities by the UK and Australia were gratefully accepted. The Pentagon and State Department were overwhelmed with many other nations' offers of forces. Most were declined as the US doubted that the forces offered would add value to the campaign. Many were not even acknowledged. This was in part a reflection of the pressure on the Pentagon staff. It was also a product of Donald Rumsfeld's displays of deep mistrust of alliances. He was to summarize this in a sound bite: the approach of the Kosovo war was to be reversed. This was not to be a coalition of equals; it was to be a US-led mission. 'Let me reemphasize that the mission determines the coalition, and the coalition must not determine the mission.'[4]

On 7 October 2001, President Bush announced that the US was conducting 'carefully targeted actions to disrupt the use of Afghanistan as a terrorist base of operations and to attack the military capability of the Taliban regime ... Our military action is also designed to clear the way for sustained, comprehensive and relentless operations to drive them out and bring them to justice.'[5]

US air and missile strikes were launched against the Taliban's conventional military capability. Royal Navy submarines fired some of the UK's small stock of Tomahawk cruise missiles. Air drops of humanitarian aid were made by giant C17 transport aircraft flying from US Air Force bases in Germany.

Afghanistan was now the main effort for US Special Operations Command (SOCOM). This comprised the US Navy's maritime special forces, the Sea, Air, Land Teams (SEALs), and supporting small boat squadrons. The US Army 'Green Berets' SOF were trained and equipped to support, assist and fight alongside indigenous forces behind enemy lines. The Army also provided three battalions of elite light infantry, the Rangers.

From early October the US began flying CIA and SOF teams into Afghanistan. Their helicopters faced considerable practical difficulties caused by distance, the mountainous terrain of central Afghanistan, the presence of Taliban air defences and winter weather. By mid-October detachments of SOF had met up with anti-Taliban forces, mainly from the Tajik and Uzbek-dominated Northern Alliance.

Bringing in precision air strikes from orbiting US Navy and Air Force jets, they created the conditions for the defeat of the Taliban by the Northern Alliance and other Afghan militias. The campaign had succeeded much more quickly than was envisaged.

There is evidence that the SAS joined this campaign.[6] General Franks' memoir shows a photograph of him conferring with the US special forces commander.[7] To one side in the HQ is a man wearing British uniform, probably from the SAS. There are credible reports of an SAS attack on a concentration of Taliban fighters in southern Afghanistan. The British do not appear to have been involved in the battle of Tora Bora, where General Franks' desire to limit US boots on the ground probably allowed Osama Bin Laden to escape into Pakistan.

The British dropped supplies to SAS troops by parachute. This needed the full-time deployment of 16 Air Assault Brigade's single air despatch squadron. The squadron comprised specially trained Royal Logistic Corps soldiers who prepared the loads for parachute despatch; packing, rigging the British Special Forces Hercules transport aircraft and finally pushing the loads from the aircraft. This was hard, back-breaking work, that required both physical strength and tight timing, and finding the drop zones at night challenged even these most highly trained pilots and aircrews of the RAF.

THE INTERNATIONAL SECURITY ASSISTANCE FORCE (ISAF)

In December 2001 an international conference convened under UN auspices in Bonn. It sought to assist the stabilization and reconstruction of post-Taliban Afghanistan. Hamid Karzai was appointed interim Afghan president and inaugurated on 22 December and a new constitution was to be drafted. At an international conference in Tokyo in early 2002 billions of dollars of international aid were pledged, as was international assistance with reconstruction, development, building new security forces and countering the narcotics industry.

The Conference agreed that it would take time to develop Afghanistan's new security forces, so a UN-mandated force would deploy to 'assist in the maintenance of security for Kabul and the surrounding area'. Tony Blair was very keen that the UK lead this force. A reconnaissance party of British officers was despatched to Kabul where it found a city with few people, no cars on the streets and in almost total darkness at night.

Some of the British troops had served in Bosnia during the civil war, when the scars of that savage conflict were all too visible. They were shocked to see that the damage to Kabul was much greater than that inflicted on Sarajevo. Many of Kabul's population had survived on international food aid for the previous five years. Government ministries were hollow shells. Competent staff had largely fled. The shattered state of Afghanistan's capital suggested that its capability as a state was at a very low level.

Over December and January, ISAF flew into Kabul to assist the Afghan authorities with the city's security. Its HQ was based on HQ of the UK's 3rd Division, commanding a British-led multinational brigade of three battalions, including 2nd Battalion the Parachute Regiment, with major French and German contributions. Many other nations offered troops. Most of these offers were of infantry, of which ISAF already had sufficient, but there were insufficient offers of engineers, logistic units, or helicopters.

The British asked to be able to call on US forces, should the mission encounter any threats that it could not handle on its own. London proposed that this would best be achieved by ISAF being subordinated to HQ CENTCOM. This was vetoed by Donald Rumsfeld, who displayed strong opposition to peacekeeping missions. The initiative was also opposed by Germany, who saw ISAF as a peacekeeping, not combat, force. This illustrated the differing national appetites for risk that would create political and military friction throughout the Afghan and Iraq wars.

ISAF's commander, Major General John McColl, directed ISAF 'to create a secure environment within Kabul, within which the developing Afghan government can gain traction'.[8] ISAF's infantry spent much time patrolling the city alongside Northern Alliance troops. Potential threats of a Taliban counterattack or fighting between rival militia groups

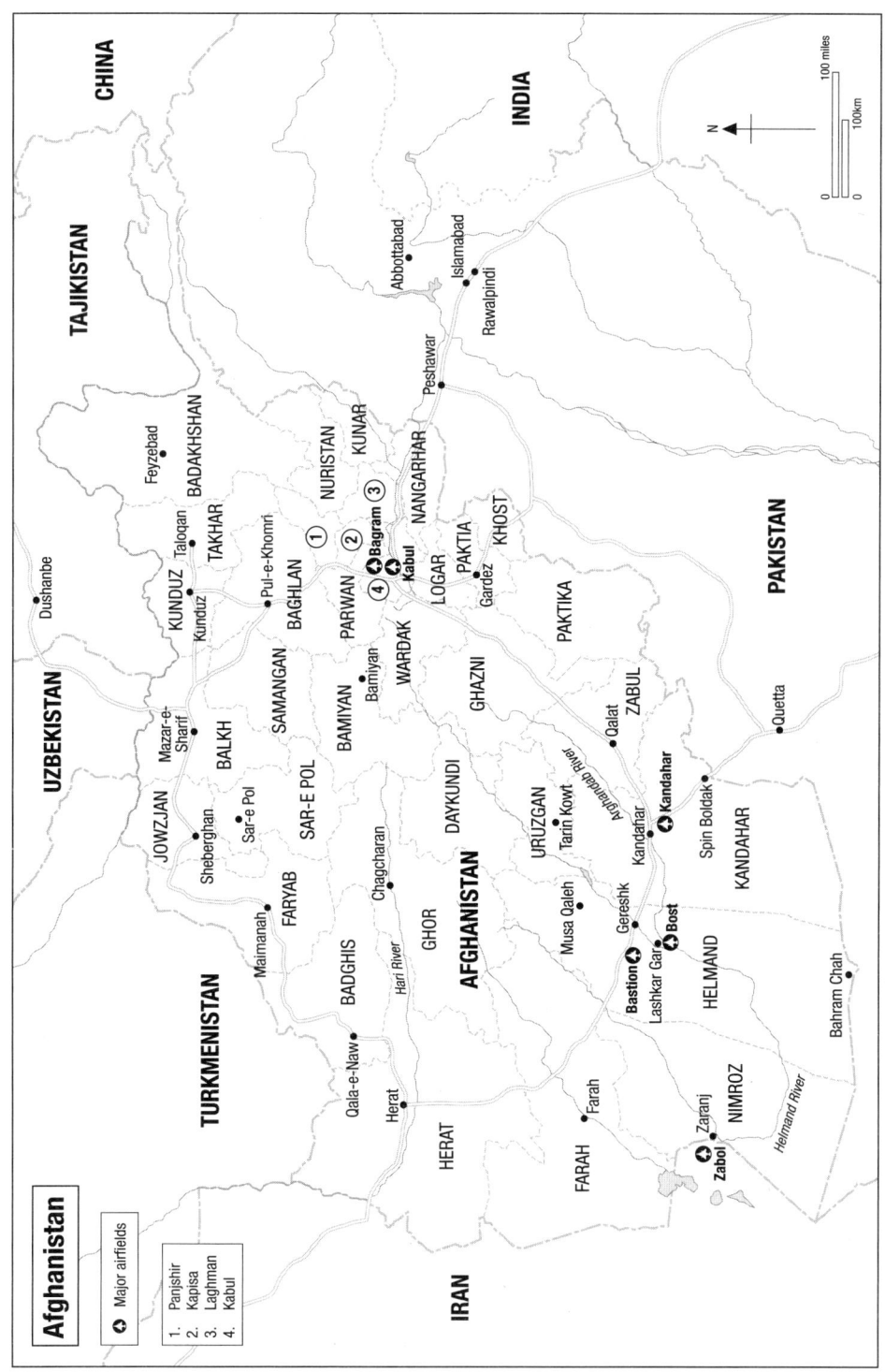

Afghanistan

⊕ Major airfields

1. Panjshir
2. Kapisa
3. Laghman
4. Kabul

failed to manifest. But there were some exchanges of small arms fire with armed criminal gangs.

McColl did all he could to support the new Afghan interim administration and Karzai, as well as the UN diplomat Lakhtar Brahimi, whom McColl treated as de facto head of the international community in Kabul. The British also provided instructors for the training of the first battalion of the new Afghan National Guard. ISAF assisted with the security for the Loya Jirga assembly of elders that elected Karzai as head of the Afghan Transitional Government.

Karzai and many Afghans wanted ISAF to increase in size and deploy beyond Kabul. McColl produced a plan to show what might be achieved with a fourfold increase in the size of the force to 20,000 troops. This was opposed by Rumsfeld and rejected by the US National Security Council. With British military planners turning their eyes to Iraq, London had no appetite to increase troop numbers in Afghanistan, instead seeking to reduce its force level there. The British handed leadership of ISAF to Turkey in mid-2002, but left a small contingent based on an infantry company in Kabul. ISAF now represented an ad hoc task force formed of a coalition of the willing.[9]

OPERATIONS *ANACONDA* AND *JACANA*

US intelligence agencies searched for any remaining Taliban, Al Qaida and jihadist forces remaining in Afghanistan. In early 2002, they detected up to 1,500 jihadist fighters concentrating in the Shah-I Kowt Valley, a mountainous region in south-east Afghanistan near the Pakistan border. On 2 March Operation *Anaconda* was mounted to destroy them. It ran into unexpected difficulties, including inadequate air/land planning, over-confidence and underestimation of the enemy, who stood and fought with unexpected determination.

When the British realized that *Anaconda* had failed, they rushed a task force of Royal Marines to Afghanistan. Operation *Jacana* saw the HQ of 3 Commando Brigade, a commando and Army artillery and engineers deploy to Bagram. This was not a rapid move as its campsite had to be cleared of unexpected ordnance. And the Army field hospital sent to Bagram was neutralized by an outbreak of norovirus. Overcoming these frictions, the Marines launched a number of search and destroy missions, without significant results.

Afghan industry, agriculture and state institutions had been very badly damaged by two decades of war. The only telephones that worked were satellite phones. Western troops, diplomats and development staff were shocked to see how poor and isolated many rural agricultural communities were. And discovering that, except in a very small elite centred on Kabul, Afghan society treated women as utterly subordinate to men was another shock to international sensibilities. To some it seemed that the further they travelled from Kabul, the further they went back in time, in both agriculture and linkages to the modern world. It was not difficult to find Afghans who had not heard of 9/11. SAS patrols in rural regions would sometimes be asked if they were Russian troops.[10]

Embassies and international organizations established themselves in a very austere environment. The CIA set themselves up in a ramshackle hotel where 'Bearded special operators and case officers with Glock pistols strapped to their thighs tramped in and out. The atmosphere was a cross between a central Asian organized crime clubhouse and a decrepit hotel in a muddy street in an old western.'[11]

Afghan warlords and militia leaders wanted to capture US and Coalition resources and military support. With insufficient understanding of the complex local dynamics, international forces unknowingly allowed themselves to be manipulated. This included warlords offering information about alleged Taliban and Al Qaida supporters. On too many occasions this led to raids on local actors who were not insurgents or jihadists but were rivals of the group providing the information.

Some of those detained by US troops or the CIA were innocent of Taliban or Al Qaida activity. Some were sent to the US military prisons at Bagram air base in Afghanistan, Guantanamo Bay, or the CIA's secret prison network. Some Afghan prisoners were subject to cruel and inhumane treatment amounting to torture. Some died of their injuries, others of deliberate neglect, fanning the flames of resentment and humiliation.

These flames were also fanned by the way in which US Coalition and private security companies' vehicles and convoys drove around, often bullying civilian vehicles off the roads, and firing warning shots. Many were under instructions not to stop in the event of an accident, no matter how serious. The private security companies hired by the US military and many embassies were if anything less restrained than US forces. A particularly egregious example was the death of an Afghan woman knocked down by a private security team on their way to meet Hillary Clinton at Kabul airport.

As soon as the Taliban were removed CENTCOM was directed by Rumsfeld to keep its troop presence in Afghanistan to a 'light footprint'. US and international forces should not be seen as an army of occupation. The US had secretly begun planning to attack Iraq. This would need considerably more ground troops than had been used to remove the Taliban. In April 2002 President Bush announced that:

> peace will only be achieved when we give the Afghan people the means to achieve their own aspirations. Peace ... will be achieved by helping Afghanistan develop its own stable government. Peace will be achieved by helping Afghanistan train and develop its own national army. And peace will be achieved through an education system for boys and girls which works ... We're clearing minefields. We're rebuilding roads. We're improving medical care. And we will work to help Afghanistan to develop an economy that can feed its people without feeding the world's demand for drugs.[12]

Afghanistan became an 'economy of force' theatre, containing about 10,000 US and coalition conventional forces and SOF. The latter joined with US funded warlords' militias to down remaining Al Qaida and Taliban forces. They conducted 'search and destroy missions' to locate and then attack Al Qaida and Taliban remnants, where intelligence indicated targets.

Resulting civilian casualties and collateral damage further alienated Afghan civilians. As there were no US HQs subordinate to the single HQ at Bagram, aggrieved Afghans lacked a local Coalition military HQ where they could seek resolution. With the exception of ISAF in Kabul, no international forces were assigned a specified area of Afghan territory as their own area of operations.

International reconstruction and development effort was largely focussed on Kabul. How then was the Afghan government capability outside Kabul to be developed? The Combined Joint Task Force (CJTF) Chief of Plans, British Army Colonel Nick Carter,[13] visited a US SOF team in Gardez. It included a vet and doctor, whose expertise was greatly appreciated by Afghans. He suggested that similar teams be deployed throughout the country to help the Afghan government extend its reach. Initially called Coalition Humanitarian Liaison Centres, these were manned by staff from US Army Civil Affairs units, assessing humanitarian needs and conduct small-scale reconstruction projects.

Carter proposed that this approach be extended throughout Afghanistan. It was, and by the end of 2002 the concept expanded to include US government civilians. The teams were re-named as Provincial Reconstruction Teams (PRTs). Deployed to provincial capitals they sought to support Afghan civilian reconstruction efforts, as well as increasing the local consent to the activities of international forces. They were multi-agency teams of military and civilian personnel, including diplomats, development agency staff and experts in other fields such as policing, agriculture and justice.

By 2004, there were nine such teams in Afghanistan. Most teams were provided by the US, but New Zealand and Germany also deployed PRTs. One was British, based in the northern Afghanistan city of Mazar-e Sharif. They varied in size, from 50 to 100 people in a US PRT, to the German PRT of 300 people; as did different national policies on development and force protection of civilians.[14]But Iraq became the US government's over-riding strategic priority. In May 2003, Rumsfeld told journalists that in Afghanistan 'we're at a point where we clearly have moved from major combat activity to a period of stability and reconstruction activities.'[15]

In late 2003, a new US-led theatre command for Afghanistan was formed: Combined Forces Afghanistan (CFC-A). Both to counter an already deteriorating security situation where Taliban attacks were slowly increasing, and to better assist the Afghan authorities and the UN, its commander, Lieutenant General David Barno, allocated responsibility for areas of Afghanistan to US military commanders. US brigades would be based in key areas of southern and eastern Afghanistan where the Al Qaida and Taliban threats were greatest. The formations would partner with the increasing number of Afghan forces and use development projects conducted by PRTs to promote popular support. Barno sought to fully integrate the US military activity with the political and development work being conducted by the US and its allies. He moved himself and his key staff into the US embassy in Kabul, to better integrate his work with that of the US ambassador, Zalmy Khalilzad.

A new Afghan constitution was written, and Karzai elected as Afghan president. Both the US and NATO considered that political and security progress was being made. But Karzai co-opted and empowered local strongmen and warlords and their militias. Some armed groups were funded and employed by the CIA. They often preyed on local civilians.

International effort to co-ordinate reform of Afghanistan's security sector saw responsibilities allocated to lead nations as follows:

- US: Afghan National Army
- Japan: disarmament, demobilization and reintegration of militias
- UK: counter-narcotics
- Germany: police
- Italy: judicial and legal system.

US-led efforts to build a new Afghan Army initially had some effect, but the new Afghan National Guard and MoD quickly fell under control of the notorious warlord General Fahim. The US had them disbanded and rebuilt from scratch. The Japanese funded a programme to disarm, demobilize and re-integrate militias. This had some success in getting warlords to hand over heavy weapons.

The German effort to rebuild the Afghan Police was inadequate. The Germans deployed 17 officers to a police academy in Kabul to run a course of three years in length. This was too small and slow, failing to meet the desperate need for police. The US State Department took over the effort, but contractors hired for the task displayed little relevant background for the task in hand. In 2005 the US military took over responsibility for training the police, but found that the service was incapable of carrying out its internal security responsibilities as a result of illiterate recruits, poor leadership and pervasive corruption.

The economic destruction resulting from decades of war meant that Afghanistan had become the world's largest producer of the opium poppy. The British effort to lead the counter-narcotics effort also ran into the sand. A plan to offer financial incentives to farmers to switch crops away from the poppy failed. A plan by British intelligence to create a paramilitary counter-narcotics unit with dedicated helicopter support, as well as a narcotics court, all manned by vetted personnel, had some success, but its effects were a drop in the ocean.[16]

THE DEFENCE REVIEW THAT NEVER WAS

Far away from the austere environment of war-ravaged Afghanistan, Defence Secretary Geoff Hoon commissioned a 'New Chapter' to the 1998 SDR. It re-examined its recommendations in the light of 9/11, domestic counter-terrorism and the early months of the intervention in Afghanistan.

It concluded that the principles of the review still applied, as did the capability judgements. But it was possible that large-scale terrorist incidents in the UK, including the use of weapons of mass destruction, could overmatch the capacity of the emergency services and, in extremis, the Regular Army. So the TA was given a role in homeland defence, through providing civil/military liaison officers and mobilizing Civil Contingency Reaction Forces (CCRFs), resulting in a modest increase in manpower and activity.

But despite its successes the Army was often overstretched, producing personnel shortages. And it constantly struggled to achieve the funding it needed. As the SDR was implemented and new operations were mounted in Kosovo and Sierra Leone, the MoD came under even greater financial pressure from an unsympathetic Treasury. A dispute between Defence Secretary Geoff Hoon and Chancellor Gordon Brown over the application of the rules of engagement for resource accounting only ended when the Prime Minister ruled in the Treasury's favour.[17] This required an immediate cut to the defence budget, and therefore a short-notice defence review. The MoD pretended that this was routine business, but none of those involved believed ministers' and spin doctors' bland and implausible reassurances.

This resulted in a 2003 White Paper setting out an adjusted policy, in which future adjustments to the force structure were signalled. in the 2004 Future Capabilities Command Paper, optimistically titled 'Delivering Security in a Changing World'. This adjusted policy acknowledged that to reflect the increased number and range of small-scale operations:

> We have effectively been conducting continual concurrent operations, deploying further afield, to more places, more frequently and with a greater variety of missions than set out in the SDR planning assumptions … a major lesson of the last five years is that the Department and the Armed Forces as a whole have to be structured and organised to support a fairly high level of operational activity at all times, not as a regular interruption to preparing for a large scale conflict.[18]

The most demanding expeditionary operations, involving intervention against state adversaries, were unlikely to be conducted without the US, either as the leader of a coalition, or in a NATO operation. Unilateral action by the UK in the most demanding expeditionary operations was unlikely. It reiterated the need for British forces to maintain the capability to lead medium-scale operations where the US was not involved, for example a European operation or one conducted by an ad hoc coalition of the willing. The paper further reduced the priority of NATO territorial defence, abandoning planning for any conventional war between NATO and Russia.

The paper seemed to assume that the future would be like the period after 1990, a mixture of short successful large-scale interventions and enduring and medium-scale peace enforcement operations. It did not foresee that that stabilization operations could turn as violent as they did in Iraq and Afghanistan, nor that such wars would inflict significant casualties and that would erode legitimacy. Too many officials and officers were basking in a warm glow of satisfaction, forgetting that the enemy gets a vote.

IMPLICATIONS FOR THE ARMY

Reversing the SDR, the size of the Army was reduced. An armoured brigade was disbanded, its place taken by a light brigade. Numbers of tanks and AS90 guns were reduced. The RAF gave up Rapier, Starstreak air defence missiles were cut by half and all ground-based air defences were concentrated in the Army.

Considerable financial savings were made against the future battlefield helicopter programme, although these were not publicized at the time. Had these reductions not been made, there would have been considerably more battlefield helicopter capability available from 2010.

MODERNIZING SPECIAL FORCES

There were improvements to Army special forces. Since the joint special forces group had been formed in 1989, the SAS and SBS had fought in two wars with Iraq, sustained their Northern Ireland and counter-terrorism commitments and supported interventions in the Balkans, Sierra Leone, Kosovo and Afghanistan. Lessons were learned. One innovation was to bring together the helicopters supporting special forces, so a joint special forces aviation wing was formed, incorporating an Army Air Corps squadron.

The special forces and Army identified further enhancements. One was to combine all their communications units into a single special forces signals regiment. Greatly improved security in Northern Ireland reduced the requirement for the Army to conduct covert surveillance in the province. But the capability was judged to be of much wider utility elsewhere, as demonstrated by the value of covert surveillance in the operations to detain indicted war criminals in Bosnia.

So the special forces group was joined by the new Special Reconnaissance Regiment. Like the Det, it drew on volunteers from across the armed forces, including women. The regiment chose to mark its formation with a parade at Sandhurst while the cadets were on leave. By all accounts it was an impressive event. Some photographs were published which showed participants from the back – protecting the true identity of surveillance operators being a key tenet of covert surveillance.

A high proportion of the new regiment came from the Royal Marines. And marines increasingly served in the SAS. In the late 2000s, a Marine office commanded the Special Reconnaissance Regiment. And ten years' later the Director Special Forces, a post previously filled by an SAS officer, was a Royal Marine.

Between 2001 and 2003 the SAS and SBS had often needed to draw on infantry support, the role performed by the parachute company in Sierra Leone, while the Royal Marines had provided close infantry support to the SBS in Afghanistan. The JRRF concept allowed any high-readiness conventional forces to support special forces. But these arrangements were ad hoc.

In contrast, the large US forces command included three battalions of Rangers. These were elite infantry supporting special forces. Tasks included raids, cordons, and reaction forces. That the Rangers provided permanently constituted support meant that they could train with the special forces they supported and use interoperable communications and equipment. This was seen as a more effective way of providing in-house infantry support than the UK's ad hoc approach. So the Director Special Forces asked for a battalion-sized unit to provide the same support.

REORGANIZATION OF THE INFANTRY

By coincidence this requirement became entangled with a long-overdue reform of the Army's infantry.[19] Since the 1998 Good Friday Agreement, Army operations in Northern Ireland had greatly reduced. Reflecting this, the MoD directed that the infantry be reduced by four battalions. The CGS, General Sir Mike Jackson, decided to reform the infantry regimental system.

The system he inherited reflected the major contraction of the Army in the 1960s. Those cuts meant that it was no longer possible to sustain an individual infantry regiment for each county or city. The Army Board encouraged regiments to merge but left much of the details to them. This resulted in a hybrid of large regiments and many single-battalion regiments. Apart from the Gurkhas, these moved every few years between roles and locations. This mechanism, known as the arms plot, was seen as adding value.

The 1991 reorganization of the infantry reduced all the large infantry regiments, apart from the Parachute Regiment. It also directed the amalgamation of some regiments, but other single-battalion regiments were left as they were for reasons that were never publicly explained. Many regiments felt bruised by this.

By 2004, the leadership of the Army felt the situation had changed. The war in Iraq had placed additional pressure on the Army's infantry. But during 2003 about a dozen battalions could not be used on operations because of planned arms plot moves. And there was a growing body of opinion in the Army that troops and their families should have greater stability, which could be achieved by reducing or eliminating infantry arms plot moves.

General Jackson was a Parachute Regiment officer. His regiment had been managed as a single entity. He saw this not only as maximizing stability for people who wanted it, but also as providing a wide range of career opportunities for the ambitious, brightest and best. The Army Board agreed with him that that small single-battalion regiments offered less to their people. So the infantry would reorganize in large regiments. The arms plot and resulting re-rolling of battalions would end.

In the face of controversy and a blizzard of lobbying by regimental veterans' groups, the necessary reorganization took place. This time the process was more transparent, with more consultation of regiments. The ability of regiments to recruit was a key factor. A detailed quantitative study used demographic data to assess this, Jackson requiring the new structure to be sustainable in the future.

The figures showed that some regiments would have difficulties sustaining their strength over the next two decades. Some of the conclusions were 'inconvenient truths' to regimental lobbyists. For example, the powerful lobby for retention of Scots infantry regiments did not reflect the evidence that Scotland would struggle to recruit more than four infantry battalions. It was not that young men from Scotland were not joining the Army. They were, but not enough wanted to join Scotland's infantry regiments. The projections were not made public.

Jackson recommended a new structure of 37 infantry battalions. But this was one more than the MoD's Permanent Secretary was prepared to fund. He and Assistant Chief of the General Staff David Richards devised a creative solution to this wicked problem – which was to assign the special forces support group role to a Parachute Regiment battalion, which would then move from the infantry to the special forces group. Civil servants in the MoD viscerally opposed the innovation, but Richards was able to persuade Defence Secretary Geoff Hoon to agree it. I worked in the MoD at the time and many civil service managers were outraged that their advice had been overruled.

The innovation was implemented and proved a great success. 1st Battalion, the Parachute Regiment became the core of the support group and was joined by Royal Marines and RAF Regiment personnel. Companies were rapidly deployed to assist special forces in Iraq and Afghanistan.

So, the three battalions of the Parachute Regiment survived, going on to play important roles in Afghanistan. The rest of the infantry did as Jackson told them, combining into multi-battalion regiments of between two and five battalions. Some new regiments were formed: the Yorkshire, Marcian and Duke of Lancaster's regiments.

Jackson was surprised that the five Scottish infantry regiments merged into a single large Royal Regiment Scotland, albeit one that retained its former regimental titles in brackets. So 1st Battalion the Black Watch became 3rd Battalion the Royal Regiment of Scotland (the Black Watch). He was particularly pleased with the Light Infantry and Royal Green Jackets: 'both regiments had a tradition of being unafraid of change and decided of themselves to combine to form the Rifles, the name going right back to the Peninsula War.'[20]

The changes in infantry regimental structures would have to take place whilst the Army was heavily committed to Iraq and increasingly engaged in Afghanistan. To administrators with tidy minds this was less than ideal. But the need to make mergers and amalgamations work without disrupting operational commitments imparted a sense of urgency that promoted the necessary changes, rather than inhibiting them. For example, when the Rifles were formed in February 2007, of its five battalions, one was in Germany having returned from Iraq three months before, and two battalions were on operation, with one in Basra Palace and the other split between Iraq and Afghanistan.

The Taliban return to Afghanistan

Some surviving Taliban fighters and leaders had melted back into rural communities in Afghanistan. Taliban members who had fled to Pakistan concentrated on survival. Pakistan's Federally Administered Tribal Areas that bordered Afghanistan provided an environment in which the writ of Islamabad and its security forces was limited.

The Pakistani military and its intelligence agency, Inter-Services Intelligence (ISI), had the dominant influence over Islamabad's foreign and defence policy. Repeated Afghan and US allegations of active support to the insurgents by Islamabad created great friction between Pakistan, Afghanistan and the US.

From 2003 the Taliban began to exploit widespread Afghan discontent with the government official's extortion and corruption and a sense of humiliation from the presence of infidel troops on Muslim soil. These discontents were reinforced by the Afghan civilian deaths and collateral damage from Coalition operations, and the threat to farmers' livelihoods posed by the counter-narcotics programme. These actions all created the conditions for a Taliban revival, which benefited from the relative security of their base areas in Pakistan. Throughout the period Taliban presence and influence in rural

Afghanistan slowly grew. Attacks on Coalition and Afghan government forces increased. By 2004, Taliban 'vanguard teams' began returning to southern Afghanistan.

Pakistan was prepared to take some action against insurgents and exhibit some co-operation with the US, particularly against Al Qaida. President Pervez Musharraf allowed the CIA to operate armed predator drones over Pakistan's tribal areas, whilst denying in public that such authorization had been granted. But key Taliban leaders and their families appeared to live openly in Pakistan.

ISAF EXPANSION

For NATO countries looking to retain military influence with the US, stabilizing Afghanistan looked like an ideal opportunity, particularly as it seemed no more dangerous than the Balkans. There were many politicians and senior military officers who feared that if NATO did not demonstrate a wider utility to both the US, it might become irrelevant and die. And the Pentagon was happy for NATO to do more in Afghanistan, to allow US troops to shift to Iraq. A consensus built up in NATO that the alliance should play a leading role in Afghanistan.

In August 2003 NATO assumed responsibility for ISAF. Having done so, the alliance and the US agreed a plan for NATO to assume security responsibility for the whole of Afghanistan. The country was divided into four sectors, and it was agreed that NATO would take them over in a counter-clockwise fashion. NATO took over northern Afghanistan in October 2004 and western Afghanistan in May 2005. These sectors appeared to be relatively stable and did not pose demanding security challenges. So, the governments of many troop-contributing countries did not need to have awkward conversations with their parliaments, media and electorates about potential risk. They portrayed their Afghan missions as low-risk peacekeeping or stabilization along the lines of the missions in Bosnia and Kosovo. Germany and other European countries wished to draw a line between the US-led counter-terrorism mission and peacekeeping and reconstruction.

CHAPTER 11
REGIME CHANGE IN IRAQ AND INITIAL STABILIZATION

FORCE GENERATION AND DEPLOYMENT

By mid-2002, a small number of British officers had begun planning with CENTCOM for regime change in Iraq, under conditions of great secrecy. The US wanted British forces to join the invasion, to avoid the image that the attack on Iraq would represent unilateral US action. It also asked for access to British bases and for UK special forces to fight. The MoD assessed that the US could defeat the Iraqi forces on their own, but it wanted to contribute not only SOF, but also a larger force package.[1] This was also seen as a way of influencing US military plans and operations, as well as reducing 'the UK's vulnerability to US requests to provide a substantial and costly contribution to post–conflict operations'.[2]

Throughout much of 2002 the US government increased pressure on Iraq to eliminate its supposed weapons of mass destruction. Prime Minister Tony Blair and Defence Secretary Geoff Hoon resisted giving any public acknowledgement that the UK would attack Iraq. The British government was attempting to balance supporting a diplomatic solution to the issue of Iraqi weapons of mass destruction, with making essential military preparations. Blair did not want to be seen to be deploying ground forces to the war until all diplomatic options had been exhausted. He was reluctant to be seen to be making overt preparations to deploy troops, including approaching British industry for additional equipment and supplies. In September 2002 air and maritime forces were offered to CENTCOM.

In the second half of 2002, the UK planned on providing a division to take part in an attack from Turkey into northern Iraq. The 1st Armoured Division would command its own 7th Armoured Brigade, with the 19th Mechanized Brigade coming from the 3rd

Division in the UK. As the small staffs in Wilton and Herford worked under special security measures to develop plans to deploy the division to Turkey and employ it in northern Iraq, considerable challenges revealed themselves. Vehicles and supplies would have to land at the Turkish port of Iskenderun, then move by road for over 400 miles to reach the border between Turkey and Iraq. This was twice the length of the route that 1st Armoured Division had moved along in early 1991. The move would take considerable time. As in 1991, deployment and logistics would require most of the Regular Army's logistic units to sustain. But with an army reduced in size by one-third since 1991, many of the transport and logistic units of the TA would also need to be mobilized.

Towards the end of 2002, the circle of knowledge was expanded to include the commanders and staffs of the brigades that were now planned to be involved. The 7th and 20th Armoured Brigades would be needed for combat and both the Army's logistic brigades, the 101st and 102nd, would be needed to move and sustain the division. In the minds of the commanders and staff officers planning the operation, the battle with Iraqi forces was unlikely to be as significant a challenge as simply getting the division to the Iraqi border with the combat supplies necessary for the division to fight.

By early January it was clear to Defence Secretary Geoff Hoon that the Turkish government was not going to agree to the use of their territory. The plan to invade northern Iraq was dropped and the US formally asked for UK land forces to fight in southern Iraq.

But UK firefighters were on strike, the Army standing in for them. The government directed that the Army's main effort be to provide emergency firefighting capabilities. As with previous firefighters' strikes, soldiers were trained to provide a limited firefighting capability using antiquated fire engines, the so-called Green Goddesses – 50-year-old vehicles that had been purchased to help mitigate the consequences of a nuclear attack. The role was challenging, but many soldiers enjoyed the positive feedback they got from the public.

Less satisfied were units that thought they might be deploying to fight in Iraq. Commanders found firefighting an unnecessary distraction from getting ready for a war that they were sure would take place. This was unsettling, particularly with a background of political and diplomatic activity and increasingly bellicose rhetoric from Washington DC, which made an attack on Iraq seem increasingly likely. In early 2003, most of the British public were in favour of the intervention. This was reflected in a parliamentary vote in February which endorsed a British role in the attack. But the size of public opposition to the war was reflected by the hundreds of thousands of protestors who marched against it.

The 1998 SDR required the Army to provide a division for a large-scale warfighting operation, moving armoured brigades at 30, 60 and 90 days' notice. But it was only on 10 January 2003 that Land Command formally tasked 1st Armoured Division to prepare for operations in Iraq. In peacetime it had three armoured brigades. The Army considered sending 19th Mechanized Brigade to Iraq as the division's second brigade. But with the shipping available and very tight deadlines set by the US, it would not reach Kuwait in time.

So only one British armoured brigade, the 7th, was sent. The brigade had spent the previous year training for operations. This was an intensely busy period, with members of the brigade spending anything up to 250 days of the year away from their barracks or married quarters. Field exercises sought to build the capabilities of battlegroups to fight. Units deployed by train to Poland for field training. Each battlegroup spent a month on the Canadian prairie at BATUS carrying out tactical manoeuvres, both with live ammunition and then with simulators fighting battles against the OPFOR. This training did not come cheap; ammunition fired on each exercise cost about £4 million at contemporary prices.

Inevitably the field exercises incurred wear and tear on armoured vehicles, increasing the demand for spare parts. With no authority yet being given by the government to purchase additional spares, it became clear that the division would need to look to itself to ensure it had sufficient spares for war. The 7th Brigade had planned a full brigade exercise. But in early autumn, it was judged that whilst the exercise would increase the formation's fighting effectiveness, the necessary consumption of spares would so reduce the size of the spare parts stockpile as to pose greater risk to the brigade's ability to move and fight in Iraq. So, with great reluctance, the exercise, the climax of the formation's training year, was cancelled.

The brigade commanded two regiments of Challenger 2 tanks with four tank squadrons each. Its two armoured infantry battalions had three companies each equipped with Warrior armoured infantry fighting vehicles. The brigade also had a regiment each of self-propelled artillery with AS90 self-propelled guns, and armoured engineers with bridge layers and minefield breaching tanks.

Under manning meant that the two armoured infantry battalions would need to be brought up to strength by each gaining another armoured infantry company. Army doctrine directed that for war armoured brigades and battlegroups should be 'square', with equal levels of tanks and armoured infantry, from which it would form four 'square' battlegroups. To achieve this, the brigade required much reinforcement. The brigade's four units – the Royal Scots Dragoon Guards, the 2nd Royal Tank Regiment, 1st Battalion, the Black Watch and 1st Battalion, the Royal Regiment of Fusiliers – were reinforced by additional tanks from the Queen's Royal Lancers and armoured infantry companies from the Irish Guards and Light Infantry. It became the largest and most lethal armoured brigade the UK had ever sent on operations.

The division was also assigned the Royal Marines 3 Commando Brigade, the UK's specialist amphibious landing force, and 16 Air Assault Brigade. Both formations were permanently at high readiness and could be deployed at 30 days' notice. The air assault brigade would deploy with two parachute battalions and an infantry battalion. The commando brigade would have two Royal Marine commandos, equivalent to an infantry battalion. Apart from an armoured reconnaissance squadron and the Marines' lightly armoured Viking all-terrain vehicles, the air assault and commando brigades had no armour. Both had only light artillery, each having a regiment of 105mm light guns and similarly lightly equipped engineers. The division's artillery, engineers, communications and logistic units provided second-line logistic support. Third-line logistic support would come from the 102nd Logistic Brigade, which was designated the Joint Force Logistic Component.

Medical reservists were mobilized. More use was made of the TA than in Operation *Granby*. This included 202 Field Hospital, which despite being formally at 30 days' notice to move was mobilized and deployed more rapidly, becoming operational in Iraq only 17 days after mobilization. Over 6,000 reservists were mobilized. Of TA personnel, some 70 per cent of those called were successfully mobilized.

In the second week of January the GOC, Major General Robin Brims, assembled 70 commanders and staff officers at the garrison cinema at Hertford, including teams from the air assault and commando brigades from the UK. Brims sought to make the planning as collaborative and collective as possible.[3]

The 1998 SDR had sought to increase the UK's strategic lift to improve the speed at which forces could be deployed. Giant C17 air transports were leased and a small fleet of roll-on roll-off ferries were purchased. But these provided only sufficient capacity to move a single 'task force' of an armoured battlegroup and its necessary logistics. Additional shipping would have to be chartered. Deploying the divisional HQ, the three brigades and the 102nd Logistic Brigade used 50 ships.

The division and its assigned brigades entered a period of intense preparation. By now the British attack on Iraq had been named Operation *Telic*. It did not take long for troops to start remarking that the real meaning of 'Telic' was 'Tell Everyone Leave is Cancelled'. Vehicles had to be prepared for the operation, with all their components in working order, requiring changing over worn-out parts, assemblies and in some cases complete vehicles. They had to be painted desert yellow. In January in Germany this was sometimes challenging, with snow and sleet washing yellow paint away after it was applied.

Armoured vehicles were loaded onto trains to take them to the post of Emden, for loading onto ships. Great effort had been made to load the ships so that vehicles and supplies would arrive shortly after the troops that would use them had landed by air. There were inevitable frictions. Many of the ships hired travelled more slowly than expected, resulting in the intricately synchronized movement plan becoming unsynchronized. But the formation staffs and units were able to use their initiative to overcome this and a host of other problems. The complete division assembled in Kuwait 70 days after the initial order.

However, provision and delivery of logistic support found it difficult to fully match the shortened timelines. The MoD knew that it had insufficient ammunition in its depots but assumed that industry would be able to provide more. In practice, industry found it difficult to do this. For example, at the start of the war, there was insufficient small arms ammunition for all the division's troops. Whilst infantry carried all the 5.56mm ammunition they needed, many sappers were issued with only ten rounds each, as were soldiers in logistic units. It was lucky that they were not ambushed by any Iraqi fighters. If they had been, there would have been avoidable British casualties.

Since the US and UK governments' arguments for attacking Iraq were based on Iraq's alleged possession of weapons of mass destruction, the most egregious example of logistic failure was inadequate supply of equipment to protect from NBC threats. All deployed troops had respirators and were required to have three protective suits. Problems with distribution and stockpiling a full range of sizes meant that many troops only had a single suit. Only 40 per cent of the necessary nerve agent detectors were available and the entire UK stockpile of residual agent detectors were found to be unserviceable. There were insufficient supplies and batteries for chemical agent monitors. Unlike many other armies, all British armoured vehicles had chemical filter systems, allowing the crews to operate without having to wear cumbersome respirators, which reduced their performance. Although stocks of filters were held in logistic depots, none reached units until after well after the war's combat phase was over. There can be no doubt that if Iraq had used chemical weapons the Army would have suffered avoidable casualties.

The 2001 Exercise *Saif Sareea 2* in Oman had shown that some of the lessons learned on Operation *Granby* had not been actioned. And other weaknesses of Army equipment had been identified. So the MoD and Treasury authorized the spending of £510 million for Urgent Operational Requirements (UORs) for the whole operation. Some purchases reflected the particular requirements of Coalition operations in a hot desert, including modifications to the AS90 gun, and others reflected the need to integrate with US forces, including the Blue Force Tracker system. Other purchases made up for the British holding insufficient spare parts. These included spares for the Challenger 2, AS90 gun, Challenger Repair and Recovery Vehicle, CVR(T) vehicles, Lynx helicopters and the RAF Chinook and Puma support helicopters.

Challenger 2 tanks were given extra protection against dust. Huge slabs of additional Chobham armour were fitted to the side of the vehicle, making them immune from the effects of RPG warheads. In retrospect, it is surprising that this armour had not been fitted to the tanks from the outset of their production, the threat from RPGs being faced by armour for the previous half century. But a joint Army/industry team fitted all the armour by 19 March.

Sufficient desert boots and camouflage uniforms were not delivered in time for the start of the war. General Brims observed that: 'desert clothing might not matter operationally, but it does matter to the soldiers. It makes them feel valued, So I went around talking to them trying to put things into perspective. At the same time, we were having to redistribute body armour and NBC kit amongst the troops and that left a pretty sour taste'.[4]

Despite the MoD requiring the Army to be capable of deploying a division to the Middle East, it had only stockpiled 9,000 desert uniforms, an insufficient quantity. In November 2002 and January 2003, it ordered 30,000 pairs of desert boots and 90,000 uniforms. Photographs and video from March and April show a significant number of troops still wearing their temperate uniforms, making them much more conspicuous than if they had the desert uniforms. Only 40 per cent of the uniforms and desert boots required were in Iraq by 13 April. Overheating of soldiers' feet in leather boots caused casualties. Numbers of the new Minimi machine guns, required to replace the inadequate light support weapons, were only 50 per cent complete by the start of the war.

INTEGRATION WITH THE US MARINES

Unlike Operation *Desert Storm*, CENTCOM deployed a full land component HQ, commanding the US Army's V Corps and the US Marine Expeditionary Force (MEF) – a corps-sized formation. It was tasked to defeat the Iraqi forces and 'remove the Iraqi regime'. Its plan was that V (US) Corps would be the main effort advancing from Kuwait to Baghdad south of the Euphrates River. North of the river the MEF was to both secure the infrastructure of the Al Rumaylah oil field and attack northwards to support V (US) Corps. The MEF main effort would be an advance on Baghdad by the 1st (US) Marine Division.

Shortly before the war began, Donald Rumsfeld told a press conference that British participation was not essential to mission success. This may have been true for the maritime and air components, but the British division doubled the MEF's strength in tanks and heavy armour, increasing the overall number of armoured brigades in the land component from three to four. Since the British contingent in the Gulf had been resubordinated from the US Marines to the US Army in 1990, the British Army and US Marines had little previous experience working together. So the British division made great efforts to integrate themselves into the MEF.

They were welcomed by the Marines, as they would be able to protect the MEF's advance to the north from Iraqi forces sallying out from Basra, thus allowing 1st Marine Division to concentrate on the advance to Baghdad. The British were given great freedom of action to accomplish this task, but they were also constrained. The MEF ordered that whatever the British did in southern Iraq, they were not to draw airpower or other resources away from the Marines advancing northwards, the MEF main effort.

The Marines were generous with the support they provided. A 60-strong air support element joined 1st Armoured Division's HQ and the battlegroups were supported by fire-control parties from their ANGLICO battalion.

CENTCOM's initially intended plan was that land forces would advance shortly after the air campaign started. In the event intelligence that the demolition of oil facilities was about to begin resulted in the land attack being advanced to the night of 20/21 May, without a preliminary air campaign.

1st Marine Division crossed the border berm into southern Iraq to capture the oil infrastructure. This contained pumping stations and 12 gas-oil separation plants. If the Iraqis wanted, these could have been blown and set on fire, with oil entering the Tigris and Euphrates rivers, so damaging one of Iraq's major industrial resources and greatly harming the country's post-war economy. British engineer specialists and EOD teams joined the Marines in successfully securing the oil infrastructure, making it safe and keeping it in working condition. The 1st Marine Division also destroyed most of the Iraqi forces in the open terrain to the west of Basra.

Concurrently, 3 Commando Brigade attacked the Al Faw peninsula, a potential launching pad from which Iraqi missiles and rocket artillery could be fired into Kuwait. It also controlled access from the sea to Um Qasr, Iraq's only port. The brigade's two commandos were augmented by the US 15th Marine Expeditionary Unit to seize the port.

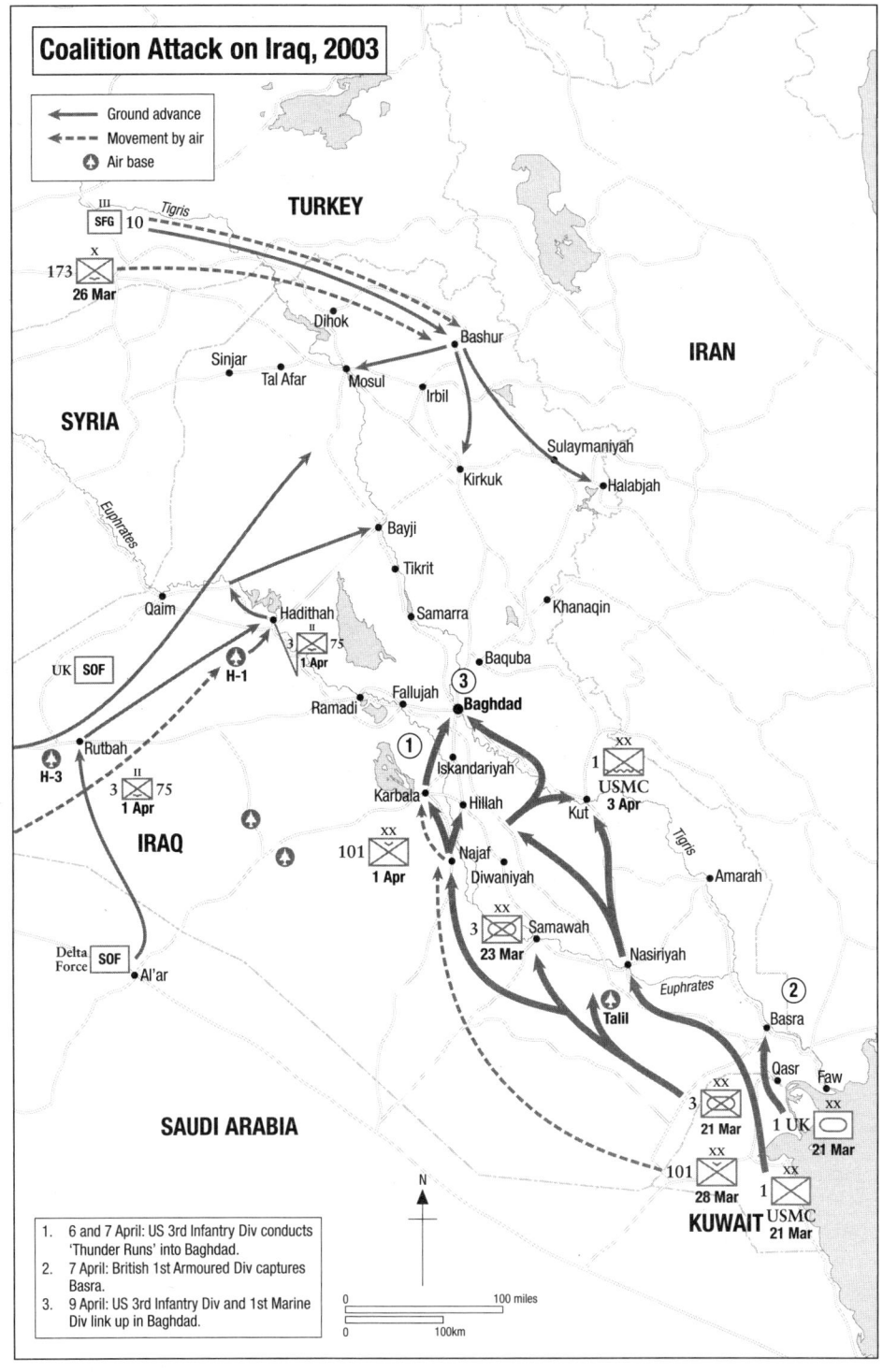

Coalition Attack on Iraq, 2003

← Ground advance
◄--- Movement by air
⊕ Air base

TURKEY

SYRIA

IRAN

III
SFG 10
Tigris

X
173
26 Mar

Dihok

Sinjar
Tal Afar   Mosul
Irbil   Bashur

Sulaymaniyah

Kirkuk   Halabjah

Euphrates

Bayji

Tikrit

Qaim   Hadithah   Samarra   Khanaqin

II
3   75
1 Apr

UK SOF
⊕ H-1

Baquba

Fallujah   ③
Ramadi   Baghdad

①   Iskandariyah   XX
⊕ H-3   Rutbah   1
Karbala   USMC
II   3 Apr
3   75   Hillah   Kut
1 Apr

IRAQ   XX   Najaf
101   Diwaniyah   Amarah
1 Apr

Tigris

Delta   SOF
Force   Al'ar   XX
3   Samawah
23 Mar   Nasiriyah

Euphrates   ②
⊕ Talil   Basra

SAUDI ARABIA   XX   Qasr   Faw
3   XX
21 Mar   1 UK
21 Mar

N   XX
101   XX
28 Mar   1
KUWAIT   USMC
21 Mar

1. 6 and 7 April: US 3rd Infantry Div conducts 'Thunder Runs' into Baghdad.
2. 7 April: British 1st Armoured Div captures Basra.
3. 9 April: US 3rd Infantry Div and 1st Marine Div link up in Baghdad.

0   100 miles
0   100km

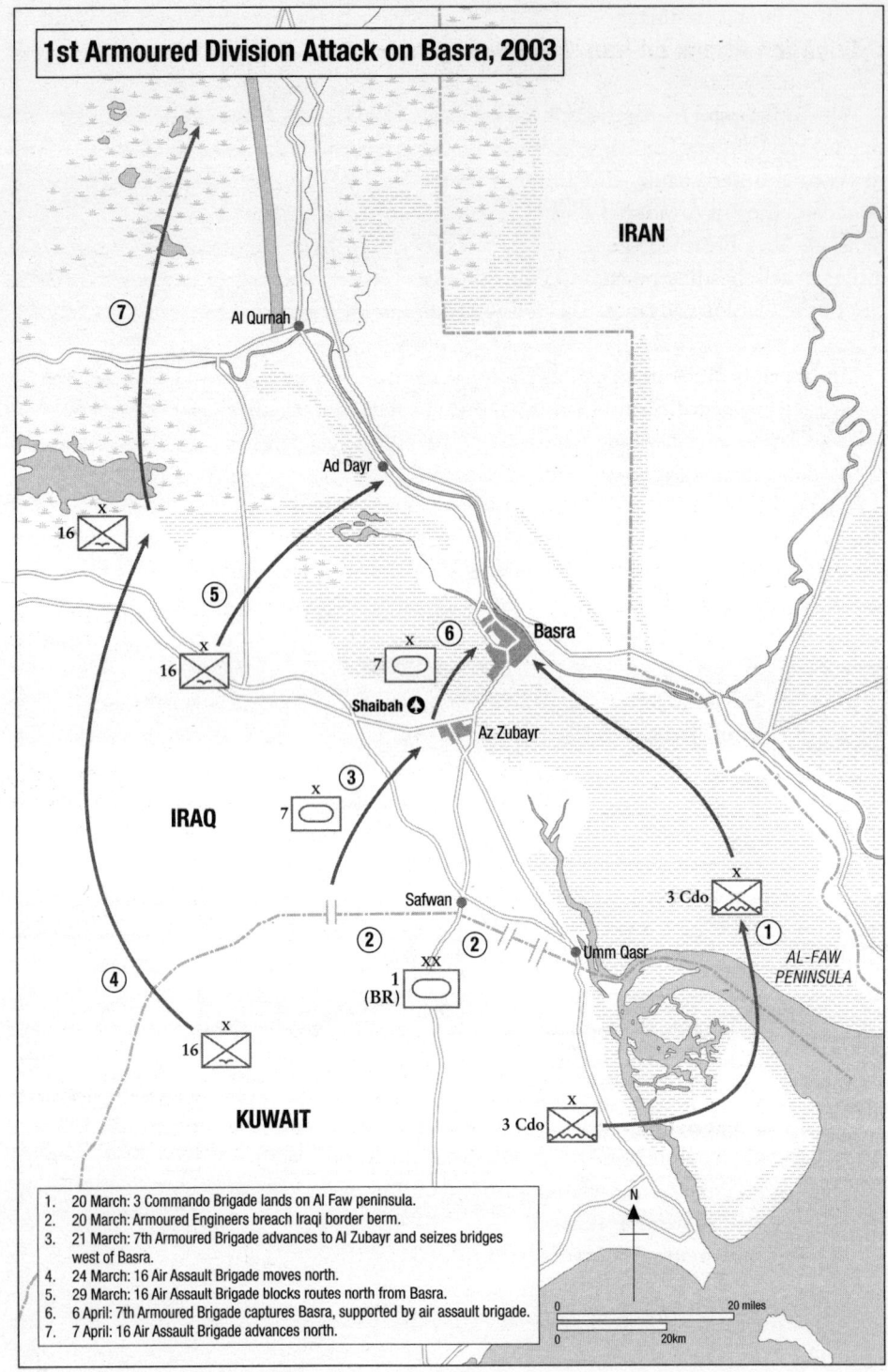

1st Armoured Division Attack on Basra, 2003

IRAN

⑦

Al Qurnah

Ad Dayr

16 X

⑤

16 X

Basra

7 X ⑥

Shaibah ⛽

Az Zubayr

IRAQ

7 X ③

Safwan

⑧ ②

② ②

Umm Qasr

3 Cdo X ①

AL-FAW
PENINSULA

1
(BR) XX

16 X ④

3 Cdo X

KUWAIT

N

1. 20 March: 3 Commando Brigade lands on Al Faw peninsula.
2. 20 March: Armoured Engineers breach Iraqi border berm.
3. 21 March: 7th Armoured Brigade advances to Al Zubayr and seizes bridges west of Basra.
4. 24 March: 16 Air Assault Brigade moves north.
5. 29 March: 16 Air Assault Brigade blocks routes north from Basra.
6. 6 April: 7th Armoured Brigade captures Basra, supported by air assault brigade.
7. 7 April: 16 Air Assault Brigade advances north.

0   20 miles
0   20km

A plan to land a commando by US Marine helicopters was aborted after a fatal mid-air collision between two US helicopters. After six hours' delay the operation was re-mounted using British aircraft.

On 21 March, 16 Air Assault Brigade moved north to relieve the US Marines 5th Regimental Combat Team as security for the Rumaylah oil fields and to protect the British division's northern flank. This allowed the 1st Marine Division to move north towards Baghdad. The 7th Armoured Brigade advanced next, attacking to protect the US Marines' flank. As they breached the berm on the border, troops were heartened by the noise of artillery shells heading north into Iraq. Some of this was attacking an Iraqi division to the east of the division's advance. The division's commander observed that:

> The intensity of the attack on them from ground floor artillery and air was ferocious. The division evaporated. Some of them surrendered but most of them scarpered. They couldn't capitulate because they had regime diehards controlling them. They actually had somebody putting a gun to their heads making commands.[5]

The US Marines had secured the western bank of the Basra canal. They were relieved by 7th Brigade, whose armoured battlegroups rapidly captured the four bridges carrying roads into Basra. These were each defended by Iraqi infantry and armoured vehicles. But attacking with Challengers, Warriors and artillery fire, the brigade quickly destroyed the Iraqi defenders.

The 7th Brigade also surrounded the smaller town of Al Zubayar. This was held by large numbers of irregular fighters, who called themselves the Saddam Fedayeen. They fired wildly at the British troops that approached the town. Starting on 25 March, armoured raids by the 2nd Royal Tank Regiment and the Black Watch were used to test the Iraqi defences and better understand their dispositions, plans and morale. Initially these met fierce resistance, with large numbers of irregular fighters putting up a high level of small arms and RPG fire. The British got the best of all these engagements. On the morning of 26 March, eight guided bombs struck an Iraqi command and control centre that the British had identified. The site was then attacked by an armoured squadron and armoured infantry. There was no resistance.

The British became increasingly bold, including sending an armoured column through the centre of the town and establishing a forward patrol base in the town's prison. After UK special forces located the Fedayeen HQ, it was attacked by a precision bomb. A counterattack by Fedayeen was defeated. Resistance crumbled, and the town was occupied on 28–29 March. To release the heavy battlegroups the town was taken over by the 1st Battalion, the Duke of Wellington's Regiment, a light role battalion that had originally deployed to Iraq to handle prisoners.

Whilst 7th Armoured Brigade probed into Basra, 16 Air Assault Brigade continued to secure the oil fields. Its northern flank saw a battle between it and an Iraqi division. Here the brigade's armoured reconnaissance squadron and artillery traded fired with Iraqi artillery, whose South African-made 155mm artillery guns outranged the smaller 105mm light guns of the British brigade. But aided by artillery locating radars and airpower, the British kept the Iraqi division away from Basra.

D Squadron of the Household Cavalry Regiment conducted forward reconnaissance for 16 Air Assault Brigade in their lightly armoured Scimitar and Striker vehicles. A major battle took place on 28 March which began with a clash with Iraqi T-55 tanks. Coalition aircraft tasked to attack the enemy instead struck D Squadron, killing one man and wounding four, one of whom was rescued from a burning vehicle by Trooper Christopher Finney. As helicopters were brought in to evacuate the wounded, cannon fire from the Scimitars and anti-tank missiles from Strikers and Army Lynx helicopters were fired on the Iraqi tanks. A leading role in this sharp engagement was played by Lance Corporal of Horse Mick Flynn. He later described firing at an Iraqi tank:

> After 60 or 70 rounds we put a number of scores and dents along his hull and turret. The crew abandoned their T-55, however we were still drawing fire from other positions. I managed to get a Lynx helicopter that had about three missiles left returning from another mission. I fired tracer to make sure the pilot could see his target. He hit it with his second shot. All in all I fired about 130 rounds.[6]

For his role in these battles, Flynn was awarded the Conspicuous Gallantry Cross.

BASRA – A MODERN SIEGE

Initially, the British had little information and intelligence on the city of over a million people. The predominantly Shia citizens were thought to have no love for Saddam Hussein or his regime, and the dictator's cousin Ali Hassan al-Majid had been given authority over both Army and paramilitary units in the city. Nicknamed 'Chemical Ali' for his role in attacking the Iraqi Kurds in 1988, he was thought to rule Basra using fear.

The British assessed that Iraqi forces would attempt to draw them to fight inside the city, where the resulting civilian casualties and collateral damage could be exploited by regime propaganda. The British were determined to minimize destruction of civilian infrastructure. The British tried not to unnecessarily antagonize Iraqi civilians, who were allowed to pass through the British checkpoints, but would exploit the protected mobility of their tanks and infantry fighting to mount raids into urban areas.

The Army applied a more developed version of the approach used to capture Al Zubayar. Deep operations would attack key targets with artillery and air strikes. Close operations would push away Iraqi forward defences. Concurrent information operations would try to reduce the will of Iraqi forces to resist, including leaflets, radio broadcasts and mobile telephone calls to Iraqi officials.

The British sought to better understand the city, the morale of the Iraqi Army forces and their control of civilians, and military positions, especially command and control nodes. They used reconnaissance patrols by British infantry and limited ground attacks by tanks and armoured infantry. British special forces infiltrated into the city, while human and signals intelligence refined the intelligence picture.

British artillery operated the Phoenix drone to provide real-time video. Over a hundred Phoenix sorties were flown over Basra, with six drones shot down by Iraqi forces. It proved particularly useful as a method of controlling artillery fire. Coalition rules of engagement allowed attack of enemy mortars and artillery detected by radar. The British chose not to do this, as the radar could give no indication of how close the Iraqi artillery was to civilians. However, the thermal camera on Phoenix was able to locate the artillery precisely. So useful was the drone, that on some occasions, rather than accept a gap in observation of key targets, the British flew the drones until they ran out of fuel and crashed.

The Iraqis established strongpoints on the western edge of Basra opposite the bridges. From 22 March to 6 April there was a contest for the control of the flat no-man's land between the two front lines. The British troops controlling the bridges were subjected to artillery and rocket attacks. Local counterattacks by Iraqi infantry and tanks were quickly defeated. The British sought to dominate the Iraqis by exchanging direct and indirect fire and by mounting raids on their positions. A sortie from Basra by 14 Iraqi tanks ran into a British armoured squadron of Challenger 2 tanks. All were quickly destroyed.

3 Commando Brigade, supported by British tanks and helicopters, engaged in hard fighting to clear the towns south of Basra and block Iraqi fighters fleeing south from the city. The commando brigade moved north to clear the town of Abu al Khasab. In Operation *James* 40 Commando were supported by commando artillery, 7th Brigade's artillery, reconnaissance vehicles of the Queen's Dragoon Guards and tanks of the Royal Scots Dragoon Guards. Their Challengers provided much intimate fire support and, in combination with the commandos' TOW missile-firing Lynx helicopters, destroyed any Iraqi armoured vehicles that presented themselves.

One of the tanks rolled onto its side. As a recovery vehicle moved to pull the stricken tank onto its tracks, more than 50 militia fighters swarmed around the vehicles, surrounding them. Although Iraqi attempts to capture the vehicles were defeated, the survivors poured heavy machine gun and rocket fire at the Queen's Dragoon Guards and REME soldiers. Because the ground was very difficult, it took two recovery vehicles to pull out the stricken tank. The battle lasted nine hours. One tank was hit by 14 RPG rounds, damaging no more than the tank's paintwork, illustrating Challenger's very high level of protection.[7]

Up to now the British had not tightly cordoned the north of Basra. On 29 March, a parachute battalion supported by tanks sealed off the north of the city and blocked the potential escape along the main road to Baghdad.

Meanwhile the fighting around the bridges, British patrols, raids, special forces, signals intelligence and the Phoenix drone were all helping the British gain an increasingly detailed picture of the Iraqi defenders of Basra. It was not without risk. Major Lindsay Graham of the Black Watch observed that:

At Bridge Four we were almost always under indirect fire from the Iraqis, usually from artillery or mortars. The protection the Warrior's armour afforded and the armaments we had enabled us to operate with impunity and not to risk our soldiers' lives unnecessarily. There were occasions when we had to dismount to fight through buildings identified as Fedayeen targets. Then we engaged the enemy, or at least convinced them that it was a bad idea to fight against us.[8]

As time went on and the British operations increased in strength and accuracy, Iraqi civilians increasingly shared information with them. To counter this, the Fedayeen militia, members of Saddam Hussein's ruling Baath Party and secret police were making ever-increasing efforts to prevent an uprising by Basra's civilians. Iraqi government-controlled media was reporting that British efforts to advance into the city were being repulsed by Iraqi forces. In fact, this was British armoured columns successfully withdrawing from the city at the end of raids. The 7th Brigade gained increasing initiative against the enemy, establishing bases on the western edge of the city. The brigade's approach was described by its commander, Brigadier Graham Binns:

> The intent for Basra was to imagine it to be a human body. What we wanted to do was to remove the head – the head being the regime – yet keep the torso whole and the patient alive by preserving the central nervous system or the infrastructure, and continuing to pump the blood around the patient – the fuel, power and water – we saved the life of the patient. But at what stage should we remove the head?[9]

On 5 April, the British thought they had located Chemical Ali and US smart bombs were used to attack him. The British thought this had succeeded. It had not, but the British felt that Iraqi resistance was crumbling. On the early morning of 6 April, the 2nd Royal Tank Regiment and Scots Dragoon Guards battlegroups were conducting more raids and the division ordered 7th Armoured Brigade to seize the city. As they advanced further, the sporadic and unco-ordinated resistance was easily brushed aside. The exception was Basra's College of Literature where stiff resistance from Arab foreign fighters from Egypt, Morocco and Tunisia required armoured infantry from the Irish Guards to fight room to room to evict them.

The city's souk was a dense network of narrow streets and alleyways. The division decided not to use the heavy battlegroups to seize it, instead planning to utilize the dismounted infantry of 3rd Battalion, the Parachute Regiment. The British planned to complete the clearance of the city the next day. But the paratroops' advance faced no serious opposition, and they were met by nothing but cheering crowds. So 3 Commando Brigade advanced to seize the southern edge of the city, capturing one of Saddam's many palaces.

Once the fighting in Basra ceased, looting began.[10] BBC journalist Caroline Wyatt watched 'looters carrying school desks, baby incubators, wires, cables – all the things that would be very useful to get the city going again'. Iraqi civilians told her that the looting was letting off steam. Like the US forces, the British had not anticipated this. Like the US, they were reluctant to use lethal force to contest the looting. The commander of 7th Armoured Brigade later stated that:

We reached the conclusion that the best way to stop looting was just to get to a point where there was nothing left to loot … we could either try and stop the looting, in which case we would have to shoot people, or we could try and prevent it but knowing that we weren't going to prevent it and take a pragmatic view … and then when we are ready we will restock it and guard it. But actually, trying to interpose ourselves was difficult.[11]

Order was gradually restored. The British adopted a stabilization mission. The media made much of the fact that, in contrast to US forces in Basra, the British had removed their helmets to replace them with the wide variety of berets and tam o' shanters of their regiments. By the end of April power and running water had been largely restored to the city. The British attempted to find local interlocutors to help with administering their sector. The divisional commander's efforts to use Iraqi tribal structures were initially successful.

We had to put somebody in charge, and we had to try and get Iraqis in charge and I would assist. So, on 7 April I met Sheikh Muzahim in a tent in the middle of the desert. He sat me on the ground for about an hour. He gave me a lecture on the law of armed conflict and the rights and responsibilities of an occupying power. He had been a brigadier in the Iraqi navy, but in real life he was a lawyer. After the lecture I said 'will you assist me in my rights and responsibilities, and can we get together a council that will run Basra Province through the difficult days ahead'. He said 'yes' and we worked together for some time, until the end of May 2003, when the de-Baathification lines were drawn and he was thrown out of office.[12]

At this moment the British troop strength in Basra was about 5,000 troops. They comprised four armoured battlegroups, a parachute battalion and a Royal Marine commando. Never again would as many British troops be present in the city.

As the exhausted troops of V (US) Corps and the MEF, including the British division, welcomed the collapse of the regime, a mixture of elation and self-confidence was felt in CENTCOM, the Pentagon, PJHQ and the MoD. A land component of four divisions, with only four armoured brigades, had attacked an Iraqi army of 14 infantry, three mechanized and six armoured divisions, comprehensively defeating them.

Twelve years after Operation *Desert Storm*, a well-trained and equipped 1st Armoured Division had again successfully conducted rapid ground manoeuvre, albeit over much shorter distances than in 1991. Compared with 1991 the division was larger, with three brigades, instead of two. Its single armoured brigade was much larger than either armoured brigade deployed in 1991.

The 1991 division had 34,000 personnel and 14,700 vehicles. In 2003 it had 32,000 troops and 15,000 vehicles. The division had deployed more quickly, in ten weeks compared with 22 weeks in 1990. This reflected the increased British strategic lift acquired since the SDR.

But the 2003 division had deployed with much less artillery, with no MLRS regiment, a single medium artillery regiment with AS90 and two light artillery regiments. The reduced amount of artillery may explain why the division was only supplied with 15,000 tons of ammunition, much less than the 147,400 tons provided in 1991. Far fewer logistic units were needed than in 1990–91. The British were able to draw on well-developed US logistic infrastructure in Kuwait, and Basra was only 80 km from the Kuwaiti border, a much shorter distance than the 350 km the division had to travel from Al Jubail to its assembly area.

The division had avoided destroying Basra by combining intelligence-gathering with raiding and had struck as Iraqi resistance was faltering. It had been a successful siege, waged with 21st-century equipment and an attitude that was the antithesis of traditional siege warfare. From the start of the war to 7 April, 31 British ground troops had been killed. Only six were killed by Iraqi fire, the remaining deaths resulting from friendly fire incidents, traffic accidents or natural causes. The British plan succeeded in destroying Iraqi conventional forces with relatively low levels of British casualties. How is this decisive success to be explained? At the end of 2023 the Army produced an analysis of the intervention. Its overall assessment was that:

> The forces which had deployed had for the most part been trained and held at high readiness and deployed into theatre rapidly. They arrived just in time to undertake operations. However, there were significant shortcomings. Critical stores and ammunition did not arrive in time … There were significant shortages of small arms ammunition in some units as they began operations, NBC filters for tanks did not arrive and there were significant difficulties with urgent operational requirements. All this represented significant risk. Fortunately, for the most part this was not realized. However British Land forces did perform well and this seems largely to be due to the way the Army and the Royal Marines select, educate, train and exercise their individual units and formations.
>
> The areas where the British Army did least well were those it practises least, in particular formation level command and control logistic support to a large deployed force and intelligence. The primary deduction is the need to continue to invest in large-scale collective training. At times during operation TELIC reliance was placed on the quality of soldiers to make up for shortcomings which should have been identified and rectified. We can do better.[13]

UNDERSTANDING THE IRAQI DEFEAT

The operation conformed to the concept of the 'three-block war', defined in 1999 by US Marine Corps General Charles Krulak as 'Contingencies in which Marines may be confronted by the entire spectrum of tactical challenges in the span of a few hours and within the space of three contiguous city blocks.'[14] The Army considered that key success factors included their well-protected armoured vehicles. Once the battlegroups realized the relative invulnerability of Challenger and Warrior, they exploited the advantage, outmanoeuvring Iraqi defenders. The 'plink, plink, plink' sounds of rifle and machine gun fire striking the outside of Challengers and Warriors could initially unnerve those inside the vehicles, but they soon gained confidence from their immunity to small arms fire and RPG warheads. And the protection afforded by helmets and enhanced body armour increased the confidence of the infantry.

British commanders assessed that the high quality of training and motivation of soldiers and officers was another major success factor. This came not only from a high standard of leadership, but also from training, operational experience and the pattern of Army careers, which included common initial training for recruits and officer cadets, mandatory career courses and widespread experience of operations, particularly Operation *Granby*, Northern Ireland and the Balkans. And the regimental identities of infantry, armoured and artillery units promoted cohesion in combat.

Most Iraqi troops displayed a much lower standard of training that the British. This was most starkly exhibited in the very low accuracy of their shooting. In contrast, the British infantry and marines, vehicle gunners and artillery crews hit many more of their targets, much more often. They saw hitting the target as central to combat effectiveness and were prepared to devote long uncomfortable hours, day after day and week after week on infantry, tank and artillery ranges in the UK, Canada and Germany, culminating in demanding field firing with live ammunition in simulated battle conditions.

Iraqi military leadership was often poor. The centralization of power by Saddam and his sons meant that the necessary co-operation between the different forces was almost completely absent. This was in stark contrast to the high degree of co-operation between land, air, sea and special forces exhibited by the Coalition. And the Coalition commanders had much more devolved authority and independence than any Iraqi commanders. General Brims was pleasantly surprised that the UK national chain of command allowed him 'complete freedom of action to conduct operations in the way I thought best'.[15] This allowed him to delegate freedom of action to his brigade commanders. He summarized his approach to command; 'Launching of a plan is top down but becomes bottom up as troops in contact find out what is really happening as opposed to what you think is happening or intelligence picture tells you is happening.'[16]

Iraqi tactics were often poor. They missed numerous opportunities to inflict greater delay and casualties on Coalition forces. Although there were instances of hard fighting by Iraqi forces, and the Fedayeen could display suicidal bravery, much of the Iraqi fighting appeared unco-ordinated. As well as an almost complete lack of integration between regular forces and the Fedayeen irregular fighters, large numbers of elementary tactical mistakes were displayed by the Iraqis, such as often failing to cover minefields and elementary obstacles with fire.

Iraq failed to block the port of Um Qasr by sinking ships and demolishing port infrastructure and to demolish the oil fields and facilities. The water obstacles that stood between Kuwait and Basra were not exploited by demolishing bridges, nor was there any effort to flood the River Euphrates. No biological or chemical weapons were used.

Iraqi forces exhibited much lower morale than British troops. The majority were conscripts, whose pay and rations were poor. There was a vast gap between officers and soldiers. Administration and logistics were permeated with corruption. For example, bribes were often required from soldiers seeking to take their leave. These factors worked against high morale.

Sometimes Iraqi units fought back. Iraqi artillery fire against the British north of Basra was accurate and effective. The Fedayeen and Baath Party militias showed greater fighting spirit, presumably because of their loyalty to the regime. Even these fell apart after the collapse of the regime. But they would return with a vengeance.

A British army at the height of its fighting power had defeated an army with much less fighting power. This followed the pattern set in the Falklands and during Operation *Desert Storm*. Over the next decade it would find itself facing much more highly motivated enemies, who were prepared to sell themselves much more dearly.

The whole Army had been up for the fight. Many were very frustrated to be held back, fearing that after the war there would be a long tail of relatively dull stabilization operations. At one stage 1st Division discovered that the best part of 2,000 troops had got themselves to Kuwait, over and above the units and individuals formally deployed there by the chain of command. This was a problem for the logistic staff, but vivid evidence of troops who wanted to march to the sound of the guns. And in Iraq, the fighting spirit of the troops was amply displayed. General Brims observed that:

> How do we have such good soldiers? Is it our training? Is it our discipline? Is it our nurturing? I think that it is everything we do from BATUS, from many operational tours to a football match, from giving them a married quarter to doing adventure training. It's about making them feel valued, giving them progressive careers and variety. Variety is important because it makes them generalist rather than specialists. Perhaps it is our values and standards; our soldiers knew the right thing to do and they did it. It is all about belonging. I am proud of an article that appeared in the *Guardian* which said 'these feral monsters become humanitarian aid workers at the drop of a helmet' ... That's my army. They dismount and fight through or they dismount and start talking with equal ease.[17]

LOGISTIC WEAKNESS

The Army assessed that there were both logistics successes and failures. Battlegroups never ran out of fuel or food and no British casualties died after receiving surgery. But even though the distances required to sustain the force were much smaller than those in 1991, there were considerable weaknesses with logistic support, particularly ammunition. The 1st Battalion, the Duke of Wellington's Regiment spent the first two days of the war with only 10 per cent of its allocated ammunition and some sappers began the war carrying only ten rounds of rifle ammunition. Brigadier Binns, commander of 7th Armoured Brigade, was greatly concerned by the lack of 30mm cannon shells for the brigade's Warrior and Scimitar fighting vehicles. He told the Iraq Inquiry that lack of ammunition was a constant cause of risk throughout the brigade's time in Kuwait and Iraq:

We couldn't find the operational ammunition for the Warrior. We knew that it had left Bicester [the logistic depot] and there was evidence that it had arrived in Kuwait, and there was a risk, a real risk, that ammunition was in such short supply that we may have fired it in training. And because the ammunition had just been taken to the range, they naturally assumed that that was the ammunition, and I thought we had fired it.[18]

Spare sparts were often in short supply. For example, 20 spare barrels for AS90 guns got lost somewhere in the supply chain. Some front-line units found that morphine and anti-malaria drugs were in short supply.

Units and brigades rapidly lost confidence in the logistic arrangements. Both 7th Armoured Brigade and 3 Commando Brigade formed special teams to travel up the logistic system to find items in particularly short supply. The team from 7th Brigade was unable to locate all the missing items, even after a visit to the logistic depot at Bicester.

Many of these problems resulted from long-term underinvestment in logistic management software, especially an asset tracking system. This made it difficult to overcome the inevitable frictions in the prioritization of loading supplies and in arrival of ships and aircraft in Kuwait. For example, the movement of combat supplies, including ammunition, depended on their being loaded onto the flat racks of the Army's DROPS Lorries. But the majority of the flat racks only arrived in Kuwait on 17 March, on the last but one supply ship.

It was fortunate that fighting was relatively short and that the Iraqi defenders displayed so many weaknesses. Had the Iraqis been more determined and competent, logistics might have been stretched close to, or beyond breaking point, particularly as many personnel arrived in Kuwait at very short notice and lacking necessary personal equipment. Brigadier Shaun Cowlam, commander of the 102nd Logistics Brigade, wrote that:

Despite the success in getting the force into theatre in half the time taken for Operation *Granby*, it was clear that poor personnel and equipment readiness across the force added significantly to both logistic and, subsequently, operational risk. Many personnel (particularly augmentees and Reservists) were poorly equipped and briefed for deployment, some arriving in theatre with no combat clothing, respirators, weapons or sleeping systems, and others not knowing which unit or location they were destined for … The lesson is that units should be equipped on deployment to the necessary scales.[19]

Logistic problems were thoroughly investigated by the National Audit Office and the House of Commons Public Account Committee, as well as through lessons learned exercises by the Army and the Defence Logistic Organisation. Whilst the MoD Permanent Secretary, Sir Kevin Tebbit, was closely questioned by the Public Accounts Committee, neither he, nor Defence Secretary Geoff Hoon, nor any logistic or procurement official seems ever to have been held to account for these logistic failures. These failures to provide the necessary equipment and ammunition in time meant that the Learmont criteria were not met in these areas.

The logistic weaknesses cost at least one soldier's life. By 2003 all British troops were issued with combat body armour made of Kevlar. Since the 1980s troops in Northern Ireland and the Balkans had been equipped with Enhanced Combat Body Armour (ECBA). This was a Kevlar vest fitted with ceramic plates. The Kevlar was optimized against shrapnel, while the ceramic plates could stop bullets at short range – something they had done several times in Northern Ireland.

There was a stockpile of this armour for peacekeeping operations. Indeed the MoD's clothing project team estimated that some 200,000 sets of ECBA had been procured and issued. But it could only locate about 30,000. And these were not despatched to Iraq before 24 March, over a week after the war had started. As there was not enough for a full division, it determined that the priority for the full armour should be the infantry as they were most likely to be exposed to enemy small arms fire. Many supporting personnel and tank crews had to use make do with standard issue body armour, without the ceramic plates.

During the fighting, a soldier was killed at a checkpoint on the edge of Al Zubayar, the first British soldier to be killed in Iraq. Sergeant Roberts was commanding a Challenger tank deployed outside Al Zubayar. While attempting to stop and search vehicles for weapons and militia he was attacked by an Iraqi civilian. The gunner of his tank attempted to fire warning shots, but instead he hit Roberts, who was killed.

An Army inquiry identified two factors that contributed to his death. Firstly, the tank machine-gun sight was inaccurate at short ranges, a factor overlooked in training tank gunners. Secondly, Roberts had previously been given a set of enhanced body armour with ceramic plates, but it had been withdrawn, to be given to an infantry unit. If Roberts had worn the enhanced armour, the bullet that killed him would probably have been stopped by the armour's ceramic plate.

In the overall conduct of the British attack into Basra, this incident, tragic as it was, would initially seem small. But it was later to become much more significant, fuelling the first wave of a tide of opinion that the British Army was being insufficiently supported by the government. This incident became a *cause célèbre*. An Army board of inquiry and the hearings by the civilian coroner made it clear that the failure to procure enough enhanced body amour directly contributed to Roberts' death. Explanations offered by Defence Secretary Geoff Hoon failed to convince his highly articulate young widow, who was much better at engaging the press and media.

FROM OCCUPYING POWER TO THE JANUARY 2005 ELECTIONS

After the invasion, the British took responsibility for Basra City and the four southern provinces: Basra, Maysan, Dhi Qar and Al Muthanna. Designated as Multinational Division Southeast, the formation was considered by the military HQ and Coalition Provisional Authority (CPA) in Baghdad to be conducting an 'economy of force' mission, whilst the Coalition main effort was in Baghdad.

The British had always planned to reduce their forces in Basra to a single brigade. So they rapidly downsized from a division of three brigades to a much smaller force. A divisional HQ would command British- and Italian-led multinational brigades, which would be joined by Dutch and Danish battalions. Having provided one of the three divisions that initially crossed into Iraq, increasing by one-third the number of armoured brigades taking part in the invasion, the British force reduced to about 10 per cent of the Coalition forces occupying Iraq. This was a much greater proportionate reduction than that made by the US forces – an early indicator that the UK was going to make a much lower military commitment to Iraq than the US would.

BRITISH STABILIZATION OF IRAQ

In Kosovo and Sierra Leone, the Army's experience of the role of the FCO and the new DFiD had been generally positive. So it expected that the reduction in military strength in Iraq would be accompanied by a significant increase in UK civilian capabilities for reconstruction and development. This expectation was not met. In 2016 the UK's independent Iraq Inquiry issued its report. It concluded that the British government's leadership of post-conflict stabilization of Iraq was inadequate.

In late 2002 and early 2003, British government planning identified that post-conflict operations would be decisive and would require a major reconstruction effort. The risks of Sunni/Shia conflict, intervention by Iran and Al Qaida were all identified. British officers engaged with US military planners reported that the US plans for post-conflict activity were inadequate, displaying concerns that the rapidly improvised US Office of Reconstruction and Humanitarian Assistance (ORHA) would be overfaced by the task.

But Prime Minister Blair chose not to place a single minister or government department in charge of pre-war planning of reconstruction. Leadership of the UK reconstruction effort was eventually given to the FCO in late March 2003, as the invasion began. An ad hoc committee was established to consider reconstruction plans, but it played no effective role in leading reconstruction.

No adequate plans had been made to fulfil the UK's obligations as an occupying power, for example in providing essential services and reconstruction in the south. No British government money had been allocated for post-conflict reconstruction. There were no plans to deploy more than a handful of British civilians to Iraq

Despite an agreement by Development Secretary Claire Short and Foreign Secretary Jack Straw that the UK should do more to support ORHA, the development department effectively opted out of doing so. Short was deeply troubled by the attack on Iraq. To the military, Short and her department displayed ingrained institutional resistance to the war. The Iraq Inquiry assessed that Short displayed 'reluctance to engage in post-conflict activity other than for the immediate humanitarian response to conflict, until it was confirmed that the UN would lead the reconstruction effort'.[20]

Blair chose to tolerate this. After her resignation in May 2003, DfID assumed leadership of reconstruction. By then the UK effort had fallen well behind the requirement in Basra and Blair's public and private rhetoric. Relations between DfID and the British military were badly damaged and would not recover for half a decade.

It rapidly became apparent to British commanders that the situation in Basra had greatly changed from that envisaged by London. The Iraq Inquiry identified that from August 2003 onwards there were several occasions when changes in the situation in Iraq required a strategic reassessment by the British government. There was no such action. The Inquiry assessed that the military leadership, specifically the Chief of Joint Operations and Chief of Defence Staff, should have argued for this. It was unclear why they did not. This is but one of many examples identified by the Iraq Inquiry of sub-optimal performance by politicians, government, departments, senior military officers and civilian officials.

For example, following a June 2003 visit to Iraq, Blair directed that the British government should return to 'a war footing' to avoid 'losing the peace in Iraq'. The Inquiry assessed that there were 'no indications that Mr Blair's direction led to any substantive changes in the UK's reconstruction effort.'[21]

At a July 2003 Cabinet meeting, Blair stated that the UK should make the CPA regional office in Basra, CPA (South), 'a model'. In a subsequent video conference Blair told President Bush that the UK would do its 'level best to meet any demand for additional resources.'[22] A senior diplomat, Sir Hilary Synnott, was called out of retirement to lead the team. But CPA (South) never had sufficient British staff or resources to provide the necessary reconstruction. This initial lack of an effective civilian organization and leadership, expertise or financial assistance in southern Iraq forced additional responsibilities onto the shoulders of Army officers, who often ran a wide variety of civilian projects and tasks, often operating well beyond their training and experience.

The Iraq Inquiry assessed that the FCO 'did not provide adequate practical support to Sir Hilary Synnott as Head of CPA (South)', and that the FCO's Permanent Secretary bore personal responsibility for this.[23] The Inquiry did not explain why inadequate implementation of a Cabinet decision, which had been declared to the US government, was tolerated by the central co-ordinating machinery of government, the Foreign Secretary, Defence Secretary or Prime Minister. Synnott wrote about the consistent failure of the FCO to adequately support the CPA (South):

> there was little evidence that the British Government as a whole saw itself as being at war. Management and oversight at ministerial and senior official level was essentially ad hoc and bore little resemblance to the highly organized arrangements for post-conflict reconstruction which had been put in place, for instance, some four years before the end of the Second World War. Blair put a constant public emphasis on the importance and urgency of making progress in Iraq. But seemingly little interested in the processes within government by which this might be brought about, he proved unable to mobilize government departments to produce the necessary results.[24]

The UK, like the US, was taken by surprise by the extensive looting and rapid deterioration of security. But the UK had little influence on the US-led CPA that was set up by the Pentagon at short notice to govern Iraq. The Head of the CPA, US Ambassador Paul

Bremer, ordered the immediate disbandment of the Iraqi security forces and exclusion of Baath Party members from public service. These actions dismantled the organizations that could have been used to support Iraqi stability and rapidly made Iraq much less stable. Britain had no influence on these decisions.

Basra was Iraq's second city, far south of Baghdad, with a distinct economy, demography and geography, and a record of secessionist ambitions. Its Shia people initially welcomed Coalition forces, but restoring public services was handicapped by the CPA's abrupt removal of Iraqi administrators. As with the rest of the country, enormous stocks of arms and ammunition were there for the taking. An early harbinger of growing Shia discontent with the British was the 24 June murder by an armed mob of six military policemen in Majar al-Kabir.

The Sunni Arab and Al Qaida insurgencies that were the main threat to US forces hardly featured in southern Iraq. But Basra's infrastructure was in a parlous state. The expectations of the population for a rapid improvement in their living conditions, and a significant failure to meet these expectations rapidly increased disaffection with British forces.

British forces represented the only security authority in the city, the Iraqi police and judicial system having collapsed. Immediately after the fall of Saddam, British troops could easily move around the city. But rioting increased as did armed attacks on the troops with small arms, rockets and roadside bombs. The city became increasingly hostile and unpredictable.

The intensity of violence was initially low, but throughout the long hot summer of 2003 the frustrations of the civilian population escalated, as did attacks by Shia militants. By the second half of 2003 the population was increasingly resorting to violence. Increasing numbers joined the Shia militias. Iraqi security force capability could not be grown fast enough. The limited Coalition and British funds available for reconstruction made little practical difference to the population and the combination of looting, lawlessness, tattered infrastructure, and electrical power shortages exacerbated discontent. In mid-August there were serious riots in Basra.

British units were required to conduct operations that covered security, governance, economy and essential services. Tasks included the re-establishment of freedom of movement and the rule of law, as well as act as diplomats, local administration advisors, infrastructure consultants and economic development advisors, all through an interpreter. The need to maintain and build the consent of the local population remained a central British military aim, but one that became increasingly difficult to achieve.

For example, before the war, Basra received electricity about 20 hours a day. By August 2003 it was receiving half that amount. This resulted from damage inflicted by looting on the electrical infrastructure, and the CPA prioritizing the electric power for Baghdad.[25] With summer heat in Basra often reaching 50 degrees, and with very high unemployment, it was unsurprising that riots ensued.

The summer heat challenged British troops. Most front-line soldiers had no access to air conditioning. And they had to deploy wearing helmets and body armour. It was only their high standard of fitness that reduced the number of casualties from heat exhaustion.

Prisoner Abuse – a Leadership Failure

In this environment 1st Battalion, the Queen's Lancashire Regiment raided a hotel in Basra. Suspects were detained and transferred to the battalion's detention facility. Over two days they were physically abused and Baha Mousa, a receptionist, died of his injuries.

Four years later, a court martial acquitted many of the perpetrators. But the subsequent public inquiry showed that this disgraceful crime was avoidable. It showed that throughout the British chain of command, there had been a systemic lack of understanding of the provisions of the Geneva Conventions. Policy and doctrine for prisoner handling and resourcing for management of detainees and interrogation were inadequate. Government policy and rules laid down after prisoner abuse in the 1970s had by 2001 been comprehensively forgotten by the MoD, the British Army and both joint and Army intelligence organizations.

The Baha Mousa Inquiry provided clear evidence that the MoD and British Army leadership had neglected its responsibilities for implementing the law of armed conflict. Compliance with the laws of war is not optional, but the Army leadership had decided it was a low priority.

So, apparently, had the UK Chief of Defence Intelligence (CDI). He was the MoD's 'process owner' for intelligence and was responsible for intelligence training. The chair of the inquiry judged the then CDI's evidence unconvincing, rejecting some of it out of hand, stating that the CDI did not have a proper understanding of what policy and doctrinal guidance applied to interrogation and tactical questioning.

That failures of policy and doctrine had built up gradually over several years did not absolve CDI of his responsibilities. But neither he nor the Army's senior leadership were ever held accountable for these failings. Key actors in the British chain of command not only failed in their duty but also made it more likely that prisoners would be abused. These self-inflicted failures contributed to a significant erosion of the legitimacy of British operations in Iraq.[26]

British Stabilization Operations in Iraq, 2004–05

The war became unpopular in the UK. Contributing factors included the failure to find weapons of mass destruction and the suicide of Dr David Kelly, an MoD weapons scientist. He had told the BBC that the government's dossier that assessed that Iraq posed an active threat of weapons of mass destruction had been 'sexed up'. This led to a sense that Prime Minister Blair and his inner circle had deliberately exaggerated the Iraqi threat. The rapid descent of Iraq into anarchy amplified increasing discontent in Parliament, the media and the public.

From mid-2003 onwards the national strategic direction given by London to the British general commanding in Basra was clear: a timetabled withdrawal from Iraq measured by troop numbers. British officers called this as 'strategy by spreadsheet'. The dilemma for the commander in Basra was two-fold. Firstly, he had to manage the imbalance in expectation between the British policy of disengaging from southern Iraq and often contradictory US direction. Secondly, he had to sustain his troops' morale. For the first time in the careers of troops in Iraq, they were fighting an unpopular war. This was reflected in the direction to reduce British casualties.

The March 2004 departure of the Spanish brigade from Multinational Division Centre South following jihadist bombings in Madrid caused a significant reduction of that division's strength. The US asked that British troops fill the gap, and that the Army assign the NATO-assigned HQ of the Allied Command Europe Rapid Reaction Corps to assume control of the whole of Iraq south of Baghdad. This request was eventually declined by the British government, in part because the MoD was planning to deploy the HQ and additional troops to Afghanistan in 2006.

In April 2004 action taken by the CPA triggered a widespread uprising across Iraq by Sadrist Shia militants aligned with Muqtada al-Sadr, the so-called Jaysh al-Mahdi (JAM). This had considerable impact in southern Iraq. On the early morning of 6 April, the JAM mounted 35 attacks on British troops in Basra and occupied government buildings. Shia fighters seized bridges in Nasirayah, the responsibility of the Italian brigade. For six days the British general commanding in Basra, Andrew Stewart, could not persuade the Italians to use force to remove the militias, offensive action being blocked by Rome. Stewart told the Italians he would send British troops to clear the militants. Rome then authorized offensive action, which was successful.

In Basra, the British employed a dual-track approach; threats to storm buildings seized by the militia whilst negotiating with key political figures. This eventually led to the withdrawal of the militants from the buildings they had seized. But this was not before Ambassador Bremer had issued a diplomatic *démarche* to the British demanding that force be used more robustly. He required the replacement of General Stewart. London supported Stewart, declining to replace him. This was the first significant military divergence between the UK and US. It would not be the last.

There was a full-scale insurrection in Maysan Province, especially in its capital Al Amarah where the single UK battlegroup experienced intense fighting.[27] A small British base in a fortified house in Al Amarah was under siege from Shia militants and was only secured through a determined defence by British infantry and use of airpower, including American AC130 gunships.

A ceasefire was eventually negotiated, but not before the battlegroup had earned more gallantry awards than any British battalion in Iraq. The Victoria Cross was awarded to the driver of a Warrior infantry fighting vehicle. At the time the British Army claimed that the fighting in Al Amarah was the most intense that any British battalion had experienced since the Korean War over 50 years earlier. This claim was correct, but over the next decade more British battalions in Iraq and Afghanistan would experience combat at equal or even higher levels of intensity.

A second Shia uprising in the summer saw significant fighting between Shia militias and Coalition forces across the country and in Basra, Maysan, Nasiriyah and Amarah. These uprisings were thwarted, again as much through political as military means.

In late 2004, the British government decided to commit a major British force to NATO operations in Afghanistan in 2006. This decision assumed that British troop levels in Iraq would have significantly reduced by then.

The security situation in southern Iraq gradually improved. The Iraqi election of January 2005 saw a significant contribution by the Iraqi security forces. This gave rise to some guarded optimism in the British government. But by then British forces had sustained 86 fatalities in Iraq.

The UK and Coalition operational directions to the British division were broadly complementary: transition of responsibility to the Iraqi forces by generating and training Iraqi units, while simultaneously supporting the development of Iraqi governance and economy. The main effort was to be 'security sector reform'.

Much of the British effort to build the capacity of the Iraqi security forces was initially similar to that mounted by the US. Training camps and training teams were established, and Iraqi soldiers and police were trained. But there was an important difference between the UK and US approach. As the US formed Iraqi military units it embedded teams of US military advisors with them, known as military training transition teams (MiTTs). These were to advise and assist the Iraqi battalions, brigades and divisions as the conducted operations.

The British chose not to do this. It appears that the decision was made by the Chiefs of Staff, influenced by concerns about force protection. With a much lower density of troops in southern Iraq, providing the same level of quick reaction forces that the US had assigned to their transition teams would have been very difficult.[28] Instead of advisors and trainers embedded down to battalion level, British advisers only visited Iraqi units in southern Iraq. Compared with the Americans, the British were far less able to understand both the strengths and weaknesses of the Iraqi forces. But at the time the British HQ in Northwood and MoD in London seemed oblivious of this greatly reduced level of situational awareness.

Other tensions developed between the US and UK militaries. British officers working in Baghdad in 2004 and 2005 noted an increasing US irritation that the British did not seem to fully appreciate the size of the American commitment, and the scale of effort and intensity of operations being conducted. Friction came from apparent British arrogance over the American approach to operations. Americans could see this as a 'we know better and we can do it better' attitude. Misunderstandings and tensions followed from attempts that were made to highlight the strengths of the so-called British way to American allies. Thomas Mockaitis noted that:

American officers [were] barraged with ungenerous, over-simplified, and often glib comparisons between their supposedly ineffectual methods in Vietnam and the allegedly superior British approach employed in Malaya. Similar comparisons between the British army's handling of Basra and the US military's alleged mishandling of the far more challenging Sunni triangle [made] American officers understandably resistant to what they [saw] as 'more British tripe'.[29]

BASRA DETERIORATES

Before the January 2005 Iraqi elections, the UK expected that there would be progress in southern Iraq. Instead, all elected local politicians strongly opposed the British presence. The victorious Islamic coalition parties failed to agree on a governor, allowing the election by default of Muhammad al-Wa'ili, whose Fadhila Party had gained only 13 of the 41 seats.

For the next four years, Wa'ili defeated all political and legal attempts to unseat him. He was linked to the black economy based on oil-smuggling, overseen by his militia within the Facilities Protection Service. The JAM and other militias carved out fiefdoms in electricity generation and the ports. Influence of Shia militias over the Iraqi security forces increased. Militias and their Iranian sponsored 'special groups' increasingly sought to gain political capital by attacking the British.

The weak Baghdad government could do little to stop this. Preoccupied with more serious threats to its existence, it showed little interest in Basra. These factors turned Basra into a kleptocracy, where armed political–criminal groups excluded the central government and the Iraqi people from power.

Previous British stabilization operations in Malaya, Bosnia, Kosovo, Sierra Leone and in Kabul had all featured a high degree of consent by most of the local population. Iraqi voters and politicians were telling the British that their troops should leave southern Iraq.

The conflict in Basra was fundamentally different to that in Anbar and Baghdad, where Al Qaida was attempting to destroy the Iraqi secular state. None of the militias in the Shia south wanted to destroy the state; they simply wanted as large a slice of the cake as possible. They were parasites that wanted to keep the host alive.

The British felt that the Iraqi Army was being successfully developed. By many metrics progress was real. But corruption remained debilitating. Commanders were frustrated that financial rules imposed by Whitehall prevented relatively inexpensive reconstruction tasks. US commanders were able to draw on a much more responsive US Commander's Emergency Relief Fund. There was no British equivalent.

For the first half of 2005, the level of violence was markedly less than in 2004. But the JAM started using Explosively Formed Projectile (EFP) roadside bombs that could penetrate all British armoured vehicles, including Challenger and Warrior. There was nothing new about EFP technology, which used explosives to form a high-energy metal slug, capable of punching through tank armour to lethal effect. Indeed, during the Cold War, the British used French-manufactured EFP anti-tank mines. Drawing on expertise provided by Lebanese Hezbollah and a supply of EFP components from Iran, Shia militias used these bombs to great effect against British vehicles. This increased UK casualties.

Many British lightly armoured 'Snatch' Land Rover 4x4 patrol vehicles were destroyed by EFPs, causing well-publicized casualties. This resulted in considerable media criticism of the government, MoD and Army for reacting too slowly. Initially the British had no technical countermeasures to the EFPs, but could only counter the threat by adapting tactics, including reducing road movement and increasing resources for force protection. This so reduced the available combat power of the British brigade, that not only was its operational effect diminished, but it also had to reduce the troops training Iraqi forces. It took months for additional armour and other countermeasures to be fielded. The then British commander, Major General Jonathan Riley, was later to observe that:

> It was borne in on me very strongly how much the collective experience of the Army of dealing with the IED threat had wasted out during the long period of ceasefire in Northern Ireland. We had forgotten institutionally how to deal with this … not just as a series of devices but as a system and how to attack the device and attack the system behind it. So as well as asking for upgrades in protection, we also began to refocus the Intelligence-gathering effort on to people who were likely to be initiating and running the networks to try and break the thing up …
>
> The armour on the Warrior and Challenger main battle tanks was upgraded very rapidly. The Snatch Land Rover was also up armoured, and I began to see the introduction of a new series of vehicles which were more effective, but these devices were of such power that there was … no technological silver bullet in this. So, we were doing what we could within the constraints of the available technology. There was nothing else around. The responses to it were therefore not just about protection against the device. They had to be about breaking the networks.[30]

It would only be in mid-2008 that the level of security forces on the streets in Basra City was sufficient to disrupt the emplacement of EFPs by Shia fighters.

THE JAMEAT INCIDENT

British government messaging that their efforts with the Iraqi forces were succeeding was rudely shattered on 19 September 2005. The Iraqi Police arrested two British special forces soldiers in civilian clothes who were conducting covert surveillance. They were detained at Basra's Jameat police station – notorious for sectarianism and human rights abuses. The police told Iraqi media that two Israeli spies had been captured. The British feared that the soldiers would be tortured, or even killed.

A British team went to the police station to negotiate the men's release. They were also taken hostage. Armoured infantry in Warriors surrounded the station. Angry Iraqi civilians gathered to confront the British. Heavy rioting resulted. Petrol bombs were thrown, a Warrior vehicle was set on fire and its commander, his uniform afire, had to evacuate his position in the turret.

The police station was forcibly entered by British armour crashing through its walls. The negotiating team were secured, but the captured soldiers were nowhere to be found. A Royal Navy helicopter over the Jameat spotted the prisoners being moved to another building. By now a force of SAS had arrived from central Iraq and rescued their comrades.

Images of the soldier escaping from a Warrior armoured vehicle, his uniform ablaze, appeared widely across the media. This and media reports of the incident contributed to increasing political, media and public perceptions that the British mission was failing.

On the Iraqi side, the Basra provincial governor broke off relations with the British. The police broke off relations with the British and the Basra Provincial Council announced a policy of non-cooperation and disengagement with the British.

The British response was to concentrate effort on implementing Transition in Al Muthanna and Maysan provinces to get the Iraqi security forces ready for Provincial Iraqi Control. This was a Coalition milestone, to be achieved when the security conditions and capability of Iraqi security forces allowed the Iraqi authorities to take over control of security. The British also stepped up intelligence-led detention operations of suspected Shia fighters.

The incident was a strategic shock. It raised serious doubts over the Iraqi Police, especially the extent to which it had been infiltrated by Shia militias. An independent review of Basra police was conducted. It was recommended that responsibility for training police in southern Iraq should pass from the FCO to the military. They increasingly concentrated on getting Iraqi Police capacity in Basra 'good enough' for security transition from British to Iraqi leadership.

The Iraqi National Referendum took place on 15 October 2005 without incident. A jointly run Iraqi–Coalition security operation was seen to be a success. But internal power struggles and malign criminal and political influences were largely invisible.

CHAPTER 12

'We Are in Two Wars and we Have Got to Win Them Both'

This compelling phrase was often used as a soundbite by senior MoD and Army leaders between 2006 and 2009, when the Army was fighting two difficult wars against unexpectedly capable and determined enemies.[1] These went well beyond the commitments that its manpower, equipment and training was resourced for by the MoD. Iraq was already unpopular. It had been hoped that the deployment to Helmand could be portrayed as a more legitimate war. But the unforeseen resistance by the Taliban and resulting casualties meant that the Afghan war became unexpectedly demanding and increasingly unpopular. Both wars administered surprises and shocks – not least the casualties inflicted by Shia militias and the Taliban. As both wars were being simultaneously directed by the MoD and fought by the Army, this chapter considers them both during this period, where the Army was placed under great strain, with resulting political impact.

The unanticipated battle for Southern Afghanistan

By the end of 2005, the US considered that despite an increase in Taliban attacks, the time was right for them to reduce forces in Afghanistan, to reinforce Iraq. In September 2006, NATO took over security leadership in northern and western Afghanistan, the most stable parts of the country. In 2006 NATO would deploy a multinational force to southern Afghanistan. Initially this would be under the command of the US, but in the autumn NATO would take over responsibility for the whole of Afghanistan, subsuming CJTF 76's responsibilities for southern and eastern Afghanistan. Counter-terrorist operations by US SOF against Al Qaida would remain under US national command, as part of Operation *Enduring Freedom*.

Many senior US officers had reservations over NATO nations' political will to take military risk, many of their armies lacking recent combat experience. But the increase in NATO strength in Afghanistan would allow US troop numbers to be reduced, so these reservations were overruled.

Prime Minister Blair, the Chiefs of Staff and the Army all wanted to play a leading role in this. They assumed that British strategy for Iraq would succeed, allowing British troops in Basra to reduce significantly from 2006, enabling rapid growth of the British contingent in Afghanistan. In making these plans the Army and MoD seem to have anticipated that Afghanistan would generate neither significant combat nor serious numbers of casualties.

Planning identified that there would be a spike in demand for key specialists such as logistics, intelligence and communications experts, but the British drawdown in Iraq would ease this. The Iraq war had also lost legitimacy with the public and media in the UK, while Afghanistan could be portrayed as a legitimate war.

The plan was for the British-led NATO ARRC HQ to deploy to Kabul in 2006, initially to command the existing ISAF in northern and eastern Afghanistan. In September 2006 it would assume responsibility for southern and eastern Afghanistan.

NATO forces in northern and western Afghanistan would not change. Southern Afghanistan had only a few US troops. The Canadians, British and Dutch agreed to fill this gap with a multinational brigade and national PRTs. Each nation would cover a province; the British would go to Helmand, the Canadians to Kandahar and the Dutch to Uruzgun. General David Richards, the new ISAF commander, used extensive analysis of both counterinsurgency (COIN) and development to design a campaign plan to support and empower the Afghan authorities. Richards intended to:

> extend and deepen the areas in which the Government of Afghanistan can safely operate in the interests of the people of Afghanistan, enabling the ANSF [Afghan National Security Forces] to increasingly take the lead in in achieving the aim ... I will seize the initiative against those who oppose the Government of Afghanistan through violent means, by using appropriate and well considered measures – including robust use of force should it be necessary – at times and places of my choosing ...[2]

A Policy Action Group was to better co-ordinate Afghan and international efforts. Chaired by President Karzai, this would be where the key military and civilian actors planned military and civilian actions for security and development and oversaw implementation, to give the president and his national security adviser the tools necessary to synchronize Afghan and international efforts. ISAF security operations were to secure Afghan Development Zones, for concentrated international and Afghan efforts to improve local governance and prosperity. PRTs would lead delivery of these non-military objectives.

This approach worked in the relatively benign areas of northern and eastern Afghanistan, but in Helmand, Kandahar and Uruzgun provinces, the Taliban were much stronger than had been anticipated, resulting in much heavier fighting than they had expected.

This resulted from inadequate understanding of the insurgents. There was little intelligence about the Taliban in southern Afghanistan and little understanding of the complex dynamics between corrupt Afghan government officials, local warlords, drug barons and tribal leaders. Nor was there understanding of how tension had been amplified by US raids on targets offered by 'friendly' warlords, who were portraying their enemies as Taliban. Nor did British planners anticipate that their interventions in these southern provinces might enmesh them in local disputes, with considerable danger of making the situation worse by exacerbating local rivalries and extant conflicts.

British planners were unaware that the Taliban in southern Afghanistan had been expending considerable effort to build up their influence and forces. They exploited several years' worth of grievances arising from the way in which local warlords had returned to power in 2002, as allies of President Karzai.

During 2004 and 2005 Taliban networks rebuilt themselves throughout southern Afghanistan. They were increasingly joined by fighters from Pakistan. Initially cautious, they used intimidation and murder to remove those who opposed them and began small-scale attacks against Afghan government forces and institutions such as district centres. Taliban-supporting Mullahs came from Quetta and Peshawar using intimidation to displace moderate mullahs. The Pakistani government repeatedly denied that it provided direct support to the insurgents, but US and Afghan officials publicly insisted that the insurgents received considerable support from the ISI, the Pakistani intelligence agency.

The Afghan Police and the National Directorate of Security (NDS), the national intelligence agency, were often captured by predatory and corrupt warlords. These factors aggravated existing frictions, fault lines and disputes amongst tribal groupings. This reinforced a sense of injustice and oppression amongst the rural population in all three southern provinces.

Meanwhile, in London, the failures in Baghdad and Basra to properly integrate military action with reconstruction and development had been a wakeup call to the British government, particularly to the three ministries involved, the MoD, DfID and FCO. A new inter-agency doctrine was developed, the Comprehensive Approach, which was intended to better integrate civil and military action, and a new inter-agency Post Conflict Reconstruction Unit was set up.

The British knew little about Helmand Province. The US had largely left it alone, apart from a PRT in Lashkar Gar, the provincial capital, and some SOF. There had been some British reconnaissance of Helmand by British SOF who found the province to be largely at peace. This was mainly the result of the revenue from opium flowing to drug barons, warlords and the Taliban. The provincial governor's personal militia enforced a brutal rule. The SAS had operated in Helmand. Their commanding officer advised that removing the governor and deploying British troops could well destabilize the province, resulting in increased violence.

British reconnaissance missions in 2005 and 2006 only scratched the surface of the complex tribal, political and economic dynamics of the province. But most of the population were illiterate, such provincial and district government as existed was in thrall to tribal and patronage networks and the police were corrupt and behaved in a predatory fashion towards the civilian population.[3]

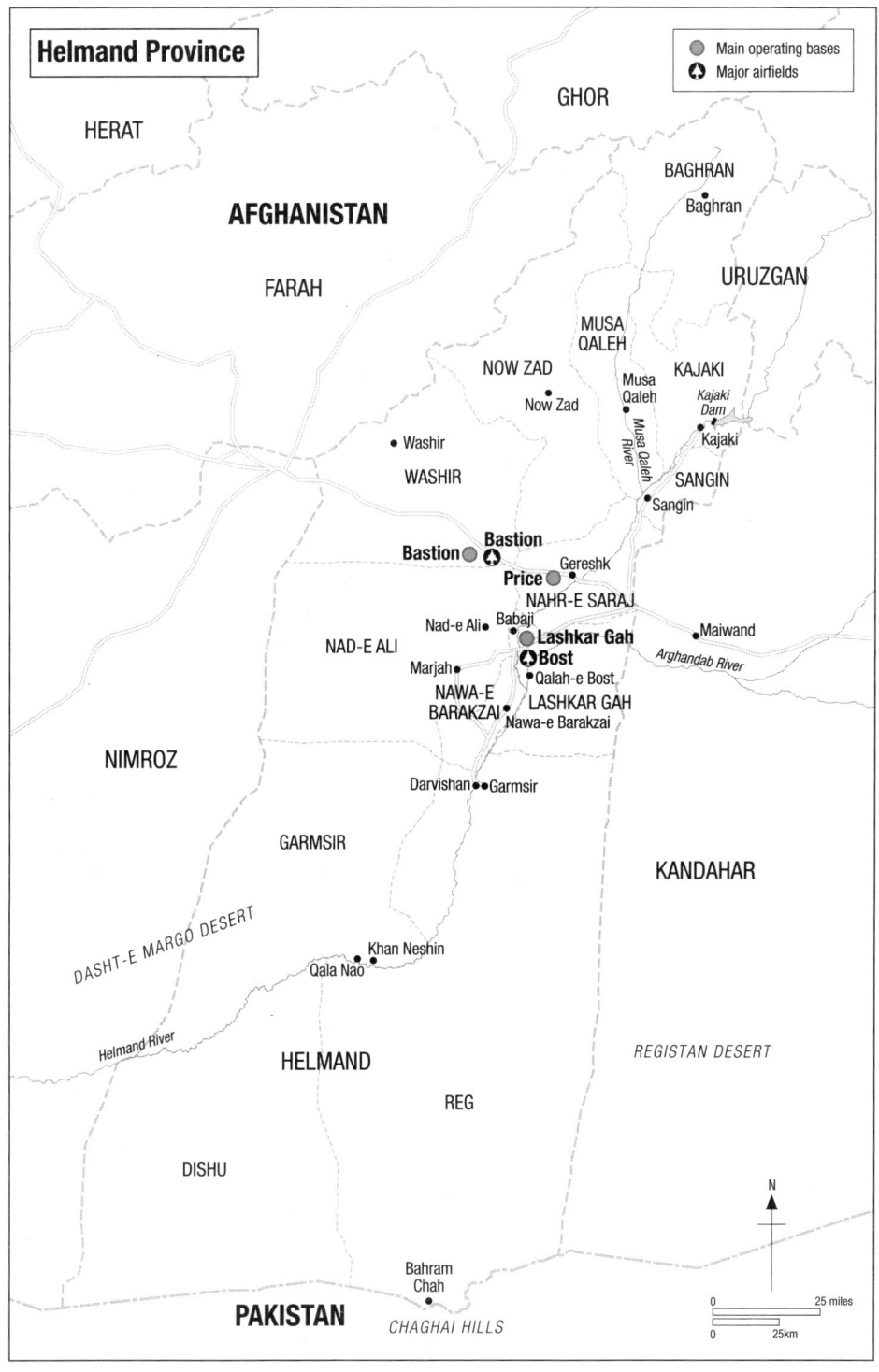

Helmand Province

- ● Main operating bases
- ⊙ Major airfields

GHOR

HERAT

AFGHANISTAN

BAGHRAN
• Baghran

FARAH

URUZGAN

MUSA
QALEH

NOW ZAD

KAJAKI

• Now Zad

Musa
Qaleh

*Kajaki
Dam*

• Kajaki

• Washir

WASHIR

*Musa Qaleh
River*

SANGIN

• Sangin

Bastion
Bastion ● ⊙
Price ● Gereshk

NAHR-E SARAJ

Nad-e Ali • Babaji •

NAD-E ALI

● **Lashkar Gah**

• Maiwand

Arghandab River

Marjah •

⊙ **Bost**
• Qalah-e Bost

NAWA-E
BARAKZAI

LASHKAR GAH

Nawa-e Barakzai

NIMROZ

KANDAHAR

Darvishan • • Garmsir

GARMSIR

DASHT-E MARGO DESERT

Khan Neshin
•
Qala Nao •

Helmand River

HELMAND

REG

REGISTAN DESERT

DISHU

N

Bahram
Chah
•

PAKISTAN

CHAGHAI HILLS

0   25 miles

0   25km

British military and civilian planners deployed to Kabul and Kandahar at the end of 2005 to produce an interagency plan for Helmand. But the commander and HQ of the brigade that would provide most of the troops for Helmand were not part of planning team.

The MoD, FCO and DfID all displayed optimism. The Defence Secretary, John Reid, told the media that this was a dangerous mission because 'terrorists will want to destroy the economy and the legitimate trade and the government that we are helping to build up'. But he also stated the 'we would be happy to go and work with the Afghan Government and leave without firing a shot'. These words were quickly overtaken by events and would return to haunt the four Labour defence ministers who succeeded him.[4]

Task Force Helmand came from 16 Air Assault Brigade. The formation would provide its HQ and 3rd Battalion, the Parachute Regiment, supported by an armoured reconnaissance squadron, combat engineers, a squadron of Apache attack helicopters and a few 105mm artillery guns. This would be complemented by a PRT. British special forces in southern Afghanistan would also increase in strength.

Command and control was over-complicated. Regional Command South would be the responsibility of a multinational brigade HQ based on the HQ of Canadian Brigadier David Fraser. The commander of the air assault brigade, Brigadier Ed Butler, would become the UK national contingent commander based in Kabul. He would answer to the UK joint HQ and hold the national 'red card' – the power to veto orders from NATO. Butler, who had personally prepared and trained his brigade, found this very frustrating, particularly as Task Force Helmand would be commanded by a colonel from outside the brigade, who had not been part of its training and preparation.[5]

The British saw Helmand's provincial governor, Sher Mohammed Akhundzada, as irredeemably corrupt and the leader of a notorious private militia. They requested that President Karzai remove him. Akhundzada was a close political associate of Karzai, but the president reluctantly complied with the British demands. Members of Akhundzada's militia now had nothing to stop them siding with the Taliban and many did so.

British forces slowly arrived in southern Afghanistan, limited by the need to simultaneously build up supplies and construct the main British base, named Camp Bastion. Although the British sent over 3,000 troops, the numbers of engineers, logistic, maintenance and medical personnel meant that its fighting elements were only a third of this number. Both the new Helmand governor and President Karzai were shocked to discover how little combat power the British had brought to Helmand.

The government had limited the funding for three years civil and military operations in Helmand to a billion pounds.[6] So the MoD had placed financial constraints on the cost of the Helmand deployment, especially on the numbers of helicopters and flying hours allocated. It seems to have assumed that there would be relatively little fighting over the five years it assumed that the operation would last. The 16 Air Assault Brigade had advised from the outset of its planning that the numbers of helicopters deployed and flying hours funded were insufficient for the operation.

This coincided with increasing Taliban attacks. Many of these targeted the government's district centres throughout Helmand. A worrying early signal was a firefight between the Pathfinder Platoon and a group of Afghan police. As the British deployed, a request from the new provincial governor led to the British deploying small groups of infantry to isolated district centres in Helmand's key towns: Sangin, Now Zad and Musa Qala.

The parachute battalion became fixed in these towns in small bases, often called 'platoon houses'. These were subject to many close assaults by large numbers of Taliban. Some bases nearly fell but considerable use of firepower of machine guns, anti-tank missiles, mortars, and precision air strikes meant that they survived.

Initially, the Taliban attacks appeared poorly executed, with waves of brave fighters attacking the British bases. Sometimes these got so close that hand grenades would be thrown by both sides. The defenders used mortars, artillery and air strikes called in 'danger close', that is so near to friendly troops that they themselves were within the radius of lethal effects.[7] This firepower caused civilian casualties and collateral damage, generating more recruits for the Taliban.

By mid-July the base at Sangin was besieged. Heavy Taliban fire meant that helicopters could only land during darkness. Troops wounded during the day had to wait until night before they could be evacuated. But even at night Taliban fire made such missions difficult, helicopters often having to abort their landings for fear of being shot down. After an attempt to parachute food supplies failed, the base was only successfully replenished by a Canadian mechanized infantry company bringing in ammunition and food inside their armoured vehicles.

Troops found themselves amid a dispute between two tribes. This, coupled with an inadequate understanding of local cultural and tribal dynamics, resulted in security in Helmand further deteriorating. The Alikozi gained advantage in a struggle over land and narcotics by misusing government appointments. Their opponents, the Ishaqzai, sided with the Taliban. The British deployment of a parachute company to support a notoriously abusive district police chief in Sangin, an Alikozi, made matters worse. Sangin would become the district where the greatest number of British casualties occurred in Afghanistan. In four years, 106 British troops would be killed there.

Unexpectedly heavy British casualties reduced the domestic popularity of the war in the UK. The Army claimed that the 2006 fighting in northern Helmand was the most intense it had experienced since the Korean War. This claim had been made previously about fighting in the 2004 Shia uprising in Iraq. But in Afghanistan the infantry had no heavy armoured vehicles. Without the use of satellite communications and air ground radios, as well as the precision firepower that attack helicopters and fighter bombers could deploy, some or all the British bases might well have fallen. Such a defeat would have had catastrophic political effects on ISAF, NATO and the British government, as well as on the Army's credibility.

There was considerable friction between the British, the Canadian-led multinational brigade HQ in Kandahar, the US-led Operation *Enduring Freedom* HQ in Bagram and ISAF in Kabul. The UK national contingent commander, Brigadier Ed Butler, seemed to see his primary loyalty as to the UK, rather than the Canadian-led brigade HQ. Butler, US Army general Ben Freakley, initially commanding land forces in Afghanistan, and General David Richards all saw the campaign from contrasting perspectives. This was exacerbated by the different personalities of the three commanders, with both Richards and Freakley finding Butler difficult to deal with. The British design for command and control reinforced these frictions rather than smoothing them out.[8]

The UK chain of command was rationalized. Butler remained national contingent commander but was moved from Kabul to Helmand to take command of all British forces there, subordinate to the direction of Brigadier Fraser. The British, Dutch and Canadians all agreed that the command framework they had agreed for southern Afghanistan needed upgrading; this required national brigade HQs to command the military operations and co-ordinate with civilian-led reconstruction, as well as the Afghan authorities and forces. The Kandahar HQ of Regional Command South would be upgraded to a multinational divisional HQ, to be commanded in rotation by Dutch, Canadian and British major generals.

As the summer faded into autumn, Taliban tactics improved. Insurgents increasingly sought to evade aircraft and artillery fire by getting as close as they could to British positions, knowing that the defenders would be reluctant to bring in friendly fire so close as to pose a threat to themselves. The British were reinforced by 800 additional troops, but movement, resupply and casualty evacuation were totally dependent on a small force of six Chinook helicopters. Helicopter flights into the British bases became increasingly hazardous. Many troops considered it a near miracle that at least one of the huge helicopters had not already been shot down.

The base at Musa Qala was at most risk.[9] The district centre that British troops occupied was less well constructed and more vulnerable than other bases in Helmand. Its helicopter landing zone was also outside its low walls. The Taliban created a formidable volume of small arms fire. Fortunately for the defenders, the Taliban fire was far less accurate than the British soldiers' marksmanship. On 6 September an attempt to evacuate casualties by Chinook was abandoned when the helicopter was repeatedly hit by Taliban fire. A later attempt, supported by fire from an artillery battery, two A10 close support aircraft, an AC130 gunship and two Apache helicopters, succeeded.

Butler decided to withdraw from Musa Qala. This caused tension with ISAF, who saw that the Taliban would claim that they had forced a British retreat. Local elders proposed a ceasefire deal that would see the British and Taliban both withdrawing from the town, to be policed by local men enrolled as auxiliary police. This was agreed by both sides. The British troops left the town in local Afghan civilian trucks – an image that illustrated the considerable limitations of British power in Helmand. The deal lasted until early 2007, when changing tribal dynamics, the sacking by Karzai of the British-supported governor and an increasing lack of trust all led to its collapse. British, civilian and Taliban lives had been saved, but the deal illustrated that the British had bitten off more than they could chew in Helmand.

Overall, the British had blunted the Taliban offensive in Helmand. Both sides had fought each other to a standstill, the British holding out in the district centres, but at the cost of major collateral damage in the towns around them. This and civilian casualties had turned many Helmand civilians against the British, increasing support for the Taliban. This greatly inhibited the ability of the British PRT to achieve more than a small proportion of its planned work. Far less British funded development was done than had been planned.

The operation used far more helicopters hours than envisaged. But additional helicopters were not sent to Helmand. Indeed, it seemed to many British officers in Helmand that until 2010 the Learmont question was not positively answered. In October 2006 the air assault brigade rotated out of Helmand, to be replaced by the Royal Marines' 3 Commando Brigade. The troops deployed were slightly greater in number.

IRAQ IN 2006 – INCREASING DIFFICULTIES

The British government agreed in January 2006 that Iraq was Britain's top overseas security priority, but it also announced plans to increase the UK role and troops numbers in Afghanistan. And this commitment increasingly meant that Iraq was in reality the lower priority.

The British continued to implement a transition strategy. This envisaged that Coalition troops would reduce their footprint as Iraqi forces became increasingly effective. They would increasingly act in 'overwatch', with their forces being able to return to support the Iraqi forces, should they become overfaced. Once Iraqi forces were sufficiently capable, they would assume the lead for security and the Coalition would declare a state of Provincial Iraqi Control. At this stage Coalition forces in that province would assume 'operational overwatch'. In March 2006, plans to reduce UK force levels in Iraq from 8,000 to 7,200 were introduced.

The transition strategy was failing in Basra. Local politicians and Iraqi forces were unwilling to confront Shia militias, which sought to gain political capital by attacking the British. Roadside bomb attacks sharply increased British casualties. The commander of the British 1st Armoured Division, Major General John Cooper, took steps to recast the campaign as one of counterinsurgency:

> I encouraged my subordinate commanders to think things through against the COIN principles, and so we used them always … If you consider 1st (UK) Armoured Division on warfighting operations, it consists of infantry, armour, guns, aviation, artillery, engineers and logistics. Which do you consider to be the most important element? None of them; it is the sum of the parts that is important; the synergy they create. It is the same with COIN; everyone is part of it; it is the sum of military operations offensive and defensive, Iraqi leadership engagement and development, the training of the Iraqi Security Forces, reconstruction operations and, just as with conventional operations, it is the synergy that comes from the sum of all of the component parts that will make the difference.[10]

The threat from an increasingly confident enemy was rising. Officials showed less interest in working with the Coalition. Corruption was widespread. The Sunni minority was leaving the south in response to a campaign of sectarian intimidation and murder.

Over the summer months, through careful work from military commanders and British diplomats, Basra's provincial council started to re-engage with the British. A joint British/Iraqi command-and-control system was established through the creation of a

Provincial Joint Coordination Centre. The British declared Provincial Iraqi Control to have been achieved in Al Muthanna Province in July, and in Dhi Qar Province in September. Both provinces were relatively stable, probably because of a balance amongst the various local political forces.

Camp Abu Naji, the main British base in Amarah, was handed back to the Iraqi Army in August 2006, but it was immediately looted by the local population. Iraqi troops did nothing to stop this, an indicator that they shared the anti-British attitude. The ransacking of the camp was widely publicized.

GENERAL DANNATT WRITES A LETTER

In summer 2006, the Army was under increasing pressure. Its structure and manpower was funded to support a single medium-scale stabilization operation. It was conducting one in Iraq, which was not going well, was inflicting casualties and was becoming unpopular. And it had just committed to another medium-scale operation in Afghanistan, which was turning out more difficult and bloodier than had been anticipated. There was considerable overstretch. Manpower that might have helped manage this additional commitment had been removed by the cuts made in the undeclared 2004 defence review.

To the Commander in Chief Land Command, General Sir Richard Dannatt, it was unclear if the MoD, Treasury or government properly understood these pressures. And even if they did, they were providing neither sufficient funding nor political momentum to adequately support the Army. He felt that 'the Army was under huge pressure and London needed to know this'.[11]

In late August, Dannatt moved to London to become the CGS. An early action was to write to Defence Secretary Des Browne setting out his assessment of the state of the Army, the support it needed and Dannatt's own role. It is worth quoting Dannatt's account of the letter:

> I began by expressing my general uneasiness with the pace of life and pressure on our people at present and described the army as 'running hot'. I was keen to stress our continuing positive attitude and flexibility but argued that the demands of the organization are currently greater than our ability to provide satisfactorily for the needs of the individual. It is individuals who are at the heart of successful operations. I was worried that the tempo of operations, short interval between tours and gaps in our ranks meant that our overall manning ran a 'severe risk akin to a cliff-edge experience'. If all manning levels were to go into freefall, our operational problems would expand exponentially. My letter went on to reveal my disquiet about certain aspects of essential equipment such as the utility and safety of some of the patrol vehicles we were using in Iraq and Afghanistan, and the availability of helicopters
>
> Our troops deserved the best and I was not convinced that they were receiving it either at the front or at home, where the standard of single and family living accommodation was extremely poor in too many parts of the Army. I was also concerned that we were not paying a fair day's pay for a fair day's fighting. Clearly greater spending on defence would go a long

way towards solving these problems, but I recognized that a significant increase in funding was unlikely. So in my letter I suggested efficiency savings and a reprioritization of resources within the Army or more widely within Defence. I reasoned that provision for possible future conflict of an unknown nature needed to be moderated in order to provide properly for what we could see and needed now for current operations. So I put it to Des Browne that responsibility including moral responsibility for decisions was becoming detached from the service chiefs.

Although charged with responsibility for the overall fighting effectiveness of the Army, today the CGS – as a result of the centralisation which so vexed me – owns so few of the decision-making levers pulled and pushed by his predecessors. Alanbrooke and Templer would have shaken their heads at my inability to determine and decide. I ended what was effectively in my manifesto with a declaration that as his chief of the general staff I fully intended not only to lead the Army, 'but to inform and explain to soldiers their families and the wider population so that they understood what we were doing and why we were doing it.' Accordingly, I stated that I required the freedom to interact with the media without constantly seeking ministerial clearance. As I put it to Des Browne, 'losing popular support at home is the single biggest danger to our chances of success in our current operations.' I knew that we had to get our message out widely.[12]

Dannatt met with Browne a month later. This conversation was unsatisfactory:

How much of my letter he understood I never really knew. He had not been in the department many weeks and if he accepted my argument about the centrality of our current operations and the critical need to succeed, he kept this well disguised. I think the wider issues passed him by completely.[13]

Dannatt embarked on an MoD-approved programme of media briefings. In October he had a wide-ranging interview with a *Daily Mail* journalist. Discussing Iraq, he described the British Army as 'part of the problem in Basra'. He said that the Army was involved in two wars and it was important to ensure that the combined commitment did not break it. Dannatt's remarks were fully in keeping with then government and MoD policy to shift forces from Iraq to Afghanistan. However, on 12 October they resulted in a banner headline across the *Daily Mail* newspaper that 'WE MUST GET OUT OF IRAQ SAYS HEAD OF THE ARMY'.

Dannatt had in fact explained government policy, but the interview was seized upon by the British media as a further argument in favour of UK withdrawal from the increasingly unpopular war. The media frenzy spun the story as direct criticism. There were many calls for Dannatt's resignation, including some voiced privately by a minority of serving officers and civil servants,[14] but he stuck to his guns.

This was a crisis in civil/military relations. A more resolute government might have sacked Dannatt. But such an action could well have blown up in their faces, particularly if Dannatt's letter to Browne had leaked, shining an unwelcome light into the dark corner of the MoD's poor leadership of the two wars and Gordon Brown's ingrained hostility to defence spending.

Dannatt had decided to influence the MoD, the Army and the attitude of the British public in a way that worked within these limitations. The evidence suggests that had UK operations in Iraq and Afghanistan and their effects on the Army received the top-level leadership that they required, Dannatt would not have had to be so outspoken. In October 2006 the Defence Board ruled that the priority of the MoD was 'strategic success in Iraq and Afghanistan'. Many officers working there wondered why it had taken so long to make this judgement.[15]

Dannatt continued to speak in public, seeking to explain the war in Afghanistan. He also suggested that towns and cities could do more to show public appreciation to troops returning from operations. His suggestion had an impact. His request was rapidly supported by many towns and cities. Over the next few years many battalions and regiments returning from Afghanistan would be invited to march through cities and towns. These events were good for the communities concerned and good for the troops marching and their families.

This coincided with a commemoration ceremony self-organized by the town of Wootton Bassett. After arrival at RAF Lyneham, the hearses bearing coffins of troops killed in Iraq and Afghanistan would pass through the town. Television news coverage created great public interest in this uniquely British event, where an unremarkable small town seemed to capture a national mood of sorrow and commemoration. At the height of the war, thousands of people from all over the UK crowded the narrow high street. To attend was a very moving, but intensely egalitarian experience.[16]

Another frustration of Dannatt's was the arrangements to support wounded troops and their families. Whilst the medical treatment of wounded troops at the Royal Centre for Defence Medicine at Birmingham University Hospital was first-class, the arrangements for the welfare of families visiting the hospital were initially inadequate. It could be argued that this was yet another consequence of MoD institutional blindness to the prospects of fighting a war resulting in significant casualties.[17]

Dannatt made himself unpopular with the Defence Medical Services' leadership about this issue. This had some impact, but more positive effects were created by the rapid formation of a new charity, Help for Heroes. Started by Bryn Parry, a former Royal Green Jacket officer, this was a self-organizing charity that raised funds and grew itself, exploiting the new opportunities provided by the internet and social media.

Dannatt led an Army initiative to better balance the relationship between the Army, MoD and society that became the Military Covenant. The concept was developed by the Army between 2006 and 2008 and increasingly gained traction both within and outside Defence.

INSTITUTIONAL FRICTION AND ADAPTABILITY

The Army had considerable experience of counterinsurgency from post-World War II colonial campaigns and from Northern Ireland. Sir Robert Thompson and General Sir Frank Kitson were both soldier-scholars who had written authoritative books on the topic. But in the late 1990s the new Joint Services Staff College had almost completely abandoned teaching insurgency and counterinsurgency, in favour of studying peace support operations. Although the Army had published relevant COIN doctrine in 2001, it was not publicized within the Army, so was not widely read. The US Army and Marine Corps had published new COIN doctrine in 2006. The British Army did not publish equivalent doctrine until late 2009, after the British had left Iraq.[18]

The Army failed to grow tactical intelligence capabilities quickly enough. It had failed to institutionalize many hard-won lessons of Northern Ireland, for example, where airborne surveillance by helicopters and fixed wing aircraft had provided decisive advantage over the IRA. The British Army had made extensive use of the Phoenix drone in March and April 2003, but having been designed for operations in Europe, the aircraft could not fly in the warmest six months of the Iraqi summer. US forces were rapidly fielding ever-increasing numbers of drones to Iraq and Afghanistan.

For the first four years of the Iraq war, airborne surveillance over southern Iraq was inadequate. Although some small Desert Hawk drones were procured for the Army, a 2004 RAF initiative to join the US Air Force's Predator force did not entitle the British force in southern Iraq to any support from the RAF's Predator. Priorities for Predator were set by the HQs in CENTCOM and Baghdad. Since southern Iraq was not a high priority, UK troops rarely saw Predators operate in their area. In 2007 the Army leased Hermes 450 drones, but British commanders in Iraq were frustrated that Iraqi and Australian troops in southern Iraq acquired drone capabilities more quickly than the British did.

Warrior vehicles had additional armour fitted to provide better protection. Warrior became the armoured vehicle of choice to send into harm's way in Iraq, both for its protection and its turret-mounted weapons, but the Army did not possess enough to have sufficient available in Basra. Between 2003 and 2006 the British were unable to deploy enough armoured vehicles with adequate protection against IEDs, so had to rely too much on inadequately protected Snatch Land Rovers.

It was not until June 2006 that Defence Secretary Des Browne and procurement minister Lord Drayson imparted much-needed urgency to the acquisition of better protected vehicles. A new vehicle, the Mastiff, entered service in December 2006. This was based on a protected patrol vehicle developed for the US Marine Corps. The British also adapted the existing FV432 APC, by upgrading it into the Bulldog, improving its power plant and fitting additional armour.

Both vehicles had greatly improved protection against RPG warheads, roadside bombs and EFP warheads. Herculean efforts were made to deploy both vehicles to Basra as quickly as possible. As Bulldogs and Mastiffs drove onto the streets, they immediately reduced casualties, reassured soldiers and emboldened commanders. Although there is much to criticize in Des Browne's handling of the war and leadership of the MoD, his decision to apply political urgency to accelerating the procurement of the Mastiff rapidly saved lives.

Why did it take so long to field the necessary new capabilities in Iraq? A major factor was that the complex structure of the MoD diffused responsibility and accountability. During the first three years of the war, it was unclear where responsibility and accountability lay for improving equipment for British forces in Iraq and Afghanistan. The Iraq Inquiry assessed that:

The Ministry of Defence was slow in responding to the threat from Improvised Explosive Devices and delays in providing adequate medium weight protected patrol vehicles should not have been tolerated. It was not clear which person or department within the Ministry of Defence was responsible for identifying and articulating such capability gaps. But it should have been.[19]

It was only public, media and political pressure that forced the MoD to display the urgency that the situation demanded. It seems to have taken the ministry too long to develop the necessary sense of urgency. A contributing factor may have been the rapid turnover of defence secretaries.

The evidence suggests that for every positive example of British military adaptation in Iraq, there were negative examples of failure to adapt. The MoD's own study of the Iraq war identified that 'In comparison with the US, the UK military was complacent and slow in recognising and adapting to changed circumstances. It took us too long to update our thinking on how to counter the type of insurgency encountered in Iraq'.[20]

There was an ingrained assumption that UK force levels in Iraq would quickly reduce. Together with the increasing unpopularity of the war, this meant that too many in the MoD and the Army struggled to find enthusiasm for the Iraq war. This problem increased considerably once British troops in Helmand became engaged in heavy fighting. These factors seemed to inhibit some people and organizations in the Army and MoD from committing to success in Iraq, disincentivizing against changing organization, process or capability. There were people and organizations in the MoD who seemed to want to dodge the questions posed by the Learmont criterion.

British military adaptability was constrained by the MoD's not being on a war footing. Air Chief Marshal Stirrup, the CDS, was widely using the phrase 'we are in two wars and we have got to win them both'. Working in the MoD at the time I attended several meetings between 2006 and 2009 where this slogan was articulated by senior leaders present. But I never saw it make any difference to the MoD as a whole. The further away from the front line some parts of the Army and MoD were, the less likely they were to suggest or support adaptations or resources necessary for success in Iraq. In the first few years of the stabilization operation in Iraq, the Army itself sometimes displayed complacency. General Lord David Richards assessed that:

> Critics say that our long experience in Ulster made us complacent about tackling insurgency elsewhere, a case of 'we've done this in Northern Ireland, so we know what to expect and how to deal with it.' As a result of our experience in Ulster, we certainly had a feel for the requirement to keep people with us and work within a political environment.
>
> But I think in Iraq, for example, too many British officers would, without realizing what they were doing, slip into a Northern Ireland mind-set. Very early on that was an appropriate response when the efficient administration of law and order along the Northern Ireland pattern was required. But once things escalated, we needed to think in new and innovative ways, in order to deal with a complex and unique insurgency and the collapse of Iraqi society. That did happen, but maybe it took longer than it should have done.[21]

GENERATING THE FORCE

Most of the Army was not working in the MoD or Army HQ in Wiltshire, but were troops in brigades, battalions and regiments kept very busy both by conducting the baseline level of routine warfighting training, and in preparing for and recovering from operational tours in both theatres.

The Army was short of battalions and regiments. The 2004 reductions of Army manpower and infantry battalions had assumed that operations would not exceed the planning assumptions. When Robert Gates became US Defense Secretary in 2006, he directed a significant increase in the size of the US Army and Marine Corps. Even though the so called 'double medium' of both Iraq and Afghanistan was well outside the MoD planning assumptions that governed the size of the armed forces, similar action was not taken for the British forces. Some with long memories recalled that when in the late 1970s the size of the Northern Ireland commitment had exceeded planning assumptions, four additional infantry battalions' worth of capability had been provided. But in the mid-2000s no such action was taken.

The Army was also short of brigade and divisional HQs. So it took a small regional brigade HQ, the 52nd Brigade, and upgraded its organization and manpower to enable it to conduct a tour in Afghanistan. It also established a new brigade HQ, 11th Light Brigade, to command Task Force Helmand for a single tour.

With only two full divisional HQs to command in Iraq, the Army had been assisted by the Royal Marines, who twice deployed their amphibious force HQ to command in Basra. Commanded by a Marine major general, this helped share the load, but its small size meant that it needed considerable augmentation by the Army.

NATO's 2007 decision to upgrade Regional Command South from brigade to divisional level created more demand for divisional HQs. To meet this, the Army re-formed the HQ of the 6th Division. It would conduct two command tours in Kandahar, each lasting a year.

These temporary organizational measures helped, but only up to a point. Far too many troops were not only conducting operational tours with their units but were also joining other units for their deployments. Mobilizing Army reservists helped, but it was judged that the level of training for front-line operations in both theatres was too demanding for TA units. The exception was medical support. Sustaining the two field hospitals at Basra and Camp Bastion would have been impossible without mobilizing TA field hospitals and large numbers of individual medical specialists.

BRITISH AND US STRATEGIES DIVERGE

While the MoD was imperfectly supporting operations in Iraq and Afghanistan and the Army was struggling to generate the required forces, British commanders in Basra were still fighting the Shia militants. The few remaining British bases in Basra were often under increasing rocket, mortar and small arms attacks, resulting in significant casualties.

Convoys carrying supplies into the British bases in the city were almost continuously attacked.

One way to regain the initiative was to conduct strike operations against Shia fighters. These often became company- and battalion-level raids, in which the longer the operation went on, the greater the fighting. So armoured vehicles, particularly Warrior, were essential.

In its six-month deployment to Basra in 2006, 20th Armoured Brigade conducted almost 70 such raids, against cells of Shia fighters, their commanders and arms dumps, with the EFP roadside bombs being a priority. The British had refined their approach to such operations. Intelligence was collected and fused at Brigade HQ. Ideally, this would be from multiple sources, including national strategic intelligence. The target would be surrounded and forcibly entered. The troops doing this had been trained in tactics by the SAS.

Once it was clear where the British were striking, Shia fighters would move quickly to attack the troops. The geography of the city meant that once the British forces closed on their targets it was easy for the JAM to work out the limited number of British withdrawal routes, to ambush the British columns as they withdrew. These used small arms, RPGs and rapidly emplaced roadside bombs. Intense fire fights resulted.

OPERATION *SINBAD*

By now the British divisional HQ in Basra was from the 3rd (UK) Division commanded by Major General Richard Shirreff. He assessed that the British had lost the initiative in the city, writing that:

> there continues to be a belief that we are carrying out some form of Peace Support Operation and that the remedies that applied to Bosnia, apply equally to Iraq. This is not the case, and the way in which hard and soft effects are balanced in a theatre like Iraq needs to be vested in one person. In Iraq, there were several unco-ordinated agencies involved in the process, including the FCO, DFID and the PRT, there was no supremo; and the consequent effect was dissipated.[22]

The security situation limited freedom of movement for both Coalition forces and British officials, with the result that no momentum could be generated. The principal task was, therefore, to restore security and Shirreff assessed that this would require forces to be concentrated on Basra, and for reconstruction to be similarly concentrated so that consent could improve. Shirreff realized that he needed more forces, in spite of the ongoing troop withdrawals. He also required the support of the British development agency, but they would not support the concept of short-term economic effect because it was believed 'it would foster a dependency culture ... indeed they believed it to be counterproductive.'[23]

So Shirreff used whatever resources he could get. Significant UK reinforcements were unavailable. The division managed to secure $87 million of US Commander's Emergency Relief Programme money from HQ Multinational Force – Iraq in Baghdad.

Operation *Sinbad* would improve security in Basra area by area. A 48-hour security 'pulse' on a small sector of Basra would establish a secure environment, during which British troops would deliver immediate improvements. During a 28-day 'pause', a high level of Iraqi Army presence would be maintained in the area and effort would be focussed on improving the Iraqi Police.[24] Longer-term reconstruction projects were to be delivered by Iraqi contractors, employing local people to lay electrical distribution cables or water pipelines, or repair roads. The Iraqi Army would then depart, and the Iraqi Police would take over responsibility for the area.

Operation *Sinbad* achieved local tactical success, but there were not enough British troops to create enough military impact to significantly change the political situation. The lack of political support from newly appointed Prime Minister Nouri al-Maliki, who was unwilling to confront the Shia militias, coupled with Iraqi security forces that were infiltrated by militants and had insufficient numbers and confidence to hold areas that the British cleared, meant that the operation only achieved a transient effect. It did not change the Basra political dynamic.

Operation *Sinbad* also did little for US confidence in the British. The October 2016 *Daily Mail* interview with General Dannatt was picked up by international and US media, making its way to the screens of US officers in Baghdad. This also did nothing for UK/US military relations, as observed by Major General Simon Mayall, then deputy commander of Multinational Corps Iraq, led by US Army general Pete Chiarelli:

> My US colleagues demanded to know if we Brits were 'on or off the bus'. My calls to London and Basra made things no clearer. Matters later came to a head when Richard Shirreff and General Nick Houghton the Chief of Joint Operations came to Baghdad to give a brief on Operation *Sinbad* and included the role that the local Iraqi 10th Division were expected to play. It was patently clear that UK and US intentions were now diverging. Pete Chiarelli was tired and irritable.
>
> Before the briefing had even begun, he said 'This is how I see it. You want to go to Afghanistan and you're dressing up the situation in Basra to justify getting out. I see no evidence whatsoever that the 10th Iraqi Division will confront JAM.'[25]

On Christmas Day 2006, British troops conducted a raid on the notorious Jameat police station, where British SOF had been held hostage in 2005. The police there had continued their malign sectarian activity. British engineers rigged the building with explosives and demolished it. But the operation was opposed by Basra's provincial council who stopped contact with UK forces in protest.

The British were now at war with the JAM. Their few remaining bases in Basra were under increasing rocket, mortar and small arms attacks, resulting in significant casualties. Convoys carrying supplies into the British bases in the city were almost continuously attacked. The year saw fighting as intense as that anywhere else in Iraq and many UK casualties, both from the intense battles in Basra and from mortar and rocket attacks on British bases. At times considerable use was made of the full range of joint fires from mortars and artillery and air strikes. Protection was improved by the issue of new Osprey body armour.

Between November 2006 and May 2007 19th Light Brigade conducted almost 130 strike operations. Many of these were mounted against militia rocket and mortar teams. By now the British had Hermes 450 drones, increasing their surveillance capability. British rules of engagement were changed to allow 'hostile intent' to be targeted. Brigadier Tim Evans, the brigade commander, explained that 'there was a conscious decision to strike early, disrupt the enemy, exploit any intelligence leads and create opportunities in order to ensure that the militia could not gain the upper hand.'[26]

Intelligence-led precision urban strike and detention operations played an important role in sustaining morale and in detaining suspects for protection. These could be very demanding. For example, a typical 2007 raid into Basra required a company at the target area and the rest of a battalion to get the force to and from its objectives: a total force of three armoured infantry companies in Warrior vehicles and a squadron of tanks. One such operation encountered 14 roadside bombs along a 4 km stretch of road alone. Vehicle columns were in almost continuous firefights.

An example of the fighting around a British convoy in Basra is described by Corporal Smith of 4th Battalion, the Rifles, based in Basra Palace at the height of the fighting. It was June 2007, his first day of a six-month tour.

After a long and hot wait in the small base we rolled out into the busy streets of Basra. Almost immediately we came under small arms fire from a very well-sited ambush. A civilian fuel tanker driver was killed, and a large crowd began to develop around the tanker which was almost immediately set alight. We broke contact and continued to the Palace but a second civilian vehicle in the convoy, a low loader, collapsed on the bridge at Red 10 – it had been badly shot up in the ambush. Also, in the initial ambush Corporal Jex Brookes the other section commander in my platoon had been hit by small arms.

The task for the rest of the small convoy was to evacuate him back to Basra Palace. My Bulldog and our lead element of Warriors were tasked with the protection of the low loader. This was my first major contact! We were now fixed by the low loader – we had to protect – all we could do was hard target the Bulldog like a dismounted Rifleman. This is where our driver Rifleman McColl really came into his own, moving us about without any command so we, the top cover and Scotty [the gunner] could concentrate on our arcs.

I was positioned with my head and shoulders out of the mortar hatches using the Bulldog as a firing platform. I was observing my arcs when I noticed the streets were emptying and the vehicle traffic decreased – an attack was imminent. I was relaying this to Scotty, when the first mortar rounds landed. They resulted in civilian casualties; I had never expected to take indirect fire on the city streets. For the next few hours, we fought a 360-degree battle to protect the disabled low loader.

I found it really hard to locate the enemy. This was a city street with corners, walls, cars, windows and rooftops. Added to that the smoke, crack and thump of small arms, RPGs and rounds banging off your vehicle all confused the situation.

We were engaging targets from as close as 25 metres away and up to 100 metres away, snap shooting and rapid fire popping up and down like jacks-in-the-box, although there was not much Scotty could do about hard targeting, waist up in his cupola as he was. I don't think we ever won the firefight; once one position was suppressed another would engage from a new or previous position. To combat this, we started to fire into likely enemy and previous positions as warning shots. The situation was getting worse. We were now taking fire from an Iraqi Police Station, which we were using as cover. Our driver 'Mac' was now showing signs of stress. He'd already fired all his pistol ammo and was shouting over the speakers that we needed to get out of here. I don't blame 'Mac' for 'stressing out'. He was on his own in his hatch, isolated from the rest of us, gunfire all around him so I pushed through to his hatch and gave him a shake and told him to just drive. Immediately he snapped out of it.

We finally got back to the Palace after more than 11 hours on the ground. The low loader was eventually denied to the enemy by Warrior 30mm fire. As we were extracting the Bulldog commanded by my platoon commander was hit by an IED, forcing another recovery. It had been an extraordinary first day in Basra. Men killed, other serious casualties, vehicles destroyed and recovered and a real test for troops on the ground.[27]

After Operation *Sinbad*, MoD officials in London argued that Basra's Shia majority made the city different from the rest of the country, and that previous efforts to stabilize it had failed to change its political dynamic. They assessed that the conflict in Basra was Shia internal competition for power and influence, rather than an insurgency against the Iraqi state. The British felt that, as they were losing legitimacy in Basra, it was now up to the Iraqi government and security forces to take the lead. As the UK had agreed to build up forces in Afghanistan, at US request, no British reinforcement of Basra was possible. Instead, troop levels would continue to reduce in Iraq to reinforce their contingent in Afghanistan, who were fighting unexpectedly bloody and difficult battles.

In early 2007 US strategy changed. It surged additional forces into Iraq to confront the insurgents. This did not increase optimism or strategic confidence in London. As UK public support for the war was decreasing with every casualty, the British declined to match the US Surge. Although evidence of the success of the Surge was reported by senior British officers in Baghdad, it seems that the UK Chiefs of Staff and the British government probably considered that the Surge would fail.

So UK and US strategic, operational and tactical approaches diverged. The British could no longer militarily 'win' in Basra. The best that could be hoped for in Basra was building up the Iraqi forces' capability and encouraging Iraqi political leaders to tackle the Shia militants. Within the MoD and army this outcome was given a sporting nickname: 'score draw'.[28]

AFGHANISTAN IN 2007

In early 2007 HQ ARRC left Afghanistan. For the rest of the campaign, US officers would command the theatre of operations. ISAF became a US-led multinational HQ. Through 2007 to 2009, ISAF continued to follow the outlines of the ARRC campaign plan. ISAF and the Afghan forces achieved some stability in Kabul and in northern and western

Afghanistan. But in southern Afghanistan, force levels were insufficient to regain the initiative over the Taliban.

MOWING THE LAWN

In Helmand, repeated British offensive operations were mounted. These greatly relied on firepower to make up for the lack of troops on the ground, creating civilian casualties and collateral damage. These operations usually cleared insurgents from the targeted areas, but there were insufficient troops to hold the area for any length of time. Sooner or later the British and Afghan forces had to withdraw, exposing to Taliban retaliation any Afghan civilians who had supported the Afghan government. Commanders called this approach 'mowing the lawn'.

As the British troop levels in Iraq slowly reduced, troop numbers in Afghanistan slowly increased, as did awareness of new counterinsurgency doctrine being used by US forces. Despite the lack of up-to-date British doctrine for this, the British sought to apply the new US COIN concept of 'clear, build and hold', by clearing insurgents from an area, holding it with sufficient security forces and then improving the local economy, security and governance to embed popular support for government control.

But the very gradual rate of increase in size of both Task Force Helmand and the Afghan security forces meant that the additional capacity to hold newly cleared terrain grew very slowly. This not only applied to the infantry and cavalry units needed on the ground, but also to the essential combat support and logistics, including EOD specialists, electronic warfare, intelligence analysts and helicopters.

The resource constraints imposed by fighting two wars with a single pool of forces and insufficient specialized capabilities applied with equal force to the US contingent in Afghanistan. But an important difference in the way both countries conducted both wars persisted: the different length of operational tours. As in Iraq, British brigades rotated through Helmand on six-month deployments. Some of the civilians in the PRTs were on longer tours, but with this came more frequent leave breaks. Only a few officers were on longer tours. As in Iraq, this reduced continuity and corporate knowledge.

In autumn 2006, the Royal Marines' 3 Commando Brigade replaced the exhausted 16 Air Assault Brigade. The Marines brought a larger force, including a unit dedicated to mentoring the Afghan Army. They also brought a group of Viking lightly protected amphibious armoured vehicles. These were used alongside armed Land Rovers as the basis of Manoeuvre Outreach Groups (MOGs), which manoeuvred through the desert to raid Taliban-controlled areas.

As the brigade arrived, local elders and the governor of Helmand negotiated additional ceasefires in Sangin and Now Zad. Both deals later collapsed, requiring a brigade operation to restore a measure of security. The brigade sent MOGs into the desert to attack Taliban positions on the edges of the lush irrigated 'Green Zone' around the Helmand River. Once the Taliban reacted to these British manoeuvres, they fought back, allowing the brigade's attack helicopters, artillery and full weight of air support to be to be applied. This approach was nicknamed 'advance to ambush'.

From April 2007 the third British brigade in Helmand, 12th Mechanized Brigade, benefited from the heavily protected Mastiff vehicle. But it would not be until after the 2009 end of the British mission in Iraq that Task Force Helmand had enough of these vehicles.

The brigade now had three infantry battalions, and a reconnaissance regiment mounted in Scimitar lightly armed reconnaissance vehicles. The Scimitars were extremely useful. With their 30mm cannon these would often be used by the British as light tanks. Not only were their weapons extremely effective, but their small size and relatively low weight meant that they could easily move along the narrow roads and tracks of the Green Zone. But their low level of armour made them very vulnerable to RPGs, land mines (of which there were many left from previous conflicts) and roadside bombs.

The brigade sought to secure Lashkar Gar, the provincial capital, with an array of surrounding company bases. The infantry spent much time patrolling in depth or attacking Taliban concentrations. Fighting could often be heavy. For example, soldiers from one of the brigade's battalions, the 1st Battalion the Royal Anglian Regiment, sometimes had to fix bayonets as they fought the Taliban at close quarters. By the end of its six-month tour the battalion had used over 20,000 mortar and artillery rounds. Death, wounds, illness and injuries reduced the battalion's strength by 20 per cent.

Despite this attrition, the overall British force level in Helmand rose, as had the number of British outposts. Holding the network of bases and cleared terrain in Helmand depended not only on the British troops, but also on the Afghan security forces. For most of the British responsibility for Helmand, they partnered with 3rd Brigade of the 215th Corps of the Afghan Army. This was organized along similar lines to a NATO infantry brigade with three *kandaks*, equivalent to light infantry battalions. Each of these had four *tolays*, equivalent to companies. A fourth *kandak* provided combat support: engineers, artillery, reconnaissance and counter-IED *tolays*.

The British developed a plan for growing the size and capabilities of the Afghan Army in Helmand. They constructed a base, Camp Shorabak, next to their main base at Camp Bastion and helped the Afghans set up a training unit there. To Helmand's Afghan Army brigade was attached an operational mentoring and liaison team (OMLT) – based on a British infantry battalion with the commanding officer responsible for mentoring and advising the brigade commander and infantry companies providing mentoring teams to Afghan battalions and companies.

The Afghan way of war was very different to the British Army's. Afghan troops were often very aggressive but usually disregarded planning and logistic preparation. But they valued the embedded British teams for the artillery and airborne firepower that they could summon, as well as their ability to bring in helicopters to evacuate casualties and bodies of dead Afghan soldiers. For example, in 2007 the OMLT was provided by the Grenadier Guards, operating in Land Rovers with little protection. Guardsmen and officers found this an extraordinary adventure.[29]

In Helmand the Afghan Police were often part of the problem, being corrupt and displaying predatory behaviour such as shaking down civilians for bribes at checkpoints and abducting and sexually abusing boys. In response, a police mentoring operation was established by 2010, as was a British-sponsored Helmand police training centre.

But increasing numbers of Afghan civilians were being killed. This increasingly irritated President Karzai, not only because of the political damage it did to him, but also because he had no authority over ISAF. For example, in late June 2007, an air strike on a village near Gereshk killed 25 civilians. Karzai bitterly criticized ISAF in public. Less than a week later another air attack killed at least 25 civilians in Helmand. These strikes were not conducted by NATO, but by US special forces as part of Operation *Enduring Freedom*.

BASRA 2007 – THE WAR AGAINST THE JAM AND THE ACCOMMODATION

The gap between US and British strategies further increased from June 2007 when Prime Minister Blair was replaced by Gordon Brown. Brown thought that 'we should end our four-year military presence in Iraq. Privately, I thought we should do so and set myself the task of leaving by the end of 2008.'[30] These views were kept from the public and media. Defence officials were horrified by Brown's idea, feeling it would have a disastrous effect on UK/US strategic relations, possibly imperilling other defence, security and intelligence co-operation, greatly damaging the so-called 'special relationship' over intelligence and defence that Britain had with the US. Within the MoD this was nicknamed the 'Love Actually' strategy, after a comedy film in which the British Prime Minister publicly criticizes a lecherous American president.

At a meeting between Brown and President Bush in 2007, Bush asked Brown to raise British troops levels. Brown declined; he was persuaded not to immediately withdraw British troops, but told Bush that British troops would leave by the end of 2008: 'I was not willing to see an endless British occupation, and I was clear that while we would not leave until security was improved, our deployments would have to be made in the British interest. Our plan was to scale down and withdraw.'[31]

But as Chancellor, Brown had been hostile to defence spending. His series of cuts to the defence budget made over the previous decade had gravely damaged his relationship with the senior military leadership. Few, if any, officials in the MoD displayed any confidence in him. Brown visibly struggled to reconcile supporting US strategy with a meaningful British military contribution and a British public, media and parliamentary opposition increasingly unsupportive of both of Britain's wars.

In 2007, the British planned to withdraw from the few remaining outposts in Basra to a single remaining base at Basra airport. This was to allow further British force reductions in Iraq, so as to enable increases in British forces in Afghanistan. The CDS, Air Chief Marshal Sir Jock Stirrup, stated that:

> we needed to break the political logjam. We needed to change the dynamic. Clearly, though, the fact that we had people sitting at locations in Basra City being rocketed and mortared, the fact that we were having to run resupply convoys to those locations that were being attacked and on which we were suffering casualties, and, politically, our forces were not being allowed to do the job for which we were in the city, that's not a sustainable position.

It is a sad fact that on military operations one sustains casualties. That's the nature of the business. But those casualties must be producing something of strategic benefit if they are to be justifiable, and they certainly weren't in the case of Basra City. But the principal rationale was actually to find a way forward politically in Basra.[32]

The continuing reductions in the size of British forces in Iraq meant that they increasingly lacked the strength to eject Shia militias from Basra. And many of the scarce intelligence and surveillance capabilities that had been used in or over Basra were being redeployed to Afghanistan. So as the year went on, the British understanding of events in Basra reduced, as did their ability to influence events in the city.

The new British commander, Major General Jonathan Shaw, thought it worth attempting to find an interlocutor with whom the British might be able to negotiate. Shaw discovered that Ahmed al-Fatusi had considerable influence over the Basra JAM. Fatusi was incarcerated in the British detention centre in Basra, having been arrested in 2005 by British troops. Shaw began negotiating with him.

These led to an 'accommodation' between the British and the JAM. The militants would cease attacks on the British, while the British would suspend their strike operations against the JAM and progressively release 120 internees, including, at the end of the process, Fatusi himself. There appears to have been an understanding that UK forces, once redeployed outside the city, would have little reason routinely to return to Basra; security within the city would be provided by the Iraqi security forces. It was hoped that this would encourage more responsible JAM elements to move towards legitimate politics and against Iranian influence.

As well as releasing prisoners, the British sought to reduce friction with the militia. They largely stayed out of Basra City and convoy movement through Basra was notified in advance to the militia. Immediately mortar and rocket attacks fell to minimal levels. Total attacks on UK forces reduced by 90 per cent. The rest of 2007 saw no further UK deaths from mortar or rocket attacks. The British transferred Basra Palace to the Iraqi forces and relocated to their remaining base at Basra airport without a shot being fired.

The British then changed their priorities from force protection to training the Iraqi Army. With indirect fire attacks greatly reduced, redevelopment work at the airport resumed, and local politicians were content to resume their visits to the British base to engage with British consular staff. With British forces no longer in the city, the people of Basra were less likely to be caught up in any crossfire.

But the Iraqi Army lacked the confidence, capability and political support to face down the militias. And the Basra police were infiltrated and intimidated by the militia. An unintended consequence of the accommodation was to consolidate the Shia militia takeover of the city. A hard-line Islamist regime was imposed. Corruption and organized crime flourished. Militia depredations ranged from widespread female dress restrictions, through the forced closure of alcohol and music shops, to brutality and murder. Basra police chief Major General Jalil later claimed that in the last three months of December, 40 women were killed in Basra for wearing make-up, not veiling, or otherwise failing to observe the narrow rulings of the hard-line local militias. British withdrawal had removed the one remaining constraint on the militias.

The British underestimated the importance of Basra as a source of revenue and arms for JAM in Iraq. For example, many of the roadside bombs and rockets used against Coalition forces in Baghdad had either been smuggled through Basra and Maysan provinces or purchased with funds raised in Basra.

The US had orchestrated a re-engagement with the Iraqi people by surging US troops into contested areas in partnership with the Iraqi security forces; while the British disengaged from the Iraqi people. As the British sector was an economy of force mission of lower priority than Baghdad this was reluctantly accepted by General Petraeus. There was a lack of appetite in Baghdad for a military confrontation with the Shia militias until the Sunni/Al Qaida insurgency had been defeated. US commanders and officials were scarred by the experience of 2004 when they had to simultaneously confront Shia uprisings and the Sunni and Al Qaida insurgencies.

But as far as the British government was concerned, the Transition Strategy still applied. In October 2007 it announced further force reductions, from 5,000 to approximately 2,500 by spring 2008. Provincial Iraqi Control of Basra Province was declared in December 2007 and British forces assumed operational overwatch.

BRITISH STRATEGIC LEADERSHIP OF THE WARS

Many Army officers, including its senior leaders, saw the MoD's strategic leadership of both wars as consistently inadequate. For example, between 2005 and 2012 the two MoD permanent secretaries came from other departments. They both sometimes appeared overfaced by the size of the MoD, its complexity and its challenges.[33] Geoff Hoon served as Defence Secretary for six years, just two weeks short of the term served by Denis Healey.

After Hoon's departure in 2005 and 2009 there were four defence secretaries in three years: John Reid; Des Browne, who was also minister for Scotland; John Hutton; and Bob Ainsworth. In a time when the US had two defence secretaries, Donald Rumsfeld and Robert Gates, the UK had five.

Reid and Ainsworth had both served as ministers of state for the armed forces, but it often seemed that Browne was not on top of his brief, particularly on Iraq and the Army. The Iraq Inquiry assessed that he displayed optimism bias.

> Throughout the UK's engagement in Iraq there was a tendency to focus on the most positive interpretation of events. One manifestation of that was failure to give weight to the candid analysis that was regularly supplied by the Joint Intelligence Committee, by some commanders in theatre, and by others that things were going wrong. The default position was to judge that negative events were isolated incidents rather than potential evidence of a trend which should be monitored and which might require a policy response. This meant that underlying causes were not always investigated and brought to light …

One of the most senior individuals displaying this tendency was Mr Des Browne, who held the post of Secretary of State for Defence from May 2006 to October 2008. Mr Browne repeatedly downplayed the negative aspects of the situation in Iraq and failed to ensure the dissemination of a full and unvarnished version of the truth on the ground in Iraq; and that the UK's policy was assessed and reviewed with due rigour based on that information. Mr Browne should himself have proposed a reappraisal of the UK's posture and tactics in Basra in 2007, on the basis of the evidence available to him. In four instances, Mr Browne gave an unbalanced account of the situation in Basra to the Prime Minister, Cabinet or Parliament:

- On 11 January 2007, Mr Browne presented Op SINBAD and the US surge to DOP(I) as being 'entirely consistent', which did not give a full picture of the substantial differences between UK and US strategy.
- Mr Browne briefed a meeting of Cabinet on 25 January 2007 that there was no disagreement between the US and UK on force levels in MND(SE), downplaying the concerns being raised by senior members of the US Administration. Mr Browne also painted an extremely positive picture of conditions in Basra, when other contemporary accounts provided a different view.
- From 28 to 31 January 2007, Mr Browne visited Iraq. After returning to the UK, he continued to stress to DOP the positive effect of Op SINBAD. Mr Browne's reassuring report did not take into account: the strength of US objections to the UK's approach; the serious risk that the UK would have responsibility without control in Basra, which was driving consideration of a continued UK presence in Basra Palace; or evidence of the dangerous situation faced by ordinary Basrawis.
- On 1 April 2008, Mr Browne gave a positive account of the reduction of corruption in the Basra police to Parliament. This painted a significantly more positive picture than contemporary reporting from those on the ground in Basra.[34]

It is probably wrong to simply blame Browne for this. In retrospect, the MoD itself sometimes displayed institutional optimism bias during this period. An over-complex structure and inflexibility in MoD decision-making added friction and delay in identifying and delivering urgent capability enhancements for Iraq and the early part of the Afghanistan operation. The Iraq Inquiry was very critical of procurement of equipment for stabilizing Iraq, including a lack of urgency and unclear accountability.[35] It assessed that delays in fielding improved surveillance, helicopter and protected patrol vehicle capabilities resulted in avoidable casualties in Iraq and Afghanistan. There is also evidence of institutional skill-fade of capabilities developed in Northern Ireland, such as counter-IED. These took too long to regenerate.

AFGHANISTAN IN 2008

Arriving in November 2007, 52nd Infantry Brigade was the first brigade to direct units to remain in the same area of operations during their tour. This had been standard practice for most of the British campaigns in Northern Ireland, the Balkans and Iraq, but since 2006, the brigades rotating through Helmand had moved battalions and companies around as required. It was only after 18 months in Helmand that the British had sufficient troops and command interest in continuity to apply the new approach.

The brigade commander, Andrew Mackay, had been greatly influenced by the new US counterinsurgency doctrine. Copies had been widely circulated around the British Army. The brigade found that within the MoD and Joint HQ there was very little understanding of the social dynamics of Helmand – its districts, towns and tribes. The brigade had to turn elsewhere to understand the province's human terrain. Assisted by the UK Defence Academy it developed a more detailed picture of the population of Helmand.

MacKay sought to reduce Taliban influence by physically ejecting them from the town of Musa Qala, which the insurgents had controlled since the 2006 ceasefire deal with the British collapsed. After encircling the town with British troops, a battalion of US paratroops landed by helicopter outside the town. With overwhelming air support, the Taliban were pushed out. The brigade then escorted Afghan troops into the town. British forces were positioned out of view and the Afghan troops were filmed and photographed raising the Afghan flag, to give the Afghan and international media the impression that the Afghan forces had played the leading role in the recapture of the town.

The British allocated £3 million for reconstruction. A new district governor was installed. He was a former Taliban leader who had changed sides. Initially, he made progress. But as time went on, he quarrelled with the district police chief, a member of a rival tribe. And his personal militia engaged in increasingly predatory behaviour towards local Afghans.

This demonstrated the way that wealth, land and power were channelled through family, tribal and criminal structures that often co-opted the flimsy government power structures at provincial and district levels. What appeared on paper to be a mechanism to national, provincial and local government was in practice more like local governance in Europe during feudal times. Musa Qala, like much of Helmand, was a perfect storm of Taliban resistance that fed off local grievances, reinforced by civilian casualties and collateral damage caused by the fighting.

In Helmand, a scheme to persuade a Taliban group to change sides and act as part of the Gereshk police succeeded, and the former Taliban were allocated a sector to patrol, the British finding them more professional than the Afghan Police. Michael Semple, an Irish expert on Afghanistan working for the EU, had used contacts with Taliban to persuade a group of insurgents to change sides. He had also persuaded several Taliban armed groups not to oppose the capture of Musa Qala, with a view to their subsequent reintegration being supported by the British.

These initiatives had been approved by the Helmand governor and by the Afghan security authorities in Kabul. But the Helmand governor Wafa then had Semple arrested, persuading President Karzai to expel him from Afghanistan. The governor had been told about Semple's work, as had many of Karzai's officials, but it appeared that none of them had shared this with the president. It may be that when Wafa realized the considerable sums of money involved did not include a percentage for him, he acted to double cross Semple.

Local attitudes were conditioned by a widespread belief that the British intended to eradicate poppy production. This was reinforced by US-funded efforts to eradicate poppy-growing in Helmand, all of which seemed to work in isolation from each other. Taliban attacks in Helmand increased in frequency and effectiveness. The Danish deployed Leopard tanks to reinforce their battalion in the British brigade. Many British troops were surprised that the Army did not do the same.

Across Helmand, the Taliban retained considerable freedom of movement outside areas that were controlled by ISAF. In these places there was an insurgent 'shadow government'. The evidence suggests that in many areas it was no more effective than Afghan local government; often it was worse. But unlike in many government-controlled areas it had an effective judicial system. This provided a harsh but effective way to resolve local disputes, particularly over land and water.[36]

The Taliban had learned lessons from their earlier battles, seeking to make more effective use of their weapons. Despite these improvements, whenever the Taliban stood and fought for more than a quarter of an hour, NATO would add extra firepower – mortars, artillery, attack helicopters and fighter bombers. Although the insurgents sometimes ambushed low-flying helicopters with machine guns and RPGs, they were never able to seriously contest NATO's control of the air. This gave ISAF the ability to use manned and unmanned aircraft for intelligence gathering, attack missions and to move troops and supplies around Afghanistan.[37]

As a result, the Taliban made increasing use of IEDs to attack NATO troops and vehicles. As NATO fielded increasingly well-protected vehicles, the size of Taliban roadside bombs increased, often producing devices of between 400 and 1,600 pounds in weight.

THE BRITISH BECOME INCREASINGLY STRETCHED IN HELMAND PROVINCE

From March 2008 until March 2009, the first two British brigades to serve in Helmand returned: 16 Air Assault Brigade and 3 Commando Brigade. With the reduction of British troops in Iraq, both brigades, which previously had deployed little more than a battalion's worth of infantry, now had a Danish battalion and five British battalions, one of which provided the OMLT as well as a company of Estonian infantry. The Estonian contingent had no national restrictions on their employment. Tallinn wanted to demonstrate the country's utility to NATO. The British received ever-increasing numbers of the heavily armoured Mastiff patrol vehicle as well as a brigade-level drone capability, the Hermes 450.

The British now embraced General Petraeus' exhortations that the main effort of countering insurgency should be protecting the people and that this required the basing of troops in the midst of their areas of operations. So much of the additional British infantry was now distributed across the irrigated areas of the Helmand River Valley in static bases. This reduced spare combat power available to be used in a more mobile role.

The British could not be everywhere. In the south of Helmand, they had no forces south of Garmser. There was evidence that newly trained Taliban would hone their combat skills by attacking the British base there.

In April 2008 the area south of Garmser was cleared by a US Marine infantry battalion with its own combat support and aviation wing. A tough battle resulted, the Taliban fighting from well-prepared bunkers that often resisted all firepower but a direct hit from a precision bomb. Marines were often on the receiving end of volleys of RPG rockets. Those Taliban that stood and fought were killed or captured. After several weeks of fighting the Taliban abandoned Garmser, which was then held by British and Afghan forces.

In October 2008 the Taliban planned to mount a surprise attack on Lashkar Gar, the Helmand provincial capital. This was discovered at almost the last minute by the NDS, just as about 400 Taliban fighters began advancing to capture the town. This was quickly confirmed by intercepted Taliban communications suggesting that they planned to attack the governor's compound and storm the prison to release jailed comrades. Mortars and rockets struck the town.

As drones and Apache helicopters were scrambled, they detected a group of Taliban advancing 'in a disciplined fashion'. As staff officers left their desks to defend the brigade HQ, Afghan police were attacked by a company-sized group of Taliban. Throughout the night Taliban were attacked by Apache helicopters, breaking off the attack only at 0400hrs. Hermes 450 drones were used to follow some back to their homes – yielding invaluable intelligence.

The British now realized there were more Taliban in central Helmand than they had assessed. They decided to clear part of the Nad-e Ali district. A battlegroup of Royal Marines, Estonian and Danish mechanized infantry and a troop of Danish Leopard tanks was given the mission to secure three walled villages, called *kalays* by the Afghans. To achieve it took 18 days of hard fighting in agricultural terrain crossed by ditches.

During the initial British attacks, the Taliban had laid relatively few IEDs. But as the British troops moved into static patrol bases the Taliban were able to plant IEDs in large numbers, ringing the bases with the bombs and restricting, complicating and slowing down British movement as well as causing almost two-thirds of British casualties. By early 2009, there had been a 40 per cent increase in IEDS detected by the British in Helmand.

In 2006 there had been considerable friction between the British brigade and the civilian-led PRT. Integration with brigade HQ was improved by an uplift of the number of civilians and by co-locating the organizations next door to each other in the same compound at Lashkar Gar, the provincial capital, with some of the military planners and the deputy brigade commander working within the PRT. It was also decided to deploy civilian stabilization advisors forward, to co-locate with the HQs of the battalions. These would be assisted by military stabilization support teams, soldiers assigned to the role, who could deploy into more dangerous environments than civilians, to act as their eyes and ears. Over the next two years the PRT became increasingly capable and integration with the military steadily improved.[38]

But for all their hard fighting, increasing commitment of resources and improving integration of the Army and PRT, the British were making only slow progress in clearing the Taliban from Helmand. Although Afghanistan had been sold to the British public as a 'necessary war', resulting heavy fighting and ever-increasing British casualties had come as another shock to the British government and people. The contentious character of the Iraq war, especially the prevailing sense that Prime Minister Blair and his spin doctors had greatly exaggerated the threat of Iraqi weapons of mass destruction, was reinforced by Iraq's apparent descent into intractable chaos. This contaminated British media and public attitudes to the fighting in Afghanistan.

MOVING TO A 'CAMPAIGN FOOTING' – OPERATION *ENTIRETY*

In the later years of the Iraq and Afghan wars senior British officers often claimed that the British Army had 'transformed in contact'. This was partly true; for example, the fielding of new equipment resulted in considerable improvements in capability. In Iraq and Afghanistan there was much tactical adaptation and learning by British troops in contact with the enemy. And there was a revolution in British battlefield medicine. But the evidence suggests that for every positive example of British military adaptation, there as many examples of failures to adapt. By the later stages of both wars the middle and senior management of the Army shared a general sense of 'we could and should have done better'. And there was much evidence that in both wars US forces often learned and adapted faster than the British did.

Some, but not all, parts of Defence developed the necessary sense of urgency and priority. If the MoD had been displaying sufficient urgency and had energized itself to providing enough support fast enough to the Army, Operation *Entirety* could well have been unnecessary.

Some parts of the British Army tried hard not to bend themselves out of shape. For example, retaining the previous campaign's default setting for individual operational tours at six months may have enhanced resilience, but it led to sub-optimal campaign continuity. Adaptation was sometimes inhibited by the MoD's centralized management of many important areas of the Army's capability. These included setting and funding equipment requirements, commanding the Iraqi campaign and managing the UK media.

But there were many areas where the Army could make its own decisions for itself. These included its structures, training, personnel policy and allocation of responsibilities. Like some parts of the MoD, not all the Army treated the Iraq and Afghan wars with the urgency they deserved. Even allowing for the unpopularity of the wars and time-consuming inflexibility and centralization imposed by the MoD, between 2003 and 2008 the British Army could have been more flexible and agile.

In 2008, the new Commander in Chief Land Command, General Sir David Richards, felt that the Army was not doing enough fast enough to make the Afghan campaign succeed. So with the agreement of General Dannatt and the Army Board, Richards placed the Army on a 'campaign footing'. Operation *Entirety* made Afghanistan the Army's main effort. This had significant impact on equipment, training and doctrine, leading to capability improvements in, for example, surveillance, counter-IED and medical support as well as mission preparation.

Activity that did not directly or indirectly contribute to success in Afghanistan was de-prioritized. Career courses were adjusted to train students in skills required in Afghanistan. For example, a new battlegroup planning course for young officers culminated with the students planning a battlegroup attack in Helmand. With only a finite number of days in a year, Operation *Entirety* meant that whilst training for Afghanistan increased, training for conventional warfighting decreased. For example, the resources and time that might have been applied to training brigades for warfighting were instead applied to the brigade mission rehearsal exercises.

BASRA IN 2008–09 – PUSH COMES TO SHOVE

The 'accommodation' initially ended attacks on the Basra airport. But once Fatusi was released from detention in December 2007 the JAM gradually restarted attacking the British, who now lacked leverage over the militia. They could have applied coercion by resuming strike operations. But the withdrawal of British troops from the city had greatly reduced situational awareness. London insisted that the Army stuck to their side of the deal, even as the JAM steadily abandoned their side.

Mortar and rocket attacks on the remaining British base at Basra airport increased. For example, on 31 January 92 rockets were fired at the base. The defences of the airport had already been increased. Improvised concrete shelters – designated Operation *Stonehenge* – survived rocket strikes. Warning radars were deployed, as were Phalanx guns. Originally procured by the Royal Navy for shooting down anti-ship missiles, these and the radars were integrated into a defence system to detect and destroy incoming mortars and rockets.

A battery of AS90 155mm howitzers was deployed to conduct counter-battery fire, but they were constrained because many of the firing points were in or close to urban areas. In conditions of great secrecy, the British rushed into service an Israeli missile: Spike NLOS. With NLOS standing for 'non-line of sight', this was an anti-tank missile with an optical sensor in the nose, allowing an operator to fly the missile to the target. Named Exactor, what use the British made of this new weapon in Iraq is unclear.

Unable to take the fight to the enemy, many troops felt intensely frustrated. Popular support for the war was draining away. This factor and the rain of rockets onto the British base unsurprisingly acted to depress morale. BBC reporter Caroline Wyatt noted that:

Every single death was one too many, as it was a war that by then very few people supported. It was very hard for the soldiers, sailors and airmen who contributed to that campaign to come back to the UK and to feel that people didn't understand what they were doing. Some troops did feel the deal and withdrawal from Basra Palace was humiliating. With troops confined to Basra air base with nothing to do and being shelled was frustrating and depressing. And they saw Afghanistan as real soldiering and real fighting. The UK people developed huge mistrust of politicians, because the public felt they had been lied to about reasons for war.[39]

The British continued to train Iraqi Army units outside the city. Together with the local Iraqi commander, General Mohan, they developed a plan for an Iraqi Army operation to clear Basra. Once Iraqi troops were sufficiently trained there would be an information operation that would seek to sow the seeds of doubt in the militia's mind as to whether they would be able to resist the Iraqi Army for ever. This would be combined with a six-week long weapons amnesty and hand back programme. Finally, there would be Iraqi Army operations against any non-compliant militia. The earliest that the operation could be mounted would be summer 2008.

The plan was briefed to US commanders in Baghdad. They agreed the concept of operations but wanted to complete their campaign to counter Al Qaida in Mosul and northern Iraq, before turning to Basra. General Petraeus and the Iraqi National Security Adviser briefed the plan to Prime Minister Maliki on 22 March. At the end of the meeting Maliki surprised Petraeus and the British by announcing that he had his own plan to clear the militia out of Basra. An Iraqi force would deploy to Basra the next day and Maliki would go there the day after.

OPERATION *CHARGE OF THE KNIGHTS*

The Iraqis named the operation *Charge of the Knights*. Despite the inspiring title, it initially lacked planning and co-ordination. It began on 25 March when a brigade of the Iraqi Army's 14th Division attacked into Basra. The formation was only partially trained. It was defeated by the militia, with most soldiers deserting. The militias struck back by raining mortars and rockets on Basra Palace, the Iraqi HQ for the operation, and attacked Iraqi Army bases in Basra, overrunning many of the installations.

The remnants of the Iraqi 14th Division were reinforced by another Iraqi divisional HQ, two additional brigades and a National Police brigade, all with their attached US mentoring teams. None of these formations had had any prior notice of the operation, arriving in Basra without informing the British and deploying straight into action. Iraqi logistic planning was conspicuous by its absence, Iraqi units arriving short of water, fuel, rations and ammunition. British logistics units helped overcome the logistic challenge, but the battle quickly posed serious tactical and reputational challenges to the British.

The British tried to influence General Mohan's conduct of the operation, but there was no doubt that it was Prime Minister Maliki who was directing operations personally from Basra Palace. An immediate point of friction were Iraqi forces' calls for artillery, helicopter and air attacks on militia positions. Fire requests would be initiated on a mobile telephone and then had to pass through several nodes, before guns or aircraft could even begin to acquire the target location. Often, by the time fire was authorized, the moment had passed, or the target had moved. In addition, many of the Iraqi requests for fire were vague

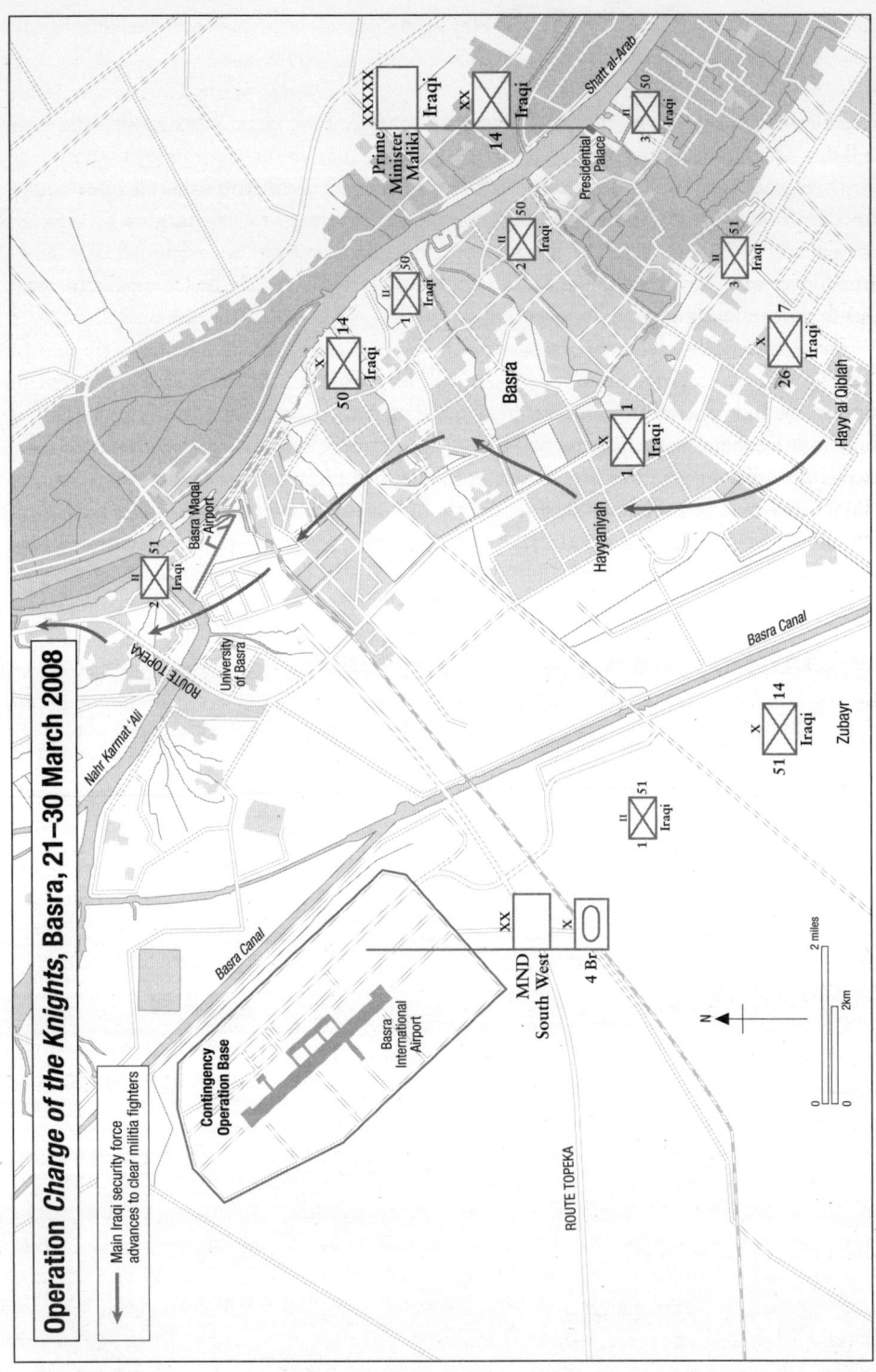

Operation *Charge of the Knights*, Basra, 21–30 March 2008

→ Main Iraqi security force advances to clear militia fighters

exhortations to attack Basra neighbourhoods, rather than specific observed targets – well outside UK and Coalition rules of engagement.

The British could not attack the targets being requested by the Iraqi forces. They had no mentoring teams deployed with Iraqi troops. There were no British attack helicopters in Basra, and all the British drones were unarmed.

There were bitter Iraqi accusations that the British were neither willing nor able to help the Iraqi troops. The start of the operation had exposed the British lack of situational awareness and resources to take the fight to the militias. Iraqis and Americans doubted the British commitment to the fight. Britain's military reputation with the US and Iraqis was rapidly and seriously dented.

The British major general commanding in Basra was away on leave. In his place was Brigadier Julian Free, commander of 4th Mechanized Brigade. Free's initial efforts to support the Iraqi operation were rebuffed by Maliki. But Petraeus designated the operation the Coalition main effort. The new US corps HQ, from XVIII (US) Airborne Corps, sent its tactical operations centre, led by the corps deputy commanding general, US Marine Major General Flynn. Flynn explained to the British that they had not had the necessary situational awareness to prevent a crisis. He and the corps HQ had come to Basra to ensure that the operation did not fail.

The US rapidly surged fighters, armed Predator drones and Apache helicopter gunships to Basra. The Iraqi formations reinforcing Basra had come with their embedded US mentoring teams, including tactical air control parties. Moving and fighting alongside the Iraqis, these were quickly able to observe, identify and engage targets by speaking directly to the attack helicopters and jets flying over Basra, and could also see images beamed directly from armed Predator drones. They quickly began striking militia fighters and militants laying roadside bombs, and orchestrated close air support to advancing Iraqi units.

The British were surprised to see the Iraqi troops and their attached US mentors being welcomed by the people of Basra. Without waiting for orders from the UK, Brigadier Free ordered the 4th Brigade to form similar mentoring teams to support the Iraqi 14th Division deployed in Basra. This worked and quickly started adding value to the battle.

General Mohan's initial impulse was to launch everything he had into the Hiyyaniyah district of Basra, a notorious militia stronghold. He was persuaded to take a more measured approach, securing the access routes into the city and then cordoning off the Hiyyaniyah. He was advised to tackle other smaller areas of resistance while simultaneously pouring humanitarian aid into the Hiyyaniyah. This enabled the soldiers of the Iraqi Army to chalk up some successes, which increased their confidence and bought consent for their actions. Colonel Richard Iron, the British advisor to General Mohan takes up the story:

> For the first time we had access to plentiful Coalition airpower with seemingly endless attack helicopters and armed Predators over Basra. The militia fought bravely, but not

intelligently, they defended in the open against Iraqi Security Force attacks to clear their roadblocks. We found it easy to identify them with drones and then destroy them one by one with Hellfire missiles.

For example, in the al-Latif area of northern Basra, the militia attempted to block the National Police brigade by establishing roadblocks and fighting positions around Qarmat Ali Bridge. We quickly identified their headquarters and resupply centre in al-Latif school and that they used a taxi to carry ammunition to their various defensive positions. We simply followed the taxi on the drone camera until we had identified all the positions and then destroyed them with missiles.[40]

The US sent a US Civil Military Operations Centre to Basra. Its rapidly funded clean-up operations and other employment, generating work. By the time the Iraqi forces deployed into the Hiyyaniyah, civilians were coming forward to point out weapons caches, criminals and hard-line militia members. Very little resistance was encountered.

A delegation of Iraqi parliamentarians flew to Iran. General Qaseem Soleimani, the commander of Iran's Quds force, brokered a ceasefire between the Iraqi forces and Sadr's supporters. This agreement, the increasing effectiveness of the Iraqi forces and the welcome given to the Iraqi troops by the people of Basra combined to greatly reduce the level of resistance to the operation.

Many of the operation's initial reverses sprang from weaknesses of the previous British approach to the city, Operation *Charge of the Knights* had created the opportunity for the Iraqi Army to conduct operations that both the Coalition and the people of Basra wanted them to conduct. By redefining the militia and Iranian-supported 'special groups' as enemies, Prime Minister Maliki changed the political dynamic in southern Iraq. Air Chief Marshal Stirrup told the Iraq Inquiry that:

> General Petraeus described this as an express train that just couldn't be stopped. It was just going down there with no plan; and just doing it is a recipe for confusion at best and disaster at worst. As it turned out, we got the best, which was confusion, but then eventually some order out of the chaos.
>
> We were cautious about reintroducing an overt UK presence on the streets, and the other very significant factor was that the Iraqis were very reluctant to have us with them because they felt we attracted fire. So, we were slower than we should have been, I think, in hindsight, in getting that mentoring going ...[41]

There is little doubt that Operation *Charge of the Knights* exacerbated pre-existing UK/US military factions. Before the operation US commanders and their staff in Baghdad had assumed that the British were sustaining the required level of operational overwatch over Basra. In fact, the level of capability that the US expected was considerably greater than that of the British and their increasingly defensive operational posture, and failure to embed British mentors in Iraqi forces contributed to insufficient situational awareness.

US divisions had multiple brigades, all of three strong battalions and large capable divisional artillery and engineers. They had aviation brigades with organic attack helicopters and considerably more transport helicopters than the British had ever deployed to Basra. By 2008 US divisions also had increasing numbers of organic drones. Throughout the campaign the British had persisted in describing their force in Basra as a multinational division. But by 2008 the so-called division had a single small British brigade.

Discovering this in the early part of Operation *Charge of the Knights*, many US officers were disappointed. Some were shocked. This disappointment was reinforced by exposure of British gaps in situational awareness, military capability and integration with the Iraqi forces. These factors reinforced the impression that while US troops had been fighting hard in the Surge, Britain had cut a weak deal with JAM and had given up fighting in Basra.

This resulted in erosion of trust between many US commanders and staff officers and the British Army. The US HQ in Baghdad and the British in Basra had drifted by mutual consent into a situation where each HQ paid insufficient attention to the other's operations. This created mistrust between the US and British military, amplified by reporting and commentary in the US and British media. In this the London press were reinforcing a long-standing narrative of an illegitimate and failing war.

The British rapid deployment of mentoring teams had some effect in countering this. Subsequent successful UK operations in Basra also restored a degree of confidence in US commanders. But between 2008 and 2014, British military credibility with the US never reached the peak established in the immediate aftermath of the overthrow of Saddam Hussein.

British influence was also reduced by national command and control. The British national commander was not the British lieutenant general in Baghdad, but the major general commanding in Basra. Usually, he saw his main responsibility as being to the British joint HQ in Northwood, rather than the US-led HQs in Baghdad. It seems that neither the UK joint HQ nor the MoD paid enough attention to the Iraq campaign as a whole.

This shows that to maximize campaign coherence and multinational unity of effort, there is a clear requirement for a single campaign plan, owned by the in-theatre operational HQ. British military influence in Iraq should have been focussed on influencing the campaign plan; and on establishing clear and unambiguous situational awareness at the theatre level. It was not.

An aggravating factor was that the length of tours in Iraq by British units and officers were usually shorter than the tours of US Army units and individuals. This disrupted continuity of command and understanding with the US Army. Peacetime process often seemed to trump the operational need. For example, even though they were only on six-month tours, British unit and brigade commanders and key staff officers were allowed to change over in mid-tour. There was an 18-month period in 2004–05 when this policy meant that the British brigade in Basra was commanded by no fewer than five different officers. In the same period US brigade sectors would have seen only two different brigade commanders.

Some British generals commanding in southern Iraq asked that 'continuity personnel' on longer accompanied tours be based in Kuwait. Despite this model having been successfully applied by the British Army in Northern Ireland, these requests were denied. This apparent 'business as usual' approach to manning undermined the effectiveness and credibility of the British with the Iraqis and with the US.

Unsurprisingly the British Army's confidence was damaged. The 'abandonment' of Basra to the JAM is the aspect of the deal which caused great unease within the British Army. For example, troops who had served in Basra before the accommodation who returned after Operation *Charge of the Knights* found that many Iraqi civilians with whom they had previously interacted were no longer in Basra. Some had fled Iraq; others had been murdered. This created a sense that the British had abandoned the ordinary decent people of Basra. And by 2008 it was abundantly clear that in many ways the British military rate of adaptation to the Iraq war had been slower than that of the US Army and Marine Corps.

AFTER OPERATION *CHARGE OF THE KNIGHTS*

The US Surge created the security and political conditions to allow Prime Minister Maliki to take on the Shia extremists and their militias. Operation *Charge of the Knights* was a decisive point. If it had failed it is difficult to see how either Maliki or the UK's strategy would have survived. Failure could also have fatally derailed US strategy.[42]

The British played an essential role in reinforcing the successes in security, not least by continuing to build Iraqi Army capability. A highly successful British mentoring mission throughout 2008 and the first half of 2009 partially restored some of the UK's military reputation with the US and Iraqi Army. But not with Prime Minister Maliki. And Basra's police were improved by a US police mentoring task force.

At the height of the war with the JAM, the British PRT had been withdrawn out of Iraqi to Kuwait, out of concern for the safely of its civilian staff. After Operation *Charge of the Knights* it returned to Basra. This meant that the British HQ could encourage and energize the Comprehensive Approach – effectively acting in support of the PRT, UK Consul General and US Regional Embassy Office.

WITHDRAWAL FROM IRAQ

In June 2009, the British handed over to the 10th (US) Mountain Division and left Iraq. But the country was not at peace with itself. And Iran had greatly increased its influence in the country. After the US withdrew, Iraqi Prime Minister Maliki stoked the fires of sectarian division against the country's Sunni minority, who returned to insurgency, this time under the nihilistic banner of Islamic State of Syria and al Sham (ISIS), the ruthless jihadi insurgents.

During the 50 years covered by this book, the four years of 2006–09 saw the highest level of operational commitment faced by the Army; and the Army's first experience of fighting unpopular wars since the 1956 Suez Crisis. The Army was bent well beyond its design limits, but somehow it did not break. Completing the Iraq mission while building up the force in Afghanistan was a major achievement. And doing so despite indifferent government and MoD strategic leadership was testimony to the Army's resilience as an organization. It took a certain bloody-minded obdurate satisfaction at all levels, from CGS down to battalions, regiments, squadrons, companies and batteries, to get through the period, possibly the most challenging years since the defeats of the early years of the Second Word War.

FAILURES OF STRATEGIC LEADERSHIP

Between 2003 and 2009 Britain's war in Iraq became increasingly unpopular with the British people, politicians and media. This greatly damaged the domestic political credibility of former Prime Minister Tony Blair. Also eroded were the reputations for competence of the British government, its defence, foreign and development ministries and the UK's intelligence services and armed forces.

How was it that the Army found itself in a war that was so problematic? The short answer is that the Prime Minister and his government did not display the necessary competence to run the war. The evidence is overwhelming.

Two internal British Army reports on the war were leaked and the third, written by this author, was declassified, as was an internal UK MoD report on its role in the war. An independent inquiry into Britain's role in the war was commissioned by Blair's successor, Gordon Brown.[43] The Inquiry was an exhaustive analysis of high-level government decision-making, comprehensively tracking the paper and email trail of advice and assessments flowing into the Prime Minister's office at No. 10 Downing Street and to the Cabinet Office, the central co-ordinating machinery of British government, as well as the relevant decisions made in No. 10 and the extent to which the decisions were implemented. It also provided analyses of decision-making in the key government departments: the FCO, MoD and DfID.

Chaired by former senior civil servant Sir John Chilcot, the inquiry reported almost seven years after it was commissioned. Chilcot never adequately explained why the inquiry lasted a year longer than the British war in Iraq. This was a source of considerable frustration to many British anti-war activists. Some parents of British servicemen killed were very disappointed that the inquiry neither declared the war illegal nor recommended the arrest of Tony Blair on war crimes charges.

The inquiry identified that prior to the invasion, the British government had an 'ingrained belief' that Iraq possessed some weapons of mass destruction. This gave rise to flawed assessments that were never adequately tested, challenged or probed. It particularly criticized the chairman of the Joint Intelligence Committee and head of the British Secret Intelligence Service for presenting weak intelligence concerning Iraq's weapons of mass destruction with excessive certainty. It assesses that 'the circumstances in which it was decided that there was a legal basis for UK military action were far from satisfactory'.[44]

In the run-up to the war, Blair had committed the UK to help the Iraqi people build a new united Iraq at peace with itself and its neighbours, in which its people should enjoy security, freedom, prosperity and equality with a government that would uphold human rights and the rule of law as cornerstones of democracy. The British government failed to achieve the strategic objectives it had set for itself both for Iraq as a whole and particularly for the four provinces of southern Iraq that it occupied:

> By 2007 militia dominance in Basra, which UK military commanders were unable to challenge, led to the UK exchanging detainee releases for an end to the targeting of its forces. It was humiliating that the UK reached a position in which an agreement with a militia group which had been actively targeting UK forces was considered the best option available. The UK military role in Iraq ended a very long way from success.[45]

The Inquiry assessed that this failure was because the scale of UK effort in post-conflict Iraq 'failed to take account of the magnitude of the task of stabilizing, administering and reconstructing Iraq, and of the responsibilities which were likely to fall to the UK'. This was because Prime Minister Blair 'did not establish clear Ministerial oversight of UK planning and preparation. He did not ensure that there was a flexible, realistic and fully resourced plan that integrated UK military and civilian contributions'.

These judgements are fully supported by the evidence. For example. from mid-2003 onwards British military commanders in Basra all sensed a profound lack of civil/military co-ordination in London, a lack of top-down leadership, and a government approach to Iraq that was under-resourced and inadequately led and co-ordinated.[46]

This is but one of many examples identified by the inquiry of sub-optimal performance by politicians, government, departments and intelligence staff, senior military officers and civilian officials. Whilst there is abundant evidence of decisions being made in No. 10, there is equally abundant evidence of follow-up action being either absent or being poorly co-ordinated. There was consistent failure to adequately monitor progress. And on many occasions politicians, government departments and senior officials not only ignored direction given by Blair, but were allowed to do so.[47] The inquiry could not:

> identify alternative approaches that would have guaranteed greater success in the circumstances of March 2003. What can be said is that a number of opportunities for the sort of candid reappraisal of policies that would have better aligned objectives and resources did not take place. There was no serious consideration of more radical options, such as an early withdrawal or else a substantial increase in effort. The Inquiry has identified a number of moments, especially during the first year of the Occupation, when it would have been possible to conduct a substantial reappraisal. None took place.[48]

In addition, the inquiry found that:

> Better planning and preparation for a post-Saddam Hussein Iraq would not necessarily have prevented the events that unfolded in Iraq between 2003 and 2009. It would not have been possible for the UK to prepare for every eventuality. Better plans and preparation could have mitigated some of the risks to which the UK and Iraq were exposed between 2003 and 2009

and increased the likelihood of achieving the outcomes desired by the UK and the Iraqi people.[49]

The evidence shows that after the successful regime change operation, the British government failed to adequately align strategic ends with the ways and means it chose to apply. A consistent failure was inadequate implementation of decisions made. Although many organizations, officials, military officers and ministers in the FCO, MoD and DfID contributed to this display of inadequate strategic competence, the single most important factor was probably the inability of Prime Minister Blair to make the decisions he had taken stick.

As war leader, Blair should be judged to be a failure. No one should have any sympathy for the considerable damage that the war inflicted on Blair's domestic political credibility. Other reputations were badly damaged, including those of the defence, foreign and development ministries and the UK intelligence services and armed forces. Whilst many other politicians, senior officers and officials must shoulder their share of the blame for British strategic failures in Iraq, the ultimate responsibility is Blair's. The Iraqi people, the British government, armed forces in general and the Army deserved better.

CHAPTER 13

Strategic Shrinkage and the Endgame in Afghanistan, 2009–14

In February 2009, the newly elected President Obama agreed to a request from the US commander in Kabul for more US troops, to reverse Taliban gains and better support the impending summer 2009 Afghan presidential elections. He despatched an additional 17,000 troops to reinforce the 36,000 US troops already there. Many of these would be US Marines, who would deploy to south-west Afghanistan, reinforcing the relatively overstretched British forces in Helmand Province. The British would concentrate on central Helmand, including its capital Lashkar Gar, while the US Marines would take over districts outside the periphery of British-controlled areas, including much of northern and southern Helmand.

Improving capabilities

By 2009 the MoD displayed the sense of urgency that appeared so lacking earlier in the Afghan war. And Operation *Entirety* had accelerated the Army's efforts to adapt to the conflict. Improvements were being made in equipment deployed to Afghanistan. Some of these, like Osprey body armour, the Hermes 450 drone, the Exactor missile and the Mastiff vehicle, were originally acquired for Iraq. Others were specific to Afghanistan.

The Army deployed its M270 MLRS to Helmand. Instead of rockets delivering bomblets over a wide area, it now fired the Guided MLRS (GMLRS) rocket. These used GPS guidance to hit target areas as small as a metre squared. With a range of 70 km these covered all of central Helmand from their base. Their 200-pound warheads could destroy trenches and bunkers, creating new tactical options. For example, a Gurkha infantry company had to attack a fortified position held by the Taliban. Locating the network of bunkers and trenches using drone surveillance allowed them all to be neutralized by a single salvo of guided MLRS rockets, greatly assisting the Gurkhas in their attack.[1]

There was also a new system to capture biometric data. This could match DNA samples taken from recovered IEDs with the DNA of detained suspects.

The 2009 withdrawal from Iraq released more special forces to reinforce Afghanistan. The same applied to British helicopters. This could not be done instantly as many helicopters returning to the UK from Basra were worn out and required refurbishing. The different threat profile and different electromagnetic environment required adjustments to the aircraft defensive aid systems. This took time: by the end of 2009 more British helicopters were arriving in Afghanistan, but not in time for the major British offensive that summer.

Operation *Panther's Claw*

In 2009, British troops in Helmand still had insufficient helicopters, drones, armoured vehicles and equipment for countering roadside bombs. The British government denied this, but troops no longer believed them.

By now, the IED was the Taliban's principal weapon. Many were laid around British bases. With insufficient helicopters to deliver food, fuel, ammunition and medical supplies, almost all of the material necessary to sustain the British battalions in the field had to be delivered by convoy. The lack of helicopters also meant that the great majority of patrols had to walk from and to their bases on necessarily predictable routes, increasing their vulnerability to Taliban bombs. Fortunately, increasing numbers of Mastiff vehicles provided much better protection.

The Army adapted in Helmand by making widespread use of handheld mine detectors and devising drills to use these to sweep the ground for Taliban bombs – given the codename 'Barma'. This reduced movement to the pace of a cautious soldier. Movement stopped completely when a bomb was found, to allow it to be dealt with by EOD experts. So convoy movement in most of central Helmand was often very slow, with accumulating risks to the infantry protecting the resupply routes from Taliban attacks and attempting to deter and disrupt the laying of yet more IEDs.

The IED threat was an ever-present danger. It required real courage to keep driving on roads and tracks and to keep patrolling the bomb-strewn fields. This was a considerable leadership challenge for the young corporals, sergeants and officers, much greater than any challenge I faced in my career. That the Army managed to continue operating in such a hostile environment was testimony to very high standards of leadership and morale.

Between May and November 2009, the British brigade in Helmand was 19th Light Brigade. In June 2009 it launched a major offensive, Operation *Panther's Claw*, to secure terrain between Helmand's two most important towns, Lashkar Gar and Gereshk, by clearing the Taliban from the central Helmand districts of Babaji and Nawa. This would be the last big British offensive operation in Helmand before the arrival of more US Marines. The brigade commander, Brigadier Tim Radford, had to limit the ambition of the operation to match the resources available to his brigade.

Months of intelligence gathering preceded the operation, which began on the night of 18/19 June with the launching of helicopter-borne British special forces' raids against identified Taliban commanders, while a dozen Chinook helicopters delivered the 3rd Battalion, the Royal Regiment of Scotland (the Black Watch) into Babaji.

The Welsh Guards advanced from the south, a push that was held up by many IEDs. The Welsh Guards' commanding officer hitched a lift with a convoy bringing supplies to his leading troops and was killed when the lightly armoured Viking vehicle in which he was riding struck a roadside bomb. Lieutenant Colonel Rupert Thorneloe was the first British battalion commander to be killed in action since the 1982 Falklands War. The next day, the helicopter carrying the brigade commander came under heavy insurgent fire and was nearly shot down.

The main advance was continued by the Light Dragoons. Normally an armoured reconnaissance regiment equipped with light armoured vehicles, they had reorganized themselves into infantry, reinforced by companies from the new Mercian Regiment. Their advance towards Babaji was as hard fought as any other British attack in Helmand. Large numbers of IEDs and tenacious resistance from Taliban fighters firing small arms and RPGs inflicted casualties and slowed the advance. The summer heat amplified the fatigue imposed by the considerable weight carried by troops. Many troops were constantly on the edge of physical exhaustion.

The Light Dragoons advanced 2 miles in two days – dealing with over 50 IEDs and incurring 30 casualties. The Black Watch were added to the advance, as was an infantry company from the battalion in Sangin. This was sufficient to overmatch the Taliban and allow the advance to resume and reach Babaji.

Operation *Panther's Claw* had of necessity been the British priority in Helmand for helicopters, drones and other surveillance capabilities. These were not available elsewhere in Helmand. So the Taliban found it comparatively easy to sew large numbers of IEDs in Sangin, resulting in further casualties. The 2nd Battalion, the Rifles in Sangin lost 15 killed in as many days.

The media and opposition parties used apparent failures to supply enough protected vehicles and helicopters to Iraq and Afghanistan as a weapon to criticize Prime Minister Gordon Brown and the governing Labour party. This caused great political difficulties.

A totemic issue was whether British troops in Afghanistan had sufficient helicopters. All the evidence was that they did not, and government attempts to persuade the media and public otherwise lacked credibility. The 2004 reductions in defence spending required by Brown had resulted in funding for new helicopters being cut. If these reductions had not been made, the UK would have had more helicopter capability in Helmand by 2009. The helicopter crews and squadrons knew this, the MoD knew it, the services chiefs knew it, but Brown persisted in denying it.

This increase in casualties inflicted by Operation *Panther's Claw* was an unpleasant surprise to No. 10. During the operation Gordon Brown made a short notice visit to

PJHQ, which exercised national command over the British troops in Afghanistan. It did not go well. Brown took the further step of telephoning Radford at 19th Light Brigade's HQ. The Prime Minister asked if the brigade had enough helicopters. Diplomatically Radford replied that he had enough helicopters for the missions he was conducting. Whether Brown understood that lack of helicopters was greatly constraining the missions that the brigade could conduct was not clear.[2]

This was the first time a prime minister had called a tactical commander since the Gorazde crisis of mid-1995. Radford could have replied bluntly, stating not only that there were insufficient helicopters, but also that this deficiency was resulting in increased casualties. Whatever the character of the conversation, had Radford, or anyone else, chosen to leak it, Brown's position would have been further damaged.

Notwithstanding this friction, the service chiefs and Brown made several efforts to explain the rationale behind the Afghan war to the British public. By then the UK media was so unsympathetic that these efforts failed. Fighting a second unpopular war was becoming increasingly difficult to justify.

THE AFGHAN SURGE, 2009–12

In June 2009, US General Stan McChrystal was appointed as the new ISAF commander. Previously leading the US SOF task force hunting Al Qaida, McChrystal found that many NATO contingents in Afghanistan had national restrictions on operations, the so-called 'caveats', reducing their utility. High levels of personnel turnover and inadequate numbers of helicopters further reduced the effectiveness of many national contingents. ISAF's various regional command HQs were fighting different wars rather than conducting a centrally directed campaign.

Afghan president Hamid Karzai was deeply troubled by the high level of avoidable Afghan civilian casualties being inflicted by ISAF. McChrystal shared Karzai's concerns, as civilian casualties were easily exploited by the Taliban. At an ISAF morning update, with regional commands linked in by video conference, he was told of an incident where ISAF had inflicted civilian casualties. McChrystal was incensed and banged the table:

> 'We're going to lose this fucking war if we don't stop killing civilians' I said, looking at the staff and at the commanders on the screen. It was uncharacteristic of me to swear during the morning update. I took a second and began again. 'I apologize for losing my temper, but we cannot continue to do this.'[3]

McChrystal directed that the campaign's centre of gravity was the Afghan population. These were to be protected from the insurgents and from excessive use of ISAF's considerable firepower. This policy was implemented by more restrictive rules of engagement and was christened 'courageous restraint'.

He wanted to improve co-ordination, both within NATO and between ISAF and the Afghan government. To improve command and control, a new subordinate HQ was formed. Subordinate to HQ ISAF, the Intermediate Joint Command ran tactical operations, exercising many of the functions of a corps HQ.

McChrystal advocated 'embedded partnering' between ISAF and the Afghan forces, aiming to combine the two forces into a single team, exploiting ISAF's combat power and technology and the Afghan forces' situational awareness. But political difficulties for the US and NATO were increased by the 2009 Afghan election, which saw flagrant ballot stuffing by supporters of President Karzai, further undermining the legitimacy of the war in NATO member states.

In December 2009 President Obama announced that a further 30,000 US troops would be sent, NATO being invited to send 10,000 more troops. Obama declared that:

> It is in our vital national interest to send an additional 30,000 U.S. troops to Afghanistan. After 18 months, our troops will begin to come home. These are the resources that we need to seize the initiative, while building the Afghan capacity that can allow for a responsible transition of our forces out of Afghanistan ...
>
> We will meet these objectives in three ways. First, we will pursue a military strategy that will break the Taliban's momentum and increase Afghanistan's capacity over the next 18 months. The 30,000 additional troops that I'm announcing tonight will deploy in the first part of 2010 – the fastest possible pace – so that they can target the insurgency and secure key population centres. They'll increase our ability to train competent Afghan security forces, and to partner with them so that more Afghans can get into the fight. And they will help create the conditions for the United States to transfer responsibility to the Afghans.[4]

Troop numbers would begin to reduce from mid-2011. This reflected the considerable war-weariness in the US, a factor similarly bearing on the British government.

The campaign would become a race against the clock: to improve security, grow the Afghan security forces, develop the capacity of the Afghan state and reduce corruption, all in time to allow Afghan security forces to take the lead in conducting security operations in all provinces by the end of 2014. The Taliban intended to frustrate these objectives, coining a slogan that whilst the US and NATO had the watches, the Taliban had the time.

Given the earlier decision to reinforce Helmand with US Marines and the political importance of Kandahar as the historic heartland of the Taliban, most of the US reinforcements would go there, to clear the main populated areas of insurgents. ISAF planned to separate the insurgents from the Afghan people, improve their security, governance and economic prospects and attack insurgent networks. Operations would be preceded by media announcements, to persuade insurgents to withdraw from the area, reducing civilian casualties.

ISAF was to 'clear' by pushing the Taliban out of the terrain they controlled and, assisted by the Afghan forces, 'hold' the cleared ground. Provision of development and services by the Afghan authorities was an essential ingredient to the 'build'. ISAF would help extend the reach of the government, improving the capacity of local officials and institutions. Only then could ISAF withdraw, confident the Taliban would be repelled by the population.

The British Army had been trying to do this in Helmand since 2007. It is not clear if the UK had any influence on McChrystal, Robert Gates, or Obama's decisions. If London did, it was not acknowledged in their memoirs, nor in any US histories of the war, both official and unofficial. Nevertheless, the government and the Army signed up to the US strategy.

OPERATION *MOSHTARAK*

McChrystal's first opportunity to use additional forces was Operation *Moshtarak*, launched by US, UK and Afghan forces in Helmand Province, to clear the insurgent stronghold of Marjah, an irrigated area to the west side of the main 'Green Zone' of agricultural terrain. It had fallen to the Taliban in 2008. The British had lacked sufficient forces to clear and hold the district.

The plan for the operation was developed by the US Marine brigade and the HQ of Regional Command South. It would also expand the British-controlled footprint in central Helmand. ISAF minimized the use of the heavy firepower available, particularly artillery and air strikes, in accordance with McChrystal's concept of 'courageous restraint'. Not only would artillery and airpower be very tightly controlled, but the plan for the operation sought to reduce the necessity for using these weapons by achieving both surprise and concentration of force.

There were no preparatory artillery or air attacks. The night air assault by 60 blacked-out US, British and Canadian helicopters, the pilots flying by night-vision goggles, successfully leapfrogged over the main Taliban defences. This was the largest air assault operation in Helmand. Tactical surprise was achieved.

The next phase of the operation was to extend Afghan government influence in the cleared areas. In the British sector, around Nad-e Ali, the subsequent stabilization operation, and the restoration of Afghan governance, was relatively successful.

Before the operation McChrystal had expected that Marjah would benefit from 'government in a box'. This term was then being used by ISAF to describe a package of measures to be taken by the Afghan authorities to promote rapid stabilization of an area cleared of Taliban. Efforts to achieve this in Marjah were problematic. Neither the Marines nor the Afghan forces initially had much understanding of the area's tribal and political dynamics. President Karzai played an unhelpful role, for example making public remarks on a visit to Marjah describing the US forces as 'invaders'. The Marines also found that, apart from the Afghan commandos, many of the Afghan forces that they had partnered with were of limited military effectiveness.

Clearance of Marjah proceeded much more slowly than planned. McChrystal was reported in mid-2010 to have described it as a 'bleeding ulcer'. The unexpected resilience of the insurgents who fought back after the initial assault indicated that, in 'clear, hold and build' operations, the 'hold' phase could be much more difficult than the 'clear'. But by January 2011 the US had achieved a measure of stability, with the centre of Marjah sufficiently stable, enjoying a thriving bazaar and resulting traffic congestion. These US and British operations eventually led to a significant improvement of security in central Helmand around the provincial capital of Lashkar Gar secured by British troops. Afghan officials routinely travelled by road, rather than by helicopter.

Up to now the Army in Helmand had been wearing desert camouflage uniforms. This worked well in the desert, but most troops were now operating in the Green Zone, and it did nothing for concealment amongst the crops and lush vegetation. A new camouflage pattern was needed that worked across the varied terrain of Helmand Province, desert, farms, trees and compounds.

Previously this had been thought impossible for any single camouflage pattern. But US special forces, followed by the SAS, had adopted a camouflage pattern developed by Crye Precision, a US company. Drawing on camouflage patterns used by the animal kingdom, this mixed green, brown, sand, black and white in an infinitely variable complex array. Crye's 'multicam' pattern was tested against many other patterns. Trials revealed that this pattern had an uncanny ability to blend into a very large range of backgrounds, more than any existing or competing patterns. A British variant of the pattern was adopted, known as 'Multi Terrain Pattern' or MTP. Once issued to all troops in Afghanistan, it was rolled out across the rest of the Army.

As with the military sweater, the Army again acted as a military uniform trend setter. The US Army rapidly followed, adopting multicam for its battle dress uniform. Over the next decade many other armies would follow this trend, either using Crye's pattern or developing a similar one of their own.

To better combat the IED threat, the Army formed a new counter-IED task force. This was based on the HQ of an engineer regiment, bringing together EOD and search squadrons, search dogs, an ECM troop to counter radio-controlled IEDs and weapons intelligence teams. The task force was initially used to clear routes, but over time its use evolved to provide counter-IED teams to company level to assist with manoeuvre operations.

Having seen the delays and casualties imposed during Operation *Panther's Claw*, the Royal Engineers asked to bring the new Trojan engineer tank to Helmand. There appeared to be some sucking of bureaucratic teeth in higher command echelons, including sensitivity that deployment of heavy armour in Afghanistan would signal British escalation. But the case was well put by the engineer staff: 'if you've got a tool use it. It might not be the right tool but it's better than having no tool.'[5] The idea was agreed, and three Trojans were flown in by giant Antonov airlifters to use their mine ploughs and rocket-propelled Python explosive hoses to breach Taliban IED belts.

In April 2010 Talisman entered service. This was a 'system of systems' to clear routes of IEDs. It used specialized armoured vehicles and expert personnel with powerful mast-mounted surveillance systems and organic small drones. It also used a remotely operated Land Rover to mount a ground-penetrating radar to detect buried IEDs and used high-mobility JCB armoured excavators to repair damage caused by IED blasts. But IEDs could still cause casualties. Staff Sergent Micky Yule, leading a Royal Engineer high-risk search team, described his encounter with an IED in late 2010:

When the shockwave tore up through me, I knew what had happened. I was blinded and deafened by the explosion but could hear gunfire as we came under attack. I couldn't work out why the bottom half of my leg wasn't there. I actually thought I might be sitting on it. My right leg was a total mess. My pelvis and arms were broken.

Sand around me was turning red and I knew I was bleeding out. I could hear my second in command dealing with the contact calling in the medical emergency response helicopter, so it fell to the two youngest members of the team to save my life. They were worried about touching my right leg in case they pulled anything off, but somehow, they managed to slow the flow of blood. They did amazingly well. I was conscious throughout and actively fighting to stay awake, sensing that if I didn't, I would probably die.

One of the guys slung me over his shoulder and carried me to a vehicle. The last thing I remember is being treated by a female medic at patrol base. I'd seen her save people on a previous incident and I felt a massive comfort hearing her voice.[6]

After Operation *Moshtarak* the Army in Helmand conducted a decreasing number of 'clear' operations, concentrating on the phases of 'build' and 'hold'. This was because all cleared areas had to be secured with more bases and checkpoints, reflecting a conscious decision to avoid 'mowing the lawn' operations.

There were still strike operations in the British areas in Helmand. But the number of troops in static roles meant that these were mostly carried out by special forces, of which more were now employed in Helmand, including US Marine Raider units and the British Army's Special Forces Support Group (SFSG).

This had played a leading role in training and advising an Afghan special forces unit. One of its parachute companies that assisted in this was led by Dan Jarvis, who later became a Labour MP.[7] There were two such British-raised special forces units in southern Afghanistan: the Commando Force 333 (CF333) and Afghan Territorial Force 444 (ATF444) units, known together as the 'Triples'. They were much more capable and much better led than the conventional Afghan Army units.

By now brigades rotating into Helmand were forming a Brigade Reconnaissance Force (BRF). This was a specially formed and trained company-sized group that could be used as a formation reconnaissance squadron might. Increasingly it was employed to conduct raids, exploiting the best intelligence available to brigade HQ. The BRF was given a high-priority allocation of scarce helicopters to achieve this, further reducing support to the rest of the brigade.

Operation *Hamkari* – the British-led clearance of Kandahar Province

After Marjah had been stabilized, ISAF's main effort switched to stabilizing Kandahar Province. Afghanistan's second city and the spiritual home of the Taliban was Kandahar, the provincial capital. Since 2006 the Canadian troops had operated in the province but had had insufficient strength to inflict a lasting defeat on the insurgents. The city of about half a million Afghans was not controlled by the Taliban, but insurgent influence was rising. The insurgents were mounting a successful operation to assassinate pro-government leaders in the city and mortar and rocket attacks were increasing.

During 2009 and 2010 reinforcing US Army brigades flowed into Kandahar, including an airborne brigade, a brigade of mechanized infantry carried in Stryker wheeled APCs, an aviation brigade with a hundred US Army helicopters and an intelligence surveillance and reconnaissance brigade bristling with intelligence-gathering systems.

By 2010, the command of ISAF's Regional Command South had rotated to British leadership, with the HQ being found from the 6th Division. Its commander, British Major General Nick Carter, saw that clearing Kandahar Province could not simply come from a physical effort to drive out the Taliban; there would also have to be a political effort to reconnect the people to the Afghan government, and intelligence gathering to better understand the province. As the city was not controlled by the Taliban, there was no need for a surprise assault. Instead, ISAF would conduct a limited reinforcement of Afghan security forces in the city. To the south of the city were agricultural districts: Panjwai, Zharai, Shah Wali Kot and Arghandab. Clearing Taliban from these districts, would be the main effort.

The operation was called *Hamkari* (from the word for 'co-operation' in Dari and Pashto). It was the largest single operation conducted by ISAF, employing over 60,000 US and Afghan troops. It was the US, NATO and Afghan main effort for 2010. Officers sometimes referred to the operation as 'the main effort of the world'. Very few British troops participated in the operation, as they were almost entirely focussed on Helmand Province. But as the planning and much of the implementation was conducted by a British-led HQ, it deserves a place in this story.

ISAF's understanding of the complex Afghan environment had greatly improved since 2006, as had surveillance and intelligence-gathering capabilities. Human intelligence has been a decisive factor in all successful counterinsurgency campaigns, but has always taken several years to develop. By 2010 it was starting to produce significant operational results in Afghanistan. These capabilities were applied to build a better picture of Taliban networks in and around Kandahar. They also generated intelligence to allow increased numbers of special forces raids against Taliban leaders in the province. Large numbers of unmanned aerial vehicles and other surveillance assets were redeployed by the US from Iraq to Afghanistan.

Incorporating lessons from Operation *Moshtarak*, the operation was designed from the outset as a combined effort by NATO and the Afghans. It began with McChrystal attempting to get President Karzai to engage with tribal elders and key figures from Kandahar, to sell the operation to his people.

A *shura* of Afghan tribal elders was held at the Kandahar Convention Centre on 4 April. Fifteen hundred people filled the building to listen to Karzai. After a wide-ranging speech in which he urged people to send their sons to join the Afghan Army, he asked the audience if they were worried about the forthcoming operation. They were. Karzai told the crowd that if they were not happy, there would be no operation. Whilst many NATO officers took this as a rebuke, McChrystal took it as a challenge, to gain more support from the key Kandahari figures.

A second smaller *shura* was held on 21 July. The requirement for the operation and its plan were briefed to the audience, with considerable emphasis on the role that Afghan forces would play. There were hard questions for Karzai, McChrystal and Mark Sedwill, the senior NATO civilian in Afghanistan, but the openly expressed sentiment of the meeting was supportive of the operation.

Between July and October 2010, Operation *Hamkari* saw heavy fighting by US, Canadian and Afghan troops to clear and hold the districts of Arghandab, Panjwai and Zharai. McChrystal was not able to preside over these attacks. In mid-summer 2010 he resigned, not for any lack of success, but because of an article published on 8 July in *Rolling Stone* magazine in which he and his staff made disrespectful remarks about the US government. He was replaced by General David Petraeus, the commander of the previous US Surge in Iraq.

The final phase of the operation was led by an Afghan Army corps HQ. At the end of 2010, ISAF declared that Operation *Hamkari* had succeeded. This operation and the earlier Operation *Moshtarak* had depended on patient tactical execution of the 'clear, hold, build' counterinsurgency approach, on sufficient density of forces and on co-ordination of military operations with reconstruction and development tasks. But the operation revealed serious weaknesses in Afghan governance capability at district level.

ISAF casualties suffered in 2010 were also the highest yet in the war. But there was a reduction in civilian casualties counted by the UN, likely the result of the more restrictive use of artillery and air strikes under ISAF's policy of 'courageous restraint'. In December 2010 ISAF reached its peak strength of 131,000 troops, from 20 NATO and 28 non-NATO nations. Ninety thousand troops were from the US, with another 16,000 employed on US national operations. Some 9,500 troops were from the UK.

SLOW PROGRESS IN HELMAND

CHANGING COMMAND

The ever-increasing flow of US reinforcements created additional demands on the HQ of Regional Command South in Kandahar. To better manage the campaign, an additional regional command HQ was formed in July 2010, with the US Marines providing the core of the new Regional Command Southwest, responsible for NATO operations in Helmand Province.

The British became junior partners in Helmand. They worked hard to integrate with the Marines, embedding staff officers in their HQ. The British joint helicopter force subordinated itself to the Marine Aviation Wing. This brought more transport and attack helicopters. It also brought the V-22 Osprey tiltrotor. By rotating its engines, it could take off and land vertically, but fly forward as an aeroplane. The Marines also brought AV8B Harrier jets, increasing the responsiveness of NATO airpower over Helmand.

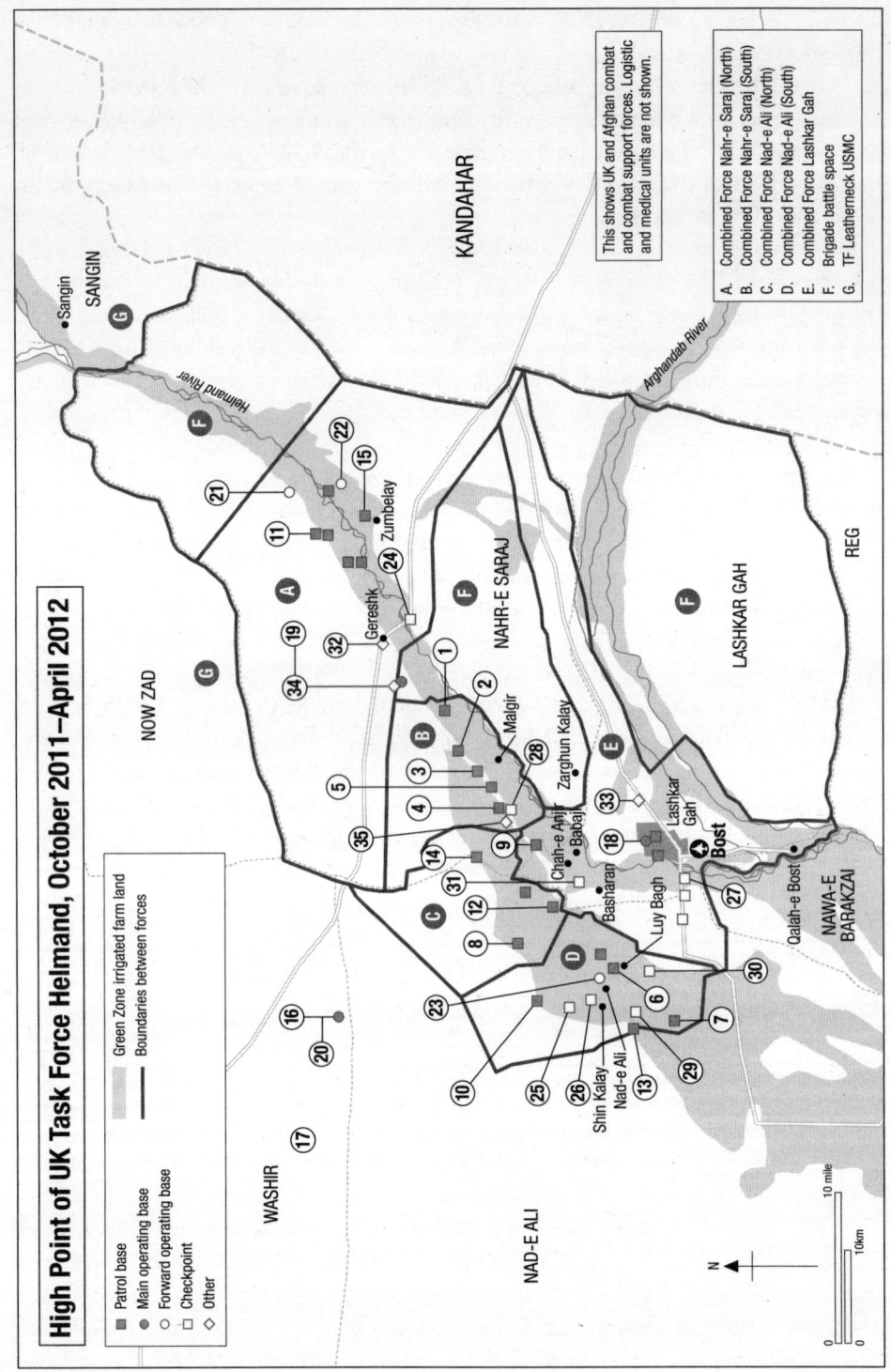

High Point of UK Task Force Helmand, October 2011–April 2012

■ Patrol base
● Main operating base
○ Forward operating base
□ Checkpoint
◇ Other

Green Zone irrigated farm land
Boundaries between forces

This shows UK and Afghan combat and Afghan combat support forces. Logistic and medical units are not shown.

A. Combined Force Nahr-e Saraj (North)
B. Combined Force Nahr-e Saraj (South)
C. Combined Force Nad-e Ali (North)
D. Combined Force Nad-e Ali (South)
E. Combined Force Lashkar Gah
F. Brigade battle space
G. TF Leatherneck USMC

KANDAHAR

SANGIN

Sangin

Helmand River

Arghandab River

REG

LASHKAR GAH

NAHR-E SARAJ

NOW ZAD

Gereshk

Zumbelay

Malgir

Zarghun Kalay

Chah-e Anjir

Babaji

Basharan

Luy Bagh

Lashkar Gah

Bost

NAWA-E BARAKZAI

Qalat-e Bost

WASHIR

NAD-E ALI

Shin Kalay

Nad-e Ali

N

0   10 mile
0   10km

Patrol bases

1. **PB 1**
   D Company 2nd Battalion the Parachute Regiment (2 PARA)
   1st Battalion Irish Guards (1 IG) team
   Afghan National Army (ANA) elements

2. **PB 2**
   HQ echelon 2 PARA
   C Company 2 PARA
   Mastiff troop 2nd Royal Tank Regiment (2 RTR)
   ANA elements

3. **PB 3**
   HQ echelon 3 PARA
   B Company 3 PARA
   C Company 3 PARA
   Mastiff troop 2 RTR
   ANA elements

4. **PB 4**
   B Company 2 PARA
   1 IG team
   ANA elements

5. **PB 5**
   B Company The Argyll and Sutherland Highlanders (5 SCOTS)

6. **PB Chilli**
   A Company 5 SCOTS

7. **PB Kalang**
   A Company 1 Royal Irish (1 R IRISH)

8. **PB Khaamar**
   A Company 3 PARA
   ANA combat elements

9. **PB Nahidullah**
   C Company The Royal Highland Fusiliers (2 SCOTS)

10. **PB Pimon**
    B Company 1 R IRISH
    7 Para Royal Horse Artillery (RHA)

11. **PB Rahim**
    4 Company 1 IG
    5 SCOTS team
    ANA 215 Corps *kandak* (battalion)

12. **PB Shahzad**
    HQ echelon 3 PARA
    B Company 3 PARA
    C Company 3 PARA
    Mastiff troop 2 RTR

13. **PB Silab**
    C Company 1 R IRISH
    1 IG team
    ANA elements
    Mamba counter-battery radar

14. **PB Wahid**
    Estonian elements
    1 IG elements
    ANA elements

15. **PB Zumbalay**
    A Company 1 IG

Main operating bases

16. **MOB Bastion**
    A Company 5 SCOTS
    12 Squadron (RAF) Reserve Node
    9 (Para) Squadron 23 Parachute Engineer Regiment
    51 (Para) Squadron 23 Parachute Engineer Regiment
    5 Squadron 22 Engineer Regiment
    52 Field Squadron
    TALISMAN (counter-IED)
    Counter-indirect fire (C-IDF) battery
    Hermes 450 unmanned air vehicle (UAV) battery
    Viking group 2 RTR
    10 Signal Regiment
    Electronic Counter Measures Force Protection (ECM-FP)
    216 (Para) Signals Squadron
    Desert Hawk medium unmanned air vehicle (MUAV)
    Brigade Reconnaissance Force (BRF)
    Joint Force Explosive Ordnance Disposal Group (JF EOD Gp)
    42 Engineer Regiment (Geographic)
    Task Force Helmand Provost Group
    Task Force Helmand Medical Group

17. **MOB Juno (location approximate)**
    Task Force 444 (Special Forces)
    Special Forces Support Group (SFSG)

18. **MOB Lashkar Gah**
    Headquarters Task Force (HQTF)
    Regimental HQ (RHQ) 7 Para RHA
    RHQ 4 Regiment Royal Artillery (4 RA)
    HQ echelon 2 SCOTS
    B Company 2 SCOTS
    Mastiff troop 2 RTR
    2 MI Bn
    D Company 5 SCOTS

19. **MOB Price**
    Danish Battlegroup
    D Squadron Household Cavalry Regiment (HCR)
    7 Para RHA
    5 SCOTS team
    Counter IED (C-IED) detachment
    ARTHUR counter-battery radar
    ANA 215 Corps elements

20. **MOB Shorabak**
    ANA 215 Corps combat support elements

Weapon Intelligence Section (WIS)
4 Military Intelligence Battalion (4 MI Bn)

Forward operating bases

21. **FOB Budwan**
    C Squadron Danish Battlegroup
    7 Para RHA elements
    1 IG teams
    ANA 215 Corps elements

22. **FOB Khar Nikah**

23. **FOB Shawqat**
    D Company 1 R IRISH
    1 IG team
    Mastiff troop 2 RTR
    ANA elements

Checkpoints

24. **CP Artillery Hill**
    ANA D-30 gun battery

25. **CP Blue 9**
    ANA elements

26. **CP Blue 17**
    ANA elements

27. **CP Bolan Shops**
    A Company 2 SCOTS

28. **CP Sabir**
    ANA elements

29. **CP Samsor**
    C Company 1 R IRISH
    ANA elements

30. **CP Shamal Storrai**
    5 SCOTS elements
    ANA elements

31. **CP Tapa Paraang**
    B Company 2 Royal Welsh (2 R WELSH)

Other

32. **Gereshk**
    Civil-military teams
    ANA elements

33. **Helmand Police Training Center (HPTC)**
    B Squadron Queen's Royal Lancers (QRL)

34. **Highway 1**
    E Squadron 1st Light Armoured Regiment
    ANA 205 Corps *kandaks*

35. **Vehicle Check Point (VCP) Dosti**
    ANA elements

There were two British organizations that the Marines chose not to supplant, but to support. The first was the British-led PRT in Lashkar Gar. By now many of its considerable earlier problems had been overcome. Some US officers and officials considered it to be as good as, if not better than, any other PRTs in Afghanistan.

BATTLEFIELD MEDICAL SUPPORT

The second organization that the Marines supported was the British-led hospital at Camp Bastion. Since its establishment in 2006, the increase in casualties had caused it to grow in size. Its 360 British staff were augmented by medics from Denmark and Estonia. When the Marines arrived, they brought with them a contingent of 50 US Navy Medical Corps personnel, known as 'corpsmen'. The hospital acquired a truly international flavour. Its capability was much more advanced than that of previous British field hospitals, including advanced technology such as CAT scanners. Improved electronic links, such as video conferencing, improved co-ordination with the home nation hospitals to which the casualties would be evacuated.

It was very effective at treating the wounded it received – not only British and NATO troops, but also Taliban and Afghan civilians. Independent assessments by the National Audit Office showed that the treatment of seriously wounded personnel was of equal levels to the best equivalent treatment in the National Health Service.

But casualties' survival rate depended on two other factors – first aid at the point of wounding and rapid evacuation. All Army personnel were trained in battlefield first aid. And additional military paramedics were deployed down to company and even platoon level, accompanying troops on patrols and other operations.

For casualty evacuation, Helmand always had an RAF Chinook helicopter dedicated to this task. The size of the aircraft's interior, equivalent to that of an underground railway carriage, allowed a large team of medics to be carried. These included an emergency specialist, anaesthetist and nurses, who could work on the patient to stabilize them in flight.

These were complemented by US Air Force Blackhawk casualty evacuation helicopters, nicknamed 'Pedro'. The passenger compartment of these was much smaller – the size was the interior of a small people carrier – so they could carry fewer medical staff. Blackhawks had built-in armour for the crew and passengers and a run-dry gearbox, and had been designed to withstand crashes. These factors, together with powerful machine guns fitted on both side doors, meant that the aircraft could fly into smaller and more dangerous landing zones than the larger, more vulnerable Chinook. US aircrew often showed great bravery in doing so. Although the Blackhawks carried fewer medical personnel, they could be quicker at getting casualties back to Camp Bastion. Many wounded British troops were successfully evacuated in these helicopters.

BRITISH LOGISTICS

By now British troop numbers in Helmand were at their highest. These generated a vast requirement for combat supplies: fuel, ammunition, food, water and spare parts. Many of these were sent by sea, arriving in the Pakistani port of Karachi. Pakistani contractors would load the freight onto their colourfully decorated trucks, known as 'jinglies' from the sound of bells fitted. These would wind their way through Pakistan, crossing into Afghanistan at the southern desert crossing point at Spin Baldak. It was likely that that the truck companies were paying protection money to the Pakistani and Afghan Taliban – one of the war's many ironies.

Urgently required supplies, such as ammunition and scarce spare parts, would be carried by military airlifters. At the height of the war, the airfield at Camp Bastion in Helmand was the fifth-busiest British airport. Contracted civilian air freighters were used extensively, and some use was made of contracted helicopters for supplying isolated bases. Supplies needed by forward British bases in Afghanistan required several 'combat logistic patrols' of a hundred or two hundred vehicles to leave Camp Bastion every week. These were mounted as combat operations, with sizeable escort forces, counter-IED teams and the full range of fire support.

To reduce numbers of troops deployed, extensive use was made of contractors to deliver supplies to military bases. As the wars progressed, increasing numbers of civilian contractors performed logistic roles 'behind the wire', including contractors providing catering, repair and support equipment and drone maintenance.

INCREASINGLY SUCCESSFUL STABILIZATION

The two brigades of US Marines took over responsibility for northern Helmand, including Sangin and Kajaki. They already held Marjah, so the British were left with the Green Zone of central Helmand, finally allowing them to achieve a relatively high concentration of force. They continued to expand their network of forward operating bases, patrol bases and checkpoints. The increasing size of the Afghan security forces meant that more and more of the checkpoints could be assigned to Afghan Army or Police detachments.

Over 2010 and 2011, the balance of military advantage slowly shifted from the Taliban to the British. An illustration of this was the success over 2009–10 of the Grenadier Guards in the Nad-e Ali area.[8] Their commanding officer, Lieutenant Colonel Roly Walker, who in 2024 became the last CGS to feature in this book, incrementally extended the network of checkpoints and bases to constrict Taliban movement in the area. The idea was to reduce the Taliban's ability to interfere with the ability of farmers to take produce to market, thus stimulating the local economy. Sappers built 20 new bases to support the Grenadiers. Walker's design also sought to exploit the insurgents' propensity to attack bases, thus bringing the fighting to the British, reducing the chances of farmers getting caught in the crossfire.

This activity was complemented by information operations and money spent on reconstruction and development. After considerable initial difficulty, the Army and the PRT had finally developed an approach that met the requirements of hard-pressed tactical commanders. A telephone 'tip line' was opened. It received many calls from farmers frustrated with the Taliban's impact on their livelihood.

There was still much fighting, the Grenadiers being involved in 1,300 firefights. They estimated that 600 insurgents had died, and that 36 civilians had also been killed. Even though the greatly improved British counter-IED capabilities and tactics were beginning to have effect, the battlegroup found over 500 IEDS; the devices still took their steady, insidious morale-sapping toll. By the end of its six-month tour the battlegroup had suffered some 15 dead and 69 wounded, including amputees. Disease and non-battle injury inflicted a further 100 casualties. This number was typical of a battlegroup living in the austere conditions of forward bases, with troops constantly moving through sewage-filled irrigation ditches.[9]

Through the rest of 2010 and 2011, the Army slowly gained more advantage over the insurgents. British casualties reduced equally slowly, although deaths, wounding and serious amputations would continue for another two years. The concentration of British troops on central Helmand was achieving results, as was deployment of ever-increasing numbers of Afghan security forces in forward bases.

More new equipment, procured for Afghanistan, arrived. This included a whole fleet of armoured vehicles. The Viking light armoured all-terrain vehicle that the Royal Marines had brought with them in 2007 was replaced by the Singaporean Bronco, which had similar performance, but had much better protection. And the end of the Iraq war released Merlin and Lynx helicopters to deploy to Helmand, complementing the additional aircraft brought by the US Marines.

British brigades in Helmand now had much better intelligence surveillance and reconnaissance capability. Surveillance was further improved by purchasing Revivor, a US tethered aerostat which carried powerful surveillance systems. Flown above British bases, it greatly extended the range at which the base could observe both legitimate and suspicious activity.

Signals intelligence capabilities, from both the Army and Government Communications Headquarters (GCHQ) were redeployed from Basra, as were tactical electronic warfare (EW) teams. And a half decade's worth of signals intelligence gathering increased the utility of these systems.

By now, the British Army had learned how to do intelligence gathering, surveillance and targeting in Helmand, rediscovering the approaches applied so successfully in Northern Ireland. A proper network of communications was built across Helmand, allowing classified information to be much more widely shared and exploited.

The integration of intelligence into operations was improved, for example, by using EW that detected insurgent activity as a cue to other systems, such as drones, to look for more evidence of the enemy. If this was confirmed, a strike by Apache or artillery would be triggered. For example, 3rd Battalion, the Parachute Regiment had great success combining EW detection of Taliban activity from the Royal Signals Light EW Troop (LEWT) with imagery from Revivor aerostats, drones and Apaches. Sergio Miller describes a particularly rapid strike:

> Some engagements were lightning quick. In one incident, a LEWT detected and fixed the locations of two insurgents known by their call signs 'Zubia' and 'Maboob'. The detection

was recorded at 1639hrs. From their transmissions it was evident the pair – loitering by the entrance of a compound – were preparing to attack a patrol. Three minutes later, a base aerostat confirmed the detection (a process known as 'PID', or 'Positive Identification', without which no strike was allowed under the rules of engagement). Simultaneously, a drone also got 'eyes on'. Authority to strike was confirmed by the local commander. One minute later, 'Zubia' and 'Maboob' were dead. The entire sequence had lasted four minutes.[10]

The Exactor missile, originally deployed to Basra, was sent to Helmand. With a man in the loop, the operator flying the Spike NLOS missile through the camera on its nose, it provided a new unique precision indirect fire capability that complemented the Guided MLRS rockets. Then Captain Johnny Mercer, an artillery forward observer, has described how, having spotted a group of Taliban at great range, he called in an Exactor missile to destroy them.[11]

The firepower of the Apache helicopter was increased by employing a new warhead for its Hellfire missile. This was a thermobaric warhead which instead of conventional explosive created a cloud of explosive vapour. The resulting explosion was very effective against insurgents in compounds, caves and bunkers.

Infantry firepower was improved. A new sniper rifle with greater range was provided.[12] Platoons were issued with a new 'sharpshooter rifle' with an improved optical sight that had greater lethal effect at longer range than the SA80 rifles. The rifles themselves were modified to make them easier to use while wearing body armour, with the addition of a forward pistol grip that could also act as a bipod.

Preparatory training for Afghanistan improved. With the Army out of Iraq, it could now relentlessly focus on Afghanistan, and the training effort was greatly boosted by Operation *Entirety*. A formation cycle was established, to make best use of the two-year interval between brigade rotations to Afghanistan.

And several new organizations were established. An Afghan COIN centre was set up. It ran the initial briefing package for brigades, delivered at the start of their training. It also developed a deep expertise of understanding of Afghanistan and sometimes acted as an internal think-tank for the CGS. The existing Lessons Learned Cell at the Land Warfare Centre was expanded.

Preparation of intelligence staff for Helmand had initially been haphazard, below the standard achieved for Northern Ireland for most of that campaign. An innovation that improved this was the formation of a dedicated Land Intelligence Fusion Centre. This provided a secure environment for intelligence staff to immerse themselves in the classified material about the area they would deploy to.[13]

David Cameron's Afghan strategy

Prime Minister Gordon Brown's handling of the Afghan war damaged his political credibility, not least as opposition leader David Cameron used the war as a way of attacking Brown in Parliament and outside. This harmed Brown's electoral prospects.

In opposition Cameron had visited Afghanistan more than any other country.[14] He decided that whilst Iraq had been the 'wrong war', Afghanistan was the 'right war' where troops were defending UK security. After the 2009 UK election and formation of the new Conservative/Liberal Democrat coalition government, Prime Minister Cameron's first activity was to chair the first meeting of the re-established National Security Council (NSC). The Army welcomed this, as co-ordination of the Iraq and Afghan wars by prime ministers Blair and Brown had been weak.

Cameron set out three strategic principles for British military operations in Afghanistan. Firstly, to accept that nation building in Afghanistan would be limited. 'A failing state would be better than a failed state', he wrote. Secondly, to build up the Afghan government and forces to handle the war on their own. Thirdly, to set a deadline for withdrawal because:

> Our military high command seemed to have settled on the idea of being in Afghanistan almost indefinitely. As we lost troops, public consent was dwindling. A date would force everyone to reach a satisfactory and stable position before support at home disappeared altogether. I was re-committing Britain to the war by making sure Afghanistan was our number one security policy priority.[15]

He worried that Britain provided only 10 per cent of ISAF's troops but bore a third of its casualties. In part this was because many other national contingents would not deploy to areas of high threat and Helmand was Afghanistan's most dangerous province. He could not influence either factor, but was determined to improve equipment in Afghanistan, which he reviewed as a 'national disgrace'. He sought to exploit the US Marines' increasing strength to concentrate British troops in central Helmand. Sangin district had seen a quarter of British casualties. Cameron insisted that it be handed over to the US Marines.

In Cameron's memoir, this is the only example of any British influence over the US conduct of the campaign. He does not mention the US Surge at all.

THE 2010 STRATEGIC DEFENCE AND SECURITY REVIEW

The NSC was the prime customer for the Joint Intelligence Committee; it improved direction and prioritization of intelligence. This was a significant improvement over the ad hoc and inadequate direction of the wars in Iraq and Afghanistan by the previous government that had caused so much unnecessary political/military friction. During the Coalition government the NSC often met to give strategic direction to operations and planning. It was used extensively to manage the UK's role in Libya and seems to have succeeded in making the MoD, FCO and DfID integrate their work by design.

The Coalition government had a poisoned financial inheritance – the damage to UK public finances inflicted by the 2008 financial crisis. It saw its top priority as that of dealing with the UK's deficit, by reducing public expenditure.

Between June and October 2010, the Coalition government both developed a new National Security Strategy (NSS) and conducted a Strategic Defence and Security Review (SDSR). The NSS analyzed the strategic context and the ends that UK defence and security policy and capability were to achieve. A leading role was played by new Defence Secretary Liam Fox. He had made a considerable effort over the preceding years to learn about defence and arrived in the MoD brimming with confidence. The NSS described using:

> all the instruments of national power to prevent conflict and avert threats beyond our shores: our Embassies and High Commissions worldwide, our international development programme, our intelligence services, our defence diplomacy and our cultural assets. We will give top priority to countering the threat from terrorism at home and overseas. We will maintain the defensive and offensive capabilities needed to deploy armed force to protect UK territory and its citizens from the full range of threats from hostile action and to meet our commitments to our allies.[16]

The SDSR set out the ways, means and resources devoted to achieving these ends. But the government's overriding priority to reduce the UK deficit required the MoD to make an 8 per cent reduction in defence expenditure, well below the average 25 per cent reduction imposed across the UK public sector. It also had to manage away a prospective £36–38 billion overspend that it had inherited from the previous government.

This 'black hole' was caused by the MoD approving new equipment projects that cost much more than the funds available. By 2008 it had been identified by the MoD staff, but successive defence secretaries failed to resolve the issue. Staff in the MoD suspected that attempts to do so were vetoed by then Prime Minister Gordon Brown, possibly as a result of rising political and media criticism of equipment allocated to UK troops in Iraq and Afghanistan.

Parliament's Public Accounts Committee concluded that the MoD displayed a 'consistent pattern of planned overspend, demonstrates serious organizational failings and a dangerous culture of optimism' and that Sir Bill Jeffrey, then Permanent Secretary, had 'not discharged his responsibility to ensure that planned and committed expenditure across the defence budget represents value for money'.[17] This illustrates that no matter how well a defence ministry is structured, it cannot be immune from the effects of sub-optimal leadership and decision-making by ministers, senior officers or officials.

To match military capabilities with available funds, the government decided that its armed forces should do less, reducing the level of strategic ambition. For example, the planning assumption for numbers of troops conducting an enduring stabilization operation was reduced from 10,000 to 6,500. Readiness was also reduced, with more time being allowed for mobilization, training and deployment. For instance, before the SDSR, the Army had been required to generate a division of three heavy brigades at six months' notice, as part of a joint force of up to 45,000 troops. This target was reduced to a joint force of 30,000 troops, including a 'best effort' division of three brigades at a year's notice.

Making these targets less demanding allowed the force structure of all three services to be shrunk. Conventional capabilities and force structure were reduced by between 20 and

30 per cent. For example, the MoD's own figures showed reductions of armoured vehicles by 35 per cent, combat aircraft by 31 per cent and battle tanks by 24 per cent, part of an overall reduction of land and air fighting equipment by 27 per cent.[18] High-readiness 'early entry' capabilities were reduced. This included shrinking the ability to conduct amphibious landings from a brigade-sized formation to a single battalion-sized commando group. The capability for a parachute landing was similarly reduced.

Complete equipment capabilities were eliminated. Doing so allowed greater savings to be achieved than simply reducing all capabilities proportionately. The troubled Nimrod MRA4 replacement Maritime Patrol Aircraft programme was cancelled, to be replaced a decade later by smaller numbers of the US P8 Orion aircraft. This left a capability gap, in part filled by other NATO countries detaching maritime patrol aircraft to the UK.

Royal Naval and RAF capabilities were greatly reduced. The two small aircraft carriers were retired early, along with the Harrier jump jets they carried, as well as the RAF's complete Harrier force. This capability gap would be temporary, as the government would continue to fund the two much larger Queen Elizabeth-class carriers, which would enter service later in the decade, as well as the F35 fighters that would fly from them. Numbers of frigates and destroyers were reduced from 23 to 19 ships. Hunter-killer submarine numbers were capped at seven and the number of logistic ships was reduced. The Royal Navy and RAF each lost 5,000 people. RAF fighter squadrons were further reduced from nine to seven and the C130 Hercules transport aircraft would be retired ten years earlier than planned.

Increases of resources were confined to improving the support to special forces and £650 million for an increased UK cyber capability for both GCHQ and a military Cyber Operations Group. An innovative new Joint Forces Command took command of the increasing number of joint organizations, such as special forces, joint training units and the joint medical command, as well as becoming an institutional advocate for joint warfare.

The review stated that the government remained 'fully committed to succeeding in the difficult mission in Afghanistan, and there will as now, be extra resources to meet the full cost of that campaign'. Afghanistan operations would be prioritized and 'in the period covered by the Review we will make no changes to Army and Royal Marine and RAF Regiment combat units involved in Afghanistan'.[19] The UK would reduce its forces in conformity with the US drawdown. Fox stated that his plans were dependent on the British drawdown in Afghanistan remaining on track. Fox also claimed that 'for the first time in a generation, the MoD will have brought its plans and budget broadly into balance'. This was over-optimistic.

IMPLICATIONS FOR THE ARMY

The size of the Regular Army was reduced by 20 per cent, some 20,000 personnel, to a new strength of 95,000. Before the SDSR it had seven deployable brigades, two deployable divisional HQs and three regular logistic brigades. These would reduce to the air assault brigade and five new 'multi-role brigades' – each containing an armoured reconnaissance regiment, tank regiment and armoured infantry, mechanized and light infantry battalions. Only one divisional HQ would be rapidly deployable, and the lower-readiness requirements meant that one of the two logistic brigades would be manned by reservists. Front-line holdings of armoured vehicles were reduced, for example heavy artillery by 35 per cent. But the 67 Apache and 60 Chinook helicopters that had proved so useful in Afghanistan were retained.

The Army aimed to make much greater use of its reserves. They were to be much more integrated into the force structure and better trained and equipped. This required reversing two decades of relative neglect of Army reserves to more than double their trained strength to 30,000. As well as the additional £1.5 billion allocated to rebuilding reserve capability over the next decade, there would need to be a significant cultural change in employers, the reserves and the Regular Army, as well as new legislation.

ARMY 2020 – A MUCH REDUCED FORCE

These plans were overtaken by events. Despite the force reductions announced in 2010, it quickly became clear that there was still a considerable shortfall in the defence budget. The outcome of an exercise to match plans with resources was announced in July 2011, resulting in further reductions to the size of the Army.

The MoD had insufficient money to afford the personnel and equipment in the force structure announced by the SDSR. The CGS, General Sir Peter Wall, was summoned by the Permanent Secretary, and told that the Army should further reduce its regular manpower to 82,000 by 2020. Wall felt that this unwelcome new reduction was too great to simply be achieved by proportionate cuts across the Army. So he commissioned Major-General Nick Carter to conduct a redesign exercise from first principles.

Announced in July 2012, the new force structure was called 'Army 2020'. The HQ ARRC would be retained – albeit at lower readiness. The Army's high-intensity war-fighting capability was reduced to a single heavy division: the 3rd, with three armoured infantry brigades. The number of deployable brigades was reduced from six to four, with armoured, engineer and artillery regiments being reduced. This broke Liam Fox's pledge that Army combat units involved in Afghanistan would be protected from change.

Formations were restructured to reflect many of the hard lessons of the Iraq and Afghan wars. But to meet the required savings targets most of these had two or three roles: not only delivering deployable combat capability, but also having a role in homeland security or international military engagement, or both.

Some innovative new organizations were formed. They included a new intelligence, surveillance and reconnaissance brigade and the 77th Brigade to conduct information operations. But there was no disguising that these reorganizations and a reduction of regular manpower reduced the Army's deployable combat power by about a third, compared with its capability in 2009. This would be partially alleviated by increasing the volunteer reserves in the TA to a trained strength of 30,000 and improving their readiness.

There were significant reductions in HQs, administration, training organizations and infrastructure.

By the time that Army 2020 was announced, an 8–9 per cent real-terms (inflation-adjusted) reduction to the defence budget since 2010 had resulted in a 20–30 per cent reduction in the UK's conventional military capability.

The Army became very concerned about the retention of quality personnel. Pay was frozen and allowances reduced, a bitter pill impossible to coat with sugar. A redundancy programme to reduce the strength of the Army saw a significant outflow of top-quality officers. The Army attributed this to accumulated overstretch resulting from fighting the Afghan and Iraq wars simultaneously, concerns about conditions of service and a sense that it was better to jump than be pushed.

Although the UK's reserves contributed significant numbers to operations in Iraq and Afghanistan, successive resource cuts had resulted in much of their capability atrophying. And the UK made less use of reserves than the US, Canada or Australia. In response to political and media pressure, Fox had appointed an independent commission to examine UK reserve forces. He accepted its assessment that reserve capability had greatly declined, and their potential was not being fully exploited. This would be reversed by enhancing the role, training and resourcing of reserves, including over £100 million per year of additional funding, so that they could play an increased role in both oversees operations and homeland security. The TA was renamed the Army Reserve.

The MoD stated that the necessary redundancy programme to reduce numbers of personnel would not affect units in Afghanistan. This was patently untrue, as I saw for myself, when I visited a brigade preparing to deploy. Redundancy greatly increased turbulence in key posts. For example, an infantry battalion lost three of its five majors to redundancy during pre-tour training.[20]

Many of the choices made in the SDSR were very controversial. UK media and politicians of all parties criticized the review as being too rushed. They seized on leaked documents and public comments by senior officers as evidence that the SDSR was already out of date. Defence commentators criticized the scrapping of aircraft carriers, Harrier jump jets and Nimrod maritime patrol aircraft, as well as personnel reductions. The US, NATO and the UK's other allies considered the forces' reductions unwelcome.

The review was trenchantly defended by Cameron and Fox. Ministers and government officials repeatedly claimed that been no 'strategic shrinkage'. This was patently absurd. No one in the Army believed this.

The House of Commons Defence Committee was unconvinced that the reduced forces were able to meet current and future commitments or retain their 'critical mass', or that 'Future Force 2020' could be delivered without increased funding. Many UK defence commentators expressed similar scepticism that the books had really been balanced, and that defence spending would be sufficient.

Fox would not have time to oversee the implementation of the review. In late 2011, he became enmeshed in a political scandal concerning an apparent conflict of interest with questionable activities of a close colleague. Fox resigned and was replaced by Phillip Hammond.

Reforming defence

Prior to the SDSR, the MoD had acquired a reputation for inefficiency, indecision and obfuscation. This was, in part, well deserved, the armed forces often complaining about over-centralization and paralyzing bureaucracy. The handling of the aircraft carrier programme was described by the Public Accounts Committee as 'a new benchmark in poor corporate decision-making'.[21] The Iraq Inquiry would later spell out in excoriating detail how the MoD had failed to provide improved surveillance and protected mobility capability quickly enough for use in Iraq.

Defence acquisition was notorious for cost-overruns and delays in delivering critical supplies to the front line, generating considerable political and media criticism. It had been subject to continuous reform since 1997. Bernard Grey was commissioned by the previous government in 2009 to propose further reforms and was subsequently selected by Liam Fox as Chief of Defence Material, responsible for spending 40 per cent of the MoD's budget.

Grey's structural reforms to Defence Equipment and Support (DE&S) were evolutionary rather than revolutionary. He identified that it was just as important to fix the MoD as a whole as to improve the performance of DE&S. Grey insisted on ruthless honesty when it came to costing equipment and logistic programmes. This was welcomed as a long overdue effort to root out the over-optimism that had bedevilled UK defence programmes in the past. But it resulted in much greater visibility of potential increases in cost.

But subsequent performance by DF&S would continue to disappoint the Army. It often became a byword for bureaucratic delay. And its handling of the Army's new Ajax armoured vehicle would fall short of the necessary effectiveness.

After the SDSR announcement Lord Levene, a former Chief of Defence Procurement, conducted an independent review into the management of defence.[22] Most of his recommendations were implemented. The MoD adopted a new management model for defence, including decentralization of budgets and authority for military capability from a much smaller ministry to the three services.

An innovative new Joint Forces Command took command of the increasing number of joint organizations, such as special forces, joint training units and the joint medical command, as well as becoming an institutional advocate for joint warfare.

A smaller defence board was to be chaired by the Defence Secretary, the sole military member being the Chief of Defence Staff. The Permanent Secretary and finance director were the other two MoD staff on the board, which teemed with civilian non-executive directors. This aimed to force the MoD to better match its plans to financial resources, so that never again would it plan to spend more than it could afford.

These were the most radical changes in the management of UK's defence since Lord Mountbatten's reforms of the early 1960s. They reversed almost 30 years of increasing centralization. They gave the Army much greater control over its equipment, structure, manpower and training than it had in the previous decade. The changes were broadly welcomed by the Army, eager to return its hands to the levers of power to optimize its capability.

APACHES STRIKE LIBYA FROM THE SEA

In December 2010, unrest in Tunisia rapidly spread throughout the Arab world. The so-called Arab Spring saw a wave of protest and rebellion erupt. Protests broke out in Libya against the role of the dictator Muammar Gaddafi. This rapidly turned into a violent conflict. When it seemed likely that government forces were heading towards Benghazi, French aircraft attacked and destroyed the armoured column leading the advance. An international operation to protect the Libyan population was rapidly improvised. Initially under US leadership, command was rapidly transferred to NATO. Initially Operation *Unified Protector* was an exclusively air operation. But as the campaign wore on it became increasingly clear that jets dropping bombs were not having sufficient effect quickly enough.

Attacks on Libyan government forces were broadened. NATO warships used naval gunfire to attack coastal targets. France and Britain deployed ship-borne attack helicopters to attack targets. They could fly much lower than the fighter bombers used by NATO and could strike different targets.

In June 2011, Army Apache attack helicopters began flying from the helicopter carrier HMS *Ocean* to attack Gaddafi-regime forces. Using Hellfire missiles and cannon fire, they conducted night attacks against regime radar and ground forces. These were successful.[23]

Apache had never been designed to fly from ships. But with considerable foresight, the Royal Marines and Army had previously identified a potential need for Apaches to support amphibious forces. This was operationalized by assigning this role to an Apache squadron. Following deck landing trials in 2005, Apaches occasionally embarked on HMS *Ocean*. This contributed to the ease in which Apaches deployed onto the carrier in 2011. And the helicopters did not need any equipment enhancements to operate over Libya. This surprised many Army officers, who were accustomed to having to upgrade or augment their equipment for Iraq and Afghanistan.

Even so, tactical adaptations were required. French president Nicholas Sarkozy was reportedly willing to accept up to 30 per cent casualties among the French attack helicopters deployed. London was much more cautious, requiring much more assurance by surveillance and reconnaissance and protection from NATO SEAD (suppression of enemy air defences) capabilities. So a new technique was evolved to allow images taken by RAF Typhoon and Tornado jets to be beamed to HMS *Ocean* to assist Apache crews in mission planning. French helicopters operated under much more permissive rules of engagement and were able to conduct more strikes.

The ghosts of British weaknesses in Basra and Helmand were slightly exorcized by the leading British role in Libya. But had the war lasted beyond September, some hard choices about military strategic priorities would have been unavoidable – for example, decisions about withdrawing attack helicopters, drones and special forces from Afghanistan. Spared of these hard choices, Prime Minister Cameron and Defence Secretary Fox insisted that the SDSR was still valid. Cameron testified to the House of Commons Liaison Committee that:

the things that we are learning reinforce the thrust behind the defence review, which was all about flexible armed forces, ease to deploy, the importance of transport and of ISTAR and drones. I suppose if there was one lesson, it is that the extra emphasis we put on ISTAR and drones will be even more necessary in future, and I would like us to go even faster on that.[24]

Previously the MoD had planned that the US would always lead any NATO combat operation and provide both combat forces and key 'enablers' such as electronic warfare and suppression of air defences. Libya saw the US withdraw from a NATO combat mission, to 'lead from behind'.[25]

Afghanistan, 2011–12

In May 2011, US special forces flew from Afghanistan to kill Osama Bin Laden in Pakistan. This removed one of the main reasons for the US presence in Afghanistan. The next month President Obama announced that the Surge had peaked and would reduce. Ten thousand US troops would depart by the end of the year with all the additional Surge troops being withdrawn by summer 2012.

In spring 2012 the Taliban declared an offensive to push back ISAF and Afghan forces. This failed, the combined capabilities and strength of the Afghan and NATO forces meaning that territory gained during the Afghan Surge was held against Taliban attacks. The additional 33,000 US Surge troops that had deployed to Afghanistan in 2010 withdrew by October 2012, leaving 68,000 US troops alongside 32,000 troops from other nations.

The Afghan Army took an increasing lead for security. Most insurgent attacks were on the edges of territory under Afghan government control, some 80 per cent of attacks occurring in 20 per cent of Afghan districts.

Insurgent attacks using IEDs fell by 20 per cent. NATO claimed to be finding and clearing more IEDs than were successfully detonated by the Taliban. But whilst 42 per cent of NATO fatalities were from IEDs, over 80 per cent of Afghan Army fatalities were caused in this way, in stark demonstration of the Afghans' lower level of counter-IED capability. This and the Afghan forces' lower numbers of armoured vehicles, helicopters and drones combined to result in their casualties doubling in 2012.

Overall, the Afghan forces assumed an increasing responsibility for security as NATO troops withdrew. But it was far from clear that there would be enough improvement in Afghan governance and a reduction in corruption to neutralize root causes of the insurgency. According to a September 2012 UN assessment:

little has changed in the underlying dynamics to mitigate a deep-seated cycle of conflict. Furthermore, a diminished international presence will have a significant financial impact in many areas that, at least in the short term, may even exacerbate predatory behaviour, with a reduced flow of money encouraging criminality.[26]

INSIDER ATTACKS

Occasional attacks on international forces by Afghan troops and police had occurred since at least 2006. A particularly unsettling attack at the end of 2009 had killed several Grenadier guardsmen, including their regimental sergeant major. Insider attacks greatly increased in 2012, when 60 ISAF troops were killed in such attacks, a 40 per cent increase compared with 2011. It was likely that war fatigue and accumulated Afghan resentment of the NATO presence were major motivating factors.

NATO and the Afghan authorities announced many initiatives to improve security against Taliban infiltration, including improved vetting and counter-intelligence. NATO troops were assigned to act as 'guardian angels' – providing armed guards for NATO troops who were training Afghans. By the end of 2012 such attacks had greatly reduced, probably as a result of the additional security measures. But insider attacks were never totally eradicated, continuing at a lower level until the end of the decade.

THE ATTACK ON CAMP BASTION

In south-west Afghanistan NATO forces reduced by about 60 per cent during 2012. September 2012 saw the Taliban mount an audacious surprise attack on the UK–US base at Camp Bastion. A large squad of well-led and motivated Taliban fighters, dressed in US Army uniforms, infiltrated through a ravine, cut protective barbed wire, penetrated the base defences undetected and reached the US Marines' aircraft shelters. They got close enough to these to attack them with hand grenades.

An ad hoc force of US Marines' maintenance personnel, US Air Force pararescue personnel and the RAF Regiment fought back with courage and determination against equally steadfast Taliban fighters. There was confused close-quarter night fighting. Two US Marines were killed, two Harrier jets destroyed, and eight other aircraft damaged.

The US Marine Corps investigation into the attack resulted in the dismissal of two Marine generals who were held accountable for the security breach.[27] Both the US investigation and an inquiry by the UK House of Commons Defence Committee illuminated with crystal clarity that the UK chain of command for the security of the base was very complex. Accountability and responsibility for base security was highly diffuse, with the British resisting subordinating their security operations to the US. This meant that:

> Insufficient attention was given to the fundamental requirement of defending Camp Bastion from external assault. We believe that this was complacent. Given that the attack took place in the British sector of the camp, British commanders must bear a degree of responsibility for these systemic failures and associated reputational damage. We note the acknowledgement by the MoD that errors were made which, collectively, created the vulnerabilities which were so devastatingly exploited by the enemy.[28]

Ironically, within two days of the attack, responsibility for base security was properly aligned. The inconvenient truth was that this was as much a clear failure by the UK military chain of command as it was of US Marine commanders. There is no evidence that any British officer was ever held accountable for these weaknesses. Some Army officers were incredulous at this deflection of blame.[29]

2012 – Operation *Olympics*

In 2005, London won the bid to host the 2012 Olympic games. A considerable amount of planning for the large-scale security operation began. From the outset this involved the armed forces. By 2009, General Sir David Richards, then Commander in Chief Land Command, stated in public that just three years out from the games, there was not enough clarity to allow him to plan for the roles the military might perform.[30] The plan that eventually developed had the police in overall charge, with games organizers searching spectators as they entered the venues, a task they contracted to G4S, a civilian security company.

General Nick Parker, Commander in Chief Land Forces, became joint commander of the operation, including events outside London, such as the sailing and windsurfing in Poole Harbour. The GOC of London District was the joint force commander of all armed forces in London. The armed forces provided air defence. With the RAF as an outer ring, prepared to intercept any hijacked or threatening aircraft, an inner ring was provided by Army and Navy Lynx helicopters carrying specially trained marksmen. Ground-based air defence was provided by the Army's Rapier and Starstreak missiles. Rapier launchers were sited in Blackheath Park, a hill in south-east London, and some man-portable Starstreak launchers were placed on the top of an East London apartment building. Special forces were deployed to provide quick reaction to any terrorist attack that might exceed the capacity of the police.

Initially, it was planned that the military would provide 6,000 personnel to assist with event security. In December 2011 the requirement was increased to 8,500 people. As the Olympics got closer the MoD and Army became increasingly concerned that G4S' arrangements appeared haphazard. It looked increasingly unlikely that the company would provide the civilian searches they were contracted to provide.

General Richards observed that the government increasingly displayed a 'bureaucratic reluctance' to acknowledge this. Government command and control arrangements were chaotic, which delayed grappling with this inconvenient truth. This meant that Prime Minister Cameron decided very late in the day to call on the only other source of rapidly trained manpower that could fill this role – up to 17,000 members of the armed forces.[31]

The Army made the biggest contribution to bridging this security gap. Ten days before the games were to start, I attended the unveiling of a memorial to the Parachute Regiment at the National Memorial Arboretum. After the service there was a reception attended by several hundred members of the regiment. Parked outside were a fleet of coaches to take troops back to their base at Colchester. As the event proceeded, I could see increasing numbers of people looking at their phones, as messages and emails arrived warning units that they were tasked with Olympic security. By the time the reception wound down, initial orders had been given. Half of those attending the function returned to barracks; the other half, comprising commanders, planners and logisticians, got onto coaches now heading for London. Not once did I hear a word of complaint, even though a significant number of those present had had their weekend and summer leave plans disrupted.

Fortunately, HQ London District had well-refined plans to deal with a wide range of emergencies, so was quickly able to arrange accommodation and feeding for thousands of troops, including at a disused warehouse in Wapping and a temporary camp in Hainault Forest. In the event the total number of troops deployed to the event was 4,700. Different events were assigned to different services and units. For example, the 1st Armoured Division provided a 900-strong security force for the cycling, running and beach volleyball events. Led by Lieutenant Colonel Charles Story, the commanding officer of 28 Engineer Regiment, the unit included two infantry companies, two armoured squadrons, and a transport squadron, engineer squadron, signals squadron and artillery battery.

Initially, the Army worried that the very short notice to conduct routine and repetitive tasks, combined with disruption of plans for summer leave, would be a blow to morale. In the event these fears were not realized. The Olympics were widely regarded as a national triumph, only equalled by the 1966 World Cup victory. Spectators were very impressed with the conduct and attitude of the military personnel, a useful reminder to the nation that the forces had a unique ability to respond to national emergencies. In retrospect, the Army's rapid deployment to provide security was a high point of its popularity.

INTERVENTION IN MALI AND NON-INTERVENTION IN SYRIA

In January 2013, jihadist rebels from northern Mali rapidly advanced on the capital Bamako. France judged that the assault might succeed and mounted a very rapid operation to defeat the insurgents. This combined long-range air attacks initially mounted from metropolitan France and rapid deployment of French Army reinforcements by air.

At that time France had less air transport capability than the UK, so the British rapidly deployed two giant C17 airlifters to fly French armoured vehicles to Mali. Many other nations offered strategic airlift. To help the French forces co-ordinate this considerable airlift operation, a British Army logistic brigade HQ deployed to Mali to assist in the rapid build-up of French and international forces. The British subsequently made a small contribution to an EU training mission.

The Arab Spring had resulted in an increasingly violent and destabilizing civil war in Syria. Following a chemical attack by government forces, the UK and US leaders agreed that a strike on the Syrian military was necessary to deter future chemical attacks by the Assad regime. David Cameron went to the House of Commons, seeking authority to conduct strikes on government forces in Syria. But Parliament voted against this. A narrow majority of MPs were unconvinced by the government's case for military intervention. Then Defence Secretary Philip Hammond said: 'there is a deep well of suspicion about military involvement in the Middle East stemming largely from the experiences of Iraq'.[32]

MPs voting against the government were expressing Iraq-influenced doubts about the intelligence that was presented. They opposed being railroaded into rapid action while UN inspectors were still at work in Syria – another Iraq parallel. Many doubted that the strikes being contemplated would have any useful effect. It was not clear if the vote was an exceptional event, the beginning of the unravelling of the last two decades of broad political consensus on defence. But it showed that Iraq and Afghanistan had deeply damaged the British political appetite for the utility of force. This was in retrospect a significant milestone. It did nothing for the US military's confidence in the British.

AFGHAN TRANSITION, 2012–14

The British effort in Helmand peaked over the period 2009–11. A combination of improved equipment, the effects of Operation *Entirety*, increasing numbers of Afghan forces and concentrating British forces meant that mostly the Taliban had been pushed away from the main towns of central Helmand. The British main effort shifted to transitioning security leadership to the Afghan forces and reducing their forces, in order to depart the province in 2014.

By now over 80 per cent of operations were led by the Afghan forces, with fewer than 10 per cent conducted solely by ISAF. At a January 2013 Kabul press conference with President Karzai, President Obama stated that after withdrawing from combat missions, the US wished to conduct 'two long-term tasks, which will be very specific and very narrow – first, training and assisting Afghan forces and, second, targeted counterterrorism missions against al Qaeda and its affiliates'.[33]

In June 2013 Afghan forces took country-wide leadership of security operations, Lashkar Gar being one of the first Afghan districts to transition. Over the next year the remaining British-controlled districts in Helmand were handed to Afghan security leadership, followed by Nar-e Saaj as the final district. British bases in Helmand Province reduced from 80 in April 2012 to five in October 2013. Most were handed over to Afghan forces, but others were abandoned. These were rapidly looted for building materials by local Afghans. By February 2014, British bases were limited to Camp Bastion and two outposts.

But fighting continued during this period. In the last two years before withdrawal from Helmand the Army expended almost 7.5 million rounds of small arms ammunition and over 8,000 artillery shells.[34] However, the main effort had switched from offensive operations to against the Taliban to defending British troops and bases and supporting Afghan forces.

The April 2014 Afghan presidential election saw security successfully provided by the Afghan forces. The two main candidates, Ashraf Ghani and Abdullah Abdullah, accused each other of industrial-scale vote-rigging. This triggered a political crisis, with Abdullah's key supporters, former warlords in the Northern Alliance, talking openly of using force to install Abdullah. A political deal was eventually brokered by US Secretary of State John Kerry, but the months of political wrangling greatly distracted the Afghan government.

For the Army, the main effort of 2014 was handing over to the Afghan forces and then withdrawing. This involved a major logistic operation to send back to the UK as much military material as could be re-employed elsewhere. This totalled 3,000 vehicles and 5,500 ISO containers. Some equipment, such as Apache helicopters, returned to UK in the bellies of the RAF's giant C17 aircraft; much returned by road through Pakistan. A new rail route was developed from Uzbekistan and then through Russia to the Baltic. This would be the last time that Russia would be helpful to the British military.[35]

Some of the equipment specially procured for Afghanistan was retained by the Army. This included the Exactor precision missile. Several vehicles were kept in service; the Jackal light scout vehicle and the heavy Mastiff APC were issued to light cavalry and some infantry battalions. The Foxhound APC was allocated to 'light mechanized' units.

The last British troops departed from Camp Bastion by Chinook helicopter on 26 October 2014, with the last Union Jack flag carried into the helicopter by an RAF wing commander. He wore full personal protection, including Osprey body armour, helmet and goggles, and the flight was protected by Apache and US Super Cobra helicopters, RAF Reaper drones and Tornado bombers.

ARMY REFLECTIONS ON THE DIFFICULT WAR IN AFGHANISTAN

Throughout its commitment to Helmand, there was great disquiet in the Army about its apparent failure to adapt quickly enough. Many wondered why it had taken so long to do so.

One factor was that the Iraq war used up so many resources and people that the bandwidth of the Army's leadership and staff was sucked away from Afghanistan. And neither the MoD nor its rapidly changing constellation of ministers imparted the necessary energy, prioritization or focussed management that the Afghan campaign required. It took the decisive effect of Operation *Charge of the Knights* to set the conditions for British withdrawal, at least two years later than the MoD's over-optimistic initial plan had assumed. The other factor was the declaration of Operation *Entirety*.

These are not sufficient to explain the apparent sluggishness. In 2015, the Army's Director Land Warfare issued a campaign study of Operation *Herrick*. A redacted version was later published as a result of a freedom of information request. It provides a balanced assessment of the strength and weaknesses of the Army's campaign.[36] One of the key judgements was that the Afghan War had come at some cost:

a total of 453 British troops have been killed during the campaign and 615 have been seriously, or very seriously wounded and a total of 2,187 were classified as 'wounded in action'. As at 2014 the UK had spent £37 billion on the campaign, and this is predicted to rise to £40 billion by 2020. The fighting spirit of this generation of British forces was tested and proven. We have an Army which is resilient, combat hardened and self-confident, and in which many individuals have demonstrated both superb professionalism and conspicuous bravery.

More critical observers would point to serious shortcomings that undermined what was always going to be a wicked problem. Such shortcomings could include systemic weaknesses in understanding the scale, nature and complexity of Afghanistan; the scale of our ambitions unmatched by the ways and means; a parochial focus on a British solution in Helmand; lengthy periods when UK land operations seemed dangerously adrift of higher direction and out of balance in ways and means; short term tactical actions that generated longer term challenges; an institutional reluctance to comprehensively and quickly adjust to operational demands; and a failure to comprehend the sheer corruption and inefficiency of some Afghan leaders – the latter running the risk of linking British forces with predatory activity and thereby undermining the narrative they were fighting so hard to encourage.

The longer-term effectiveness of the ANSF [Afghan National Security Forces] in Helmand will prove the principal measure by which the legacy of the UK military presence on Operation HERRICK will most likely be judged.

After 2021 this judgement would be uncomfortable.[37] But it seems to have been given a stiff ignoring by the MoD and government.

CHAPTER 14
A DECADE OF DEFEAT, DECLINE AND DISRUPTION

When combat operations in Afghanistan ceased in 2014, it seemed to many that the UK was sick of being embroiled in frustrating, bloody, unpopular and unsuccessful wars. Many in the Army thought that it would be set for another period of low operational pressure and a level of small-scale operations – most probably building capacity of other nations and some small peacekeeping operations.

In fact, there was great geo-strategic turbulence and an ever-increasing threat to the UK and its interests from viruses, terrorism and Russia. This had profound implications for the Army, including a return to boots on the ground conducting forward defence in Europe. But troop numbers continued to fall.

The 2022 Russian attack on Ukraine was the tipping point. The MoD and government were forced to acknowledge that the Army's equipment was increasingly out of date, although they denied that its strength had become too small. Shortage of funds meant that Army capability was declining below critical mass. In 2025, the new Labour government initiated a new strategic defence review and made a modest increase in defence spending. It was not clear whether either initiative would prevent the Army from reaching a tipping point of irreversible decline.

2014 – THE 'BLOOD YEAR'

UKRAINE – THE CURTAIN RISES

In early 2014 a popular uprising threw out the Ukrainian president. Kyiv's citizens were in favour of a close relationship with the West and the EU, which he opposed, as did Russian president Vladimir Putin. Quickly, Russian forces staged a relatively bloodless coup in Crimea, Moscow then annexing the peninsula as part of Russia. The Kremlin then orchestrated an uprising against Kyiv in the Donbas region of eastern Ukraine. This led to land battles with Ukraine's armed forces, including pitched battles in urban areas, the shooting down of a Malaysian airliner and intense barrages of Russian artillery rockets that stopped a counterattack by Ukraine's elite airborne troops in its tracks.

Europe eventually negotiated the Minsk Agreement between Ukraine and Russia. This had the effect of freezing the front lines in place. But hostilities continued, albeit at a lower level.

The Army provided training to Ukrainian forces. Operation *Orbital* began in early 2015. For the next seven years small Army training teams travelled to Ukraine. Training topics included infantry, counter-IED, logistics, medical, planning and leadership. The Army felt that it had helped the Ukrainian Army shift its commanders from using a Soviet-style authoritarian approach towards employing the British approach of more delegated command. This was complemented by the deployment of retired senior officers as mentors to Ukrainian forces. In September 2020, 16 Air Assault Brigade sent 250 paratroops to jump into eastern Ukraine alongside Ukraine's 80th Air Assault Brigade.

BOKO HARAM IN NIGERIA

From 2010 onwards, Nigeria had faced a growing insurgency from Boko Haram, a jihadist group. In 2013 the group seized a British hostage and a rescue effort mounted by the SBS failed, with the death of the hostage.

Boko Haram's April 2014 mass kidnapping of 276 schoolgirls from Chibok caused international outrage. The UK deployed a Sentinel surveillance aircraft, followed by Tornado reconnaissance jets. Prime Minister David Cameron stated that the RAF had located some of the missing girls in a forest. But when Cameron offered UK military assistance to rescue them, Nigerian President Goodluck Jonathan refused. Cameron observed that 'the problem was a weak government and corruption. The Nigerian Army was so hollowed out by venal, politically appointed generals, that it was incapable of participating in operations with UK assistance.'[1]

In London, the NSC diagnosed the Nigerian government and forces as being hollowed out by malign patronage and corruption. It chose to embark on a long-term training effort to improve the capability of Nigeria's intelligence agencies and armed forces. Building on an existing British military training team a protracted programme of military assistance was delivered from 2015 onwards. This involved between 130 and 300 troops in Nigeria. Much of this was provided by 7th Infantry Brigade and the 2nd Battalion, the Royal Anglian Regiment.

2014 – ISIS ERUPTS IN SYRIA AND IRAQ

After the US withdrew combat forces from Iraq in December 2011, Prime Minister Maliki increasingly indulged in sectarian repression of the Sunni minority, whilst hollowing out the Iraqi security forces through malign political patronage. A toxic combination of discrimination, deliberate neglect and increasing repression increasingly disenfranchised and alienated the Sunni minority. Meanwhile the remnants of Al Qaida in Iraq took up arms against the Assad regime in Syria. Rebranding itself as the Islamic State of Syria and al Sham (ISIS), it carved out territory from the central town of Raqqa to the Iraqi border. In summer 2014 it defeated Iraqi forces in western Iraq, the bloodthirsty jihadists conquering a third of Iraq's territory and marching on Baghdad.

The ISIS advance was stopped by Grand Ayatollah al-Sistani declaring a fatwa against ISIS and encouraging Iraqi men to take up arms to do so. And Iran activated the Shia militias it sponsored, to the same effect. The RAF conducted humanitarian supply drops and delivered arms to Kurdistan by Hercules, as well as air reconnaissance missions.

In September 2014, President Obama formed a US-led international coalition against ISIS and began a campaign of air and missile strikes against ISIS in both Iraq and Syria. The US made its support conditional on the resignation of Prime Minister Maliki, who was replaced by Haida al-Abadi, a less confrontational figure. Washington led an international political, military, intelligence and information campaign to degrade ISIS' military capabilities by attacking its command and control, the way it used the internet for propaganda and its ability to raise funds from trading in oil and smuggled antiquities.

The RAF did not initially join US air strikes on ISIS. It was only after the murder of British and US hostages, apparently by a jihadi of UK origin, resulting in a formal request for assistance by the Iraqi government and parliamentary assent, that RAF Tornados flew from Cyprus to strike ISIS in Iraq.

US advisors helped the Iraqi government build the capability of selected Iraqi Army and police formations for a counteroffensive against ISIS. Obama made it clear that the US would not deploy ground forces to directly combat ISIS. It would be Iraqi, Kurdish and Syrian 'boots on the ground', supported by US firepower and advisors. But US special forces launched helicopter-borne raids on ISIS and worked with Iraqi government forces and with Kurdish militias. Concurrently Iran sought to build the capabilities of the popular mobilization units, by providing arms, equipment and training, all co-ordinated by the presence of Iranian military advisors.

Lieutenant General Simon Mayall formulated a plan for a British military contribution to the war against ISIS. This included providing training teams to Iraqi government forces and the Peshmerga. Once the units had been trained, British military advisors would accompany the units into combat. This seemed to have Prime Minister Cameron's initial approval, but the provision of military teams to accompany the Iraqi and Kurdish forces into battle was not implemented.[2] The Army despatched some training teams to assist Iraqi government security forces. At its peak the training mission saw some 900 British personnel in Iraq, the great majority from the Army. But the government ruled out any conventional Army participation in fighting on the ground. In his autobiography David Cameron demonstrates clear pride in Britain's role in helping to combat ISIS in Syria and Iraq. He saw it as a template for wider overseas operations:

That meant avoiding putting western troops on the ground where possible, taking time to understand the situation, working with and through allies. That was what I called 'smart intervention'. It aimed to avoid the radicalization and backlash at home that had been unintended consequences of earlier interventions.[3]

These principles made sense. But they had the consequence of Britain doing less on the ground in Iraq and Syria than US or French forces. Inevitably this reduced British military influence with the US.

By late 2014 the expansion of ISIS in Iraq was halted. In 2015 and 2016 Iraqi government formations and militias moved over to the offensive, recapturing Tikrit in April 2015, Ramadi in March 2016, and Fallujah in June 2016. In October 2016 Iraqi forces began attacking Mosul. About 5,000 ISIS fighters had extensively fortified the centre of the city, creating fighting positions, obstacles and tunnels. With some 94,000 Peshmerga, Iraqi government troops and police involved this was probably the largest single ground battle since 9/11 and one of the largest and longest battles of any war since 1945. ISIS proved determined defenders, making great use of IEDs, improvised armoured vehicles and small drones for observation and attack, and constantly seeking to encircle and cut off government forces.

President Obama relaxed his constraints forbidding US Army boots on the ground. Iraqi Army and police formations attacking Mosul were closely accompanied by US military advisors. At the peak of the battle these were supplied by a US Army brigade providing parties of advisors and fire controllers that assisted Iraqi formations with planning and called in fire support. This included precision bombs and missiles from Coalition aircraft, fire from US Army Apache helicopter gunships and shells and guided rockets fired by US artillery units. The French Army also deployed an artillery battery to support the fighting. After Mosul was captured, French artillery fire supported Kurdish forces fighting against ISIS in Syria.

In contrast, the closest the British Army came to the battle in Mosul was a team of Royal Engineers who advised Iraqi sappers building a bridge well outside Mosul. There were no British Army advisors accompanying Iraqi troops in Mosul, no British Apache helicopters flying alongside US Army Apaches, nor any troops from the Royal Artillery joining US and French artillery firing on ISIS. When asked why this was the case, MoD officials could not offer an adequate explanation.[4]

COUNTERING EBOLA IN SIERRA LEONE – OPERATION GRITROCK

In late 2014 West Africa was threatened by a large-scale outbreak of Ebola. This virus causes haemorrhagic fever. It is spread by contact with bodily fluids of an infected person, making it highly contagious and very lethal. The disease was rapidly spreading and threatened to overwhelm the fragile health system of Sierra Leone.

In September 2014, London intervened to prevent this. A combined joint interagency task force was sent to Sierra Leone. Headed by a DfID official, it comprised a significant military effort from all three services, commanded by 104th Logistic Brigade led by

Brigadier Steve MacMahon. A civil/military combined joint interagency task force (CJIATF) was formed.

On arrival it found that efforts by the UN, World Health Organization and Sierra Leonean government were all failing. Indeed, some epidemiological analysis of data conducted by the British suggested not only that the disease was out of control, but also that it could not be brought under control. The one light on the horizon was that the country's military were still very well respected throughout the country, as was the defence minister.

The CJIATF carried out a quick assessment. Two days after arriving it recommended to President Koroma that he form a National Ebola Response Centre. This was designed to co-ordinate the national response to the disease and to support the president in making the necessary strategic decisions. The British played the leading role in setting it up and it was initially staffed by British military and civilian staff from the CJIATF, though rapidly joined by Sierra Leone Army personnel including the defence minister, who ran the operation for the Prime Minister. An instrumental role was played by two British lieutenant colonels, already serving in the country as members of the small international training team. The effort in Freetown was complemented by newly established District Ebola Response Centres (DERCs) in each of the county's 14 districts.

The CJIATF strategy consisted of three phases: 1 – contain and protect; 2 – expand and influence; and 3 – eradicate. The Army was heavily involved in all of these. With assistance from Sierra Leonean sappers, the Royal Engineers built six UK-funded 100-bed Ebola treatment units and provided engineer support to the other treatment units run by the government and non-governmental organizations.

At the height of the operation Royal Engineer experts were running contracts to the value of £23 million and directing a civilian workforce of 1,470 people as well as a squadron of Sierra Leonean combat engineers. The British military helped set up and run two Ebola training academies in Freetown to train healthcare workers and other staff. The British military were joined by international contingents, including troops from Ireland and Canada. Norway and the Netherlands provided airlift.

There was a major gap in public understanding of the disease, especially of how traditional Sierra Leonean funerary practices of washing the dead provided an ideal opportunity for the virus to spread. Brigadier MacMahon saw the most important part of the mission as being an information operation to dispel ignorance, spread advice on treatment and isolation and engage community leaders.

Given the horrifying character of the disease and its high mortality rate, it was essential to sustain the morale of healthcare workers and the British military by being able to provide rapid and high-quality treatment to any who contracted the disease. So the military built a 20-bed Ebola treatment unit for infected healthcare workers, and a forward field hospital in Freetown. Further medical backup was provided by a full hospital and surgical capability aboard RFA Argus, which also carried Merlin helicopters.

The initial deployment saw a peak of 1,000 military personnel carrying out these operations. There was a particular need to collect and dispose of dead bodies, which in some places were littering the streets. This unpleasant and dangerous task was one in which the Sierra Leonean Army played a major role, including providing security to protect medical workers, guarding quarantine zones, and assisting British engineers. Many international civilian personnel praised them. One told Chatham House that:

> The Sierra Leonean military stand out as the group of people who went above and beyond on a daily basis. They just got on with the job. They were the only people, and I mean the only people, who worked seven days a week, and they never complained. They would be in there doing the day-to-day co-ordination, at the district and the national level, with nobody else in the office.[5]

The British Army took great satisfaction from this. It had been supporting, advising and training the Sierra Leonean Army for the previous 15 years. Its great effectiveness in this most testing of national challenges was proof that this long-term investment had created an effective, politically neutral force.

After five months, cases were declining from a peak of 500 a week. The effort shifted to mass elimination of remaining infection pockets. Both DfID and the military were able to withdraw from districts and scale down to a footprint of about 250 personnel. But a spike in cases in May 2015 saw the military surge back into the capital and the districts. This succeeded and the focus shifted to an intelligence-led approach to quarantine and eradication. On 7 November 2015 the World Health Organisation declared Sierra Leone free of Ebola, and the last eight personnel left Sierra Leone in mid-November.

This was the second time that the British Army had deployed to counter a major health emergency, the first being the foot and mouth outbreak in the UK in 2001. In many respects it was a model interagency operation, with clear leadership from the government, prompt decision-making by the NSC and a common purpose, motivated by an imminent threat. Much of the success was due to the leadership of the international and joint forces contingent, provided by the logistic brigade commander and HQ.

THE 2015 STRATEGIC AND SECURITY DEFENCE REVIEW

In 2014, former US Defence Secretary Roberts Gates told the BBC that 'with the fairly substantial reductions in defence spending in Great Britain, what we're finding is that it won't have full spectrum capabilities and the ability to be a full partner as they have been in the past'.[6] He reflected growing concern in the Pentagon over the continual reduction in the size of British forces.

This was refuted by Prime David Cameron, who said that the UK had 'a massive investment programme of £160bn in our defence industries, in our equipment' and that 'we are a first-class player in terms of defence and as long as I am prime minster that is the way it will stay'.[7] But Gates was correct to say that the overall level UK defence capabilities had reduced, lessening the UK's ability to be a military partner to the US. For example, 13 frigates (down from 17 in 2010), three tank regiments (down from six in 2010) and seven fighter squadrons (down from nine in 2010) could not carry out the same number of tasks, either in peacetime or in war, as could be performed in 2010. As British military readiness had been reduced, they could not be mobilized and deployed as quickly as previously.

Cameron's public statements on military capability, and those of his chancellor and defence ministers, often appeared oblivious of the reductions in both readiness and force structure. They ignored two 'inconvenient truths'. The first was that the UK's potential military opponents had not been standing still. Not only had potential adversaries in the Middle East and Asia Pacific been increasing their defence budgets and modernizing their forces, but more advanced military equipment had been proliferating globally, including amongst anti-Western states, such as Iran.

Secondly, the growing cost of military technology often led to reductions in platform and unit numbers. Although improved technology can make those platforms or units considerably more capable, it often cannot compensate for numerical reductions.

Hosting the 2014 NATO Summit in Wales, Cameron publicly encouraged NATO members to halt an overall decline in Alliance defence spending. But in the 2015 election campaign, neither he nor any of his ministers was prepared to commit the UK to meeting NATO's 2 per cent of GDP defence spending target beyond 2015. Their line was that this was a matter for an SDSR to be held after the next election.

The 2015 Conservative Party election manifesto said that 'we have strengthened Britain's influence in the world'.[8] This *might* have been true for diplomacy, development aid, and intelligence. With a significant reduction in the size of the armed forces, it did not apply to defence. The reduction in size of all three services meant that they had far less redundancy and flexibility than before. They moved closer to critical mass in many areas of capability. Then Chief of Defence Staff General Sir Nicholas Houghton stated publicly that: 'unattended our current course leads to a strategically incoherent force structure: exquisite equipment, but insufficient resources to man that equipment or train on it. This is what the Americans call the spectre of the hollow-force.'[9]

The manifesto proposition was contradicted by strong evidence of strategic caution. This includes the September 2013 parliamentary vote vetoing UK strikes on Syria, the decision to have only a small non-combat presence in Afghanistan after 2015, and the relatively small size and limited role of the Army's contribution to the campaign against ISIS. Reductions in conventional forces and the Conservative party's refusal to commit to meeting NATO's 2 per cent of GDP defence spending target, did nothing to strengthen UK military influence with the US, in NATO, and further afield.

In September 2014, General Sir Nick Carter became CGS. He had an ambitious programme to modernize and reform the Army, launching many initiatives. A business consultancy was brought in to assist with this. Carter also sought to improve the Army's intellectual foundations. An in-house think tank was set up – the Centre for Historical Analysis and Conflict Research – and officers were attached to the London's main defence and security think tanks.

Carter wanted to improve the Army's corporate identity. One measure was to insist that officers of the rank of colonel and above cease to display the identity of their previous regiment but wear a single pattern of general staff uniform. Carter also sought to improve the quality of the Army's senior leadership, including by establishing mandatory training for all newly promoted major generals.

The combined NSS and SDSR[10] announced by David Cameron in November 2015 assessed that the threats to the UK and its interests had increased since the previous 2010 review. He stated that the UK needed 'to deter state-based threats, tackle terrorism, remain a world leader in cyber security and ensure we have the capability to respond rapidly to crises'. Launching the review, Cameron celebrated the UK's ability to simultaneously meet the NATO 2 per cent of GDP defence spending target and the UN target of 0.7 per cent of Gross National Income on development aid. The review emphasized the armed forces' requirement for strong cyber defence and for advanced cyber offensive capabilities, to support national and coalition operations.

The threat of terrorist attacks in the UK was increasing. ISIS had been particularly successful in using the internet to propagate propaganda, and there was evidence that more people were becoming self-radicalized online. There were significant increases in armed counterterrorist police and the staffing of MI5, MI6 and GCHQ, probably the biggest single increase in UK intelligence agencies since World War II.

A contingency plan to release armed police from static guarding functions to respond to terrorist attack was developed. Operation *Temperer* planned for up to 5,000 troops providing armed guards at key sites such as Downing Street, Buckingham Palace, Parliament and nuclear power stations. The plan was activated after the May 2017 Manchester Arena bombing and the September 2017 bombing at Parsons Green tube station in London.

Defence engagement, the use of the armed forces to achieve influence, including by partnership, capacity building and training, was made a core funded defence task. The Army was to re-role four infantry battalions into 'specialist infantry battalions', optimized for this role.

The review clearly signalled that readiness and ambition were to be rebuilt. For example, the Army returned to its pre-2010 target of generating a division-sized force at six months' notice, instead of the 2010 target of a year. The target for a large-scale deployment of a joint force of division size, or air and maritime equivalents, would increase from 30,000 troops to 50,000 troops by 2025. And the review had much emphasis on deploying more troops faster and at greater distance, with Defence Secretary Michael Fallon stating that the UK is 'going to be more assertive – delivering more missions in more places'.

The size of the Army remained at 82,000. There was no additional new equipment for the Army, but the review funded the programme to upgrade the Warrior infantry fighting vehicle and replace the elderly CVR(T) family with new Ajax scout vehicles. The new intelligence surveillance and reconnaissance brigade and 77th Brigade (designed to conduct modern information operations) were both to further develop their capabilities, particularly to counter hybrid warfare.

Two of the planned armoured infantry brigades would still be fielded, but they would be joined by two new 'strike brigades'. These would be capable of rapid action over long range and a brigade was directed to run an experimentation campaign to assess the new role. The concept was originally buried in the review report, but the weekend before the announcement No. 10 decided to apply additional spin, talking up the strike brigade as a new eye-catching initiative.[11]

Seen as a British equivalent of US Army Stryker brigade combat teams, their key armoured vehicles would be Ajax armoured reconnaissance vehicle and a new wheeled mechanized infantry vehicle. They would be formed from one of the three existing armoured infantry brigades and an infantry brigade.

AFGHANISTAN DETERIORATES

In December 2014 ISAF was replaced by NATO's Operation *Resolute Support*, a 12,000-strong non-combat mission for training, advising and assisting the Afghans, and improving the effectiveness of the defence and interior ministries, Afghan SOF, military intelligence and the Afghan Air Force. US and NATO air forces were generally not available to support Afghan troops (other than SOF) on the ground. It was initially planned that this mission would halve in strength by the end of 2015, reducing completely by the end of 2016.

In keeping with Prime Minister Cameron's aversion to the Army taking part in combat, no British troops joined any of the US and NATO advisory teams that were based at regional hubs such as Kandahar. This was good for minimizing political risk to No. 10 and the MoD, but was bad for sustaining British military influence with the US military in Kabul.

The British government assigned the Army to take on two NATO missions in Kabul, with about 350 troops. The first was to support the new Afghan officer academy. Dubbed 'Sandhurst in the Sand', this provided foundational training to young Afghan Army officers. The other was to assist with the security of NATO forces in Kabul, a task that was quickly nicknamed 'Armoured Uber' by soldiers as it involved ferrying officers and officials around the city.

From 2014, US and British politicians and senior military officials expressed guarded confidence that the Afghan security forces would continue to neutralize the Taliban. But successive Taliban campaigns increased control over rural areas and captured important rural district centres and key provincial capitals, while at the same time conducting high-profile attacks in Kabul and other important cities. Taliban control over rural areas slowly increased.

COLLAPSE OF GOVERNMENT CONTROL IN HELMAND

With the withdrawal of combat forces from Helmand, the British media greatly reduced reporting of events there. But after 2014, the Taliban steadily gained control of almost all of the province. The initial Afghan security forces' response was hasty and poorly co-ordinated, as key districts fell to the Taliban. If the British government or MoD were concerned or even interested in this, they showed no outward sign.

In early 2015 the Taliban killed Helmand's effective police chief, significantly reducing co-operation between the Afghan government forces in the province. Over the next year the Taliban made significant advances. A key weakness was that the fighting strength of the Afghan Army's 215th Corps was much lower than it should be, owing to a 'ghost soldier' scam, where corrupt commanders siphoned off salaries of non-existent soldiers; and equipment and ammunition was sold to the Taliban.

It was no coincidence that in October 2015 President Obama announced a change in US strategy – declaring that he would keep the 9,800 American troops still in Afghanistan in place throughout 2016, saying that doing so would 'allow us to sustain our efforts to train and assist Afghan forces as they grow stronger – not only during this fighting season, but into the next one. By the end of 2016, we will maintain 5,500 troops at a small number of bases, including at Bagram, Jalalabad in the east, and Kandahar in the south.'[12] He was responding to a request from Kabul to press the pause button on the US drawdown.

In early 2016 a US Army battalion was deployed to Helmand to provide increased support to the Afghan forces. In May 2016 the Taliban mounted a major offensive, with assassination teams killing government commanders in their homes. The insurgents used specially trained elite mobile strike groups to mount attacks, while local Taliban militias secured captured ground. The Taliban captured many army and police checkpoints.

To disrupt this, US air strikes in Helmand greatly increased. But these did not break the Taliban advance, which came within a few miles of the provincial capital of Lashkar Gar. Many of the districts in Helmand Province fell under Taliban control, with the Afghan government having little influence beyond the immediate vicinity of the provincial capital.

In a blaze of publicity over 800 US personnel, Marines and contractors replaced the US infantry battalion at the turn of the year. They re-trained Afghan battalions and helped the Afghan Army plan a series of counterattacks. One was directed at the Taliban-controlled town of Sangin, where so many British and US casualties had been inflicted. The counteroffensive benefited from air support, including the Afghan Army's recently introduced Scan Eagle short-range drones. The US Marines also fired GMLRS rockets to support the Afghan troops.

But none of the attacks inflicted a decisive defeat on the Taliban. Following a late 2017 US media report explaining how drones and airpower were being employed in Helmand, the Taliban adjusted their tactics to better conceal themselves from the air, including ceasing the use of radio communications to neutralize signals intelligence gathering.

RETURN TO PEACEKEEPING OPERATIONS

The SDSR envisaged that the end of Afghan operations would allow the Army to return to UN peacekeeping operations. A total of £500 million was allocated to this. Most of this funded an Army contingent's deployment to join the UN mission in South Sudan, a mission chosen by the government over the advice of the MoD, who considered that there were more important UN missions to support.[13] An engineer regiment formed the core of the mission, which lasted for the funded five years.

It was an unfamiliar role in a vast operating area with a challenging climate and poor infrastructure. The sappers built two new field hospitals for the UN and conducted numerous infrastructure maintenance and improvement projects. An innovation, welcomed by the UN, was the conduct of women's self-defence courses by female sappers.

Following on from its assistance to the 2014 French mission to combat jihadis in Mali, the Army sent forces to join the complementary UN stabilization mission in the country. This was separate from the remaining French counter-terrorism mission. The force was a small battlegroup of infantry in Foxhound APCs and light cavalry. But a military regime seized power and required international forces to depart in 2022. Although largely unremarked upon by the British media, this was a defeat for the French-led international effort to stabilize the country.

RETURN TO FORWARD DEFENCE – AN ARMY TRIPWIRE IN ESTONIA

As a result of the 2014 Russian attack on Ukraine, NATO increased exercises in Eastern Europe. From 2016 this was complemented by a forward deployment of land forces to the Baltic states and Poland, consisting of four multinational battlegroups. This was the Enhanced Forward Prescence (EFP) initiative, designed to increase deterrence against a Russian attack.

Canada led the battlegroup in Latvia and Germany the battlegroup in Lithuania. The US led the battlegroup in Poland, to which a British light cavalry squadron was attached. The main British effort was Estonia. In 2016, the country felt very vulnerable. Not only was it small and close to Russia, but its necessarily small armed forces were at that time relatively light in combat power, with no tanks and few modern armoured vehicles. But as the Estonian company that joined the British in Helmand showed, the Estonian troops had no shortage of courage and determination. This was demonstrated both in Afghanistan and by Kaja Kallas, the country's Prime Minister. She and other Estonian leaders had grown up when the country had been part of the Soviet Union and therefore had a deep distrust of Moscow.

The Army deployed a battlegroup to Estonia. Led by an armoured infantry battalion or armoured regiment HQ, it initially included British tank squadrons, armoured infantry companies, engineer squadrons, artillery batteries and the full range of other combat support and logistics, totalling around a thousand troops. It was joined by smaller contingents from France, Belgium, and many other NATO armies.

The Army prepared battlegroups as if they were going to war. Over 12 months before deployment, time was allocated for individual and collective training. Initially this climaxed with complete battlegroups deploying to Canada for Exercise *Prairie Storm* at BATUS. As BATUS was run down, this training migrated from Canada to the Sennelager Training Centre in Germany and to Estonia itself.

The initial deployment in 2017 was into an unknown area of operations, with much uncertainty about the mission. The first engineer squadron commander observed that 'we had no idea what we were really stepping into, and what reaction it would have in Moscow'.[14] Throughout their six-month tours, battlegroups were at extremely high readiness to deploy very quickly to counter a surprise Russian attack. They were rapidly integrated into the Estonian Army's plans to defend the country.

This required the battlegroups to understand the terrain they would move and fight over to develop and refine tactical plans. In this and many other ways the battlegroups in Estonia returned to many of the approaches that the Army had practised in the Cold War, albeit with many more modern vehicles, equipment and weapons. From commanding officer to driver, gunner and rifleman, troops rediscovered the skills of fighting in woods and forests that had been second nature in the 1980s. Winters in Estonia could be cold, very cold, so the arts of living and fighting in extreme cold weather that had been so important to those required to operate and fight in Norway and Bosnia were taught and practised.

The Estonian terrain was an especial challenge. There were many woods, forests and marshes. In the iron grip of deep winter, the soil would freeze solid, making digging almost impossible. The British therefore learned to make defences out of timber and solid ice – known as icecrete. Drawing on experience as far back as World War II, the engineer squadrons developed new ways of using their new Titan, Trojan and Terrier armoured engineer vehicles to provide close support to companies and squadrons. They took advantage of major NATO exercises in the region to conduct live demolitions, to an extent achievable nowhere else, including blowing up complete bridges.

Collective training culminated in an annual Estonian national exercise, *Spring Storm*. This tested the Estonian defence plan and NATO's ability to reinforce the country. For example, the 2023 exercise saw participation not only by most of the Estonian Army, but also by troops from Canada, Denmark , France, Germany, Italy, Latvia, Lithuania, Poland and the US. The Queen's Royal Hussars battlegroup was joined by troops from the Light Dragoons' light cavalry and HQ 7th Light Mechanised Brigade Combat Team.

THE 2018 NOVICHOK ATTACK

Since the 1980s the UK had considered and practised how it might respond to terrorist use of chemical, radiological or nuclear weapons. The details of cross-government plans and capabilities to achieve this were classified, but they involve the experts at the MoD's chemical, biological and nuclear defence research centre at Porton Down, as well as RAF and Army capabilities.

Much of this expertise and personnel was used in the response to the March 2018 Russian military intelligence attack using Novichok, a nerve agent, against Sergei Skripal, a defected Russian spy, in Salisbury. The intensely toxic nature of Novichok posed a major risk to public safety, as shown when contact with it made a police officer and two civilians seriously unwell, one of whom, Dawn Sturgess, later died.

Wiltshire Police led the security response, while the recovery was led by the Department for Environment, Food and Rural Affairs (DEFRA). The Joint Military Commander was Colonel Andrew Davis from the Army HQ for the south-west. Police and military command nodes were deployed at Frome police station and Porton Down, and the HQ of the joint task force was assembled at the Defence chemical, biological, radiological and nuclear (CBRN) training centre at Winterborne Gunner.

The task force was commanded by a wing of the RAF Regiment, an HQ that had not previously practised deployed command and control. The Army contribution included Falcon Squadron Royal Tank Regiment, the Army CBRN reconnaissance capability and troops from two engineer regiments, two transport regiments and a signal regiment.

After initial chemical reconnaissance, 12 sites had to be decontaminated, tasks lasting from one to three months. This required complete removal of every single object that might have been exposed to the nerve agent, including much of the interior and roof of the house that had been 'ground zero'. As military decontamination techniques were geared to washing away contamination, an option not available in Salisbury, new techniques had to be devised. And operating in the enclosed personal protective equipment during a long hot summer was a real challenge to soldiers and commanders.

The operation lasted for a year. It included 250 different tasks, including the removal and disposal of 31 contaminated vehicles and 28 shipping containers of contaminated material. That it concluded without any chemical casualties was a remarkable achievement that it would be too easy to take for granted.

THE 2020 COVID PANDEMIC

Another strategic surprise was the 2020 outbreak of COVID-19 and the subsequent pandemic. The lockdowns and other preventive measures had a profound effect on the Army, not least with many troops not required for duty being sent home. But the Army still had to sustain its forces at high readiness and generate forces for operational deployments, such as the battlegroup in Estonia. By taking precautions and carefully managing the risk, essential commitments could still be managed. It helped the Army that the great majority of its people were at a high standard of personal fitness and people with asthma had not been recruited.

As the emergency developed, the Army and MoD found themselves contingency planning to support the civil authorities. An early government initiative was to guard against the National Health Service (NHS) being overwhelmed by rapidly constructing additional COVID treatment facilities, called Nightingale Hospitals. The military, particularly the Royal Engineers, provided much expertise and labour to support this.

Whilst military capabilities were well understood in the Home Office and DEFRA, they were less well understood in other government departments. Many of these did not have adequate plans for a widespread national emergency. So military planning teams were offered and deployed. At the height of the pandemic there were at least five such teams, headed up by brigadiers in other government departments. And the Army's Regional Command was mobilized, deploying dozens of military planners to assist local resilience forums.

A high-readiness military reaction force was formed, with 20,000 people from the three services. Few of them were initially used and the size of the force was eventually reduced. As the capability to conduct public testing ramped up, the military deployed troops to help get the programme started before it was handed over to contractors. The military also invented the concept of mobile testing units that could be rapidly deployed where the need was greatest.

The Army's Joint Helicopter Command set up aviation task forces to rapidly transport key personnel around the country. They had particular value in aerial evacuation of COVID patients from remote areas to intensive care units. And 77th Brigade, the Army's information operations formation, assisted the Cabinet Office in identifying and countering online rumours and deliberate disinformation.

Military HQs, staff officers and planners continued to offer a capacity to simultaneously manage current operations and plan for future operations. These capabilities were often lacking in government departments and their agencies. They proved invaluable. An example was the running of a Whitehall cross-government wargame that simulated a winter 2020 COVID crisis, to help the government test its plans.

The evidence submitted to the UK's independent COVID inquiry paints an extremely unflattering picture of government leadership of the crisis, with many weaknesses flowing directly from the leadership style of Prime Minister Boris Johnson. The military support was the opposite of this – calm, considered and co-ordinated. This flowed directly from the training of commanders, HQs and staff officers to produce plans and command operations under the pressure of war. These qualities had also been on display in the foot and mouth crisis and campaign against Ebola in Sierra Leone.

But Johnson's decision to set up a national vaccine task force was highly successful. The military embedded ten planners in the task force and distributed 170 more across the UK's regions. It also assigned over 120 troops to a vaccine quick reaction force as well as preparing 80 vaccination centres in Scotland.

This was the third time in this period that the Army had fought a virus, foot and mouth in 2001 and Ebola in 2014 being the previous occasions. Increased globalization, urbanization and the possibility of malign actors using genetic engineering to weaponize viruses suggests that the 2020 pandemic will not be the last such Army operation.

The 2021 Integrated Review

Between 2010 and 2020 the UK's independent National Audit Office had repeatedly judged the future equipment plans of the MoD to be 'unaffordable'. It was becoming increasingly clear that of the three services, the Army had the highest proportion of obsolete equipment, particularly its armoured vehicle fleet. Of its planned modernization programmes, both the Warrior upgrade programme and the new Ajax scout vehicle were subject to great delay and cost escalation.

The 2015 SDSR tasked the Army to deliver a modernized warfighting heavy division by 2025, consisting of two armoured infantry brigades and a strike brigade. In late 2020 Army and MoD evidence to the House of Commons Defence Committee stated that the division would only consist of a single armoured infantry brigade and an 'interim manoeuvre support brigade', the latter with some new Ajax vehicles and infantry travelling in Boxer and Foxhound armoured personnel carriers (APCs).[15]

The MoD said it was unable to meet the 2015 SDSR target because its budget 'did not fully resource the army to achieve this output within this timeframe'. More simply put, it did not have enough money to fund what it said it was going to do. Development delays to the Ajax armoured reconnaissance vehicle and a very slow delivery rate for new Boxer APCs further compounded the issue. And the division's three armoured cavalry regiments were then equipped with Scimitar light armoured reconnaissance vehicles. Delivered in the early 1970s, the Scimitars were obsolescent. There were also abundant indications that the stockpiles of spares and ammunition needed to deploy more than one armoured infantry brigade did not exist.

When asked in 2020 if a British war-fighting division would be capable of 'overmatching the forces of a peer opponent such as Russia', Minister for Defence Procurement Jeremy Quin replied 'absolutely.'[16] This assessment ran counter to the MoD's own evidence. A Russian tank division would have three times as many tanks as the British division and would overmatch the British division's anti-tank weapons by a factor of ten. Chaired by MP Tobias Ellwood who appeared in Chapter 7, the Defence Committee saw through the minister's unjustified optimism bias, assessing that:

> were the British Army to have to fight a peer adversary – a euphemism for Russia – in Eastern Europe in the next few years, whilst our soldiers would undoubtedly remain amongst the finest in the world, they would, disgracefully, be forced to go into battle in a combination of obsolescent or even obsolete armoured vehicles, most of them at least 30 years old or more, with poor mechanical reliability, very heavily outgunned by more modern missile and artillery systems and chronically lacking in adequate air defence. They would have only a handful of long-delayed, new generation vehicles, gradually trickling into the inventory, to replace them.[17]

Between 2020 and 2025, it became clear that UK military capability was heading towards another funding crisis. A major factor was that many equipment programmes, including land, naval and nuclear capabilities, had escalated greatly in cost. Many analysts of UK defence were pessimistic, assessing that yet more significant military capability reductions would be required to balance the defence budget. Their pessimism was confounded by the November 2020 statement by Prime Minister Boris Johnson, in which he proposed increasing the defence budget by £16.5 billion over four years.

In 2020, the government decided that it would expand the approach of previous defence and security reviews. To reflect the even wider range of security challenges the UK faced, it would conduct a wide-ranging study into intelligence activity, foreign policy, development and defence.

In March 2021, Boris Johnson launched the Integrated Review of Security, Defence, Development and Foreign Policy. 'Global Britain in a Competitive Age'[18] saw the UK as an 'international actor that brings together the levers of UK power and influence in a more co-ordinated way'. The review assessed that that the international order was becoming more fragmented, characterized by increasing competition between states, and that 'defence of the status quo is no longer sufficient for the decade ahead'. It described competition from countries such as China, Iran and Russia – as well as from non-state actors such as the Islamic State – as occurring above and below 'the boundary between peace and war'. It proposed that the UK should respond by taking a more proactive approach to shaping the international order by further integrating the armed forces with other government agencies.

Threats to the UK and to its allies from other states were growing and diversifying. The review stated that Russia 'will remain the most acute direct threat to the UK'. The Euro-Atlantic region and NATO were critical to UK's security and prosperity. The UK's commitment to European security would be 'unequivocal'. British forces would continue to be deployed to Estonia and Poland as part of NATO's 'tripwire', a term that had not been used in a British government document for some time. The review increased the size of the UK's nuclear-warhead stockpile after a long period of reductions of warhead numbers.

The US was seen as the UK's 'indispensable ally' and pre-eminent partner on security, defence and foreign policy and it was stated that defence co-operation between the two 'is the broadest, deepest and most advanced of any two countries in the world'. Military partnerships were to increase, especially with France, Germany and the UK-led Joint Expeditionary Force group of European nations: Denmark, Estonia, Finland, Latvia, Lithuania, the Netherlands, Norway and Sweden.

The review proclaimed a 'tilt' towards the Indo-Pacific, including increased engagement with India and with the Five Power Defence Arrangement with Commonwealth members Australia, Malaysia, New Zealand and Singapore, as well as collaborative development of a new fighter by the UK, Italy and Japan.

The consequences for the armed forces were spelled out in a subsequent MoD command paper, 'Defence in a Competitive Age'.[19] More UK forces were to be deployed both across Europe and globally, and for longer periods, for capacity-building missions and to counter terrorist, hybrid, grey-zone and proxy threats; for example, by training, advising and accompanying partner nations' forces on operations, a role assigned to the Royal Marines and the Army's new Ranger Regiment. Overseas basing in Germany, Cyprus, Gibraltar, Kenya, Oman and Singapore was to be expanded. This announced extensive plans for modernization and restructuring, and saw the Royal Navy having an especially important role in future conflicts, calling for increases in maritime capability and reductions in air- and land-based forces in favour of investments in advanced technology. It also set out cuts to both personnel and legacy equipment in the Army and RAF in particular.[20]

The UK was to deploy 'a greater and more persistent presence' in the Indo-Pacific than any other European country', although the review seemed not have noticed that France already had around 4,000 military personnel based in the region:[21] an elementary mistake that the MoD should have spotted.

This drove the 2021 deployment of the Royal Navy's new carrier task group for exercises in the region.[22] It was also a driver for the formation of the AUKUS strategic alliance between Australia, the UK and the US, for co-operation with Australia over its next generation of nuclear-powered attack submarines.[23]

There would be significant investments in warships and the Tempest fighter aircraft – and in modernizing aging Army equipment. It would emphasize future rather than current military capabilities, by moving away from obsolete 'sunset' capabilities to 'sunrise' capabilities – including networking, the exploitation of data, artificial intelligence and an increasing number of robotic and autonomous systems. Strategic Command would become a hub for innovation, including creating a 'digital backbone', a high-capacity data network to be used across the three services.

When probed on the wisdom of cutting conventional weapons to fund emerging technology, Prime Minister Boris Johnson told Parliament that 'the old concepts of fighting big tank battles on the European landmass … are over'.[24] This statement may or may not have reflected briefings to Johnson from the MoD, but it was evidence that dealing with a major land war was not a high priority. The main effort of the review seemed not to be on high-intensity conflict, but more on 'operating'. This was operations short of major war, from humanitarian and peacekeeping operations, to confronting hybrid, threshold and grey zone threats. Throughout there would need to be training and support to Britain's allies and partners, including those engaged in stabilization and counterinsurgency.

In his call for raising defence spending in November 2020, Johnson also declared that his ambition for the Royal Navy was for it to be 'foremost in Europe'.[25] But neither he nor the review explained the strategic rationale for the decision to increase maritime capabilities at the expense of land and air capabilities, which would be reduced.

Numbers of RAF aircraft were reduced. Eight Chinook heavy-lift helicopters would retire, as would all 14 C130J Hercules medium-transport aircraft that supported special forces, their role being assumed by the larger A400M Atlas. It was claimed that improving the availability of the 25 Atlas would cover the ensuing gap.

This significant reduction in transport aircraft and helicopters rested uncomfortably with the emphasis placed in the Integrated Review on increasing the UK's global presence, with more forces operating in more places. When tackled about this in public both ministers and senior RAF officers appeared in denial that the reduction in airlift would have any impact on operational capability. Very few Army officers believed this. No independent military analysts did.

THE FUTURE SOLDIER PROGRAMME – DOING MORE WITH LESS, AGAIN

Of the three services, the Army entered the review with the highest proportion of its equipment either obsolete or nearing obsolescence. The MoD claimed the Army would receive more funding for equipment modernization than the Royal Navy or RAF.

The Army announced that its capability changes would be part of an all-embracing change programme called Future Soldier. This was the first time such a change programme had been given a simple, unifying title.

The Army's manpower was to reduce from 82,000 to 72,500 regular troops, its smallest size for over two centuries. Some officials argued that the reduction, however, was less significant than it might appear because the Army had been operating below its planned-personnel figure for some years. The reserve was to be enhanced and assume an increased national resilience role, although it would not increase in size.

There was more demand from allies and partners for training of special forces, from both armies and paramilitary forces. To help meet this requirement, some of the existing special forces' training and advisory roles were to be assumed by special operations-capable Army and Royal Marine units. The existing 'specialized infantry battalions' raised to train, advise and accompany partner forces in high-threat operations would form a new Ranger Regiment in a new special operations brigade. To form the new regiment, four existing battalions were transferred out of the infantry, becoming the 1st to 4th battalions of the Rangers. A new security forces assistance brigade would be created for less-demanding capability partnering roles. Both brigades' units would be much smaller than normal infantry battalions.

The 3rd Division would remain a heavy formation optimized for high-intensity warfighting. It would shift its capabilities in favour of both protection and deep battle, reducing its ground-manoeuvre capability from three to two armoured brigades. These would comprise a mixture of heavy and medium armour. They would also have their combat support and logistic units placed under command. This would apply to all the Army's manoeuvre brigades, which would all be designated 'brigade combat teams', a term commonly used by the US Army.

A new deep reconnaissance strike brigade would combine all the division's artillery with two armoured reconnaissance regiments. Its purpose was to engage the enemy with greater precision at longer range, using its organic artillery, as well as drawing on the Army's drones, Apache helicopters and electronic warfare capability. This was to increase attrition of the enemy at greater depth, making the close battle by the armoured brigade combat teams easier and 'anticlimactic'. The Army's electronic-warfare and air-defence capabilities were to double in size.

The previous strike brigade concept for a medium-weight formation was dropped. This much-heralded idea that featured so heavily in the 2015 SDSR appeared to have been abandoned without explanation. When I asked senior Army officers to explain this, they equivocated, often changing the subject. It may be that wargaming and operational analysis showed that the lack of tanks in the proposed strike brigades greatly reduced their combat power.

The Army retained the 1st Division, comprising the security force assistance brigade, air assault brigade and two light infantry brigades. One of these, the 7th Light Mechanized Brigade, was a full combined arms formation, with its infantry battalions travelling in Foxhound light armoured patrol vehicles procured for use in Afghanistan. It also had a light cavalry regiment equipped with the Jackal scout vehicles, also procured for

Afghanistan. Its artillery, engineers and logistics had some wheeled armour but mostly travelled in soft-skinned vehicles. This was a formation with high potential utility provided it did not have to fight an enemy with greater firepower and more armoured vehicles in open terrain. The other brigade, the 4th Light Brigade, had regular light infantry battalions and light cavalry. But the formation's artillery and engineers came entirely from the Army Reserve. This greatly reduced its readiness for combined arms combat operations.

The size of the infantry was again reduced. Some of this was achieved by reducing the size of the battalions in the security assistance and special operations brigades. But the size of the Army's regular light battalions fell and the infantry overall became more dependent on mobilization of reserves to reach the strength necessary for operations.

The Integrated Review promised a programme of modernization of Army equipment. This included new model Apache attack helicopters, already joining the Army Air Corps, new Boxer wheeled infantry carriers, and a much-needed update to ageing Challenger tanks. The Army welcomed these investments. But its armoured warfare capability would be greatly reduced by the review.

REDUCING ARMOURED WARFARE CAPABILITIES

After the Army received the protected patrol vehicles so essential for Iraq and Afghanistan, the number of other new armoured vehicles entering service was greatly reduced. One was Foxhound, a small wheeled APC designed not only for Afghanistan, but also to be used more widely. It was employed in the later stages of the Helmand campaign, then in Kabul, on NATO exercises and in UN operations in Mali.

The British Army invented the tank in World War I. In World War II the Army fielded many innovative specialized armoured vehicles to breach the many obstacle belts in Hitler's Atlantic Wall. In doing this, the Army invented the concept of armoured engineers, sappers equipped with specialized armoured vehicles to help armoured units move, breach obstacles and fight.

The Royal Engineers needed a family of new armoured engineer vehicles for the new century. The long-obsolete Combat Engineer Tractor was replaced by Terrier, an armoured earthmover. This was the first armoured vehicle specifically designed to fit inside the new A400M transport aircraft. It was also the first armoured vehicle to be designed from the outset as a 'drive by wire' vehicle, the crew controlling using electronic commands rather than mechanical linkages. This allowed another innovation – remote operation, using a games console-style controller. But the Army seemed not to promote this innovation, in public at least.

Two new engineer tanks entered service, based on the Challenger 2 chassis. Trojan was optimized for breaching obstacles, including minefields, while Titan was a bridge layer. The three vehicles provided welcome improvement to close support engineering for armoured formations, although fully exploiting the three new vehicles in training was greatly hampered by shortages of spare parts. The other limiting factor was the small number of vehicles. The Army's operational requirement was for 88 Terrier, of which 65 were produced, and 45 of each type of engineer tank, of which 33 each were procured. Having less than the required level of armoured engineers will constrain armoured manoeuvre in the future.

The armoured engineer vehicles had another significance. After the last vehicles were delivered, the UK stopped manufacturing armoured vehicles. This symbolized the reduction in the industrial base that supported the Army; which was a reflection of the considerable reduction in the Army's size.

With the decision to cut an armoured brigade, one-third of the Army's Challenger 2 tanks would be retired. The remaining 143 tanks were to be upgraded. The Challenger 3 programme would replace the British rifled 120mm gun with the Rheinmetall 120mm smoothbore gun, requiring a new turret. The Israeli Trophy active protection system would be fitted to the tank. Fielded by the Israeli Army a decade earlier, fighting in Gaza had demonstrated the system's ability to destroy incoming anti-tank warheads including the Kornet missile. Trophy would undoubtedly improve the survivability of British tanks.

Since 2010 the Army had been planning to modernize its Warrior infantry fighting vehicles. Firepower would be increased by replacing the 30mm Rarden cannon with a 40mm gun. This would use 'case telescoped' ammunition, an innovation that greatly reduced the size of both gun and ammunition. It would also have a programmable multi-role high-explosive shell that could set to airburst above the enemy, greatly increasing its utility as a suppressive weapon. To accommodate the gun, the upgraded Warrior would require a new larger turret. Development of the vehicle was subject to several years' delay. Lockheed Martin, the contractor, admitted that this was their responsibility and funded the additional costs.[26]

The Integrated Review cancelled the programme. Warrior would be replaced by the Boxer wheeled APC. The Boxers would be armed only with externally mounted machine guns and grenade launchers. Armoured brigades would therefore lose the best part of a hundred turret-mounted cannon. This would greatly reduce brigade firepower, making the formations considerably less capable of destroying enemy light armoured vehicles. And in the attack the infantry would have much less organic fire support.

The Army had invested considerable effort in developing Warrior in the 1980s, transforming the capability of infantry in its armoured formations, from mechanized to armoured infantry battalions. The success of this enhancement had been demonstrated in Iraq in 1991, where Warrior-equipped companies were able to keep up with Challenger-equipped armoured squadrons and used their organic firepower and night sights to destroy defending Iraqi bunkers and light armour. During the difficult UN operations in Bosnia, Warrior had been the main British armoured vehicle deployed, its protection and firepower being used to defend aid convoys and British positions. Warrior's wide utility was again demonstrated in 2003–2009 during fighting in Basra. It was at the fore in the heavy fighting against Shia militants in southern Iraq and the Taliban in Afghanistan.

This battle-proven capability was to be abandoned. To many British defence commentators and Army officers with experience in armoured warfare, this decision was literally incomprehensible. When questioned in public, senior Army officers could offer no credible defence of the decision, other than bland statements that 'we will fight differently'. It seemed that the Army was abandoning the hard-won experience of almost

30 years of operations. And there was no evidence that any other major army in the world was planning to go in a similar direction. Indeed, across NATO many armies were modernizing their infantry fighting vehicle inventories. For example, the US Army was planning to replace its Bradleys with a similar capability, Germany was replacing its Marders with the Puma, and Sweden was updating its CV90s. No other NATO army planned a similar abandonment of its infantry fighting vehicles.

Conversely the Integrated Review decided to double down on investing in the new Ajax family of armoured reconnaissance vehicles. This was the only survivor of the Army's ambitious programme for a new family of medium-weight armoured vehicles – the Future Rapid Effects System (FRES). The concept was developed between 2001 and 2003.

FRES had two roles. Firstly, to replace the wide range of light and medium armoured vehicles in a host of supporting roles across armoured and mechanized units. Secondly it would develop fighting vehicles that could be transported by air to achieve rapid effect, thus bridging the gap between the Army's existing heavy forces and light forces. The Army had been very impressed with the US Army's speedy procurement of Stryker wheeled APCs to fulfil this role.

The FRES programme was subject to considerable bureaucratic friction, resulting in delay upon delay. MoD Defence Equipment and Support insisted on a two-year study by a systems house. The added value of this step was not clear. The project got as far as trials of wheeled APCs. But the MoD withdrew funding. Some of the money went into protected vehicles for Iraq and Afghanistan, but much of the resource necessary for the programme seemed to get swallowed up into the MoD's decision to fund new aircraft carriers.

Ajax had a troubled and delayed development history. Shortly after the review, development of Ajax had to be suspended as excess noise was damaging the hearing of soldiers using the vehicle.

An independent review was commissioned.[27] This revealed that the Ajax programme was a textbook example of mismanagement and miscommunication. There was plenty of blame to go round – to General Dynamics, the manufacturer, to DE&S, to the Defence Science and Technology Laboratory and to the Army itself. None of the four parties had properly communicated with each other. It had taken the commanding officer of the Armoured Trials Development Unit to act as an internal whistleblower about the hearing damage – at some personal risk to his career.

The report exposed shocking examples of apparent incompetence. But the only sanction applied was non-payment of General Dynamics until the programme was back on track. No officers, officials or managers were named in the report, and no one appeared to have been held to account for inadequate performance.

AFGHANISTAN FURTHER DETERIORATES

By 2017, the Taliban had recaptured much of the rural terrain cleared at such human and financial cost in the 2010–11 Surge. In August 2017 the iconoclastic new US President Donald Trump announced a new US South Asia Strategy. It aimed to bring America's longest ever war to a close. It concluded that the withdrawal of all US and NATO mentors away from Afghan forces had been like 'pulling the training wheels off too early'.

Trump declared that 'conditions on the ground, not arbitrary timetables will guide our actions from now on', and that the US would 'fight to win'.[28] The strategy sought 'to conclude the war in Afghanistan on terms favourable to Afghanistan and the United States'. This had to convince the Taliban that they could not win, to push them to negotiate a settlement with the Afghan government. The strategy had three lines of action: military, financial and legitimacy. Pakistan would also be pressured to cease supporting insurgents. The military effort would seek to roll back gains the Taliban had made since 2014.

US military advisors were redeployed back to Afghan Army formations. They could use airpower much more freely to support Afghan security forces. By the end of 2019, the additional troops and increased bombing blunted the increasingly effective Taliban offensive, but the additional US military effort did not increase terrain under Afghan government control. Despite persistent briefings by US officials that US strategy was succeeding, the war was at a stalemate.[29]

The Pentagon's assessment of the state of security in Afghanistan noted numerous weaknesses in the Afghan forces.[30] These included recruit training, with trainees arriving at their units malnourished and inadequately trained, poor command and leadership, logistics and pervasive weaknesses in management. Overall, the Afghan forces had a personnel shortage of 12 per cent, and were struggling to retain key specialists including pilots, aircraft mechanics, technical specialists and SOF.

The Afghan forces lacked the combat power to clear territory held by the Taliban, who were slowly but gradually increasing their control over rural districts. Too many Afghan troops were guarding highly vulnerable static checkpoints. When attacked, too many were abandoning their positions or deserting. And the Afghan special forces, the most capable component of the Afghan military, were being persistently misused as conventional infantry reaction forces, suffering heavy casualties in the process.

In late 2019, US advisors assessed that the Afghan Army Corps in Helmand had only 40 per cent of its intended strength. The Afghan forces in Helmand and Kandahar provinces had largely collapsed and the Taliban's position in Helmand had continued to improve. Eighteen of the 20 districts in Helmand either were controlled by the Taliban or had major Taliban presence. These included the districts of Babaji, Marjah, Nad-e Ali and Sangin that had previously, at great effort and significant casualties, been cleared of Taliban by British troops and US Marines.[31] Although neither the Afghan nor British governments acknowledged this, the Afghan forces were on course for irreversible decline. The Afghan governance and security forces capability built in Helmand had been insufficiently robust and self-sustaining to survive on their own.

TALIBAN STRENGTHS VERSUS AFGHAN GOVERNMENT AND SECURITY FORCES' WEAKNESSES

The Taliban's 'battle of the narrative' became increasingly important, often as important as the armed conflict itself and sometimes more so. The Taliban had a simple message: that they, and not the 'puppet regime' in Kabul, were the legal government of Afghanistan; and that they were waging a just war to expel foreign infidels from Afghan soil and restore the Islamic Emirate. This had great effect both inside and outside Afghanistan, encouraging their supporters, fundraisers and potential recruits.

The Taliban's offering to the Afghan people in the districts that their forces controlled was to provide security and facilitate dispute resolution in Sharia courts. It did not pledge to improve agriculture, health, education or infrastructure in the way that international stabilization efforts did. By contrast, the US and NATO forces, and their many national development agencies, attempted to help the Afghan government to do many things, none of which they usually did well, while the Taliban usually carried out their two simple objectives well. The Taliban were able to match their words with deeds much more effectively than the Afghan government or international forces could. This was a major factor in their success.

The Afghan forces had become so hollowed out that they would not survive the Taliban's 2021 offensive. As well as the superiority of the Taliban's message over that of the Afghan government, NATO, the US and the UK, other key factors contributed to the subsequent Taliban victory.

The US, UK and NATO set goals for Afghanistan that were unrealistic and over-ambitious. This was the product of over-optimism that followed the unexpectedly rapid 2001 defeat of the Taliban government, multiplied by inadequate understanding of Afghanistan at all levels – national, regional, provincial and district. The military and civilian strategies, campaign plans and tactics used were often inadequately adapted to the true conditions in Afghan districts and provinces.

The US and its allies usually described the war at the strategic, operational and tactical levels as an insurgency by the Taliban against the Kabul government. In reality, it was a complex and multifaceted civil war. Local tribes, drug gangs, criminal networks, warlords, politicians at all levels and individuals holding Afghan government political and security appointments all sought to promote their interests by aligning with external actors, including the US, NATO, the Afghan government and the Taliban. Force was often used to promote the armed actors' interests. This would often be in pursuit of local advantage, including over water, land, narcotic activity or long-lasting tribal grievances.

At the national level, presidents Karzai and Ghani sustained their political position by appointing powerful Afghan actors to national, regional and local political positions. This empowering of actual and potential malign actors further complicated the situation and reduced US and NATO freedom of action. The sponsoring and support of warlords and militias by the CIA and US SOF also undermined the unity of effort. Neither Karzai nor Ghani set up an effective mechanism to lead and manage the Afghan government's war effort – a weakness for which the Afghan people paid the price.

The considerable weakness of Afghan government structures and officials at the province and district level were insufficiently improved during the Afghan Surge. The Surge was probably far too short an initiative to materially improve Afghan governance. When the districts that were prioritized by the international forces for clearance operations and development efforts transitioned to Afghan government control in 2014, the ability of the Afghan authorities to provide development and services at the district level and the Afghan security forces' ability to provide security were gradually overmatched by an emboldened and resurgent Taliban, whose control of rural areas inexorably grew.

PRESIDENT TRUMP'S DOHA AGREEMENT

President Trump made a strategic pivot to negotiations with the Taliban. On 29 February 2020 the US and Taliban signed the 'Agreement for Bringing Peace to Afghanistan between the Islamic Emirate of Afghanistan which is not recognized by the United States as a state and is known as the Taliban and the United States of America',[32] the Doha Agreement. This declared a bilateral ceasefire between the Taliban and US forces. The Taliban would 'prevent any group or individual in Afghanistan from threatening the security of the United States and its allies, and will prevent them from recruiting, training, and fundraising and will not host them.' US and allied forces would withdraw from the country 14 months after the agreement.

The agreement envisaged 'the formation of the new post-settlement Afghan Islamic government as determined by the intra-Afghan dialogue and negotiations.' These negotiations would begin by 10 March 2020. By this date the Taliban were to release 1,000 prisoners, and 5,000 Taliban fighters held prisoner by the US and Afghan government would be released. The US also declared that it would begin diplomatic action to lift UN sanctions on the Taliban and that it and its allies 'will refrain from the threat or the use of force against the territorial integrity or political independence of Afghanistan or intervening in its domestic affairs.'

The agreement gave the Taliban decisive political and military advantage over the Kabul government, whose position was greatly weakened. It gave Presidents Trump and Biden a way out of the war. Many Afghans saw this for themselves, and civilian and military morale and confidence started to deteriorate.

THE TALIBAN'S VICTORY CAMPAIGN

Prior to 2021, the US and UK urged President Ghani to withdraw Afghan troops and police from the many isolated checkpoints dispersed across rural areas surrounding provincial capitals. They also recommended that the Afghan forces concentrate on the defence of key towns, cities and Kabul. This way they hoped that the government could fight the Taliban to a stalemate. It does not seem that Ghani heeded this advice.

In early 2021 new US President Joe Biden announced that the US military would withdraw from Afghanistan by the 20th anniversary of the 9/11 terrorist attacks. The evidence suggested that the UK had no impact on the decision. Given that the US forces in Afghanistan had seen no UK boots on the ground outside Kabul, it was hardly surprising that UK had earned itself negligible influence on US decision-making.

UK Defence Secretary Ben Wallace briefly proposed that the UK assemble a coalition of NATO states to replace US troops. On paper the UK could have found the necessary forces. The operation would have needed a brigade and special forces on the ground and a force holding Kabul or Bagram airfields. Sustaining this would have required an airbridge, probably mounted from the Gulf. It would also have needed extensive surveillance and guaranteed airborne firepower.

Such forces could have been found by the UK, but doing so would have greatly reduced the UK's capability to mount any other overseas operations. It would have been very difficult for the UK to fill gaps left by withdrawal of US logistic and intelligence support. There was little support for this idea, either within Whitehall and No. 10 or with the UK's allies. The subsequent UK operation to evacuate civilians from Kabul was dependent on US military capabilities, including intelligence, air traffic control, defence against rocket attacks and precision air strikes.

Biden's announcement was a great blow to the morale of Afghan government forces. Washington, London and Kabul may have thought that the Taliban would not start its offensive before the final withdrawal of US forces in September 2021. In the event the Afghan security forces collapsed much more quickly than either Washington or London expected.

The Taliban had planned its offensive at the tactical, operational and strategic levels. Its opening move of seizing border crossing points in western Afghanistan deprived the Afghan government of revenue from taxing trade. This was rapidly followed by attacks in eastern and northern Afghanistan. These offensives pre-empted any efforts that the former warlords of the Northern Alliance might have made to mobilize their militias. The subsequent fall of Kandahar, Afghanistan's second city, decisively weakened the government's position.

After their initial success in attacking Afghan government forces in isolated rural outposts, Taliban insurgents would negotiate with their enemies, either directly or through interlocutors such as tribal elders or local politicians. The insurgents sometimes successfully secured a surrender; on other occasions they offered not to attack if the government forces abandoned their positions.

Throughout the spring and early summer of 2021, the Taliban's 'victory campaign' gathered momentum. It was exploited and reinforced on social media. Videos of Taliban fighters attacking were followed by images of abandoned government fighting positions; next came imagery of Taliban forces taking control of urban areas and empty government buildings, and finally there followed uplifting footage of shops and schools re-opening. This was an effective information operation, showing the Taliban as tough and militarily effective, and, at the same time, magnanimous to those who surrendered, and effective at imposing stability after the fighting had moved on. Afghan and international journalists reported from areas captured by the Taliban, projecting images of security and normality. The Ghani government's response was much less effective, not least in failing to demonstrate a sense of urgency.

The US conducted a few air strikes against the Taliban, with little effect. But without any troops on the ground the US had only a limited idea of their locations and did not want accidentally to bomb Afghan troops. None of the US' allies, including the UK, joined any of these air attacks.

Even so, from the outset of the Taliban offensive the US had the option of mounting a large-scale air offensive that would have attacked many Taliban targets all over the country. This could have administered a disruptive shock to the Taliban offensive. Combined with a US demand that the Taliban cease fire, it might have given the insurgents pause for thought. The US seems to have chosen not to use its full military muscle to change battlefield dynamics.

The speed of the Taliban advance and collapse of the Afghan government forces took the MoD, FCO and No. 10 by surprise, Prime Minister Boris Johnson having declared in Parliament on 8 July that there was 'no military path to victory for the Taliban'. There was.

The Taliban advance continued, with both Lashkar Gar and Kandahar falling. By early August Kabul was surrounded. Afghan government officials and wealthy Afghans had for some days been departing the country by air. Civilians panicked. The media showed disturbing images; of Afghans fighting each other for seats on departing civil airliners and of civilians grabbing hold of a giant C17 transport aircraft, only to fall to their deaths.

Afghan Air Force aircraft carried over 500 Afghan military personnel to Uzbekistan. On 15 August Afghan President Ashraf Ghani fled Kabul by air. The will to fight of the few remaining Afghan government forces collapsed, and the Taliban occupied the capital. Half of the insurgent fighters were carrying US-made M16 rifles captured from the Afghan Army.

OPERATION PITTING

Both the US and UK military had been contingency planning for an evacuation operation. With the unexpectedly rapid collapse of the Afghan forces, these plans were rapidly activated. The same day, the commander of US CENTCOM met the Taliban in Doha to establish a 'deconfliction arrangement' through which the US and Taliban would co-ordinate the air evacuation from Kabul. As he did so, the leading troops of Operation *Pitting*, the British evacuation operation, arrived at Kabul airport.[33]

The US 82nd Airborne Division took charge of the airport with some 6,000 US troops on the ground, leading the security and evacuation operation. By the time they arrived the Afghan forces had collapsed. So the US were forced to negotiate with the Taliban in Kabul. These did not attack the US or British troops, but even so, a suicide bomber got into the crowds of desperate Afghans, killing US Marines. The British were extremely lucky to have not suffered any serious military casualties.

The UK rapidly deployed 1,000 troops, mostly from 16 Air Assault Brigade, including 2nd Battalion, the Parachute Regiment (2 Para). A hundred flights by RAF Hercules and newly acquired A400M Atlas transport aircraft carried out 15,000 Afghans deemed to be eligible by the British government. The operation was dependent on both US command and control, force protection and drones, as well as tactical co-operation with the Taliban.

Ironically, 2 Para had been the first British battalion into Kabul after the 9/11 attacks. It was a double irony that Taliban fighters and US and UK troops found themselves co-operating on the ground, in an effort to manage the crowds of Afghans seeking places on the departing flights. A ring of Taliban checkpoints around the airport sought to protect against any attack on the evacuation operation by ISIS, the terrorist group having proclaimed that the Taliban had become allied to the US.

Although the British evacuation benefited from advanced planning and reconnaissance, it rapidly became extremely challenging. The British and American paratroopers and marines flown into Kabul struggled to control the desperate crowds of Afghan citizens attempting to flee the country. Security depended on an accommodation with the Taliban, which set up checkpoints controlling civilian access to the airport. This was uncomfortable for many British troops, but they made it work. A paratrooper of A Company 2 Para described the unanticipated situation as he arrived:

> There was a big crowd of civvies who were standing off from us and all of a sudden they went dead quiet. Then an Afghan with an AK47 emerged out of the crowd and started telling them to move back. As soon as we saw him we all dropped onto our belt buckles. My finger was on the trigger. We were on Card Alpha rules of engagement, so we couldn't just drop him because he was holding a weapon, he needed to pose an immediate threat to life, and right now he wasn't.
>
> More of them started to emerge out of the crowd. Some had RPGs. They were only 15 metres away. I was thinking that they must be trying to clear the civvies to make way for some kind of attack on us, but then this Delta Force guy comes flying down on a motorbike shouting 'Don't fire don't fire! Friendly Taliban!' No one had told us that a deal had been made. I don't know how it didn't go to shit.[34]

The British ambassador, Laurie Bristow, 2 Para, and the Joint Force HQ did all they could in very difficult circumstances, to stop the operation 'going to shit'. Indeed, Bristow considered the military advice he received on the ground 'far more useful than anything I received from London'.[35] Many British troops at the airport thought that the government was failing to properly lead and co-ordinate the evacuation, especially when it came to rapidly identifying Afghan citizens eligible for evacuation to the UK and communicating with them. London seemed to provide insufficient strategic leadership and co-ordination.

To no one was this more evident than to the paratroopers dealing with the crowds of desperate Afghans. A leading role in evacuation was played by Private Fahim, an Afghan citizen who had joined the Parachute Regiment. As well as communicating with Taliban fighters, he greatly assisted 2 Para's efforts to identify eligible evacuees in the crowds. He observed the desperate plight of the crowd of Afghan civilians:

> There was screaming. People were crushed, people were crying or shouting for help. Anyone could understand they were desperate and scared, but I understood every word that they were shouting and begging. On top of this the Taliban were firing warning shots I had a few come really close.
>
> I felt helpless. Officers cried on my shoulder. There was blood sweat and tears from all ranks. Everyone had a nervous breakdown at some point. Every day of it was non-stop tragedy. People were shouting 'help me'. We couldn't help everyone and some of the more deserving people got left behind. Requirements and what paperwork was needed would

change, it was very frustrating, outlets were doing their best but they're not experts on documents

Lads passed through deserving people who wouldn't have got through otherwise, for bureaucratic reasons. It took about an hour for the Home Office personnel to process one family and they'd only sent two people. Once they'd arrived, the number of people we were getting out actually slowed down. If it had been that way from the beginning, we'd have got no more than 1000 out. It was about using common sense.

I knew first hand from my own family's experience that they were not exaggerating about the threats. People were crying that they would die that night if I didn't help them, but sometimes there was nothing I could do. I think about those people now. Is he dead? Is he alive? [36]

The British government's ability to manage the crisis buckled under the pressure of the large number of requests to evacuate Afghan civilians who had assisted the British in some way. The Foreign Commonwealth & Development Office (FCDO; it had replaced the FCO in 2020) was supposedly in the lead for deciding who should be evacuated. But it was incapable of deciding quickly enough. Its crisis cell was rapidly overwhelmed by the large numbers of requests for evacuation made by desperate Afghans who had worked for the British, both directly and indirectly, and their many British supporters. The leadership of the FCDO gave an impression of being missing in action, with Foreign Secretary Dominic Raab working from a Mediterranean holiday hotel. Although Raab eventually returned to London, his Permanent Secretary, the department's professional head, spent the whole crisis on leave. [37]

AN UNFINISHED RECKONING

The Afghan government and their forces had been comprehensively defeated. War is a zero-sum game and the Taliban had won. The US, the UK, NATO and the Afghan government had lost.

The military credibility of the US and UK were greatly weakened. For the many veterans grappling with physical and mental disability and the families of the dead and wounded, the defeat was a kick in the teeth.

There was no sugar-coating this pill. It was a bitter blow for all the Afghans who had sided with the international effort to reconstruct and stabilize the country. And Afghan women's rights to employment and education were rapidly removed by the Taliban government.

Their victory gave comfort to many of the adversaries of the US and its allies: Al Qaida and other jihadists, Russia, China and those who funded and supported the Taliban, including in Pakistan. It was a strategic inflection point for the US, akin to the 1975 fall of Saigon. But this time the UK had also been defeated. The defeat of the US and its allies and apparent chaos of the evacuation may have encouraged the Kremlin.

Whitehall and Parliament went into strategic shock. There was a justified sense of outrage expressed in an emergency debate in Parliament. Many MPs, especially military veterans, roundly criticized Prime Minister Boris Johnson and his government for the apparent chaos of their response.

The British government seemed to deny this 'inconvenient truth'. The aftermath of the Afghan evacuation saw a curious lack of strategic reflection in public by the British government, the MoD and the armed forces. The Iraq Inquiry had forensically examined the British war in Iraq, showing how the UK failed to achieve its strategic objectives; but Afghanistan was a defeat of even greater strategic impact.

The House of Commons Defence and Foreign Affairs Committees pulled no punches in their reports investigating the British evacuations, particularly the apparent failures of the FCDO. For example, there was a strong suspicion that an aircraft full of animals had only found its way to and from Kabul because of personal intervention by the Prime Minister and/or his wife. The Foreign Affairs Committee concluded that:

> The hasty effort to select those eligible for evacuation was poorly devised, managed, and staffed; and the department failed to perform the most basic crisis-management functions. The lack of clarity led to confusion and false hope among our Afghan partners who were desperate for rescue. They, and the many civil servants and soldiers working hard on the evacuation, were utterly let down by deep failures of leadership in Government. We are full of praise – in particular – for the personnel on the ground in Afghanistan during Operation *Pitting*, who implemented a chaotic policy to the best of their ability.[38]

So chaotic were the FCDO's decision-making processes that the House of Commons Defence Committee's inquiry was unable to determine who, if anyone, decided to grant a British animal welfare charity a scarce slot at Kabul airport to evacuate its animals. The media suspected that this was decided by Prime Minister Boris Johnson, an assessment that was never convincingly rebuffed. It is very difficult to find any evidence of positive strategic leadership by Johnson adding any value to the diplomats or military personnel in Whitehall or Kabul. And the Defence Committee reminded the government of the inconvenient truth that more blood and treasure had been lost in Afghanistan than in Iraq:

> The UK contribution to the war in Afghanistan took the lives of 457 UK armed forces personnel and injured thousands more, and cost more than £27 billion. The evacuation from Afghanistan in August 2021 resulted in 15,000 people being brought to the UK but left many behind. It is therefore of critical importance that the UK Government conduct an open, honest and detailed review of the UK's involvement in the country. This review should include military operations and political decisions covering the full timeline of the UK's involvement, from the terrorist attacks of September 11th 2001 and the invocation of Article 5 of the Washington Treaty, to the evacuation from Kabul in August 2021.[39]

The committee called for a national inquiry into Britain's war in Afghanistan. This recommendation was given a stiff ignoring by the government and the opposition Labour party. Why was this? Was it because such a report would have produced many uncomfortable conclusions of failures of political and strategic leadership by multiple prime ministers, defence secretaries and other ministers of both Conservative and Labour parties, and by senior officers and officials across the MoD, FCDO and DfID? It would have been as excoriating as the Iraq Inquiry, likely more so.

That such an inquiry has not been commissioned represents a conspiracy of negligence by both main political parties – a symptom of a degree of collective institutional denial. But without recognition of defeat by the Taliban, how could the government, MoD and Army be compelled to confront their failures and learn lessons? Would this deliberate institutional complacency be the handmaiden of subsequent strategic defeats?

In the absence of such an inquiry, the best reflection of the chaotic collapse of Afghanistan was made by Laurie Bristow, the final UK ambassador to Kabul. He assessed that:

> the rhetoric of Global Britain was failing to paper over some uncomfortable facts about the UK. The limit of our influence over US thinking was stark. So was our inability to act independently of the USA. The decisions to end the NATO military presence were made in Washington. We in the UK did not agree with the decision to withdraw the NATO forces or with the way it was done. Every person I met with experience of Afghanistan was aghast at Trump's dismal deal with the Taliban and then at Biden's botched execution of the withdrawal. But the UK was a junior partner, and we did not have an equal voice in US decision-making. The fact that we thought the military withdrawal unwise and badly thought through did not change US policy.
>
> Equally important, no one had managed to convince the Americans that the UK had a better strategy and no one – not the military not the diplomats not the intelligence agencies had done so for 20 years. Senior retired people criticized the absence of a strategy, invariably neglecting to mention their own role at the time in devising and executing strategies of the past, which had failed to pacify Helmand, eradicate opium, bring about gender equality, or create the conditions for a political settlement. For the UK it was uncomfortable for the limits of our influence on US decision-making to be exposed so graphically. But this did not tell us anything we did not already know if we chose to admit it. It was a wakeup call.[40]

But the UK's political leaders preferred to press the snooze button.

STRATEGIC SHOCK – THE 2022 RUSSIAN ATTACK ON UKRAINE

During 2021, Russian president Vladimir Putin increased his vitriolic messaging that Ukraine was a fake country that should never have seceded from Russia. And he condemned NATO and what he considered to be a Western-dominated European security architecture that need to be re-set to Russia's advantage. Over the winter of 2021/22, the UK and US increasingly warned that intelligence showed Russian formations concentrating in assembly areas around Ukraine, from which they could rapidly attack the country. This was complemented by Maxar, a US satellite imagery company, publishing satellite photos that convincingly supported the narrative from London and Washington. These warnings were not acted upon by many European countries, nor did they deter Russia.

The odds appeared to stack in Russia's favour. The Kremlin had much larger armed forces that had benefited from over a decade's additional funding, a sustained modernization programme and success in its wars in Georgia, Ukraine and Syria. Many Western intelligence agencies predicted that Ukraine would quickly be defeated, General Sir Mark Carleton-Smith, the CGS, subsequently saying that UK Defence Intelligence had thought that a Russian victory might take a week.[41]

In early 2022, both Prime Minister Johnson and Defence Secretary Wallace determined to strengthen Ukraine's military capability. A detachment of Rangers from the newly formed special operations brigade was rushed to Ukraine to train its Army on the new NLAW anti-tank missile. The US also supplied Javelin and Stinger missiles. There is evidence that these man-portable weapons were chosen not only because they would be of use in countering the initial Russian attack, but also because their simplicity and small size meant that they would be of great value to any Ukrainian resistance movement that would fight on after the likely Russian victory.

When the Russian attack began, Putin appeared confident that Ukraine would be rapidly defeated, with minimal Russian casualties.

Although many Western defence analysts expected a rapid Russian victory, the initial Russian main attack to capture Kyiv failed. It was clear after the end of the first month of the war that the Russian war machine had failed to subdue the country. Under the charismatic leadership of President Zelensky, Ukrainian forces put up an unexpectedly resolute and effective defence, imposing more delay on Russian forces than many military analysts, including myself, expected.

The war invalidated the superficial optimism of Prime Minister Boris Johnson's 1991 statement that 'the old concepts of fighting big tank battles on the European landmass … are over'.[42] Inconveniently for him, the Ukraine war saw many tank battles and intense artillery barrages. Although drones had high utility for both sides, so had conventional land warfare capabilities, including infantry, armoured vehicles and artillery. Without a mechanized brigade stationed in Kyiv, the city could well have been overrun in the first week of the war.

THE ARMY'S RAPID RESPONSE

After Russia attacked Ukraine, the UK rapidly reinforced NATO forces in Europe. Over the rest of the spring and summer, most of the 12th Armoured Brigade was sent at short notice from Salisbury Plain to Eastern Europe. This included a tank squadron to Scandinavia, doubling the Army force in Estonia, an armoured battlegroup to Poland and an air assault brigade task force of helicopters and paratroops in Macedonia. The British logistic and training facility at Sennelager, in west Germany, was activated.

The Army deployed more forces more rapidly to more parts of Europe than any other army in Europe. From 2022 onwards the Army participated in increased NATO field exercises, including spending a year providing the lead land elements of NATO's Very High Readiness Joint Task Force.

In the aftermath of the Russian attack, there was change at the top of the Army. General Carleton-Smith was replaced as CGS by General Sir Patrick Sanders. He immediately established his authority over the Army by publicly criticizing 3rd Battalion, the Parachute Regiment for lapses in discipline. These included unruly behaviour in Macedonia and allegations of a sex orgy at their Colchester barracks. An operational tour by the battalion was cancelled.

This action administered a necessarily bracing shock to that particular battalion. With the Russian attack on Ukraine having greatly increased the chances of war in Europe, the senior leadership of Defence and the government were forced to take a hard look at the ability of the armed forces and the Army to fight. There could be no more equivocation, or hiding behind soundbites, however carefully crafted by spin doctors.

An early indicator was Operation *Mobilise*. General Sanders directed the Army to concentrate on improving its readiness for war. Much was made of this in his speeches and those by other senior Army officers. But hard details on measures taken by the Army were conspicuously absent from the public domain. This may well be because the actions taken under the operation were of necessity classified.

But it is hard to avoid the conclusion that if the Army had been fully ready for war, Operation *Mobilise* would not have been necessary. As with the 2008 Operation *Entirety* to urgently optimize the Army for the Afghan war, the implication is that if the MoD had been fully committed to supporting the Army, including providing adequate resources, Operation *Mobilise* would not have been necessary. That neither the Royal Navy nor the RAF conducted such an exercise is further confirmation that their readiness was greater than the Army's.

In public, Sanders emphasized that land power had been decisive in defending Ukraine. He was careful not to publicly contradict defence policy. But he showed a pragmatic advocacy of making the most of conventional land warfare capability, as exemplified by his statement that 'you can't cyber your way across a river'.

This reinforced justified scepticism that no amount of investment in 'sunrise' capabilities such as drones and cyber can replace the combat capability of conventional weapons, such as warships, tanks and fighters. If the first two years of the Ukraine war show anything, it is that to fight a modern land battle armies need all the traditional tools in the box and need them at sufficient scale to fight prolonged battles. The need for large-scale stockpiles of ammunition and spare parts was graphically demonstrated.

The government made a major commitment to provide weapons and training to the Ukrainian forces. Operation *Interflex* became a large-scale operation to train Ukrainian troops. By the end of 2024 over 50,000 Ukrainians had completed training. This included basic training of recruits and specialist training for Ukrainians who would operate British equipment.

The training used up a significant proportion of the UK's ranges and training areas. This significantly reduced collective training opportunities for the Army. The cancelled exercises did not appear to have moved overseas.

A squadron of Challenger 2 tanks was donated to Ukraine. To provide sufficient spare parts, stocks were withdrawn from the Army's remaining tank regiments, depressing

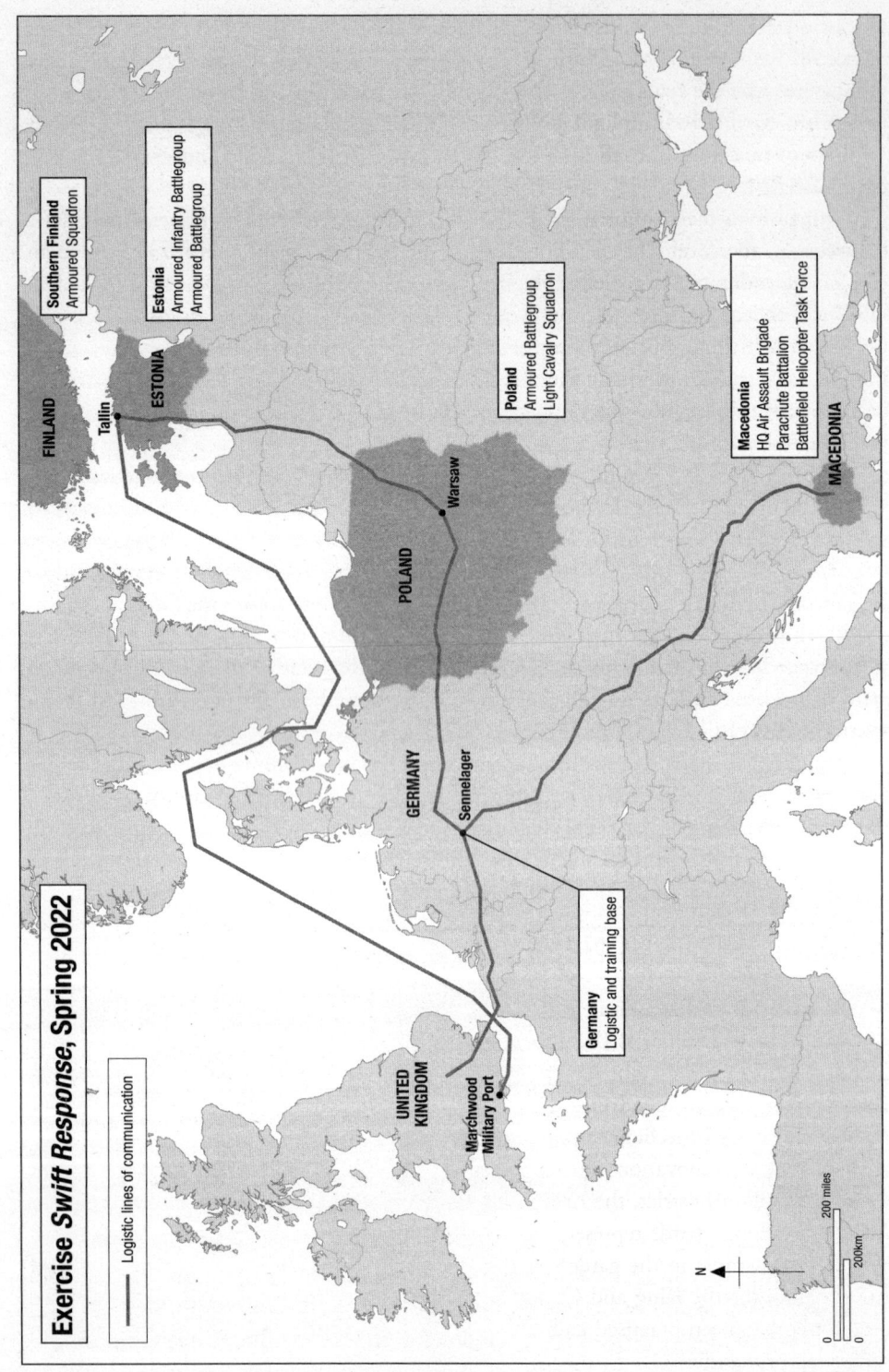

Exercise *Swift Response*, Spring 2022

— Logistic lines of communication

Southern Finland
Armoured Squadron

Estonia
Armoured Infantry Battlegroup
Armoured Battlegroup

Poland
Armoured Battlegroup
Light Cavalry Squadron

Macedonia
HQ Air Assault Brigade
Parachute Battalion
Battlefield Helicopter Task Force

Germany
Logistic and training base

FINLAND

Tallin

ESTONIA

POLAND

Warsaw

GERMANY

Sennelager

MACEDONIA

UNITED KINGDOM

Marchwood
Military Port

N

200 miles

200km

0

0

readiness. All the Army's serviceable AS90 guns were donated to Ukraine, along with most of the Army's stockpile of 155mm shells. To fill the gap, 14 Swedish Archer guns were purchased, with the remaining close support batteries in the 3rd Division retraining on the far less capable 105mm light gun.

These were significant reductions in the Army's capability. But troops saw the need, particularly when they had contact with Ukrainian trainees, who within a few weeks, would deploy to their country's highly lethal front line. What disappointed troops and their commanders were the ever-lengthening gaps between donation of Army equipment to Ukraine and potential replenishment of the missing capability.

One small consolation was the performance of the NLAW anti-tank missile. It was unique amongst man-portable weapons in that it was programmed to fly over the target vehicles, firing downwards at the thin top armour. This made it highly effective at destroying Russian tanks. The NLAW was widely praised by Ukrainians from front-line infantry to President Zelensky.

A collaborative development by UK and Sweden and manufactured in Belfast, the system had a long pedigree. In the early 1990s, the Army assessed that the warhead needed to penetrate frontal armour on future tanks would be so heavy as to make any infantry weapons too heavy to carry. So a programme to demonstrate the technology was funded. By the mid-1990s a prototype missile was successfully fired against target tanks.

NLAW was widely exported. This made it a rare example of a 21st-century British land weapon serving with the Army to have achieved export success. In the past many British systems had been purchased by foreign armies. For example, the 105mm light gun, 81mm mortar and CVR(T) light armoured vehicles had been widely exported in the 1970s, as had the Chieftain tank. But in the 21st century very little land military equipment was being manufactured in the UK, let alone being exported. The reduction in the size of the Army had led inexorably to a considerable reduction in the size of British defence industry manufacturing equipment for foreign armies.

A ROYAL INFLECTION POINT

The Army made contributions to the 2022 funeral of Queen Elizabeth II and the 2023 coronation of King Charles III. The latter event featured some innovations.[43] Firstly, to better synchronize the eight bands playing on the march from Westminster Abbey to Buckingham Palace key drummers and commanders were 'wired for sound', with unobtrusive noise-cancelling earphones playing a 'click track'.

Secondly, an innovation was suggested for the coronation by the garrison sergeant major of London District, the Army's top expert on drill and state ceremonial. This was for the marching guards representing many of the Army's regiments and the other two services to assemble in the garden of Buckingham Palace. There they performed a final Royal Salute for the King and Queen followed by three cheers. Although much of the ceremonial had been practised and rehearsed, this new idea could not be. In the event it succeeded brilliantly.

Finally, the event involved many troops based outside London. Many of these travelled into the city by rail, then marched with their bands through early morning London. After the event they returned to barracks in the same way. This was a great surprise to many Londoners and tourists, who found themselves up close to the Army in an unanticipated way.

The whole operation was masterminded by HQ London District, the capital's standing military HQ. It used the same organization that had planned and conducted the military security for the Olympics – an illustration of the flexibility and versatility of the Army's regional HQs.

2023 – the Integrated Review 'refreshed'

In July 2023, the MoD 'refreshed' the 2021 Integrated Review in a Defence Command Paper.[44] This reflected the strategic shock administered by the Ukraine war. It assessed that that UK security had deteriorated more quickly than anticipated. The government prioritized NATO, with armed forces 'optimized to war-fight in the Euro-Atlantic and in defence of our homeland'. This was a significant change from the previous review, which prioritized peacetime operations.

The modest military 'tilt' to the Indo-Pacific was to be sustained. Previously advocated by Boris Johnson, this policy was enthusiastically promoted by the Royal Navy.

The UK would collaborate with Italy and Japan in the Global Combat Air Programme to develop a new fighter jet, and with Australia and the US in the AUKUS partnership to develop nuclear submarines and other advanced military technology. The share of the defence budget assigned to these programmes would grow greatly over future years. There was no sign of similarly increased collaborative investments in future land warfare technologies.

None of the reductions in forces' manpower ordered in 2021 was reversed. The Army was to increase its partnership with Estonia, to be able to rapidly reinforce the battlegroup based there to brigade strength. Defence spending was set to increase to 2.27 per cent of GDP by 2024–25, with a government aspiration to increase defence spending to 2.5 per cent of GDP, subject to affordability.

The Army had concluded from the fighting in Ukraine that to fight a modern high-intensity land war it needed to improve its air defences and its ability to find and strike deep targets using drones, electronic warfare and long-range rockets. These were sound assessments. But providing these essential capabilities would require more money.

General Sanders served only two years as CGS, when most of his recent predecessors had served over three years. There were media reports that plain speaking by Sanders about the Army's capability weaknesses had upset Defence Secretary Ben Wallace.

The Army continued to support NATO, not only sustaining the forward deployed battlegroup in Estonia, but also joining NATO exercises. In 2024, it made a major contribution to Exercise *Steadfast Defender*. A total of 90,000 NATO troops took part in the exercise, which brought together existing German and Polish national exercises under the NATO banner.

The British Army contributed some 16,000 troops, from 7th Light Mechanised Brigade, 12th Armoured Brigade, 16 Air Assault Brigade, 101st Logistic Brigade and the HQ of 3rd Division. They operated alongside Estonian, Polish and US units. The British logistic and training base in Germany was activated by 104th Logistic Brigade. Operations included seizure of an airfield in Estonia by a parachute battalion, followed on by air landing infantry and an MLRS rocket launcher, and river crossings in Poland by the armoured and mechanized brigades and British M3 ferries.

Mobilization, movement and deployment provided useful validation of its plans to deploy to Eastern Europe. And the brigade exercises practised multinational tactical interoperability. But having deployed a division's worth of brigades, it was surprising that after the NATO exercises finished, the formations did not come together on a European training area for a full divisional exercise. I asked senior officers why this did not happen. I did not receive a convincing reply. Whether this reflected a failure of ambition or the constraints of having insufficient logistic stockpiles or funding was unclear.

NATO'S INCREASING REQUIREMENTS FOR THE BRITISH ARMY

Following the Russian attack on Ukraine, NATO's 2022 Strategic Concept, agreed at NATO's Madrid Summit, agreed a new NATO Force Model. This was to:

> provide a larger pool of high readiness forces across domains, land, sea air and cyber, which will be pre-assigned to specific plans for the defence of Allies. It will improve NATO's ability to respond at very short notice for any contingency, and enable Allies to make more forces available to NATO on an assured basis ... When fully implemented, the NATO Force Model will provide well over 300,000 troops at high readiness.[45]

NATO developed a strategic plan for deterrence and defence of the Euro-Atlantic Area, complemented three joint force commands' plans to conduct operational-level joint campaigns, executed by their land, sea and air component commands. From these, the NATO military staff developed National Capability Targets setting out the forces at readiness required from each NATO state. The total number of forces required by NATO for the deterrent and defence plans appears to be between 30 and 50 per cent larger than those required by NATO before 2022. For example, the requirement for the new Allied Reaction Force is more demanding than that for the previous Very High Readiness Joint Task Force.[46]

In March 2025, Admiral Pierre Vandier, NATO's Supreme Allied Commander Transformation, suggested that these new targets were likely to represent a 30 per cent increase on their predecessors.[47] Speaking in London in June 2025, the new NATO Secretary General Mark Rutte stated that:

> Russia is reconstituting its forces with Chinese technology, and producing more weapons faster than we thought. In terms of ammunition, Russia produces in three months what the

whole of NATO produces in a year. And its defence industrial base is expected to roll out 1,500 tanks, 3,000 armoured vehicles, and 200 Iskander missiles this year alone. Russia could be ready to use military force against NATO within five years.

Our decisions on defence spending are driven by NATO's battle plans and capability targets. They define what forces and capabilities Allies need to provide. And last week, NATO Defence Ministers agreed ambitious new targets. The exact details are classified but we need:

A 400% increase in air and missile defence. We see in Ukraine how Russia delivers terror from above. So we will strengthen the shield that protects our skies. Our militaries also need thousands more armoured vehicles and tanks. Millions more artillery shells. And we must double our enabling capabilities, such as logistics, supply, transportation, and medical support.[48]

The exact requirement that NATO asked the British Army to supply was classified. But it included the British leading a 'strategic reserve corps' of at least two divisions, an HQ and corps combat support brigades.[49]

This reflected an Army strength – the capabilities of the HQ ARRC and its signal brigade. In late 2024 more brigades were assigned to the corps. These included the 1st Aviation Brigade, with 50 new top-of-the-range Apache helicopters, making it the most powerful European attack helicopter formation. A 'theatre sustainment' logistic brigade was assigned, as were medical and military police brigades. Corps combat engineering capability would be provided by 8th Engineer Brigade, artillery and air defence by corps artillery and air defence groups.

In contrast, most of the other NATO multinational corps provided by European armies did not appear to have the sufficient organic corps level combat support, including artillery, engineer, and air defence brigades.[50] Compared with these formations, HQ ARRC was more capable of fighting a corps-level battle to improve the success of its divisions, albeit having less such capability than a US Army corps.

The remaining NATO requirements for the Army were classified. But there were credible reports that the Army had told the MoD that to supply the full range of forces required by NATO would require an Army of 90,000 regular troops. It would need to be supported by a significantly larger stockpile of ammunition and spare parts. At the time of writing, it was unclear whether with its current resourcing the Army would be able to meet NATO's requirements.

THE GREAT DISRUPTIONS OF 2025

In February 2025, the new US government of President Donald Trump administered strategic shocks to the UK, NATO and Europe. Vice President JD Vance used the Munich Security Conference to voice outspoken criticisms on the character of European culture and politics. Defense Secretary Pete Hegseth told the conference that the US was de-prioritizing its military commitments to conventional defence of Europe, instead prioritizing homeland defence and countering China.

Trump attempted to strike a peace deal between Ukraine and Russia. The remarks of Trump and his senior officials suggested that the US government had pivoted in favour of Russia. These worries were increased by a public confrontation with President Zelensky in the Oval Office and the temporary withdrawal of US intelligence support to Ukraine. In Trump's efforts to negotiate an end to the war in Ukraine, he and his advisors often seemed to favour Russia.

European states and the UK found these events deeply worrying. European governments increasingly feared that in the event of a Russian attack on Europe, the Trump government would not necessarily honour NATO's Article V guarantee that an attack on one member of NATO was an attack on all the alliance. Europe finally woke up to its cumulative neglect of hard power and defence spending.

The UK mounted a diplomatic effort towards engineering a rapprochement between Zelensky and Trump. Just before his first call on the White House, Prime Minister Starmer announced that the UK needed to change its national security posture by delivering the biggest increase in its defence budget since the end of the Cold War. The UK would move faster to increase defence spending. This would increase to 2.5 per cent of GDP by 2027. It would further grow to 3 per cent of GDP 'in the next parliament'. The increase would be funded by cuts in spending on overseas aid.[51]

The Army was encouraged to hear Chancellor Rachel Reeves argue in public that 'as we spend that money on that defence and security … we use it in a way that can also help stimulate the economy, and particularly to revive some parts of the country that do often feel like they're left behind.'[52] This appeared to reverse the Treasury's ingrained hostility to defence spending, but only time would tell if this would change their behaviour.

Starmer and French President Macron mounted an initiative to safeguard any peace deal between Ukraine and Russia. London and Paris would develop and lead a 'coalition of the willing' to defend a deal in Ukraine and 'guarantee the peace'. This would not be a traditional UN peacekeeping mission that emphasized impartiality, minimum use of force and consent. Instead, 'defending' and 'guaranteeing' any peace agreement would require a force capable of deterring Russian military attacks on Ukraine, requiring it to be capable of high-intensity combat leading.

If the force had a large land component, it would be likely that both France and UK would play a leading part. In 1996 the British Army had easily generated the forces for the NATO IFOR, a multinational division, including a full armoured brigade and division troops. It was far from clear that it could rapidly generate the same forces again.

THE ARMY IN 2025 – UNREADY FOR WAR?

Was the Army ready for war? Could it 'fight tonight'? Evidence suggested that there were considerable weaknesses in Army readiness. This was exposed by the 2024 House of Commons Defence Committee Report 'Ready for War?'.[53] It demonstrated multiple capability shortfalls across the armed services, placing considerable limitations on UK readiness. Weaknesses included declining manning levels and a lack of medical capability.

Whilst small-scale non-combat operations might not be constrained, UK readiness for medium-scale and large-scale high-intensity warfighting appeared to require considerable improvement, not least to deliver the UK forces assigned to NATO.

Since 9/11 the Army had been only partially modernized. It had received new digital communications, the Apache helicopter, itself recently upgraded, the Wildcat scout helicopter and the new family of armoured engineer vehicles. Some of the adaptations made for Afghanistan had been embedded in the Army, including updated small arms, the Guided MLRS rocket, the Spike NLOS missile and Jackal and Foxhound light patrol vehicles.

The inconvenient truth was that the Army was the least modernized of the UK services. It still had hundreds of obsolete armoured vehicles, dating from the 1960s and 1970s. In contrast, the RAF's oldest Typhoon fighters entered service in the early 2000s and the Royal Navy's oldest warship, HMS *Lancaster*, was commissioned in 1992. The US Army, French Army and many European armies had more modern and capable armour, including the US M2 Bradley, Swedish CV90 and French VBCI infantry fighting vehicles, as well as Leopard 2 tanks and more modern artillery. And the British Army was the only army in NATO giving up infantry fighting vehicles. Some key front-line equipment had been donated to Ukraine. This included all the Army's AS90 155mm self-propelled guns. And the 2021 decision to abandon armoured infantry capability by retiring Warrior infantry fighting vehicles greatly reduced the lethality of armoured brigades and battlegroups.

There is much more to readiness than just equipment. Being ready to fight also requires stockpiles of spare parts and ammunition. Even before the Ukraine war there were many pointers that there were insufficient stockpiles for more than a few days of high-intensity warfighting without running out of vital supplies.

The Army needs to be supported by adequate medical capability. This is so the lightly wounded can be returned to battle. It supports the moral component. Knowledge that the wounded will be rapidly evacuated and treated, as well as looked after in hospital, and that they and their families will receive the necessary, medical and welfare support, boosts morale.

So the most astonishing part of the Defence Committee report was an admission that there was insufficient medical capability to support operations. Given the difficulty that inadequate family support at the Royal Centre for Defence Medicine at Birmingham University Hospital caused the government between 2006 and 2010, this capability weakness was alarming. Equally alarming was the apparent lack of urgency displayed by the MoD in seeking to rectify this deficiency.

Readiness also requires the force to be fully manned with sufficient people, all properly trained. Omens here were all inauspicious. At the end of 2024, Army manning appeared to be on a downward trajectory. And a minister's response to a parliamentary question showed that the Army had a surprisingly high proportion of troops with a health condition that prevented their deployment on combat operations outside the UK. Of an Army manpower target of 72,5000 personnel, over 16,000 troops were 'medically not deployable' or 'medically limited deployable', some 22 per cent of all troops.[54] Public comments by ministers indicated that there was no credible plan for an all-out mobilization of the Army reserves.

This illustrated that the greatly reduced size of the Army created risks. The force that fought in Operation *Granby* in 1991 had been generated from an Army of 155,000 troops. This had 15 all-regular ground manoeuvre brigades made up of nine armoured brigades, four infantry brigades, an airmobile brigade and an airborne brigade.

The reduced Army of 110,000 troops that followed the 1991 Options for Change contractions sustained the brigade-sized force that served in Bosnia with the UN, and the larger intervention for the NATO IFOR in 1996. Having five armoured or mechanized brigades, and airborne and airmobile brigades, it was then able to sustain the brigade-sized British contingent in Bosnia from 1997 to 2001 and the brigade-sized contingent in Kosovo from 1999 to 2003.

The same Army generated the large division deployed to Iraq in 2003. Afterwards the Army had gone beyond the defence planning assumptions to sustain two large brigades on demanding simultaneous operations in Iraq and Afghanistan, the so-called 'double medium commitment'. To prevent the Army being stretched to breaking point, the Afghanistan commitment had needed to be sustained by using the Royal Marines' commando brigade and forming two additional ad hoc brigade HQs: 52nd and 11th Light Brigades.

Since then, the Army has reduced in size by a third. An Army of 72,500 troops would have much less redundancy. It *might* be able to generate a single division of about 30,000 troops, for a one-off intervention. But it would struggle to sustain other operations, both concurrently, or subsequently. The Army now had only four all regular combined arms ground manoeuvre brigades – 7th Light Mechanized, 12th Armoured, 16 Air Assault and 20th Armoured.[55] With the requirement to deploy a brigade to Estonia in war, it is hard to see how more than a single British warfighting division could be mobilized.[56]

The Army still has many strengths. It has many competent self-motivated soldiers and officers. The middle and senior management of the Army had many people who had served through the difficult wars in Iraq and Afghanistan and had not been found wanting. But the combat experience that had tested people under fire had ceased in 2013. So the Army in 2025 has very few people under the age of 35 who had fought against the Iraqi militias or the Taliban.

The Army still has good individual training, from basic recruit training, through NCO and officer courses. Until 2003, it had conducted a high level of collective training, at battlegroup and brigade level. This made sure that units could deploy to an operational theatre to conduct demanding combined arms manoeuvre. British Army success against the Iraqi forces in 1991 and 2003 were built on these very strong foundations.

But from 2005 onwards the Army was forced to abandon brigade training for war, in order to prepare forces for Iraq and Afghanistan. After the Iraq war ended, battlegroup training at BATUS resumed. But after 2020 this unique training facility was abandoned. The Army said that training for heavy battlegroups would move to Oman. Some exercises took place, but the level of armoured warfare training in Oman was much lower than had been achieved in Canada. Although some brigades took part in NATO exercises, these, by their multinational character, were less demanding than those the Army had previously run for brigades, in Germany, Canada and Poland.

This matters, not just as a symbol of reduced military aspiration and funding but also because it is a key element of the Army's military capability and credibility, particularly with the US military. After 2014, as it reduced its forces in Iraq and Afghanistan, the US Army resumed conducting demanding brigade-level field exercises. Ten armoured brigades a year rotated through the US National Training Centre at Fort Irwin and light brigades regularly trained at the Joint Readiness Training Centre. In the same period, the British Army never achieved that level of training.

In early 2025 the Army conducted a brigade exercise for 4th Light Brigade, including two of its battlegroups, where the force was thoroughly tested against a demanding OPFOR on Salisbury Plain. This appeared to be the first such exercise for at least two decades. If sustained by further such exercises this would be an important step in rebuilding Army collective training.

The US, NATO and the UK's other key allies are all well aware of these weaknesses, not least from reporting by their attachés in London, as are Russia and China. This reduces UK military credibility and influence. The MoD often states that, for NATO operations, these weaknesses can be ameliorated by allied military contributions. But many NATO capability weaknesses, such as long-range indirect fire, air defence and munition and spare part stockpiles, are such that they cannot be used to compensate for UK capability weaknesses. This is another example of an MoD statement that not only flies against the evidence, but is not credible to those in the Army.

Until these capability weaknesses are rectified, deploying British Army units and formations to fight carries increases risk of avoidable casualties and mission failure. In a shooting war, these weaknesses would mean that British brigades would take greater casualties and be slower to achieve their missions than better equipped and trained US brigades. These factors are what most worries US generals who might have to fight alongside the British. Failing to be able to 'fight tonight' carries the risk of mission failure, inflicting such damage to the credibility of the armed forces and MoD that the British public would lose confidence in their competence and value for money. If British forces suffered avoidable casualties or defeat, the nation might suffer such a strategic shock that it chose to move away from having anything other than token armed forces.

CHALLENGES TO THE MORAL COMPONENT

In the 2020s, the Army's moral component seemed to be under challenge. There were several incidents of disgraceful behaviour, including evidence of bullying, harassment, racism and sexism. A major general was court-martialled for fraud and three brigadiers commanding brigades were removed from command for misconduct. The Defence

Secretary expressed his displeasure to the Army Board and in February 2021 an Army-wide study period, Operation *Teamwork*, was held to discuss these problems and ways to overcome them. These were unprecedented events.

A female officer cadet committed suicide at the Royal Military Academy Sandhurst in 2019. The findings of an Army board of inquiry into her death was published in mid-2022, over two years after the event.[57] Investigation showed that she had alcohol misuse issues and had self-harmed. An instructor had taken sexual advantage of her. What the inquiry did not appear to ask was how was it that an instructor felt that breaking rules to have sex with a trainee was acceptable. Equally disturbing were dangerous levels of miscommunication between various staff at Sandhurst. The CGS, General Sanders, apologized to the cadet's family. If disciplinary action or sackings occurred at Sandhurst this was not made public. The incident did nothing to help the Army recruit women.

Although the Army's moral component was damaged by the death of Baha Mousa in Iraq, the service seemed to come out of Afghanistan with its moral component in pretty good order. A wounded Taliban captive was murdered by a Royal Marine, but that was a disciplinary matter for that part of the Royal Navy.

But there was disturbing evidence of potential unlawful killings by SAS troops in Afghanistan. These are subject to an independent inquiry. Unlike some other armies, the British have always insisted that elite forces engaged in secret operations are no more exempt from domestic law or the law of armed conflict than conventional forces. Abandoning this principle would cross a line into institutional illegality and immorality.

Another serious challenge to the moral component was the very poor standard of the Army's accommodation. Throughout the whole of this period the Army's living accommodation was systematically underfunded. Although there was much work to upgrade accommodation in barracks for single troops and married quarters, the cold reality was that the demand greatly outpaced both the supply of new modern accommodation and the requirement for repairs and maintenance.

The poor standard of accommodation was an open sore. The Army and MoD's apparent inability to find enough funds for this greatly undermined their credibility with troops living in deteriorating conditions. To make matters worse, maintenance was often performed too slowly and below the required standard. For all the MoD's celebration of the armed forces, the apparent mismanagement and underfunding was a morale black hole, inexorably dragging down the welfare and commitment of too many troops and their families.

In the mid-1990s most forces' family accommodation had been sold and leased back. The funds realized from the sale could, if spent on the accommodation, have made a positive difference, but that did not happen. This was one of the worst deals for the taxpayer ever made by the MoD. In 2024 the married quarters were repurchased by the MoD.

ENGAGING WITH THE FUTURE

Despite these difficulties in generating combat power, between 2023 and 2025 the Army sought to better set out its path to a future Army. The limitations of the Army exposed by the Ukraine war made clear weaknesses in the 2021 Integrated Review. So the Army set out to devise a new concept for fighting modern land wars. This would not only incorporate the key lessons of the Ukraine war, but would examine how the Russian way of war could be better countered – a revisiting of the conceptual foundations of development of doctrine, concepts and equipment in the 1980s.

Led by Major General James Bowder, the Director Futures (the post itself a recognition of the need to better plan for the future), a new 'Land Operating Concept' was developed.[58] This envisaged surveillance, drones, artillery and precision missiles in a new 'recce-strike' function, better exploitation of data and electronic warfare and more robust logistics.

The concept was developed over a year. As it evolved it was subject to extensive review by allied armies and leading UK think tanks. Evidence was gathered through a series of wargames that tested new ideas. This innovation itself catalyzed other innovations, including applying the concept's principles to develop new designs for the Army's structure.

By now the CGS was General Sir Roly Walker, who had commanded the Grenadier Guards in Helmand 15 years earlier. In 2024, Walker articulated an ambitious concept that the Army would double its lethality in three years and treble it by 2030, all without additional resources. Key to this would be learning from Ukraine's tactics, especially using many armed and unarmed drones, and exploiting better data, networked communications and emerging artificial intelligence technology. If the Army could locate enemy forces earlier, analyze and decide more quickly and attack at longer range, it could destroy more targets, more quickly and further away.

In parallel the Army made a significant effort to better innovate. An annual Army Warfighting Experiment brought in industry to try out new technologies under simulated battle conditions on Salisbury Plain.

A new Experimentation Task Force was formed to conduct trials of new technology and tactics. At the core of this was a light infantry battalion. This followed the previous examples of Experimental Mechanized Force in the 1920s and the 6th Airmobile Brigade in the 1980s. It quickly got to work, for example in 2023 conducting practical experiments to trail the recce-strike concept at battlegroup level, particularly the potential use of tactical drones to achieve this.

The force twice deployed to the US to exercise as part of Project *Convergence*, the US Army's ambitious programme to exploit emerging technology. In the harsh desert of the US Army's National Training Centre it tested new technologies and tactical thinking against the NTC's unforgiving OPFOR.[59]

This featured extensive use of drones, for both surveillance and attack. Experimental robotic armed ground vehicles were also used. These provided screen and guard forces without any troops in them – to see if a unit's first battle could be entirely fought by machines. First person view armed drones, which had proven particularly useful in the hands of both Russian and Ukrainian troops, were particularly useful – not least in attacking enemy drone control stations. Using these tactics, the experimental battlegroup mounted a very successful defence of the main town in the training area. These recent field trials had encouraging results that augured well for the feasibility of General Walker's ambitious plan.

The 2025 Strategic Defence Review – the last chance to stop further decline?

The 2023 Integrated Review had an ambition to improve readiness, including by increasing logistic stockpiles and investing in ammunition production. Defence Secretary Ben Wallace understood the importance of these measures. But despite his efforts to balance the defence budget, and to get Prime Minister Boris Johnson to pledge extra money for defence, the MoD's plan for future equipment still remained greatly in excess of the available funds. In December 2023 the independent National Audit Office identified major weaknesses in the affordability of the future equipment plan – a funding gap of up to £16.9 billion.[60]

The new Labour government took power in summer 2025. It inherited a defence budget of 2.3 per cent of GDP. This included very large sums for nuclear capabilities, both submarines and deterrent, costs that had escalated greatly over recent years. This and the considerable costs of the ship building, aerospace and guided missile programmes meant that the funding for other conventional capabilities and the Army was being increasingly squeezed out of the budget.

Evidence of this was an autumn 2024 MoD decision to cut military capabilities, including the early retirement of transport helicopters, Watchkeeper unmanned aerial vehicles, a frigate, two tanker vessels and both landing platform docks – this measure greatly reducing amphibious capability. This suggested that the MoD had institutional memory loss.

Had it forgotten the desperate shortages of transport helicopters and drones in Afghanistan, and the resulting operational difficulties and avoidable casualties? Or that the 1982 landings of the commando brigade on the Falklands would have been impossible without the two landing ships? The Royal Navy had now abandoned the ability to land a brigade from the sea. In the event of the Falkland Islands being recaptured by Argentina, an amphibious landing would become much more difficult than it had been in 1982.

These decisions were evidence of a defence budget under severe pressure. As was a mid-2024 MoD edict that new spending of more than £50,000 had to be personally approved by a minister – a recipe for delay, if ever there was one.

John Healey, the new Defence Secretary, was frank, stating that whilst the armed forces were able to conduct peacetime operations, such as evacuations and peacekeeping, they lacked the necessary capabilities to fight a war.[61]

On 2 June 2025 Prime Minister Keir Starmer proclaimed that The United Kingdom's SDR[62] heralded a 'new era for defence and security'. The review recognized the armed forces' limited capacity for high-intensity warfare, including that their medical capabilities had 'long been subject to neglect and underfunding.' Many troops felt that this judgement applied more broadly to the Army as a whole.

Despite these 'inconvenient truths', the review offered an ambitious vision. The armed forces would focus on a 'NATO First' policy. It set out a plan for a 'high-low' equipment mix, reshaped forces and a reinvigorated defence industrial base that would act as an engine for economic growth and prosperity. Given the threat environment, it noted that 'business as usual' was not an option.

It conspicuously failed to set a target date for the armed forces to be ready for war with their current capabilities. It required the restoration of 'the UK's ability to deter, fight, and win – with allies – against states with advanced military forces by 2035', ten years in the future. It did not provide justification for another decade's delay in rebuilding combat capability. But other nations and NATO were assessing that should the Ukraine war end, Russia could rebuild its offensive capabilities in half a decade or less.[63] There was no such assessment in the SDR.

The review noted the Army had donated a significant proportion of its equipment and ammunition stockpiles to Ukraine. It endorsed the existing plans to acquire Ajax scout vehicles, Boxer APCs, and Challenger 3 tanks, but not its plans to acquire new medium artillery to replace the AS90 guns gifted to Ukraine, nor to fill the capability gap caused by abandoning armoured infantry.

Funding would be key to implementation. The review was conducted 'within the budgetary context of a transition to 2.5% of GDP' from 2027, with an ambition to spend '3% of GDP on defence in the 2030s if economic and fiscal conditions allow'. It would be very unlikely that this would fully fund either restoring readiness or the existing equipment programme, so short-term savings would probably be required. Indeed, the MoD would be required to make £6 billion of savings over the next five years. This could well include more reductions in Army capabilities.[64]

Even with the relatively modest defence budget increase to reach 2.5 per cent of GDP, the MoD probably could not afford all the capabilities to meet its NATO obligations. This would probably require a defence budget closer to 3.5 per cent of GDP. And if the UK wanted to have an effective air and missile defence capability to defend its homeland there would be considerable additional costs.[65]

Given the overhang of unfunded plans identified in 2023, it was very difficult to see how further significant capability cuts could be avoided. Although the Prime Minister and Defence Secretary exuded optimism about increasing defence spending, close reading of the review showed considerable cautious conditionality. The phrase 'when funding allows' was applied to an increase of the defence budget to 3 per cent, and to many other potential enhancements, including a modest increase of size from 72,500 to 76,000 troops and a 20 per cent increase in the size of Army reserves. Shortly after the SDR, NATO heads of government agreed that NATO's current target for members to spend 2 per cent of GDP on defence should rise to 3.5 per cent of GDP by 2035 to fund 'core defence requirements, and to meet the NATO Capability Targets', with another 1.5 per cent of GDP to be spent to 'protect our critical infrastructure, defend our networks, ensure our civil preparedness and resilience, unleash innovation, and strengthen our defence industrial base'. This was supported by the Prime Minister. Whilst the measure could assist with meeting the SDR's target to achieve full warfighting capability in a decade in the future, it would be of no assistance in restoring readiness or managing the serious short-term funding challenges that threatened to further erode current capabilities.[66]

The review set out the Army's war roles:

1. Contributing to national defence and resilience plans through an enhanced Standing Joint Command (UK) and its nationwide network of Joint Military Commanders. In war, additional capabilities will be required to support the protection of critical national infrastructure.

2: Deter and defend in the Euro-Atlantic: providing one of two Strategic Reserve Corps to NATO, ready to deploy rapidly from the UK to anywhere in the Euro-Atlantic area. HQ ARRC would command this formation, comprising two divisions enabled by 'corps-level capability'. The Army must also sustain its contribution to NATO's forward presence in Estonia and Poland.

3: Shape global security: delivering essential 'train, advise, assist, and accompany' missions with key allies and partners. [67]

The review called for the Army to be 'bolder in its ambition, seeking to increase lethality ten-fold'. It did not set out any evidence that this was achievable. Given that the Army's previous ambition was for a three-fold increase in lethality by 2030, a further seven-fold increase in lethality seemed more like an optimistic soundbite than an evidence-based assessment.

CAPABILITY GAPS AND NEW OPPORTUNITIES

The Army's 2025 capabilities fell short of meeting these requirements. HQ ARRC commanded logistic, engineer, and attack helicopter brigades, but lacked the full artillery, air defence and intelligence and surveillance brigades that were integral to the US Army's corps.

The 3rd Division, the Army's mechanized division, had only two armoured brigades. It remained the only NATO armoured division without dedicated infantry fighting vehicles.

The 1st Division had the air assault brigade, a light mechanized brigade and an infantry brigade whose engineers and artillery were Army reserve units. The latter formation was assigned to wartime reinforcement of Estonia, so would not be available to the reserve corps. It also had little regular artillery, falling short of a full deep strike brigade equivalent to that in the 3rd Division, and much of its logistics was provided by the Army Reserve. So, providing NATO with a high readiness British light division of three regular combined arms brigades would be very difficult.

To provide a fully capable strategic reserve corps, the Army would need to have one and a half extra infantry brigades, as well as additional artillery, air defence and intelligence and surveillance forces – a total of four and a half brigades. This would probably require about 15,000 more troops.

To meet the SDR's requirements, most of the Army's reserves would probably need to be mobilized to support the corps, particularly logistic and medical units and people. So, fully meeting the Army's NATO requirements would leave very few regular or reserve troops for home defence and resilience, let alone provide any strategic reserve formation.

How could these gaps be filled? Ideally by rebuilding the Regular Army's size to at least 90,000. Also, by increasing the size of the Army Reserve and restoring its readiness to the level it had in the Cold War. The 1980 and 1984 corps exercises described in Chapters 2 and 4 showed that the Territorial Army could do this. There should be no insuperable obstacles to doing this again.

Is there an alternative approach that would allow the Army to deliver the additional capabilities required by the SDR, without increasing its size by a quarter? There is – using advanced technology to reduce manpower required by units and formations.

This concept has the potential to enable smaller units and brigades to have equal or even greater effect than current forces, possibly allowing the Army's force structure to grow within its manpower ceiling. Even so, given the Army's 2025 weaknesses in force structure, logistic stockpiles, collective training, readiness and manning, it is difficult to see how this ambition could be achieved without a significant additional increase in funding.

This story ends with the Army poised at a tipping point between future decline or restoration of capability. Despite the encouraging language and imaginative vision of the 2025 Strategic Defence Review, the Army's future rests on a knife edge. With adequate funding and political support, further decline could be halted, and the Army could rebuild its combat capability and military credibility. Will the government give the British Army a fighting chance of success? Or will the Army's capability and utility continue to fall? In August 2025 the answers to these questions are unclear.

POSTSCRIPT

HOW THE ARMY CAN SUCCEED IN THE FUTURE

During this half century, the Army earned its pay for the government and British people in Northern Ireland, Zimbabwe, the Falklands, the Balkans, Sierra Leone, twice in Iraq and in Afghanistan, in evacuating British citizens from imminent danger, in acting as a backstop to the public sector during many civil emergencies, in conducting three operations in which it helped fight a lethal virus.[1] It twice played a major role in NATO's deterrence, firstly during the Cold War and secondly in reassuring Eastern European nations who felt directly threatened by Russia after 2022 and in providing equipment and training to Ukraine's troops.

It usually did this with minimum fuss and an institutional thirst to get its units and formations on operations, where its people could test themselves against challenges greater than those simulated in training. Too often it did this whilst under-resourced, or given inadequate leadership by defence ministers, or both. On many operations, including Northern Ireland, the 1991 Gulf War and the intervention in Bosnia, this did not undermine mission success.

Too many times, prime ministers, defence ministers and MoD officials made statements that contradicted the experiences of troops, often apparently drafted by officials wearing rose-tinted spectacles. Topics for this optimism bias often included the arrival of new equipment, maintenance of barracks and hosing, and terms and conditions of service. Too often there would be rhetorical declarations that the British Armed Forces were the best in the world – when troops knew otherwise. The Army already had a carapace of dry humour that could thicken into a weary cynicism. This happened too often, especially during the Iraq and Afghanistan wars, where inadequate strategic leadership by prime ministers and defence ministers directly contributed to avoidable casualties and strategic defeats. No-one should have been surprised when hints of discontent of the Army and its troops rippled into the public domain.

What does journey tell us about the factors that make the Army succeed and thrive, or those that damage the organization?

The Army exists to fight on land. All else revolves around this. From 1975 to 2025, the British Army retained this singularity of purpose. In the Balkans, Iraq and Afghanistan it encountered allied armies who seemed unwilling to fight. They may have lost fighting spirit through excessive focus on peacekeeping, or through national reluctance to use force, but these armies had little utility when the bullets started flying.

Without the high standards of leadership and morale necessary to make people willing to do two things that go against human nature – to move into danger and to kill other people – an army is incapable of fighting. The central vehicle to prepare for this is training, individual and collective. In the Cold War, the Army's high level of collective training allowed the testing of plans, doctrine, people and equipment, showing that collective training can be an accelerator of change.

Training and operations test people. This allows people to be selected for promotion – a Darwinian activity. When it works well, it maximizes the chances of the right people filling leadership roles. But people can always surprise us, some performing exceptionally well, others struggling, failing or going off the rails. This should be a 'truth universally acknowledged' of military organizations, but the key factor is whether too many people are failing. So, the Army's leadership needs to be taking a very close interest in its people and their performance.

ADAPTATION AND INNOVATION

The Army's story is one of innovation in peace and adaptation on operations, both successful and unsuccessful. This section identifies the factors that promote or inhibit these essential activities.

Military hierarchies and institutional deference can inhibit innovation, as can peacetime management practices, including processes for budgets, management and procurement. These factors can reinforce the status quo, frustrate the upward flow of initiatives and ideas, inhibit urgency and slow innovation. Organizations can resist change, being reluctant to bend themselves out of shape, amplifying cultural factors that resist innovation.

The Army is infused with heritage and tradition. These add value to the moral component, but can also inhibit innovation and adaptation, by anchoring organizations and people to a static image of the past, promoting resistance to change.

The Army must have ingrained institutional curiosity about recent and current conflicts, as well as lessons to be learned from its allies, partners, and competitors and from the public and private sectors. It has recognized that it must anticipate the future and react to unexpected challenges and display a culture of enthusiastic continuous improvement across the lines of development.

Troops working on the front line often understand their challenges better than those above them. They can be a key source of ideas. Units and formations, including senior leaders, should constantly seek to understand front-line operations, and the factors that inhibit their effectiveness. This requires a high standard of meaningful internal communication. The most important factor for promoting innovation is leadership. All commanders should see identifying, encouraging, and leading innovation to be essential to success. They should explain the reasons for change, communicate effectively and identify and remove blocks to innovation.

Bottom-up innovation can have considerable effect. But it cannot succeed without the engagement, encouragement and enthusiasm of leaders, as well as implementation mechanisms that deliver the necessary changes. Top-down innovation works best when it is driven by the most senior leaders imparting direction and encouragement. Commanders, leaders and managers should lead this by integrating top-down direction and initiatives while at the same time capturing and exploiting bottom-up innovation. Political engagement and support greatly increase the chances of innovation succeeding.

Innovators are 'entrepreneurs of battle', as vital to the Army as commercial entrepreneurs are to business. Some people are better at promoting innovation and creating a 'culture of encouragement' than others. The Army must identify people with a talent for innovation and exploit that talent. There should be visible rewards for innovative people and organizations and active prevention of blocking processes and behaviours. Leaders and managers who obstruct innovation should be discouraged and, where necessary, discarded.

What does an innovative army look like? It is actively seeking to better 'engage the future'. It has senior leaders providing energy, encouragement, and enthusiasm to identify and implement changes. It recognizes that although technology can assist with innovation, the key challenges are leadership, culture, and mental and organizational agility. It is easier to focus innovation when there is an identified opponent and plans to counter them, both in peace and war, as shown by the Army in the Cold War and Northern Ireland. Collective training generates many useful insights that can be exploited. Whilst much training and experimentation can be conducted in simulated environments, there is no substitute for testing capabilities in field conditions against a challenging opposing force. There is also value in inviting external advice from 'critical friends' outside the Army.

What does an adaptable army look like? Most military operations pose unanticipated challenges. Both sides compete in a battle to adapt more quickly, a multi-domain dynamic extending across the full range of the conflict. The more innovative and adaptive the enemy, the greater these challenges. A 'lessons learned loop' is required to identify and implement the necessary adjustments, working top down, bottom up and sideways, across organizations. Technological adaptation will be essential, but the Army and MoD should recognize that technology can take longer to change than other lines of development, especially doctrine, tactics, and training. Close co-operation between intelligence, scientific, equipment, operations and training staff is also essential. This was exhibited in the Northern Ireland campaign.

CHANGING THE ARMY

These approaches to innovation and adaptation are essential to the Army's future ability to fight. But war and preparing for war is itself another Darwinian activity, as this account illustrates. The Army was not static in this period – but in a constant state of change. What factors help the Army change, to adapt to operations, or to innovate in anticipation of future conflict?

Success needs political alignment between the Army, defence ministers and governments that understand the Army. Where this alignment is absent, accumulated headwinds and frictions can reach a threshold where the Army's senior leadership can go into a defensive crouch, seeking to minimize damage.

Success depends on political support. Not just from the defence secretary, but also from the cabinet, chancellor and prime minister. Some successful change was initiated by politicians, as was the case with George Robertson and Geoff Hoon. In other cases, the Army identified the need to change that exploited political agendas and opportunities. This applied to the 1981 Nott Review and the 2002 SDR New Chapter.

A high level of mutual confidence between the Army, defence ministers and government is essential. Whilst George Robertson and Tony Blair supported the Army, this did not extend to Chancellor Gordon Brown, resulting in a mutual loss of confidence when Brown became Prime Minister. Confidence can be eroded by ministerial micro-management, such as the behaviour of Tom King's office that so vexed the Army before the Gulf War of 1991.

The chance of a change programme succeeding also requires political competence. Given the apparent variation of motivation, political weight and competence of ministers, the CGS and his team must devote time, energy and a wide range of interpersonal skills to engaging ministers. Conversely civil/military crises, such as the 2006–09 tension with the government over Iraq and Afghanistan, can be extremely damaging and erode mutual trust and inhibit change.

Anticipation of change is essential. Before the 1981 Nott Review, the Army had a very clear idea of its weaknesses, with Project Mercury identifying the necessary adjustments to the force structure. The Army got the necessary changes endorsed by the review. Before the 1998 SDR, the Army had identified the measures needed to rebalance its capabilities. This shows that the Army needs to be constantly assessing its capabilities against current and future operations, developing a menu of relevant enhancements and changes to apply, should the strategic opportunity present itself.

Sufficient resources to deliver change are vital. The Army's evolution in the Cold War and Northern Ireland campaigns shows that change is more straightforward when the Army's capabilities are optimized against a clearly identified enemy, area of operations, mission and plan. The Bagnall Revolution was focussed on a main enemy that drove warfighting capability – Warsaw Pact forces. Military operations in Northern Ireland were assisted by a sharp focus on the IRA. Operation *Entirety* was exclusively focussed on the Army's role in southern Afghanistan.

Sense of urgency is a success factor. Such a sense must be shared and communicated to all those implementing Army changes, and the partner organizations that support them. In 1999, the Army was unlucky that the new and unforeseen operations in Kosovo and Sierra Leone had to be conducted before the Army had implemented the changes required by the 1998 SDR, particularly growing the manpower of the Army and additional logistics, engineering and signals capabilities. But from 2008, Operation *Entirety* greatly accelerated the rate of change necessary for the Army to improve capability for Afghanistan. This suggests that when conducting change programmes, the default setting should be to implement the changes as rapidly as possible.

Doctrine can act as an agent of change, particularly if senior leaders are seen to apply it. Bagnall saw modernized doctrine as a central vehicle for change and used it as such. Commanders across the Army took notice and made visible efforts to understand and apply doctrine, encouraging subordinates to do so. The Bagnall reforms illustrate that doctrine can be written quickly, Promulgating it, applying it, ensuring it is understood throughout the Army and creating a quorum of shared understanding takes longer. In the Cold War, the Army had the advantage of a high level of exercise activity that allowed doctrine to be rapidly tested and adjusted.

But success can lead to institutional inertia and over-confidence. This appears to have contributed to complacency in the MoD between 1998 and 2008. The Army needs to find ways of guarding against any warm glow of success leading to conservatism and stasis. Having an outsider take a fresh look at issues, capabilities and problems can help achieve this. This was demonstrated by General Bagnall's review of the Army's role in Northern Ireland.

Strategic shocks, such as 9/11 and the Russian attack on Ukraine, can result in very rapid changes in defence policy. The Army will always have to conform with current defence policy. But to be better prepared for the future it should not allow defence policy to become a cage that restricts thinking about the future. The Army will be better placed to react to such rapid changes if it has a strong foundation of thinking about the spectrum of conflict on land and the way its character is evolving – a foundational pillar of the Army as a profession.

When resources are short, there will be increased competition between the three services. Even so, the more collaborative the three services can be, the greater the chance of the right changes being made and of successful change implementation. There must be harmony between the Army and the other services, rather than competition.

Continuity of senior leadership has been a success factor. For example, Bagnall's successive three roles as corps commander, army group commander and CGS provided the big ideas and leadership that did so much to change the Army. He also carefully selected his successors. The CGS' powers of patronage can both support or inhibit continuity and change.

THE VITAL ROLE OF STRATEGIC LEADERSHIP

Both in peace and war, the Army's success has rested on the formulation and execution of strategy by its leaders, the MoD and the government. This required strategic ends need to be balanced with the necessary ways and means to achieve the outcomes required.

In the Cold War, these outcomes were achieved by the Army making its contribution to deterring an attack by the Warsaw Pact. And ends, ways and means were broadly in balance in Rhodesia/Zimbabwe, at the Iranian Embassy and in the Falklands War. Although the Army succeeded in the Gulf in 1991, ways and means had to be rapidly re-balanced away from the accepted practices of the Cold War.

In Northern Ireland between 1970 and 1977, an inadequate strategy made the situation worse, making the Army's job more difficult. But thereafter, ends, ways and means were in balance and conditioned by governmental and Army strategic patience.

These factors were also in balance in the interventions in Bosnia, Kosovo, Sierra Leone and in Afghanistan in 2001 and Iraq in 2003. But afterwards, the stabilization of Iraq and Afghanistan saw increasing misalignment between ends, ways and means, resulting in strategic failures. The principal responsibility for this lies with the political leadership, or lack of it, by prime ministers, chancellors, and defence ministers. But the Army was sometimes guilty of over-optimism, over-promising and under-delivering, as well as moving too slowly to make necessary adaptations.

The decline in Army capability from 2014 onwards results from similar strategic misalignments and inadequate leadership. Major factors include the continual shrinkage of the defence budget and the Army's share of it, together with over-complex, slow and inadequately led new equipment projects.

The government, the MoD and the Army will need to rapidly up their game. Getting these factors right will maximize the chances of the Army succeeding both on operations and as a living, growing institution. The last 50 years have provided plenty of evidence of success and also times when these factors have been weak and absent. To succeed over the next 50 years will require much more than good luck; it will need leadership and co-operation in No. 10, Whitehall, the MoD and Army HQ. It will also require the understanding and support of the British public. Writing in 2007, Sir Max Hastings assessed that the British Army:

> still represents one of our finest national institutions. But it will not remain so unless we the British people afford to it the attention, resources and respect which it so richly repays. We shall not deserve future military triumphs to add to those of the past, unless we provide those who secure them for us with the means to sustain their great heritage.[2]

SELECT GLOSSARY

ACE	Allied Command Europe
ANGLICO	Air Naval Gunfire Liaison Company. These provided teams of specially trained and equipped US Marine Corps personnel who were experts in controlling and co-ordinating fixed and rotary wing air support, naval gunfire and artillery. They were allocated to 7th Armoured Brigade in 1990 and 1st Armoured Division in 2003
APC	Armoured personnel carrier
ARRC	Allied Rapid Reaction Corps
BAOR	British Army of the Rhine, the overall command for Army formations in Germany from 1945 to 1992. Its largest formation was 1st British Corps, abbreviated to 1 (BR) Corps. It also commanded the Army contingent in West Berlin and British Support Command, the formation that organized logistic supply and reinforcement of Germany in war
Battlegroup	A term used by many NATO armies to designate a battalion-sized combined arms grouping, usually formed around an infantry or armoured battalion. The US Army used task force as a similar term
BATUS	British Army Training Unit Suffield. An immense training area in Canada, where all battlegroup weapons could be fired
Bradley	US Army infantry fighting vehicle
CDS	Chief of the Defence Staff
CENTCOM	US Central Command
CERP	Commander's Emergency Response Programme. A US military fund that allowed commanders to spend money on short-term reconstruction projects
CGS	Chief of the General Staff. The head of the Army

CJTF	Combined Joint Task Force. A multinational and joint HQ. Many were formed during the wars, with a wide variety of names, such as CJTF Mountain, or CJTF 76
CMF	Commonwealth Monitoring Force
COIN	Counterinsurgency
Combat supplies	Term applied to the types of supplies necessary for a land force to move and fight; principally ammunition, fuel, food, water and spare parts
Commando	This had three meanings. Firstly, it applied to a Royal Marine or Army soldier or officer who passed the demanding commando course. Secondly, the battalion-sized infantry units of Royal Marines were called commandos, for example 40 Commando Royal Marines. Thirdly, it was used as part of the name of the two Army units that were part of 3 Commando Brigade, Royal Marines, for example, 29 Commando, Light Regiment Royal Marines
CPA	Coalition Provisional Authority
CVR(T)	Combat vehicle reconnaissance (tracked)
DFiD	Department for International Development
DROPS	Demountable rack offload and pickup system. A heavy lorry carrying a flat rack on which were loaded combat supplies. It could self-load or unload the flat rack. It was introduced by the Army in the early 1990s
ECM	Electronic countermeasures
EFP	Explosively formed projectile
EOD	Explosive ordnance disposal
FCO	UK Foreign and Commonwealth Office. It was replaced in 2020 by the Foreign, Commonwealth and Development Office
GOC	General officer commanding. Term usually used for major generals commanding a division
GPMG	General purpose machine gun. The British version of the highly successful FN MAG 58 belt-fed 7.62mm machine gun. From 1985 it was replaced as an infantry section weapon by two light support weapons. Throughout the period, it was fitted to many armoured vehicles and used from a tripod in its sustained fire (SF) role
GPS	(US) Global Positioning System

HQ	Headquarters
IED	Improvised explosive device
IFOR	Implementation Force. NATO Implementation Force in Bosnia 1995–96
IISS	International Institute of Strategic Studies
IRA	Irish Republican Army
ISAF	International Security Assistance Force
ISI	Inter-Services Intelligence. The Pakistani military's secret intelligence agency, with a role in covert operations
ISIS	Islamic State of Syria and al Sham
JCO	Joint Commission observer
JFHQ	Joint Forces HQ. As a generic term this applies to any HQ commanding a joint force. From the late 1990s the UK fielded a national JFHQ. Part of PJHQ. It was held at very high readiness to conduct joint intervention operations. It has commanded many non-combatant evacuation operations
KFOR	Kosovo Force
KLA	Kosovo Liberation Army
LSL	Landing ship logistic
LSW	Light support weapon. A variant of SA80 designed to provide supporting fire, with a longer barrel and bipod
MEF	Marine expeditionary force. A term used by the US Marine Corps. In autumn 1990, 7th Armoured Brigade joined the MEF commanding 1st (US) Marine Division in eastern Saudi Arabia. In 2003, 1st Armoured Division was assigned to an MEF. Its HQ was equivalent to a US or British corps HQ, albeit one with a dedicated air wing of fighters, helicopters and transport aircraft
MLRS	Multiple launch rocket system
MoD	Ministry of Defence
National Guard	The US Army and US Airforce both have National Guard formations – reserve units, staffed by part time personnel
NATO	North Atlantic Treaty Organization
NBC	Nuclear, biological and chemical
NCO	Non-commissioned officer
NEO	Non-combatant evacuation operation
NITAT	Northern Ireland training advisory team
NORTHAG	Northern Army Group
OMLT	Operational mentoring and liaison team

OP	Observation post
OPFOR	Opposing force. At the beginning of this period field exercises would be conducted against a simulated enemy – referred to as the enemy. As time went on, this term was replaced by the US term OPFOR. From 1995 onwards, exercises at BATUS in Canada would feature simulated combat against a permanent OPFOR, based on an armoured regiment, using vehicles modified to look less British and more like Soviet-style armoured vehicles
P Company	The selection tests for admission to the Parachute Regiment and airborne forces
Panzer	German term for tank
Panzergrenadier	German term for armoured infantry – literally tank grenadier. The equivalent British term was armoured infantry
PJHQ	Permanent Joint Headquarters
POMCUS	Prepositioning of materiel configured in unit sets
PRT	Provincial reconstruction team
RAF	Royal Air Force
Rarden	A 30mm cannon fitted initially to Scimitar and Fox reconnaissance vehicles in the 1970s. It was chosen as the main armament of the Warrior infantry fighting vehicle. It was optimized to defeat enemy light armoured vehicles. It had a revolutionary design which was made smaller than similar contemporary weapons
REFORGER	Return of forces to Germany. Throughout the 1970s and 80s, the US Army pre-positioned equipment and vehicles in large storage sites in West Germany. Exercise *REFORGER* regularly practised sending US troops top use this equipment, including the deployment of 2nd (US) Armoured Division to take part in Exercise *Spearpoint*
Regular	Shorthand for Regular Army, used to signify that the people, unit or formation were not from the Territorial Army (TA), later the Army Reserve
REME	Royal Electrical and Mechanical Engineers Corps
Republican Guard	An elite component of the Iraqi ground forces
RM	Royal Marines
Rounds	A term for bullets or shells
RPG	Rocket-propelled grenade

RUC	Royal Ulster Constabulary
RUF	Revolutionary United Front (Sierra Leone)
SA80	Small arms for the 1980s. The Army's 5.56 assault rifle introduced to service in 1986
SACEUR	Supreme Allied Commander Europe
SAS	Special Air Service Regiment. The Army's original special forces
SBS	Special Boat Service. The Royal Marines' maritime special forces
Scout	An Army light helicopter capable of carrying five people and firing SS11 anti-tank guided weapons
SDR	Strategic Defence Review
SEAL	Sea air land. The US Navy's maritime special forces
SF	Special forces. UK term embracing the SAS, SBS, SRR, SFSG and their assigned RAF and Army aircraft
SFOR	NATO Stabilization Force in Bosnia from 1997 to 2004
SFSG	Special Forces Support Group. A battalion-sized group providing specialist support to other UK special forces. Formed in 2006, it comprises 1st Battalion, the Parachute Regiment, a company of Royal Marines and a sub-unit of the RAF Regiment
Shura	A word in the Dari language for a consultative meeting. These would be called by Afghan and NATO military commanders and officials to consult local communities
SLA	Sierra Leone Army
SLR	Self-loading rifle. A British variant of the Belgian designed 7.6mm FN FAL rifle. Unlike all other users' FN rifles, the British Army version could not fire bursts
SOF	Special operations forces. US term for their wide range of special forces. Throughout this period the term was increasingly used within NATO
Spearpoint	General title for Cold War-era field training exercises conducted by 1 (BR) Corps
Special Branch	Term used by police forces in the UK and former British colonies to describe police intelligence. Co-operation with RUC Special Branch was a particularly important element of Army operations in Northern Ireland
Spetsnaz	Soviet, and later Russian, special forces
SPG	Self-propelled gun. Term generally applied to armoured vehicles on which were mounted artillery pieces

SRR	Special Reconnaissance Regiment. Special forces unit conducting covert reconnaissance and surveillance. Formed in 2005 out of 14 Intelligence Company, the sub-unit conducting covert plains clothes surveillance operations in Northern Ireland
SS11	An anti-tank guided missile that in the 1970s was fitted to the Army Scout light helicopter
T-55, T-62, T-72, T-84	All models of Russian tanks employed by the Soviet Army in East Germany. Also employed by combatants in Bosnia and Kosovo, and by Iraqi forces
TA	Territorial Army. This was formed of units and sub-units manned by reserve soldiers and officers. In 2012 the title was replaced by the term Army Reserve
Task force	The US Army uses this term to describe battalion-sized combined arms groupings, similar to NATO battlegroups. Also used to describe various ad hoc groupings. Term also used by US and NATO SOF to describe battalion-sized groups. Also used to describe the UK forces of all three services that conducted the Falklands War
TOW	Tube-launched, optically tracked, wire-guided
UDR	Ulster Defence Regiment
UKLF	United Kingdom Land Forces
UN	United Nations
UNAMSIL	UN Mission in Sierra Leone
UNMOS	UN military observers
UNPROFOR	UN Protection Force
UOR	Urgent operational requirement. Equipment urgently needed for operations, subject to a rapid staffing process in the MoD
USAF	United States Air Force

Select Bibliography

General histories

Carver, Michael, *Britain's Army in the 20th Century*, Macmillan, 1998

Carver, Michael, *The Seven Ages of the British Army*, Beaufort Books, 1984

Carver, Michael, *Tightrope Walking: British Defence Policy Since 1945*, Hutchinson, 1990. The best single-volume history of the topic. Carver was CGS 1973–75 and CDS 1973–76.

Chandler, David and Beckett, Ian, *The Oxford History of the British Army*, Oxford University Press, 2003

Chappell, Mike, *The British Army in the 1980s*, Osprey, 1987

Dannatt, Richard, *Boots on the Ground: Britain and Her Army since 1945*, Profile Books, 2016

David, Saul, *All the King's Men: The British Redcoat in the Age of Sword of Musket*, Viking, 2012

Fraser, David, *And We Shall Shock Them: The British Army in the Second World War*, Hodder and Stoughton, 1982

Hastings, Max and the Imperial War Museum, *The British Army – The Definitive History of the Twentieth Century*, Cassell, 2007

Holmes, Richard, *Soldiers: Army Lives and Loyalties from Redcoats to Dusty Warriors*, HarperCollins, 2012. A thematic history of the British Army, its constituent parts, its people and their culture

Mallinson Allan, *The Making of the British Army*, second edition, Bantam, 2011. The best single-volume history of the Army ever written

McInnes, Colin, *Hot War Cold War*, Brassey's, 1996. A thematic analysis of the British Army's evolution from 1945 to 1995, with an emphasis on capability, doctrine and operations. Chapters on Northern Ireland, BAOR and Operation *Granby* are especially useful.

Smith, D. G., *The British Army 1965–80*, Osprey, 1977

Strachan, Hew, *The Politics of the British Army*, Clarendon Press, 1995. An excellent history of the topic from 1689 to 1991.

Strawson, John, *Gentlemen in Khaki and Camouflage*, Pen and Sword Books, 2009. An illuminating and entertaining history of the Army since 1900.

Tanner, James, *The British Army Since 2000*, Osprey, 2016

The Cold War

Barker, Dennis, *Soldiering On: An Unofficial Portrait of the British Army*, Sphere, 1988

Beevor, Anthony, *Inside the British Army*, Chatto and Windus, 1990. The Army at the end of the Cold War.

Dewar, Michael, *A Day in the Life of the British Army*, David and Charles, 1990. The Army in 1989/90.

Rogers, H. C. B., *The British Army Today and Tomorrow*, Littlehampton Books, 1979. A portrait of the Army in the late 1970s.

Stanhope, Henry, *The Soldiers*, Hamish Hamilton, 1979. A snapshot of the Army in the late 1970s

Storr, Jim, *Battlegroup! The Lessons of the Unfought Battles of the Cold War*, Helion, 2021

NORTHERN IRELAND

Edwards, Aaron, *The Northern Ireland Troubles 1969–2007*, Osprey, 2023. An excellent short summary of the campaign.

Hamill, Desmond, *Pig in the Middle: The Army in Northern Ireland, 1969–84*, Methuen, 1985. An excellent history.

Lewis, Rob, *Fishers of Men*, Hodder and Stoughton, 1999. An account by an Army human intelligence collector.

Matchett, William, *Secret Victory: The Intelligence Operations that Beat the IRA*, Matchett, 2016

Rennie, James, *The Operators*, Century, 1996. A good description of selection and training can be found in an apparently accurate account of the author's training for duty time with the Det in the 1980s.

Taylor, Peter, *Brits*, Bloomsbury, 2001.

THE FALKLANDS WAR

Bijl, Nicholas van der, *Nine Battles to Stanley*, Leo Cooper, 1999.

Delves, Cedric, *Across an Angry Sea: The SAS in the Falklands War*, Hurst, 2018

Ely, Nigel, *Goose Green: The Decisive Battle of the Falklands War – by the British Troops who Fought it*, Lume Books, 2020

Ethel, Jeffrey and Price, Alfred, *Air War South Atlantic*, Sidgwick & Jackson, 1983

Fitz-Gibbon, Spencer, *Not Mentioned in Despatches … The History and Mythology of the Battle of Goose Green*, Lutterworth Press, 1995

Fox, Robert, *Eyewitness Falklands*, Methuen, 1982. As a journalist Fox took part in the Battle of Goose Green. A vivid account.

Freedman, Lawrence, *The Official History of the Falklands Campaign*, Routledge, 2005. The essential foundation.

Hastings, Max and Jenkins, Simon, *The Battle for the Falklands*, Pan Macmillan, 2022. Hastings was a journalist who embedded himself with the Marines, Paras and SAS and Jenkins is an expert political commentator. The 2022 edition has a reflective commentary from 40 years after.

McManners, Hugh, *Forgotten Voices of the Falklands* War, Ebury Press, 2007

O'Connell, James, *Three Days in June*, Monoray, 2021. The battle of Mount Longdon.

Thompson, Julian, *No Picnic: 3 Commando Brigade in the South Atlantic, 1982*, Pen and Sword Books, 1992. The operations of the commando brigade in the Falklands War told by its commander. Includes the role of the brigade's Army units.

OPERATION *GRANBY* – THE 1991 LIBERATION OF KUWAIT

Benson, Nicholas, *Rats' Tails: The Staffordshire Regiment at War in the Gulf*, Brassey's, 1993

Billière, General Sir Peter de la, *Storm Command*, HarperCollins, 1995

Cordingley, Patrick, *In the Eye of the Storm: Commanding the Desert Rats in the Gulf War*, Hodder and Stoughton, 1996

McManners, Hugh, *Gulf War One: Real Voices From the Front Line*, Ebury Press, 2010

McNab, Andy, *Bravo Two Zero*, Bantam, 1993

Milner, Laurie, *Royal Scots in the Gulf: 1st Battalion the Royal Scots on Operation Granby 1990–91*, Pen and Sword Books, 1994

Powell, Des and Lewis, Damien, *Bravo Three Zero*, Quercus, 2022

Ryan, Chris, *The One That Got Away*, Century, 1995

White, Major General Martin (ed.), *Gulf War Logistics: Blackadder's War*, Brassey's, 1995

THE BALKANS

Barry, Ben, *The Road from Sarajevo: British Army Operations in Bosnia, 1995–1996*, The History Press, 2016. The commanding officer's account of battlegroup operations in Bosnia at the end of the UN mission and beginning of NATO operations.

Bell, Martin, *In Harm's Way*, revised edition, 1996. A personal account by a fearless BBC journalist who did much to explain the terrible war in Bosnia.

Bildt, Carl, *Peace Journey*, Weidenfeld & Nicolson, 1998. A very good account of the political efforts to create a ceasefire in Bosnia and of the role of the NATO Implementation Force.

Borger, Julian, *The Butcher's Trail: How the Search For Balkan War Criminals Became the World's Most Successful Manhunt*, Other Press, 2017

Clark, Wesley K., *Waging Modern War*, Public Affairs, 2001

Kent-Payne, Vaughan, *Bosnia Warriors: Living on the Front Line*. A company commander's account of UN operations in Bosnia in 1993.

Ripley, Tim, *Operation Deliberate Force: The UN and NATO Campaign in Bosnia 1995*, Centre for Defence and International Security Studies (CDISS), Lancaster University 1999. The definitive account of the military resolution of the war in Bosnia.

Stewart, Bob, *Broken Lives*, Harper Collins 1993. A personal account by the commanding officer of the first British battalion into Bosnia.

SIERRA LEONE

Dorman, Andrew, *Blair's Successful War: British Military Intervention in Sierra Leone*, Ashgate, 2009

Fowler, Will, *Certain Death in Sierra Leone: The SAS and Operation Barras*, Osprey, 2010

IRAQ AND AFGHANISTAN

Bailey, Jonathan, Iron, Richard and Strachan, Hew (eds), *British Generals in Blair's Wars*, Ashgate, 2013

Bristow, Laurie, *Kabul: Final Call*, Whittles Publishing, 2024

Caddick-Adams, Peter and Thomas, Graham, *The Fight for Iraq January – June 2003*, Army Benevolent Fund, 2003. An excellent photographic record of the capture of Basra.

Dodge, Toby, *Iraq: From War to A New Authoritarianism*, International Institute for Strategic Studies, 2013

Farrell, Theo, *Unwinnable: Britain's War in Afghanistan, 2001–2014*, Bodley Head, 2017. An excellent single volume history of the topic, written by Britain's most expert academic.

Giustozzi, Antonio, *The Taliban at War 2001–2018*, Hurst and Co, 2019.

Holmes, Richard, *Dusty Warriors: Modern Soldiers at War*, HarperCollins, 2016. An accomplished historian, Holmes well describes the battles fought by 1st Battalion, the Princess of Wales's Royal Regiment during this period.

Jowett, Adam, *No Way Out: The Searing True Story of Men Under Siege*, Sidgwick & Jackson, 2018

Ledwidge, Frank, *Losing Small Wars: British Military Failure in Iraq and Afghanistan*, Yale University Press, 2011

Malkasian, Carter, *The American War in Afghanistan: A History*, Oxford University Press, 2021. An excellent history, which contains very useful material on the conflict in Helmand and an excellent assessment of the strength and weaknesses of the British effort.

Mansoor, Peter, *The Surge*, Yale University Press, 2013. Prides a US perspective on Iraq in 2007 and 2008, including Operation *Charge of the Knights*.

Martin, Mike, *An Intimate War*, Hurst, 2017

McChrystal, Stan, *My Share of the Task: A Memoir*, Portfolio/Penguin, 2013

Mercer, Johnny, *We Were Warriors*, Pan, 2018. An account of a tough tour in Afghanistan by a commando artillery officer, who subsequently became an MP and Veterans Minister.

Miller, Sergio, *Pride and Fall: The British Army in Afghanistan, 2001–2014*, Osprey 2024. An excellent single volume history of the topic, written by a former officer.

Ripley, Tim, *Operation TELIC*, Telic-Herrick Publications, 2014. The best single-volume history of the British Army in Iraq from 2003 to 2009.

Simpson, Emile, *War From the Ground Up: Twenty-First-Century Combat as Politics*, Hurst, 2010

Streatfeild, Richard, *Honourable Warriors; Fighting the Taliban in Afghanistan – A Front-line Account of the British Army's Battle for Helmand*, Pen and Sword Books, 2016

Synnott, Hilary, *Bad Days in Basra: My Turbulent Time as Britain's Man in Southern Iraq*, I B Tauris & Co Ltd, 2008

Tootal, Stuart, *Danger Close*, John Murray, 2010. An account by the commanding officer of 3rd Battalion, the Parachute Regiment's deployment to Helmand in 2007.

Wood, Levison and Jones, Geraint, *Escape from Kabul*, Hodder and Stoughton, 2023

BIOGRAPHIES AND MEMOIRS

Carver, Michael, *Out of Step*, Hutchinson & Co, 1989. The great majority of the book covers events before this period. But it has a first-person account of Carver's role as CGS during the early years of the Northern Ireland campaign and invaluable insights into the 1975 defence review.

Chapman, Chip, *Notes From a Small Army*, John Blake, 2013. A light-hearted memoir by a Parachute Regiment officer who served from the Falklands War to the era of global counterterrorism. The most amusing book on this list.

Dannatt, Richard, *Leading from the Front: An Autobiography*, Bantam, 2010

Billière, Peter de la, *Looking for Trouble*, HarperCollins, 1995. Useful material on the SAS in the 1981 Iranian embassy siege, the Falklands War and Operation *Granby*.

Ely, Nigel, *Fighting for Queen and Country: One Man's True Story of Blood and Violence in the Paras and the SAS*, Lume Books, 2020. Despite the sensationalist title this is an excellent memoir of service in the Parachute Regiment, including the Falklands War, and the SAS.

Flynn, Mick, *Bullet Magnet*, Weidenfeld & Nicholson 2010. Flynn was decorated for bravery in both Iraq and Afghanistan.

Guthrie, Charles, *Peace, War and Whitehall*, Osprey, 2021

Hennessy, Patrick, *The Junior Officers' Reading Club: Killing Time and Fighting Wars*, Penguin, 2010. A particularly vivid account of mentoring the Afghan Army in Helmand in 2007.

Hoon, Geoff, *See How They Run*, Unicorn, 2021. Half of the book covers his six years as Defence Secretary.

Jackson, Mike, *Soldier: The Autobiography*, Bantam, 2007

Jarvis, Dan, *Long Way Home: Love, Life, Death, and Everything in Between*, Little Brown, 2020. A humble and informative memoir by a Parachute Regiment officer who later became a politician.

Kitson, Frank, *Bunch of Five*, Faber & Faber, 1977. Not a memoir so much as four autobiographical case studies of counterinsurgency and peacekeeping. Perhaps the best book by any British practitioner of COIN.

Mayall, Simon, *Soldier in the Sand*, Pen and Sword Books, 2020. Not only a useful account of the making of the modern Middle East, but also full of useful vignettes of the British Army between 1980 and 2015.

Mulligan, Owain, *The Accidental Soldier: Dispatches from Quite Near the Front Line*, Fox Lane Books, 2025. A darkly humorous, self-depreciating account by a TA officer commanding a cavalry troop in Iraq.

Ratcliffe, Peter, *In the Eye of the Storm: 25 Years in Action with the SAS*, HarperCollins, 2000. Perhaps the most useful of all recent SAS memoirs.

Reynolds, Mike, *Soldier at Heart: From Private to General*, Pen and Sword Books, 2013

Richards, David, *Taking Command*, Headline, 2014

Tillotson, Michael, *The Fifth Pillar: The Life and Philosophy of the Lord Bramall*, revised paperback edition, Sutton Publishing, 2006

REGIMENTS AND FORMATIONS

I have found these books particularly useful:

Ferguson, Gregor, *The Paras 1940–84*, Osprey, 1984

Goldsack, Mark (ed.), *'Second to None': A Portrait of The Light Infantry*, Third Millenium, 2011

Loyd, William, *Challengers and Chargers. A History of the Life Guards 1945–92*, Leo Cooper, 1992

Macintyre, Ben, *The Siege*, Viking, 2024. An authoritative, readable account of the SAS at the 1981 Iranian embassy siege.

Mallinson, Allan, *Light Dragoons; The Making of a Regiment*, Pen and Sword Books, 2009. One of the best written of all regimental histories.

McNish, Robin, Charles Messenger and Paul Bray, *Iron Division: The History of The 3rd Division 1809–2000*, third revised edition, Ian Allan, 2000. A very useful account of the division's organization, training and operations.

Ogorkiewicz, Richard, *Tanks*, Osprey, 2018. The definitive history of tanks by a leading international expert. Contains very useful analysis of the Chieftain and Challenger.

Parker, Tony, *Soldier, Soldier*, Faber, 1983. A snapshot of the Royal Anglian Regiment at the height of the Cold War

Pringle, Andrew (ed.), *Swift and Bold: A Portrait of the Royal Green Jackets 1966–2007*, TMI Group, 2007

Ripley, Tim, *16 Air Assault Brigade: Britain's Rapid Reaction Force*, Pen and Sword Books, 2008. A very useful history of the brigade and the helicopters of the Joint Helicopter Command, including operations in Macedonia, Afghanistan and Iraq.

Royal Engineers Historical Society, *History of the Corps of Royal Engineers*, Volume XIII Institure of Royal Engineers 2024

Stone, David, *Cold War Warriors: Story of the Duke of Edinburgh's Royal Regiment (Berkshire and Wiltshire)*, Pen and Sword Books, 1998

Strawson, John, *A History of the SAS Regiment*, Secker & Warburg, 1984

Zulueta, Paul de, and Doughty, Simon, *Those Must Be the Guards, The Household Division in Peace and War 1969–2023*, Osprey, 2023. An excellent history of an influential group of regiments in peace and war.

NOVELS

Campbell, Barney, *Rain*, Penguin, 2016. The story of a young officer in a cavalry regiment in Afghanistan.

Clarke, A. F. N., *Contact*, expanded edition, Clarke Books, 2012. An autobiographical account by a young officer in the Parachute Regiment who served in Northern Ireland in the 1970s.

Judd, Alan, *A Breed of Heroes*, Simon and Schuster, 1981. A young infantry officer in Northern Ireland in the early 1970s.

Parker, Harry, *Anatomy of a Soldier*, Faber & Faber, 2016. The story of an infantry officer in Afghanistan.

Trollope, Joanna, *The Soldier's Wife*, Simon and Schuster, 2013

EQUIPMENT

Dunstan, Simon, *Challenger Main Battle Tank 1982–97*, Osprey, 1998

Dunstan, Simon, *Challenger 2 Main Battle Tank 1987–2006*, Osprey, 2006

Foss, Christopher, *Warrior Mechanised Combat Vehicle 1987–94*, Osprey, 1996

Foss, Christopher and Dunstan, Simon, *Scorpion Reconnaissance Vehicle 1972–94*, Osprey, 1995

Grant, Neil, *SA80 Assault Rifles*, Osprey, 2016

Houghton, Steve, *British Sniping Rifles Since 1970*, Osprey, 2021

Musgrave, John, *Firepower: Making 21st Century Warfare Decisive*, Riverside Publishing, 2023

SA80 (Small Arms for the 1980s): The Sorry Saga of the British Bulldog's Bullpup: an essay posted on the History of War website. http://www.historyofwar.org/articles/weapons_SA80.html#8

Suttee, William, *Chobham Armour: Cold War British Armoured Vehicle Development*, Osprey, 2022

PAPERS, REPORTS AND DOCUMENTS

'Concepts of Land/Air Operations in the Central Region: I. A lecture given at the RUSI on 23 May 1984 by General Sir Nigel Bagnall,, KCB, CVO, MC, COMNORTHAG', *RUSI Journal*, July 1984

Iron, Richard, 'Rapid Intervention and Conflict Resolution: British Military Intervention in Sierra Leone 2000–2002', Australian Army Occasional Paper Conflict Theory and Strategy Series 003 February 2019 https://researchcentre.army.gov.au/library/occasional-papers/rapid-intervention-and-conflict-resolution-british-military-intervention-sierra-leone-2000-2002#:~:text=Leone%202000%2D2002-,Rapid%20Intervention

%20and%20Conflict%20Resolution%3A%20British%20Military%20Intervention%20in%20Sierra,success %20for%20Western%20military%20intervention

'Operation Banner: An Analysis of Military Operations in Northern Ireland', British Army Code 71842, July 2006. Report published on the Operation Kenova website, https://www.opkenova.co.uk/

'Operation Banner Primer: An Account of the British Military's Deployment to Northern Ireland, 1969–2007', Kings College London Centre for Defence Studies, February 2022. Report published on the Operation Kenova website, https://www.opkenova.co.uk/

'Operations in Iraq – An Analysis From a Land Perspective', British Army Code 71816, 2004. https://www.scribd.com /document/29888389/Operations-in-Iraq-An-Analysis-From-a-Land-Perspective

'Operations in Iraq January 2005–May 2009: An Analysis from the Land Perspective', British Army, 29 November 2010. https://assets.publishing.service.gov.uk/government/uploads/system/uploads/attachment data/file/55732 6/20160831-FOI0700377396Redacted.pdf

'Stability Operations in Iraq (Op TELIC 2-5): An Analysis From a Land Perspective', British Army Code 71844, July 2006. https://www.scribd.com/document/44712515/Uk-Stbility-Operations-in-Iraq-2006

The Baha Mousa Public Inquiry Report, Volume One, Part III, 2011, https://www.gov.uk/government/publications/ the-baha-mousa-public-inquiry-report

The Gulf War: Volume 1, special issue of the British Army Review, Winter 2020. https://www.army.mod.uk/media /11016/bar_gulf_war-vol1-final.pdf

The Iraq Inquiry. https://webarchive.nationalarchives.gov.uk/20171123123237/http://www.iraqinquiry.org.uk/

'The Ajax Lessons Learned Review', Ministry of Defence, March 2022. https://www.gov.uk/government/publications /the-ajax-lessons-learned-review

Brown, Lieutenant General Chris, 'TELIC Lessons Compendium', MoD UK. https://assets.publishing.service.gov.uk /government/uploads/system/uploads/attachment_data/file/16787/operation_telic_lessons_compendium.pdf

Director Land Warfare British Army, 'Operation HERRICK Campaign Study', 2015. Redacted copy on MoD website https://www.gov.uk/government/publications/foi-responses-published-by-mod-week-commencing-11-january -2016

Mueller, Karl P. (ed.), *Precision and Purpose: Airpower in the Libyan Civil War*, RAND Corporation, 2015. Chapter 6 by Christina Goulter is particularly useful. https://www.rand.org/pubs/research_reports/RR676.html#:~:text =The%20study%20details%20each%20country's,potential%20model%20for%20the%20future.https://www .rand.org/pubs/research_reports/RR676.html#:~:text=The%20study%20details%20each%20 country's,potential%20model%20for%20the%20future

Ross, Emma, Welch, Gita Honwana and Angelides, Philip, 'Sierra Leone's Response to the Ebola Outbreak Management Strategies and Key Responder Experiences', Chatham House Centre on Global Health Security, March 2017 https://www.chathamhouse.org/sites/default/files/publications/research/2017-03-31-sierra-leone -ebola-ross-welch-angelides-final.pdf

Ucko, David H., *When Intervention Works: The Instructive Case of Sierra Leone*, War on the Rocks website, 31 August 2016. https://warontherocks.com/2016/08/when-intervention-works-the-instructive-case-of-sierra-leone/

Vincenti, G., Royal Army Medical Corps, 'Stress Reactions to Simulated Battle Conditions', *British Army Review*, Number 85, August 1986

VIDEOS

Defence of the Realm: Mission Angola, an account of the early 1990s British mission there. Found on the BBC Player streaming service. Archived as part of the BBC Four Armed Forces Collection. https://www.bbc.co.uk/ programmes/p00fgp7j/episodes/player

Evacuation, a documentary film by British broadcaster Channel 4, which is an excellent portrait of Operation *Pitting*. https://www.channel4.com/programmes/evacuation

Reforger 87/Exercise Certain Strike 1987 Documentary, by Andy McIlone who participated in the exercises with the Grenadier Guards. https://www.youtube.com/watch?v=9jZSUwp0FsU

IMPERIAL WAR MUSEUM ARCHIVE

Falklands – The Land Battle Part 1: The Landings, Army Department Film C1577 1984 https://www.iwm.org.uk/collections/item/object/1060028063

Falklands – The Land Battle Part 2: Towards Stanley, Army Department Film C1578 1984 https://www.iwm.org.uk/collections/item/object/1060028064

Falklands –The Land Battle Part 3: The Final Battle, Army Department Film C1579 1984 https://film.iwmcollections.org.uk/record/32704

ROYAL ENGINEERS YOUTUBE CHANNEL

The Gulf Conflict | Part 1 | Defensive Operations https://www.youtube.com/watch?v=_ERyeepGe-w

The Gulf Conflict | Part 2 | Preparation for War https://www.youtube.com/watch?v=LzsSyczps6w

The Gulf Conflict | Part 3 | The Liberation of Kuwait https://www.youtube.com/watch?v=Ce0UdoUOpDY

ENDNOTES

INTRODUCTION

1   Williamson Murray, *Military Adaptation and War: With Fear of Change*, Cambridge University Press, 2011.
2   Two books that have served as role models for this work are:
    Saul David, *All the King's Men; The British Redcoat in the Age of Sword and Musket*, Viking, 2012.
    David Fraser, *And We Shall Shock Them: The British Army in the Second World War*, Hodder and Stoughton, 1983.

CHAPTER 1: NAMING OF PARTS

1   *Joint Doctrine Publication 0-20 UK Land Power*, sixth edition. Published by the UK Development Concepts and Doctrine Centre October 2023. https://www.gov.uk/government/publications/uk-land-power-jdp-0-20
2   Ben Barry, *The Road from Sarajevo: British Army Operations in Bosnia 1995–1996*, The History Press, 2016, p. 35–38.
3   General Sir Simon Mayall, *Soldier in the Sand*, Pen and Sword Books, 2020, p. 104.
4   These are medals for bravery and leadership under fire. The majority of recipients are Army personnel, but the numbers include Royal Marines, Royal Navy and RAF. The Air Force Cross and Distinguished Flying Cross are awarded to pilots and aircrew of all three services.

CHAPTER 2: THE CRUCIBLE OF THE COLD WAR (1)

1   William Loyd, *Challengers and Chargers: A History of the Life Guards 1945–92*, Leo Cooper, 1992, p. 62.
2   Loyd, *Challengers and Chargers*, pp. 109–110.
3   John Strawson, *Gentlemen in Khaki and Camouflage*, Pen and Sword Books, 2009, p. 261.
4   Barry, *The Road from Sarajevo: British Army Operations in Bosnia 1995–1996*.
5   Mike Reynolds, *Soldier at Heart: From Private to General*, Pen and Sword Books, 2013, p. 212.
6   Reynolds, *Soldier at Heart*, p. 213.
7   Andrew Pringle (ed.), *Swift and Bold: A Portrait of the Royal Green Jackets 1966–2007*, p. 143–144.
8   Report from British Strv 103 trials at BAOR, 1973, published on Swedish tank archives website. http://tanks.mod16.org/2015/04/02/report-from-british-strv-103-trials-at-the-baor-1973/
9   Robin McNish, Charles Messenger and Paul Bray, *Iron Division: The History of the Third Division 1809–2000*, Ian Allan, 2000.
10 Statement on the Defence Estimates, 19 March 1975, p. 52.
11 House of Commons Library. A guide to Previous UK Defence Reviews July 2024 page 16. https://commonslibrary.parliament.uk/research-briefings/cbp-7313/
12 Personal communication from an officer in the Military Secretary's staff, 1975.
13 Norman L. Dodd, 'British New Look Divisions Tested in Exercise Spearpoint', *Militaire Spectator*, Broese / Vrijens, August 1977.

14   Presentation on the covering force by Major General Vickers attended by the author June 1979.

15   Field Marshal Lord Bramall (ed. Robin Brodhurst), *The Bramall Papers: Reflections on War and Peace*, Pen and Sword Books, 2022

16   Frank Kitson, 'The New British Armoured Division', *RUSI Journal*, March 1977.

17   Garry Johnson and Christopher Dunphie, *Brightly Shone the Dawn: Some Experiences of the Invasion of Normandy*, Frederick Warne, 1980. A short compilation of battle vignettes of D-Day and the Normandy campaign based upon the Army Staff College Battlefield Tour of the late 1970s.

18   The BBC recorded the event. The programme *Review of the British Army* could, at the time of writing, be found on the BBC iPlayer app at https://www.bbc.co.uk/programmes/p00k22j0

19   General Sir Mike Jackson, *Soldier: The Autobiography*, Bantam, 2007, p. 85.

20   *Armed Forces Magazine*, Issue 2, 'The British Army'.

21   Michael Tillotson, *The Fifth Pillar: The Life and Philosophy of the Lord Bramall*, revised paperback edition, Sutton Publishing, 2006, pp. 226–30.

22   Hansard 4 November 1980. Statement by Lord Strathcona and Mount Royal, Minister of State MoD.

CHAPTER 3: RAPID INTERVENTION (1)

1   This section draws on the following:
      General Sir Willam Jackson, *Withdrawal from Empire: A Military View*, Batsford, 1986, pp. 252–56.
      Paul de Zulueta and Simon Doughty, *Those Must Be the Guards, The Household Division in Peace and War 1969–2023*, Osprey, 2023, pp. 155–56.
      Tillotson, *The Fifth Pillar*, p. 235.
      Brigadier John Learmont, *Reflections from Rhodesia*, RUSI Journal, December 1980.

2   Tillotson, *The Fifth Pillar*, p. 235.

3   See Colin Kaye, Mission Extraordinary *Zimbabwe – Rhodesia*. British Army Review, August 1980.

4   Goldsack (ed.), '*Second to None*', p. 83.

5   De Zulueta and Doughty, *Those Must be the Guards*, p. 157.

6   There are far too many bad books about the SAS. The best introduction is John Strawson, *A History of the SAS Regiment*, Secker & Warburg, 1984.

7   Ben Macintyre, *The Siege*, Viking, 2024. An excellent account of the siege and its participants: terrorists, police, intelligence personnel and the hostages. As complete a picture of the hostage drama and its resolution by the SAS assault as it is possible to produce.

8   'Admiral Sir Henry Leach: First Sea Lord who convinced Thatcher that Britain must recapture the Falklands', Obituary, *The Independent*, 2 May 2011.

9   Roderick Macdonald, *Managing Chaos: the Falklands Campaign 1982*, RUSI Journal, May 2022.

10   This section is based on several sources: the Official History and the accounts by Cedric Delves and Peter Ratcliffe of the Pebble Island raid. The planned SAS raid on Argentina is described by Ratcliffe on pp. 433–34 of the Official History and in the book *Exocet Falklands: The Untold Story of Special Forces Operations* by Ewen Southby-Tailyour, Pen and Sword Books, 2014. The assessment of potential adverse diplomatic consequences of the planned attack is mine alone.

11   Based on Captain Wight's citation published at https://www.specialforcesroh.com/index.php?threads/wight -aldwin-james-glendinning.31220/#google_vignette. The patrol is also described in Nicholas van der Bijl, *Nine Battles to Stanley*, Leo Cooper, 1999.

12   Thompson, Julian, *No Picnic: 3 Commando Brigade in the South Atlantic, 1982*, Pen and Sword Books, 1992, p. 65.

13   *Falklands – The Land Battle: Part 2: Towards Stanley*, Army Department Film C1578 1984. https://www.iwm .org.uk/collections/item/object/1060028064

14   Julian Thompson, *The Royal Marines. From Sea Soldiers to a Special Force*, Pan Books, 2001, p. 567.

15   Hugh McManners, *Forgotten Voices of the Falklands War*, Ebury Press, 2007, p. 273.

16   Julian Thompson, *Ready for Anything: The Parachute Regiment at War 1940–1982*, Weidenfeld & Nicolson, 1989, p. 336.

17   Thompson, *Ready for Anything*, p. 341.

18   The Scots Guards traditionally retained the now obsolete historical designation of Left Flank and Right Flank for two of their companies.

19   This account is based on John Kizeley, 'The Land Campaign: A Company Perspective' in Badsey, Stephen, Havers, Rob and Grove, Mark (eds), *The Falklands Conflict Twenty Years On: Lessons of the Future*, Frank Cass, 2005.

20 Kizeley, 'The Land Campaign'.

21 'The Falklands Campaign: The Lessons' (Command 8758), UK Ministry of Defence, December 1982.

22 'The Falklands Campaign: The Lessons', p.17

23 Jeffrey Ethel and Alfred Price, *Air War South Atlantic*, Sidgwick & Jackson, 1983.

24 I saw this for myself in 1988–89.

25 Allan Mallinson, *The Making of the British Army*, second edition, Bantam, 2011, p. 563

26 Cedric Delves, *Across an Angry Sea: The SAS in the Falklands War*, Hurst, 2018, p. 180.

27 I served in the battalion at the time.

28 Brigadier Sir Tony Wilson obituary, *The Times*, 10 February 2025. https://www.thetimes.com/uk/article/brigadier-sir-tony-wilson-obituary-x8vfd8626#:~:text=Brigadier%20Sir%20Tony%20Wilson%20Bt,we%20are%20publishing%20one%20now.

29 Private conversation with officer involved in programme.

CHAPTER 4: THE CRUCIBLE OF THE COLD WAR (2)

1 I attended such lectures at Osnabruck and the Army Intelligence Centre in 1982, on the junior staff course at Warminster in 1984 and at the Army Staff College in Camberley in 1987.

2 See: BRIXMIS IN THE 1980s: THE COLD WAR'S "GREAT GAME" by Major General Peter Williams CMG OBE. Privately published report.
Steve Gibson *BRIXMIS: THE LAST COLD WAR MISSION*. The History Press, 2018.

3 De Zulueta and Doughty, *Those Must be the Guards*, p.129

4 Pringle, *Swift and Bold: A portrait of the Royal Green Jackets*, p.143

5 This section draws on numerous sources including the Dictionary for National Biography entry for Sir Nigel Bagnall, written by General Sir John Waters.

6 Corps Battle Notes, HQ 1 (BR) Corps 1981 reference zz2/81, Author's collection.

7 Guthrie, *Peace, War and Whitehall*, p. 78.

8 Guthrie, *Peace, War and Whitehall*, p. 151.

9 Guthrie, *Peace, War and Whitehall*, pp. 146–50.

10 This section is based on Captain B.W. Barry, 'An Airmobile Battalion', *British Army Review*, Number 79, April 1985.

11 'Tactical Training', Undated note signed by Lt Gen Nigel Bagnall referenced COM/28/001, Author's collection.

12 General Sir Richard Dannatt, *Leading from the Front: An Autobiography*, Bantam, 2010.

13 Jim Storr, *Battlegroup! The Lessons of the Unfought Battles of the Cold War*, Helion, 2021.

14 Captain G. Vincenti, Royal Army Medical Corps, 'Stress Reactions to Simulated Battle Conditions', *British Army Review*, Number 85, August 1986. It is possible that "G. Vincenti" is a pseudonym.

15 Herforder Pils is a German Beer. "Dhobi" is Army slang for laundry – a term learned in India.

16 April 2016 blog posting by @Ravenser on the Think Defence website. https://thinkdefence.wordpress.com/2016/03/25/nato-knew-throw-party/

17 Hansard 22 October 1984.

18 'Operation *Lionheart* Initial Impressions'. Document held by House of Commons Library.

19 Dialogue witnessed by the author 1988.

20 'Concepts of Land/Air Operations in the Central Region: I. A lecture given at the RUSI on 23 May 1984 by General Sir Nigel Bagnall, KCB, CVO, MC, COMNORTHAG', *RUSI Journal*, July 1984.

21 Direction repeated to the author by senior British and NATO officers in 1987.

22 A good impression of the exercise can be found in the film *Reforger 87/Exercise Certain Strike 1987 Documentary*, by Andy McIlone, who participated in the exercises with the Grenadier Guards. https://www.youtube.com/watch?v=9jZSUwp0FsU

23 A well-researched account of the development, trials and tribulations of the SA80 in its first decade can be found in *SA80 (Small Arms for the 1980s): The Sorry Saga of the British Bulldog's Bullpup*, an essay posted on the History of War website. http://www.historyofwar.org/articles/weapons_SA80.html#8

24 This section is based on a number of accounts, including that in Robin McNish, Charles Messenger and Paul Bray, *Iron Division*, Ian Allan, 2000.

25 The exercise is described in Walter Bohm, *White Rhino 89*, Tankograd Publishing, 1989.

26 The exercise is described in Carl Schulze, *Key Flight '89: The Last Cold War Exercise in BAOR*, Tankograd Publishing, 2009.

27 Witnessed by the author from 1990 onwards.

28 The author wrote the draft section discussing air manoeuvre.

29 The principles of *ADP Operations* were put to good use in 1995–96 when the then Brigadier Richard Dannatt and the author planned NATO operations in Bosnia.

Chapter 5: Operation *Banner*

1 This chapter draws on the following:

'Operation Banner: An Analysis of Military Operations in Northern Ireland', British Army Code 71842, July 2006. Report published on the Operation Kenova website, https://www.opkenova.co.uk/

Desmond Hamill, *Pig in the Middle: The British Army in Northern Ireland*, Methuen, 1975.

'Operation Banner Primer: An Account of the British Military's Deployment to Northern Ireland, 1969–2007', Kings College London Centre for Defence Studies February 2022. Report published on the Operation Kenova website.

Aaron Edwards, *The Northern Ireland Troubles*, Osprey, 2023.

The memoirs of Generals Guthrie, Jackson, Dannatt and Richards.

2 "Tony Makepiece Warne Exceedingly Lucky, Sidney Jary Limited, 1993, pp. 38–40.

3 'Operation *Banner*', British Army Code 71842.

4 The Baha Mousa Public Inquiry Report, Volume One, Part III, 2011, pp. 9 and 10. https://www.gov.uk/government/publications/the-baha-mousa-public-inquiry-report

5 'Operation *Banner* Primer', p. 58–59.

6 'Operation *Banner* Primer', p. 188.

7 Hammill *Pig in the Middle*, p. 141.

8 'Dicks', or more often 'dickers' described lookouts for terrorists and insurgents. Term initially used in Northern Ireland, later applied in Iraq and Afghanistan.

9 Goldsack (ed.), '*Second to None*', p. 36.

10 Andrew Pringle (ed.), *Swift and Bold: A Portrait of the Royal Green Jackets 1966–2007*, p. 120.

11 Frank Kitson, *Gangs and Counter-gangs*, Rockliff, 1960; Frank Kitson, *Low Intensity Operations*, Faber & Faber 1971. Kitson's later book *Bunch of Five*, Faber & Faber, 1977, is one of the best books on the topic of counterinsurgency – ever.

12 Statement by Frank Kitson to the Bloody Sunday Inquiry, 18 February 2000.

13 Hammill, *Pig in the Middle*, p. 121.

14 A credible account, approved by the MoD, of the work of the Force Research Unit is Rob Lewis, *Fishers of Men*, Hodder and Stoughton, 1999.

15 Operation *Kenova* Inquiry at https://www.opkenova.co.uk/

16 BBC TV Documentary *Once Upon a Time in Northern Ireland. Episode 2. Do Paramilitaries Lie Awake at Night?* https://www.bbc.co.uk/iplayer/episode/p0fhvtp4/once-upon-a-time-in-northern-ireland-series-1-2-do -paramilitaries-lie-awake-at-night

17 Minute from Defence Secretary to Prime Minister dated 1973. TNA DEFE 25/282. Available at acre.com

18 A good description of selection and training can be found in James Rennie, *The Operators*, Century, 1996, an apparently accurate account of the author's training for duty with the Det in the 1980s.

19 See Andy McNab, *Immediate Action*, Corgi, 1995. The author describes his attachment to the Det from the SAS.

20 'Operation *Banner* Primer', pp. 51–52, 82–86.

21 The incident is described in General Sir Peter de la Billière, *Looking for Trouble*, HarperCollins, 1995, pp. 315–16, and Hamill, *Pig in the Middle*, pp. 229–31.

22 William Matchett, *Secret Victory: The Intelligence Operations that Beat the IRA*, Matchett, 2016.

23 Jackson, *Soldier*, pp. 112–13.

24 'Operation *Banner*', British Army Code 71842, pp. 8-5–8-7.

25 Jackson, *Soldier*, pp. 120–22.

26 This section uses material in Hamill, *Pig in The Middle* and insights provided by a staff officer present at Mrs Thatcher's meeting with the Army.

27 Quoted in an interview with Morrison in *An Phoblact*, 1 June 2015. https://www.anphoblacht.com/contents/25032

28 'A Soldier's Tribute: Major-General Alastair Duncan CBE DSO', Forces TV website, 30 August, 2016. https://www.forcesnews.com/services/tri-service/soldiers-tribute-major-general-alastair-duncan-cbe-dso

29 Field Marshal Lord Guthrie, *Peace, War and Whitehall*, Osprey, 2021, p. 29.

30 Personal conversations with author.
31 'Operation *Banner*', British Army Code 71842, p. 77.

CHAPTER 6: OPERATION *DESERT STORM*

1   Defence (Options for Change), a statement by Defence Secretary Tom King. Hansard 25 July 1990.
2   Patrick Cordingley, *In the Eye of the Storm: Commanding the Desert Rats in the Gulf War*, Hodder and Stoughton, 1996, p. 7.
3   Paul W. Westermeyer, *Liberating Kuwait: US Marines in the Gulf War, 1990–1991*, History Division, US Marine Corps, 2014, pp. 47–49, 70–74. Available at www.usmc.edu
4   Hugh McManners, *Gulf War One: Real Voices from the Front Line*, Ebury Press, 2010, pp. 77–78.
5   A remark attributed to General Sir John Chapple CGS in 1991, when asked by officers why it had been so difficult to generate forces and equipment for Operation *Granby*.
6   Sources used are *The Gulf War: Volume 1*, special issue of the *British Army Review*, Winter 2020, https://www.army.mod.uk/media/11016/bar_gulf_war-vol1-final.pdf; and Air Marshal Sir Kenneth Hayr, 'Logistics in the Gulf War', *RUSI Journal*, Autumn 1991.
7   Robert H. Scales, *Certain Victory: The US Army in the Gulf War*, Brasseys, 1993.
8   Rupert Smith, 'A Commander Reflects', *Journal of Military Operations*, March 2016. https://www.tjomo.com/article/a-commander-reflects/
9   Major General Martin White (ed.), *Gulf Logistics; Blackadder's War*, Brasseys, 1995.
10 *The Gulf War: Volume 1*, pp. 21–22.
11 Laurie Milner, *Royal Scots in the Gulf: 1st Battalion the Royal Scots on Operation Granby 1990–91*, Pen and Sword Books, 1994, p. 110.
12 'The Gulf War: The Land Battle', Major General Rupert Smith, *RUSI Journal*, February 1992.
13 Andy McNab, *Bravo Two Zero*, Bantam, 1993; Chris Ryan, *The One That Got Away*, Century, 1995; Des Powell and Damien Lewis, *Bravo Three Zero*, Quercus 2022, Peter Ratcliffe, *In the Eye of the Storm: 25 Years in Action with the SAS*, HarperCollins, 2000.
14 McChrystal, Stan, *My Share of the Task: A Memoir*, Portfolio/Penguin, 2013, p.53.

CHAPTER 7: BLOODY BOSNIA

1   'Address Before a Joint Session of the Congress on the Cessation of the Persian Gulf Conflict March 6, 1991', Public Papers of the Presidents of the United States: George H. W. Bush (1991, Book I), US Government Publishing Office. https://www.govinfo.gov/content/pkg/PPP-1991-book1/html/PPP-1991-book1-doc-pg218-3.htm
2   A phrase used by Professor Richard Holmes in a letter to *The Times* of 23 May 1991. It concluded as follows: 'Unless the secretary of state for defence moves quickly, he risks ending up with an army that is not "smaller and better", just "smaller but bitter"'. The phrase was widely used within the Army in the early 1990s.
3   Ministry of Defence, *Front Line First: The Defence Cost Study* (London, HMSO, 1994). See https://researchbriefings.files.parliament.uk/documents/RP94-101/RP94-101.pdf
4   John Major, *John Major: The Autobiography*, HarperCollins, 1999, p. 545.
5   Martin Bell, *In Harm's Way*, revised edition, Penguin, 1996.
6   Personal communication by senior British officer.
7   Bob Stewart, *Broken Lives*, HarperCollins, 1993 is the personal account by the Cheshires' commanding officer.
8   Briefing by Lieutenant Colonel Duncan, Warminster, 1994.
9   Obituary Major-General Alastair Duncan, *The Times*, 26 July 2016. https://www.thetimes.com/article/major-general-alastair-duncan-nrwnfkxhc
10 Obituary Major-General Alastair Duncan, *The Times*, 26 July 2016. https://www.thetimes.com/article/major-general-alastair-duncan-nrwnfkxhc
11 Bell, *In Harm's Way*, p. 193.
12 Jan Willem Honig and Norbert Both, *Srebrenica: Record of a War Crime*, Penguin, 1996.
13 Private communication.
14 Tim Ripley, *Operation Deliberate Force: The UN and NATO Campaign in Bosnia 1995*, Centre for Defence and International Security Studies (CDISS), Lancaster University, 1999.
15 Ripley, *Operation Deliberate Force*, p. 177.

16 John Major, *The Autobiography*, Harper Collins, 1999, p. 545.

17 A post operation lessons seminar at PJHQ the author attended in late 1996; author's interview with senior British commanders planning the operation; '"High-Risk" Secret Plan To Withdraw British Troops From Bosnia Revealed', BFBS Forces News, 31 December 2019. https://www.forcesnews.com/news/high-risk-secret-plan-withdraw-british-troops-bosnia-revealed; 'The Secret British Plan to Abandon Bosnia as Srebrenica Fell', Middle East Eye Website, 2 April 2021. https://www.middleeasteye.net/big-story/operation-screwdriver-secret-british-plan-abandon-bosnia-srebrenica-fell

18 One of the officers involved went on to work for me.

19 Personal communication with former British battalion commander.

20 A full account of 2 LI's operations in Bosnia is found in the Barry, *Road From Sarajevo*.

21 Part of foreword by Martin Bell, in Ben Barry, *The Road from Sarajevo*, The History Press, 2016, p.7.

22 Tobias Ellwood became MP for Bournemouth. He was also a minister in the MoD and a very successful chair of the House of Commons Defence Committee.

23 From notes written by David Livingston, quoted in Barry, *Road From Sarajevo*, p. 139.

24 Jackson, *Soldier*, p. 212.

25 Dannatt, *Leading From the Front,* p. 173.

26 General Wesley K. Clark, *Waging Modern War*, Public Affairs, 2001, p. 87.

27 Clark, *Waging Modern War*, p. 97.

28 The company came from 2nd Battalion, the Royal Green Jackets. Described in Pringle (ed.), *Swift and Bold*.

29 There is an excellent account of this campaign in Julian Borger, *The Butcher's Trail: How the Search For Balkan War Criminals Became the World's Most Successful Manhunt*, Other Press, 2017.

30 Borger, *Butcher's Trail*, Chapter 3; Barry, *Road From Sarajevo*, Chapter 14.

31 Carl Bildt, *Peace Journey*, Weidenfeld & Nicolson, 1998, pp. 302–03.

CHAPTER 8: KOSOVO

1 CGS Letter to the Army, in Factsheets Annex of Strategic Defence Review White Paper, July 1998.

2 Guthrie, *Peace, War and Whitehall*, p. 231–32.

3 Private conversations between the author and MoD and intelligence officials.

4 Jackson, *Soldier*, pp. 238–39.

5 This section is based on the author's experience, both during the Kosovo War and at a number of military briefings afterward, and also on General Clark's memoir *Waging Modern War*, pp. 301–23, and two newspaper articles: 'Kosovo Land Threat May Have Won the War' by Dana Priest, *Washington Post*, 19 September 1999 and 'Revealed: The Secret Plan to Invade Kosovo' by Julian Borger and Patrick Wintour, *The Guardian*, 18 July 1999.

6 'Revealed: The Secret Plan to Invade Kosovo', *The Guardian*, 18 July 1999.

7 Clark, *Waging Modern War*, p. 304–05.

8 Jackson, *Soldier*, p. 288.

9 Jackson, *Soldier*, p. 272.

10 Extracted from Jackson, *Soldier*, pp. 272–74.

11 Jackson, *Soldier*, p. 274.

12 Clark, *Waging Modern War*, p. 399.

13 'It is simply the right thing to do', transcript of Tony Blair's speech in Chicago, *The Guardian*, 27 March 1999.

14 Guthrie, *Peace, War and Whitehall*, p. 241.

15 De Zulueta and Doughty, *Those Must Be the Guards*, p. 273.

16 Guthrie, *Peace, War and Whitehall*, p. 240.

CHAPTER 9: RAPID INTERVENTION (2)

1 Brigadier Mike Wharmby's short account Operation *Gabriel* can be found at https://paradata.org.uk/content/4663300. It contains an admirably concise account of the background to the genocide.

2 An excellent BBC documentary film was made of the early stages of the mission. *Defence of the Realm: Mission Angola* is often found on the BBC Player streaming service. Archived as part of the BBC Four Armed Forces Collection. https://www.bbc.co.uk/programmes/p00fgp7j/episodes/player

3   Primary Responsibility and Primary Risks: ADF Participation in INTERFET, Australian Army Land Warfare Centre. Also David Richards, *Taking Command*, Headline, 2014.

4   This section is based on the following sources
     Richards, *Taking Command.*
     Guthrie, *Peace, War and Whitehall.*
     Richard Iron, 'Rapid Intervention and Conflict Resolution: British Military Intervention in Sierra Leone 2000–2002', Australian Army Occasional Paper Conflict Theory and Strategy Series 003 February 2019. https://researchcentre.army.gov.au/library/occasional-papers/rapid-intervention-and-conflict-resolution-british -military-intervention-sierra-leone-2000-2002#:~:text=Leone%202000%2D2002-,Rapid%20Intervention %20and%20Conflict%20Resolution%3A%20British%20Military%20Intervention%20in%20Sierra,success %20for%20Western%20military%20intervention
     Will Fowler, *Certain Death in Sierra Leone: The SAS and Operation Barras*, Osprey, 2010. Andrew Dorman, *Blair's Successful War: British Military Intervention in Sierra Leone*, Ashgate, 2009.

5   Richards, *Taking Command*, pp. 135–36.

6   Richards, *Taking Command*, p. 137.

7   The 1996 BBC TV documentary film on the Pathfinder Platoon is archived as part of the BBC Four Armed Forces Collection, *Phantom Platoon.* https://www.bbc.co.uk/programmes/p00fgprc

8   Guthrie, *Peace, War and Whitehall*, p. 223.

9   Tim Collins, *Rules of Engagement*, Headline, 2005, p. 12.

10   Fowler, *Certain Death in Sierra Leone*, p. 39.

11   Fowler, *Certain Death in Sierra Leone*, p. 47.

12   Fowler, *Certain Death in Sierra Leone*, p. 47.

13   Conversation with the author, 2000.

14   Iron, 'Rapid Intervention and Conflict Resolution', p. 116.

15   Iron, 'Rapid Intervention and Conflict Resolution', p. 103.

16   UN Security Council Resolution 1313, 4 August 2000 [on extension of the mandate of the UN Mission in Sierra Leone (UNAMSIL)]. Archived at UN Digital Library. https://digitallibrary.un.org/record/420042?ln=en&v=pdf

17   Iron, 'Rapid Intervention and Conflict Resolution', p. 140.

18   Private conversations between the author and several senior Army officers.

19   Iron, 'Rapid Intervention and Conflict Resolution', p. 131.

20   US ambassador, quoted in Iron, 'Rapid Intervention and Conflict Resolution', p. 141.

21   David H. Ucko, *When Intervention Works: The Instructive Case of Sierra Leone*, War on the Rocks website, 31 August 2016. https://warontherocks.com/2016/08/when-intervention-works-the-instructive-case-of-sierra-leone/

22   Guthrie, *Peace War and Whitehall*, p. 253.

23   Guthrie, *Peace War and Whitehall*, pp. 253–54.

24   Angelique Chrisafis, 'How the brigadier has mopped up chaos and won farmers' support', *The Guardian*, 30 March 2001.

CHAPTER 10: RAPID INTERVENTION (3)

1   'Toppling the Taliban', RAND Corporation, 2015. https://www.rand.org/content/dam/rand/pubs/research _reports/RR300/RR381/RAND_RR381.pdf

2   Multiple Sources report this. A detailed account is found in Michael Gordon and Bernard Trainor, *Cobra II: The Inside Story of the Invasion and Occupation of Iraq*, Pantheon Books, 2006, pp. 15–17.

3   Speech to Congress 20 September 2001. https://georgewbush-whitehouse.archives.gov/infocus/bushrecord/ documents/Selected_Speeches_George_W_Bush.pdf

4   US Department of Defense October 18, 2001 News Briefing – Secretary Rumsfeld and General Richard Myers. https://usinfo.org/wf-archive/2001/011019/epf508.htm

5   Presidential Address to the Nation. http://georgewbush-whitehouse.archives.gov/news/releases/2001/10 /20011007-8.html

6   Off the record conversation with UK special forces officers.

7   Tommy Franks, *American Soldier*, HarperCollins, 2004, between pp. 174 and 175.

8   Theo Farrell, *Unwinnable: Britain's War in Afghanistan, 2001–2014*, Bodley Head, 2017, p. 98.

9   There is a good account of the genesis and early role of ISAF in Theo Farrell, *Unwinnable*, pp. 92–100.

10   Author's conversations with British SOF commanders.

11   Steve Coll, *Directorate S*, Allen Lane, 2018, p. 116.

12   President Bush Speech, 22 April 2003, Virginia Military Institute. http://www.presidency.ucsb.edu/ws/index
     .php?pid=73000

13   Later to return to Afghanistan as Commander Regional Command South in 2010 and Deputy Commander of
     ISAF in 2013. Subsequently Chief of the General Staff, then Chief of the Defence Staff.

14   Based on numerous sources, including a visit to the UK PRT in Helmand Province May 2009. See also Carter
     Malkasian and Gerald Meyerle, 'Provincial Reconstruction Teams: How Do We Know They Work?', US Army
     Strategic Studies Centre, 2009. Available on the Library of Congress website: https://www.loc.gov/item/2023692660

15   CNN report 1 May 2003. See http://edition.cnn.com/2003/WORLD/asiapcf/central/05/01/afghan.combat/

16   Private briefing to author by UK officials.

17   Geoff Hoon, *See How They Run*, Unicorn, 2021, p. 106.

18   'Delivering Security in a Changing World: Future Capabilities' (Command 6269), Ministry of Defence, July 2004.

19   This section is based on Jason, *Soldier*, pp. 346–55 and Dannatt, *Leading From the Front*, pp. 227–31. As
     Deputy Colonel of the Light Infantry, the author was involved in the creation of the Rifles and read all the
     papers and evidence provided by the Director of Infantry.

20   Jackson, *Soldier*, p. 351.

CHAPTER 11: REGIME CHANGE IN IRAQ AND INITIAL STABILIZATION

1   This section draws extensively on the Iraq Inquiry. https://webarchive.nationalarchives.gov.uk
     /20171123123237/http://www.iraqinquiry.org.uk/

2   Iraq Inquiry Executive Summary, 6 July 2016, p. 121.

3   These and other observations by Brims are drawn from an unpublished interview conducted by the Land
     Warfare Centre in 2003. Referred to as 'LWC Interview'.

4   Brims, LWC Interview, p. 3.

5   Major Peter Caddick-Adams and Graham Thomas, *The Fight for Iraq January – June 2003*, Army Benevolent
     Fund, 2003, p. 45.

6   Caddick-Adams and Thomas, *The Fight for Iraq*, pp. 75.

7   Operation *James* and the battle to recover the stranded tank are described in Tim Ripley, *Operation Telic*,
     Telic-Herrick Publications, 2014, p. 117.

8   Caddick-Adams and Thomas, *The Fight for Iraq*, pp. 86–87.

9   Caddick-Adams and Thomas, *The Fight for Iraq*, p. 94.

10   Paragraph based on BBC Radio documentary *The Reunion: The Battle for Basra, 6 April 2008*, broadcast 1 April
     2018. Archived at https://www.bbc.co.uk/programmes/b09xctwq

11   The Report of Iraq Inquiry, Section 9.1, March–22 May 2003, p. 154. https://www.gov.uk/government/
     publications/the-report-of-the-iraq-inquiry

12   BBC Radio documentary *The Reunion: The Battle for Basra, 6 April 2008*, broadcast 1 April 2018. Archived at
     https://www.bbc.co.uk/programmes/b09xctwq

13   'Operations in Iraq: An Analysis from a Land Perspective', British Army Code 71816, 2004, pp. 6-1 and 6-2.

14   General Charles C. Krulack, *The Strategic Corporal: Leadership in the Three Block War*, US Marine Corps
     Gazette, January 1999. https://apps.dtic.mil/dtic/tr/fulltext/u2/a399413.pdf

15   Brims, LWC Interview, p. 9.

16   *The Reunion* documentary.

17   Brims, LWC Interview, p. 9.

18   Iraq Inquiry, Volume 6, paragraph 564.

19   Iraq Inquiry, Volume 6, paragraph 472.

20   Iraq Inquiry, Volume 6, p. 533.

21   Iraq Inquiry, Volume 6, p. 535.

22   Iraq Inquiry, Volume 6, p. 95.

23   Iraq Inquiry, Volume 6, p. 535.

24   Hilary Synnott, *Bad Days in Basra: My Turbulent Time as Britain's Man in Southern Iraq*, I.B.Tauris & Co Ltd,
     2008, p. 252.

25   Evidence given to Iraq Inquiry by Major General Andrew Stewart. http://webarchive.nationalarchives.gov.uk /20171123123302/http://www.iraqinquiry.org.uk/the-evidence/witness-transcripts/

26   Baha Mousa Public Inquiry Report.

27   Richard Holmes' book *Dusty Warriors: Modern Soldiers at War*, HarperCollins, 2016, well describes the battles fought by 1st Battalion, the Princess of Wales's Royal Regiment during this period.

28   The reasoning behind this decision was one of several issues that the Iraq Inquiry chose not to explore.

29   Thomas Mockaitis, *The Iraq War*, US Army War College, 2007, p. 11.

30   Iraq Inquiry, transcript of evidence given by Lieutenant General Sir Jonathan Riley. http://webarchive.nationalarchives .gov.uk/20171123123620/http://www.iraqinquiry.org.uk/the-evidence/witnesses/r/lt-gen-jonathon-riley/

CHAPTER 12: 'WE ARE IN TWO WARS AND WE HAVE GOT TO WIN THEM BOTH'

1   Term used by Air Chief Marshal Sir Jock Stirrup, UK CDS. Witnessed on two occasions by the author.

2   Jonathan Bailey, Richard Iron and Hew Strachan (eds), *British Generals in Blair's Wars*, Ashgate, 2013, pp. 218–19.

3   An excellent summary of the growth of the Taliban in Helmand and southern Afghanistan is found in Farrell, *Unwinnable*, Penguin, 2017, and Carter Malkasian, *War comes to Garmser*, Hurst, 2013.

4   FactCheck: a shot in Afghanistan? Channel 4 News. https://www.channel4.com/news/articles/uk/factcheck %2Ba%2Bshot%2Bin%2Bafghanistan/3266362.html

5   Farrell, *Unwinnable*, pp. 169–71.

6   Farrell, *Unwinnable*, p. 155.

7   *Danger Close* is also the title of a vivid account of 3rd Battalion, the Parachute Regiment's 2006 battles in Helmand, written by the then commanding officer, Stuart Tootal; John Murray, 2010.

8   Farrell, *Unwinnable*, pp. 169–72. Also Richards, *Taking Command*, Chapters 11–13.

9   A gripping account of the defence of the isolated British base at Musa Qala by the commander of an ad hoc infantry company thrown together to defend the outpost is to be found in Adam Jowett, *No Way Out: The Searing True Story of Men Under Siege*, Sidgwick & Jackson, 2018.

10   Evidence given to the Iraq Inquiry by Lieutenant General John Cooper, 15 December 2009. https://web.archive.org/ web/20160716225704/http://www.iraqinquiry.org.uk/media/230141/2009-12-15-transcript-rollo-cooper-s2.pdf

11   Dannatt, *Leading from the Front*, p. 236.

12   Dannatt, *Leading from the Front*, pp. 237–38.

13   Dannatt, *Leading from the Front*, p. 247.

14   Author's experience in MoD.

15   Dannatt, *Leading from the Front*, pp. 249–63

16   I saw this for myself in October 2009.

17   Dannatt, *Leading from the Front*, pp. 270–78.

18   'Army Field Manual Volume 10 Counterinsurgency', British Army Code 71876, October 2009. This avoidable delay is explained by Colonel Alex Alderson's PHD thesis: The validity of British Army counterinsurgency doctrine after the war in Iraq 2003-2009, Cranfield University Library. https://dspace.lib.cranfield.ac.uk/items/ b7dfd3bb-b35c-4638-8d2e-c52b405bb5be

19   Iraq Inquiry, Sir John Chilcot's public statement, 6 July 2016. http://webarchive.nationalarchives.gov.uk /20171123124608/http://www.iraqinquiry.org.uk/the-inquiry/sir-john-chilcots-public-statement/

20   UK MoD Iraq lessons compendium. https://assets.publishing.service.gov.uk/government/uploads/system/ uploads/attachment_data/file/16787/operation_telic_lessons_compendium.pdf

21   Richards, *Taking Command*, p. 300.

22   Evidence given to the Iraq Inquiry by Lieutenant General Richard Shirreff, 11 January 2010. https://web.archive .org/web/20160717194013/http://www.iraqinquiry.org.uk/media/95138/2010-01-11-Transcript-Shirreff-S2.pdf

23   Evidence given to the Iraq Inquiry by Lieutenant General Richard Shirreff, 11 January 2010.

24   International Police Advisers were provided by Armor Group, a private security company, to provide advice and mentoring to the Iraqi Police Service.

25   Simon Mayall, *Soldier in the Sand*, Pen and Sword, 2000 p. 239.

26   Operations in Iraq January 2005–May 2009: An Analysis from the Land Perspective', British Army, 29 November 2010, p. 51. https://assets.publishing.service.gov.uk/government/uploads/system/uploads/ attachment_data/file/557326/20160831-FOI07003_77396_Redacted.pdf

27 'The Report of the Baha Mousa Inquiry by Rt Hon Sor William Gage', 8 September 2011, Volume 1, pp. 9–11; see also Volume 2, pp. 460–637. https://www.gov.uk/government/publications/the-baha-mousa-public-inquiry-report

28 Author's observations in UK Ministry of Defence, 2006–07.

29 An insightful account of the role of the Grenadier Guards' OMLT role is to be found in Patrick Hennessy, *The Junior Officers' Reading Club: Killing Time and Fighting Wars*, Penguin, 2010.

30 Gordon Brown, *My Life, Our Times*, Vintage, 2018, p. 213.

31 Brown, *My Life, Our Times*, pp. 260–61.

32 Evidence given to the Iraq Inquiry by Air Chief Marshal Sir Jock Stirrup, 1 February 2010. https://webarchive.nationalarchives.gov.uk/20171123123302/http://www.iraqinquiry.org.uk/the-evidence/witness-transcripts/

33 Observed by the author in both MoD and the IISS.

34 Iraq Inquiry Section 9.8. https://www.gov.uk/government/publications/the-report-of-the-iraq-inquiry

35 Iraq Inquiry Executive Summary: 'Between 2003 and 2009, UK forces in Iraq faced gaps in some key capability areas, including protected mobility, Intelligence, Surveillance, Target Acquisition and Reconnaissance (ISTAR) and helicopter support. It was not sufficiently clear which person or department within the MoD had responsibility for identifying and articulating capability gaps. Delays in providing adequate medium weight Protected Patrol Vehicles and the failure to meet the needs of UK forces in MND(SE) for ISTAR and helicopters should not have been tolerated. The MoD was slow in responding to the developing threat in Iraq from Improvised Explosive Devices (IEDs). The range of protected mobility options available to commanders in MND(SE) was limited. Although work had begun before 2002 to source an additional PPV, it was only ordered in July 2006 following Ministerial intervention.' Iraq Inquiry Executive Summary. https://www.gov.uk/government/publications/the-report-of-the-iraq-inquiry.

36 Farrell, *Unwinnable*, p. 365.

37 The account of Taliban adaptation and weaknesses is based on discussion in Antonio Giustozzi, *The Taliban at War 2001–2018*, Hurst and Co, 2019, Chapters 5 and 6.

38 Author's observations from 2009 visit to Lashkar Gar and Sangin.

39 BBC Radio documentary *The Reunion: The Battle for Basra, 6 April 2008*, broadcast 1 April 2018. Archived at https://www.bbc.co.uk/programmes/b09xctwq

40 Richard Iron, 'Basra 2008: Operation Charge of the Knights' in Bailey et al (eds), *British Generals in Blair's Wars*, p. 197.

41 Evidence given to the Iraq Inquiry by Air Chief Marshal Sir Jock Stirrup, 1 February 2010. https://webarchive.nationalarchives.gov.uk/ukgwa/20171123123302/http://www.iraqinquiry.org.uk/the-evidence/witness-transcripts/stirrup

42 The reputational consequences of Operation *Charge of the Knights* for the UK and its wider lessons are discussed in Chapter 3, pp. 3–5.

43 Iraq Inquiry. https://webarchive.nationalarchives.gov.uk/20171123123237/http://www.iraqinquiry.org.uk/

44 http://www.iraqinquiry.org.uk/the-inquiry/sir-john-chilcots-public-statement/

45 Iraq Inquiry Chairman's Statement, 6 July 2016. http://www.iraqinquiry.org.uk/the-inquiry/sir-john-chilcots-public-statement/

46 Author's interviews 2009–10.

47 See pp. 134–35 of the Iraq Inquiry Executive Summary, for analysis of weaknesses in UK decision-making and implementation in the post-conflict period.

48 Iraq Inquiry Executive Summary, p. 110.

49 Iraq Inquiry Executive Summary, p. 136.

Chapter 13: Strategic Shrinkage and the Endgame in Afghanistan, 2009–14

1 Operational briefing at Land Warfare Centre 2009.

2 Private conversation with several British officers. Also Farrell, *Unwinnable*, pp. 272–73.

3 McChrystal, *My Share of the Task*, p. 310.

4 Speech archived on White House website. https://obamawhitehouse.archives.gov/the-press-office/remarks-president-address-nation-way-forward-afghanistan-and-pakistan

5   Royal Engineers Historical Society, *History of the Corps of Royal Engineers*, Volume XIII, Institute of Royal Engineers, 2024, pp. 329–30.

6   History of the Corps of Royal Engineers, Volume XIII, p. 340.

7   Described in Jarvis' excellent memoir *Long Way Home: Love, Life, Death, and Everything in Between*, Little Brown, 2020.

8   This is well described in Sergio Miller, *Pride and Fall: The British Army in Afghanistan, 2001–2014*, Osprey 2024, pp. 439–43.

9   Miller, *Pride and Fall*, p. 442.

10   Miller, *Pride and Fall*, p. 486.

11   Johnny Mercer, *We were Warriors*, Pan, 2018, p. 301.

12   An excellent book on the topic is Steve Houghton, *British Sniping Rifles Since 1970*, Osprey, 2021.

13   Author's visit to the unit late 2010.

14   This section is drawn from David Cameron, *For the Record*, HarperCollins, 2019, pp. 165–68.

15   Cameron, *For the Record*, p. 166.

16   UK National Security Strategy, p. 27. https://www.gov.uk/government/publications/the-national-security -strategy-a-strong-britain-in-an-age-of-uncertainty

17   See House of Commons Public Accounts Committee 2010 report 'Managing the Defence Budget and Estate', summary at http://www.publications.parliament.uk/pa/cm201011/cmselect/cmpubacc/503/50302.htm

18   'Vehicle & Aircraft Holdings within the scope of the Conventional Armed Forces in Europe Treaty', UK MoD Defence Statistics (WDS), 2015 edition. https://www.gov.uk/government/uploads/system/uploads/attachment _data/file/423149/CFE_2015.pdf

19   SDSR Factsheet 15: Afghanistan. UK Cabinet Office, https://www.gov.uk/government/publications/the -strategic-defence-and-security-review-securing-britain-in-an-age-of-uncertainty

20   Visit to a brigade at the start of Afghanistan training in 2012.

21   The Commons Committee of Public Accounts report on the Ministry of Defence (MoD) major projects 2010, 22 February 2011, https://committees.parliament.uk/committee/127/public-accounts-committee/news /176754/mps-report-on-ministry-of-defence-major-projects-2010/

22   'Defence Reform. An Independent Report into the Structure and Management of the Ministry of Defence June 2011 by Lord Levene of Portsoken'. https://www.gov.uk/government/publications/defence-reform-an -independent-report-into-the-structure-and-management-of-the-ministry-of-defence--2#:~:text=In%202010 %20the%20Secretary%20of,2011%2C%20setting%20out%2053%20recommendations.

23   Based on Karl P. Mueller (ed.), *Precision and Purpose Airpower in the Libyan Civil War*, RAND Corporation, 2015; pp. 170 and 171 in Chapter 6 by Christina Goulter are particularly useful. And on Rob Weighill and Florence Gaub, *The Cauldron NATO's Campaign in Libya*, Hurst, 2018.

24   'House Of Commons Oral Evidence Taken Before The Liaison Committee, The Prime Minister, Tuesday 17 May 2011'. https://publications.parliament.uk/pa/cm201012/cmselect/cmliaisn/608/11051702.htm

25   Ben Barry 'Libya's Lessons', *Survival*, September 2011. International Institute for Strategic Studies https://www .tandfonline.com/doi/full/10.1080/00396338.2011.621622#d1e146 and Press statement introducing the IISS Strategic Survey 2011 at http://www.iiss.org/publications/strategic-survey/strategic-survey-2011/press-statement/

26   'The Situation in Afghanistan and its Implications for International Peace and Security', Report of the Secretary-General to the UN General Assembly 13 September 2012. https://unama.unmissions.org/sites/ default/files/sg_report_to_sc_as_published_13sept12.pdf

27   'Accountability Determination of US commanders for the 14–15 September attack on the Camp Bastian, Leatherneck and Shoraback complex, Helmand Province, Afghanistan', Department of the Navy, 30 September 2013. https://www.hqmc.marines.mil/Portals/142/Docs/CMC%20Memo%20for%20the%20 Record%20in%20Bastion%20Investigation.PDF

28   'Afghanistan – Camp Bastion Attack', House of Commons Defence Committee, 26 March 2014 https:// publications.parliament.uk/pa/cm201314/cmselect/cmdfence/830/830.pdf

29   Views expressed to the author in private by a number of officers.

30   House of Commons Defence Committee, The Defence Contribution to UK National Security and Resilience, Examination of Witnesses (Question Numbers 189–99), General Sir David Richards KCB CBE DSO ADC GEN and Brigadier James Everard OBE, 27 January 2009, https://publications.parliament.uk/pa/cm200809/ cmselect/cmdfence/121/9012702.htm

31   Richards, *Taking Command*, p. 311.

32   Quoted in 'Syria Crisis: No to War, Blow to Cameron', *Daily Telegraph*, 30 August 2013.

33   'Joint Press Conference by President Obama and President Karzai', 11 January 2013. Archived by White
       House at https://obamawhitehouse.archives.gov/the-press-office/2013/01/11/joint-press-conference-president
       -obama-and-president-karzai
34   Miller, *Pride and Fall*, p. 522.
35   Briefings by senior British officers; Miller, *Pride and Fall*, p. 519.
36   Director Land Warfare, 'Operation HERRICK Campaign Study', 2015. Redacted copy on MoD website. https://
       www.gov.uk/government/publications/foi-responses-published-by-mod-week-commencing-11-january-2016
37   A useful recent analysis of British failures to stabilize Helmand is by Dr Tom Galloway, 'Social capability and
       the lessons of Helmand Province', Global Insecurities Centre University of Bristol. Published by the Centre for
       Historical Analysis and Conflict Research, February 2025. https://chacr.org.uk/2025/02/05/in-depth-briefing
       -87-social-capability/

Chapter 14: A Decade of Defeat, Decline and Disruption

1   Cameron, *For the Record*, pp. 545–46.
2   Mayall, *Soldier in the Sand*, p. 290.
3   Cameron, *For the Record*, p. 605.
4   Question posed by author at MoD briefing.
5   Emma Ross, Gita Honwana Welch and Philip Angelides, 'Sierra Leone's Response to the Ebola Outbreak
       Management Strategies and Key Responder Experiences', Chatham House, March 2017, p. 17.
6   'Military cuts mean "no US partnership", Robert Gates warns Britain'. http://www.bbc.co.uk/news/uk-25754870
7   'David Cameron dismisses Robert Gates' defence cuts warning'. http://www.bbc.co.uk/news/uk-25763902
8   Conservative Party Manifesto 2015, p. 75. https://www.conservatives.com/Manifesto
9   Lecture by General Sir Nicholas Houghton GCB CBE ADC Gen, Chief of the Defence Staff, UK Ministry of
       Defence and the Royal United Services Institution, 18 December 2013.
10   'National Security Strategy and Strategic Defence and Security Review 2015', MoD website, 25 November
       2015. https://www.gov.uk/government/publications/national-security-strategy-and-strategic-defence-and
       -security-review-2015
11   Before and after the launch of the review the author was besieged by defence journalists who wanted to better
       understand the concept.
12   'Transcript of President Obama's statement about Afghanistan', 15 October 2015, *Stars and Stripes*. https://
       www.stripes.com/news/transcript-of-president-obama-s-statement-about-afghanistan-oct-15-2015-1.373441
13   Off the record conversations with senior MoD officials.
14   History of the Corps of Royal Engineers, Volume XIII, p. 490.
15   'Oral evidence: Progress in delivering the British Army's armoured vehicle capability, HC 659, Tuesday 20 October
       2020. Witnesses Jeremy Quin MP, Minister of State, Minister for Defence Procurement, Air Marshal Richard
       Knighton CB, Deputy Chief of Defence Staff (Military Capability), Ministry of Defence, Lieutenant General
       Christopher Tickell CBE, Deputy Chief of the General Staff, British Army, and Chris Bushell, Director General
       Land, Defence Equipment & Support', House of Commons Defence Committee. https://committees.parliament.
       uk/oralevidence/1068/html/ 'Written evidence submitted by the Ministry of Defence. HCDC Inquiry: Progress in
       delivering the British Army's armoured vehicle'. https://committees.parliament.uk/writtenevidence/12523/html/
16   'Oral evidence: Progress in delivering the British Army's armoured vehicle capability, HC 659', House of
       Commons Defence Committee, Tuesday 20 October 2020.
17   'Obsolescent and Outgunned: The British Army's Armoured Vehicle Capability', House of Commons Defence
       Committee Report. 14 March 2021. Conclusion at https://publications.parliament.uk/pa/cm5801/cmselect/
       cmdfence/659/65908.htm#:~:text=Were%20the%20British%20Army%20to,or%20even%20obsolete%20armoured
       %20vehicles%2C See also House of Lords Library report Warfighting capability of the British army 3rd (UK)
       Division 4 July 2022. https://lordslibrary.parliament.uk/warfighting-capability-of-the-british-army-3rd-uk-division/
18   Integrated Review of Security, Defence, Development and Foreign Policy. 'Global Britain in a Competitive
       Age'. British Government, 16 March 2021, https://www.gov.uk/government/publications/global-britain-in-a
       -competitive-age-the-integrated-review-of-security-defence-development-and-foreign-policy
19   https://publications.parliament.uk/pa/cm5801/cmselect/cmdfence/659/65903.htm#_idTextAnchor000
       https://www.iiss.org/blogs/military-balance/2021/08/uk-special-operations-brigade

20   'Defence in a Competitive Age'. British Government March 2021. https://www.gov.uk/government/publications/defence-in-a-competitive-age

21   The Military Balance 2021. International Institute for Strategic Studies 2021. 2021: French Polynesia (900) + New Caledonia (1,450) + La Reunion (1,700).

22   'UK Carrier Strike Group: meeting Indo-Pacific expectations?', IISS Military Balance Blog. https://www.iiss.org/blogs/military-balance/2021/08/uk-carrier-strike-group-indopacific

23   'UK, US AND Australia launch new security partnership', UK Prime Minister's website.

24   '17 November 2021 – Oral Evidence from the Prime Minister', House of Commons Liaison Committee. https://committees.parliament.uk/event/6247/formal-meeting-oral-evidence-session/

25   PM statement to the House on the Integrated Review: 19 November 2020. https://www.gov.uk/government/speeches/pm-statement-to-the-house-on-the-integrated-review-19-november-2020

26   'House of Commons Defence Committee, Written evidence submitted by Lockheed Martin UK', 20 September 2020. https://committees.parliament.uk/work/460/default/publications/written-evidence/

27   The Ajax Lessons Learned Review', Ministry of Defence, March 2022. https://www.gov.uk/government/publications/the-ajax-lessons-learned-review

28   Remarks by President Trump on the Strategy in Afghanistan and South Asia, August 21, 2011. https://www.whitehouse.gov/briefings-statements/remarks-president-trump-strategy-afghanistan-south-asia/

29   Private conversation with State Department and Pentagon officials, autumn 2018.

30   'Enhancing Security and Stability in Afghanistan', US Department of Defense, December 2018. https://media.defense.gov/2018/Dec/20/2002075158/-1/-1/1/1225-REPORT-DECEMBER-2018.PDF

31   Andrew Quilty, 'Static War: Helmand after the US Marines' return', Afghan Analysts Network, 23 April 2020. https://www.afghanistan-analysts.org/en/reports/war-and-peace/static-war-helmand-after-the-us-marines-return/

32   Published on the US State Department website. See https://www.state.gov/wp-content/uploads/2020/02/Agreement-For-Bringing-Peace-to-Afghanistan-02.29.20.pdf

33   There are two good books on the operation: Levison Wood and Geraint Jones, *Escape from Kabul*, Hodder and Stoughton, 2023; and Laurie Bristow, *Kabul: Final Call*, Whittles Publishing, 2024. The documentary film *Evacuation* by British broadcaster Channel 4 is an excellent portrait. https://www.channel4.com/programmes/evacuation

34   Wood and Jones, *Escape from Kabul*, p.131.

35   Bristow, *Kabul: Final Call*, p.138.

36   Wood and Jones, *Escape from Kabul*, pp. 148–49.

37   'Missing in action: UK leadership and the withdrawal from Afghanistan, House of Commons Foreign Affairs Committee', May 2022, p.20.

38   Missing in action: UK leadership and the withdrawal from Afghanistan, House of Commons Foreign Affairs Committee', May 2022, p.52.

39   'Withdrawal from Afghanistan', House of Commons Defence Committee, 10 February 2022. P20 https://publications.parliament.uk/pa/cm5803/cmselect/cmdfence/725/report.html

40   Bristow, *Kabul: Final Call*, p.193.

41   General Sir Mark Carleton-Smith speaking at Policy Exchange, 12 April 2022. https://policyexchange.org.uk/events/security-and-the-role-of-land-power/

42   '17 November 2021 – Oral Evidence from the Prime Minister', House of Commons Liaison Committee. https://committees.parliament.uk/event/6247/formal-meeting-oral-evidence-session/

43   De Zulueta and Doughty, *Those Must be the Guards*, pp. 186–90.

44   'Defence's response to a more contested and volatile world', Defence Command Paper 2023, UK MoD website, 18 July 2023. https://www.gov.uk/government/publications/defence-command-paper-2023-defences-response-to-a-more-contested-and-volatile-world

45   NATO Infographic New NATO Force Model. https://www.nato.int/nato_static_fl2014/assets/pdf/2022/6/pdf/220629-infographic-new-nato-force-model.pdf

46   This paragraph draws on private discussions with NATO officials.

47   https://www.defensenews.com/global/europe/2025/03/14/nato-to-ask-allies-for-30-capability-boost-top-commander-says/

48   Building a better NATO. Speech by NATO Secretary General Mark Rutte at Chatham House – London, United Kingdom, 9 June 2025. https://www.nato.int/cps/en/natohq/opinions_235867.htm

49   Private conversations with senior Army officers.

50   An IISS assessment of NATO Land forces is in 'The Future of NATO's European Land Forces: Plans, Challenges, Prospects', June 2023. https://www.iiss.org/research-paper/2023/06/the-future-of-natos-european-land-forces/

51   Hansard 25 February 2025.

52 Rachel Reeves vows to use defence spending to support UK's 'left behind' industrial towns. *The Guardian*, 4 March 2025.

53 'Ready for War', Report by the House of Commons Defence Committee, 4 February 2024. https://committees .parliament.uk/work/7654/armed-forces-readiness/publications/

54 'One fifth of armed forces not fit to fight, admits MoD', *The Times*, 23 December 2024.

55 In "British troops employ lethal new tactics in California". Soldier Magazine. May 2025. https://soldier.army .mod.uk/issues/may-2025/updates/rise-of-the-machines

56 Private conversation with senior UK and NATO officials.

57 Service Inquiry into the death of a Service Person discovered in their Single Living Accommodation at the Royal Military Academy Sandhurst (RMAS) on 6 February 2019. MoD website, November 2022. https://www .gov.uk/government/publications/service-inquiry-into-the-death-of-a-service-person-discovered-in-their-single -living-accommodation-at-rmas-on-6-february-2019-november-2022

58 'The Land Operating Concept – A New Way of Winning', *British Army Review*, Number 185, pp. 6–10. https://chacr.org.uk/2023/08/31/the-british-army-review-185/

59 'Army announces new way of winning future wars', Posting on British Army website 16 September, 2023. https://www.army.mod.uk/news/army-announces-new-way-of-winning-future-wars/

60 National Audit Office The Equipment Plan 2023 to 2033 Date: 4 Dec 2023 page 7 https://www.nao.org.uk/ reports/equipment-plan-2023-to-2033/

61 British Armed Forces "not ready" to fight a war and deter invasion, John Healey admits', *Daily Express*, 24 October 2024. https://www.express.co.uk/news/politics/1966831/Army-Navy-not-ready-war-air-Russia

62 UK MoD The Strategic Defence Review (SDR) 2025 - Making Britain Safer: secure at home, strong abroad Updated 5 June 2025. https://www.gov.uk/government/publications/the-strategic-defence-review-2025 -making-britain-safer-secure-at-home-strong-abroad/the-strategic-defence-review-2025-making-britain-safer -secure-at-home-strong-abroad

63 Assessments included

The International Institute for Strategic Studies assessed that – were a ceasefire to take place in Ukraine in 2025 – Russia could be in a position to pose a significant military challenge to NATO allies, particularly the Baltic states, as early as 2027. IISS report Defending Europe Without the United States: Costs and Consequences May 2025 page 8.

Danish Intelligence Outlook 2024 published January 2025 assessed that if the war in Ukraine ended, Russia would be able after 5 years to launch a large-scale attack on NATO. https://www.fe-ddis.dk/en/produkter/Risk _assessment/.

NATO secretary General Mark Rutte, speaking in London warned that "Russia could be ready to use military force against NATO within five years". Building a better NATO. Speech by NATO Secretary General Mark Rutte at Chatham House 9 June. 2025

64 Private conversations with MoD officials.

65 This analysis is informed by off-the-record conversations with UK defence officials and IISS analysis. See also Malcolm Chalmers, 'UK Defence Spending Decisions Can't Wait for the Strategic Defence Review' RUSI, 9 September 2024 https://www.rusi.org/explore-our-research/publications/commentary/uk-defence-spending -decisions-cant-wait-strategic-defence-review and Matthew Savill, 'Starmer Shows His Hand on Defence Spending', RUSI, 25 February 2025 https://www.rusi.org/explore-our-research/publications/commentary/ starmer-shows-his-hand-defence-spending

66 The Hague Summit Declaration issued by the NATO Heads of State and Government participating in the meeting of the North Atlantic Council in The Hague, 25 June 2025. NATO website, 25 June 2025 https:// www.nato.int/cps/en/natohq/official_texts_236705.htm

67 UK SDR 2025, section 7.3 Land Domain.

POSTSCRIPT

1 I would like to thank Brigadier John Ridge of the MoD's Defence Innovation Unit and Brigadier Will Strickland of the Army Concepts Branch for commissioning research that helped inform this chapter.

2 Sir Max Hastings, and the Imperial War Museum, *The British Army – The Definitive History of the Twentieth Century*, Cassell, 2007, p. 21.

INDEX

References to maps and keys are in **bold**.